Legal Executions After Statehood in North Dakota, South Dakota, Wyoming, Montana, Idaho, Washington and Oregon

Also by R. Michael Wilson

Legal Executions After Statehood in Arizona, Colorado, Nevada, New Mexico and Utah: A Comprehensive Registry
(McFarland, 2011)

Legal Executions in the Western Territories, 1847–1911: Arizona, Colorado, Idaho, Kansas, Montana, Nebraska, Nevada, New Mexico, North Dakota, Oklahoma, Oregon, South Dakota, Utah, Washington and Wyoming
(McFarland, 2010)

Legal Executions After Statehood in North Dakota, South Dakota, Wyoming, Montana, Idaho, Washington and Oregon

A Comprehensive Registry

R. MICHAEL WILSON

McFarland & Company, Inc., Publishers
Jefferson, North Carolina, and London

Also of Interest

Wells, Fargo & Co. Stagecoach and Train Robberies, 1870–1884: The Corporate Report of 1885 with Additional Facts About the Crimes and Their Perpetrators, revised edition.
James B. Hume and John N. Thacker.
Edited and expanded by R. Michael Wilson
(McFarland, 2010).

Library of Congress Cataloguing-in-Publication Data

Wilson, R. Michael, 1944–
Legal executions after statehood in North Dakota, South Dakota, Wyoming, Montana, Idaho, Washington and Oregon : a comprehensive registry / R. Michael Wilson.
p. cm.
Includes bibliographical references and index.

ISBN 978-0-7864-6126-4
softcover : 50# alkaline paper ♾

1. Executions and executioners — West (U.S.) — Chronology.
2. Capital punishment — West (U.S.) — History. 3. Criminal justice, Administration of — West (U.S.) — History. I. Title.
HV8699.U6W547 2011 364.660978 — dc22 2010047902

British Library cataloguing data are available

Manufactured in the United States of America

McFarland & Company, Inc., Publishers
Box 611, Jefferson, North Carolina 28640
www.mcfarlandpub.com

To those too oft forgotten:
THE VICTIMS

Table of Contents

Preface

Half the world's countries have abolished the death penalty, but in the United States the administration of the death penalty persists as one of the most controversial ethical and practical issues of American jurisprudence. Capital punishment has been under attack in America for a dozen decades and one day may become a relic, the details only to be found in those literary museums known as historic encyclopedias. I was drawn to a study of western case histories because the work of documenting these thrilling events has proven so daunting that few have undertaken the task. Those who have examined capital punishment in the West, however, have limited their efforts to mere lists or to documenting a constrained geographical area and time period. An examination of the death penalty in the early days of the West is an important aspect of the debate over capital punishment, and nothing less than one hundred percent of the executions in one hundred percent of the West gives us a basis for drawing meaningful conclusions.

In June 2009 sixteen jurisdictions among the United States had no death penalty statute in effect: Alaska, Hawaii, Iowa, Maine, Massachusetts, Michigan, Minnesota, New Jersey, New Mexico, New York, North Dakota, Rhode Island, Vermont, West Virginia, Wisconsin, and the District of Columbia. Kansas, New York and New Hampshire had not executed a person since 1976, when the U.S. Supreme Court restored the death penalty, and Illinois currently has a moratorium on death sentences. As 2009 came to a close Colorado, Kansas, Maryland, Montana, Nebraska, and New Hampshire were considering statutes abolishing the practice, at least in part because of economic considerations, but these are the states which have the fewest prisoners on death row. Since 1976 there have been nearly twelve hundred executions in the United States, reaching a high of ninety-eight in 1999 but decreasing to thirty-seven by the end of 2008, and two-thirds of those put to death were executed in just five states: Florida, Missouri, Oklahoma, Texas, and Virginia. It seems only a matter of time before these high rate capital punishment states begin to question the propriety of executing human beings and opt for a term of life in prison.

This work contains the details of all the crimes resulting in executions in the seven northwestern American states after they attained statehood: Idaho, Montana, North Dakota, Oregon, South Dakota, Washington, and Wyoming. With this information one is able to see practices and patterns which lead to two logical conclusions: (1) the death penalty is no deterrent to murder. Regardless of the number of public executions, "cold-blooded, pre-meditated, first-degree murder with malice" proliferated in the West. If there is a justification for the infliction of death as a punishment it must be to prevent future murders by the same miscreant; and (2) if capital punishment is to continue in use we must come to realize that the U.S. Supreme Court got it wrong when they ignored the fact that when a hanging or shooting is done properly death is nearly instantaneous, and any agonies perceived are in the eye of the beholder.

The research for this book relied primarily upon contemporary newspapers. Other sources included court records and diaries or personal accounts. The work has been arranged with the researcher in mind, with case histories presented chronologically by state. Each case history is headed by the name of the condemned and the date of execution. Specific sources are listed at the end of each case history, and a general bibliography and comprehensive index is provided.

Introduction

The English custom of hanging criminals came to America with the pilgrims and the practice of hanging criminals moved west with the pioneers. The sentence of death was imposed exclusively for the crime of "cold blooded, premeditated murder," or murder in the first degree, with only a few exceptions and hanging was the most common form of execution. During the early days executions were thought to be a deterrent, so gallows were built a distance from the jail, allowing for a solemn procession exhibiting the condemned man on his way to his execution. Soon it became apparent that this caused difficulties, so scaffolds were built closer to the place of confinement.

When the law changed to require that gallows be built inside an enclosure, and the hanging be a private affair, scaffolds were consistently built adjacent to the jail. The sheriff of each county was responsible for executions and he invited at least one physician and might invite the district attorney, lawmen, a coroner's jury of six to twelve reputable citizens, ministers of the gospel, and a number of relatives or friends requested by the condemned. The condemned was provided access to religious comfort and many condemned men chose to be baptized into a religion during their final hours. Before the fatal moment arrived the condemned was offered a hearty meal; he washed, shaved and dressed in a new dark suit or other attire of his choosing provided by the county, state or federal authority; and the death warrant was read to him in his cell or at the place of execution. He might be provided an alcoholic beverage or drug to help him brace up for the ordeal. The prisoner was escorted by several men who provided support in case he faltered, and he was followed closely or led by his religious advisor if he had one.

The condemned was placed on the trapdoor where his wrists and arms, knees and ankles were pinioned. At some point during the proceedings he was given an opportunity to speak to the crowd. When his speech was finished the final preparations were completed including a black hood pulled over his head or a blindfold tied over his eyes. It was then but a moment before the trap was sprung or the order to fire was given. A physician was required to be in attendance to pronounce the moment of death, when the body was deposited into a coffin. People of the west were familiar with death by gunshot but hanging continued to be a mystery and preoccupied the interest of the public, so at times articles were published explaining the sensations experienced. Of course there was no opportunity to ask the subject of a legal hanging as the law required that they be "hanged until dead," but failed suicides by hanging and scientific study provide insight into the sensations. As early as April 16, 1869, the *Walla Walla Statesman* published an article entitled "How It Feels to Be Hanged."

> We are told that hanging, if successful — that is, if it breaks the person's neck — is the most sudden death a person can die. It ruptures the spine in the immediate neighborhood of the medulla oblongata, and thus breaks up communication of the nerve force, or vital power, to the organs that carry on the human machinery. If the man's neck is not broken the

> first action of the cord is to close the trachea, or windpipe, and thus stop the supply of air. It also compresses the large veins in the neck which return blood to the heart — the jugulars — but does not entirely compress the large arteries that carry blood to the brain, for these lie deep. The immediate physiological effect is congestion of the brain — a congestion not dissimilar in its commencement from the congestion of drunkenness, which is generally regarded as agreeable, and the consequences of this congestion — a consequence that perhaps follows in three minutes after the pressure of the cord is felt — is the total abolition of conscious sensation. The man may struggle and writhe in a way terrible to see, but these struggles are like those of convulsions generally — painful only to the beholder.
>
> Therefore, if a man is hanged successfully, he feels only the one sickening sensation of the plunge before he gets to the end of the rope; three seconds of horror. If he is hanged successfully by strangulation, he feels the same three seconds, and in addition, between the pressure of the cord and the deep congestion of the brain, three minutes of swimming, drowsy, uncertain uneasiness — at worst, three minutes and three seconds; and this is all we give of misery to murderers.
>
> Compare with this the pain that man suffers before he dies from an ordinary illness — the drawn out wretchedness of his three weeks of fever, the days of agony with rheumatism, and the bent-forward, restless nights before this rheumatism finally brings his damaged heart to a standstill; the months of slow death entailed by a cancerous stomach; in fine, compare the history of any disease with the short shrift of hanging, and then reflect that our humanity now obliterates the murderer's three minutes and three seconds by the use of chloroform. Really it is a fine age, and if a man is tired of this world and wants to get out on easy terms, the thing for him to do is to cut his neighbor's throat and be hanged under chloroform.

One of the main criticisms of hanging as a means of execution was that the condemned's neck was, all too often, "unbroken and he would perish by the long and painful process of strangulation." John Burns, however, spoke from personal experience in refuting that perception. He recalled,

> Some time during the [Civil] war, ruffians who desired to be thought [bush] whackers, came upon me at my house, intending to compel me to give up some money I was supposed to have. I had none, and told them so, but they did not believe me and their next move was to cut a cord out of a bedstead, tie one end around my neck, throw the other over a joist overhead, and pull me up till my feet were clear of the floor. This they did four times, questioning me between whiles. I lost consciousness every time as soon as my feet left the floor but felt no pain at any time, and after the second hoist I meant to sham continued insensibility when they let me drop again, since to lower me they just let go the rope and I fell to the floor, but this was beyond my power. My first consciousness was that I had raised my body to a sitting position, which put shamming out of the question. I experienced no pain when the rope tightened, nor when I was suspended, nor after I was released, except the soreness caused on my skin by the chafing of the rope. I weighed about two hundred pounds, which insured that the rope was fully tightened each time."

Dr. D. S. Lamb, an ex-surgeon of the United States Army, studied the subject of hanging and in 1894 reported in the *St. Louis Globe-Democrat*:

> DEATH BY HANGING —
>
> The Three Different Stages Through Which the Victim Passes
>
> I have made the subject of death by hanging a long study. From my observations during my experience in the army I feel justified in saying that death by hanging is the most exaggerated of all modes. It may be immediate and without symptoms but the subject must pass through three stages before death.
>
> In the first stage the victim passes into a partial stupor lasting from thirty seconds to two minutes, but this is generally governed by the length of the drop, the weight of the body, and the tightness of the constriction. There is absolutely no pain in this stage; the feeling is rather one of pleasure. The subjective symptoms described are intense heat in the head, brilliant flashes of light in the eyes, deafening sounds in the ears and a heavy numb feeling in the lungs. In the second stage the subject passes into unconsciousness and convulsions

> usually occur. In the third stage all is quiet except the beating of the heart. Just before death the agitation is renewed, but in a different way from that in the second state. The feet are raised, the tongue has a peculiar spasm, the chest heaves, the eyes protrude from the orbits and oscillate from side to side, and the pupils dilate. The pulse can, in most cases, be felt ten minutes after the drop.
>
> I once knew a man who was desirous of ascertaining if there was any suffering by hanging and in order to find out he placed a rope around his neck and stepped off a bench, intending to step back again, but he became immediately unconscious and would have died in a few minutes had it not been for the timely arrival of a friend. He said he experienced all the feelings that I mentioned in the first stage.

This three stage process depended upon the rope being properly knotted and adjusted. The knot was carefully positioned on the left shoulder just behind the jaw so that it would press upon the carotid artery, cutting off blood to the brain which resulted in unconsciousness in a few seconds. This positioning of the knot forced the head to snap backward and dislocate the vertebrae. Ideally, during a legal hanging, the spine would be dislocated between the first and second or the second and third cervical vertebrae and the spinal cord would be severed, or at least severely compressed, cutting off all sensation to the torso and extremities.

Before one execution by hanging the trapdoor gallows was described as "ready and in fact every detail for the execution has been carefully arranged. The gallows is of the regulation pattern, very strong built, and has a drop of six feet. The rope is of best quality hemp, and 1½ inches in size."

In fact, there was no regulation design for gallows. Each sheriff, when required to do so, hired a local carpenter to design and build a gallows for his county. The trapdoor and release mechanism were of particular concern and the drop, the distance a man would fall, had to be calculated correctly. The distance a particular man should drop was determined by a mathematical formula based upon his weight where a one hundred ninety-six pound man required a six foot drop and, for each deduction of seven pounds in weight, two inches were added. Scaffolds of the trapdoor design, paid for with county funds, were usually disassembled and stored for reuse. Another type of gallows used a heavy weight as a "counter poise" so that, when the weight was dropped, the condemned man was jerked-up with such suddenness it dislocated the man's vertebrae.

Hemp was used almost exclusively for a hangman's rope because the strands were longer and stronger than flax, the other commonly available material at that time. The hemp material was beaten until soft and then twisted into strands, and three strands were then twisted around a central strand called "the heart" to form a rope. A very thick rope was ordered from the manufacturer so that, even after stretching, it was still thick enough to prevent it from cutting into the neck of the condemned person. Upon arrival the rope was soaked in water and stretched to remove elasticity, and then it was tested for the condemned's weight, usually by dropping a comparable weight through the trapdoor to the required distance or by jerking up the equivalent weight of the condemned man. The loops of a hangman's noose were not a set number but seven loops were most often used, though on occasion a hangman might use as few as five or as many as thirteen loops. The point where rope grated on rope was lubricated with grease, soap, or wax to make the strands slide more easily and cinch tightly.

Lethal gas as a means of execution was first considered after such gases were used during World War I. The first state to adopt the use of lethal gas was Nevada and the first execution occurred on February 8, 1924. The protocol for an execution by lethal gas is relatively standard throughout the states. The state will construct an airtight steel chamber with windows within which is affixed a steel chair with straps attached. As the moment nears the condemned is instructed to breathe deeply when the fumes reach his face, and if the condemned fails to follow this instruction it can result in a period of six or more minutes of violent convulsions. In preparation an executioner will place a pre-determined quantity of potassium cyanide or sodium cyanide crystals (or pellets) into a container under the seat or at the back of the chair. The prisoner is then brought in and he may already be wearing an eye mask. He is seated in the chair and the straps are applied to his chest, waist, wrists, and ankles and a stethoscope may be taped to his chest or electrocardiograph skin electrodes are attached to monitor his heart beat. In some states the prisoner may be given an opportunity to speak to witnesses before the eye mask is pulled on.

The chamber is then sealed and the curtains are drawn back while an executioner opens a valve allowing sulphuric or hydrochloric acid to flow into a container below the container holding the cyanide crystals. A switch, lever, button, or key is then activated, dropping the crystals into the acid. The chemical reaction creates a white cloud of lethal hydrocyanic (hydrogen cyanide) gas which rises to fill the chamber and envelope the prisoner. Death may be nearly instantaneous or the prisoner may take six or more minutes to die. After the prisoner's vital signs cease, the chamber is flushed with anhydrous ammonia and then all the gases are purged by fans and processed through special "scrubbers" which utilize water as a neutralizer.

In five to fifteen minutes guards can enter the chamber to remove the body and the chamber may be ready for reuse within a half hour. A doctor, usually the prison physician, officially pronounces the person dead and the remnants of the poisonous gas on the remains must be neutralized with a bleach solution before the body is handled by an undertaker. The remains are then disposed of by prior arrangement or by law.

Lethal injection began to replace or serve as an alternative to other forms of execution in many states. In the early days there was a two chemical protocol but it was soon replaced by a three chemical protocol. The prisoner would be brought into the execution chamber and strapped to a gurney. The executioner would be in place in a control room to maintain his anonymity while medically trained personnel inserted an intravenous cannulae (IV) in each arm, the second a back-up in case the primary IV failed. At this point, typically, the curtains are drawn open for the witnesses to view the condemned person, who can then make a statement. At a signal the executioner would begin administration of the drugs: sodium thiopental to induce sleep; pancuronium bromide to restrict respiration, which in time would cause death by asphyxiation; and potassium chloride to quickly stop the heart. The heart beat of the condemned is monitored and when all vital signs cease a doctor pronounces death.

In executions by electrocution there is a direct application of a strong electric current sufficient to cause brain death. The prisoner's head and one leg are shaved so that electrodes can be attached, allowing the current to flow through the body. The prisoner is strapped securely to a chair and the current is fed through the electrode attached to the head in an intensity of more than one thousand five hundred volts, and the charge exits at the electrode attached to the leg. There may be as many as three to four jolts of electricity lasting up to a minute each, which ensures death. The body may change color and the flesh may burn during an electrocution.

Frequency of Executions

In the West defendants were condemned to death only when they were convicted of murder in the first degree, with few exceptions, even then many convicted murderers were sentenced to prison terms. Other murderers eluded the executioner through suicide, by escaping from imprisonment never to be heard of again, by obtaining a second trial on appeal and being acquitted, or by being convicted of or pleading to a lesser degree of crime. In numerous instances death sentences were commuted to a life term in prison and, even when the evidence clearly showed every element necessary for a conviction of murder in the first degree, juries might bring in a peculiar verdict such as murder in the second degree or manslaughter.

Most executions were successful, according to newspaper accounts, but it was not the embarrassment of bungling that promoted privacy in executions. Early executions were intentionally as public as possible as this was believed to deter other would-be murderers. However, in the mid–1870s the phenomenon of privacy during executions swept through the West and territories and states required that gallows be constructed within a wall or enclosure of high board fencing, or have a special building erected or selected for the purpose. The laws were often very specific in excluding and including citizens of the jurisdiction as witnesses, and the number of invitations was greatly limited.

Executions State by State

Before Idaho became a state on July 3, 1890, there were twelve men hanged during fourteen executions in the Idaho Territory. After statehood twelve men were hanged during eleven executions. On January 6, 1994, lethal injection replaced the noose for the execution of Keith E. Wells, the only man executed by that method and the last execution in Idaho.

Before Montana became a state on November 8, 1889, fifteen men were hanged during thirteen executions, and after statehood fifty-five men were hanged during forty-eight executions. On May 10, 1995, lethal injection replaced the noose for the execution of Duncan McKenzie, the first of three men executed by that method.

Before North Dakota became a state on November 2, 1889, there were two men hanged in separate executions, and after statehood there were six men hanged in individual executions.

Before Oregon became a state on February 14, 1859, six men were hanged during five executions, and after statehood one hundred men were executed during eighty-four executions. The gas chamber replaced the noose for the execution of Leroy McCarthy on June 20, 1939. In all, eighteen men would be asphyxiated in sixteen executions before lethal injection was used to execute Douglas F. Wright on September 6, 1996, the first of two men executed by that method.

Before South Dakota became a state on November 2, 1889, there were four men hanged in separate executions, and after statehood there were nine men hanged during nine individual executions. South Dakota abolished the death penalty in 1915 but reinstated it in 1939; it was abolished again from 1977 to 1979. On April 8, 1947, George Sitts became the only condemned man in South Dakota executed by electrocution. On July 11, 2007, Elijah Page became the last man executed in South Dakota, and the only man executed by lethal injection.

Before Washington became a state on November 11, 1889, there were twenty men hanged during fourteen executions, and after statehood ninety-three men were hanged during ninety-one executions. Washington retained hanging as the mode of execution until October 13, 1998, when Jeremy Sagastegui became the first of two men executed by lethal injection.

Before Wyoming became a state on July 10, 1890, there were seven men hanged during seven individual executions, and after statehood there were thirteen men hanged during individual executions. By the time Perry Carroll was scheduled to die on August 13, 1937, the gas chamber had replaced the noose. Four more men would die by asphyxiation before the gas chamber was replaced by lethal injection for the execution of Mark Hopkinson on January 22, 1992.

IDAHO

Idaho was considered a part of the "Oregon Country" when it was acquired from Great Britain in 1846. A dispute persisted over the northern boundary of the Oregon Country between the parallels of 42° and 54°40', which had been under joint control of the United States and Great Britain, and included the area between the northern border of California and the southern border of Alaska. Although there was a strong movement in America to claim the 54°40' boundary for the United States, Alaska's southern boundary agreed to by Russia, President James K. Polk surprised everyone when, on June 15, 1846, he agreed to the parallel of 49° to separate the United States from Canada. This agreement gave the United States sole control over the area that would become Idaho. The Idaho Territory was established on March 4, 1863, and Idaho was admitted as the 43rd state on July 3, 1890.

Ellington, James
May 27, 1896

James A. Ellington was born near Barnesville, Georgia, on March 7, 1853. Ellington left home when twenty years old and up until 1891 tramped around the central states. In that year he tired of the hobo life and settled in San Luis Obispo, California. In 1894 Ellington moved to Los Angeles, where he met fifty-six-year-old Charles Briggs, who convinced him to go into a roof painting partnership in Boise, Idaho. They moved there in November and almost immediately began to quarrel over money.

On December 20 the two men passed on 13th Street, and Ellington suddenly whirled about and shot Briggs in the back. The shot brought people from their homes and they saw Briggs and Ellington wrestling, the gun still in Ellington's hand. A second shot grazed Briggs' head and a third passed through Briggs' hand. An officer was running toward the men, so Ellington grabbed Briggs' watch and ran into the foothills. The wounded man was carried to Dr. George Collister, who confirmed that Briggs had been shot in the back. Briggs lingered for five days and made an antemortem statement naming Ellington as his murderer, then died on Christmas day 1894.

Ellington was captured in Emmett on January 22 and brought to Boise. During the return trip he said he had attacked Briggs because "I just wanted to shoot him down to my size." Ellington was arraigned on a charge of murder and his trial began on February 4, 1895. Ellington testified that Briggs had often threatened to kill him and on the day Briggs was shot the defendant had demanded money owed him, but Briggs attacked him with a knife and he shot in self-defense. However, the evidence proved otherwise. Ellington was convicted of first degree murder after six days of testimony and brief deliberations by the jury. Ellington was sentenced by Judge Richards to hang on May 17, 1895. An appeal was filed so the Supreme Court stayed the execution, but the justices affirmed the lower court's decision on December 12, 1895. During the next term of court on April 6, 1896, Judge Richards sentenced Ellington to hang on Wednesday, May 27, 1896. On May 20 his application for a commutation of sentence to life imprisonment was heard by the Board of Pardons and denied.

The night before his execution Ellington went to bed at 11:00 P.M. and slept until 5:00 A.M. He remarked that he had not passed a more peaceful night for some time, which may have accounted for his healthy appetite at 7:00 A.M. when served breakfast. Deputy Sheriff Hugh Fulton then read the death warrant, and when Fulton exited the cell Bishop Glorieux entered with two sisters, who administered the sacrament and then prayed with the condemned man. Next came Frank Martin and J. R. Wester, his attorneys, his former religious advisor the Reverend D. M. Reynolds, and several members of the Women's Christian Temperance Union, who all prayed with Ellington. Barber Parke followed and shaved the condemned man, so when the *Statesman* reporter entered the narrow cell there was hardly room to stand. Outside the cell were the men who had been invited to witness the execution, among them two doctors who monitored Ellington's condition. When the condemned man seemed to weaken they prescribed a stimulant and it was administered.

At 9:15 A.M. Sheriff Moseley moved the witnesses into the house of execution, a small structure in the corner of the courthouse yard. Deputy sheriff Kelly stood at the door of the house admitting only those with permits while other deputies enforced the rope barricade which had been stretched around the structure. At 9:17 A.M. deputy Fulton called Ellington from his cell and took his right arm while Father Glorieux took his left. As they stepped into the yard Ellington looked around and groaned in anguish, so Fulton said softly, "Brace up, Jim." As they walked to the scaffold deputies Ralston and Smith fell in behind with the reporters at the rear of the procession. When the prisoner wavered Father Glorieux whispered words of encouragement. Ellington was escorted onto the trapdoor and was asked if he had anything to say and he responded, "No, not a word." He shook hands with everyone on the scaffold, giving attorney Martin his two written statements, and when he came to deputy Ralston of his death watch he said, "Be a good boy, George."

While Ellington's arms were being pinioned he said farewell to the crowd and tried to justify his crime. He began to weaken again, so Father Glorieux stepped forward and offered a crucifix for him to kiss. He repeated this several times and each time it seemed to brace up the condemned man. Deputy Fulton placed the noose and cinched it tight, then carefully positioned it under the prisoner's left ear. Ellington took that opportunity to say," Make everything safe, boys. Make no mistake of it. Don't have it to do over again." Fulton pulled the black hood over Ellington's head, but failed to secure the draw string, and Sheriff Moseley pushed the lever that pulled the bolts and the trap was sprung at 9:21 A.M.

As Ellington heard the bolts operating he cried out, "Oh, my God!" The condemned man dropped seven feet and, as the body fell, air caught the hood and it flew off the prisoner's face. It seemed as if the condemned man's head would be ripped off but the fall only broke his neck, and there was no convulsive movement. He was pronounced dead in nine minutes and cut down six minutes later. A coffin had been placed beneath the scaffold and it was pulled out so Ellington's remains could be deposited, and the body was turned over to undertaker Glover. A brief service was held in the undertaker's parlor that evening, and a graveside funeral service was conducted at 10 o'clock the following morning when Ellington's remains were interred in the Catholic cemetery.

Idaho Daily Statesman (Boise): May 23, 1896; May 27–28, 1896.

Larkins, James S.
April 30, 1897

Josie Hill was a notorious prostitute, prepossessing and quite popular. In 1893, Hill left Salt Lake City, Utah, for Idaho with a man named Callahan. On the road a masked highwayman killed and robbed Callahan, who had been flashing a large bankroll before leaving Salt Lake City, and Hill was suspected of being implicated in some way but was acquitted at trial. Sid Larkins had been a particular friend of Hill and it was also suspected he might have been the highwayman, but there was never enough evidence to bring him to trial.

James Sidney "Sid" Larkins had been born in Utah on February 15, 1860, and when he turned eighteen he began railroading on freight and passenger trains for the Northern Pacific Railroad. He soon learned gambling and decided to make his way by that trade. Most of his playing was for others, on a salary, and he never stooped to cheating or swindling. His associations led him to become a moderate drinker, but on occasion he would over-indulge and would afterward blame this condition for his criminal acts.

After Hill was released from jail at Salt Lake City she established a sporting house on the outskirts of Idaho Falls, Bingham County, Idaho, in an area known as "the Island," and Larkins moved there. Larkins was among the steady clientele for Hill, but Larkins believed their relationship should be more exclusive. Hill resisted his proposals and responded by denying Larkins access to her favors and her house. At 6:00 A.M. Christmas day Larkins went to Hill's house and found Lennie Vernon and George Coulter there. Perhaps because it was a holiday Hill admitted him and, as he removed his hat, she turned toward her other guests. Larkins, without warning or hesitation, pulled his pistol and shot Hill in the back. The bullet passed through but did not exit and lodged beneath the skin of her abdomen. Larkins rushed out of the house and tried to shoot himself without effect, so he continued his flight from the scene.

News of the shooting spread quickly and deputy sheriff Boyes and constable Clyne sent men in every direction, and after searching four hours one party discovered the fugitive three miles north of town on the west bank of the Snake River. Larkins lay unconscious with a four inch gash across his throat and he had lost a lot of blood, but the cold weather kept him from bleeding to death. Drs. Mitchell, Pendleton and LaRue had dressed Hill's wound while the pursuit was in progress, and they announced that Hill's chance of recovery was slight. When Larkins was brought in the doctors used only six stitches to close the neck wound and then turned him over to the officers. Larkins was lodged in jail but he was not yet charged, as Hill's condition was being closely monitored. When Hill survived three days it appeared that she would fully recover, so Larkins' examination was postponed until she could testify. However, Hill took a turn for the worse and died on January 9, 1896. Larkins was then charged with murder. Larkins was held over for action by the grand jury, indicted, tried and convicted at the spring term of the District Court, and sentenced to hang. An appeal was filed and it took a year to dispose of the matter, and the petition for commutation of sentence was denied. The date for Larkins' hanging was set for April 30, 1897.

Larkins slept well the night before his execution but arose early to host a large number of visitors, and he was in good spirits. At 8:30 A.M. Sheriff Coltman read the death warrant to Larkins in his cell. At 10:00 the Reverend Yost arrived and engaged the prisoner in prayer for an hour before the sheriff called Larkin from his cell. The sheriff led the procession with deputies Hafer and Winn on either side supporting the prisoner. The gallows had been constructed next to the jail just outside Larkins' window, and deputy DeKay waited on the scaffold near the lever which activated the release mechanism.

The condemned man mounted the stairs and took his position beneath the noose where his arms and legs were pinioned and the noose was adjusted, and then the sheriff asked if he had anything to say. Larkins responded, "My friends. A Savior died for you and for me. He was not surrounded by friends as I now am. I believe you who are here are all my friends. Accept him as your Savior. He is mine. I bid you a long farewell." When Larkins finished the black hood was pulled on and Sheriff Coltman said, "Good-bye, Sid," as he signaled DeKay. The lever releasing the heavy counter poise weight was thrown at 11:07 A.M. and

Larkins was "twitched-up" four feet into the air breaking his neck, and in eight and one half minutes he was pronounced dead by Drs. Moore and Mitchell. Larkins hanged a few minutes longer, was cut down, placed in his coffin, and buried that afternoon.

Blackfoot News (Blackfoot, ID): December 28, 1895; January 11, 1896; April 24, 1897; May 1, 1897. *Idaho Statesman* (Boise): December 26, 1895; January 9, 1896; April 30, 1897; May 1, 1897

St. Clair, Herman C.
June 24, 1898

Herman C. St. Clair, not his real name but he would give no other, was born on October 4,1849, in Tahlequah, capital of the Cherokee Nation (now in Oklahoma). He joined the U.S. Navy in 1864 and served until 1876. As soon as he was mustered out of the Navy he enlisted as an Indian scout for the Army of the West and served with General George Crook on the Yellowstone survey. He was with General Nelson Miles when he chased Sitting Bull's band in the north central part of the United States. In 1879 he was deployed to Idaho to serve under Colonel Reuben Bernard in the 1st Cavalry, Company G, and was involved in several skirmishes with Indians. At Deep Creek he received a minor wound to his arm and was on Wood River in 1880 and 1881.

During his military service he received three awards for bravery, but after he mustered out he went to California, where he became involved with sporting women, whiskey and cards. This led him into a life of crime; he served terms in California's Folsom and San Quentin Prisons under the alias Eugene St. Clair. When he was released from his last prison term he went to British Columbia, where he met John Decker in 1896. In October 1897 Decker and St. Clair started for Mexico in a wagon owned by Decker. Decker paid for everything from more than $1200 he carried in a belt, as St. Clair had no money. They traveled to Van Wyck in Long Valley, Idaho, and stayed Thursday night, October 21, in the abandoned Jerry Lester cabin two miles from town.

The following day St. Clair went into Van Wyck alone and showed a considerable amount of money, which he began to spend freely. He had a .38-caliber six-shooter which he tried to trade, but without success. When questioned about Decker he said his companion had gone on to Boise with a freight train, but none had left Van Wyck recently. St. Clair's drunken debauch continued into Saturday and liquor loosened his tongue so that he made remarks that aroused suspicions. A party of men went to the Lester cabin on Sunday, October 24, to search and were careful to give St. Clair no indication what they were about.

There appeared at first no sign of Decker nor of a struggle but as the search widened they located a wagon track leading through the tall grass into a gulch. They followed the trail and where it ended they found evidence that something heavy had been unloaded from the wagon bed and dragged through the grass. They followed that trail two hundred yards and found Decker's body wrapped in a blanket, with double wrapping about the head; a rope around the dead man's neck had been used to drag the body. The search party left the body undisturbed, returned to Van Wyck and arrested St. Clair, but gave no clue to the charge. They took their prisoner to the cabin and then worked him up the gulch searching for Decker. They allowed him to discover the body, carefully watching for any reaction which would give away his guilty knowledge, but he showed only surprise. He recognized the body but when accused of the murder he protested his innocence. The party threatened lynching, which unnerved St. Clair and, though he made no confession, he made several conflicting statements which supported the belief he was guilty.

St. Clair was taken to Idaho City by officers and as soon as he was out of danger of a lynching he resumed his usual braggadocio. St. Clair was examined, held over for the grand jury, and indicted. The trial, which began on November 11, took seven days even though the defendant refused to take the stand and would not allow his attorney, Karl Paine, to enter an insanity plea. On November 18, 1897, the jury, after brief deliberations, found St. Clair guilty of first degree murder. Two days later the judge sentenced him to hang on January 14, 1898. On January 12 an appeal was filed with the Supreme Court, which served as a stay of execution. On May 10 the decision of the lower court was affirmed, and on June 14, 1898, St. Clair was sentenced to hang in ten days; the application for a commutation of sentence sent to the governor was denied.

During St. Clair's imprisonment he tried to escape by sawing through a three-quarter inch thick bar. He slid through the opening and made his way to the rear door of the jail, which had been built in 1868 and served as the state's prison for some time, and there the prisoner was confronted by jailor James McQuillan. St. Clair brandished a knife and tried to take McQuillan's pistol, but he had seriously underestimated the deputy. McQuillan fought desperately to retain his gun and St. Clair was shot through the jaw, breaking the bone and carrying away part of his tongue and several teeth. McQuillan wrestled St. Clair's knife from his grip and in the continuing struggle the prisoner was stabbed fifteen times, nine wounds being deep and two of these penetrating the prisoner's lungs. St. Clair was so badly wounded that he had no choice but to give up, but he survived.

As the fatal day approached, St. Clair continued to assert his innocence but admitted he had buried Decker's money belt and most of the money near Joe Robbins' barn "when I heard two men planning to rob Decker." He said he thought the money might still be there and suggested that these two men had probably gone through with their plan and killed Decker while trying to learn where the money was hidden. He refused to name the person who had aided in his attempt to escape by providing the file and knife, nor would he provide names and addresses of relatives so they could be contacted.

He told Guy Flenner, the reporter for the *Statesman*, that he looked forward to his fate philosophically and said, "I am losing no sleep. No use to worry now; I might as well laugh as cry; my fate is fixed and there is no way to avoid it. I am a fatalist and believe that whatever is to be. I intend to perform my part next Friday. Being so weak I don't think I will be able to walk up the steps of the scaffold without assistance. If I was not to be hanged I could not go up without being helped, or at any rate I would have to go very slowly and stop to rest more than once before reaching the top." He said that if his fate was not to hang he would soon die from infection in his jaw wound, and showed the reporter that the cut to his wrist had severed the cords and left his hand misshapen and his fingers useless. His form, "once sturdy as an oak, was emaciated," according to Flenner, "and his step was feeble. Irregular whiskers about two inches long covered his face, which was pale as death in contrast to his red whiskers. He looked like a walking corpse...."

A week before the execution, the invitations, bearing a mourning border, were sent to a number of witnesses and read:

> Idaho City, Boise county, Idaho.
> June 15th 1898.
> Mr.____. You are requested to be present at the execution of H. C. St. Clair on June 24th, 1898 at 10 A.M. at Idaho City, Idaho
> J. A. Lippincott
> Sheriff
> Not Transferable

The prisoner slept little his last night, finally dozing off at 12:30 A.M. but waking at two o'clock. He again fell asleep after 6:00 A.M. and had to be awakened at 9:30 for breakfast in the jail corridor. He ate a hearty meal of soft items to accommodate his shattered jaw, which included poached eggs, minced meat, strawberries and cream. He appeared calm and composed when he returned to his cell after breakfast and began dressing in a new suit of clothes. At 10:10 A.M. Dr. Warren Newell of Idaho City, Dr. A. C. Lippincott of Boise, and Dr. E. E. Maxey of Caldwell examined the prisoner and found his pulse at 106, but it was reduced to 96 in five minutes by the administration of a whiskey toddy and a small dose of morphine. The prisoner then asked for a little more time and he was granted eight minutes. At 10:23 Sheriff Lippincott announced that the time had arrived, so St. Clair grabbed his vest and coat, stepped out of his cell and finished dressing in the corridor. Deputies McQuillan, Elder Smith and Clay Mosher applied the straps to St. Clair's arms, and the prisoner carefully smoothed out his clothing while they worked. When the chest strap was secured he complained, "That's too tight, old man; I want it so I can breathe good." When they were done he examined the work and announced, "Why, that's good enough for anybody."

Sheriff Lippincott was beside the prisoner with one deputy in front and two behind as they walked to the gallows. At the scaffold the deputies offered assistance in climbing the stairs but St. Clair declined, saying, "Never mind. I can walk up there." He ascended the thirteen steps and stood on the trapdoor facing east. Mosher touched St. Clair's shoulder, as he was preoccupied looking over the scene, and he turned his head to accommodate adjustment of the noose. Mosher cinched the noose, which had been obtained by the sheriff from California's San Quentin prison along with the black hood. St. Clair complained the noose was too tight so it was loosened slightly. The prisoner glanced over the crowd as if preparing to make a speech, but finally spied Guy Flenner, the *Statesman* reporter, and said, "Good-bye, old man; take good care of yourself." Mosher then pulled on the black hood, followed by the condemned man's final words, a muffle, "Good-bye, everybody!"

The sheriff and deputy Smith each stood at a lever, one a dummy. When Mosher waved his hand the trap was sprung and the prisoner fell six feet. The three doctors immediately attended the dangling man and reported that they felt no pulse at thirty-eight seconds but continued to monitor his vital signs until they pronounced him dead in eight minutes. St. Clair's neck had been broken by the fall and he hung motionless. The body was cut down and carried into the jail where the black covered casket awaited the murderer's remains. The cap was removed and it was found that the rope had cut through the skin, but most of the blood came from the jaw wound which had been reopened by the drop. The prisoner had protested an autopsy but one was performed. His brain was removed and some features of abnormality were discovered, though not described by the doctors. They found on his body fifteen knife wounds and two bullet wounds, as well as a number of tattoos apparently acquired while in prison. The undertaker then took charge of the remains and that afternoon Herman St. Clair was buried on the hill near the city cemetery next to the grave of murderer Simeon Walters. The painted headboard bore the simple inscription: "H. C. St. Clair. Hanged June 24, 1898, for the murder of John Decker."

Idaho World (Idaho City): June 24, 1898. *Statesman* (Boise, ID): June 24–25, 1898; August 30, 1925.

Rice, Edward
November 30, 1901

Matt Mailley, a harmless old man, owned and operated a cigar store in Wallace, Idaho, and had converted the back storeroom into his living quarters. On the morning of September 4, 1900, he was found dead with the back of his head crushed and his throat cut, and the store had been robbed of several hundred dollars. Covering the face of Mailley was a handkerchief and by the laundry mark it was traced to Edward Rice. Forty-two-year-old Rice was only five feet seven inches tall but he was stocky, weighing nearly two hundred pounds, and he had made a concerted and obvious effort to befriend Mailley.

Rice had no money nor the means of earning any before the murder but afterward he began spending freely and within a few days had spent several hundred dollars. A barkeeper recalled that Rice had come to his saloon on the evening of September 3 and bought several drinks. The barkeeper recalled telling Rice of fresh blood on his trousers so Rice hurried out and bought a new pair. All these facts led to suspicion that Rice had murdered Mailley. He was arrested, his room was searched, and the bloody trousers were found hidden behind the wainscoting. He was indicted for the murder and tried at the fall term of the District Court. The jury, after brief deliberations, found Rice guilty of first degree murder and he was sentenced to hang on December 31, 1900.

The prisoner was taken to the penitentiary on November 11, 1900, to await the date of his execution, but the sentence was stayed pending review by the state's Supreme Court. It took many months to dispose of the motions and appeals but eventually the Supreme Court upheld the lower court's decision, and the application for a commutation of sentence was denied. Rice was then taken to Wallace, where he was resentenced to hang on November 30, 1901.

W. E. Borach, who had met Rice at the trial of Paul Corcoran in northern Idaho, interested himself in the matter of the condemned man's sanity and had an informal examination conducted by the prison physician and two assisting doctors. Two of the physicians certified that he was insane, based upon his bizarre behavior and his one attempt at suicide in which he had hidden a knife from the guards and tried to slash his throat. The third physician refused to sign the certificate, but this was enough for Governor Frank W. Hunt to convene a meeting of the Board of Pardons. During testimony one of the certifying doctors said that he could not say if Rice was insane, but felt strongly that he was a pervert. Based upon this testimony, and the third doctor who testified that Rice was not insane, the governor refused to interfere with the execution and announced that if there were to be any intervention it would have to originate in the courts.

At 7:30 A.M. on November 30, 1901, buggies and carriages began arriving at the penitentiary. Warden Charles E. Arney and deputy warden Tom Martin received Father G. M. van der Velden, the physicians, reporters, officials, and the others invited as witnesses, but only the priest, reporters and a few officials were allowed in the cell corridor during the reading of the death warrant. The priest donned his robes and entered the cell at the head of the small procession. Rice was dressed in a new cutaway suit of black with standing collar, blue tie and white shirt and appeared quite pale. The death watch was still on guard as the warrant was read:

In the District Court of the First Judicial District of the state of Idaho.

State of Idaho vs. Edward Rice.

To the Warden of the State Penitentiary of the State of Idaho:

Whereas, on the 5th day of November, 1900, the said court in the above entitled action made and entered a judgment in said action whereby it was ordered, adjudged and decreed that the said defendant, Edward Rice, should suffer death; and

Whereas, said judgment in said action was, on the first day of June, 1901, duly affirmed by the Supreme Court of the state of Idaho; and

Whereas, Saturday the 30th day of November, 1901, between the hours of 8 o'clock A.M., and 2 o'clock P.M. of said day, was by said court on the 4th day of October, 1901, designated as the day on which said judgment shall be executed.

Now, therefore, you, the said warden of the state penitentiary of the state of Idaho, are hereby commanded to execute said judgment on Saturday, the 30th day of November, 1901, between the hours of 8 o'clock A.M., and 2 o'clock P.M. of said day within the walls of the said penitentiary of the state of Idaho, in the county of Ada, in said state of Idaho by hanging the said Edward Rice by the neck until he, the said Edward Rice, shall be dead.

Done in open court this 4th day of October, A. D. 1901.

A. E. Mayhew, Judge

Attest:
Horace M. Davenport, Clerk
by Charles A. Erwin, Deputy.

While the death warrant was being read Rice kept clutching at his collar as if it was too tight. When the reading concluded, a prayer was offered by the priest, and many present joined in. The priest then asked Rice if he had anything to say and the condemned man answered, "I have much to talk about, but there is lots of time, Father." The priest, somewhat taken aback by the response, blurted out, "Oh no! There is no time! The death warrant has been read." There followed a moment of awkward silence before the warden and his deputy formed the procession and led the march to the gallows. Edward Rice, prisoner number 788, followed the two prison officials with the priest at his arm; the spectators formed a line two by two behind them. The procession moved at a slow, deliberate pace in consideration of the solemnity of the occasion. Upon reaching the scaffold the warden, deputy warden, prisoner, and Father van der Velden, followed by the attendant guards, climbed the stairs single file while the witnesses took their places about the scaffold. The gallows was enclosed within white muslin to ensure that no one who was not invited could view the gallows or the execution. Rice took a position two steps behind the trapdoor and Father van der Velden resumed his prayers. When he concluded Warden Arney bade Rice good-bye and the condemned man responded, "Good-bye Mr. Arney, there is no hurry; there is lots of time."

The condemned man, without prompting, took two steps forward, which centered him on the trapdoor, and a guard removed his collar. His arms were pinioned at the elbows, his legs at the knees. He was then given an opportunity to speak and his last words were, "I have that about me which will protect me; I am afraid of no harm. I don't think you are doing right to put me out of the world. There is lots of time." The noose was placed over Rice's head, cinched and positioned. The priest extended the crucifix and Rice kissed it, and then the black hood was pulled over his head. Warden Arney asked the four guards, "Are you ready," and when they answered yes he said, "Proceed!" Each pulled a lever, including three dummies, the trap was sprung, and the prisoner dropped five feet, five inches, breaking his neck. There followed a spasmodic upraising of his left hand, a twitching of the fingers, and a heaving of the breast. The prison physician monitored Rice's pulse and pronounced him dead in a few minutes, and in a few minutes more the guards lowered the body into a coffin and carried it into one of the small buildings on the prison grounds. Rice was buried in the prison cemetery at noon with eight guards as pall bearers and Father van der Velden delivering a simple service.

Idaho Daily Statesman (Boise): November 30, 1901; December 1, 1901.

Connors, James
December 16, 1904

Charles Lennon was born and raised in Massachusetts. As soon as he was old enough he left home and tramped America adopting the name James Connors, which he thereafter insisted was his true name. On September 25, 1904, Connors was in Idaho near Blackfoot when he and two other tramps decided to rob the Japanese section gang at 5:00 P.M. Connors was armed with a six-shooter when the three robbers took over one of the section houses and, after picking over the valuables on the victims' persons, they chased the railroad crew out of their quarters. Section foreman W. E. Fitzgerald watched the robbers while he sent his daughter to bring deputy sheriff E. P. Sweet. When Sweet arrived he and Fitzgerald approached the Japanese section house and Connors waved to Sweet to enter. As the deputy crossed the threshold the robber raised his pistol and, without warning or provocation, shot Sweet in the forehead. The ball entered the deputy's brain and he fell in the doorway.

Connors jumped over Sweet's body to chase Fitzgerald and the foreman, who was unarmed, ran to a second section house and locked the door. Connors fired through the door twice, broke it open, cornered Fitzgerald and shot him three times. Then, with his pistol empty, he pistol-whipped Fitzgerald into unconsciousness. Confident that Fitzgerald was dead, or soon would be, he jumped through a window and started down the tracks toward town, reloading his pistol as he walked. By then Connors was alone, as his two companions had fled after he fired the first shot, and they would never be identified.

A number of citizens armed themselves and were charging to the sound of the gunshots when they encountered Connors. The robber took cover behind a rail car as the citizens fired at him and he returned their fire. Connors continued the gunfight until deputy sheriff W. W. Kinney brought him down with a load of buckshot, and he was lodged in the Blackfoot jail with serious, but not fatal, wounds. Deputy Sweet died an hour later and Connors was charged with his murder. Fitzgerald was expected to die as well, but he surprised everyone by fully recovering. On September 28 deputy Sweet was driven to the cemetery followed by a large procession paying their respects. As the funeral procession proceeded a large number of the men began to form a plan to lynch the murderer, obtained a rope, and made a rush for the jail. However, many responsible men rushed ahead to warn the deputies and a number of them were deputized to defend the jail. The mob was held at bay until they could be dissuaded from their purpose and dispersed.

Connors was indicted by the Bingham County grand jury, tried and convicted of first degree murder, and during the trial he behaved with brazen indifference. He was delivered to the penitentiary to await his execution. His time at the prison was marked by a rebellious attitude, and he had to be disciplined by confinement in the "dark cell." The appeals process was finally completed and the application for a commutation of sentence was denied. Only during the last several days did Connors display any sign of penitence, but he refused any religious consolation. On the day before his execution the prisoner was shaved, bathed, and allowed to choose his meals. He slept well through his last night and as soon as he awakened he arose, dressed and lit his pipe. He refused breakfast and an offer of liquor, saying, "I was a pretty good fellow when I was sober. Whiskey brought me where I am and I don't want any more of it."

At 6:00 A.M. on Friday, December 16, 1904 the warden read the death warrant to Connors in his cell and with the warden leading, one guard on either side and Father Fuchs following, the procession started for the scaffold. The condemned man climbed the stairs without assistance, centered himself on the trapdoor, and stiffened his arms against his sides for the straps to be applied. While the prisoner's arms and legs were being pinioned Father Fuchs asked, "Have you anything to say, any message for your father or mother?" and Connors replied, "No sir! I have nothing to say." The large number of witnesses was disappointed that Connors never confessed nor asked for nor granted forgiveness. The noose was cinched and positioned, the black hood was pulled on and in the next instant, at 6:15 A.M., the trap was sprung. Connors broke his neck in the fall so that in ten minutes Dr. Van Note pronounced him dead. After hanging a few minutes more the body was cut down, taken directly to the prison cemetery and buried without service or prayer, as was his request.

Idaho Falls Times: September 30, 1904. *Idaho Republican* (Blackfoot): September 30, 1904. *Idaho Statesman* (Boise): December 16–17, 1904.

Bond, William H. H.
August 10, 1906

Charles Daly lived at 414 North Third Street, Boise, Idaho, with his wife Jennie. William Henry Hicks Bond, known to his friends as Fred, lived with the Dalys. Bond was born in Cornwall, England, in 1871 and three Bond brothers came to America and continued west, two settling in Butte, Montana, and William continuing on to Boise, Idaho.

Over time a relationship developed between Jennie Daly and Bond and they became intimate. On the evening of October 5, 1904, Jennie Daly and Bond were sitting in the parlor during the late evening hours discussing how they would get rid of her husband. Charles Daly came home from work, kicked off his shoes and, finding the two in that compromising situation, asked, "Jennie, do you love Fred?" and when she answered yes, her husband said, "Do you hear that Fred? Then its all over between me and my wife." Charles Daly said he was going to leave and sat down to put on his shoes when Bond shot him once. Charles Daly appeared dead so Bond and Jennie Daly began concocting and rehearsing their explanation and alibi. Three hours later Charles Daly began to show signs of life so Bond took a hatchet and struck him several blows on the head and then, just to be certain, shot him twice through the heart. When Mr. Daly failed to show up for work the next morning his absence was investigated, his body found, and Bond and Mrs. Daly were arrested on suspicion. Jennie Daly quickly confessed and turned state's evidence. As part of her deal she was convicted only of manslaughter and sentenced to serve a brief prison term.

Bond was indicted on a charge of first degree murder and at trial, based upon his lover's testimony and the physical evidence, he was found guilty, sentenced to hang, and delivered to the prison to await his execution. It took many months to dispose of the appeals and the application for commutation, but finally the date of execution was set for August 10, 1906. His attorneys, Silas W. Moody and K. I. Perky, tried one last time for a reprieve but it failed, as the plea made no showing which the court nor the jury had not fully considered. On the Thursday before his execution Bond acknowledged that all hope was lost and became despondent, but by evening he had braced up after spending a long period in his cell with Dr. I. F. Roach, his spiritual advisor.

The prisoner bathed and shaved during the afternoon, ate a hearty supper, and spent the evening talking with fellow condemned prisoner Rudolph Wetter. During the late evening hours Bond sorted through his personal effects and wrote a long letter to one of his brothers in Butte, then retired. Bond was restless until midnight, then slept but arose again at 1:00 A.M. and did not sleep again until 2:30. At 5:00 A.M. he woke again, arose and dressed. He ate a hearty breakfast and then was visited by Dr. Roach. At 6:00 A.M. Warden Whitney, accompanied by guards Rich and Ackley, prison physician Collister and Adjutant Hawke of the Salvation Army, appeared at the door of Bond's cell. The warden requested that Bond stand while the death warrant was read, and when he finished the warden offered his hand and said, "Good-bye, Fred," and Bond grasped it tightly and responded, "Good-bye warden. I want to thank you for the way you have treated me here." Turning toward the cell door he called out, "Good-bye boys, all of you." Warden Whitney asked, "Are you ready, Fred?" and Bond answered, "Yes! I am ready." As they started the procession, Rudolph Wetter, who had been reprieved during the night, called out, "Good-bye, old man."

Guards Rich and Ackley walked on either side of the condemned man but he needed no support. The warden and Dr. Roach led, Adjutant Hawke and Dr. Collister following. Once on the scaffold Bond was told where to stand and which direction to face, and he obeyed instantly, centering himself on the trapdoor facing the twenty-three witnesses. The warden asked Bond if he had anything to say, and the prisoner responded that he would die bravely, believing in God. The straps were applied, the noose positioned, cinched and adjusted. Bond then, in anticipation of the black hood, said to the small crowd, "Well, God bless you all. May the Lord have mercy on my soul." The black hood was then pulled on as the warden had his foot poised over the bolt release, but he hesitated when Bond moaned, "God! God, have mercy on my soul! Oh, God, hear my prayer! God, hear my dying words!" When he ended his entreaty, at 6:11 A.M. the trap was sprung and the condemned man fell five feet, breaking his neck. Dr. Collister recorded Bond's pulse and after six minutes pronounced him dead. The body was cut down, the straps were removed, and the body was deposited in its casket. The black hood was left in place when Bond was buried in the prison cemetery later that morning.

Idaho Statesman (Boise): August 10–11, 1906.

Seward, Fred
May 7, 1909

Clara O'Neill, a lovely twenty-year-old, moved to Moscow, Latah County, under the alias of Grace Wilson, preferring to use an alias rather than her maiden name of Reese. She had recently been divorced from her husband, Wallace, and, having to support her three-year-old invalid child, had turned to a sporting house in Palouse, Washington, for a brief period. She decided to seek a more honorable employment than prostitution and moved to Moscow, Idaho, for a fresh start. Fred Seward, a "tin horn, dinner-pail saloon swamper" who had lived off O'Neill's meager earnings in Palouse, followed her. He was particularly infatuated with O'Neill and wanted her to go to Bovil and "rustle" for him again, but O'Neill refused and this made Seward angry.

On October 12, 1908 O'Neill was on her way to Spokane to bring her daughter to Moscow, where Dr. W. H. Carithers was prepared to care for her medical needs. Seward walked with her toward the train depot and they quarreled as Seward tried one last time to convince O'Neill to be his woman. He intended to succeed or to kill her and then himself if she rejected his proposal. She again rebuffed him. As they passed the storage house, he grabbed her left arm and pulled her inside the building. He held her arm tightly as he pulled a .32-caliber Colt automatic pistol and shot her three times at close range. Two bullets were fired into her breast and the third bullet ranged through her temple, passing entirely through her skull and slightly wounding Seward in his left arm, and O'Neill died instantly. The murderer then placed the gun to his head and fired, but the bullet glanced off the skull bone so that the wound was not fatal but took out his right eye and rendered him so senseless that he could not fire again. However, being conscious, he took out his knife and cut his own throat but missed the arteries.

Seward was arrested, treated, and had sufficiently recovered in three days to appear for his examination, he was held over for the grand jury, indicted, and tried in December. His defense was that O'Neill was trying to cut his throat, but the claim of self-defense was not proven. Seward was found guilty of first degree murder, sentenced to hang on February 17, 1909, and delivered to the prison. Governor James H. Brady granted two reprieves so that the Board of Pardons could review the details of the case. They could find no justification to interfere, but appeals did not delay the proceedings.

As the days passed Seward seemed to weaken, but the Reverend Chalafant spent a great deal of time with him and he braced up. Warden Snook would not admit the curious to the prison, and of those who had some legitimate purpose he admitted only those Seward agreed to see. On the day before the execution Seward seemed anxious to get it over with and said, "I am ready to go. I have faith in the hereafter and am satisfied of my forgiveness."

The warden was determined to have a successful operation and thoroughly checked everything personally. The trapdoor was tested on Thursday and a sack of sand was suspended by the rope for an extended period to ensure it would handle the weight of the condemned man. Warden Snook did not issue invitations until the 5th and limited the number of witnesses to fifty men. The gallows had been erected in the yard one hundred feet from the door to the cells and it was veiled with canvas so that it could not be seen from the surrounding hill tops. The other prisoners were kept locked in their cells that day until the execution was over.

The condemned man slept soundly throughout his last night under the watchful eyes of guards E. P. Merritt and T. C. Gregory. He arose early and ate a light breakfast before 6:00 A.M., and then dressed in a brown checkered suit and a soft white shirt, but no vest or tie. At 7:00 A.M. the Reverend Chalafant arrived and remained in seclusion with the prisoner until Warden Snook appeared at the cell door at 8:00 A.M. He told the warden, "I will have nothing to say on the scaffold but you may say for me that while I have made a failure in life I have hope for the life to come. God has forgiven me and I have peace."

Seward stood while the warden read the two page death warrant. The warden, deputy warden Rich and guard Ackley, who were on either side, escorted Seward to the yard where he climbed the stairs unassisted. Warden Snook, the Reverend Chalafant and F. R. Shaw, representing the Seward family, awaited his arrival, and the condemned man was offered an opportunity to speak to the witnesses but only shook his head. He stood on the trapdoor while his arms and legs were pinioned, and he was asked to move slightly, and swayed as he did but kept his balance. When the deputy warden adjusted the noose Seward said, "Rich, make a good job of it." As the black hood was pulled on the reverend said a brief prayer and Seward was heard to mumble a response a moment before the trap was sprung. At 8:09 A.M. Seward dropped seven feet and Dr. George Collister, the prison physician, grabbed one wrist and Dr. J. B. Lewis, former county physician, grabbed the other. At 8:17 A.M. both doctors agreed that the prisoner was dead and Collister gave the signal. Deputy warden Rich cut the rope and guards Stone, Kramer, and Martin lowered Seward's remains into his coffin, where Dr. Collister examined the body and declared that Seward's neck had been broken in the fall. The lid was then fastened down and the coffin placed upon a low wagon used for hauling in the yard. The remains of Seward were taken directly to the prison cemetery followed by half the witnesses, where four guards lowered the coffin into the grave and the Reverend Chalafant recited a short prayer.

Star-Mirror (Moscow, ID): October 22, 1908; May 7–8, 1909.

Arnold, Noah
December 19, 1924

On May 31, Sheriff W. L. Kirkpatrick tried to arrest C. I. Moore, whose real name was Noah Arnold, at Sand Point, Idaho, on suspicion of a hotel robbery at Idaho City. Arnold resisted arrest, drew his pistol, and seriously wounded the sheriff. Arnold fled and rendezvoused with Mike Donnelly and the two career criminals went to Hope, Idaho. They needed a stake so on July 16, 1923, they entered the store of William A. Crisp, and Arnold, gun in hand, ordered the storekeeper to raise his hands. Crisp complied but Arnold was not satisfied and said, "Put up your hands or I will bore you." Once Crisp's hands were raised to Arnold's satisfaction the two robbers cleaned out the till and the safe, but then Arnold went after Crisp's watch. Crisp refused to give it up. A brief struggle followed and Arnold, who could have easily overpowered the aged storekeeper, shot Crisp twice in the abdomen and he died of the wounds.

Arnold went to Great Falls, Montana, while Donnelly went to Sand Point. Donnelly was soon arrested on suspicion of being involved in the Crisp robbery-murder and he was lodged in the Sand Point jail. He quickly wrote a letter to Arnold at Great Falls telling him of the developing situation.

Sheriff Kirkpatrick had recovered from his wounds sufficiently to travel to Great Falls and there, with the help of local lawmen, identified and arrested Arnold on August 6. Kirkpatrick brought his prisoner to Bonner County and lodged him in jail. Arnold insisted that it was Donnelly who shot Crisp and said he only stood by and watched, but soon after Arnold arrived a mob took him from his jail cell. They carried their prisoner far out into the country, put a noose around his neck, and pulled him up several times. Each time they would drop him, and when he regained consciousness they would question him, and he finally confessed to all the details, including the fact that he had shot Crisp. Arnold claimed that his true name was Robert Ford, another Noah Arnold alias, and the mob as agreed returned him to his cell to await trial.

In October Arnold and Donnelly were indicted, tried, and convicted of the murder of Crisp, but Donnelly turned state's evidence and was only sentenced to a term of life in prison. Arnold was sentenced to hang in late November 1923. An appeal was filed on November 2 which stayed the proceedings. After a year, the state Supreme Court affirmed the lower court's judgment and sentence. Judge W. F. McNaughton sentenced the prisoner to hang on December 19, 1924. A campaign then began to have the Board of Pardons and Governor C. C. Moore consider a commutation of sentence, and the Reverend G. W. Williams of the African Methodist Church of Boise made the presentation on December 2. The board declined to intervene and preparations for the execution proceeded.

The execution was scheduled for minutes after midnight and Arnold spent his last day in good spirits, fully resigned to his fate through the efforts of the Reverend Williams. The reverend prayed with the condemned man until Warden J. W. Wheeler arrived at the cell door and read the death warrant. The warden then retired to the scaffold to await the prisoner, who was escorted from his cell by the Reverend Williams and one guard. The prisoner ascended the stairs alone and said to the fifty witnesses, "I am not guilty of the murder of W. A. Crisp, but I am willing to pay the penalty." He was then quickly prepared with his wrists and arms, knees and ankles bound, the noose adjusted, and the black hood pulled over his head.

At 12:18 A.M. the prisoner was moved onto the trapdoor, where his weight activated the automatic trigger. Water flowed from an upper bucket into a lower bucket and when the weight of the upper bucket was decreased to a certain weight, which took ninety seconds, the trap was sprung. Arnold dropped and broke his neck in the fall and prison physician Dr. George Collister pronounced him dead in nine minutes. The body hung long enough to ensure he would not revive and was then cut down and deposited in the coffin provided by the state, and buried in the prison cemetery that morning. After Arnold's remains were in the grave a guard disclosed that during the day before his execution Arnold had admitted murdering five people, but still denied killing Crisp.

Idaho State Journal (Pocatello): December 2, 1974. *Billings Gazette* (MT): December 30, 1924. *Helena Daily Independent* (MT): August 7, 1923; December 21, 1924. *Ogden Standard Examiner* (UT): November 2, 1923; December 4, 1924; December 19, 1924; February 9, 1936.

Jurko, John
July 9, 1926

On June 25, 1924, seventy-year-old A.B.W. Vandermark repossessed the Cozy Billiard Parlor in Twin Falls, Idaho, and that evening he invited John Barber, E. W. Richard and A. E. Dickson to play cards at his new establishment. At 10:00 P.M. forty-year-old John Jurko, a Twin Falls barber, entered the parlor with his wife and immediately began arguing with Vandermark. The two men had been engaged in a partnership in the billiard parlor since February but in May, Vandermark dissolved the partnership and began legal proceedings to take sole ownership. However, the argument was not over a partnership gone bad nor over the repossession of the billiard parlor, but was over some remark that Vandermark was supposed to have made regarding Mrs. Jurko. Vandermark had, according to Jurko, told his wife that she was too good for her husband and that she should leave him, and she had just told her husband of the remark that morning.

Vandermark arose from his chair and stood by it, cards in hand, as he denied making the remark and ordered Jurko to leave. Jurko suddenly drew his six shot .32-caliber automatic pistol and fired all six rounds, six bullets striking Vandermark's body and five exiting, and he bled to death in minutes. Mrs. Jurko fled when the first shot was fired and it would take days to find her. Immediately after the shooting, and without waiting to see Vandermark's condition, Jurko started for the sheriff's office to surrender but along the way he met Chief of Police P. C. Herriman and surrendered to him, and handed over his empty pistol.

Jurko was lodged in jail while Coroner Dr. P. J. Grossman summoned a jury and held an inquest, and the coroner's jury found that Jurko had killed Vandermark. He was charged with murder and at his examination he was held over for action by the grand jury. In early September Jurko was indicted and his trial began in Judge W. A. Babcock's courtroom on September 18. After three days of testimony and six hours of deliberations the defendant was convicted of first degree murder. Two days later Judge Babcock sentenced him to hang on November 14. The motion for a new trial was denied. He was delivered to the state prison at Boise to await his execution. However, an appeal was filed with the state Supreme Court which stayed the judgment. The aggressive appeals process continued until March 1926, when the Supreme Court affirmed the lower court's decision. In May, Judge Babcock resentenced Jurko to hang on July 9, 1926. Jurko's last hope was an application for executive clemency filed with the Board of Pardons, which met on July 7, but they refused to interfere.

Jurko, during his final days, resigned himself to his fate with the help of the Reverends C. E. Burgess and A. C. Tunnell, and they were with him that final night. As the minutes ticked away Jurko received the local newspaper reporters and said, "Tell the people never try to take a person's life. This crime I did was pushed on me. This man broke my heart; I lost my head, and killed him. For this I must die. I want to thank Twin Falls friends for their efforts to save my life and also the prison officials for the treatment given me here." After the reporters left the Reverends held their final prayer service in Jurko's cell and when they concluded Warden J. W. Wheeler asked if he desired to have the death warrant read, and Jurko replied, "Suit yourself, go ahead and read it." When the warden concluded Jurko said, "No mercy, no justice! But I forgive everyone."

After the warden had gone to the scaffold the procession formed, with a reverend on each arm of the condemned man, and at five minutes past midnight they escorted him to the foot of the stairs and then retired. Jurko ascended alone and was met by the warden and two guards and was asked if he wanted to speak to the fifty witnesses. He stepped to the railing and said, "I am no criminal. I ask the Lord to give me a better justice in the next world." Jurko's wrists and arms, knees and ankles were then pinioned, the black hood was pulled over his head, and the noose was adjusted. At 12:13 A.M. he was guided onto the trapdoor where his weight activated the automatic trigger, and for the next ninety seconds water could be heard trickling from an upper bucket into the lower one until the trap was sprung. As soon as the body appeared two guards stepped forward to steady it, and then prison physician Dr. George Collister began monitoring his vital signs. Jurko was pronounced dead at 12:25 A.M. and then the body was cut down and deposited in its coffin.

Ogden Standard Examiner (UT): June 26, 1924; November 8, 1924; April 22, 1925; July 9, 1926. *Salt Lake Tribune* (UT): May 15, 1926.

Powell, Troy; Walrath, Ernest
April 13, 1951

On Monday evening, May 8, 1950, sixty-five-year-old Newton Wilson was in his quarters at the rear of his Boise grocery store. Before Wilson retired twenty-year-old Troy Powell and nineteen-year-old Ernest Walrath broke in and snuck up behind Wilson. Walrath struck Wilson over the head with his pistol, knocking him senseless, and then Powell struck him numerous times with a slungshot, a sock filled with rocks. Wilson was unconscious, lying on the floor face down, when Walrath pulled a butcher knife with a ten inch blade and stabbed him in the back seven times, leaving the blade imbedded with the final thrust. Wilson never regained consciousness and bled to death where he lay. The two robbers then ransacked the store and living quarters but were only able to find $12 in Wilson's pockets. They fled and changed their clothes before calling Barbara Cooter, and the three drove to the river while singing popular songs along the way as if on a holiday adventure.

Once at the river the two men threw their bloody clothes into the water and then returned to Boise. In the morning a clerk, who was unable to gain entry and suspected something was amiss, called the police, who forced entry and found the dead body of Wilson. About the time the body was being discovered, Cooter, who characterized herself as an "unwilling witness," called the police and told them of the murder and that they could find Walrath at the service station where he worked part-time and they could find Powell at his parents' home. The two men were arrested and as soon as they were behind bars they both confessed, but Justice of the Peace J. M. Lampert postponed their arraignment to May 18 at the request of the defense attorneys. When the defendants appeared in court they pled guilty again and sentencing was set for June 16 in Judge C. E. Winstead's Boise courtroom. Judge Winstead sentenced the men to hang at the Idaho State Penitentiary on August 2. An appeal based on the trial record and sentence stayed the execution for nearly a year, but finally the state Supreme Court affirmed the judgment and sentence of the lower court and the two murderers were sentenced to hang on April 13, 1951.

During their final days both condemned men turned to religion, but up to their final hours they kept hoping for some relief from the courts or the governor. When they were informed that there would be no respite or reprieve they spent their time with their clergymen, Powell with the Reverend Martin Sumner, Jr., and Walrath with the Reverend Hartzell Cobb. The two reverends had just completed their final prayer session when Warden L. E. Clapp appeared at Walrath's cell door minutes before midnight. The warden read the death warrant and then Walrath was escorted sixty feet into the execution chamber, with the Reverend Sumner holding his arm, and he climbed the stairs onto the temporary gallows. He had been offered a sedative earlier but only pointed to his Bible and said, "The only medicine is there."

He was positioned on the trapdoor and prepared by Ada County Coroner Clyde Summer and his assistants. Walrath's wrists and arms, knees and ankles were strapped securely, the noose was adjusted, and when the black hood was brought out he said, "Lord Jesus, receive my spirit." The black hood was pulled over his head at 12:11 A.M. and the trap was immediately sprung. Walrath dropped, breaking his neck in the fall, and the three physicians in attendance pronounced him dead at 12:22 A.M.

While the body was being cut down, deposited in a coffin and the straps removed, Warden Clapp went to Powell's cell and read the death warrant. While they waited for everything to be readied Powell said, "I am going like a man and when I go I know beyond a shadow of a doubt that God is with me. I am happy to know that in a few minutes I will be entering the Kingdom of Heaven. There is no blood on my hands." He was then conducted into the execution chamber, where the same process was completed. When the black hood was produced Powell said, "I know I'm right with God." The cap was pulled over his head at 12:40, the trap was sprung, and ten minutes later the three physicians pronounced him dead. His body was cut down, placed in a coffin, and removed from the execution chamber. Later that day the families of both deceased murderers called at the prison and removed the remains to local undertaking parlors.

Idaho State Journal (Pocatello): May 11, 1950. *Independent Record* (Helena, MT): April 13, 1951. *Ogden Standard-Examiner* (UT): April 13, 1951. *Post-Register* (Idaho Falls, ID): June 16, 1950. *Salt Lake Tribune* (UT): May 10, 1950; April 13, 1951.

Snowden, Raymond A.
October 18, 1957

On Saturday evening, September 22, 1956 Cora Lucyle Dean, a forty-eight-year-old divorcee, drove into Garden City, Ada County, Idaho, and went to the Hi-Ho Club where she met thirty-five-year-old Raymond A. Snowden. The couple seemed to have much in common, so after an evening of drinking and chatting they left together shortly after midnight. The couple walked a short distance to an isolated spot in the driveway of a paint factory, where Snowden made sexual suggestions to Dean. When she rejected his advances he became violent, loud and threatening and pulled from his pocket a knife with two blades, opened the longer blade and said, "take your pick, Honey, rape or death." When Dean continued to resist and kicked Snowden, he cut her throat from ear to ear and, as she bled to death, he carefully inserted the blade at the back of her neck, probed for her spinal cord, and severed it. He then inflicted twenty-seven more wounds to her dead body, some as he cut away portions of flesh and ate it.

On Sunday morning a twelve-year-old boy was pedaling his bicycle between the Garden City buildings collecting bottles for their deposit, and he discovered the mutilated body. The authorities were called and Detective Frank Boor, upon learning of the wound to the spinal column, recalled an incident from months earlier where a man had threatened to cut the spinal cord of his ex-girlfriend. He tracked down the man and arrested Snowden on Monday, September 24. The prisoner was questioned closely by officers for eight hours and that evening he broke down and confessed to the killing, but said it was hazy and all he could remember clearly was eating Dean's flesh. He recalled taking some items of her blood soaked clothes but said he threw them into a trash barrel, and the clothes were never found. He said he then went to downtown Boise and threw the knife into a sewer, so a search was begun for the murder weapon and early Friday morning it was found. Patrons at the Hi-Ho Club were questioned and they positively identified Snowden as the man who left the club with Dean.

The prisoner was charged with murdering Dean and at his arraignment on October 5 he pled not guilty, but two weeks later on advice of his newly appointed attorney he changed the plea to guilty. On October 26 Snowden was sentenced by Judge M. Oliver Koelsch to hang on December 7, 1956. The judge said the crime "was utterly devoid of any extenuating and mitigating circumstances." Even though the defendant had pled guilty his attorney filed an appeal, which stayed the execution, and over the next year the case was argued on several grounds, including insanity and trial error. On October 24, 1956, Dr. Dale Cornell, a psychiatrist, testified that Snowden was sane but his attorney proposed that Snowden had acted upon an uncontrollable impulse and therefore could not premeditate a murder, a requirement for a conviction in the first degree, so Snowden should be guilty of second degree murder at most. The prosecuting attorney, Blaine Evans, countered that the killing "involved skillful mutilation and a well planned attack which meant that Snowden did to this woman exactly what he wanted." The claim of insanity, the attorney's primary strategy, was dismissed. The appeal on trial error was heard on July 24, 1957; the state Supreme Court denied the appeal, and on September 9, 1957, Judge Koelsch sentenced Snowden to hang on October 18.

As the final day approached Snowden resigned himself to his fate. On Thursday he was served his last supper, a broiled lobster, and then he spent his final hours in religious conversation with prison chaplain Orville Stiles. Warden L. E. Clapp arrived at the cell door before midnight and read the death warrant, and then the prisoner was escorted sixty feet from his cell into the death chamber. The warden asked the condemned man if he had anything further to say and Snowden told the small group of witnesses, "I can't put into words what I want to say." His wrists and arms, knees and ankles were then strapped, the noose was adjusted, the black hood was pulled over his head, and he was moved onto the trapdoor at 12:05 A.M., where his body weight activated the automatic trigger. Water from an upper bucket trickled into a lower bucket and in forty-eight seconds, when the upper bucket was decreased to a certain weight, the trap was sprung. The body dropped and three physicians, including the prison's doctor and two consulting physicians, monitored vital signs and pronounced Snowden dead at 12:20 A.M. The body was then cut down, examined and it was determined his neck had been broken in the fall. His remains were then put into the coffin provided by the state. The warden had wired relatives to make a claim for the body, if they desired, but they declined. On Saturday Snowden's body was buried in the prison cemetery after a brief service by the Reverend Stiles, with two state officials as witnesses and six convicts acting as pall bearers, the only people in attendance.

Idaho State Journal (Pocatello): September 25, 1956; October 24, 1956; October 17–18, 1957. *Post-Register* (Idaho Falls, ID): September 28, 1956; October 1, 1956; April 15, 1957; September 9, 1957; October 10, 1957; October 21, 1957.

Wells, Keith E.
January 6, 1994

On December 20, 1990, twenty-seven-year-old Keith Eugene Wells was on parole for armed robbery. That evening he went to the Rose Pub in Boise, Idaho, taking along a baseball bat (later he described himself as "a predator on the prowl for prey"). He leaned the bat against the bar and leisurely drank a few beers. Twenty-three-year-old John Justad, another patron, went to the bathroom and in a few moments Wells picked up the bat and followed. Wells waited outside the bathroom and when Justad came out Wells bashed in his skull, killing him. The barmaid, twenty-year-old Brandis Rains, heard the commotion and went to investigate and Wells then crushed her skull, killing her as well. Wells, when arrested, said, "It was time for them to die."

He was tried in April 1992, convicted of first degree murder, and sentenced to die by lethal injection. He declined to have an appeal filed, but an appeal was filed with the U.S. Supreme Court on his behalf. In the winter of 1993 he asked that the appeal be dropped and the Supreme Court voted seven to two to reject the appeal, and Wells was sentenced to die at Idaho's Maximum Security Institution on January 6, 1994. A last minute effort to save his life, filed against his wishes, was a motion questioning his mental competency which was submitted to a federal judge, but the motion was rejected hours before the execution.

Wells refused to make a statement on his final day but was allowed to telephone a news anchorwoman. He asked her to tell the victims' relatives that he was sorry. At a late hour he was marched into the execution chamber and he lay down on a gurney. He was strapped down and a combination of three drugs was administered by a doctor: sodium thiopental to induce sleep; pancuronium bromide to restrict respiration, which in time would cause death by asphyxiation; and potassium chloride, which quickly stopped the heart. While the execution was taking place the prisoners staged a protest by screaming, stomping their feet, and beating upon the bars of their cells. After Wells was pronounced dead his body was deposited into a coffin and he was buried the following day.

Pharos-Tribune (Logansport, IN): January 6, 1994. *Progress* (Clearfield, PA): January 6, 1994.

MONTANA

Eastern Montana, comprising about 80 percent of the state, was acquired by the United States as part of the Louisiana Purchase in 1803. The first Europeans to enter Montana were Meriwether Lewis and William Clark in 1805, and two years later the first fur trading post was established, though the first white settlement was not founded until 1841. The eastern portion of Montana became part of Missouri in 1812, Nebraska in 1854, and the

Dakotas in 1861. Western Montana, comprising 20 percent of the state, was acquired along with the Oregon Country in 1846; and it became the eastern portion of Washington Territory in March 1853, then became the eastern part of Idaho when that territory was formed; and finally was united with eastern Montana when the Montana Territory was organized in 1864. Montana was admitted as the 41st state on November 8, 1889.

King, Thomas
June 6, 1890

Thomas King worked in the mines of Colorado for a number of years before moving to Montana, where he worked at Granite for a short period before moving to Elkhorn during the latter part of 1889. On the evening of November 28, 1889, King and his friend George Peters went to a ball given under the direction of Matthew Fogerty. The men seemed to invite a row and persisted in waltzing together to the embarrassment of all present. Fogerty objected and finally stopped them after some heated words were exchanged. Shortly after 3:00 A.M. King and another man danced together and when Fogerty tried to stop them, Peters rushed in to take a hand. However, before a fight could begin King stepped back and put his hand on his revolver, but did not draw it. This had the effect of breaking up the dance and all but a few men went home.

After the second-floor hall was cleared, Fogerty and a man named Connors started for Ecklund and Colberg's Saloon across the street, but found King and Peters waiting at the foot of the stairs. Peters wanted to fight but Fogerty told him he would see him later. King and Peters followed the two men to the saloon and Peters again tried to instigate a quarrel, so Fogerty and Connors left for Lloyd's Saloon. King and Peters followed in a few minutes and at the bar Peters pulled off his coat and announced, "You are no man, but I am." A friend of Fogerty's rushed at Peters but was thrown to the floor, and then Fogerty and Peters fought. They worked their way across the saloon and out into the street, Fogerty getting the better of Peters as the fight progressed. Once outside Peters ran down the street to get away from Fogerty and avoid a thrashing. Fogerty followed with King close behind, but Fogerty lost his footing on the snow and, in trying to keep his balance, spun around and found himself facing King. King pulled his Smith and Wesson six-shooter and, without hesitation or warning, shot Fogerty. The bullet took effect in Fogerty's side and he died in a few minutes.

King and Peters then went to their cabin on the edge of town where they were soon discovered and arrested. King and Peters were indicted by the Boulder County grand jury on January 14, 1890. George D. Greene was appointed counsel for King, and his trial began two weeks later. The defendant claimed that he had been struck over the right eye a moment before the killing and he did not see who hit him, but he was stunned and did not intend to shoot when he drew his pistol. He testified that he intended to club Fogerty but the pistol discharged accidentally. The jurors rejected the defense and on January 30 they returned a verdict of guilty of murder in the first degree. A motion for a new trial was denied and Judge Galbraith sentenced King to hang on March 27, 1890. An appeal to the Supreme Court stayed the execution until May 2, when the lower court's judgment and sentence was affirmed, and then Acting Governor John E. Rickards granted a respite until June 6 so that Governor Joseph K. Toole could review the case. Attorney Greene petitioned for a commutation of the sentence but the governor denied the petition and found no cause to interfere.

During King's time in jail he became acquainted with Maggie Devere, who was serving a sentence for helping another woman escape. They became friends before she was released on a court order on June 3 and she returned the next day to visit King, and tried to slip a small folded paper into his hand. The bindle was seized by the guard and found to contain six and one half grains of morphine, more than enough to kill him, and the next day Sheriff Halford found in King's cell a spoon with the handle sharpened to a razor's edge, so his death watch was increased to a twenty-four hour guard at his cell door. The prisoner spent his last days smoking constantly and chatting with Frank Perry, his death watch guard. He sent a telegram to Father Palladino of Helena asking him to join Father Follett, his religious advisor for the past several weeks. King carefully prepared his statement of three pages, attorney Greene writing it out for the illiterate prisoner, and then Greene agreed to read the statement on the scaffold.

At midnight Sheriff Halford and a reporter from the *Independent* visited and remained until 2:00 A.M. and the sheriff related how George Bryson, the wife murderer hanged on August 9, 1899, had bravely met his fate, and King showed intense interest in the anecdote. It was observed that once death became a certainty it eased the terrible suspense and made the long confinement more bearable, and King conceded that was true in his case. When advised to go to the gallows like a man he replied, "I will do the best I can." King could not sleep his last night and it was daybreak before he laid down, fully dressed, for a few hours' rest. King's breakfast was served early but he had no appetite and could not even drink his coffee. He entertained a reporter and a few visitors and during the intervals chatted continuously with his guards.

The three quarter inch cotton rope had been carefully stretched over several days and that last morning deputies oiled the rope to ensure it would slide easily and cinch tightly. A crowd of men and boys gathered about the jail at an early hour and nearly one hundred spectators had found cracks in the rough board fence through which they had a perfect view of the gallows. Only forty persons were allowed inside the enclosure and at 10:30 A.M. the invited witnesses were still arriving by train. Father Follett was among them and he went directly to King's cell and administered the last sacrament of the church, and King made his confession, which seemed to brace up the condemned man. At 11:00 A.M. Sheriff Halford appeared at the cell door and read the death warrant and history of the respites. When the reading concluded King, who had been staring at the floor, raised his eyes and said, "I am prepared to meet my God." His statement was then read by Attorney Greene. In it he said he was guilty of the act but not the intention. When Attorney Greene finished reading King drank a cup of whiskey.

There was a delay while the last preparations were completed in the yard. The prisoner used the time to shake hands with all present, the last being the Chinese cook who ran up the stairs to say farewell to his friend. The undersheriff handed King a boutonniere of germana leaves and blossoms, which he put in the buttonhole of his coat. At 11:06 A.M. the sheriff, who had gone to the jail yard, returned to announce that all was in readiness and the procession began. The sheriff led, King behind with a deputy on each arm, and last came Father Follett and Attorney Greene. When King first saw the gallows he hesitated for a moment, then continued onto the platform and stood under the noose. The sheriff and undersheriff pinioned his arms and legs as Father Follett stood at his shoulder whispering words of religious support and encouragement, and then the noose was adjusted and the black hood was pulled on.

King clenched his fists as the priest murmured a prayer and Sheriff Halford pulled the string that signaled the executioner inside his canvas enclosure. An axe severed the rope restraining the two hundred fifty pound weight of tin and it dropped at 11:16 A.M., jerking the condemned man three and one half feet into the air. Drs. Fletcher of Boulder, Reddell of Elkhorn, and the coroner of Jefferson County monitored his pulse until it ceased in nine minutes, and six minutes later King was pronounced dead. The way was then cleared for John Borkin, the photographer, to set up his equipment and after a photograph was taken, twenty minutes after the drop, the body was cut down. The noose had cinched so tightly around King's neck that it had to be cut off before the doctors examined the body and determined that the condemned man's neck had not been broken, but that the spinal cord had been severed. King's body was turned over to undertaker J. R. Paradise, who prepared it for burial. King was laid to rest in the Catholic cemetery shortly before 1:00 P.M.

Independent (Helena, MT): June 5–7, 1890.

Antley; La-la-see; Pascale; Pierre Paul
December 19, 1890

In the fall of 1887 a party of six Kootenai Indians started from Pleasant Valley to go to the Tobacco Plains to attend a dance given by their tribe. The party included Antley, Antoine, John Annon, Kocaia, Jerome, and Dominic, "all young bucks fired with the spirit of their ancestors." After the first day of dancing the six men camped near Wolf Creek for the night. They soon discovered there was a party of three white prospectors — named McDonald, Seeley, and Thompson — camped nearby. No sooner had the prospectors been discovered than one of the Indians proposed that they kill the whites. John Annon, Jerome and Antley crept to within a few paces when Annon raised his rifle and fired twice, killing two prospectors, and when the third prospector fled he was pursued by Antley and brutally murdered.

Word of the murders spread quickly among the mining camps and the miners of Demersville organized a posse. They quickly captured Jerome and John Annon, who were promptly hanged from the nearest tree without the benefit of a trial. The other fugitives managed to elude capture until the late summer of 1890 when a determined sheriff's posse tracked down and captured the remaining four Indians, with help from Kootenai chief Eneas, known among the whites as "Big Knife." After the four were in jail they were questioned and it was found that Antoine, Kocaia and Dominic had counseled against the evil act, but Antley confessed his part in killing the third miner. Antley was tried at the fall term in Judge Marshall's court at Missoula. After only ten minutes of deliberation the jurors convicted him of first degree murder. He was sentenced to hang on December 19, 1890, and nothing would delay the proceedings.

On September 1, 1887 La-la-see and Pierre Paul, two Kootenai Indians, after a day of hunting spent the night with three other Indians at La-la-see's teepee on the Flathead reservation in Montana. In the morning La-la-see, as he was watering their horses, saw two white prospectors stop nearby and build a fire to cook their breakfast. La-la-see hurried back to the teepee and suggested, "Let's go out and kill them." They formed a plan and one of the Indians approached the prospectors as they were seated about their campfire finishing their meal. The Indian asked where they were going and the two men said Missoula. They soon started off and as soon as they turned their backs La-la-see shot one man and Pierre Paul shot the other, the rifle bullets tearing through their bodies and killing them instantly. The two murderers weighted the bodies with rocks and threw them into the Rock River. The bodies were found by a woman who was threatened by the murderers if she should reveal the crime and perpetrators, but in the summer of 1888 she notified the authorities and the other three natives agreed to testify about what they had seen.

The two fugitives were sought for several years and were finally arrested in the summer of 1890 with the help of Kootenai chief Eneas. La-la-see and Pierre Paul were tried in Judge Marshall's Missoula courtroom at the fall term and on Saturday, November 8, they were convicted of first degree murder and sentenced to hang on December 19, 1890. Neither appeal nor application for clemency would delay the proceedings.

In the spring of 1889 an Indian named Pascale and a prospector named J. M. Dunn traded horses and Pascale later demanded that they trade back, but Dunn refused. Pascale then rode along with Dunn until they reached Angel Hill, where he fell behind and shot Dunn in the back, took both horses, Dunn's outfit, and all the money Dunn had about him. He hid Dunn's body in the brush and fled with his plunder.

It was not until one year later that Dunn's remains were discovered by Antoine Finley, a member of the Pend d'Oreille tribe, and the body was identified by remnants of clothing found with the skeleton. Pascale was suspected so Finley went to the Kootenai Indian camp and told Pascale of finding the remains, and the Indian immediately boasted that he had killed Dunn, saying, "I killed him just like I would a grasshopper." Finley told the authorities and Pascale was arrested by Sheriff Harton and, though the Indian murderer readily admitted his crime, he then claimed the killing was in self-defense. Pascale was tried at the fall term of Judge Marshall's court, convicted of first degree murder, and sentenced to hang on December 19, 1890. Neither appeal nor petition for executive clemency delayed the execution.

During their last day the condemned men were visited by a priest, but Antley and Pascale refused to listen to his prayers or pleadings while La-la-see and Pierre Paul listened intently. On their final night the condemned still had hope of clemency but finally word came that they would not be saved and they became morose and sullen. They awoke that final morning in a better spirit, until their black suits were delivered to their cell. Antley weakened as he dressed in his burial clothes and he was quickly revived with stimulants, but the others held up well.

The gallows had been built within an enclosure of high board fencing and two hundred witnesses were assembled inside by 10:00 A.M. when the four condemned men were escorted from the jail onto the scaffold. They were aligned on the single trapdoor beneath the nooses and each, in turn, had his wrists and arms, knees and ankles bound, the noose adjusted and a black hood pulled over his head. At 10:44 A.M. Sheriff Harton sprang the trap and the last of the four was pronounced dead in twenty minutes, and the bodies were cut down three minutes later. The bodies were given to Chief Joseph, who planned to take the remains to St. Ignatius for burial.

Inter Mountain (Butte, MT): December 19, 1890. *Standard* (Ogden, UT): December 20, 1890. *Xenia Daily Gazette and Torchlite* (OH): December 20, 1890.

Burns, John
December 16, 1892

Early on Saturday, August 13, 1892, two tramps arrived in Missoula on an eastbound train. John Burns and a man who called himself Lyons, but whose real name was Gannon, spent nearly all their time at the gaming tables and by evening of the following day they had lost nearly all their money. Burns tried to pawn a watch at one of the prominent saloons but was turned away. Sometime shortly after midnight, while a fire raged in town, Lyons tried to sell a valuable ring to Paul Goldenbogen, but he thought the ring might have been stolen so he had Lyons arrested. At 4:00 A.M. Goldenbogen was standing in front of the Exchange Saloon when John Burns approached and asked why he had informed on Lyons. As Goldenbogen was answering Burns pulled a pistol and shot him, the bullet striking Goldenbogen in the right side. The wounded man reeled towards the front of the sidewalk where Maurice Higgins, Frank Smith and Tom Black were standing. The three men turned at the sound of the shot and, as they looked at Burns, he fired again. The second bullet struck Higgins a little to one side of the center of his forehead and Higgins fell on his face on the sidewalk. Goldenbogen exclaimed, "I am shot, too!" and fell across Higgins' body.

Burns, after firing the second shot, ran eastward with Black in close pursuit, but the tramp held up his pistol and threatened Black, who was unarmed, so he had to let Burns escape. However, he watched Burns run to the corner of the Hammond block and turn toward the bridge. Sheriff William Houston quickly arrived on the scene and took up the chase at Black's direction. When the sheriff reached the bridge he saw Burns at the other end, but when he got to the other side of the river he lost sight of the fugitive. He searched but could find no sign of Burns, so he started back to town.

When he got to the bridge he saw Burns, this time crossing back into town, and he again pursued the murderer. At the center of the north span he saw Burns passing the Hammond block. Once across the bridge he saw the fugitive, still some distance away, enter the Concordia Saloon but immediately exit. Black joined the sheriff and identified the man being chased as the shooter. They followed Burns around the corner onto Main Street, caught up with him two doors west of the *Missoulian* newspaper office, and arrested him. He had no gun on his person and it was never found, so it was supposed he had thrown it in the river.

Maurice Higgins, brother of Missoula's Mayor Frank G. Higgins, was just a boy but he was a member of the town's fire department. On the evening of August 14 a terrible fire had started at the rear of the Blue Front Saloon on Front Street. Before the flames were extinguished the conflagration had consumed the Rogers Hotel, the Hawkes Stable, and a dozen other buildings. Higgins had been on the front line fighting the fire and afterward joined two fellow firemen to discuss their success in stopping the further spread of flames, and that was the only reason young Higgins was standing in front of the Exchange Saloon at that early hour.

After being shot Higgins was taken to the family residence where two surgeons carefully cut into his skull to extract the bullet, but could not find it. The doctors claimed that the wound would have been immediately fatal to most men, but young Higgins had a strength and vitality that sustained him for eight hours, and he died at noon. Goldenbogen was taken to Sister's Hospital where he had recovered sufficiently by 11:30 A.M. to have a short visit. Sheriff Houston brought Burns to the hospital and the wounded man positively identified him as the one who shot him and Higgins. Burns fainted when brought face-to-face with his victim. By the time Burns was returned to his cell Maurice Higgins was dead, and he was charged with his murder. Burns was indicted and arraigned, and trial was set for September 12 for jury selection, with testimony beginning two days later. The defendant was positively identified by Sheriff Houston and by Charles Moore, the night bartender at the Headquarters Saloon, as well as by Smith and Black. Goldenbogen was brought in on a stretcher and he identified the defendant as the man who had shot him and murdered Higgins. Burns' defense was that they had arrested the wrong man and his partner was a man named Haywick, not Lyons, so he had no motive for the shooting. He said that he and Haywick had been watching the fire during the early hours of the conflagration but then went to a house of ill fame and had just left when they heard two shots fired some distance away. Lyons was brought in and testified that his partner was named Brown, not Burns, and that it was Brown who had shot Higgins. However, the mysterious Brown and Haywick were conspicuously absent in court, as were the sporting ladies Burns claimed to have been with during the murder. The case went to the jury during the afternoon hours of September 16 and by 10:00 P.M. they had found Burns guilty of first degree murder.

On September 20 the judge sentenced Burns to hang on November 11, 1892. On October 5 Burns' attorney filed a motion for a new trial based upon an error and it was sustained on October 12. Burns' second trial began on October 17 and lasted ten days, a much longer trial, though the evidence was substantially the same. The jury retired after 4:00 P.M. on October 27 and at 5:05 P.M. on October 28 Burns was again found guilty of first degree murder. The judge, on November 5, sentenced Burns to hang on December 16, 1892. Neither appeal nor application for executive clemency delayed the proceedings.

The trapdoor gallows was assembled well in advance of the date, the same gallows used to hang four Indians two years earlier, and the hangman's rope was the same used to hang

Pierre Paul. The drop was set at seven feet and this entire contraption was built within an enclosure, and on the eastern side was a door which connected, through an enclosed passageway, to the east door of the jail. When Burns was first convicted he found a packet of morphine left by the previous occupant of his cell and considered taking a lethal dose but lost his nerve. As the day of his execution approached his thoughts turned to escape, and he had one of his many visitors pass him a fine toothed saw and a packet of a sleeping drug. A close watch had been placed on Burns after his first conviction and it was kept up, Al Weinrich during the day and "Old Man" Nobles at night. It was the habit of Nobles to eat supper at midnight and wash it down with a glass of water from a pitcher which stood on a stand in the room.

On Tuesday, December 13, shortly after eating his supper, Nobles began to feel unusually drowsy. He fought off the sleepiness as long as he could but finally dozed off. Burns then started sawing at the cell door but Sheriff Houston, a very light sleeper, awoke at the slight but peculiar noise and came from his quarters to investigate. Burns heard the sheriff coming and hid the saw blade but kept the handle to make it seem as if he had thrown the blade out the window. Burns was taken to a regular cell at the front of the jail and guarded by another deputy until Weinrich came on duty at his regular hour.

Burns had been angry with the sheriff and one of his deputies but said he no longer held a grudge over their part in his conviction, and told a deputy, "You can't blame me for trying to escape. It was a matter of life and death with me and, of course, I would take all chances to escape." Nobles was very sick the following morning and vomited freely from the drug. After the substitute death watch guard was relieved by Weinrich, he returned to search Burns' room and found the nine inch saw blade, with teeth on both edges, hidden in the broom, and Nobles was replaced on death watch duty. On Burns' final full day he was shaved by barber Simpson at 7:00 P.M. and at 10:00 P.M. all the prisoners were locked in their cells and were soon asleep, indifferent to the fate of Burns.

Burns had sent for Mayor Higgins, and the brother of the murdered boy expected a confession or at least a plea for forgiveness, but by the time he arrived Burns had changed his mind and would say nothing. Burns had previously threatened that a person, whose identity he would not divulge, would avenge his death on the mayor; he told the mayor he did not want revenge and would try to have it stopped. Burns would eat nothing at 10:30 P.M. and at midnight refused to sleep. At 1:00 A.M. he again refused to eat but half an hour later requested whiskey, which was denied. From 2:00 to 3:30 A.M. the prisoner talked incessantly but said little of importance, then laid down and in half an hour was asleep.

He awoke at 6:00 A.M. and ate several oranges, which gave him an appetite, so he ate a hearty breakfast soon afterward. At 9:00 A.M. the *Missoulian* reporter returned and within minutes was joined by a priest who had been Burns' religious advisor for weeks. The priest administered communion and conferred the acts of contrition and faith, hope, and charity. At 9:30 A.M. Al Weinrich gave Burns a drink of whiskey and the prisoner requested to walk to the scaffold with a cigar in his teeth.

The fatal hour had finally arrived and Burns was marched to the gallows, assisted by the priest. Once on the platform he turned to the small crowd and said, "Well, boys, I bid you farewell." The sheriff slipped the noose over his head and adjusted it under the left ear, and next the straps were quickly applied to his arms and legs. The priest, to distract him, talked to him during the entire time he was being prepared. Sheriff Houston asked, "Jack, is there anything more you wish to say?" and Burns replied loudly, "No, let her go!" He then said in a low tone, "Make a good job of it, Bill." The black hood was quickly pulled over Burns' head and the attendants retired from the platform, the sheriff being the last.

When the sheriff stepped down the first step he hesitated for a moment and gave a short kick, there was a rattle as the trigger was pulled and the trap was sprung. The condemned man broke his neck in the fall but there were two slight heaves of his chest before the body hung motionless. After hanging a sufficient time to ensure death, Burns' remains were cut down and placed in the coffin provided by the county. The body was taken to Flynn's undertaking parlor and the following day at 2:00 P.M. he was buried in the Catholic cemetery.

Missoulian (MT): December 21, 1892.

Anderson, Robert A. July 13, 1894

Emanuel Fleming lived alone in a cabin on the outskirts of Livingston in Park County and was known to carry a few dollars at all times. About April 5, 1894, twenty-eight-year-old Robert A. Anderson, alias Bob Fields, and his sixteen-year-old partner, William Mortimer, went to Fleming's cabin intending to rob and murder him. They were scared off so they postponed their plan for two weeks. On the night of April 19, Anderson and Mortimer broke into Fleming's cabin while he was away. Mortimer, armed with a double-bit axe, hid behind the door while Anderson sat on the bed with his revolver at the ready.

When Fleming entered the dark cabin at 9:00 P.M. he sensed the presence of someone and called out, "Who is there?" Mortimer immediately struck him on the head with the axe, but the glancing blow was not sufficient to knock him down, so Fleming turned and ran out of the cabin, crying for help. Anderson followed as far as the door and shot Fleming four times, one bullet ranging through his bowels inflicting a fatal wound. Several residents in that part of town heard Fleming's cries and the four gun shots and two men saw Fleming running from his cabin, but the assailants left by a rear door or window and were not seen.

Fleming was taken to the doctor where he lingered for one day before dying. During the time the dying man languished he said that he thought one of his assailants was Anderson. This surprised many as a search had been made for the assailants shortly after the deadly attack and Anderson, and his partner Mortimer, had joined the posse. Anderson was immediately arrested and Mortimer, who was known to have been in his company that evening, was arrested soon afterward. The two prisoners were kept apart and closely questioned and Mortimer finally weakened and confessed.

Anderson was brought to trial at the May 1894 term of the District Court, where Mortimer turned state's evidence and testified to the details of the crime, and a great deal of circumstantial evidence was also submitted corroborating Mortimer's testimony. Anderson denied any part in the killing and testified that he only learned of the murder later that night when Mortimer told him about it and begged Anderson not to give him away. The jury was out only ninety minutes before returning a verdict on the first ballot finding Anderson guilty of first degree murder. On May 23 Judge Henry sentenced Anderson to hang on June 23.

Mortimer, in consequence of his young age and cooperation, was allowed to plead guilty to murder in the second degree and was sentenced to a prison term. Anderson's attorney, a Mr. Fox, had ably defended his client and then did all he could to get a new trial but, when this failed, he requested that Governor John E. Rickards come down from Helena and make a personal investigation of the case. The governor granted a respite to July 13, examined every detail of the record, and then declined to interfere further.

On July 12 the gallows and rope were tested and determined to be in good working order. County attorney Miller visited during the afternoon before the execution to obtain a statement, but Anderson continued to deny any part in the murder. The prisoner was also visited by the Reverend Fowler, his spiritual advisor, who helped him brace up for his ordeal. The condemned man never showed any sign of fear or weakening, and when Anderson's attorney came that evening he repeated his denial of guilt.

His aged mother, who had been with him throughout the trial, sat with him until 2:00 A.M. when she bid him farewell for the last time. After she left he slept for one hour and at 3:00 A.M. Anderson arose and dressed in a new black suit with a button-hole bouquet on the coat and called for coffee, after which he enjoyed his last cigar. At 3:10 A.M. Sheriff Conrow entered his cell and read the death warrant and, when finished, the Reverend Fowler entered and stayed with Anderson to the end. At 4:40 A.M. the prisoner said, "Well, I guess the time is about up; they will soon be satisfied now." As the authorities prepared for the march to the gallows Mortimer asked to see Anderson. The condemned man was taken to the cell of his accomplice and the youngster begged his forgiveness, and Anderson forgave him. While passing through the corridor another prisoner held for murder said, "It's too bad that you have to go this way," and Anderson replied, "Oh, that's nothing; we all have to go sometime or another."

At 5:00 A.M. the prisoner, accompanied by Sheriff Conrow, the Reverend Fowler, and deputies Davies and Millard, stepped into the jail yard and immediately climbed onto the platform of the scaffold. Anderson stepped onto the trapdoor and deliberately centered himself beneath the noose. The sheriff personally pinioned Anderson's arms to his sides and his legs just below the knees. The Reverend Fowler read a short passage of scripture and delivered a prayer for the condemned man, and when the reverend finished the sheriff adjusted the noose, pulled on the black hood, and asked Anderson if he was ready. The condemned man replied, "Ready when you are. Good-bye, Conrow. I have nothing to say."

The sheriff responded "Good-bye" as he stepped to the left and touched the trapdoor release lever at 5:08 A.M. The body dropped eight feet and then turned slowly three times. Anderson drew up his legs, straightened them, and then there was no further movement, and in nine and one half minutes Drs. Wells, Shawks, Alton and Campbell pronounced Anderson dead. The body was cut down at 5:34 A.M., examined, and it was determined that his neck had been broken in the fall. Anderson's remains were turned over to his family for burial.

Livingston Enterprise (MT): July 14, 1894. *Miner* (Butte, MT): July 14, 1894. *Inter Mountain* (Butte, MT): July 14, 1894.

Osnes, John H.
July 13, 1894

Twenty-five-year-old John H. Osnes, a burly Norwegian, had been a resident of Montana since 1890. He was generally known around Fort Benton as a worthless sort who worked short intervals for several sheep men and others, but enjoyed the respect of none. His friends Ole Lilledall and Eric Carlson, also Norwegians, returned to Fort Benton on March 29, 1894, after a brief visit to Illinois. Osnes believed that Lilledall had a large sum of money he carried on his person so he immediately began to plot how he could lure Lilledall outside the settlement to murder and rob him.

The two men left together and Osnes returned alone on Sunday evening, April 1. A number of people were suspicious, especially Carlson, so Osnes was arrested on the assumption that he had dealt foully with Lilledall. A search was organized and the murdered man was found in a coulee, his throat cut and his head crushed beyond recognition, and the body had been robbed of all valuables. Osnes narrowly escaped being lynched and was held for trial.

Osnes was charged with the murder of Lilledall and tried in May by Judge DuBose in the District Court of the Tenth Judicial District. The defendant took the stand and testified to the details of the killing, and admitted that after Lilledall was dead he searched carefully for the money he believed his victim had but found only $2.25. He was convicted of first degree murder and sentenced to hang on June 29, and a motion for a new trial was denied. On June 18 Governor John E. Rickards received a telegram from Secretary of State Edwin Uhl forwarding a plea from the Swedish and Norwegian minister asking for a commutation of Osnes' sentence to life imprisonment. The governor responded, "Evidence in case of Osnes shows one of the most atrocious [crimes] ever committed in State. So far no extenuating circumstances have been submitted for my consideration. On proper showing will grant respite but cannot grant petition wired on face of evidence in court. Governor, Montana."

On June 26 Thomas W. Murphy, Osnes' defense attorney, informed the governor that the case had been appealed to the state's Supreme Court. The following day the petition for a respite was granted by the governor to July 13. On Monday, July 9, the Supreme Court upheld the lower court's judgment and sentence and Osnes was scheduled to hang on Friday, July 13, 1894. Thomas Murphy's final plea for a commutation of sentence, which had been forwarded to the governor on July 12, was rejected.

Sheriff O'Neil had the scaffold erected the week previous and all was in readiness. The prisoner seemed unconcerned about his fate and spent his last days indulging in coarse jokes, singing or sleeping. The prisoner was finally convinced to receive religious counsel and two days before his execution Osnes embraced the Catholic religion. Thereafter he was attended by Father Follet who stayed with him the final twelve hours and accompanied him onto the scaffold. On Thursday the Reverends Clowes, Gamble and Carlson joined Father Follet, but Osnes showed no sign of weakening and refused to repent or confess. On his final evening the prisoner was visited by Sheriff Hamilton and deputy Dwyer of Cascade County and, when asked how he felt, he said, "I feel away up, I don't feel that anything's going to happen," and his expressions to everyone were full of bravado and levity.

On Friday morning, July 13, at 9:00 A.M. the witnesses gathered inside the enclosure in the jail yard, including nine lawmen and four newsmen among the other citizens. At 9:45 A.M. the prisoner sent word to Judge DuBose that he would like an interview, so the judge hurried to the jail where Osnes asked if the judge thought he had been accorded a fair and impartial trial. When Judge DuBose said that he had, Osnes turned upon his heel, walked to the other end of the cell, and talked to the priest, ignoring the judge entirely. A few minutes after the judge left Sheriff O'Neil entered the cell and read the death warrant and respite of the June 29 execution date. When the reading was concluded a belt was strapped around the prisoner's waist, but the two attached straps for his wrists were left unbuckled. The cell door was swung open and the brief march to the scaffold began with the doomed man walking beside Father Follet, followed by the sheriff and deputies.

They passed out a side door of the jail to the north part of the jail yard and entered the enclosure by a door specially installed for that purpose. Osnes' eyes swept over the crowd, taking in everything at a glance. "Good-bye, Sam," was his last public statement, said to his cousin he spotted among the crowd. The condemned man climbed the stairs and took his place on the trapdoor. He inspected the noose and then stamped his slippered feet upon the trapdoor to ensure it was solid. Father Follet prayed and then produced a crucifix, which he pressed to the lips of the condemned man. The prisoner whispered something to the priest then looked to Sheriff O'Neil as if to say, "I am ready!"

The black hood was pulled on, then the prisoner's wrists and arms, knees and ankles were pinioned, and as soon as the noose was positioned and cinched tight the sheriff and two deputies stepped to one side behind a black curtain. One of them, concealed to remain anonymous, touched the lever controlling the staple that held the trapdoor. There was a sliding noise followed by a dull crash as the trap was sprung at 10:02 A.M. The prisoner gave a few convulsive twitches and in four minutes he was pronounced dead. Seventeen minutes later Drs. Atkisson and Crutcher ordered the body cut down, and the prisoner's remains were placed in a coffin provided by the county. He was buried that afternoon.

Great Falls Tribune (MT): July 14, 1894. *State of Montana vs. John H. Osnes.*

Christie, Calvin J.
December 21, 1894

Calvin J. Christie, alias J. A. Adams or Calvin J. Black, was born in Aurora, Illinois, but moved in 1875 with his parents to St. Paul, Minnesota, where his father soon died and his mother remarried. Christie ran away from home and in time became a noted St. Paul thief. He started his criminal career at age twelve when he joined a gang of pickpockets who generally eluded the police, except when they met over a store on Wabash Street to divide their loot and argued so violently that the police were called. Even then they avoided conviction through able counsel, but on those rare occasions when a conviction was obtained the sentences were light due to their youth.

As Christie matured he undertook safe-cracking under the tutelage of Bill Donaldson, the noted Boston cracksman. After a safe-cracking job in Hinckley, Minnesota, Christie returned to St. Paul and joined a gang consisting of "Kid" Adams, the Green brothers and "Half-breed" Bourke. Christie was caught and convicted of robbing a jewelry store and, under the alias J. A. Adams, spent thirteen months of a five year prison term before being transferred to the insane asylum. Christie, it was learned too late, could sham a convulsive fit at will, which baffled the medical staff at the prison. He remained at the asylum for another thirteen months before he escaped. He hopped a freight train to St. Paul but, knowing it was not safe for him there, continued on to Montana, where he adopted the alias Charles J. Black. He became a painter and sign writer but was always looking for some criminal opportunity.

He proposed to rob the bank at Columbia Falls and needed a woman to execute his plan, but could find none willing to participate. He finally found another criminal opportunity when, on the evening of April 28, 1894, at 5:30 P.M., Lena Cunningham left Columbia Falls for her home three miles north of town. Christie hurried ahead of her and lay in wait, and when his victim reached the point on her route where he was hiding, he approached her and struck a heavy blow to her head. She fell out of her carriage and he then inflicted a number of additional blows, but was scared off before he could rifle the body for the money and valuables he knew she carried. Cunningham's neighbor was driving his cattle home by that same route at 6:00 P.M. and discovered the prostrate form of a woman lying in a pool of blood. Cunningham was alive but unconscious and, even with the terrible wounds to her face and head, he recognized her and sounded the alarm.

Cunningham soon died of her wounds without regaining consciousness. Christie returned to town and joined the posse that was hastily formed to search for the assailant, but he had been seen leaving town just before Cunningham and heading in the same direction. The shoe prints leading from the scene of the assault were peculiarly marked, and they matched Christie's shoes exactly. Blood was found on Christie's clothes and Dr. William Bullard confirmed that it was human blood. Other men furnished further links that formed an irrefutable chain of circumstantial evidence. Christie was arrested and held for trial at Kalispell. There were strong feelings that Christie should be lynched, but he was instead brought to trial. He was convicted of first degree murder and sentenced to hang on September 28, 1894, but appeals and petitions delayed the date to December 21.

Christie made several attempts to escape and only a week before the fatal day a bottle of nitric acid was found in his pocket. He was unable to sleep two nights before his execution and played cards with his death watch guards until daybreak. He dreaded the last meeting with his mother, Mrs. Brumley, and this made him anxious. His mother and step-father called at the jail at 2:00 P.M. Thursday but she was denied entrance to the cell, possibly because a few days earlier she had insisted that her son would never hang; it was a precaution to have her sit outside the cell door under a close guard. The scene was a sad one with the son and grief-stricken mother praying, then crying together. Mrs. Brumley nearly fainted when it came time to leave and afterwards Christie paced in his cell and cried periodically. Soon after the meeting with his mother he braced up and slept soundly the night before his execution.

On his final morning the prisoner arose at 7:00 A.M. when called by Sheriff Joseph Gagner. Christie ate a hearty breakfast of eggs and oysters and then the Reverend Fisher remained with the prisoner all morning, offering prayers periodically, but Christie refused to confess and continued to protest his innocence. Promptly at 10:00 A.M. the sheriff opened the cell door, informed Christie that his time had arrived, and read the death warrant. The prisoner put on his coat and bid farewell to all the prisoners and guards, then marched to the gallows with a smile on his face. He joked with the sheriff as the straps were being adjusted, saying, "That's too tight, Joe, you will squeeze the oysters." The sheriff asked Christie if he had anything to say to the one hundred fifty witnesses gathered in the jail yard, but the prisoner turned his eyes skyward and proclaimed, "I am the happiest man on earth today. I would not trade my faith in Jesus Christ for all the gold and pardons that could be stacked in this jail yard." He then offered a brief prayer and concluded by saying his final words, "Let her go!"

The noose was adjusted and the black hood pulled on as the Reverend Fisher offered a brief prayer. At 10:07 A.M., at the same moment the Reverend said "Amen," the trap was sprung. A two hundred pound weight dropped and the condemned man was jerked up. Christie's neck was so thoroughly broken that the body seemed to hang only by the skin of the neck. Coroner Cummings and Dr. Ghent announced that Christie's pulse had ceased in a few minutes and in ten minutes Christie's remains were cut down and lowered into his coffin. Undertaker Bradley took charge and drove the casket to a potter's field, where Christie was buried.

Butte Miner (MT): December 21–22, 1894.

Pugh, Clay
July 1, 1895

Clay Pugh was a twenty-five-year-old miner who had been employed at Anaconda. On July 4, 1894, he went to Butte, caused some trouble, and landed in jail. When searched it was found he had $100 sewn into his shirt, and as soon as he was released he went to Washington State but found no opportunities there and returned to Montana. On October 5 Pugh tried to "beat his way" on the No. 5 ore train of the BA&P railroad. Chauncey W. West, a man respected by all, was the conductor and therefore in charge of the train, which was bound for Anaconda. West noticed Pugh and told him that No. 5 was an ore train and it was company policy not to carry passengers, but after some discussion West suggested that Pugh could pay the fare and that would probably satisfy the company. Pugh said he had no money and just needed the ride to Anaconda to look for work, so West told him again to get off. Pugh promised he would disembark before the train left the depot at 10:15 A.M., but Pugh remained on the platform of the caboose. After the train was underway West saw that Pugh was still on it. The conductor did not want to put him off in an isolated spot so he waited until the train reached the dump of the Isele Mine, where he said to Pugh, "I thought I told you that you couldn't ride." Pugh replied, "Well, I am here now and I propose to stay." The train was near the road house when West signaled the engineer to stop, caught hold of Pugh and tried to push him from the rear platform of the caboose. Pugh resisted and told West, "You are not man enough, you son of a bitch, to put me off." West struck a light blow to Pugh's face and succeeded in pushing him off the train. West turned and started into the caboose when Pugh yelled, "I'll fix you right now!"

Pugh pulled a revolver from his hip pocket and fired once, the bullet taking effect in West's back to the right of the lumbar region. West fell on the platform of the caboose face down and Pugh shot him in the back again, this time to the left of the lumbar region. Pugh put the revolver back into his pocket and ran south, forded Silver Bow Creek, ran up the tracks a short distance, and then struck out for the foothills. West was carried into the road house where he found several friends and said to them," This is what a man gets who tries to do what is right." At noon he was removed by ambulance to Murray and Freund's Hospital where physicians at once examined him.

The doctors were confused by the two wounds, thinking them to be an entry and exit wound from a single bullet, so at 3:00 P.M. they removed one bullet but were afraid to probe for another due to West's deteriorating condition. Upon finding the first bullet, the doctors realized that there were two wounds and that either bullet might have passed through the liver and stomach, so West's chances of recovery were deemed slight. At 3:30 P.M. the county attorney was sent for and he transcribed an ante-mortem statement, and West died soon afterward.

When the shooting occurred two women were watching from the road house and marked the path Pugh took. M. L. Holland was working at the Isele Mine when he heard the shooting and went to investigate. The women told him the direction Pugh had fled so he returned to the mine for his buggy and took along J. R. Odgers, who had an old pistol but only one bullet. They caught up with their man and when they were close to Pugh, about one half mile from the road house, Holland fired his one round. Pugh, believing they had at least five more, surrendered without resistance. The prisoner was brought back to the road house and the sheriff was telephoned, while two men with rifles ensured that Pugh would not flee again. Deputy sheriff Elderkin soon arrived, took custody of the prisoner, and lodged him in the county jail. His personal effects were inventoried and he was found to have $53.50 in coin in his pockets and $50.00 in bills sewn into his clothing, so he could easily have paid the fare for riding the train.

Pugh was indicted but his attorneys, Campbell and English, obtained a change of venue from Silver Bow County to Jefferson County. After brief deliberations the jurors brought in a verdict of guilty of first degree murder and Judge Showers sentenced Pugh to hang on June 17. A respite was granted by Governor John E. Rickards while the Supreme Court considered the matter, but the lower court's decision was affirmed and the justices refused to interfere further; the application for a commutation of sentence was quickly denied by the governor.

As the day of his execution approached Pugh left instructions with his death watch to write his brother in Walla Walla, Washington, and asked the Reverend G. W. Blythe to inform his mother in Iowa of his death. The death warrant was read to Pugh in his cell before 10:00 A.M. on July 1, 1895, and a few minutes past 10:00, Pugh, dressed in a neat suit of black and wearing a black hat, walked from his cell into the jail yard with Sheriff Gilliam on his right and deputy Halford on his left. Undersheriff Sherlock led the way to the scaffold. When Pugh was in place on the trapdoor, the Reverend Blythe read the fourth verse of the twenty-third Psalm and then made a few remarks while the straps were being applied to Pugh's wrists and arms, knees and ankles. Sheriff Gilliam pulled on the black hood and adjusted the noose as Pugh spoke his last words through the cloth, asking the sheriff to "put it on good and tight and pull it up."

Although everything was in readiness there was a delay of several minutes before the signal was given, and the trap was sprung at 10:28 A.M. Pugh dropped forty inches and the sound of a loud crack signified the breaking of his neck. Drs. Lebcher and Vawter monitored Pugh's pulse and pronounced him dead in nine minutes, but the body hung eight minutes more before being lowered into a plain casket bearing the simple inscription, "At Rest." Pugh's remains were immediately conveyed to a potter's field at the poor farm and buried.

Inter Mountain (Butte, MT): October 5, 1894; July 1, 1895.

Cadotte, Joseph
December 27, 1895

Joseph Cadotte, who had a reputation as a hard character, had been out wolfing for several weeks with Oliver Richards, better known in the region as Oliver Grandchamps. After disposing of their wolf skins they returned to the Henault Ranch in the Tetons not far from Fort Benton. Richards and Cadotte had been interested in the same girl for some time but Richards was favored by the young lady and Cadotte, who was jealous of Richards, resolved to do away with his competition.

On June 15 Richards, unarmed, was sitting in a cabin mending a bridle when Cadotte appeared on the outside and thrust a Winchester through a broken window. Seeing the rifle pointed at him, Richards at once fled out the door and made a break for the Henault cabin, but Cadotte stepped around the corner and, taking deliberate aim, shot his trapping partner in the back from fifteen paces. Cadotte then watched the prostrate form for several minutes to see if there was any sign of life and, upon seeing none, mounted his horse which he had saddled and picketed nearby. Cadotte fled north taking with him a Winchester rifle and one full belt of cartridges.

On July 7 Cadotte was captured on the Flathead reservation by the Indian police. He said that he and Richards had been quarreling over the division of the proceeds of the season's wolfing. He said,

> We were wolfing, Oliver and I, and had caught about $44 worth of skins when we went to Fort Benton. Oliver owed me for a wagon he sold that belonged to me, and I kept all of the money we got for the wolves. He got very drunk and spent some money that had been entrusted to him and he wanted me to give him enough to square it. I could not do it, as I had bought a buggy and spent my money. We came back to the home of his mother and sister and the next day renewed the dispute and [he] began to quarrel with me, and twice I made him put away a knife that he flourished. Then he started for the house, and I called for him to stop three times, but he would not, then I killed him. I thought he was going to get his gun, so I killed him in self-defense. He was a big man and weighed two hundred forty pounds; I tried every way to satisfy him, and told him I would go wolfing with him again, but he would not agree to go.

Cadotte was only five feet, seven inches tall and weighed one hundred forty five pounds with an Indian's countenance. Cadotte was indicted, tried, and convicted of first degree murder, as there were several eye witnesses to the killing and none corroborated his claim of self-defense. He was sentenced to hang but an appeal delayed the execution. The plea for a new trial was based upon the prosecuting attorney's statement that brought to the attention of the jury a birthmark, a ring around the defendant's neck: "We, too, are superstitious, and it is an old saying, and by some believed to be true, that a man to hang is known by his neck," but the defense attorney had taken no exception at the time. On December 9, 1895, Justice DeWitt, speaking for the Supreme Court, affirmed the lower court's decision saying the statement, though reprehensible, had not been prejudicial. Cadotte's date of execution was re-scheduled for December 27, 1895.

For several days before his execution Cadotte spent his time writing to his friends and acquaintances, and he also wrote a final statement regarding his trouble with Richards. He blamed his Indian nature for being unable to control his resentment and his reliance upon violence to settle perceived injuries, and as the moment approached he expressed hope that they would not delay one minute. Cadotte had not spoken to Sheriff George B. McLaughlin since he was convicted because the sheriff had testified that the defendant had threatened to kill him. Cadotte denied the accusation and on the morning of his execution the prisoner sent for the sheriff, admitted the threat and begged his pardon, which was given. The sheriff made every effort to grant his request for an expeditious execution and had completed all preparations by 9:00 A.M., a full hour early.

The scaffold was of the counter poise weight design and had been erected at the rear of the county jail, where twenty witnesses had assembled inside an enclosure. Father Folette spent the morning with the prisoner and precisely at 10:00 A.M. the two men received the sheriff at the cell door for the reading of the death warrant. Cadotte's wrists were bound behind his back before the march to the scaffold began, and the prisoner exited the jail with the priest at his side. When they arrived at the gallows Cadotte examined the structure and, as he stepped beneath the noose, batted it with his head. He examined the rope, which was 1½ inches thick and nicely greased, and he stated his approval. The prisoner's knees and ankles were pinioned once he was in position, but when the black hood was presented he decided to make a brief statement and detailed the crime, insisting the motive was a quarrel over money, and ended with a simple "Good-bye!" He requested that the silk scarf around his neck be removed and this was done.

The black hood was pulled on and the noose quickly adjusted, and as soon as the prisoner was prepared the signal was given and Sheriff McLaughlin, at 10:10 A.M., pulled the bolt. The four hundred sixty pound weight dropped and the prisoner's body shot upwards three feet, then dropped back until his feet dangled twelve inches above the platform. Cadotte's head fell forward, his neck broken in two places, and not a tremor was perceived. Dr. Atkinson pronounced Cadotte dead in six minutes but the body hung nine minutes more before the sheriff cut down the prisoner's remains and placed them in the coffin provided by the county. The sheriff delivered the body to the undertaker and Cadotte was buried by friends later that day.

Inter Mountain (Butte, MT): December 27, 1895. *Butte Miner* (MT): December 28, 1895. *River Press* (Fort Benton, MT): June 22, 1895; July 13, 1895; December 14, 1895; December 28, 1895.

Biggerstaff, John
April 6, 1896

Water Street was the seedy section of Helena, Montana, in 1896 and gangs of urchins crowded dirty alleys and sidewalks and freely used highly offensive language toward everyone they met. None but the lowest class congregated on Water Street, where the houses were squatty and contained every sort of character. Mrs. Mathews, a woman of poor reputation, lived in one of these houses, and Mrs. Houghton, whose alias was Mrs. Bowhay, and her daughter Emma frequently visited Mathews. William Biggerstaff and Richard Johnson visited Mathews often, and Biggerstaff lived in the house next door. Biggerstaff was married, but was separated from his wife, and was so enamored with Houghton and Emma that he had at times been "criminally intimate" with the mother. However, Richard Johnson was similarly interested in the two women.

Houghton moved into Biggerstaff's house and lived there for some time when, on the night of June 8, 1895, she gave permission to Emma to sleep over at Mathew's house. After 4:00 A.M. Johnson showed up in a drunken condition and in a few minutes Johnson's friend Richard Smith came in. Several minutes later Biggerstaff, seeing the two men at Mathews' house and being concerned for Emma, joined them and Houghton soon followed. Mrs. Houghton told her daughter to get up but Emma said she was sleepy and wanted to remain in bed. Johnson intervened and ordered Emma to get up and go home and made some other remarks that angered Biggerstaff. He told Johnson to leave the girl alone and also that he had no business ordering her to do anything.

After a brief argument Biggerstaff left through the back door and in a few moments Smith and Johnson also started out the back door. Smith halted their progress and said to Johnson, "Look out! Here comes Biggerstaff with a gun." They both jumped back inside and put their shoulders to the door. Biggerstaff forced the door open a few inches, pushed his pistol into the opening, and fired one bullet into the house. Smith, still holding the door, wrestled with Biggerstaff for the pistol while Johnson rushed across the room and picked up an old gun from the corner. Smith let go of the door and stepped back, allowing Biggerstaff to enter the house, and Johnson immediately struck him on the shoulder with the barrel of the gun. Johnson and Biggerstaff then clenched and a second shot was fired. They fell to the floor together, Johnson on top. In a few moments Biggerstaff crawled out from under his victim, put his pistol into his pocket and walked out.

Smith then checked Johnson and found that he was mortally wounded, and Johnson bled to death in minutes. Biggerstaff was arrested, convicted, and sentenced to hang. The appeal for a new trial and application for commutation of sentence delayed the execution for many months but all efforts failed.

On the day before Biggerstaff was to hang, Houghton, who had since moved to Butte, came to visit but could not gain admittance. This caused the prisoner to break down considerably and it was later learned that he had depended upon her to smuggle in poison for him to cheat the hangman. A short time later Biggerstaff's wife visited and bade him farewell. A good night of sleep completely restored his nerve, so, in the morning, he ate a hearty breakfast and then spent every remaining minute with Father Day. When the time arrived the death warrant was read to the prisoner in his cell and his wrists and arms were pinioned.

The gallows had been erected next to the jail so the duration of the procession was but three minutes, and Biggerstaff bade farewell to the prisoners as he passed their cells. He stepped out into the yard and climbed the stairs with a firm tread, and he was smiling as he stepped under the noose and nodded to several faces he recognized in the crowd of four hundred spectators. He said, "I hope all present are my friends. I forgive all. I hope all now forgive me. Good-bye!" The prisoner's knees and ankles were being pinioned while he spoke and, when he finished, the black hood was pulled over his head and the noose was adjusted. At a signal a deputy behind a screen pulled the lever and the great weight fell. Biggerstaff was jerked up only six inches but it had been so sudden that his neck was broken. He was pronounced dead in eight and one half minutes, his remains were cut down and placed in a coffin, and delivered to his wife for burial.

Inter Mountain (Butte, MT): April 7, 1896.

Gay, William
June 8, 1896

William Gay lived with his family in Castle, Meagher County, Montana. He had taken up some land that later came within the town limits of Castle as the town grew, and this particular tract was coveted by many people because it lay in the path of the proposed Montana Midland Railroad. It was the only tract not owned by the Castle Land Company and a man named Benson filed a claim on Gay's land and finally gained possession of it. The civil case resulted in bitter feelings on the part of both parties, each of whom had a large circle of friends. Each faction, as the civil case was pending, circulated every manner of derogatory story. Most were dismissed outright, except for the allegation that Gay had sexual relations with his daughter Ella. Gay was arrested and charged with incest, the case was tried before Judge Henry, and Gay was acquitted.

Gay's brother-in-law, a man named Gross, owned a ranch six miles below Castle. On April 4, 1893, Gross resisted the service of a search warrant served by Constable C. E. Westbrook, and he was arrested and bound over to stand trial. Gross, accompanied by an officer, set out to secure bonds for his release and they stopped at the Gay home. While there Gross affected his escape, and on April 24 Gay's arrest was ordered by the sheriff for stealing goods in Wyoming. Gay was not at home so the officer began searching the wooded area nearby and Gay, it was alleged, shot at him twice and ordered him to clear out.

Four days later another attempt was made to arrest Gross and Gay when officers saw the two fugitives struggling to get a hay wagon out of a mud hole. They hid and patiently watched for their opportunity as the fugitives freed the wagon, drove it to the barn, unloaded the contents, removed the hay rack, and installed the wagon box. Gay and Gross had only driven two hundred yards when the officers rose up, guns in hand, and ordered the men to throw up their hands. Gross was busy controlling the team but Gay grabbed his rifle, jumped to the ground and hid behind a wagon wheel, and opened fire on the posse. The lawmen dove for cover and in the confusion the fugitives managed to escape again.

On May 8 the fugitives were seen near the Durst Ranch so another posse was formed and started after the fugitives, spotting their quarry near Gross' ranch and closely pursuing them. After riding several miles Gross and Gay were run to ground and ordered to surrender, but instead they chose to shoot it out and Gay went down with a terrible wound to his leg. When the posse began to close in, posse man Rader was shot. During the excitement that resulted the two fugitives again escaped and Rader died of his wound soon afterward. Several days following the murder of Rader, Sheriff O'Marr and seven deputies started out after the fugitives, and on May 12 they surrounded the pair hiding in the brush of Musselshell Creek. As the posse worked their way through the heavy underbrush deputy James Macke was shot in the body. Once again in the confusion the fugitives escaped. After suffering intensely for two days Macke died of his wound.

The search for the two murderers continued but Gross was never captured. Gay was recognized at Needles, California, in December 1894, arrested and returned to Montana. He was indicted, tried, convicted of murdering Macke, and sentenced to hang. The petition for a new trial in the District Court was denied and the appeal was turned down by the state Supreme Court, and the U.S. Supreme Court refused to interfere or grant a stay on the application for a writ of error. Next came scores of petitions imploring Governor John F. Rickards to commute the sentence to life imprisonment, and Gay's daughter Maude visited the governor and asked him to visit her father. All papers were in the governor's hands on the Saturday before the execution when he visited Gay in his cell, and the condemned man insisted that if he was given time he could produce additional evidence and witnesses in his favor. The governor assured the prisoner, "I am giving your case the most earnest consideration it is possible for me to give it; and, while I do not wish to delay the matter longer, if I find I cannot settle the question to the satisfaction of my own mind in the time I have, I will grant the respite." Governor Rickards did settle the matter to his satisfaction and refused to intervene.

Sunday night, Gay's last, the prisoner suffered terrible anguish and could not sleep a minute. He sent for the governor but Rickards refused to visit him again. When day broke Gay had to be assisted in putting on the new suit of clothes provided. He had not eaten anything for twenty-four hours and had so weakened that he had to be revived by hypodermic injections of stimulants. The death warrant was read to him in his cell at 10:00 A.M. and then it took nearly an hour to get him braced up for the ordeal, but finally he summoned all his strength just to make the walk to the gallows. Once in position upon the platform Gay denied that he had shot Macke and forgave all, but expressed bitterness toward Sheriff McKnight of Meagher County, and only forgave him when urged by the priest. Several men came forward to shake his hand before his arms were pinioned, and they were closely watched so they could not provide anything with which the condemned man could commit suicide. The noose was adjusted and as the black hood was perched atop Gay's head he wanted to say something more, and he yelled out, "I am murdered! You witness a murder!" The black hood was then pulled down and secured and in but a moment, as the clock struck 11:00 A.M., the bolt releasing the counter poise weight was pulled and the great weight dropped. Gay's body shot up one foot, breaking his neck. Not a muscle in his body moved. He was pronounced dead in seven and one half minutes and Gay's remains were cut down at 11:10 A.M. The body was placed in its coffin and conveyed to the Catholic church for services, and he was buried in the church cemetery the next morning.

Inter Mountain (Butte, MT): June 6, 1896; June 8, 1896.

Salmon, Thomas
January 27, 1899

Thomas Salmon was the ex-president of the Miner's Union and took part in the strike of July 1898. In September he was discharged by William O'Connor, superintendent of the Red Lodge Coal Mines in Red Lodge, Montana. That night he borrowed a revolver and the next morning went to O'Connor's office to demand reinstatement, and when O'Connor refused, Salmon shot him to death. After the murder Salmon was expelled and denounced by the union, and he was arrested, charged with murder, and indicted. He was tried at the fall term of the court, convicted of first degree murder, and sentenced to hang on January 27, 1899. The appeals process and applications for executive clemency sent to Governor Frank Steunenberg did not delay the execution.

On Salmon's last day he retired at 8:00 P.M. and finally fell asleep at 11:00. He slept soundly until 5:00 A.M., when he arose and ate a hearty breakfast. Salmon was an atheist to the last and stated he did not need any "sky pilot" to show him how to die. In the presence of a few friends and jail officials he preached his own funeral service. When the sheriff announced that his time was up the condemned man told the lawman to proceed with the execution and to "do the thing up quickly." He said he did not want to stand out in the cold and shiver and have people say he trembled through cowardice. He said, "the weather is cold on earth and there is a probability of it being warmer in the land to which I am about to journey."

Salmon and his escorts walked to the scaffold at a rapid pace and Salmon ran up the stairs ahead of the sheriff. As he was being prepared he said,

> Gentlemen, you are assembled here this morning to pay your respects to a friend who is to go to that everlasting shore where many have gone before but none have ever returned, and none ever will. In a few minutes the trials and tribulations of this life will be over for me. With these few remarks you can then consign this body to the earth from which I think I came. If any of you follow my body to the cemetery don't uncover your heads and thus contract colds and pneumonia. It is a barbarous habit, and I hope you will protect yourselves, and by so doing you will please me. Gentlemen, I wish all my friends an everlasting farewell.

The trap was sprung only a few minutes after the condemned man appeared in the jail yard and his neck was broken in the fall. In fifteen minutes he was cut down and placed in his coffin, and within the hour he was interred in a potter's field without any form of service.

Inter Mountain (Butte, MT): December 21–22, 1899. *Butte Miner* (MT): January 28, 1899.

Allen, Joseph H.
September 14, 1899

In June 1898 J. S. Reynolds, also known as J. H. Leach, and Joseph H. Allen left Shoup, Idaho, and went to Lewis and Clark County, Montana, to find work shearing sheep. They planned, once the season ended, to continue on to British Columbia to hunt and trap through the winter. They worked first for Warren Gillette, then Si Cooper, and finally for W. W. Martin, but while working at Martin's sheep ranch three of their four horses wandered off. Reynolds loaded part of their camp outfit on Allen's buckskin and the two men set off in search of their lost animals, one belonging to Reynolds and two to Allen. The two men separated for a while but rendezvoused some distance from the Martin ranch, followed a creek to a point near Emil D. Keller's ranch west of Mitchell and camped Sunday night, July 24. Stephen Arnold, an employee of Keller, saw the men in camp quarreling. They stopped their argument as he approached but resumed arguing after he left a few minutes later.

The next day Arnold, in going over the same ground, saw traces of blood. He searched and found Reynolds' body in the bushes wrapped in a blanket with the head enclosed in a sack. When he removed the head wrap he found a gaping bullet wound above the dead man's right eye and powder burns on his forehead, Reynolds' trousers had been taken. Widening his search, Arnold found a blood-stained sack of flour in the stream. The coroner examined all the evidence and concluded that Reynolds was probably asleep and resting his head on the flour sack, using it as a pillow, when Allen placed his pistol close to Reynolds' head and fired a single bullet through his brain.

Allen had fled to William John's place on the Montana Central Railroad line where he cashed a check for $26.58, payable to Reynolds, by forging the name of the murdered man. He ate breakfast before continuing on to Helena on the Montana Central freight, then traveled westward working for or stealing rides on freight trains until he arrived at Oakland, Oregon, near his birthplace. Sheriff Thomas Davidson of Lewis and Clark County distributed circulars giving Allen's description and offered a reward of $250 for his capture. Oakland's postmaster, T. G. Ruth, recognized Allen from the circular, contacted Davidson, and on August 13, 1898, Ruth had the fugitive arrested.

Sheriff Davidson went to Oakland and brought Allen to Helena, and during the trip the prisoner readily admitted the killing but insisted it was in self-defense. He said, "Reynolds was a stronger man and I was afraid of him." Allen was held over at his preliminary hearing, indicted, and brought to trial in Judge Henry C. Smith's court on November 10, 1898. The jurors, on the first ballot two days later, stood ten to two for a conviction of first degree murder. After eight more hours in deliberations they brought in a unanimous guilty verdict and three days later Allen was sentenced to hang on January 12, 1899.

The motion for a new trial was denied and the matter was appealed to the state Supreme Court. The justices affirmed Judge Smith's decision on July 3, 1899, and this action was immediately followed by two petitions to Governor Robert B. Smith pleading for a commutation of sentence. While the petitions were being considered, Judge Smith, on July 17, resentenced Allen to hang on September 14, 1899. Governor Smith denied both applications for commutation so, on the day before Allen's execution, his mother, Lena Allen, with Mrs. Charles Dahler and Helena Clarke, pleaded with the governor for a respite of a few days, but he refused to intervene. On Wednesday the gallows was tested with weights, and the sheriff announced that the execution would take place at 9:00 A.M. and that none without an invitation would be admitted. In fact, the sheriff planned the execution for 6:00 A.M. and this ruse, he hoped, would keep the crowd to a minimum.

On his final night Allen retired at midnight after spending the evening bidding farewell to his mother and friends and, after the jail closed, he wrote several letters. The death watch reported that he slept soundly until 5:00 A.M. when Father O'Brien and jailor Marsh woke him. He dressed in his new suit of black and ate a hearty breakfast and after the meal he smoked his last cigar as he received his final spiritual consolation. When offered he refused any form of stimulant.

Just before 6:00 A.M. Undersheriff Haley stepped to the door of Allen's cell and read the death warrant and, when finished, Allen responded, "All right!" The straps were then applied to his wrists and arms and the prisoner said to Sheriff Davidson, "Now, Tom, let's get out and have this over as soon as possible." The sheriff escorted the condemned man out of the jail into a drizzle where a hundred witnesses waited, including a number of lawmen more interested in how the job was done. A square of carpet was positioned on the scaffold and Father O'Brien, with a hand on Allen's shoulder, positioned the condemned man beneath the noose. The noose was brought down and adjusted by the sheriff and Mr. McFarland drew it tight. Allen's legs were then pinioned and all was in readiness, as a black hood was not used at the request of the condemned man.

The sheriff raised his hand and the executioner, concealed behind a curtain, pressed the lever that released the four hundred fifty pound weight at 6:07 A.M. The body shot upward and then settled down. Allen's eyes were closed and the protuberance under the right ear confirmed that his neck had been broken. Drs. Riddell and Fleming monitored Allen's pulse, which fluctuated for six minutes, then slowly decreased until Dr. Riddell pronounced him dead in eighteen minutes. At 6:30 A.M. Allen's remains were lowered into the coffin provided by the county, and later that day he was buried in the Catholic cemetery.

Inter Mountain (Butte, MT): September 14–15, 1899.

Brooks, William C.
November 24, 1899

William C. Brooks, was discharged from the U.S. Army in 1895 and moved from Fort Custer to Billings, Yellowstone County, Montana, with his wife, Jennie C. Brooks. Brooks was obsessively jealous and suspected his wife of infidelities, so over the next three years the couple quarreled constantly and officers of the law were frequently called by neighbors to quell the disturbances.

On November 18, 1898, the fighting reached a crescendo when William C. Brooks pulled a revolver and fired one shot, the bullet striking his wife in the breast. Jennie C. Brooks grabbed the gun and they wrestled for control but she soon weakened from her wound and lost her grip on the pistol. She fled out of the house and across the street, where she collapsed from the loss of blood. Her husband followed closely and, once she lay helpless, he placed the muzzle to her ear and shot her through the brain. As soon as the fatal shot was fired William Brooks ran to a small barn and four more shots were heard, but he had ineffectually tried to take his own life and inflicted only one minor flesh wound. Neighbors rushed in and restrained him until officers arrived; he was arrested and lodged in jail.

Brooks was indicted for murder and his trial began on February 6, 1899. His defense was insanity, but an examination by competent physicians proved the plea to be a ruse. He was found guilty of first degree murder, and on February 10 the defendant was sentenced to hang on March 17. Various appeals and petitions stayed the sentence but all efforts finally failed. On October 26, Judge Loud re-sentenced the murderer to hang on Friday, November 24, 1899.

During the time Brooks was in jail he spent all his time praying and singing a sort of incoherent mixture of the hymns, "Saved by Grace," "Jesus Died for Me," and "I Am Going to Glory." He ate a hearty supper on his final night and then spent a quiet evening before he was put to bed at 7:00 P.M. His death watch reported that, while he did not sleep much, he was not restless. He arose before 5:00 A.M. and spent his time singing and praying. The Reverend Clark of the Congregational Church and the Reverend Ople of the Methodist Church visited but were turned away when he refused to see either minister. Jailor Harding then brought his breakfast but he refused to eat. At 7:00 A.M. Sheriff George W. Hubbard, his deputies, attending physicians, and newspaper reporters assembled in the corridor and the prisoner was brought out for the reading of his death warrant. The procession then formed and walked to the gallows, Brooks singing all the way.

The prisoner declined to say anything to the spectators but motioned to the sheriff that he wanted to pray, then knelt on the carpet for several minutes of silent prayer. Upon rising he took his position on the platform where his wrists and arms, knees and legs were pinioned. He continued singing as the sheriff adjusted the noose and ceased only when jailor Harding pulled the black hood over his head. The heavy counter poise weight fell at 7:03 A.M. and Brooks was jerked up with such suddenness that it broke his neck. A few muscle twitches of the lower limbs were the only signs of life, and these lasted only a few moments, and at 7:15 A.M. Drs. E. P. Townsend and Rhinehart pronounced him dead. The body was cut down, placed in the plain coffin provided by the county, and given to undertaker Smith. Coroner Townsend, assisted by Drs. Rhinehart, Clark and Hogan, performed an autopsy that afternoon and determined that Brooks' brain showed no abnormalities, corroborating the finding that his insane behavior had been a ruse.

Butte Miner (MT): November 19, 1898; November 24–25, 1899. *Inter Mountain* (Butte, MT): November 24, 1899.

Calder, William W.
March 18, 1900

William Wallace "Billy" Calder, his younger brother "Jimmy," and James Eli "Dee" Fisher lived on a ranch a few miles from the Musselshell River in southeastern Fergus County, Montana. In Billings, Lewiston and other settlements in the area these three men had a reputation as petty crooks, and Billy was considered the leader. On September 24, 1898, the three men went to the sheep ranch of Farquhar McRae, which was a few miles from their ranch, intending to murder him and steal his flock of seventeen hundred sheep. The plan was to have Billy engage McRae in friendly conversation and, while thus preoccupied, Fisher was to shoot him in the head. When they arrived McRae was herding a portion of his flock and Billy, as agreed, distracted him in conversation, speaking of the fine condition of his sheep and congratulating him on his prospects. However, Fisher seemed immobilized as Billy signaled several times to shoot McRae. When Fisher failed to move Billy, with an oath, snatched the rifle from his hands, put it to McRae's head and shot him once, killing the sheepman instantly. Once McRae fell Billy kicked the body and said, "'Tis no more than killing the dogs to kill him." They stripped the dead man of all his valuables, tied a rope to the body, and dragged it to the cabin yard.

Fisher, embarrassed by his inability to act, then announced that he would kill McRae's herder, John Allen, so that they could get the rest of the sheep. Fisher left but returned shortly saying, "She's off," meaning he had killed Allen. The three men then dragged Allen's body to the cabin yard where they wrapped McRae's body in a quilt, wrapped Allen's body in a tarpaulin, and then cached both bodies in an old chimney on the ranch. They spent the night in the cabin, which gave them time to ransack it for any valuables that might be hidden there.

The next morning they hitched up McRae's team to his wagon, placed both bodies beneath a load of bacon, ham, flour, and dried and canned fruit, piled on their plunder and drove toward Forsyth in Custer County. They drove the sheep with them and along the way asked everyone they met if they had seen McRae, explaining that the sheepherder had sold them his flock and had promised to help them load the sheep at Forsyth. They were confident that this ruse would serve as an alibi.

When the murderers reached the Musselshell they camped beside the river and built a big fire of drift wood. They removed the bodies from the wagon, cut them into pieces and threw the body parts into the fire, which was kept up until nothing but calcined bones, buttons and buckles remained. These remnants they threw in the river before proceeding on to Forsyth.

News of McRae's disappearance did not reach Lewiston until a week after the murders. The Calders and Fisher were immediately suspected, so a posse started out and caught the three fugitives at Forsyth. The river was dragged where there had been an unusually large fire on the bank and the bones and buckles were recovered. Once the murderers were lodged in jail, Jimmy, the weakest of the three, was promised that he would be punished by imprisonment for a term of only two years if he would tell the truth, so he confessed every detail, and the Calders' mother, Mrs. Sam Smith, also gave testimony against Billy.

On March 25, 1899, Billy Calder was convicted of murder in the first degree and six days later Dee Fisher was also convicted. Both defendants were sentenced to hang on May 12, 1899, and both men appealed. Dee was granted a new trial, which was to be held at Fort Benton in July, but the Supreme Court denied Billy's appeal. On March 10, 1900, Judge Dudley DuBose brought Billy into court and asked him if he had any reason why sentence should not be imposed upon him, and he responded with a lengthy harangue citing every possible reason he could think of, all of which had been considered and disposed of by the Supreme Court. The Judge then said that he had sentenced too many men to hang and that a long wait for an execution was not a kindness. He said, "I believe that the shorter the time is, the better it is for him and the better for the state. Viewing it in that light — a kindness to you — I have made the time very short." He then proceeded to sentence Billy to hang on Friday, March 16, 1900, between the hours of 9:00 A.M. and 5:00 P.M., only one week from that date.

After the convictions Jimmy Calder recanted his testimony. Billy, it was clear, was lost, but by changing his testimony Jimmy believed he could save Dee Fisher. He claimed now that he and Dee had been some distance from the ranch in a coulee when the killings occurred and had not taken part in the butchery, and that Billy alone had killed both men. As a consequence he was scheduled to be tried on a charge of first degree murder. Fisher was tried first on April 24, 1900, but the jury deadlocked eleven for acquittal and one for conviction and death, and after four hours of deliberation they compromised and acquitted Dee Fisher. Jimmy Calder was tried next but the charge of murder was dropped and he was tried for perjury, based upon the circumstance that he had testified under oath to two completely conflicting stories and one had to be perjurious. Billy was convicted and sentenced to serve six years at the state prison in Deer Lodge. He served his time as a model prisoner and was released on July 30, 1904.

The execution of Billy Calder was the first legal execution in Fergus County. The gallows had been assembled in advance and was of the twitch-up design. A twitch-up gallows drops a counter poise weight attached to the end of the hangman's rope opposite the noose, and in this case the weight was a large box which could hold anything with an aggregate weight sufficient to jerk the condemned off a low platform. Sheriff Thomas Shaw selected scrap iron, which was readily available, and had batches weighed until the accumulated weight was three hundred eight pounds. The gallows had been constructed to accommodate two men, in the belief that Fisher would hang with Billy, but now the second pulley, through which the hangman's rope would have been laced, dangled unused. The sheriff had not witnessed a hanging previously and wanted to take no chances, so he had the dirt excavated a foot deep under the platform, and a rope was tied to one corner of the platform covering the depression. If, after the condemned was jerked up, the stretching of the rope or Billy's neck left his feet touching the platform it could be pulled out allowing a foot of clearance.

During the last few days of life Billy mellowed and accepted the religious teachings of the Presbyterian Reverend Albert Pfaus, expressing a belief in God but avoiding any discussion of the possibility of a future existence. On Wednesday, March 14, Billy asked for a meeting with his brother Jimmy, and then severely criticized him for lying about Fisher's part in the killing of Allen. Billy's mother visited him at 9:30 on the morning of his execution and, as she left, his last words to her were, "I forgive you for all you ever did. Good-bye."

After she left Father James A. Vermaat and the Reverend Pfaus joined the prisoner. The priest offered to hear the condemned man's final confession, but Billy declined. When Sheriff Shaw began reading the death warrant Billy interrupted and asked him to hurry, as he was concerned he might lose his nerve. Straps were brought out and each wrist was pinioned to a thigh, then a large strap bound his arms at the elbows. As soon as he was bound the sheriff left for the gallows, as it was his duty to release the weight, and he took his position behind a curtain on the right side of the scaffolding.

The prisoner walked to the gallows with Undersheriff Lincoln P. Slater guiding him by the arm and they arrived at 10:35 A.M. The prisoner nodded to several faces he recognized among the witnesses but made no remarks of significance, as the condemned man was expected to make a confession but again refused to do so. Outside the twelve foot wooden fence surrounding the jail yard three hundred spectators had assembled but could see nothing of the execution. Billy took his place under the noose, then turned to face the crowd and complained, "The sun is shining in my eyes." Slater quickly pinioned Billy's legs at the knees and ankles, the noose was positioned and cinched, and the black hood was readied.

Billy was then given the opportunity to address the witnesses. He looked over the seventy spectators, which included lawmen, the attending physicians and newspaper reporters, before he said, "Well, boys, I bid you all goodbye. I have told Mr. Johns all I could tell. All I can say now is that I am innocent." The black hood was pulled on and the drawstrings tightened, and in a moment, at 10:41 A.M., the cord supporting the weighted box was cut. The great weight dropped, jerking the condemned man skyward two feet and breaking his neck. The body rebounded and came to rest with Billy's feet four inches above the wooden platform, so it was not pulled away. The body convulsed almost immediately and then, after a few minutes, twitched several more times before becoming still.

Dr. H. H. Wilson, who had been standing close and watching the preparations, waited three minutes before stepping forward to search for a pulse and found a strong heartbeat. He conferred with two other attending physicians who were there to witness the activities, then checked the pulse every few minutes until, at ten minutes, the pulse was beginning to weaken. Over the next four minutes the body visibly relaxed as Billy clenched and unclenched his hands until he was pronounced dead at 10:55 A.M. After hanging five minutes more, the body was cut down and lowered into a coffin, which had been stored around the corner of the jail and brought forward. The noose and hood were removed and the lid closed before six men carried the coffin to a hearse outside the jail yard, where Billy's mother waited to take charge of her son's remains. The hearse was driven to Hobensack and Stoddard's Funeral Parlor and prepared for burial. The following morning William Wallace Calder was laid to rest in the little cemetery just west of Lewistown.

Butte Miner (MT): March 17, 1900. *Fergus County Argus* (Lewiston, MT): March 12–13, 1900; March 17, 1900; March 21, 1900.

Hurst, Joseph C.
March 30, 1900

Joseph C. Hurst, on the evening of December 23, 1898, followed Dominick Cavanaugh through the alley to his stable intending to rob him. He had a brief friendly conversation with his victim and when Cavanaugh turned to shut the stable door Hurst struck him with an iron bolt. Cavanaugh fell to the ground crying out twice, and this caused a woman in the alley near Steele's House to cry out as well. As Hurst looked toward the woman he struck at Cavanaugh again, but hit the ground and broke off the bolt's head. The woman fled so Hurst struck Cavanaugh several more blows, killing him. While looking for the end of the bolt he saw the Myers boys at the end of the alley coming toward him and he fled without the opportunity to rob the dead body.

Hurst was soon arrested, tried at the spring 1899 term of the District Court, and convicted of first degree murder. He was sentenced to hang but the sentence was stayed pending an appeal before the state Supreme Court. This process lasted nearly a year but finally the lower court's decision was affirmed and at the spring term Hurst was sentenced to hang on Friday, March 30, 1900. The petition for a commutation of the death sentence was denied.

During the morning before the execution, Governor Robert B. Smith was visited by Hurst's father, W. S. Hurst, with the prisoner's mother and sister, but the governor "was like a stone wall" and nothing more could be done. That afternoon the prisoner was visited by his wife and two little boys, his parents, brothers and sisters. He was very cool and talked freely with anyone admitted. He spent some time with the Reverend Henry Warman, Pastor of the M.&E. Church of Glendive, and this helped Hurst to remain composed throughout Friday morning. Just before 2:00 P.M. he was taken to a Catholic church where the Reverend Father Claude M. Ebner of Dickson, North Dakota, gave him religious consolation.

Father Ebner went with Hurst to the scaffold at 2:20 P.M. The prisoner was placed on the trapdoor and his limbs were pinioned before he spoke to the crowd of seventy-five men, saying, "Gentlemen, this is a terrible, terrible mistake, terrible mistake. I forgive you all the same as Jesus did."

The black hood was pulled on, the noose adjusted, and the trap was sprung at 2:28 P.M. Drs. J. H. Hunt of Glendive and F. S. Gray of Miles City reported that respiration ceased in five minutes and pronounced Hurst dead ten minutes later. The body was cut down after hanging a few minutes more and deposited in a coffin provided. Ex-attorney general Haskell had inquired of the prisoner what disposition should be made of his body and Hurst asked to be buried in his wedding suit. The body was dressed accordingly and later that afternoon turned over to his wife, father and mother to be taken to Wadena, Minnesota, for interment.

Inter Mountain (Butte, MT): March 29–30, 1900.

Pepo, William
April 6, 1900

On June 25, 1898, two Germans stopped at the ranch of August Kropp ten miles from Pondera, Montana. The three men spent the day conversing in German and the travelers said they had come from north of the border to look for work. Kropp told them he had no work for them so they asked directions to Choteau and left after supper. Kropp warned them that the Muddy River was high so they should take the longer route by way of the bridge and, if they decided not to press on at that late hour, told them they would find an old, unoccupied cabin just beyond the bridge. The men, carrying bundles of belongings wrapped in quilts, traveled seven miles to the cabin, which was still twelve miles from Choteau, and settled in for the night.

The cabin, which was located on F. Truchot's hay ranch, had an opening for a window in the south wall and the door was in the east wall near the corner. In the middle of the room was one bunk made of common boards and the two men spread their bedrolls there. At some time during the night one of the men arose, careful not to disturb his traveling mate. He stood near the door and, using a heavy club, bludgeoned the sleeping man to death. He rifled the man's belongings, taking the best from both bundles, left the rest, and fled. The next day the murderer stopped at the ranch of William Chalmers, where he talked with a German woman employed there, and she gave him directions to Choteau. The man, who talked in a rambling manner as if something weighed heavily on his mind, slept there that night and got an early start at daybreak. He never arrived in Choteau and it was supposed he had turned off at Burton and went to Collins, where he could catch the train east.

On June 29, Robert Davis, who was in charge of haying operations for Truchot, went to the unoccupied cabin to get mower sickles he had stored there. When he pushed open the door he saw a large pile of bedding covering the partially decomposed body of the murdered man. The deceased was lying on his back on the side of the bed next to the door with his head slightly turned away. The right front part of the skull above the temple was entirely crushed and three pieces of the skull had imbedded in the brain.

Every detail was carefully recorded to help in identifying the man: the height of the dead man in life was five feet six inches and his hair was dark brown; he wore a size thirty-seven coat and pants thirty-two at the waist. The items left in the cabin were described and among them was a size forty Ulster overcoat, labeled *Samuel Bros., Ludgate Hall, Syduiham House, London.* In the overcoat was a well worn book containing shorthand notes, a long list of Blackfoot Indian names and terms with their meaning in English, various accounts of items purchased and labor performed with horses and cattle, many addresses and some poems, but nothing to indicate the owner's name.

A clothier examined the apparel and determined that none of it had been purchased below the border, and said that the Ulster overcoat was much too large for the murdered man. Sheriff Hagen thought that the dead man's identity might be learned by writing to the addresses in Winnipeg, Fort Steele and Pincher Creek, Northwest Territory. The accounts showed that the man had been engaged a considerable portion of the past three years in the vicinity of Standoff and McLeod, and this was investigated. The sheriff had deputy S. Y. Penrod send out letters, and he received a response dated July 18, 1898, from A. Ross Cuthbert, inspector for the Northwest Mounted Police:

> Dear Sir: G. A. Mills of this district has handed me your letter (per S. Y. Penrod) enclosing account of finding a body of a murdered man in F. Truchot's house by Rob. Davis. The memorandum book found containing the entries quoted in your letter I, as well as G. A. Mills and others, identify as the property of one William Pepo of this place, now absent.
>
> Pepo, whose description is attached, has served several sentences here for theft, having completed his last sentence (inflicted by myself) in January. Then he went to Mucleod where he worked until the end of May, as you will see by attached letter, which he wrote to a friend here, and subsequently went to Montana. I am now endeavoring to ascertain if he left Mucleod with any one, presumably the murdered man. In the event of his returning here, let me know if you desire any steps to be taken.

Inspector Cuthbert then described Pepo as, "fair, light blue or grey eyes, aged 40 years, powerfully built, height about 5 feet 8 inches, bald headed, sharp features, not bad looking, had beard and mustache when here. Is a German and speaks English perfectly. Is well educated for a laboring man. Has done journalistic work and writes shorthand." Inspector Cuthbert later learned that Pepo had left McLeod with a German named James Plath and informed the sheriff that Plath had not been heard of since. A description of Plath matched the deceased. Pepo, in height, was about the same as the murdered man, but his weight was much heavier, being about one hundred eighty pounds, and Pepo's breast measured forty inches while his victim was a slimly built man.

The sheriff wrote all these facts to Governor Robert B. Smith requesting that a reward be offered for William Pepo; the governor responded by posting the $250 reward for his apprehension. Reward circulars with Pepo's description were widely distributed. On September 16, 1898, Sheriff Hagen and August Kropp went to Batavia, Minnesota, to identify a man jailed there. He was of the same height and build as Pepo and there were other similarities but the long hair on the sides of his bald head had been trimmed and his heavy beard had been shaved clean. He had spoken German to the Minnesota sheriff when arrested but when Hagen and Kropp arrived the prisoner claimed to be Irish, and every effort by Kropp to converse with the prisoner in German failed.

The suspected murderer was held at Batavia until further information could be sent from the Northwest Territory. During the early days of 1899, William Pepo was positively identified and brought to Choteau County for trial. At the spring term of the District Court Pepo was tried and convicted of first degree murder. He was sentenced to hang but an appeal and the petition for commutation of sentence delayed the execution for nearly a year. Both efforts finally failed and he was sentenced to hang on April 6, 1900.

Pepo's last night was spent chatting with his guards and newspaper reporters until midnight. He several times declared he was innocent but would not argue the matter in any respect. He smoked for the greater part of the evening and at midnight expressed a desire to retire, complaining that there was not much time left. Pepo slept soundly until 5:30 A.M. and the sheriff had some difficulty arousing him. He dressed and then refused breakfast, and the death warrant was read to him in his cell. The condemned man marched from the jail at 6:00 A.M. requiring no support. He surveyed the forty witnesses that had gathered to see him die and then looked up at the sun just breaking over the high board fence surrounding the gallows. He smiled at the deputies binding his legs and moved about to help them do their job. The noose was adjusted and just before the black hood was pulled on, the prisoner was asked if he had anything to say, and he replied, "I have nothing to say; you are hanging an innocent man."

The hood was pulled down and then Sheriff Hagen raised his hat and a deputy, concealed behind a curtain, cut the restraining rope releasing the one thousand pound weight at 6:09 A.M. Pepo was jerked about thirty inches into the air breaking his neck, then settled back to rope's end. He was pronounced dead twelve minutes later and ten minutes after that his remains were cut down. The body was placed in a plain coffin provided by the county and buried in the Choteau County cemetery at 3:00 P.M. with the resident Methodist minister conducting a brief ceremony. Pepo left two letters, one written to the Reverend C. E. Cunningham and one addressed to a female friend, but in neither was there any word of a confession. He never divulged his true name or any history further back than six years previous to his execution.

Butte Miner (MT): April 7, 1900. *Inter Mountain* (Butte, MT): April 8, 1900. *Teton Chronicle* (Choteau, MT): July 1, 1898; July 29, 1898; August 5, 1898; September 16, 1898; September 23, 1898.

Lucey, Daniel
September 14, 1900

Daniel Lucey, sometimes spelled Lucy, was born in County Kerry, Ireland, in 1858 but came to America with his parents when a small child. The family settled in Boston where Lucey, when a teen, served a three year apprenticeship with a plumber. As an adult he moved west, enlisted in the army and was assigned to the 13th Infantry, serving from 1882 to 1886. He then transferred to the 6th Cavalry and fought in the Apache Wars, but in 1889 he was ordered to do plumbing work as a part of his duties, so he deserted and took up mining in Arizona. He drifted from one mining camp to another and finally left for Butte, Montana, arriving in 1890. He remained in the vicinity of Butte moving from one mining job to another, usually under an alias because the circumstances under which he lost one job prevented him from getting the next, and his favorite alias was Dan Sullivan.

Patrick L. Regan was a thirty-two-year-old miner well known in Butte. He was initiated into the Miner's Union in March 1895 and worked at the Anaconda and other mines during the next three years. Regan saved several hundred dollars and in August 1898 he decided to go to the Coeur d'Alene country. Daniel Lucey was familiar with that country and convinced Regan they could "share the perils" of the trip, but Lucey had no money so Regan would have to fund the expedition. On September 2 the two men packed intending to catch the train, and Lucey seemed to own almost nothing so Regan packed some of his clothes in Lucey's valise. Lucey managed to delay Regan long enough to miss the train and then proposed they walk to Silver Bow Junction west of Butte where he knew the keeper of a lodging house and where, he claimed, he could get them first class accommodations. He said that the next day they would proceed by train, and when they reached Rocker, Lucey urged Regan to buy a bottle of whiskey. Getting a late start ensured that the two men would arrive at Silver Bow Junction after dark so when they reached that place there were no vacancies. Lucey proposed they continue to Gregson Springs, eight miles farther west and a shorter trip than returning to Butte. Gregson Springs was well known as a place where one could find lodging, food or drink at any hour so Regan agreed. When the two men reached Silver Bow Canyon thirteen miles west of Butte, a few miles east of the Springs, Lucey picked up jagged three-cornered rock and knocked Regan down and then crushed his skull. It had rained during the day and the stream was swollen and filled with heavy silt and debris, so Lucey dragged the body two hundred yards, through a barbed wire fence that scratched his face, and threw the body into the stream. He was confident that the body would be covered with silt and sink, and by 5:00 A.M. Lucey was seen walking alone eastward along the railroad tracks.

He carried a valise into Schiffman's Saloon, ordered a whiskey and paid with a $20 gold piece. He was wet, one leg of his trousers was badly torn, and his face was scratched and bleeding. He stayed several hours, drinking the entire time, then went to the depot to buy a ticket on the train to Anaconda. He threw down his money but when a man came in and announced that a body had been found, and that murder was suspected, Lucey hurried out without his change, ticket, or valise. Lucey cut across country two miles to Stuart and then went on to Anaconda. When the newspaper arrived in Anaconda he read the account of finding the body, went to his room and lit the lamp, then told the lodging house keeper he would be back, went out but never returned.

The account Lucey read in the newspaper stated that at 8:00 A.M. section foreman Henderson and some hands were making repairs on the track of the BA&P Railroad at a point where Silver Bow Creek winds to within a few feet of the tracks. Henderson's attention was attracted to an object in the creek and he investigated, finding the body of a dead man partially submerged. The silt of the stream had permeated the clothing and caused it to sink, but this also lodged it against an obstruction where it had remained until the water subsided to expose it. The body was unrecognizable but the injuries and turned-out pockets strongly suggested that he had been the victim of robbery and murder.

The crew searched and located the scene of the killing at the east end of the canyon, where they found a pool of blood and several bloody stones. There was a trail where the body had been dragged. A few coins, dropped by the murderer in his hasty search of the victim, were found in the grass thirty feet from the creek. The coroner was notified and the body was removed to Butte. Mike Regan, Patrick's brother, identified the body and said he had left the previous evening with a man named Sullivan. The search for Regan's traveling companion began and the fugitive was soon identified as Daniel Lucey, so rewards were posted for his arrest and the fugitive's description was circulated by the sheriff of Silver Bow County:

> I will guarantee a reward of $300 for the arrest of Dan Lucy [*sic*], alias Dan Sullivan, who murdered Patrick L. Regan in Silver Bow canyon on the night of September 2, 1898.
>
> This murder which stands as an exceptionally horrible one, committed for the purpose of robbery, has aroused an intense feeling in the city of Butte, and all citizens are eagerly awaiting news that will tell of the arrest of the murderer. The description of the man is as follows: Height about 5 feet 9 inches; weight about 170 pounds; light complexion; wore sandy mustache when last seen; has full face and blue eyes; age about 37 years; wore a suit of dark clothes with vest to match; he may have a scratch or scratches on his face as a result of the encounter with Regan; is square built and has the appearance of an ordinary looking working man; has followed mining; has been a sailor and soldier; usually has not

> much to say in company; is a heavy drinker and is liable to be found around saloons.
>
> I desire your earnest co-operation in hunting for the above described person, and in addition to the reward mentioned you will receive the thanks of the city of Butte if you are successful in your endeavor to arrest and hold the man wanted.

The circular resulted in a number of sightings and several arrests, but each time the person arrested was cleared and released. However, in April 1900 Lucey stopped in a saloon at Cripple Creek, Colorado, where the bar was tended by a man who formerly lived in Butte. He recognized Lucey and called a policeman, who at first refused to take action, but when the barkeep made the arrest and grappled with Lucey, the officer stepped in and lodged the fugitive in jail. Lucey had avoided detection by staying among the hobo and criminal element and they objected to Lucey's extradition, but when the Butte officer pulled his six-shooter he was allowed to take his prisoner out of town. When Lucey arrived in Butte he was still wearing the same trousers worn during the murder except that the tear had been sewn. While awaiting trial he discarded the trousers, obtained a pair of overalls, and cut off the tattered leg and managed to dispose of it, though a remnant of the trousers was found under his mattress.

Lucey was tried in Judge Clancy's courtroom in August 1899, convicted of first degree murder, and on August 26 he was sentenced to hang. His attorney then excused himself from the case and attorney B. S. Thresher filed an appeal with the state Supreme Court, which stayed the execution. The Supreme Court took nearly a year to affirm the lower court's judgment and sentence, and then on August 14, 1900, Judge Clancy sentenced Lucey to hang one month later. Thresher's efforts to obtain a commutation or respite from Governor Robert B. Burns failed.

On the Wednesday before his execution the condemned man sent for James Hayes, clerk of Judge Clancy's court, and said he would give the clerk a statement that evening. In the meantime Lucey was visited by a priest who convinced him to forego a public statement, so Hayes was turned away when he came at 7:00 P.M. Before 8:00 P.M. a man and lady called upon Lucey and later he said that she was his only relative in Butte. Late Thursday, Lucey asked that his execution the following day be delayed until 11:00 A.M., instead of 8:00 A.M. as originally planned, and the sheriff granted his request. At 10:00 P.M. Undersheriff Murphy gave the jailor the new suit of clothes for Lucey, and a half hour later the prisoner was visited by C. F. Kelly, deputy chief to the county's district attorney. Next came the sheriff's wife, her daughter and a Miss O'Neill who comforted the prisoner. The jail closed at 11:00 P.M. and Lucey knelt beside his cot and prayed until 11:40 P.M. when he drank a glass of beer and then laid on his bed, reading his prayer book until he fell asleep at 12:45 A.M. Lucey awoke at 4:00 A.M. but did not rise until 7:30 A.M. when two Catholic sisters called upon him and remained until 10:00. A half hour later Fathers DeSiere and Harrington joined him and later Fathers Battens and McGlynn arrived.

The counter poise gallows had not been used for a year and had been stored in the courthouse basement. It had been inspected and found to be as good as new but was not erected in the southwest corner of the jail yard until Thursday. The executioner would be hidden behind a six foot board fence. At 11:00 A.M. the death warrant was read to Lucey in his cell and the procession to the gallows began with Father DeSiere on his right and Father Harrington on his left, dressed in their priestly vestments, and two other priests walked behind. Lucey held a crucifix tightly in his right hand and never released his grip. He stepped onto the matting covering a platform two feet wide, two and one half feet long and four inches high and took his position beneath the noose, facing the crowd. The process of pinioning his arms and legs began immediately and while the deputies worked Lucey said to the witnesses, "Well, ladies and gentlemen: The only statement I have to make is that I was convicted by the *Anaconda Standard* through prejudice. I also blame the county attorney. I want to thank all my friends for the way they have treated me while I have been in here and I thank the good fathers and sisters for the wonderful things they have done for me. I forgive all and beg to be forgiven. I am ready and willing to die."

The priests then prayed for him and each kissed him. The black hood was pulled on and the noose adjusted and in but a moment, at 11:11 A.M., the counter poise weight was dropped. Lucey's neck was broken as his body was jerked three feet into the air, then settled back so that his feet dangled a foot above the platform. County physician Dr. P. J. Sheeran and Dr. T. J. Murphy announced that the prisoner's heart ceased to beat at 11:16 A.M. and after hanging a few minutes more the body was cut down and turned over to undertaker Sherman for burial.

Once the body was prepared the doors of Sherman's undertaking parlor on East Park Street were thrown open and throngs of curious people lined up to see Lucey's remains. During the first hour six hundred twenty-five people passed through single-file, but it was still some time before the doors could be closed. Services were performed that evening and again in the morning, and Lucey's remains were then taken to the cemetery and buried.

Lucey, before his death, would not comment on the numerous unsolved murders in the area but he became a strong suspect after his conviction. These murders included a man found killed and left in an old mine shaft west of Missoula Gulch a year earlier. A bullet-riddled body was found about the same time near Brown's Gulch two miles from Silver Bow Junction. The body of old man Schwab, with a single fatal bullet wound, was found in a tunnel near the old West Side Roadhouse. Although Lucey might have had a hand in these and several other murders for robbery, he almost certainly murdered Tim Leary in Silver Bow Canyon in October 1896. However, none of these murders were ever solved.

Inter Mountain (Butte, MT): September 3, 1898; September 5, 1898; September 10, 1900; September 13–14, 1900.

McArthur, James
September 6, 1901

James McArthur, sometimes spelled MacArthur, alias James Fleming, was a career criminal when, in 1899, he was nearing the end of a prison term at the penitentiary in Deer Lodge, Montana. Clinton Dotson was registered at the prison and assigned to his cell; Dotson had been sentenced to a life term for the murder of Eugene Cullinane in American Gulch, which was fifteen miles north of Avon. Dotson had been at American Gulch visiting his father, Captain Oliver Dotson, and was captured several days after Cullinane's body was found. He was in the company of Ellis Persinger and Oliver Benson and all three men were arrested, tried and convicted of murder.

Dotson concocted a scheme which would earn pardons for himself and for the two men convicted with him. He told McArthur he had robbed a train in Wyoming and cached $15,000 of the loot, and promised McArthur half if his cell mate would perform the necessary tasks to get him released. McArthur, who had poor prospects at best, believed his cellmate's story and agreed to the plan. Dotson told his plan to Benson and Persinger, each serving a ten year term, and promised that it would get them pardoned. Persinger told the warden the details of Dotson's plan but the scheme seemed so bizarre and unprecedented in the annals of crime that Persinger was not believed.

As soon as McArthur was released he traveled to Washington Gulch where Captain Dotson had moved after his son was convicted of a murder in American Gulch. McArthur carried a message from the captain's son and befriended the seventy-three-year-old man. He stayed with the captain which gave him an opportunity to study his host's handwriting, and he traveled with the captain to various places over the next few weeks. On January 8

McArthur and the captain stopped at the saloon of Becky Ferris. McArthur, under the influence of liquor, proudly related the details of the scheme and Ferris warned the captain, but he would not believe her.

On January 10 the captain contracted smallpox and was sent to the pesthouse in Helena where he remained until February 13, but meanwhile McArthur returned to the captain's cabin and began to make preparations. He did not fear discovery or interference, as the captain was a newcomer to the gulch and was rarely visited by the other old timers. The interior of the cabin was divided into two rooms by a plank partition so McArthur cut a square hole in a plank about five feet above the floor and covered it with a cloth, so the back room would remain darkened. On the morning of February 1 McArthur went to the cabin of Herman Ruther and borrowed a bottle of ink, which he returned that evening. Throughout the period from January 12 to February 15 McArthur was seen at the captain's cabin, and smoke from the stove showed that the cabin was occupied, but no one investigated.

Captain Dotson returned home from the pesthouse on February 15, 1901, and a few minutes after he entered his cabin a shot was heard by several neighbors. At 2:00 P.M. the stranger who had been living at the cabin left southward towards Avon, frequently looking back. McArthur was next seen passing the home of Michael Killey a mile south, and a mile farther on he passed two men who knew him. He reached Avon at 6:00 P.M. where a half dozen men recognized him. Three days later the body of Captain Dotson was found, shot through the head and lying in the east front room. On a wash stand were two handwritten documents, one a will and the other a confession, and the position of the body and circumstances were supposed to look like a suicide. A gun was fastened to the wall pointing in the direction of the body and a string was attached to the trigger, passing backward around a nail, the end of the string had been dropped between the captain's feet, and one shell in the gun was empty.

A careful examination of the scene revealed that the body had not fallen at that spot, as a large pool of blood was found in the northeast corner, and had been carefully concealed. A trail of blood ran from the pool to where the body was found, showing the captain had been moved after death, and the hair on the back of the captain's head was turned backward, revealing he had been dragged by his feet. The documents on the wash stand were not in the captain's handwriting and later experts would testify that these two documents were written with McArthur's hand, but poorly disguised to appear as if the captain had written them. The will left everything to Clinton Dotson, the captain's son then in prison. The confession said that the captain and son-in-law Ed Cachelin murdered Eugene Cullinane and that Cachelin took Cullinane's watch to Helena and hid it in the bedtick of Clinton Dotson's wagon, which had resulted in the conviction of three innocent men, and guilt and remorse had driven the captain to suicide. There were other matters in the confession which further pointed to McArthur as the author.

McArthur was well-schooled in the tramp's method of traveling unseen on trains and he could have easily avoided capture, but he had developed a fondness for one of Mr. Berry's daughters, lingered at the Berry ranch in Missoula County, and was apprehended there. McArthur, when arrested, talked freely of the details of the crime and Clinton Dotson's part in it, and testified in equal detail at his trial. He was convicted of first degree murder and sentenced to hang by Judge J. M. Clements of Helena.

In the southeast corner of the jail yard a sixteen foot board fence was erected enclosing five thousand square feet. The scaffold was the same on which Daniel Lucey had hanged on September 14, 1900, and it had been thoroughly tested, and in the northeast corner of the enclosure diagonally in front of the gallows a stand had been erected for the press. McArthur was visited on the morning before his execution by spiritual advisors the Reverend Phelan of Helena and the Reverend Aikens of

Philipsburg. The prisoner declared he would give no trouble, but later said that the officers would never take him from his cell.

He was watched closely because he vowed after his conviction that he would cheat the hangman, and two weeks prior to his date with the executioner he had tried to commit suicide. He used a needle, the only implement he could obtain, to sever several arteries in his wrist and thumb. Once weakened from the loss of blood he gave up, became ill, and was bedridden for two days under a doctor's care. He constantly tried to get visitors to bring poison and made other feeble attempts at self-destruction so, at times, he was double-ironed.

By midday Thursday, however, McArthur was "as jovial as a man at a fair" when he greeted the newspaper reporter. The morning paper had said McArthur treated death as a joke and he responded, "Could I regard death as a joke, could any man? It is a serious thing; I am going to meet my Maker because people want me to. I am innocent of the crime for which my life must pay the penalty. But, who cares?" He said that his friends would clear his name and that his brothers Will from Butte and John from Lisbon, South Dakota, were then in town. He confided to Sheriff McMahon and Undersheriff Dee that he had a wife and two daughters in South Dakota and said, "They never wanted for anything when I had anything to give them. Why, once I held a man up in Helena and took $400 from him and expressed every cent of it to my family, going broke myself."

On McArthur's final night he was watched by Charles Aspling and Frank Comstock. He stayed up all night talking with the two deputies who had been locked in his cell. Several times he called for whiskey and the drinks braced him up. The *Inter Mountain* reporter called at 2:00 A.M. and McArthur warned, "Don't sleep too late, you must be here on time to see me jerked." When day broke the prisoner yelled to the jailor, "Come on, McMahon said I was to be up early for breakfast. He said 5 o'clock. Come on there and get breakfast for me, you fellows have got to hang me at 10 o'clock." However, breakfast was delayed until after McArthur received Holy Communion from Father Phelan and two Sisters of Charity at 8:00 A.M., after they had erected an altar under the north jail window where they talked and then baptized the prisoner into the Catholic faith. This was followed by a mass and then Father Phelan, after hearing McArthur's confession, gave him the last sacrament.

After the father and sisters left the prisoner grew moody, and as he was shaved he began complaining about every inconsequential matter. He ate a hearty breakfast at 8:30 A.M. and then his brothers were admitted. During the visit, the condemned was man dressed in his burial clothes, a neat fitting black suit with turned down collar and a black bow tie. He continued to protest his innocence and now accused Perry Ouchley and Ed Cachelin of his crime. His brothers insisted he was never married but he persisted in saying he had two daughters, now claiming they were living in Amboy, Illinois. As the fatal moment approached McArthur was visited by Fathers Phelan, Aiken and Thompson, who prayed with him. At 10:08 A.M. Sheriff McMahon read the death warrant and this seemed to settle the prisoner. The procession to the gallows followed at 10:15 A.M. with Fathers Phelan and Thompson leading; next came the prisoner with Father Aiken on his right and the sheriff on his left, and they were followed by Undersheriff Dee and the two death watch guards. As they passed Clinton Dotson's cell McArthur's accomplice asked, "Won't you forgive me, Mac?" and McArthur replied, "I can say good-bye but I can't forgive," but then at the strong urging of Father Phelan he forgave the man who had placed him in this predicament. Dotson then "collapsed and cried like a small child."

It had stormed from 9:00 P.M. the previous night until 4:00 A.M.; snow had fallen and melted, so now it was cold and wet in the jail yard and heavily overcast. As McArthur stepped into the yard he hesitated for a moment to examine the gallows, then glanced at the crowd of one hundred fifty witnesses before he walked to the platform and took his place beneath the noose. "Friends," he called out, "I want your attention for a few moments. I am about to meet my Maker. I am here to die an innocent man. I have been wronged and God knows it. I forgive everybody. I go with a clear conscience to meet my Maker. I thank you for your attention and am now ready to meet my Maker. Good-bye all!"

Sheriff McMahon waited until he was done speaking and then pinioned his arms and legs, and McArthur assisted in adjusting the noose and black hood by tilting his head. When all was prepared at 10:20 A.M. the restraining rope was cut and the three hundred twelve pound weight dropped. McArthur was jerked into the air and the condemned man's neck was neatly broken, so that the body displayed neither a convulsion nor a twitch. In fifteen minutes county physician Dr. J. H. Owens and Drs. Glass and Dodds could feel no pulse, so at 10:43 A.M. they pronounced him dead. McArthur's remains were lowered into a basket and turned over to undertaker Bien for preparation. One hour later the body of James McArthur was interred in a plot provided by Warden Conley.

Inter Mountain (Butte, MT): April 3–5, 1901; September 5–7, 1901. *Butte Miner* (MT): April 3–5, 1901.

Dotson, Clinton
April 4, 1902

Oliver Dotson had earned his nickname "Captain" during his youth while commander of a Mississippi river boat. Later he drifted to South Dakota where he lived for many years and, though an eccentric, married and raised a large family. At age sixty-seven he moved to American Gulch, fifteen miles north of Avon, Montana, and three miles west of Washington Gulch along the Northern Pacific rail line. Both gulches had been prosperous placer mining camps a quarter of a century earlier but now only old timers who had hung on when the gold played out lived there. Captain Dotson and his son-in-law, Edward Cachelin, mined the placers and did well enough to fill their cupboard and have a few dollars left over.

In 1899 Captain Dotson's son Clinton and his grandson Oliver Benson came from South Dakota for a visit. They stayed several weeks then started for Helena with a span of small horses and a wagon. A few days after they left, the body of Eugene Cullinane, a neighbor of Captain Dotson, was found brutally murdered and Dotson's son and grandson were suspected. Two days after the grisly discovery the two suspected murderers, and a third man named Ellis Persinger, were arrested near Bozeman still driving the same team and wagon. In the bedtick of the wagon was found Cullinane's watch, taken when he was killed, and all three men were charged with murder. The watch proved to be the strongest item of evidence against them, as they could not explain how they had possession of it if not involved in the murder. They were convicted and Benson and Persinger received ten year prison terms while Clinton Dotson was sentenced to life.

At the prison Clinton Dotson shared a cell with James McArthur, who was about to be released. Dotson convinced McArthur that he had robbed a train in Wyoming and cached $15,000 of the loot. He promised to pay McArthur half that sum if he would perform a task for him. McArthur, a long time criminal and frequent convict, appreciated the ingenuity of Dotson's plan and the payoff, so he agreed.

Dotson then made the mistake of telling Persinger the details of his plan to get the three murderers out of prison and Persinger told the warden, but his story seemed so implausible that he was not believed. Dotson and McArthur had conspired to kill Captain Oliver Dotson and make it look like a suicide, and leave two forged documents — a will leaving everything to Clinton Dotson and a confession to the murder of Cullinane. The confession would say that Ed Cachelin followed Clinton Dotson's wagon and hid the watch in the bedtick at the direction of Captain Dotson. Clinton was certain that the latter document would be believed, would prove his innocence, and would gain him a pardon. McArthur carried out the plan but in a manner so slipshod that the captain's death was immediately recognized as murder with McArthur as the author of the crime and the forgeries.

On February 16 McArthur sent a coded letter to the penitentiary stating that the work was done. When arrested McArthur readily confessed to every detail of the crime and implicated Clinton Dotson as his co-conspirator. James McArthur and Clinton Dotson were tried separately for the murder of Captain Dotson, McArthur first. Judge J. M. Clements of Helena presided over both cases and Dotson was convicted of first degree murder, and on July 20 he was sentenced to hang on September 6, 1901. He obtained a respite while the state Supreme Court considered his sentence, and after it was affirmed he was re-sentenced on March 24, 1902, to hang on April 4. There followed a deluge of letters requesting commutation, including a letter from a mother of nine children claiming to be Clinton Dotson's wife and another letter from one of those children, a twelve-year-old girl. For days before his execution Dotson expressed a horror of the crowd, saying, "I don't mind to die, but I do hate to face the crowd that will be here to see me go through this awful ordeal. If it was not for that I wouldn't care."

On the day before his execution Dotson slept until 10:00 A.M. and awoke with a surly attitude. The Reverend A. B. Martin arrived to provide spiritual comfort and sat with him while he ate a hearty breakfast. Sheriff McMahon ordered the suit of clothes that Dotson would wear on the scaffold and J. E. Maple of Butte took the prisoner's measurements. During the remainder of the morning and early afternoon Dotson continued to hope for clemency but word came at 4:00 P.M. that Governor Joseph K. Toole refused to interfere. Dotson had refused to talk until he heard from the governor but then said, "I will give it up. I have fought this thing off as long as I can, and until I am tired and weak." During his last evening Dotson ate a hearty supper and drank whiskey until he started chatting freely with reporters. He told a bit of his history, smoked several cigars, and stroked his graying beard as he talked. When asked about his part in his father's murder he said, "I am ready to die but I am innocent of my father's death. I go hoping that people who have had it in for me will think of me kindly as they can. But I am innocent. That is all."

That night Undersheriff Dee and Charles Aspling were placed in his cell to ensure that he did not take his own life. The prisoner did not fall asleep until 4:00 A.M., after he was given whiskey. It did not sit well at first and he became sick but finally fell asleep. He was awake at 6:00 A.M. and an hour later the Sisters of Charity arrived for prayer services. Breakfast was brought but he could not eat and had only coffee. Father Phelan arrived at 10:50 A.M. and they were joined by the Reverend Martin, and the clergy provided support when Sheriff McMahon arrived at 11:20 A.M. to read the death warrant. When the sheriff concluded Dotson called for whiskey and drank enough to brace up, and then the procession formed and proceeded to the gallows.

Five hundred people surrounded the scaffold on April 4, 1902, when Dotson took his place on the platform. He was asked if he had anything to say but he declined. At 11:26 A.M. the straps were applied to his arms and legs and the noose was adjusted. It took only two minutes from the time he stepped onto the gallows to the moment when the black hood was pulled over his head, and the signal was immediately given to cut the restraining rope. A three hundred twelve pound counter poise weight dropped and Dotson's body shot upwards, breaking his neck in the sudden jerk. Drs. J. H. Owens and E. F. Dodds monitored Dotson's heart beat and pronounced him dead at 11:43 A.M.. Dotson's remains were lowered, the rope cut, and the body was turned over to M. Bein and Son, undertakers. That evening Dotson was buried next to co-conspirator James McArthur in a plot provided by Warden Conley.

Inter Mountain (Butte, MT): April 3–5, 1901; September 5–7, 1901. *Butte Miner* (MT): April 3–5, 1901.

Martin, James
February 23, 1904

Charles Lennox and James Martin were tramps, and on the evening of May 19, 1902, they found themselves stranded at Silver Bow Junction on their trip east. They spent most of that day drinking in the saloon and at 9:00 P.M. they stepped out onto the railway platform and saw John R. Williams, a brakeman, walking toward them. When the brakeman came abreast of Martin and Lennox they ordered him to put up his hands, but instead of obeying, Williams struck Lennox, knocking him off the platform onto his back. Williams turned to flee and was shot in the back, the bullet ranging upwards only slightly, and the following day this proved to be a fatal wound. Before he died Williams said it was the larger of the two men who had shot him and this would have been Lennox, who had been knocked to the ground.

Meanwhile Martin and Lennox had fled and hid in a boxcar on the Oregon Shortline. Two days later they were arrested at Dillon and charged with Williams' murder. Two pistols were found in the lining of the boxcar, so it was clear that both men were armed at the time of the robbery and murder. As soon as the two prisoners arrived at the Silver Bow jail, Lennox confessed and said that Martin had shot the brakeman, but when confronted with Lennox's statement, Martin denied that he shot Williams. The officials of the county attorney's office relied upon the physical evidence and determined that, from the angle of the wound and Lennox's position on his back below the platform, he could not have fired the fatal shot. However, Lennox's confession was voluntary, without inducement or promise, so he was given no immunity from prosecution.

Both men were charged with and indicted for first degree murder. Martin and Lennox were convicted, sentenced to hang, and appeals followed for both. In August, while their appeals were pending, Martin and Lennox managed to escape from jail. The men separated and Martin, in three days, had made his way to a point fifteen miles north of Walkerville, but he was in poor health from hunger and thirst, so he found it necessary to stop at a cabin for food. While he ate deputy sheriff McKenna appeared and arrested him without resistance. Lennox was never again seen or heard of in the state. Martin, upon his return to jail, was kept in one of the principal corridors under constant observation while his appeal was being decided. When the appeal was denied in early January 1900 Martin was moved to a death row cell. Martin's attorney, Thomas Morrin, applied for a rehearing, and when that was refused the Women's Christian Temperance Union and the Florence Crittenton Society took his case to Governor Joseph K. Toole, requesting a commutation of sentence to life in prison on the grounds that Martin's health was so poor that he would soon die in prison, but the governor refused to interfere.

Late Monday afternoon Martin began to make his final preparations for his Tuesday execution. He bathed in the sheriff's living quarters, dressed in his burial clothes, and then asked to see the gallows and, in the company of the sheriff, looked it over carefully. As soon as night fell the courthouse and jail became a scene of subdued activity but remained the center of curious attention. Between 8 and 9 o'clock the Reverend Bovard baptized Martin into the Methodist faith and afterwards women named Wedlake, McCullough, Johns and Woodberry sang and prayed with him for an hour. At ten o'clock Sheriff John J. Quinn asked him to set the hour of his execution and he requested 4:30 A.M. The reverend and women left before eleven o'clock and from then until 1:00 A.M. Martin passed the time smoking and visiting with friends and with his favorite death watch guard, David Keefe. He ate a light meal of tamales and coffee with Keefe and jailor Dolan while other officers dropped in to talk with him. Salvatore Franchеschi, another murderer, bade him good-bye.

Soon afterward Wedlake and Johns returned and prayed with him until 4:17 A.M. When they left they took away the flowers that decorated his cell, and wept unabashedly. Mrs. Bovard followed and prayed with the prisoner, after which he called for the deputies and bade them all farewell. When he came to deputy sheriff McKenna, who had tracked and captured him after his escape, he said, "Good-bye Jack; God bless you."

Long before the hour set for the execution a large crowd had assembled in the jail yard. They surged forward toward the gallows only to be pushed back again and again by deputies and extra policemen hired for that purpose. At one point the surging mass nearly broke down the railing around the gallows, so the crowd was pushed into the courthouse, but they pushed forward into the yard again. The executioner could not get through the crowd of spectators so Sheriff Quinn, who was determined to protect the hangman's identity, ordered the crowd moved outside of the enclosure and, after some effort, the gates were closed behind them. The hangman took his place behind the curtain, the gates were reopened, and the crowd surged forward one last time.

At 4:30 A.M. Sheriff Quinn appeared at Martin's cell door to ask if he was ready and the prisoner said he was. His arms were pinioned and the procession began from the jail down to the yard and onto the platform. Once under the noose Martin chose to sing and pray, as there was some delay in finding deputy Pelletier who was to read the death warrant. Martin struck up "Rock of Ages," which was followed by a short prayer and then the Reverend Bovard invited the condemned man to sing again, and he chose "There is a Land that is Fairer than Day." While Martin sang the second hymn deputy Pelletier was found and escorted through the crowd to the gallows. The Reverend spoke his last words of encouragement and then Martin said, "My friends, I hope to meet you over there in a land that is fairer than day. Good-bye. God bless you!"

The death warrant was read as Martin's legs were being pinioned and the sheriff then stepped forward, and it took but a moment to drop the noose over the prisoner's head, then cinch and position it beneath his left ear. Martin's hands twitched nervously, clenched and unclenched repeatedly, and his head swayed back and forth. He cast his eyes skyward and then looked at the crowd when he smiled and said, "Good-bye, my friends, Good-bye. God be merciful. God is all wise and God is good. He will forgive me!" The sheriff paused until Martin finished his last statement, then pulled on the black hood. The sheriff took a quick step to the door of the executioner's chamber and slapped the canvas twice. This was followed by the sound of snapping cord; the three hundred fifty pound counter poise weight fell at 4:46 A.M., jerking the condemned man into the air two and one half feet before the body settled back to rope's end.

The body was swinging so the sheriff stepped forward with Dr. Donnelly and each took hold of a wrist to steady it. Martin pulled his knees up, straightened them, twitched his fingers while a shudder passed through the body, and took ten deep breaths before his breathing slowly decreased and ceased in three minutes. At 5:01 A.M. Dr. Donnelly said, "Sheriff, I think your man is dead." The crowd was requested to exit but, when they lingered, they were compelled to leave by a force of deputies. After the crowd was outside the enclosure, and the gates closed, two deputies stepped forward and took Martin's body in their arms. The hanging rope was then cut at the weight to release tension, the body was lowered into the undertaker's basket and the noose was removed.

Martin's remains were taken to Richards' undertaking establishment and prepared for burial. He was placed in a cloth covered casket with a silver breast plate inscribed "At Rest" donated by the undertaker. The casket was next taken to the chapel where anyone could have a last look at the murderer, and the funeral service was scheduled for Saturday at 11:00 A.M. The deceased was dressed in a black serge suit, bloucher shoes, and a black necktie, and a small crucifix was pinned to his lapel. There was hardly a mark on Martin's neck though his face had a slight purple hue, so he appeared more like a man who died a natural death. Following the service James Martin was laid to rest in the city cemetery.

Inter Mountain (Butte, MT): February 23, 1904.

Mott, Louis H.
March 18, 1904

Louis H. Mott and his wife owned a laundry business in Missoula; and it had been a successful enterprise and had supported them and their two daughters. Mott developed a drinking habit and it grew on him until he turned to drugs to try to control it. The business suffered, so the Motts sold out and tried to start again at several places, only to return to Missoula. At various times they saved up considerable money only to have Mott squander it on his addictions. Mott had also developed the habit of abusing his wife, and as his condition deteriorated he began to accuse her of various infidelities, but any who knew them believed she was faithful to her husband.

In January 1904 the Motts were in Missoula where they had re-established their laundry business at the old location. Only through Mrs. Mott's industriousness and frugality had they made a success of the enterprise. She sold the business and their home on the second floor on January 2, 1904, and Louis was enraged when he returned home during the afternoon of January 4, much under the influence of liquor. He accused his wife of plotting against him. She made every effort to explain the situation during a wordy discussion, then to escape his harangue she fled into the kitchen with her two daughters.

When Louis sent nine-year-old Alice and four-year-old Ethel into the hall, saying he wanted to play cards with them, Mrs. Mott began to fear he might harm her, so when Louis walked to the end of the hall at the entrance to the kitchen she went out onto the little landing at the head of the rear stairs. This platform was separated from the kitchen hall by a glass paneled door and Louis went to the door with pistol in hand and shot five times through the glass, and three bullets struck his wife. Mrs. Lockhart, the cook, heard the shooting and thought Louis had shot himself but found him with the pistol in his hand as if he was about to commit suicide. She wrested the pistol from his grip and only then did she see that Mrs. Mott lay wounded on the rear landing.

Mrs. Mott staggered to her feet and down the stairs where she fell, unable to go further. She was rushed to Sister's Hospital and every effort was made to save her but she died in two hours. Mott was immediately placed under arrest and jailed. He said at that time something about "another man" and that it was time he did something about it. He said he tried to finish the job but "the gun wouldn't go." He was tried and convicted of first degree murder at the next term of the court and sentenced to hang. There was no motion for a new trial nor an appeal to the Supreme Court. A petition was sent to Governor Joseph K. Toole seeking a commutation of the sentence to life imprisonment, but he refused to interfere.

On the night before his execution the prisoner was given an opportunity to inspect the gallows, the same which had been used to execute James Martin at Butte a month earlier, and he approved of the preparations. The prisoner did not sleep during his last night but spent his time writing letters and conversing with his spiritual advisors. Father Macklin had spent nearly the entire night with him and during that time baptized him into the Catholic faith. At 5:00 A.M. two Sisters of Charity came to pray with him and remained for twenty minutes. Shortly before 6:00 A.M. Sheriff Thompson appeared at the door to his cell and the body straps were loosely applied so that he could still use his limbs, and then the procession to the gallows began.

The condemned man, with Sheriff Thompson by his side, led the way with Undersheriff Sterling and deputies Gagnon and Watson behind, and Father Macklin in the rear. The crowd had been gathering since 5:00 A.M., and when the gates were opened forty-five minutes later two hundred spectators jammed through to the railing, ten feet from the platform. Still, this crowd barely filled half the space provided for the witnesses. The executioner, who would remain anonymous, was already in position behind a curtain. The condemned man was escorted through the cells and the procession descended to the ground floor, hence into the jail yard and to the gallows which was within the high stockade adjoining the jail.

The prisoner took his place under the noose and, without hesitating for a breath, raised his hands to command silence, "Now gentlemen, I have a few words to say to you." He claimed that there were extenuating circumstances and dishonest methods used to bring about his conviction and insisted that they would some day learn the truth. Next he turned his eyes skyward and said, "Almighty God!" but paused, looked down at the deputies binding his legs and told them it was too tight and they were making him fall. When all the straps were in place the prisoner turned his head skyward again and completed the statement he had begun earlier, saying, "Almighty God, into thy keeping I now resign my spirit. Citizens of Missoula, good-bye."

The black hood was pulled on and the noose positioned and cinched tight and, as the bells of the Catholic Church began to toll at six o'clock, the restraining rope was cut and the heavy counter poise weight dropped. The body was jerked into the air and there was not a quiver, as his neck had been broken. Drs. Buckley, Brown and McCullough pronounced him dead at 6:13 A.M. but the body hung a few minutes longer before being cut down and placed in the coffin provided by the county. Louis Mott was buried that afternoon following a service at the Catholic church.

Inter Mountain (Butte , MT): March 17–18, 1904.

Metzger, Herbert H.
May 5, 1905

Homer P. Ward lived alone in a cabin located between White Sulphur Springs and Neihart on Sheep Creek, several miles from any settlement. He built a house and barn, and he worked hard to improve his property. He had just invested a great deal of time and effort meticulously caulking the logs of his house with moss by driving it into the chinks with a wooden wedge and mallet, and the cabin was nearly air tight in preparation for Montana's severe winter weather.

On November 21, 1904, Thanksgiving eve, twenty-eight-year-old Herbert H. Metzger snuck up on the cabin, peeked through the east window, and found Ward seated at his table eating a meal with his back toward the window. Metzger fired a single shot through the window pane, the bullet taking effect in the back of Ward's head killing him instantly. The shot put a small hole in the glass pane and blew parts of Ward's skull forward, and the leaden ball made another small hole in the west window pane directly opposite the east window. Metzger entered the cabin, put the body on the bed, and ransacked the cabin. He took a number of Ward's personal items including Ward's hat, and discarded his own very distinctive hat. He covered the body with old newspapers and saturated the bed, bedding and body with kerosene, then lit the pyre with a match and fled, but stopped to set fire to the small barn as well. He was certain that the entire cabin, including the body and his hat, would be burned to ashes, hiding the crime and his identity.

However, the cabin was so airtight that the fire quickly consumed all the oxygen and was smothered, and Ward's body was blackened but not consumed. The fire created such a perfect vacuum that two kittens in a box beneath the stove were smothered, and the two bullet holes in the windows and the slight spaces around the door did not admit enough air to save them or fuel the flames. Ward's remains were discovered on Thanksgiving day and the bullet holes in the glass panes, the half eaten meal, the place where the body fell and was dragged to the bed, the bits of skull and brain matter spattered about, the missing property, and all other circumstances told a story of murder for robbery. In the ashes the men found a .30-.30 shell casing, which curiously had not been discolored by the flames.

Officers spent the next several days investigating but had developed no leads until a twelve-year-old boy living with Frank Petite identified the hat belonging to Metzger. This fixed the crime on him, so Major James F. Keown of Bozeman with deputy sheriffs George Williams and John Payne left for the Belt Mountains where the fugitive had gone. They followed Metzger's trail to the camp of Alex Orict near Niehart, arriving on December 4, and in Orict's cabin they found Ward's harness and bear skin coat, so they detained Orict. Metzger arrived within a few hours wearing Ward's hat and carrying Ward's rifle and both men were arrested. Orict was quickly cleared of any complicity, as the work had clearly been done by one man, and all the evidence pointed to Metzger.

The trial began on March 23, 1905, and the defendant testified in his defense, and it may have been a slip of his tongue which convicted him. He insisted he had never been in Ward's cabin and said that Ward's hat had been given to him by a man he did not know, and whom he had met on the road a few miles from the Ward cabin, but said, "I tried the hat on and it was too small. I took the paper out of the hat band and threw it on the floor." Later when he tried to correct "floor" to "grass" it only drew attention to his error. Metzger was convicted of first degree murder, the jury deliberating only two hours, and he was sentenced by Judge Edwin K. Cheadle to hang on May 5, 1905. At his request his attorney did not file a motion nor an appeal for a new trial and Metzger refused to ask for a commutation of sentence or clemency in any form. Although he had no money nor friends in the area he could have written to his family in Ohio for funds, but he refused. He insisted he was innocent and first tried to fix the blame on Orict, but when that failed, he tried through innuendo to shift the blame to others, but the circumstantial and physical evidence had been conclusive and his claims were dismissed.

By April 28 Sheriff C. H. Sherman had posted the invitations. As the date approached for the execution Metzger entertained many visitors but all those who came were merely curious and not particularly sympathetic. He spent his time smoking and chatting with his death watch guards. He had developed a good rapport with Undersheriff George Williams, and they exchanged anecdotes about hangings. Williams found Metzger crying one morning but the prisoner insisted that he was only melancholy thinking about his family, not his impending death.

On Wednesday, May 3, the carpenter was busy building the gallows and erecting the board fence and the sounds of hammer and saw visibly wore on the prisoner's nerves. The gallows was tested on Thursday and found to be in perfect working condition, and the rope had been soaked in soap and water and stretched for several days using a two hundred pound sack of sand, and this weight was also used in testing the apparatus. The pulleys were thoroughly oiled and checked, as this was the same gallows used to hang James Martin on February 23, 1904, at Butte, Silver Bow County, and they wanted to be sure everything worked. The counter poise weight measured only ten by seven by thirteen inches and weighed three hundred ten pounds and was composed of lead encased in tin. The gallows frame was securely braced to the wall of the jail and another brace was placed against the upright beam nearest the noose. The apparatus was assembled inside a forty-two by thirty-two foot enclosure and a railing had been built ten feet from the gallows, to keep back the small crowd of witnesses. A canvas tent was pitched near the post which supported the weight so that the weight and release were concealed from view and the identity of the person who activated the contrivance would remain anonymous.

Two days before his execution Metzger sent a note to Thomas Newman, a barkeep friend, saying, "Please fill this bottle with whiskey and charge it to my account.—Herbert H. Metzger." Newman, with characteristic generosity, opened an account on a clean page of his ledger and sent back word that the prisoner's credit was good until 5 o'clock Friday evening. That morning the prisoner was given a letter from his sister, Ida Young Pierce of Ohio, asking him to come home. He was not much affected by the note and wrote back saying nothing of his situation, and gave his response to the Reverend H. G. Wakefield of Lewiston to post. Wednesday evening three musicians went to the jail with banjo, guitar and harmonica and played a number of tunes for the prisoner, and one ragtime jig prompted Metzger to say, "I'll go to Hell sure if I keep pace with that," and he became nearly hilarious and called out, "Let's have another drink."

During those final days the Reverend Wakefield spent many hours with Metzger, though he did not support the clergy generally and thought them all hypocrites. On Thursday the Reverend arrived early to offer religious consolation but Metzger refused to see him. The prisoner said, "I do not care to talk to him and I want no one to pray for me," but he did consent to seeing a reporter who had agreed to record and publish his statements. Metzger, as he had done before, tried to shift the blame to Alex Orict and said he would have told his story on the witness stand but he feared that he would get a life sentence and preferred to hang.

Later that morning two "women of the town," his only female sympathizers, visited and spent several hours in conversation. On the prisoner's last night J. L. Dilworth sat with him until 3:00 A.M. and then Metzger retired. He arose at 7:00 and dressed for breakfast, and afterward the sheriff opened the jail and the prisoner talked with his many curious visitors. The jail closed for the noon meal and Metzger ate a hearty chicken dinner, then lay down on his cot and napped. The sheriff woke the prisoner at 2:30 P.M. and read the death warrant and Metzger said, "I never lose any sleep over a little thing like this, and I won't lose any hereafter. I feel sorry for the officers; they look like they are going to be hung. I felt like joking when the warrant was read."

Undersheriff Williams entered the cell and said, "Well, Metzger, are you ready?" and he replied that he was. Williams asked, "Do you want a drink first?" and he replied, "I don't give a damn! What have you there? Are you going to put a harness on me?" Metzger put on his coat and, as the leather belt was placed around his waist, Metzger said, "George, God bless you," and then, "Good-bye, Sherman." He called for another drink and it was given, the glass filled to the brim. While he was being prepared a reporter asked, "Have you anything you want us to say for you?" and the prisoner replied, "Give my best wishes to those who have come to see me. A man never knows who his friends are until he is in trouble."

The reporter asked him about that shiny shell casing found in the cabin, which had never been explained, and he replied, "Now it was strange that shell should have been found inside. The first thing a man would do who fired that shot would be to eject another cartridge into the magazine." The reporter suggested that possibly the shell caught in the murderer's clothing and was thus carried in. "No! No!" Metzger responded with another slip of the tongue, "I always wore a sweater up in the mountains there and it could not have caught in that."

The walk to the gallows was made quickly. The condemned man took his place beneath the noose; the sheriff placed it over his head, positioned it behind his left ear, and cinched it tight. Undersheriff Williams, at the same time, applied the straps to the prisoner's ankles and knees. The black hood was pulled on and the sheriff stepped behind the canvas. There was the sharp rap of the clevis followed by the sound of the weight striking the earth at 2:45 P.M. Coincidently the school bell rang for the afternoon recess hour just as Metzger was jerked into the air, then fell back until his toes dangled eighteen inches above the platform. The body convulsed, hands clenched, and his shoulders drew upwards.

The Reverend Wakefield offered a prayer for the murderer's soul as his life ebbed away and Drs. J. M. Kumpe and John Stephens checked his pulse, and in eleven and one half minutes they pronounced him dead. Metzger's neck had not been broken but the spinal cord had been severed. A pine coffin, painted black and with white metal handles, was brought forward and the body was cut down and deposited while the rope was cut into pieces and distributed to the witnesses as souvenirs. Metzger's remains were interred in the city cemetery before sundown.

Inter Mountain (Butte, MT): May 5, 1905. *Meagher Republican* (MT): December 2, 1904; December 9, 1904; December 23, 1904; March 24, 1905; March 31, 1905; April 28, 1905; May 5, 1905.

Lu Sing
April 20, 1906

In 1892 a beautiful Chinese woman married Low Quong, whose family owned the influential Low Quong Chung Company in San Francisco. After the marriage the newlyweds moved to Portland, Oregon, where they lived for fourteen months. The woman then ran away from her husband and lived with a man in Payette, Idaho, for six months. Next she went to Dillon and lived with a Chinese man. It was about that time she learned that the company to which her husband belonged had offered a reward of $600 to any Chinese who would kill the man with whom she was living.

She began to move about often, finally ending in Salt Lake City, Utah. There she met Tom Sing and went with him to Butte, Montana. After two weeks in Butte they moved to Bozeman, where Tom Sing bought a laundry and they settled down. He had been in business for two years in October 1905 and was very well liked and had become a leading citizen in the Chinese community, even though he had cut off his queue (braid) and wore American clothes. The woman had taken Tom Sing's name and believed that her constant moving about for some time had left a cold trail, or at least that in the long period of her absence the company had revoked the reward offer, so she never told Tom Sing there was a price on his head. However, she asked him to always take his meals at home.

Lu Sing, a fifty-year-old Chinese man also known as "Hobo" Sing but not related to Tom Sing, arrived in Bozeman in early September 1905. He worked at several Chinese restaurants for his board. Some said he had been banished from Butte some time ago for being a bad character. On October 1 Lu Sing went to the Reverend M. L. Rickman of the Baptist Church in Bozeman and asked him to address a letter to a Chinese man in San Francisco. The reverend could not understand the name and suggested he take the letter to Tom Sing. Lu Sing threw up his hands and became very excited, saying, "No, Tom Sing bad, bad man," and then tore the letter to shreds.

On October 3 Tom Sing entered Young Sing's restaurant on Main Street near Rouse Avenue and ordered his usual breakfast of ham and eggs. He was served on a meat block in the kitchen, so he pulled up a box for a chair. When everyone in the kitchen was again preoccupied with their work Lu Sing walked behind Tom Sing, seized a hatchet that lay beside the meat block and struck Tom Sing on the head six times so rapidly that he completed the last blow before his victim could fall to the floor. A Chinese cook heard the blows being struck but by the time he turned the attack had ended. However, he saw Lu Sing standing over the body with the bloody hatchet still in his hand. He rushed Lu Sing, threw his arms around him and called for help. Several other Chinese workers then assisted in disarming and holding the prisoner until policeman "Dad" Williams could be summoned. Tom Sing died in his wife's arms fifteen minutes later without regaining consciousness.

Lu Sing was arrested for murder and jailed. Later that day he was turned over to Sheriff E. M. Reynolds, who moved him to the steel cage cell in the county jail. Lu Sing, when questioned, said he was in the restaurant drinking a cup of coffee when he saw a black cloud descend from the heavens between him and Tom Sing. When the cloud lifted Tom Sing was dead. Lu Sing was tried at the November term of the court and after less than two hours in deliberations the jurors convicted him of first degree murder. He was sentenced to hang but the usual appeals and petitions stayed the execution. While he was in jail nearly five thousand people visited to look at the murderer. When it became clear that there would be no clemency or respite granted by Governor Joseph K. Toole, Lu Sing tried to starve himself to death, but his death watch guards forcibly fed him soup.

On the day before his execution Lu Sing was given a plain black suit of "citizen's clothes." He slept little during the evening and at 10:00 P.M. ate heartily before he dressed in his new clothes. May Bon Shing Gout, the Chinese interpreter from Helena, read the death warrant to him in his cell before 1:00 A.M. and then the gates to the jail yard were opened and a crowd of one hundred seventy-five men, including fifteen Chinese men, surged in under the electric lights and took seats on the walls and piles of lumber. A few minutes after 1:00 A.M. the undersheriff and the jailor strapped Lu Sing's arms to his sides and led him out to the gallows. Once in place Lu Sing called for the interpreter and denied his guilt, again blaming the black cloud.

Sheriff Reynolds adjusted the noose while Lu Sing's legs were being pinioned, the black hood was pulled on and the signal given, and though. Lu Sing tottered, he was supported for a moment until the restraining rope was cut. The counter poise weight dropped and the condemned man, while making a guttural sound, was jerked into the air and the body rebounded until his feet dangled fourteen inches above the platform. The shock did not break the prisoner's neck so it took fifteen minutes for Lu Sing to strangle to death, and then Drs. L. E. Safly and Ragsdale pronounced him dead. The body was then cut down and taken to the undertaker's establishment. After Lu Sing's remains were removed curiosity seekers rushed forward and cut the rope in pieces for souvenirs. Only the quick action of the officers saved the gallows from the same fate.

Inter-Mountain (Butte, MT): April 21, 1906.

Fuller, Miles
May 18, 1906

Henry Callahan, a civil war veteran born in 1843, was a placer miner who had lived in Butte, Montana, for quite some time. In 1904 Callahan lived in a cabin south of Silver Bow Creek. In 1897 Callahan's friend, Adolph Schwade, had been murdered and Callahan accused Miles Fuller of the crime, but there was never enough evidence to arrest Fuller. Thereafter the two men became mortal enemies. In 1904 Miles Fuller lived in a cabin south of Silver Bow Creek behind the Colorado Smelter, not far from Callahan's cabin. Fuller was also a placer miner but he had come to Butte some considerable time after Callahan.

On October 24, 1904, Callahan was returning to his cabin through the old, isolated brickyard at about 6:00 P.M. Fuller was stalking Callahan, and H. J. Warfield later said that on the night of the murder he saw Fuller watching Callahan from concealment near the School of Mines. Fuller must have hurried ahead of Callahan, cut him off, and started walking toward him in the direction of town because when the two men came face to face Fuller pulled his revolver and shot at Callahan three times. One bullet penetrated Callahan's breast, then ranged upwards tearing open his throat and severing the jugular vein. Another bullet entered the left eye and lodged in Callahan's brain. The third bullet missed, but either of the other two wounds were fatal. Fuller, however, was not satisfied, so he laid his pistol on the ground, rolled Callahan onto his back, and slashed his throat twice.

George Olnquist and William Symons were passing nearby, heard the shots and rushed to the scene. They were near enough to see Fuller fire the third shot, then lean over the body for a moment before he realized the two men were approaching. Fuller fled before the two witnesses reached Callahan, who was already dead, but they found Fuller's revolver beneath him where the murderer had placed it before rolling Callahan's body onto it.

The authorities were notified and Sheriff Quinn arrested Fuller at his cabin at 8:00 P.M. A fire had recently been started in the stove and Fuller's overcoat lay on his bed where he had thrown it, yet he told the sheriff he had been home two hours. The next day he changed his story and said he got home at 5:00 P.M. and started a fire, then started a second fire just before the sheriff arrived. At the inquest, in addition to the testimony of Olnquist, Symons, Warfield, and the sheriff, another man testified that Fuller told him he would kill Callahan before the end of the year; another witness related that on an earlier occasion Fuller had entered Callahan's cabin and tried to kill him by putting strychnine in his sugar, but this tampering had been discovered. Fuller, in his defense to the last accusation, stated that he knew too much about poison to use strychnine for that purpose and recommended arsenic.

Fuller was indicted, tried, convicted of first degree murder, and sentenced to hang. A motion for a new trial was made and overruled, and his attorneys immediately appealed to the state Supreme Court, and the justices' delay in affirming the lower court's decision left Fuller in jail for more than a year and a half. Finally the court affirmed the judgment and sentence of the lower court, so a petition was sent to Governor Joseph K. Toole asking for a commutation of sentence, but in the meantime Fuller was sentenced to hang on May 18, 1906. The governor, after careful consideration of the case, refused to interfere.

On the Wednesday before his execution Fuller went to bed at 3:00 A.M. and slept soundly. On Thursday Sheriff Quinn made a half dozen visits to Fuller's cell to discuss the time for his execution but the condemned man was indecisive. Finally Sheriff Quinn told Fuller it would be best to have the execution at or before 6:00 A.M. "No, No," Fuller protested, "I want to wait till later." The sheriff said, "But if you wait till later there will be a big crowd, and it will make a spectacle of you." Fuller whined, "I don't care. I don't care if they do come. I want to live as long as I can." The sheriff then told Fuller to be ready at 5:00 A.M. and that settled the matter.

On Thursday evening a large crowd gathered at the jail asking to see the prisoner and Fuller said, "Oh, let them come in," so the doors were flung open and more than one thousand people filed through, including a large number of women. Among the crowd were friends of Fuller and they were allowed to step out of line, shake his hand, and bid him farewell. Finally he grew weary and at his request the doors were closed, leaving a large disappointed crowd outside. Fuller's attorneys, Judge John Lindsay and E. S. Booth, then arrived to arrange his funeral and they settled on undertaker White and Krebs. They advised their client not to make a statement on the scaffold and he agreed. They also arranged for the disposal of his personal effects and he named several friends he wanted to receive certain items.

Fuller did not sleep well his last night and at midnight he ate a light meal. Newspaper reporter Joe Dufors, his death watch guard, spent the night in or near the cell and the Reverend F. H. Gwynne, his spiritual advisor, stayed with the prisoner all night, praying and singing hymns. Finally Fuller laid down to sleep but awoke at 3:00 A.M. and asked the time, and when told he said, "I suppose they will be ready for me soon. The time passes quickly." When dawn broke the prisoner was awake so the Reverend Gwynne resumed his prayers while Fuller lay on his cot staring at the cell window. They were joined by the Reverend Williams and the two clergymen administered the Holy sacrament and read scripture to Fuller before offering a prayer for mercy upon his soul.

The condemned man tried to relax and smoke his last cigar until the ministers told him the time was near, and then he dressed in the black suit provided by the sheriff but declined to wear the white shirt. At 4:00 A.M., from his cell window, Fuller could see the men already taking their seats along the wall of the jail yard and remarked that they might have to wait until noon, then resumed smoking his cigar. He called for a cup of coffee but refused breakfast, and afterwards had a drink of liquor at the suggestion of the ministers. His death watch officers were Jack Leonard, F. E. Hartshorn, and Joe Dufors and they bid him good-bye, and Fuller cried as he shook their hands. When asked what advice he would leave he told the Reverend Gwynne that he would advise men to obey their parents because they would not lead them astray, but said he had been raised by strangers.

At 4:30 A.M. Sheriff Quinn inspected and rigged the gallows: the rope was threaded through the pulleys and attached to the counter poise weight, which was lifted to its resting place on one of the posts. The noose was measured so that it hung down to the height of a man's shoulders and allowed for eighteen inches of slack. Before 5:00 A.M. two thousand people had gathered and many sat on the rear and side walls and blocked the courthouse door, but were held back from the jail yard. Two women had come early enough to secure excellent positions to view the execution, but thought better of it and left.

At 5:00 A.M. the executioner, masked and dressed to conceal his identity, moved quickly from the jail's kitchen door to the executioner's black shed and disappeared inside. County physician J. A. Tremblay and his assistant Dr. Maillett arrived and paced outside the cell door until, at 5:10 A.M., jailor John C. Sullivan and the sheriff came to the cell and the sheriff entered. He removed his hat and sat while Fuller finished singing a hymn, then said, "Well, Miles, you might as well stand up and I'll read this form to you." It was the death warrant and its reading signified that Fuller's time was up. The sheriff asked Fuller if he would speak on the scaffold and he declined.

Deputy sheriff Burke came in during the reading and when the sheriff concluded he strapped Fuller's arms. The procession then began with Sheriff Quinn taking one arm and Burke the other as jailor Sullivan swung the cell door open and they descended into the jail yard through the jail's kitchen door, only ten paces from the gallows. A force of deputies went ahead clearing the way, and the clergy and newspapermen followed the prisoner.

When the doomed man saw the noose he said, "Oh, My God!" The prison pallor, stoop of age, venerable beard, and squinting eyes unaccustomed to direct sunlight all made Fuller look older than he was. As soon as Fuller was beneath the noose his legs were strapped and Sheriff Quinn pulled Fuller's beard aside to position and adjust the noose, and when the noose was cinched Fuller complained, "Don't pull it so tight, please." When the prisoner saw the black hood in the sheriff's hand he said, "Don't put that cap on, boys," but the hood was pulled on and he again groaned, "Oh, My God!"

As the condemned man spoke these last words the sheriff called, "Let 'er go!" and the executioner cut the restraining rope with his knife. A four hundred pound weight fell at 5:23 A.M. and the condemned man was jerked up, breaking his neck, and when the body settled Fuller's toes dangled six inches above the platform. The ministers had stood by the gallows during the execution but all had been done so quickly, about two minutes from cell to jerk, that there was not time for a final prayer. Dr. Tremblay monitored Fuller's pulse and pronounced him dead in eight minutes. When the body was cut down it was taken to the undertaking rooms of White and Krebs at the Knights of Pythias Hall on South Main Street and prepared for burial, and many curious people went there to look at Fuller's remains. The funeral service by Dr. Gwynne was held Saturday at 2:00 P.M. in the undertaking rooms, with burial in Mt. Moriah Cemetery afterwards, all expenses borne by the undertakers.

Inter Mountain (Butte, MT): May 18, 1906.

Rock, George J.
June 15, 1908

George J. Rock was sent to prison from Dawson County on March 16, 1905. He was convicted of murder in the second degree for shooting Ed Corl, the man who had supplanted him in the affections of his wife. While in prison he tried to commit suicide but, failing in that, decided to escape. Chief deputy Robinson was murdered during the attempt to escape by Rock, William Hayes, C. B. Young and Oram Stevens. All four of the men were charged with first degree murder, but Young turned state's evidence and received a life sentence and Stevens was found not guilty. Hayes was convicted and sentenced to hang with Rock but his execution was delayed to April 2, 1909, by an appeal. Rock pled guilty so Judge Winston deferred passing sentence on Rock to allow him time to withdraw his plea, but Rock refused to act and was sentenced to hang on June 15, 1908. He refused to file an appeal or submit a petition for clemency and seemed anxious to die, saying, "I have thrown the dice and lost."

On Rock's last night he read several chapters of the Bible before retiring at 9:00 P.M. He slept soundly until 6:00 A.M., when he arose and ate a hearty breakfast. During the late morning hours Fathers McCormick and Moran and the Reverend Jewett attended to Rock's religious needs but, aside from reading the Bible, the condemned man showed no repentance. He refused opiates and stimulants and seemed eager to have the execution proceed.

At 1:25 P.M. Sheriff Fifer read the death warrant to Rock, with ministers and deputies present, and then Rock's wrists were strapped behind him by the sheriff and the march began from Rock's cell in the old wing of the prison to the gallows in the northeast corner of the penitentiary yard. Father McCormick of Deer Lodge was on his right and Father Moran of Anaconda was on his left; next came Sheriff Fifer, Undersheriff Joseph Larsen, deputy sheriff Selloens and the Reverend Jewett of the Methodist Church at Deer Lodge. Rock took his place on the platform and not a word was spoken by anyone, and even the three hundred spectators watched in total silence. The prisoner's ankles were strapped together while Sheriff Fifer positioned the noose. The black hood was pulled on and in a second the restraining rope was cut and, at 1:30 P.M., the four hundred pound counter poise weight fell and the condemned man was jerked into the air. However, Rock's neck was not broken so it took ten minutes for him to strangle to death.

Drs. Nye and Lee pronounced him dead at 1:40 P.M. and after hanging a while longer Rock's remains were cut down by prison contractors, who took charge of the body. He was buried in the convict's cemetery that afternoon.

Inter-Mountain (Butte , MT): June 15, 1903.

LeBeau, Frederick
April 2, 1909

On June 16, 1908, Frederick LeBeau, a forty-five-year-old Canadian, was traveling with Joe Hobbins when they stopped at the Yoakum Ranch two and one half miles from Fortune in Flathead County, Montana. They bought food but then argued with William F. Yoakum, who ordered them off his property. The following day the two travelers returned to buy food again and this time, on the way, they discussed killing the Yoakums. Once at the ranch the men argued over the asking price for the food so William refused to sell them food and again ordered the two men off his property. LeBeau, without warning, drew his pistol and shot the old man in the abdomen. He then walked up to his victim as he lay writhing on the ground, put the muzzle of his revolver to William's head, and put a second ball into his brain. Riley R. Yoakum, William's son, rushed to help his father and he and LeBeau engaged in a face-to-face shootout, and Riley was so painfully wounded by LeBeau that he committed suicide.

Scott Grubb went to the Yoakum Ranch on June 19 and found the bodies, so he covered them and sent word to bring officers and a coroner from Kalispell. A search of the ranch house revealed a great deal of money and other valuables unmolested, which ruled out robbery as a motive. Absent any indication to the contrary it was believed the father and son, who were known to have violent tempers, had quarreled and killed each other, so a coroner's jury brought in a verdict in accord with that suspicion.

LeBeau fled to Canada while Hobbins went on to Whitefish. Two weeks later, while drinking heavily, Hobbins remarked that he knew something of the crime. He was arrested and he quickly confessed all the details and provided a description of LeBeau. Though he was disbelieved he was jailed while the officers reopened the case. When LeBeau returned to the United States on July 29 he was recognized and arrested at Eureka and then brought to Kalispell. LeBeau told a story close in detail to Hobbins, except in his version Hobbins did the shooting while he was an innocent bystander. He claimed that when the shots were fired he ran and Riley Yoakum fired several shots after him. He dropped behind a fence and thought that Hobbins believed him dead, so he waited until Hobbins left and then made his way to Canada, where he stayed several weeks.

LeBeau first pled guilty but quickly withdrew that plea, was tried and found guilty of first degree murder when the jury disbelieved his story. He was sentenced by Judge Erickson to hang while Hobbins was sentenced to a long prison term. LeBeau's appeal for a new trial was denied by the state Supreme Court, so Governor Edwin L. Norris was petitioned to grant a commutation on the grounds that LeBeau was insane, based upon a variety of bizarre behaviors. The condemned man was examined by Dr. Scanlan and pronounced sufficiently sane for the execution to proceed. The governor refused to interfere, and the date for the execution was set for April 2, 1909.

As the time for LeBeau's execution approached he was nearly in a state of nervous collapse. Two hours before the time set, Senator Long, the prisoner's defense attorney, was called to help brace up the condemned man. Once Long was present the sheriff read the death warrant, but the prisoner objected vehemently until assured that it was required by law. Throughout the reading he objected to the use of the term murder. When it was read to him, he struck out at the paper. He complained several times that he was sick and was once seized with a fit of vomiting. The reading, which began at 7:04 A.M., was finally completed after many delays and when LeBeau was told it was time to go, he suddenly composed himself and said he was ready.

LeBeau's hands were strapped to his side and he protested until Senator Long convinced him that it was required. The prisoner then begged that Long accompany him, but the senator declined until the sheriff asked him to join in the procession. At the gallows LeBeau insisted that he be allowed to climb the steps unassisted. He stopped halfway up and pushed off his shoes, commenting that he was not a murderer and did not intend to die with his shoes on. Once atop the scaffold the prisoner stepped directly onto the trapdoor and glanced around before the noose was adjusted. He cried out, "Oh God, man, that's tight." He then asked for Long to come up and shake hands, which the senator did. LeBeau looked out over the crowd and said, "You may have seen a good many hangings, but you never saw one like this. Mr. Long, I want you to see that I get a good funeral." He protested his innocence several times as his legs were being pinioned and his final words as the black hood was drawn over his head were, "I'm not guilty!"

The trap was sprung at 7:22 A.M. and there was one convulsive movement before the body hung still and lifeless. In seven minutes Drs. Campbell and Taylor announced that LeBeau's heart had stopped. The body was allowed to hang fifteen minutes before being lowered into a basket and delivered to Coroner Waggener. LeBeau's remains were taken to Demersville and buried in the town cemetery.

Inter Mountain (Butte, MT): April 1–2, 1909.

Hayes, William A.
April 2, 1909

William Hayes was sentenced in Chouteau County to serve ten years at the state prison in Deer Lodge for robbery. He had been a well-behaved convict and was due for release on March 11, 1911. On the morning of March 8, 1908, at 8:15 A.M. Frank Conley, one of the prison's contractors, opened the "prison court" which provided an opportunity for prisoners to voice their grievances. Chief deputy Robinson escorted eight prisoners into the hallway outside Conley's office: M. O. Howell, W. W. Brown, William A. Hayes, George J. Rock, Oram Stevens, C. B. Young, and two others. Howell was first to appear before the court; Brown next, and he was just leaving when Conley heard a scuffle in the hallway and found that Rock had struck deputy Robinson with a slungshot and cut him with a knife. In a moment Hayes rushed into Conley's office waving the knife, jumped the rail, grabbed Conley and said, "If you don't let us out of here we will cut your head off."

Conley pulled his revolver, shot Hayes in the head, and the prisoner fell. Just then deputy Robinson came in and said, "My God, Frank, they have got me." Robinson was followed closely into the room by Rock so Conley said, "Get out of my way, Robinson," and shot Rock over Robinson's shoulder, then shot the convict a second time. By then Hayes had recovered from his wound, arose and started slashing at Conley, so he shot him again and he fell. Conley's gun was empty so he picked up Hayes and threw him into the hallway, and the wounded convict stumbled out into the yard.

By the time Conley returned to his office Rock was straddling Robinson and slashing him. Conley picked up a chair and hit Rock on the head and he went down again. Conley started toward Robinson to give him aid but Rock got up and slashed Conley's neck, so the contractor knocked him down again, this time with the butt of his pistol. As Rock fell he cut Conley's leg and yelled out, "Come on Jack! We have got them!" but guard Carver rushed in and knocked Rock unconscious.

Conley, Hayes and Rock recovered from their injuries while fifty-five-year-old Robinson died. Robinson was considered one of the best officers at the prison and was survived by a wife and five children. Hayes, Rock, C. B. Young and Oram Stevens were charged with first degree murder. Young turned state's evidence and received a life sentence and Stevens had not been involved in the attack, so he was found not guilty. Hayes pled not guilty and went to trial, was convicted and sentenced to hang beside Rock on June 15, 1908. Hayes filed an appeal which stayed the execution but the lower court's decision was affirmed on February 26, 1909. He was then sentenced to hang at the Deer Lodge prison on April 2, 1909.

On Thursday the convict took his last bath and was being shaved when Sheriff Neville visited and they had their final talk about the execution. The prisoner declined to make any statement on the scaffold, and refused to tell his real name, saying only that William Hayes was an alias. He said, "Try and make a good job of this if you can, Sheriff, as I do not want to suffer any more than is necessary." Neville assured the condemned man he would do all he could to have the execution move along speedily and smoothly. Hayes ate a good supper, then remarked, "I feel happier tonight than ever before in my life. I have no complaint to make and am at peace with the world, which will soon see the last of me. By this time tomorrow morning my troubles will all be over and I know what the future has in store for me. I am not afraid to meet my God, whom I have been taught is all-merciful and forgiving."

He retired at 9:00 P.M. and was asleep by 10:30, and death watch guard James Johnson said the condemned man slept soundly until called a little before 6:00 A.M., and as soon as he arose he dressed in the new black suit provided by the warden. It seemed ironic that Hayes would spend his final hours in the same room where Robinson was murdered, but he was conducted to Conley's office where Father Landry said mass and then the prisoner received Holy communion for the last time, with three Sisters of Charity and three other women in attendance.

He refused breakfast so Sheriff Neville proceeded with reading the death warrant, and then Undersheriff Tom Mullen adjusted the belt that secured the prisoner's arms. Hayes complained that the belt might cause problems walking but Sheriff Neville insisted that it be put on, so Hayes resumed praying as the procession began. The march to the scaffold took only one minute, with Father Landy walking with the prisoner; he remained at his side, praying to the last. Tom McTague was on the other side of Hayes while the sheriff, undersheriff, and deputy Allan Williams followed closely behind, and prison officials and newspapermen brought up the rear.

On the platform Hayes took his place under the pulley with the noose dangling in his face. His knees were quickly strapped, the noose cinched in position, and the black hood was pulled on without anyone asking the prisoner if he had anything to say. The sheriff then tapped on the canvas curtain which hid James Beaton, who cut the restraining rope. The three hundred eight pound counter poise weight dropped at 8:02 A.M. and Hayes' body shot upwards and then dropped back down. His neck was not broken so his hands and feet twitched convulsively for several minutes and he clutched at the bottom corners of his coat. Drs. W. G. Nye and J. H. Garberson began monitoring Hayes' pulse and at 8:05 A.M. they pronounced him dead. The body hung fifteen minutes more before being cut down and placed in the prison-built coffin provided, his hands still tightly clenching the bottom corners of his coat. Four convicts carried the coffin to the prison cemetery located south of the penitentiary. Father Landry held a brief service before the grave was filled in, and at the head of the mound was placed a small wooden headboard inscribed, "William Hayes, Hanged."

Inter Mountain (Butte, MT): April 1–2, 1909.

Fahley, Leslie; Hall, Henry; Gibson, Harrison
February 16, 1917

On October 6, 1916, Michael Freeman, using the alias Levings, along with C. E. Campbell and L. Sitzwell, who were looking for harvesting work, climbed aboard a boxcar when the train was stopped near Nihill, Meagher County, Montana. Already aboard were nine other hobos and in the darkness, as the two men tried to find a place to lie down, one of them stepped on the hand of another. He jumped up, called out to the others, and in a moment there was a general brawl which quickly escalated to a shooting scrape when Leslie Fahley, Henry Hall and Harrison Gibson pulled their pistols and began shooting wildly. Freeman, who was silhouetted in the light of the door, was shot to death while Campbell was shot four times. Another man was wounded seriously but not fatally, and still another was slightly wounded.

After the shooting ceased Sitzwell was attacked and badly beaten about the head and body, and he was unconscious when found. The nine hobos were arrested and lodged in the jail at Judith Gap while the killing of Freeman was investigated. The three guilty parties were quickly singled out from the nine prisoners, moved to the jail at the county seat at White Sulphur Springs, examined, and held over for action by the grand jury. The three men were indicted in December, tried, found guilty of first degree murder, and sentenced to hang on February 16, 1917. Neither appeal nor application for executive clemency would delay the proceedings.

The single trapdoor gallows was built in the jail yard at the county courthouse in White Sulphur Springs, and was enclosed within a high fenced enclosure to ensure privacy. When it came time for the hangings the death warrants were read to the prisoners in their cells, and then they were brought out one at a time, and each man in turn took his place on the trapdoor and declined to speak to the witnesses. Wrists and arms, knees and ankles were pinioned, the noose was adjusted, and the black hood was pulled over each head without delay, and then the trap was sprung. The time between hangings was about twenty minutes, and as the attending physician pronounced each man dead the body was cut down and placed in the coffin provided by Meagher County. When all three men were in their coffins the lids were nailed down and they were loaded onto a wagon, driven to the potter's field section of the Meagher cemetery, and buried.

Bismarck Daily Tribune (ND): October 7, 1916. *Journal* (Stevens Point, WI): October 8, 1916. *Review* (Decatur, IL): February 16, 1917.

Fisher, Frank; O'Neill, John; Powell, Sherman A.
January 14, 1918

In October 1916 Thomas Higgins was on his way home to Butte, Silver Bow County, Montana, when he saw two men robbing Frank Sullivan at gunpoint. He went to Sullivan's rescue but one of the robbers, Frank Fisher, shot him dead and then the two robbers fled. Fisher and John O'Neill, alias Ray Gullich, were quickly captured, as Sullivan provided a detailed description, and they were lodged in the county jail. They were tried and convicted of first degree murder at the spring term of the District Court and the motion for a new trial was denied. The two prisoners were sentenced to hang but an appeal stayed the execution. The case was finally disposed of by the state Supreme Court in 1917 when they affirmed the trial record and sentence of the District Court, and then in December 1917 a second appeal was denied. On December 14, Judge John V. Dwyer sentenced Fisher and O'Neill to hang on January 14, 1918. Applications praying for executive clemency were quickly denied, so there was no further delay in the proceedings.

Sherman Powell and J. A. Montgomery, employees of the Great Northern Railway dining car service, were playing cards but the game ended when there was a heated dispute over the winnings. Later Montgomery was found dead in his bed, with his throat cut so deeply he was nearly decapitated. Powell was arrested and held for action by the Silver Bow County grand jury, indicted, and at trial he was found guilty and sentenced to hang. The case was delayed by appeals but finally on December 14, 1917, Judge John V. Dwyer sentenced Powell to hang on January 14, 1918, with two other condemned men sentenced earlier that day. Applications praying for executive clemency were denied so there was no further delay in the proceedings.

The gallows was built within an enclosure in the jail yard at Butte and Sheriff John O'Rourke sent out invitations to selected lawmen, simply worded: "Your presence at Butte, Montana, on the morning of January 14, in the year of our Lord one thousand nine hundred and eighteen is desired to witness the execution of John O'Neill, Frank Fisher, Sherman Powell."

One hundred witnesses were in attendance when the three men were escorted into the jail yard at 4:35 A.M., and outside the enclosure more than one thousand men had gathered and clamored for admittance but the Washington Artillerymen with fixed bayonets, reinforced by police and deputy sheriffs, kept them from tearing down the fencing. The death warrants had been read to the prisoners in their cells minutes earlier so there would be no delay on the scaffold, and as soon as they stood upon the triple trapdoor their wrists and arms, knees and ankles were pinioned and the nooses were adjusted. When asked if they had anything to say Fisher declined to speak, O'Neill and Powell only said goodbye to the witnesses, and then the black hoods were pulled over their heads.

Just as the trap was sprung at 4:40 A.M. Powell fainted, but all three men dropped straight down breaking their necks. Powell was the last to be pronounced dead by the attending physicians at 4:47 A.M. and then the bodies were cut down, deposited in the coffins provided, and buried in the potter's field section of the Butte cemetery that afternoon.

Capital Times (Madison, WI): January 14, 1918. *Northwestern* (Oshkosh, WI): January 14, 1918. *Eau Claire Leader* (WI): January 15, *1918. La Crosse Tribune* (WI): January 10, 1918. *Ogden Standard* (UT): January 14, 1918.

Guellae, Juan
April 12, 1918

At 10:30 P.M. on December 16, 1917, police officer Enos Nelson was called to the Little Terrace Saloon between Minnesota Avenue and First Avenue South in Billings, Montana, on a complaint that one of the customers was brandishing a handgun and creating a disturbance. When he arrived he found that the gunman had fled out the back door into the rear alley, so Nelson stepped out the back door to see if he could see the gunman. Juan Guellae, after leaving through the back door when he learned the police had been called, hid behind a fence and lay in wait. When Officer Nelson appeared he shot him five times at close range, four bullets striking Nelson in the arm and shoulder and the fifth bullet striking his forehead just above the right eye. Guellae, whose gun had been emptied into the officer, fled before another officer arrived. Nelson was found lying face down in the snow and rushed to St. Vincent's Hospital in a police patrol wagon, but he died in an hour.

Guellae was pursued and cornered, and he managed to wound another officer before a patrol sergeant shot him in the stomach with a shotgun. The prisoner was taken to the hospital for treatment, lodged in jail, and he had recovered sufficiently for his examination in January. He was held over for action by the grand jury; in February he was indicted and his trial began immediately in Judge Charles Taylor's courtroom in Billings. Guellae was convicted of first degree murder and on February 19, 1918, he was sentenced to hang on April 12. Neither appeal nor application for executive clemency to the governor would delay the proceedings.

Yellowstone County Sheriff Stone W. Matlock was responsible for the execution and he relied upon Undersheriff Guy A. Willis to see that everything went smoothly. The sheriff designed a solemn invitation, bordered in black, which read: "Mr. ____, Your presence is requested at Billings, Montana on the morning of Friday, April twelfth, in the year of our Lord Nineteen Hundred and Eighteen, to witness the execution of JUAN GUELLAE." It required an R.S.V.P.

The gallows was built off the second floor tier of the jail, measured a yard square, and allowed for a drop of six feet, and the thick manila rope was tied to an iron hook imbedded in the ceiling. Guellae, who had come north from Mexico in 1910, was a Catholic, so he was attended by Father J. Phillip Aushutz during his final days. On the morning of April 12 he was awakened at 3:00 A.M. and served breakfast, and after finishing his last meal the sheriff read the death warrant to him in his cell. He was brought out at 3:50 A.M. and placed on the trapdoor protruding out over the first floor jail corridor, but he declined to speak to the forty-five witnesses gathered below.

Undersheriff Willis strapped his wrists and arms, knees and ankles, pulled the black hood over his head, and adjusted the noose. Willis said, "He stood like a statue" while Father Aushutz prayed for his soul and when he announced, "In the midst of life we are in death," the lever was pushed by Sheriff Matlock and the trap was sprung at 4:05 A.M. Guellae dropped breaking his neck in the fall and there was no perceptible movement after fifteen seconds. A physician was in attendance and after he determined the heart beat had ceased, he pronounced Guellae dead. The body was then lowered to the floor below and given to Father Aushutz for burial in the Catholic portion of Billings' cemetery.

Billings Gazette (MT): April 12, 1953; June 3, 2007.

Lane, Alfred
September 3, 1920

On April 26, 1920, homesteader Harry Theade endorsed a check for his neighbor Alfred Lane to settle a debt, but when Lane tried to cash the check it was refused. Lane returned to Theade's ranch twenty-two miles north of Forsyth, Montana, to discuss the matter, but they could not come to a resolution. Theade turned and started into the cellar and as he was going down the stairs Lane shot him in the back three times, killing him instantly.

Lane stayed in the area for several days but finally on May 3 he realized he was suspected and about to be arrested, so he took to the hills, where he hid for seventy-two hours. Sheriff Grierson, fourteen hours after Lane fled, went to Lane's ranch to arrest him and discovered he was gone. He organized a posse and they searched some very rough country. The sheriff realized he might never find Lane by that method, so he made certain the fugitive could not obtain any food nor supplies until, driven by hunger, Lane surrendered on May 6. The prisoner then made several incriminating admissions before and after he was lodged in the Forsyth jail. He was tried at the summer term of the District Court, convicted of first degree murder, and sentenced to hang on September 3, 1920. During the forty days he was in jail he was attended by a priest, who would be with him up to the last moment. The proceedings were not delayed by appeal nor by application for executive clemency.

The gallows was built within an enclosure in the Forsyth jail yard and when the moment arrived the death warrant was read to Lane in his cell, and then he was marched out of the jail and onto the trapdoor. His wrists and arms, knees and ankles were pinioned and the noose adjusted, and all the time he and his priest prayed in unison. When asked if he had any statement for the witnesses he replied that he bore no grudge because of his execution and wished to "leave no enemies behind when I leave this world."

He kissed the crucifix that was held to his lips before the black hood was pulled over his head, and the trap was sprung. Lane broke his neck in the fall and the attending physician monitored his vital signs until his heart ceased to beat, then pronounced him dead. The body was cut down, placed in the coffin provided, and buried in the Forsyth cemetery.

Billings Gazette (MT): May 7. 1920. *Ogden Standard-Examiner* (UT): September 3, 1920.

Yiek, Albert
August 26, 1921

Twenty-nine-year-old Albert Yiek, sometimes Yeik, rode into Monida, Montana, on the evening of April 20, 1920, put up his horse and saddle, and made a bed in the loft of the barn behind the Summit Hotel. Early the next morning the hotel's chore boy found Yiek asleep and recognized the saddle and horse as belonging to his father, who lived in Idaho. The boy telephoned his father, who in turn notified the Idaho authorities of the theft. The Idaho authorities then telephoned Beaverhead County's fifty-year-old Sheriff Cyrus King Wyman at Dillon requesting that he go to Monida and arrest Yiek. Wyman called ahead and general store manager John B. Egan gave Yiek some menial job to occupy his time and keep him in Monida, and Yiek wore his chaps continuously but no one seemed suspicious of this odd behavior.

After Wyman arrived he went to the general store and arrested Yiek, but the prisoner asked to go to the barn and get his jacket, and the sheriff consented. As they reached the barn Yiek pulled a .32-caliber pistol from beneath his chaps and he shot Sheriff Wyman in the stomach and, as the lawman spun about, Yiek shot him in the back. Yiek ran to his horse, mounted, and rode at a dead run down the main street of Monida. A clerk, James Robbins, rushed out of the Monida Mercantile Store with his rifle, ran to the barn and through a crack in the boards shot at the horse. Robbins inflicted a minor wound on the horse's cheek but this cut the reins and set the animal bucking. The murderer, thrown from his saddle, then ran afoot into the snow-covered hills surrounding the town and by 7:00 P.M. a posse was organized from men in Monida, Dillon, and Lima.

While the posse was getting organized one of Monida's citizens kept watch of Yiek with binoculars, and later he was easily tracked to a vacant farmhouse two miles northwest of Monida. The farmhouse was surrounded by sixty heavily armed, angry men and they riddled the building with pistol and rifle bullets. Yiek returned fire until he was out of ammunition, but Yiek had taken refuge in the basement and was not wounded, so as soon as the shooting ceased he surrendered. He stepped out pleading, "Let the law take its course." Monida had no jail so Yiek was held in a room at the hotel under a heavy guard until he was transferred to the county jail at Dillon the following day, to prevent a lynching.

As soon as Yiek was behind bars he tried the "insanity dodge" and kept up his bizarre behavior throughout the trial, but Drs. Scanland and Bolton of Warm Springs examined him and found him sane. When arrested Yiek had given the name C. E. Davis, and on May 17 his trial began in Judge J. C. Smith's courtroom under that alias.

On May 19, after only forty-seven minutes of deliberations, the jurors found him guilty of first degree murder and fixed his punishment at death. On May 24 Yiek was sentenced to hang on June 25 and returned to jail, where he was heavily shackled and a guard was posted over him because of his history of escapes. Yiek had been sent to prison for two years and during his stay escaped three times, and in all served ten years for his original crime and three escapes. Yiek's attorney filed a notice of appeal on June 14 which stayed the execution and the case dragged on for a year, but on May 23, 1921, the state Supreme Court agreed to hear arguments in the case on June 3. The justices affirmed the lower court's judgment and sentence on June 7 and denied a new trial. The date for execution was then set for August 26, 1921. The application to Governor Dixon for executive clemency was denied on August 24 and Yiek began preparing for his death.

During his final days Yiek was visited often by Father Foley and Father Gallagher, and they helped the condemned man maintain his composure. Yiek's appetite did not begin to fail until his last two days, but he had been losing weight and looked haggard, though he never lost his desire for conversation. His sleep became broken and he slept less as the date approached, but he made no requests for opiates nor stimulants. By August 17 the invitations has been sent out to the witnesses and the contract for building the gallows had been awarded to R. T. Wemple. The gallows was constructed in parts but not assembled until August 24, and tested the following day, and a pit was dug beneath the low platform to allow for a six foot drop. The fourteen foot high fenced enclosure was erected between the courthouse and the jail by the end of the week previous to the execution, and it was illuminated with electric lights. Outside the enclosure a tent was pitched to house the executioner and keep his identity secret, and the rope release ran through a hole in the fence. On Thursday Sheriff Daniel Mooney assigned deputy Sam Ditty to stay in the cell with Yiek, and they played cards and joked all day. Ditty was replaced by Undersheriff Ross and chief of police Nelson for the night shift, and the prisoner was visited by his attorney several times. He was served his last supper at midnight and then his brother visited him twice, and when William weakened the condemned brother assured him, "You have done all that you could, there is no need to fuss about it."

At 3:30 A.M. Sheriff Mooney and several deputies entered Yiek's cell and read the death warrant, and after the sheriff concluded with the statement of the sentence of death Yiek said, "I am going to surprise you fellows and a lot of people in Dillon. I am going to die like a man. There will be no trouble. I will be game." The officers returned to the sheriff's office to await the proper time, but in ten minutes Yiek rang the alarm bell and told them, "I am ready, if you are, let's get this thing over with." He was told to wait and at 4:00 A.M. the witnesses were admitted to the courtyard, took their places at the scaffold, and in a half hour the officers entered the cell again. Yiek came forward, raised his arms to assist the officers in adjusting the harness of straps, and said, "Let 'er go!"

As soon as the harness was in place Father Gallagher of Butte gave him the last rites and the procession started with deputy Ditty leading the way and Sheriff Mooney on one arm and Undersheriff Ross on the other, with Father Gallagher following. Once the prisoner was in the courtyard he looked about and said,

"You have quite an audience, you must be going to pull off a grandstand performance." Yiek climbed the seven steps to the platform, took his place on the trapdoor, and the officers quickly strapped the harness about his arms and legs, but Yiek complained, "Dan, that's a little tight about my legs," so these were loosened. Next the noose was placed around his neck and cinched but Yiek said, "Loosen it a little, I want to speak," and as soon as the noose was loosened he said, "I am going to die like a dead game sport. That's all. Goodbye!" The witnesses had expected a confession but there was none, and he turned to the officers and said, "I am ready."

He shook hands with the officers on the scaffold and when the noose was again cinched tight he yelled out, "Let her go!" His wrists were bound, the black hood was pulled over his head, and the trap was sprung at 4:39 A.M. Yiek fell, breaking his neck, and Drs. R. H. Ryburn and W. H. Buchen pronounced him dead eight minutes later, at 4:47 A.M. The witnesses were ushered out while the coroner's jury signed the death certificate and the body was lowered, the noose removed, and the remains delivered to the Brundage Undertaking Parlor. After the body was removed the gallows was taken down, the pit filled in, the enclosure fence removed, and by 9:00 there was no sign that an execution had taken place. Father Gallagher held a funeral service at 11:00 A.M. in the undertaking parlor and at noon the body was driven to the potter's field in the Mountain View Cemetery and buried.

Billings Gazette (MT): April 22, 1920. *Dillon Examiner* (MT): April 23, 1920; August 17, 1921; August 24, 1921; August 26, 1921; August 29, 1921. *Evening Republican* (Mitchell, SD): April 22, 1920. *Independent* (Helena, MT): May 23, 1921. (Yiek's hanging provided courtesy of the Lima Historical Society).

Vuckovich, Joseph
February 17, 1922

Joseph Vuckovich, alias Joe Wins, and Jerry Shea were feuding over their competing bootlegging businesses in Missoula, Montana. On the evening of February 12, 1921, Shea's wife was shot in the head and died instantly, and the evidence indicated that it was Vuckovich who had murdered her. Mrs. Shea and Vuckovich had been having an affair, apparently unknown to her husband, and it was supposed that she had decided to end the relationship. Vuckovich remained at large for several days but finally he was arrested and lodged in the Missoula jail. Vuckovich was indicted, pled not guilty, and his trial began in mid–March in Judge Lentz's District Court room.

The defense tried to show that it was Jerry Shea who had shot his wife out of jealousy when he learned of her infidelity, but he denied any knowledge of the affair with Vuckovich. When this failed the defense changed its tactics and tried to prove that Mrs. Shea had committed suicide, but the state countered with testimony from Coroner Dr. Charles H. Marsh who had removed the bullet from the head of the deceased, and then showed that the bullet and the expended shell casing found at the scene came from Vuckovich's gun. The defendant was found guilty of first degree murder and sentenced to hang on May 27.

On April 30, 1921, he expressed confidence that he would be granted a new trial when the matter was argued on May 15, but in any case if the motion was denied an appeal would immediately be taken to the state Supreme Court, which would act as an automatic stay of execution until the matter was heard. The motion for a new trial was denied and the appeal taken. The Supreme Court heard the case and in late December affirmed the lower court's judgment and sentence, and then on January 7, 1922, the justices denied a request for a rehearing. The date for the execution was set for February 17, 1922, and his attorney filed motions for *habeas corpus* and for the right to appeal to the U.S. Supreme Court, but these were denied.

By February 3 his friends were circulating petitions to ask for executive clemency for Vuckovich, but on that date Sheriff G. A. Cole had also begun erecting the gallows within an enclosure on the courthouse lawn. On the day before the execution a telegram was sent to

Governor Joseph M. Dixon asking for a reprieve and stating that petitions were prepared for submission containing over five thousand signatures of county residents asking for a commutation of sentence. The governor responded by telegram: "While deeply appreciating the responsibility involved, I have been unable to find the extenuating circumstances that would justify me in interfering with the verdict of the jury."

Vuckovich spent a restful last night and had to be awakened from a deep sleep at 5:00 A.M. He made his preparations and Sheriff Cole appeared at his cell door at 6:00 A.M. to read the death warrant. He was then escorted into the enclosure and onto the scaffold. Inside were two hundred witnesses but outside there was a strong force of armed guards who had been posted throughout the night to ensure no one tampered with the gallows or the enclosure. As soon as Vuckovich was in place on the trapdoor, his wrists and arms, knees and ankles were bound and the noose was adjusted. Sheriff Cole then asked if he had anything to say and the condemned man responded, "I pray to God and Jesus Christ that they take the one who got me into this and take him and punish him worse than I got punished this morning. Of course, I am losing my life as innocent as any man that ever was here." The black hood was pulled over his head and the sheriff sprang the trap at 6:11 A.M. Vuckovich dropped breaking his neck and Dr. Charles H. Marsh monitored vital signs until he pronounced him dead ten and one half minutes later. The body was then cut down, placed in the coffin provided, and buried in the Missoula cemetery at the expense of his many Serbian friends.

Anaconda Standard (MT): January 7, 1922; February 2, 1922; February 9, 1922; February 17–18, 1922. *Independent* (Helena, MT): February 14, 1921; March 26, 1921; April 30, 1921.

Bolton, Glenna; Reagin, Joseph
February 9, 1923

There had been a number of break-ins at ranch houses thirty-five miles southwest of Sheridan, Treasure County, Montana, and forty-year-old undersheriff Irving Keeler believed he knew the identity of the burglar. Keeler, with the sheriff, deputized two ranchmen, and at 10:00 P.M. on Friday, December 9, 1921, they went to the home of Glenna M. Bolton and found the stolen property in a bunk house occupied by twenty-one-year-old Joseph Reagin. The sheriff returned to Hysham for an arrest warrant for Reagin and Bolton and left Keeler and the deputies to guard the property. Keeler went into the house and was talking with Bolton and his wife, who was confined to bed with a broken leg, when Reagin suddenly appeared at the door with a .45-caliber revolver in hand and a red handkerchief tied over his face. Keeler called Reagin by name and the burglar immediately shot the undersheriff, killing him. Reagin then went to the bunk house and forced the two deputies, at gunpoint, to burn the incriminating stolen goods before he fled into the hills.

Soon a posse of one hundred men were scouring the hills around Hysham for the murderer, but at 3:00 A.M. Reagin went to the Pope's ranch and stole a rifle and ammunition, then returned to his hiding place. As the investigation continued it became clear that Reagin had an accomplice in the burglaries, and had been tipped off about the lawmen's presence, and this accomplice was identified as Bolton.

Reagin was soon captured after a fierce gun fight, in which the fugitive's knee was shattered by a rifle bullet, and he was lodged in the Hysham jail where Bolton soon joined him. At their examination the two men were held over for the grand jury, indicted, and tried at the January term of the District Court. Both defendants were found guilty of first degree murder and sentenced to hang in February, but appeals to the state Supreme Court stayed the executions. The case was argued in the fall and on October 19, 1922, the judgment and sentence of the lower court was affirmed for Reagin, and then on November 13 the court affirmed the judgment and sentence for Bolton as well. The date for their execution was fixed at February 9, 1923, and nothing further would delay the proceedings.

A gallows which would accommodate one man at a time was built in a high board enclosure within the jail yard at the Treasure County seat of Hysham. The Reverend G. B. Nye had access to the two condemned men during their final days, and he had a positive influence on them as the fatal moment approached. After 3:00 A.M. on their final day Sheriff Phil Isaac and undersheriff W. E. Williamson appeared at the cell doors and read the death warrants, which had only arrived at 2:50 A.M.

Bolton was selected to go first. He was taken out and marched into the enclosure and onto the platform. Snow was falling as he addressed the small number of witnesses and he thanked the officers for their kindness to him while in the jail and for everyone's kindness to his mother and sisters. His wrists and arms, knees and ankles were bound and the noose was adjusted while he was talking, and then the black hood was pulled over his head. At 3:41 A.M. the trap was sprung and he broke his neck in the fall, and at 3:49 the attending physician pronounced him dead. The sheriff had already returned to the jail for Reagin while the body was being cut down and deposited in the coffin provided by his family.

Reagin appeared in a few minutes, took his place on the trapdoor and was prepared in the same manner. When asked if he had anything to say, he shouted, "Good-bye! I hope to meet all you men on the other side of the blue. So long." As the black hood was being drawn over his head he again shouted, "Good-bye men!" The trap was sprung at 3:54 A.M. and Reagin's neck did not break in the fall, so it took sixteen minutes for him to strangle to death. After the attending physician pronounced him dead he was cut down and deposited in the coffin provided by Treasure County. Bolton's remains were turned over to his family for burial but Reagin's remains were not claimed, so he was buried in an obscure section of a potter's field later that day.

Billing Gazette (MT): December 11, 1921. *Independent* (Helena, MT): November 14, 1922. *Lincoln State Journal* (NE): February 10, 1923. *Ogden Standard-Examiner* (UT): February 9–10, 1923.

Harris, Monte; Harris, William
April 20, 1923

On November 25, 1921, shortly after midnight, the morning after Thanksgiving, Cyril Schilling was clerking at the front desk of his Harrison Hotel at 2610 Harrison Avenue in Butte, Montana, when he heard a rap on his side door and found four men awaiting entry. After Monte Harris, William Harris (not related), Earl McCoy and George Beach entered, William Harris brandished a revolver and ordered Schilling to raise his hands, and Schilling said, "For God's sake don't shoot, you can have everything in the house." However, without hesitation, Harris shot him dead and rifled his pockets, then the four men went into the dance hall and robbed all the men and women of their money and jewelry. The men ran outside and fled in an automobile.

The following day deputy sheriff Jack Kelly, "Doc" Porter, and William Curran located the men hiding in a vacant house on Wall Street. Kelly had the house surrounded. The fugitives were so badly outnumbered and outgunned they had to surrender. Five men were lodged in the jail at Butte but one proved an alibi and was released, and at their examination the four remaining prisoners were held over for action by the grand jury. They were indicted, demanded separate trials, and all four were found guilty of first degree murder in February 1922. McCoy and Beach were sentenced to serve life terms in prison and the two Harris defendants were sentenced by Judge Lynch to hang in April, but a notice of appeal stayed the executions.

On December 15, 1922, the *Helena Daily Independent* newspaper announced that the appeal of Monte Harris would be argued on January 5, 1923, and that the appeal of William Harris would be argued shortly thereafter, and when both appeals were denied the date for their execution was set for April 20, 1923. Neither appeal nor applications for executive clemency would delay the proceedings further.

On Wednesday both men were baptized into the Catholic religion and then confessed to the hold-up. William Harris admitted he had fired the fatal shot and insisted that Monte Harris was innocent of the murder. As they awaited their execution the condemned men could hear the gallows being erected in the jail corridor near the front door, which provided a six foot drop. Before 3:00 A.M. on April 20 Sheriff Larry Duggan and Undersheriff Dale Robinson appeared at the cell doors and read the death warrants to the prisoners. They were then taken out and walked the short distance onto the gallows, where they took their places on the trapdoor.

As they were being prepared, Monte Harris, when asked if he had anything to say to the fifty witnesses, said, "I die an innocent man. I have nobody left but my mother. I worship her. I wrote a letter to her and I want someone to promise me faithfully and honestly that they will deliver it to her." Assistant Chief of Police Mike O'Donell took the letter and promised to deliver it just as John Duggan finished adjusting the noose, and Monte Harris said, "Make a good job of it Johnny." All this time William Harris, who had made a statement hours earlier and declined to speak on the trapdoor, stood silently listening to the priest pray for their souls.

The black hoods had been dispensed with by the sheriff "so there will be no delay after the nooses are adjusted." The trap was sprung at 3:08 A.M. and both men broke their necks in the fall, and were pronounced dead by the attending physicians seven minutes later. The bodies were then cut down and deposited in the coffins provided. Monte Harris' letter was read and in it he asked that he be given a Christian Science service and burial, so on Saturday his last request was fulfilled and, though they had both been baptized Catholics, William Harris was given the same funeral service, and then the remains of both men were buried in the Butte cemetery.

Billings Gazette (MT): November 27, 1921. *Anaconda Standard* (MT): February 24, 1922. *Independent* (Helena, MT): December 15, 1922; April 24, 1923. *Montana Standard* (Butte): December 15, 1963. *Ogden Standard-Examiner* (UT): April 20, 1923. *Salt Lake Tribune* (UT): April 21, 1923.

Danner, Seth O.
July 18, 1924

In early October 1920, John and Florence Sprouse announced that they were moving from Britton, South Dakota, to Washington State to live with John's mother. They went as far as Marshall County and visited with family for several days, then said they had to hurry back to Mobridge where they were to meet another couple who was going to travel west with them — Seth and Iva Danner. On June 8, 1923, the bodies of the Sprouse couple were found buried in shallow mud-hole graves along the Yellowstone trail in Central Park near Bozeman. Seth Orrin Danner and Iva Danner were arrested on suspicion of murder, as they were the last people to see the Sprouses alive, and Iva quickly confessed, blaming her husband for the murders while the two couples were camping in the park in November 1920.

During the investigation it was found that Seth had stolen the automobile that John Sprouse had purchased in South Dakota for the trip, and had sold it at Three Forks; the couples had known each other at Britton in 1920; and Iva was a step-daughter and cousin to her husband. After Iva and Seth Danner were charged with murder Seth tried to shift the blame onto Florence's ex-husband as "the mysterious man who might have committed the crimes at Central Park, if there were any crimes committed."

Unfortunately for Danner's defense it was discovered that Florence Sprouse had been a widow when she remarried. Seth Danner was tried in Judge B. B. Law's Bozeman courtroom at the fall term and his new defense was that John Sprouse had been intimate with Iva Danner and that John's wife had killed him out of jealousy, and then tried to kill Iva Danner, but Florence Sprouse was killed in self-defense. The jury dismissed the testimony as implausible and in contradiction to the evidence, so they convicted Danner of the first degree murder of Florence Sprouse. Danner was sentenced to hang but a notice of appeal stayed the execution. The state Supreme Court considered the matter until May 26, 1924, when it affirmed the lower court's judgment and sentence and denied the plea for a retrial. The date for Danner's execution was then set for July 18, 1924. Applications for executive clemency were sent to the governor from Danner's attorney and from two of his sisters, but these were denied.

A death watch was placed over the condemned man several weeks prior to his date with the hangman and that was when Danner began studying the Bible with great devotion. He adopted the Catholic faith and was baptized into the religion, and was attended by one or both of two priests almost continuously. On his final day he ate three hearty meals, the last about midnight, and then talked with his death watch guards and the priests until Sheriff James Smith appeared at his cell door at 2:00 A.M. to read the death warrant. He was taken out, marched into the enclosure built in the Bozeman jail yard, and took his place on the trapdoor at 2:04 A.M.

His wrists and arms, knees and ankles were pinioned, the noose was positioned, and he was asked if he had anything to say to the witnesses, who consisted of two priests, a physician, four deputies, sixteen reputable Gallatin County residents, and a newspaper reporter. Danner said, "I bear no malice to anyone. I have made my peace with my Savior and will go to Him with the assurance that I am fully prepared. I hope that all of you will follow my example. I have nothing more to say." The priest then offered him a crucifix to kiss and the black hood was pulled over his head. At 2:15 A.M. the trap was sprung and Danner dropped, breaking his neck, and in four minutes the attending physician pronounced him dead. The body was cut down, deposited in the coffin which had been stored nearby, and taken to a local funeral parlor to await the arrival of his family, who would see to his burial.

Billings Gazette (MT): May 27, 1924; July 19, 1924. *Independent* (Helena, MT): June 23, 1923; August 19, 1923.

Walsh, Roy
February 15, 1925

Albert S. Johnson operated a general store in Renova, Jefferson County, Montana. On the evening of June 26, 1923, he heard a knock at the front door and was anxious to accommodate his regular customers so he opened the door, but he found two masked and armed men who commanded him to raise his hands. He refused and one of the men fired a single round from a rifle which struck him in the neck. The two men then fled and Johnson was rushed to the hospital in Butte, but he died twenty-four hours later.

Arthur Hughes, a miner, was arrested on June 28, and as soon as he was behind bars he confessed to the robbery and informed on his partner Roy Walsh, and said it was Walsh who fired the fatal bullet. The search for Walsh was brief and that afternoon, though armed, Walsh was surrounded and he surrendered without a fight. Both men were indicted but Hughes turned state's evidence and later pled guilty to manslaughter and was sentenced to serve a term of eighteen to thirty-six years.

At his trial on July 27 Walsh was found guilty of first degree murder and sentenced to hang, but while he was being held in the jail at Boulder, Montana, he used his razor to fashion a padlock key from a piece of hardwood, escaped, and remained free for four months. His photograph was widely circulated and he was identified as a recent arrival at the Missouri state prison, where he had been sentenced for breaking into a cabin. He was extradited to Montana and the new date for his hanging was set for June 16, 1924. An appeal was filed which stayed the execution until, on

Christmas eve, the state Supreme Court denied the appeal and set the new date for execution at January 14, 1925.

In December, while Walsh's appeal was pending, Hughes had declared it was he and not Walsh who fired the fatal bullet. This confession was taken under review and dismissed after interviews with both prisoners on December 29 proved the statement implausible and a ploy to save Walsh, and on January 13 the new date for Walsh's execution was set for February 15, 1925. Walsh's final hope for relief was a reprieve or commutation of sentence by Governor John E. Erickson but the governor responded to the petition on February 14 and, after relating the details of the case, he wrote, "No new evidence has been submitted, and no mitigating circumstances suggested upon which to base an order of commutation. In view of the atrocity of the crime committed and in view of the record in the case, I do not feel justified in interfering with the verdict of the jury and the judgment of the courts. Petition denied."

On Friday evening the twenty-four-year-old condemned man spent his time writing a long, rambling discourse urging boys to avoid the pitfalls into which he had fallen, and praised the horse "as a faithful servant of man and an example of fidelity and duty." He had refused all religious counseling, though he had spoken with a priest and a Methodist minister, and declined to have any clergy with him on the gallows. Late in the evening he was informed that the governor had refused to intervene and then he laid down on his cot for a nap. At 1:30 A.M. Sheriff John W. Mountjoy and Undersheriff Knight appeared at his cell door, awoke him and after he asked, "Are we starting back to Missouri?" the sheriff read the death warrant.

Walsh was taken out of his cell, marched into the Boulder jail yard and onto the gallows. He took his place on the trapdoor where his wrists and arms, knees and ankles were bound and the noose was adjusted. He was asked if he had anything to say and he made a brief speech, concluding, "I wish the world well." The black hood was pulled over his head and at 1:43 A.M. the trap was sprung. Walsh dropped six feet and broke his neck, and he was pronounced dead six and one half minutes later. The body was then cut down and deposited in the coffin provided. Later that day he was buried in an obscure part of the Boulder cemetery, without a graveside service.

Billings Gazette (MT): February 17, 1925. *Independent* (Helena, MT): January 1, 1925; February 14–16, 1925.

Vettere, Tony
October 1, 1926

At 9:15 P.M. on November 22, 1925, Tony Vettere met John Deranja a mile from Meaderville in Silver Bow County, Montana, and shot him in the left side with a load of buckshot, killing him instantly. At 10:00 P.M. Tony Vettere found Joseph Cicarelli standing in front of the Favero house in Meaderville, a suburb of Butte. Cicarelli was talking to Antone Favero when Vettere called out "Joe Cicarelli" and without any hesitation fired two shotgun blasts at the men. Cicarelli received a fatal load of buckshot in his right shoulder and he bled to death in minutes. Favero received a load of buckshot in the abdomen and was rushed to the hospital at Murray, where he told his sons that it was Vettere who had shot him, and he died at midnight.

The police were investigating the Meaderville shootings when they learned that at about 11:00 P.M. a man hiding in the shadow of a building had fired five pistol shots at Angelino Gucciono as he was walking down a Butte street with Lisa Marselli. Gucciono dropped to the ground when he heard the shots and Marselli ran to a nearby house, with Vettere running after her, and when she was admitted he broke out several windows before he fled. The following day Vettere, unarmed, was discovered hiding in a gully eight miles from town and he was arrested by Undersheriff Dayton O. Robinson and deputies John Duggan and Bill Byers. They learned that Vettere had some difficulty with Cicarelli a few years earlier when Vettere had become too familiar with Cicarelli's wife, but there had been no difficulties between Vettere and any of the other men.

Witnesses at the inquest on November 25 testified that Vettere was seen in the vicinity of the Favero home about 10:00 P.M. carrying a shotgun, Favero's sons testified to their father's dying declaration, and deputies testified that they found shotgun shells in Vettere's house loaded with the same size shot as that removed from the bodies. The coroner's jury returned separate verdicts in the deaths of Ciccarelli and Favero, finding Vettere responsible for each killing. Vettere, who refused to take the witness stand, was returned to his cell to await action by the grand jury.

The defendant was indicted in late February 1926, tried in Judge Jeremiah J. Lynch's District Court room in Butte, convicted of the first degree murder of Favero, and on March 16 he was sentenced to hang on May 7. His attorney had already filed a motion for a new trial in District Court but it was denied, and then he filed an appeal with the state Supreme Court which stayed the execution. The Supreme Court heard arguments in the case in early August, affirmed the lower court's judgment and sentence, and denied Vettere a new trial. On August 27 the date for his execution was set at October 1, 1926, but his attorney then raised the issue of sanity. When the condemned man was determined to be sane, his attorney petitioned the governor but Governor John E. Erickson refused to grant executive clemency.

During his final days Vettere was visited by Father J. M. Gilmore but his reaction to the priest was so violent he was not permitted to be with the prisoner alone. On September 30 the prisoner asked to see Judge Lynch, but he refused to visit the man in his cell. Vettere would not rest that final evening and paced his cell, tensed as if ready to spring, and when the deputies entered the corridor Vettere yelled out, "Where all these men come from." Undersheriff Robinson entered his cell at midnight to take him into the corridor for the reading of the death warrant but Vettere pulled a three foot piece of pipe from his bed clothes and attacked the undersheriff. Robinson backed out of the cell with Vettere close behind, and in the corridor of the jail Vettere pulled out a makeshift knife made from a spoon and, flailing about with the pipe in one hand, tried to cut the officers. He yelled, "You can shoot me but you won't hang me," and said, "I kill every man who come here. Get Judge Lynch. I want kill him," and then, "Viva Mussolini!" Sheriff Larry "Jack" Duggan demanded the pipe, but Vettere refused saying he would kill everyone. Two canisters of tear gas were brought in and he was sprayed from two sides, and the officers finally managed to herd him back into his cell, where he was gassed for fifteen minutes.

He was finally overcome by choking, dropped his weapons, and retreated onto his cot. The deputies then rushed in, overpowered him, and his wrist and arms, knees and ankles were bound with straps. He was carried onto the gallows and as he stood on the trapdoor he recovered his senses and began cursing everyone. The black hood was pulled over his head and the noose adjusted at 12:20 A.M., and the trap was immediately sprung. Vettere dropped, breaking his neck, and he was pronounced dead at 12:28 A.M. The body was then cut down and surrendered to the doctors for an autopsy, and his brain was taken for study. The remains were then taken to the Duggan Funeral Parlor, owned by the sheriff, and when Vettere's cousin said there were no funds for the burial the sheriff volunteered to pay for the burial in the Holy Cross cemetery, without any religious service. On October 6, the day of the funeral, Drs. J. E. Dobos and H. A. Maillett announced that after an examination of Vettere's brain he was found to be sane.

Anaconda Standard (MT): March 12, 1926. *Billings Gazette* (MT): November 24, 1925; November 26, 1925; October 1, 1926. *Havre Daily News-Promoter* (MT): May 24, 1926; October 1, 1926. *Independent* (Helena, MT): November 23, 1925; March 17, 1926; October 1, 1926; October 3, 1926; October 5–6, 1926.

Schlaps, Ferdinand
May 20, 1927

On Saturday, May 1, 1926, Antone "Tony" Geisler was working in the barn on his farm twenty miles west of Homestead in Roosevelt County, Montana, near Biem, when he was confronted by eighteen-year-old Ferdinand Schlaps. The farmhand, who had worked for Geisler for a year, aimed a single barrel shotgun at his employer and demanded that Geisler give him the twenty-five dollars Schlaps knew was in his pockets. Geisler refused, so Schlaps fired a charge of buckshot into Geisler, reloaded and fired a second load, killing him. After taking the money from Geisler's pockets he reloaded the shotgun and snuck up to the kitchen window where Ludmilla Geisler was working. He took aim through the window and fired, the load of buckshot striking her in the shoulder. She ran to the closet and shut and locked the door, so Schalps remained quiet for some time to give the impression he had fled. After a while Ludmilla Geisler, knowing she needed medical attention or she would bleed to death, cautiously crept from her hiding place. She saw Schlaps a moment before he fired and pleaded for her life, but Schlaps ignored her and fired a load of buckshot into her abdomen, killing her. He dragged her body outside, cleaned up the blood in the house, and waited for darkness.

After the sun set he loaded the bodies into the trunk of Geisler's new automobile and drove nineteen miles to the Muddy River in Sheridan County, then threw in the bodies. On Sunday morning a rancher went to the river to haul water, discovered the bodies caught in debris along the bank, and notified Sheridan County Sheriff Rodney Salisbury. While the sheriff organized a posse he made a brief inquiry which pointed directly to Schlaps as the murderer, and within a few hours he was arrested at his brother's farm ten miles from the murder scene. Schlaps was lodged in the Great Falls, Montana, jail and at first he denied killing the Geislers, but he soon broke down and confessed the details of the murders to Sheriff Rodney Salisbury, saying he wanted Geisler's new automobile. He repeated his confession at the inquest later that day.

On May 4 he was taken to Wolf Point and lodged in the Roosevelt County jail, where he confessed several times, and then on May 12 he dictated his confession before witnesses and signed it. On May 17 he appeared before Judge S. E. Paul, who appointed Eric Moun of Poplar as his attorney and set May 26 as the date for Schlaps' hearing. On May 26 the defendant pled not guilty and was held over for action by the grand jury, and he was indicted in early July.

His trial for the murder of Ludmilla Geisler began in Judge Paul's courtroom on July 8. His defense was that he had a low mentality, but he had been tested by a teacher on May 22 and determined to have the mentality of an eighteen-year-old boy. Though his behavior was not typical, his cell mates testified he seemed, at least, reasonably normal. The evidence, especially the many consistent confessions, was overwhelming. Schlaps was found guilty of murder in the first degree and sentenced to hang on September 25, 1926, but his attorney filed a notice of appeal which stayed the execution. The grounds for the appeal was again his low mentality, his difficulty with the language, which put in question his confession, and evidence of the murder of Antone Geisler at trial, though he was being tried only for the murder of Ludmilla Geisler. The state Supreme Court, after careful consideration, affirmed the judgment and sentence of the lower court and Schlaps' date of execution was rescheduled for May 20, 1927. Neither appeal nor application for executive clemency from Governor Erickson would delay the proceedings further.

The gallows had been erected in the jail yard within an enclosure so that the walk to the structure would take only a minute. During his final days Schlaps had become fully resigned to his fate, so he was fully composed when, at midnight, the death warrant was read to him in his cell. He was then taken out and, in a driving rainstorm, escorted onto the scaffold. He took his place on the trapdoor and declined to speak to the small crowd of witnesses, but he moaned continuously as the straps were applied to his wrists and arms, knees and ankles, and the noose was adjusted. The black hood was pulled over his head at 12:10 A.M. and the trap was sprung immediately. Schlaps dropped four and one half feet, breaking his neck, and this was followed by a few convulsive movements of his legs before he hung lifeless and was pronounced dead by the attending physician. The body was then cut down, deposited in a coffin, and given to his family for burial.

Anaconda Standard (MT): May 3, 1926. *Billings Gazette* (MT): May 4, 1926; July 22, 1926; May 21, 1927. *Havre Daily News-Promoter* (MT): July 7, 1928; May 20, 1927. *Independent* (Helena, MT): May 18, 1926.

Davisson, Rollin
November 6, 1929

Rollin Davisson, a laborer with a rich history of service to Yellowstone park, lived in a cabin near Livingston, Montana. He had a dispute with his employer over a fifty cent discrepancy in his wages and on Wednesday evening, August 21, he went to the police station to ask for help from police chief Peter Holt, but Holt refused to intervene between Davisson and his employer.

In the station was traffic officer Martin Zollman, curio dealer J. P. Evans, and city treasurer Robert Ballie. After a brief argument with Holt, Davisson suddenly pulled a concealed revolver and shot Holt once through the heart while he sat in his chair, killing him instantly. Zollman then tried to restrain Davisson and during the struggle the officer was shot in the chest once, a mortal wound, and then Davisson tried to shoot Evans and Ballie but the gun jammed. Clyde Neal, a fireman, heard the shots, rushed to the scene, and beat Davisson unconscious with a piece of cement block. Zollman died within minutes and Davisson was locked in a cell charged with two counts of murder. The following day county health officer Dr. J. E. Stuart examined the prisoner and pronounced him sane; and that evening Masonic funeral services were held for Zollman and then his remains were sent to Milwaukee for burial. On Friday, as the coroner's jury found that both police officers had died at the hands of Davisson, Holt's family was making arrangements for his burial at Livingston.

In late September Davisson was indicted and tried at the fall term of the District Court and on September 20, after deliberating only thirty-five minutes, the jurors found the defendant guilty of the first degree murder of Holt and left the sentence to the discretion of the judge. Davisson's defense had been insanity, but the defense had called him as a witness, which proved his sanity. Davisson was brought into court on September 25 and sentenced to hang on November 6. There was an effort to have Governor Erickson commute his sentence to life in prison but Davisson opposed the action saying, "No use in doing that. It would be unjustified if the governor did change the sentence to life imprisonment. Anyway, I would rather die than live in prison the rest of my life."

Davisson was held in the jail at Livingston and on his final night he slept soundly after reading a magazine until a late hour. He was awakened by his guards at 6:00 A.M. and served breakfast and at 6:55 a deputy sheriff read the death warrant. Davisson was then escorted out into the jail yard enclosure and onto the scaffold where his wrists and arms, knees and ankles were bound and the noose adjusted. He was asked if he had anything to say. He told the fifty witnesses, "I have just one request to make. Bury me in Montana. Don't give my body to any of my relatives. They have never done anything for me and are not entitled to my remains." The black hood was pulled over his head at thirty seconds after 7:03 A.M. and his old friend Sheriff Gilbert sprang the trap. He dropped, breaking his neck, and he was pronounced dead at 7:05 A.M. by county health officer Dr. Stuart. After the body was cut down, County Coroner G. H. Selby took charge and buried Davisson in the Mountain View cemetery.

Billing Gazette (MT): August 23, 1929. *Ogden Standard-Examiner* (UT): August 23, 1929; September 21, 1929; November 6, 1929.

Hoffman, George
August 29, 1933

Just before midnight Wednesday, September 21, 1932, George Hoffman, a forty-four-year-old itinerant barber, broke into the cigar store of George Burrell in Choteau, Teton County, Montana. His sole purpose was to rob Burrell, a cripple from birth who walked with a cane or a chair, pushing the chair in front of him until he needed to sit down. It was his habit to push the chair to his calendar each night at midnight and change the date. Hoffman snuck up behind Burrell and while he was distracted with the calendar Hoffman struck him on the back of the head with a piece of pipe, knocking him unconscious. Hoffman then rifled the cash drawer and the pockets of Burrell finding $70, but the cigar store owner began to regain his senses, so Hoffman took the cord from the telephone, tied a knot, placed it around Burrell's neck with the knot over the artery on the right side, and strangled him to death.

The body was discovered the next morning when an employee arrived to open the store, and Burrell's chair was found in front of the calendar. Hoffman was arrested on suspicion that he was involved in the murder, or at least knew something of it, and he was lodged in the jail at Choteau. Officers then went to Hoffman's hotel and found the stolen money hidden beneath the bathtub. Sentiment ran so high in Choteau that Hoffman was transferred to the county jail at Great Falls to prevent a lynching. While en route to Great Falls on September 24, Hoffman confessed the details of the murder to undersheriff J. L. Billings and Teton County attorney Bert I. Packer. At Great Falls he confessed again, this time to Cascade County deputy attorney Arthur Jadine and Judge J. J. Greene.

Hoffman was tried at the fall term of the Teton County District Court at Choteau, found guilty of first degree murder, and sentenced to hang. His court appointed attorney filed a notice of appeal, which stayed the execution, but after months of delay the state Supreme Court affirmed the judgment and sentence of the District Court. Hoffman's date of execution was set at August 29, 1933. Hoffman's brother John S. Hoffman then filed an application with Governor Frank H. Cooney praying for executive clemency based on the condition of their eighty-two-year-old mother, but the governor could find no legitimate grounds to grant a respite or a commutation of sentence.

Teton County had not had a hanging for decades and had no gallows. They found it more economical to borrow one from Silver Bow County and have it brought by truck two hundred fifty-nine miles to Choteau. Once it arrived it was erected in a vacant warehouse near the jail, to save the cost of constructing an enclosure.

Hoffman, during his final days, showed little emotion or concern over his pending doom, even when visited by his ailing mother and several brothers. He had tried to keep his situation secret from his mother and when he learned that she had been told he said, "There's only one person on earth lower than me, and that's the one who told this affair to my mother." He was visited by Father J. F. Schulte of St. Luke's Church and, though the condemned man was pleasant, the priest found he had little influence on Hoffman, who said, "I would like to have a little more time to think it [salvation] over."

On his final morning Hoffman awoke at 3:00 A.M., dressed, and was served breakfast. The death warrant was read to him in his cell and at 4:25 A.M. he was escorted the short distance into the warehouse and onto the gallows by newly elected Sheriff J. L. Billings and the jailer. Daybreak was quickly approaching as he stood on the trapdoor and gazed down at the one hundred seventy-five witnesses gathered beneath him. His wrists and arms, knees and ankles were bound, the noose adjusted, and he was asked if he had anything further to say, but he declined. At 4:40 A.M. the black hood was pulled over his head and the trap was sprung. Hoffman dropped four and one half feet, breaking his neck, and in three minutes his heart ceased to beat and he was pronounced dead by the attending physician. The body was cut down and taken to the Choteau morgue for an autopsy. On Wednesday, August 30, there had been no claim for the remains so plans were being made to bury Hoffman in an obscure corner of the Choteau cemetery in an unmarked grave.

Inter Lake (Kalispell, MT): September 26, 1932. *Independent* (Helena, MT): September 25, 1932; August 5, 1933; August 13, 1933; August 27, 1933; August 30–31, 1933. *Ogden Standard-Examiner (UT)*: August 11, 1933.

Zorn, Henry
April 24, 1935

On the evening of August 10, 1934, twenty-five-year-old Henry John Zorn, alias Miller, arrived in Billings, Montana, and checked into a local hotel. He left his suitcase at the hotel when, on the following night, he boarded a freight train for Miles City, Custer County, Montana. He arrived at 11:00 P.M. and went directly to the industrial school, which he had burglarized in 1929 and had been sentenced to serve a five year prison term. He was again burglarizing the office of school superintendent A. C. Dorr when just after midnight faculty member Lester C. Jones entered, interrupting his work opening the safe. Zorn fired four shots at Lester, killing him instantly, fled, and as soon as he was outside he saw a freight train heading east and boarded.

Because of his previous burglary at the school, Zorn was under suspicion, and after his fingerprints were matched with those at the scene Sheriff Edgar Taylor circulated his description widely. Zorn jumped off the freight train before reaching Terry and walked ahead a mile, so when officers made a thorough search of the train they missed him, and he boarded the same train after it left Terry. He left that train at Fargo, North Dakota, and boarded another headed west, but on August 15 he learned there was an intensive manhunt for him so he doubled back to Minneapolis, Minnesota and sent a telegram to Billings to have his small black suitcase forwarded to him. The authorities were notified of the request so a telegram was sent to Minneapolis asking the authorities to watch for Zorn, and he was arrested a half hour later as he checked at the express office for his suitcase.

Zorn did not fight extradition and was taken by two officers on the train from Milwaukee to Roundup, arriving at 4:30 A.M. on Thursday, August 23, and from there by automobile he was driven to the Yellowstone County jail. He arrived at the jail at 6:00 A.M. and later that day he dictated a twenty page typewritten confession in the presence of a large crowd of officials, then signed the document.

Zorn, who had been identified by his alias up until time of trial, was found guilty of first degree murder during the fall session of the Custer County District Court at Miles City. He was sentenced to hang. His court appointed attorney filed a notice of appeal, which stayed the execution, and the case was reviewed by the state Supreme Court. The justices disposed of the matter in February 1935 when they affirmed the lower court's judgment and sentence and set the date for Zorn's execution at April 24, 1935. Applications for executive clemency were sent to Governor Frank H. Cooney by Zorn's attorney, but as the date neared the governor was out of the state and the matter was delegated to Acting Governor E. Elmer Holt. The acting governor found no grounds for interfering with the execution, and ignored death threats which came to his attention days before the execution.

During his final days Zorn was attended by the Methodist Reverend George Reid and had fully resigned himself to his fate. Late on his last evening he stated, "I am going out with no revenge or hatred for anyone. I know that I am going to a better world." His mother, Josephine Adams, sat with him and wept almost continuously, but by midnight she had become hysterical and had to be removed. She asked that she be given the body for burial. After she left, her son said, "A good mother," then said, "I want to thank the people of Montana for their loyalty to and interest in my behalf. I have no bitterness in my heart for anyone. I am going with a clear conscience."

The gallows had been built within a corner of the Custer County jail structure and this made for cramped quarters once the fifty witnesses were in place. All the other prisoners had been moved to the city jail, so Zorn was the only occupant that night. Sheriff Edgar Taylor went to Zorn's cell after 1:00 A.M. and read the death warrant and then, with the Reverend Reid on his arm, Zorn was escorted into the corridor and onto the platform. He took his place on the trapdoor and was twice asked if he had anything to say, and each time he shook his head. His wrists and arms, knees and ankles were bound, the noose was adjusted, and the black hood was pulled over his head as the Reverend Reid prayed for his soul. At 1:27 A.M. the trap was sprung and Zorn dropped to his death, breaking his neck in the fall. Several physicians were in attendance and they pronounced him dead in fourteen minutes. The body was then cut down, placed in the coffin provided, and delivered to the local funeral parlor where the body would be prepared to accompany Josephine Adams to Butte for burial.

Montana Standard (Butte): August 14, 1934. *Billings Gazette* (MT): August 24, 1934. *Inter Lake* (Kalispell, MT): April 24, 1935.

Criner, George
October 16, 1935

On the evening of August 7, 1935, police chief Joseph Sullivan and seventy-six-year-old officer James Fraser were called to the Miles City, Custer County, Montana, home of thirty-six-year-old George Criner and his common-law wife, Mary Allsup, to intervene in a raucous fight. They had been arguing over possession of a diamond ring and the argument escalated into an attack on Allsup. When the officers entered they found that Allsup had been slashed horribly with a two-bladed pocket knife and had wounds on her forehead, face, and body, and her clothes had been slashed and nearly torn off. The house was in a shambles, the walls of the bedroom were splattered with blood, and the entire house was littered with broken furniture. Criner was still agitated and threatening so Fraser pulled his pistol, but Criner wrestled it from his grip and, with Fraser now unarmed, Criner shot Sullivan. Fraser started for his patrol car but Criner followed and shot him in the back of the head, killing him instantly.

While Criner was occupied murdering Fraser, Sullivan dragged himself to the house next door and telephoned for reinforcements. Sheriff Edgar Taylor with several deputies rushed to the house and found that Fraser was dead, and that Allsup and Sullivan were seriously wounded. Criner was still at home and he surrendered to the sheriff without further resistance. The wounded were rushed to the hospital. Allsup died the following day, but Chief Sullivan was reported in satisfactory condition. After a long period recuperating he fully recovered.

A half hour after Criner was arrested a large angry crowd surrounded the jail, but they dispersed without any violence when Sheriff Taylor allowed a four man delegation to search the jail and determine that the prisoner was not there. The sheriff, anticipating trouble, had the prisoner taken to Billings and delivered to the Yellowstone County jail at 2:00 A.M. for safekeeping.

The coroner's jury was convened after noon the day following the murders. Criner was found responsible for two deaths, and the prisoner was held over for action by the grand jury. On August 9 Criner confessed to murdering Fraser and Allsup. At an early hour on August 15, Criner, wearing an "Oregon boot" foot restraint, was delivered to the Custer County jail at Miles City. Later that day he was arraigned before Judge S. D. McKinnon and he pled not guilty on the advice of his court-appointed attorney, W. B. Leavitt. He was tried and found guilty in September and sentenced to hang on October 16. Neither appeal nor application for executive clemency would delay the proceedings.

During his final days he was attended by the Reverend Walter Smith and had resigned himself to his fate. His last wishes were that the ring, over which they had fought, would be given to the reverend and that $32.50, all the money he had, be used to buy a headstone for Mary Allsup. His appetite had not been affected by his pending doom and he ate a hearty dinner of chicken and a supper of steak. The Reverend Smith talked with Criner at 8:30 P.M. and returned just before he was to make his walk to the gallows, the same on which Henry Zorn had died recently and which was again erected in the southwest corner of the jail.

Sheriff Taylor appeared at the cell door at 1:00 A.M. and read the death warrant, and then Criner was escorted the few feet to the gallows by the sheriff and the Reverend Smith. He took his place on the trapdoor without prompting and as he was being prepared, with limbs bound and noose adjusted, he was asked if he had anything to say to the fifty witnesses. He replied, "I am sorry for what I done." At 1:14 A.M. the trap was sprung and Criner dropped through, breaking his neck. County Physician A. R. Varco monitored his vital signs and pronounced him dead in only a few minutes. The body was then cut down, deposited in the coffin provided, and later that day he was buried in the Miles City cemetery following a brief service by the Reverend Smith. His grave remained unmarked, but a nice stone was erected over the grave of Mary Allsup.

Billings Gazette (MT): August 9, 1935; August 16, 1935. *Inter Lake* (Kalispell, MT): August 8, 1935; October 16, 1935. *Independent* (Helena, MT): October 16, 1935. *Ogden Standard-Examiner* (UT): August 9, 1935.

Robideau, Franklin
January 15, 1938

Mike Kuntz managed the Occident Elevator at the Russell Miller Milling Company in the Columbus Wheat Basin. On the Friday evening following Thanksgiving, November 26, 1937, Franklin Robideau found Kuntz, his wife, and their five-year-old son Lawrence at the grain elevator and they began arguing over the wheat Robideau had in the elevator. Robideau claimed one hundred eighty bushels more than he had been credited and when the matter could not be resolved, they all got in the Kuntz automobile and drove several miles to an isolated spot. Robideau later said that they were "going to shoot it out," but as soon as the two men stepped out of the automobile Robideau pulled a pistol and shot Kuntz dead, then turned his gun on Kuntz's wife and without warning or hesitation shot her dead as well. He then beat the little boy into unconsciousness, and believed him dead or dying. He loaded the bodies into the automobile, drove back to the grain elevator, drove the vehicle inside, and locked the doors.

Robideau returned home and went about his business as if nothing had happened, but in the morning the little boy regained consciousness and managed to walk to a nearby village store and report that he could not wake his mother or his father. The people investigated, discovered the dead bodies, and notified the authorities. Based upon the boy's statement Robideau was arrested, but he tried to shift blame onto two squatters living near the company, and when this failed he told several inconsistent stories. He appeared before Judge Ben Harwood on December 11 and pled guilty to shooting Mike Kuntz, but denied killing his wife or beating the child. The judge accepted his plea and on December 15 he sentenced Robideau to hang on January 15, 1938. Nothing would intervene to delay the proceedings.

The facilities at Columbus were less than substantial, so the condemned man was taken to Billings and lodged in the jail there. As soon as he arrived in Billings, Robideau confessed to both killings and said his true name was Joseph L. Liberty, an escapee from a New York prison. During his final month he was attended by the Reverend H. S. Tool of Columbus, who helped him accept his fate. Early on his final day at Billings he told the sheriff, "My book is all written and I'm closing the last chapter tonight."

At 11:45 P.M. Friday evening, January 14, Robideau was driven forty-five miles to Columbus, handcuffed to Undersheriff Ed O'Connell. He said before they started, "Well boys, I'm glad its over," and he remained in good spirits throughout the trip, laughing and joking with his guards. They drove their automobile right into the Columbus machine shop, which had been converted into the death chamber, and he stepped from the vehicle right at the foot of the stairs to the platform, ascended, and took his place on the trapdoor. The death warrant had been read to him earlier and he had emphatically refused to speak to the witnesses, including more than forty lawmen, so his limbs were bound and the noose adjusted.

The black hood was pulled over his head by Sheriff Murphy at 1:10 A.M. and the trap was sprung. Dr. A. V. Blackstone waited beneath the gallows and monitored vital signs until he pronounced Robideau dead at 1:27 A.M. The body was then cut down, deposited in a coffin, and held until his wife could complete funeral arrangements at Columbus.

Billings Gazette (MT): January 16, 1938. *Bismarck Tribune* (ND): January 17, 1938. *Independent* (Helena, MT): January 4, 1938; January 15, 1938.

Simpson, W. L.
December 30, 1939

Twenty-year-old Robert O. MacDonald and eighteen-year-old Gerald E. MacDonald, brothers, worked for fifty-year-old W. L. "Lee" Simpson on his Golden Valley County ranch near Ryegate, Montana, fifty miles from Lewiston. On April 11, 1938, as the two hired hands were sleeping Simpson snuck up on Gerald and crushed his skull with the blunt end of an ax, then quickly shot Robert to death with his rifle when he awoke. Simpson and his wife put both bodies in their car, drove to the golf course at Roundup, and buried one body in a shallow grave beneath a pile of rocks and stuffed the other body into a rock crevice.

On April 14 two men from the Livestock Production Credit Association visited the Simpson ranch. Believing they might be looking into the murder of the MacDonald brothers, Simpson drove them off at the point of a rifle though no shots were fired. The two men reported the threatening behavior to Sheriff Elmer J. "Red" Dolve and he drove to the Simpson ranch with deputy Arthur "Buzz" Burford, arriving at 5:30 P.M. As soon as they stepped from their car Simpson began shooting at them from the second story window of his stone ranch house, and the first bullet went through Burford's arm while the second bullet put a hole in the sheriff's hat.

They took cover behind their automobile and engaged in a blazing gun battle for four hours, and several hundred rounds were exchanged. After dark the sheriff crawled to cover behind a pile of rocks behind the ranch house while Burford, who had been wounded seven times during the exchange of shots, was unconscious from loss of blood and was left under cover behind their vehicle. In a few minutes Simpson came out of the house, walked around the sheriff's vehicle and sent a single rifle bullet through Burford's head, killing him. As soon as the sheriff heard the shot he stepped out and emptied his rifle in the direction he believed Simpson was standing and Simpson returned several shots and, though they were nearly point-blank for a rifle range, none scored a hit. Simpson retreated to his house while the sheriff ran to his automobile and drove into Ryegate for help.

When Sheriff Dolve returned with a posse he found that Simpson had fled in a farm truck and had left Mrs. Simpson and their two children behind. Dolve then sent the posse in all directions to search for the murderer of Burford, but they could not find a clue to his whereabouts. In the morning Simpson telephoned Sheriff Guy Tullock at Lewiston and said, "I want to talk to you about something that has happened." Tullock arranged a meeting, arrested Simpson without incident, and lodged him in the Lewiston jail. As soon as Simpson was behind bars he confessed to killing the MacDonald brothers and told where the bodies could be found. When asked why he had killed them he replied, "I'll get up to that. I'll tell you later." He then provided a list of sixteen names of persons who were "trying to steal my land" and were "marked for death" and he spoke of "being framed," but Sheriff Tullock believed the killings were somehow related to the arrest and conviction of two men for killing of one of Simpson's cows the previous year.

Sheriff Tullock contacted officers at Roundup and they found the bodies of the MacDonald boys, dressed only in their underwear. Simpson was taken to the prison at Deer Lodge for safekeeping, to prevent a lynching at Ryegate, and he was charged with three counts of murder. While at the prison he attempted suicide by slashing his wrists with a piece of broken glass, and one wound became so infected that his right arm had to be amputated above the elbow.

In early September Simpson was returned to Ryegate, indicted, and his trial for deputy Burford's murder began in Judge W. L. Ford's courtroom on September 6. It took three days to seat a jury. Testimony began on September 9 and the prosecution's case was a simple presentation of overwhelming evidence while defense attorney A. G. McNaught concentrated on proving self-defense and insanity. A jury deliberated briefly before returning a verdict of guilty of murder in the first degree. The motion for a new trial was denied and Judge Ford sentenced Simpson to hang in October 1938, but a notice of appeal stayed the execution. The state Supreme Court considered the matter for more than a year before the justices finally denied the appeal and affirmed the judgment and sentence of the District Court. On December 1 Judge Ford sentenced Simpson to hang on December 30, 1939. An application for executive clemency based on the sanity of the condemned man was then submitted to Governor Roy E. Ayers, and on December 21 he scheduled a hearing on the issue. Early on December 29 Governor Ayers rejected the appeal for clemency without comment.

As soon as Simpson was told of the governor's denial of his appeal for clemency, he asked Sheriff Dolve to summon the Baptist Reverend E. L. Mills of Roundup, and the reverend was with the prisoner all afternoon. The gallows, brought from Forsyth, had been erected in an enclosure created by building two high fences between the jail building and an adjacent building, and access to the platform stairs was directly through a ground floor window of the courthouse. After midnight the first of five hundred witnesses began to arrive and filled the large enclosure; meanwhile Simpson dressed in his burial clothes of dark trousers and a gray shirt. At 2:00 A.M. Sheriff Dolve went to Simpson's cell and, in company with the Reverend Mills, read the death warrant.

Simpson was taken out and escorted to the window, he stepped through, and climbed the stairs onto the gallows. The Reverend Mills held his left arm and deputy Verne Meigs was on his right but he needed no support, and Sheriff Dolve had gone ahead and was awaiting him on the platform. Once Simpson stepped onto the trapdoor the Reverend Mills announced, "By special request of Mr. Simpson I will offer a brief prayer," and when he said "Amen!" Dolve warned the witnesses to remain silent when Simpson spoke. Dolve then prompted Simpson, who said, "I want to praise God. I am being taken out of this world of sin tonight and I feel confident that you people will meet me all up there. God bless you all. Pray for my loved ones. That is all." While he spoke his wrist and arms, knees and ankles were bound and when he concluded the black hood was pulled over his head and the noose adjusted, and he complained, "Don't choke me!"

The trap was sprung by Sheriff Dolve at 2:14 A.M. and Simpson dropped straight down, breaking his neck in the fall. Coroner Dr. E. R. Fouts and Dr. A. A. Bennett of Roundup monitored his vital signs and pronounced him dead at 2:30 A.M. His body was cut down and taken to the Ryegate mortuary where his remains were prepared for burial, though no arrangements had yet been made. His wife and two children were in Missouri and made no claim for the remains so Simpson was buried in the Ryegate cemetery the following day after a graveside service by the Reverend Mills.

Montana Standard (Butte): April 16, 1938; December 22, 1939; December 30–31, 1939. *Independent* (Helena, MT): September 10, 1938; November 24, 1939; December 2, 1939.

Coleman, Phillip, Jr.
September 10, 1943

The sister of Andrew J. Walton, an eighty-one-year-old living in Helena, Montana, went to his home on Sunday morning, July 4, to check on him and found him lying on the floor in a pool of blood, his head crushed by some blunt instrument. She called the authorities and Walton was rushed to the hospital, but he died the next day without regaining consciousness. The evidence indicated he had been attacked on the night of July 3 but there were no clues to the murderer. The coroner's jury found, on July 9, that he had been "killed by a severe beating by persons unknown," and he was laid to rest in the Helena cemetery the following day.

On Saturday, July 24, thirty-nine-year-old Lewis Brown and twenty-nine-year-old Phillip "Slim" Coleman arrived separately at Lothrop, a section station thirty miles west of Missoula on the Northern Pacific line, and were hired onto the crew by forty-nine-year-old Carl W. Pearson, the rail section foreman. That night both men decided they did not want to stay at Lothrop and Coleman told Brown, "I need $200 and I am going to have it." The two men devised a plan to rob Pearson. Coleman went to the section foreman's home long after they had retired, awoke Pearson and said that Brown was ill and needed help. Pearson left his thirty-year-old wife, Roslyn, in bed, took a bottle of aspirins and a flashlight, and hurried out behind Coleman. As soon as he was in the front yard Brown struck him in the head from behind, inflicting a mortal wound. Coleman then returned to the house and stabbed Roslyn to death while she lay in bed. Brown searched Pearson while Coleman searched the house, and after they met in the yard they quarreled over the division of plunder and then separated. Brown took a freight train to Missoula and Coleman stole the Pearsons' automobile, and it was discovered at Drummond twenty-eight miles east of Missoula and seventy-eight miles from the murder scene.

At 11:00 A.M. seven-year-old Richard Pearson went to his mother's room to wake her and when he could not he started for the home of neighbor Vera Winsper, then found his father lying in the yard. He told Winsper he could not wake his parents and she called Sheriff Robert D. McLean, who found in checking the section house that Coleman and Brown were absent. Their descriptions were circulated and Brown was arrested in Missoula the following morning. Coleman, who first tried to give a false name, was also arrested the following morning at Idaho Falls, Idaho, identified as the fugitive, returned to Missoula, and lodged in jail with Brown. Brown persisted in denying any part in the Pearson murders but due to similarities in the Walton murder, particularly the manner of bludgeoning the victim, he was questioned but denied any knowledge of that murder as well.

Both men were charged with murdering the Pearsons — Brown charged with murdering Carl Pearson and Coleman with murdering Roslyn. They were indicted and tried at the summer term of the court and both men were found guilty of first degree murder as charged in the indictments, but the murder of Roslyn had been particularly brutal and the body was badly mutilated. Brown was only sentenced to serve life in prison but Coleman was sentenced to hang on September 10. There was no relief for Coleman from appeals nor applications for clemency.

Coleman had shunned any religious counseling up until Monday, September 6, when he was baptized into the Catholic faith, and his priest then encouraged him to bare his soul through confession. On Thursday afternoon Coleman spoke with Governor Sam C. Ford by telephone and was told there would be no relief from the executive office so. On Thursday evening, he summoned Sheriff McLean and confessed to killing Walton. He said that he was staying in Helena and knew Walton, and had been drinking quite a bit. On the evening of July 3 he decide to rob the old man and he had access to the cabin next door to Walton's house, and there he found a hatchet. He said, "I went in and slugged him with the dull end of the hatchet and then looked for money. There wasn't but 12 cents. I lit out and met up with a soldier who was riding in a car. Him and me headed for Livingston but we got to Logan and then came back a ways and went to Butte." He said they soon parted and he claimed the soldier had stolen the car, but could give no more information on him. He asked the sheriff to keep his confession secret in case the governor had a last minute change of heart and decided to grant a reprieve or commutation.

The gallows had been built in the jail corridor and at 7:00 A.M. the sheriff appeared at Coleman's cell and read the death warrant. The prisoner was taken out and escorted the short distance to the gallows by his priest, where a handful of witnesses awaited his arrival. He shook hands with each witness and said he had "no hard feelings," and, "I'd like to get it over with as soon as possible." He climbed the stairs and took his place on the trapdoor where his wrists and arms, knees and ankles were quickly strapped, the noose was adjusted, and the black hood was pulled over his head. At 7:11 A.M. the trap was sprung and the prisoner dropped to his death, breaking his neck in the fall. The attending physicians monitored his vital signs and in nine minutes pronounced him dead. The body was cut down, placed in the coffin provided, and delivered to the priest. He was buried in the local cemetery in the forenoon, following a brief service.

Billings Gazette (MT): July 10, 1943; July 26–27, 1943; September 11, 1943. *Independent* (Helena, MT): September 10, 1943.

McKenzie, Duncan P.
May 10, 1995

Twenty-two-year-old Duncan P. McKenzie, living near Conrad, Pondera County, Montana, purchased a used pickup truck in January 1974 to celebrate his release from prison after serving three years for assaulting a woman. He commented several times that he always "broke-in" his vehicles by having sex in them, said he preferred school teachers, and insisted he had one in mind.

McKenzie worked at a seed company north of Conrad, not far from the Pioneer one room country school. On Tuesday, January 22, twenty-three-year-old Lana Harding, the pretty brunette school teacher who lived alone in the teacherage near the school, failed to report for her classes. Investigation showed that there had been a violent struggle in her living quarters so Sheriff Walter Hammermeister organized a search, and the following day the partially clothed body of Harding was found in a snowy field four miles northwest of the school, two hundred yards from the frontage road. She had been raped, choked, beaten, a rope was tied around her neck, and the right side of her head was smashed open. Her remains were taken to Great Falls for an autopsy but meanwhile McKenzie was arrested and lodged in the Pondera County jail. His truck had been seen headed toward that field on Monday night and his bloody gloves were found near the murder scene. Blood was found in the truck bed along with purple fibers matching Harding's sweater, and Harding's brain matter and blood were found on an auto part in the truck bed.

McKenzie insisted that he was innocent but he was easily convicted of kidnapping and first degree murder on February 1, 1975. On February 23, Judge R. J. Nelson sentenced the prisoner to hang on April 30, 1975, at the prison in Deer Lodge. McKenzie fought against his execution by every means at his disposal and he avoided execution eight times over the next two decades, but when all avenues of relief were exhausted he chose lethal injection over the gallows.

As the day neared McKenzie asked Governor Marc Racicot for clemency, saying that he felt sorry for the Harding family, but "I can't come to you and beg forgiveness for something that I didn't do." On Saturday May 6 the Board of Pardons recommended against granting further relief, and the governor refused to intervene.

At 11:40 P.M. McKenzie was taken from his cell. He wore headphones playing country western music, which had been his last request, and he was allowed to listen to Marty Robbins during the execution. Before the walk to the execution chamber began the prisoner had been cooperative and joked with the staff, but when asked if he had anything to say he merely shook his head. He was taken into the execution chamber and strapped to a gurney. The executioner was already in the control room, so he would remain anonymous as the witnesses took their positions outside the chamber windows.

Medically trained personnel inserted an intravenous cannulae (IV) into each arm, the second a back-up in case the primary IV failed. At a signal from the warden, just after midnight, the executioner administered the drugs: first, sodium thiopental to induce sleep; second, pancuronium bromide to restrict respiration, which in time would cause death by asphyxiation; and third, potassium chloride which quickly stopped the heart. McKenzie lay still throughout the process, and only the songs of Marty Robbins could be heard in the silence of the chamber. The prison doctor closely monitored vital signs and pronounced him dead. The body was removed and buried the following day.

Billings Gazette (MT): February 8, 1974. *Garden City Telegram* (KS): May 10, 1995. *Havre Daily News* (MT): March 16, 1977. *Independent Record* (Helena, MT): January 24, 1975. *Indiana Gazette* (PA): May 8, 1995. *Syracuse Herald-Journal* (NY): May 10, 1995.

Langford, Terry A.
February 24, 1998

In 1988 twenty-two-year-old Terry Allen Langford, a drifter from North Carolina, went to Montana determined to become a "mountain man" in the Rocky Mountains and live off the land. He arrived in Ovando by bus on the fourth of July weekend and found his way to the home of the Blackwoods. He hid in the garage overnight and raided their garage refrigerator, and he also ransacked their pickup truck and found a loaded .22-caliber rifle. In the morning he took the Blackwoods hostage, forcing forty-eight-year-old Celene Blackwood to tie the wrists of her husband Ned. He marched them at gunpoint into the house, where he bound Ned to a rocking chair, then he bound Celene and lay her on the couch. He guarded his captives for several hours, calmly talking with them. He then shot Ned in the back of the head with a single bullet from the rifle, killing him instantly, then shot Celene in the left ear. Celene did not die immediately from the gunshot wound so he cut her throat.

Langford was soon captured and within hours he confessed and begged for the death penalty. However, at his arraignment he pled not guilty and was tried and convicted on two counts of first degree murder, but he would never explain why he killed the Blackwoods. He said, "Every day I lay my head on the pillow, I ask myself what happened," and said of the Blackwoods, "We were getting along fine. They were really nice people." Langford was sentenced to die but over the next nine years he vacillated between demanding death and fighting for his life. As late as Monday night, February 23, 1998, less than twenty-four hours before his execution, he petitioned Governor Marc Racicot for a delay, but it was denied.

Before midnight on February 23 the death warrant was read to Langford in his cell, and then he was escorted into the execution chamber. He was strapped down on a gurney before medically trained personnel inserted an IV in each arm, the second IV in case the primary

IV failed. The executioner took his place in the next room, from which he would administer the drugs while remaining anonymous, and then the curtains to the viewing area were opened. Langford was asked if he had anything to say but he declined. It was after midnight so the warden ordered that the three drug combination be administered: sodium thiopental to induce sleep; pancuronium bromide to restrict respiration, which in time would cause death by asphyxiation; and potassium chloride which stopped his heart within minutes. In a few minutes the prisoner was asleep and his breathing became labored, and then in a few minutes more he lay still. The doctor in attendance checked his vital signs and pronounced him dead, and then the witnesses retired. The body was removed and delivered to an undertaker for preparations as had been previously arranged.

Salina Journal (KS): February 25, 1998. *Sitka Sentinel* (AK): February 24, 1998. *Stars and Stripes* (U.S. Military): February 25, 1998.

Dawson, David T.
August 11, 2006

On April 18, 1986, David and Monica Rodstein, both thirty-nine, with their fifteen-year-old daughter, Amy, and eleven-year-old son, Andrew checked into room 149 at the Airport Metra Inn on Main Street in Billings, Montana. Twenty-eight-year-old David Thomas Dawson, a methamphetamine addict, had already checked into room 151 next to the Rodsteins, but registered under the name John Monroe. The Rodsteins were moving to Atlanta but Monica, Amy and Andrew were planning an early start the next morning to visit with Monica's mother in Nebraska, then they would join David in their new home in Georgia.

At 4:30 A.M. Amy had just packed belongings into her mother's automobile and was returning to the room when Dawson came up behind her carrying a duffel bag with a gun clearly visible inside. He forced her into room 149 and said to the Rodsteins, "Calm down. I need your money. We are going to the next room." Dawson took them into room 151 and turned up the volume on the television, then hung the "Do Not Disturb" sign on the door. Dawson pulled out the gun and ordered everyone to lie face down on the floor. He taped David's wrists behind and his ankles and then taped a sock in his mouth as a gag. When he went to Monica she pleaded with him, but he bound and gagged her in the same manner, and then he did the same to Andrew.

Dawson forced Amy to help him transfer all their belongings from room 149 and from the automobiles to room 151 and then he carefully wiped down room 149 with a towel to remove any fingerprints. Dawson next bound and gagged Amy and then he went through the belongings, taking all the money, traveler's checks, credit cards, identification, and other valuables. When that was done Dawson injected David with a substance and told him, "You will all be asleep and I can just leave. You will be found by the maids or somebody, and I will leave word at the desk." He then stood up Amy and ordered her to face the wall, but she heard her mother become agitated when Dawson prepared to inject her and he told her, "Calm down. Everything will be fine. Before you know it, I will be gone and you will be back to your life."

However, it was at that time that Dawson, using a cord torn from the telephone, strangled David and Monica. He moved their dead bodies to the rear of the room, stored them under the sink, and covered them with a bed spread. When Amy was allowed to turn around Dawson told her they were sleeping. Later that day he removed Andrew's gag and forced him to drink some fluid, "to put him to sleep." Dawson took Amy along as he moved both of the Rodsteins' automobiles to the rear of an adjacent store, and when they returned to the room Dawson packed the Rodstein belongings he planned to keep into their suitcases. Dawson gave Amy a glass of the same mixture he had given Andrew, but when he was distracted she poured it out and pretended to sleep. At some point Dawson strangled Andrew with the same telephone cord he used to murder David and Monica and he put Andrew's body with his parents. Dawson kept Amy captive two days and during that time he made a number of trips, taking her along, but she never tried to escape, as she feared he would retaliate against her family, not knowing they were already dead. Dawson then put Amy in the bathroom and let the family dog, Tigger, keep her company.

The Rodsteins were missed by the morning of April 19 and a search began, and that evening their automobiles were found by patrolmen. Late on April 19 officers Gary Hatfield and Steve Lund were sent to investigate the disappearance of the Rodsteins. They first checked with former neighbors and took one along to identify the automobiles, and they all arrived at the inn just before 11:00 P.M. where the clerk insisted that the Rodsteins had left, though they had not checked out.

When they searched room 149 they found it empty. But the Rodsteins could not have left without their automobiles, so the officers began questioning everyone at the inn. They talked with Dawson, and he acted suspiciously, and they saw him going in and out of his room several times in a short period of time. After talking with everyone Hatfield went to Dawson's room and he answered the door wrapped in a yellow towel, though he had been seen fully dressed only a few minutes earlier. Hatfield said he wanted to check the room so Dawson flung the door open and stepped aside, then called back into the room, "Amy, they are here to help you. You are going to be okay," then turned to Hatfield and said, "She is in the bathroom."

Hatfield noticed the three dead bodies on the floor covered by a bed spread, with their feet sticking out, as he stepped in. He found Amy in the bathroom, unharmed, and she later said, "I thought that the next person that opened the door would be Dawson to kill me, or do something. It was very horrible, very scary." Officer Lund, with another officer, arrived and took custody of Dawson while Hatfield took Amy to the police station and interviewed her over the next few hours. Items found in Dawson's baggage suggested he may have planned to sexually abuse his captives but he had not done so.

In March 1987, Dawson was tried in Judge Diane Barz' Yellowstone County courtroom, the jurors deliberated for fourteen hours before they convicted the defendant of three counts of deliberate murder, four counts of kidnapping, and one count of robbery. A month later he was sentenced to die at the state prison in Deer Lodge. For the next eighteen years every legal manipulation was used to delay the execution but finally in 2004 Dawson fired his court appointed attorneys and demanded that he be put to death. Still the American Civil Liberties Union (ACLU) and various church organizations fought to save his life, against his wishes. When questioned by Judge Gregory Todd the condemned man said, "All I have is twenty years preparing to be executed. Enough is enough. There has to be an end." His date for execution was set for August 11, 2006, but, up to a few hours before his execution, efforts were still underway to stop the execution.

On August 10 Dawson ate his final meal at 5:30 P.M. and then just before midnight the death warrant was read to him in his cell. He was shackled and escorted into the single wide trailer that had been transformed into an execution chamber at the prison. Twelve witnesses were already seated as he was strapped to a gurney, and then medically trained personnel inserted two IVs into his arms, one a back-up in case the primary IV failed. Warden Mike Mahoney entered the chamber exactly at midnight and asked if Dawson had anything to say, and when the prisoner replied, "No!" the warden signaled for the drugs to be administered: sodium thiopental to make him sleep; pancuronium bromide to restrict respiration, which could cause death by asphyxiation in time; and potassium chloride to stop his heart. At 12:01 Dawson snored, his chest rose and fell, he lifted his right index finger, and then his fingers curled loosely into his palms before he lay still. Five minutes later the coroner stepped forward on a signal from the warden and with his stethoscope listened for a heartbeat and then shined a light into Dawson's eyes before announcing, "David Dawson has been pronounced dead at 12:06 A.M., August 11, 2006."

Billings Gazette (MT): December 15, 2005; August 6, 2006; August 10–11, 2006. *Independent Record* (Helena, MT): August 6, 2006; August 11, 2006.

NORTH DAKOTA

Approximately two-thirds of the region that became North Dakota was acquired from France in 1803 as part of the Louisiana Purchase. The northeastern part of the region was acquired from Great Britain in 1818. However, to say this vast area belonged to the United States is misleading, as Native American tribes were well established and strongly defended their lands. In 1812 British colonists tried to establish the Red River settlement at Pembria but it failed, and forty years later Charles Cavaler brought settlers to Pembria and established an agricultural colony.

The Dakota Territory was established in 1862 and, in spite of the dangers, the territory was opened to homesteading on January 1, 1863. The railroads arrived in 1871 and the period from 1878 to 1886 was labeled the "Dakota Boom." The Dakota Indians fought this intrusion for two decades but were eventually overwhelmed. On November 2, 1889, the Dakota Territory was divided into the states of North Dakota and South Dakota and North Dakota became the 39th state.

Bomberger, Albert F.
January 19, 1894

Albert F. Bomberger was born on February 18, 1871. At age seventeen he left his home in Lebanon City, Pennsylvania, and began working his way west. In December 1892 he arrived at the Krieder farm southeast of Cando, where he was hired as a farmhand by Daniel Krieder. He was treated as part of the family and given a bedroom on the second floor of the house. Mr. and Mrs. Krieder had eight children, the oldest being a pretty fifteen-year-old girl named Annie. Bomberger soon became hopelessly infatuated with Annie and made several indecent proposals.

On July 4, while drinking heavily, he formed a plan to visit Annie's second floor bedroom on the evening of July 6. He carried out his plan after midnight but was scornfully rejected again. This time, because of his persistence, Annie threatened to call her parents, who slept on the first floor. Bomberger retreated to his room, located next to Annie's bedroom, to brood over being rebuffed.

On the morning of July 7, as the farmhand began his chores, he resolved that he would murder the Krieder family and outrage Annie. Bomberger went into the house, took the double barreled shotgun and shells, and went looking for Daniel. He found his victim asleep in his bedroom and shot him full of buckshot from one barrel. He next went into the kitchen where Mrs. Krieder was preparing breakfast and shot her to death. The stairs to the second floor were in the kitchen so he proceeded up to the childrens' rooms. He ordered Annie, twelve-year-old Aaron, five-year-old Eva, and three-year-old Henry into his room while he went about his work. He next shot the eleven-year-old girl named Merby. Nine-year-old Mary and seven-year-old David were shot next with a single load of buckshot fired into each child.

Bernice, thirteen years old, jumped from a second story window and ran to the barn but Bomberger followed. He intended to kill her there but she begged so piteously to see her family again that he dragged her back into the house and let her see each dead body. As Bernice looked over the bodies of her brother and sisters Bomberger noticed that Mary, the second child he had shot, was still alive, so he took a butcher knife and cut her throat. Then, as Bernice crouched in a corner with her hands thrown over her face, he shot her dead from close range. Bomberger next took Annie to her room and raped her.

While the murderer was preoccupied, Aaron, Eva, and Henry escaped and hid among the farm buildings, but Bomberger had lost interest in killing them. Instead, he dragged Annie to the barn and raped her again, then ordered her to the house to make his breakfast. He saddled his pony before he went into the kitchen, but he had lost his appetite. He forced Annie to hand over $50 of the family's funds and ordered her to pack a lunch. He herded Annie back to the barn where he forced her into a loft, bound her, and then fled north toward the international border.

Annie was freed by the other children after the murderer rode off and she walked into Cando to report the crime. Sheriff John McCune of Cando was soon on Bomberger's trail and captured him without resistance at Deloraine, Manitoba, on July 8. A large number of Cando's residents were intent upon lynching Bomberger but Sheriff McCune eluded them at Cando, and took his prisoner by way of Devil's Lake to Grand Forks where the local sheriff lodged the prisoner in jail. A contingent of Cando residents then started for Grand Forks, for the same purpose so the sheriff at Grand Forks, to prevent further bloodshed, decided to remove his prisoner to Fargo. However, when he got to the Winnipeg junction he learned that the "mob" consisted of only nineteen prominent citizens of Towner County, so he returned his prisoner to Grand Forks.

In November Bomberger was returned to Cando to stand trial. The party left Grand Forks in a special car on the St. John train, passed Devil's Lake where a crowd had gathered but made no demonstration, and then at Church's Ferry took a wagon the last seventeen miles to Cando. Upon arriving in town the sheriff took his prisoner to the Congregational Church, avoiding a large crowd, and Bomberger had his preliminary hearing before a justice of the peace. The next morning, November 21, the grand jury met and returned nine indictments for murder in the first degree. Bomberger was held under close guard in a small room above the church so he would not have to be transported through the streets of Cando, and the church would be used for the trial because the courtroom could not hold the large number of spectators expected. The prisoner was brought down before noon to have the indictments read, and the trial began at 1:30 P.M.

The murderer was only charged with the killings of Bernice and Mary at his first trial, as these were considered the strongest cases of premeditation. Bomberger had no attorney so J. O'Brien of Devil's Lake was appointed to represent the defendant, and then the court recessed for one hour. The court reconvened at 2:35 P.M. and Bomberger pled guilty, the entire proceeding taking only fifteen minutes. The district attorney asked the judge to allow him to call the county coroner to testify to the post mortem examination, to enlighten the judge as to the enormity of the crimes. After the testimony concluded the court adjourned until 5:00 P.M. on Thursday, November 23. When the court reconvened the judge sentenced the prisoner to be hanged on January 19, 1894.

The scaffold was erected by Elmer Judd in a small meadow one mile north of Cando, a half mile north of the Shanley Slaughter House, and adjoining the William McDonald place on the east — just north of the road running east and west between sections 17 and 20. This place was chosen because the elevated ground surrounding the meadow provided a good view for any who desired to witness the execution. The scaffold was enclosed by a seven foot fence twenty-four feet square, more to hold back the crowd than to obstruct their view, as the platform of the gallows was twenty feet above the ground. From the platform of the scaffold the condemned, if he chose to look, could plainly see the Krieder farmhouse.

The prisoner was kept in a room on the second floor of the courthouse. A mattress on the floor served as a bed for Bomberger and three death watch guards were with him constantly, because there were no bars on the courthouse windows. The prisoner spent his days playing cards and smoking his pipe. He maintained a hearty appetite and slept "as peacefully each night as a man whose mind is at ease with himself and all mankind."

On the day before his execution Bomberger remarked, "I wish I had not pled guilty." Sheriff McCune answered, "You've got no kick coming, Bomberger, you were given a chance to plead and plenty of time to think about it beforehand." Bomberger replied, "Yes, I know what you say is so, and I have no kick coming on the way I was used, and the show given me. It would probably have been the same thing in the end, yet I cannot help wishing that I had pled not guilty."

"During his final days many women visited, mostly the curious but also several sympathizers, but the condemned man was too much taken up with his own thoughts to pay any attention. Newsmen began to arrive in town on January 17 and several tried, but failed, to get an interview with the prisoner. On the morning of the execution a representative of the *Fargo Forum* requested to photograph Bomberger but he objected. He ate a hearty dinner at noon, then smoked his pipe until Sheriff McCune came at 12:45 P.M. with a bowl of water and a clean pair of socks. After bathing Bomberger returned to his chair in the auditor's office where the sheriff read the death warrant. Bomberger had nothing to say in response and refused the services of a clergyman, saying about his faith, "I do not know what I believe." The sheriff informed Bomberger that the time set for the execution, 1:30 P.M., was near at hand and that he should finish dressing.

The prisoner put on his vest and coat and walked out of the courthouse to the waiting sleigh. He took his seat between two county sheriffs and was driven into the enclosure at the gallows. The prisoner was given an opportunity to shake hands with the official witnesses near the gallows and bid them farewell, then he walked up the stairs and took his place on the trapdoor. From that vantage point he could see the crowd of over one thousand spectators on the surrounding hills. Sheriff McCune quickly pinioned the prisoner's arms and legs and adjusted the noose, then asked if he had anything to say. Bomberger responded in a loud, clear voice, "Gentlemen, I have a few words to say before I leave. I committed the crime and am sorry for it, and I hope no one here will ever follow in my footsteps. I want no clergyman on the scaffold with me. Good-bye, all!" A reverend who had visited the prisoner in his room several times called out, "Albert, look to Jesus!" and Bomberger replied only, "Thank you."

The black hood was drawn over his head and with the words, "Good-bye Jack (to McCune); good-bye Sheriff," the bolt was drawn and at 1:33 P.M. the trap was sprung. Bomberger fell eight feet, his shoes clearing the ground by only six inches. There were three doctors in attendance and they immediately stepped forward, announced that the prisoner's neck was broken, and recorded his pulse. In fourteen minutes, 1:47 P.M., Bomberger's heart ceased to beat and he was pronounced dead. The body was cut down and placed in the coffin provided by the county, then carried to the courthouse, where hundreds of curious citizens passed by to view the remains of the mass murderer. Bomberger was buried in the public cemetery one mile east of Cando at dusk. Later a telegram was received from his parents requesting that the body of their son be sent to Pennsylvania for burial.

Plaindealer (Grand Forks, ND): January 19, 1894. *Grand Forks Herald* (ND): January 17, 1894; January 20, 1894.

Jenkins, Ira O.
September 14, 1900

James Jenkins and his son Ira operated the Casino Coal Mine near Wilton, North Dakota. On March 19, 1900, they reported finding August Stark, one of their employees, dead in the mine. The body was frozen when delivered to the coroner but after the examination was completed it was determined that the body had been dragged a considerable distance after death, suggesting foul play. The two Jenkins men were questioned and they told conflicting stories, so both were charged with Stark's murder. The state's prosecuting attorney, Edward Allen, believed that Ira had killed Stark and brought Ira to trial in May, and Ira's father testified that his son admitted to him that he had killed Stark during a robbery. Ira testified that his father had murdered Stark by strangling him but, when doctors testified that the dead man had not been choked, the jury found Ira guilty of first degree murder and recommended the death penalty. On May 28 Judge Walter Winchester sentenced Jenkins to hang at Bismarck on September 14, 1900. Neither appeal nor petition delayed the proceedings.

During the evening before the execution Ira and his father were brought together and the son asked if his father was going to "help him out by admitting his guilt." The father said he could not and was subjected to a torrent of oaths and verbal abuses. Ira Jenkins retired late but slept well and was awakened at an early hour. Breakfast was served at 4:00 A.M. because the execution had been scheduled between 5 and 7 o'clock, but by 5:00 A.M. a thunderstorm formed and the heavy rain caused a delay. From the moment the prisoner arose he engaged in a tirade of vulgarity, profanity and blasphemy and refused to show any feeling of remorse, sorrow or fear, and continued to protest his innocence.

The witnesses had begun to gather at the jail between 2:00 and 4:00 A.M. and waited patiently for the sheriff to begin the process. At 8:00 A.M. the death warrant was read to the prisoner in his cell and when Sheriff Bogue concluded, Jenkins asked, "Is that all?" He then asked for the form so that he could show his contempt for it. His wrists were cuffed and his arms strapped to his sides and the procession formed at 8:05 A.M. Jenkins climbed the steps onto the platform in a drizzling rain as he called out greetings to several people he recognized below, and when he was allowed to speak he said, "I see down there a great many people who are anxious to see me hung. I see a great many young men down there, and to them I want to say that liquor did this." When he paused his legs were bound and, when he began again, a confession was expected, but the crowd was disappointed when instead he berated his attorney and protested his innocence once again. When Jenkins paused a second time the noose was adjusted and the black hood was pulled over his head. Through the dark cloth he yelled out, "I am an innocent man!"

It was 8:14 A.M. when all the preparations were completed and in a moment the trap was sprung and the prisoner fell, breaking his neck. In nine minutes Dr. Matchan pronounced him dead and then the body was cut down and placed in the coffin stored beneath the platform. The body was examined and it was observed that there was little distortion or disfigurement of Jenkins' features. The remains were taken to the home of relatives for burial the following morning at 10:00 A.M. Jenkins had written his confession and hid it in his pants pocket to be found afterward. The deceased left a wife and an infant child and there was a great deal of public sympathy for them.

Bismarck Daily Tribune (ND): September 15, 1900.
Minot Optic (ND): September 15, 1900.

Thorpe, Hans
September 14, 1900

Hans Thorpe was in his thirties in 1898 when he moved to Minot, North Dakota. He had been a seaman for some years traveling around the world and then worked on the railroads, which took him through a great part of the country. In Minot he met and courted Ida Johnson, a girl still in her teens, but she was so taken with this man of great experience that she soon married him. Within a year, however, the marriage was experiencing great difficulties, primarily because Thorpe was insanely jealous every time his wife was out of his immediate presence. He was a man who believed his wife a chattel and considered her unfaithful whenever she was not with him.

On the evening of December 1, 1899, Ida went next door to visit with Mrs. Johanson. Thorpe had been on a week long spree and when he discovered that his wife had left their house he took his pistol and followed her. When he entered the Johanson house he pulled his revolver and, without comment or hesitation, shot Ida in the head twice, killing her instantly. He then turned the gun on himself and fired one round, the bullet destroying his right eye and scarring his face but causing no fatal wound.

Neighbors heard the shots and called the authorities, who arrested Thorpe and lodged him in jail, where he survived after receiving medical care. Thorpe's trial began in late April 1900 and he was convicted of first degree murder. Judge David Morgan sentenced him to hang on May 10, but appeals and petitions for a commutation of sentence delayed the execution to September 14, 1900.

During the time Thorpe was in jail he refused any religious consolation. He said he did not believe that either a priest or a preacher could do him any good. On his last night Mr. McClure, representative of *The Optic*, called and found the sheriff's wife preparing a wreath of natural flowers in the form of an anchor. Jailor Thompson admitted the reporter to cage number 1, which faced the corridor, and joined George Whinney, master mechanic of the Great Northern, who was visiting the condemned man. The prisoner complained of some misinformation published in the newspaper but commended the laws of the United States and North Dakota. Then he said, "Before I go into eternity I hope there won't be a sphere of grass grow on my grave until certain parties get their just dues for the dirty and inhuman work they have done to me and my wife, and if there is such a thing as a person's ghost coming back, I will surely come." He then said he did not get justice from man but hoped to get it from the Almighty.

The scaffold had been designed and erected by Judge Murray outside the city limits a half mile southeast of the Ward County Courthouse at one of the most picturesque places in the Mouse River Valley. The site was hemmed in on the right by a long range of crescent shaped bluffs and on the left by the elm covered river banks, and an early frost had just started to turn the color of the leaves.

On the fatal morning clouds began to form at 1 o'clock and at 2:00 A.M. rain began to fall. At 4:00 A.M. those who would witness the execution made their way through the mud, relying on the lightning flashes to light their way, and in an hour all were present in the hallway of the jail. At 5:50 Sheriff M. Carroll came from his room and was joined by District Attorney Johnson, who held the death warrant. They woke the sleeping prisoner and told him the fatal hour had arrived. Thorpe yawned and said, "All right, I am ready."

Thorpe quickly dressed in a gray suit and white shirt, black neck tie and sailor's cap, then listened to the reading of the death warrant. The cell door was thrown open and the procession began at 6:04 A.M. The prisoner was placed in a buggy and driven to the gallows. When he arrived he was greeted by a huge crowd which had gathered outside the enclosure. He made a short address, restating what had already been said, and then entered through a door in the fence. Once on the platform he shook hands with Judge Murray, Sheriff Carroll, chief deputy Sykes, District Attorney Johnson, and several others. Sheriff Carroll asked Thorpe if he had anything to say, so he walked to the rail and glanced over the crowd. Seeing the newspaper man he said, "Say, McClure, will you now take back what you said about my collapsing? I won't kick even when the rope is fixed. McClure, so far as polities are concerned!" The sheriff tapped the prisoner on the shoulder and said, "Your time has come."

Thorpe was led to the center of the platform and positioned on the trapdoor. His arms and legs were pinioned, the noose adjusted, and the black hood pulled on by the sheriff. The sheriff toyed with the frills of the black hood to distract the prisoner while deputy Sykes stood with knife poised over the cord holding the trap lever. At a prearranged signal from the sheriff the cord was cut and Thorpe dropped through at 6:30 A.M. The body swung around four times before Dr. Crokat of Minot and Dr. Windell of Bowbells steadied the remains and began checking for a pulse. In ten minutes they pronounced him dead and in eight minutes more, at 6:48 A.M., Thorpe's remains were cut down and placed in a handsome coffin. The body was immediately driven to the burying grounds and buried.

Minot Optic (ND): September 14, 1900.

Bassanella, Jacob L.
February 20, 1903

Jacob Lewis Bassanella and his younger brother Joseph Bassanella were active desperadoes in North Dakota at the beginning of the twentieth century. In March 1901 the boys were together when Jacob shot and killed farmer Axel Anderson in a Great Northern boxcar at Grand Forks. The boys fled but were quickly caught and jailed. They denied their guilt and on May 22 escaped. Joseph was caught near Glasgow, Montana, in mid–June and returned to Grand Forks. He was tried, convicted of first degree murder, and sentenced to life in prison.

In late May 1901 James Smith, an inoffensive young man, appeared at Washburn explaining that he had just returned from the war in Spain. He found steady work at odd jobs to support himself. In March 1902 a wealthy farmer named Anton Hylinger was murdered with a shotgun. Smith was immediately suspected and within a few days he was lodged in jail. He managed to escape in September but was soon captured at Fort Yates and taken to the Burleigh County jail at Bismarck, a far more substantial structure than the jail at Washburn. Still, he managed to escape for a brief period in October but was arrested in time to appear at his trial in Washburn in early November.

Smith was found guilty of murder in the first degree and on November 10 he was brought into court for sentencing. He surprised Judge Walter Winchester when he confessed to the murder of Hylinger, and then disclosed that he was the fugitive Jacob Bassanella. The prisoner, regardless of his name, was sentenced to hang on February 20, 1903. Bassanella was again held in the Washburn jail and, though extra precautions were taken, he nearly managed to escape again. Thereafter a twenty-four hour death watch was maintained.

The gallows was built in the northwest corner of a twenty by twenty foot enclosure adjoining the McLean County jail on the north side of the yard. During his final days the prisoner was attended by Fathers Clemens and Lewis. They were with him most of his final full day until he retired at an early hour. He slept until midnight, when he was awakened and served his last meal. The death warrant was read to the condemned man in his cell and at 3:55 A.M. he was led out to the scaffold. He walked at such a quick pace that the guards had to hurry to keep abreast. After climbing nine stairs he took his place on the trapdoor and Sheriff Gradin prepared him for the drop by pinioning his arms and legs. As the black hood was produced he said, "Wait a minute, I may want to say something," then paused before he said, "Gentlemen and young men, let this be a warning to you and do not follow in my steps."

When he paused again the black hood was pulled down and the noose adjusted. Through the dark cloth he said, "Here, fix that knot, do a good job, gentlemen, don't make a botch of it." It seemed he was about to continue his statement of warning to the witnesses when the trap was sprung and he dropped six feet. Bassanella was short and heavily built, with a thick muscular neck, so that the drop which had been carefully calculated did not break his neck and the prisoner drew up his legs three times before resting motionless. Dr. Quain of Bismarck and Dr. Dillon of Washburn recorded the dying man's pulse and in seven and one half minutes pronounced him dead. Bassanella's remains were cut down and placed in a coffin provided by the Catholic church.

In the dead man's pocket was found a signed statement which said: "I, Jacob Lewis Bassanella, to whom it may concern; I make this statement before I'm executed. I'm justly punished according to law. I freely confess of the crime committed at Grand Forks of which my dear brother Joseph was innocently convicted of and to be doomed for life at the Bismarck pen. I am wholly responsible for the crime. I made the plan and carried out myself. It is my wish to have my body turned over to the Rev. Father Clemens of Bismarck." The confession was dismissed as false and self-serving. In accordance with the prisoner's last request, his remains were give over to Father Clemens to be taken to Bismarck for burial the following day.

On March 14, 1908, Joseph Bassanella with another convict tunneled their way out of the penitentiary and Joseph headed north with some idea of avenging his older brother's death. He was recognized at a point seventeen miles from Washburn and during a shoot-out he was killed by a bullet through his brain.

Bismarck Tribune (ND): February 21, 1903.

Ross, William R.
March 6, 1903

William Robert Ross was born on July 24, 1873. When he was four years old his family began moving about Minnesota and North Dakota and when he was fifteen years old they settled at Pendroy in the Mouse River Valley. He moved about the area for several seasons during which time his mother died and he married Annie Barisch when they both worked for Mr. Schwartz. After a period of some hardship, several times resolved by stealing calves, cows and horses, he was caught and served a year in prison. Ross sent his wife to Malta, Montana, to keep house for his father and he joined them as soon as he was released. He took several jobs but soon moved closer to town and began stealing cattle and horses in partnership with the man who was running their old liquor shop in Towner.

Carl Hanson, a man Ross had known in Minot some years earlier, came to town and they went to work for Ed Tiegerson on his ranch. In the fall, when some horses went missing, Tiegerson told Ross to bring them back if he found them. Ross searched and found several horses and brought them back, only to find that Hanson had left with another of Tiegerson's horses. They were about to file a complaint when Hanson returned and said he had found the rest of Tiegerson's herd. Ross joined him in going to Willow City on July 5, 1902.

Hanson, according to Ross, had never found the missing stock but wanted Ross to go with him to steal a particularly fine string of horses belonging to Thomas Walsh, an elderly farmer. The men could have easily taken the horses but Ross feared that Walsh would sound the alarm and have lawmen on their trail within hours, and he knew they would have to move slowly with the herd. Ross decided that he must kill Walsh so he took his rifle, snuck into the house and shot Walsh while he slept. He intended to bury the body, as he had done previously when he murdered Napolean LeMay, but lost his nerve and would not re-enter the house.

He went to Towner, then Harvey, and then to Fessenden, where he finally found a buyer for Walsh's horses. Ross met Schwartz, the man he used to work for, and was recognized and arrested as his description had been widely circulated and a reward was offered. The authorities had focused on Ross immediately and after some close questioning Ross confessed to the crime and implicated Hanson.

Ross was brought to trial at Bottineau in August, convicted of first degree murder, and sentenced to hang on December 5, 1902. As the date approached, however, Ross confessed to another murder. He said he and Carl Hanson were working on a ranch near Delta when they met Napolean LeMay camped with several fine horses. Ross said that when LeMay refused to trade, Hanson shot him in the back while Ross distracted him, and they buried the body in a nearby dry well. They took the horses and disposed of them, dividing the spoils. This disclosure earned Ross two respites while the matter was investigated, but finally the date for Ross' execution was scheduled for March 6, 1903. Hanson was arrested and denied being involved in either murder, but there was sufficient evidence to implicate him and he was convicted of murder in the first degree. One week before Ross' execution Hanson was sentenced to life in prison.

In his final days Ross converted to Catholicism and was baptized by Father C. M. Turcotte, who then administered the last sacrament. On his last evening Ross ate a hearty supper and his appetite did not fail him the next morning. He dressed in his dark suit and spent two hours sequestered with Father Turcotte, and then called for William Murray from Minot, to whom he gave his personal belongings and instructions for their distribution. He wrote out a lengthy statement in which he admitted some crimes, denied others, but mainly commented on his new found Catholic faith.

The gallows had been built beside the Bottineau courthouse and was entirely enclosed for privacy. At 1:00 P.M. the condemned man listened as the deputy state's attorney Bowen read the death warrant and the two reprieves. He shook hands with all in his presence including his attorney. He nearly broke down when the straps were applied to his wrists and arms in the cell, but Father Turcotte whispered words of support and this helped him brace up. At 1:13 P.M. he was escorted to the scaffold by Father Turcotte and Sheriff Gardner, where the priest offered a prayer for the condemned man's soul. Ross was then allowed to speak to the witnesses and he said, "I am sorry for all the sins that I have done and I ask forgiveness from all that I have harmed and I forgive all those who have harmed me. I have told the truth all the way through." As he paused, Judge Murray of Minot asked, "Willie, who killed LeMay?" and Ross replied, "Carl Hanson." Ross then concluded, "I bid one and everybody good-bye."

His legs had been pinioned and the noose adjusted as he spoke. As the black hood was presented he kissed the cross offered by the priest and as the hood was pulled over his head he said, "May God forgive me for all my sins." At 1:16 P.M. the trap was sprung by Sheriff Gardner and Ross' body dropped eight feet, breaking his neck. Drs. McKay, Dochterman and Lemieux recorded his pulse and pronounced him dead in eleven minutes. The body was cut down and placed in a coffin, viewed by the coroner's jury, and then released to undertaker Greiner for processing. Ross' face appeared natural and the only sign of his manner of death was a slight rope burn on his neck. He was buried the following day at Bottineau.

Bismarck Tribune (ND): March 7, 1903. *Bottineau Courant* (ND): March 6, 1903.

Rooney, John
October 17, 1905

During the early morning hours of August 26, 1902, the three Sweet brothers were camped on the grade near the tracks of the Chicago, Milwaukee and St. Paul Railroad on Fargo's west side. Three masked men approached stealthily and, with guns drawn, tried to rob the Sweets. One of the Sweet brothers slipped down behind a bush but John Rooney, one of the robbers, fired at him and ordered him out into the open. The Beaton family lived one hundred twenty-five yards away and one of them came out at the sound of gunfire and, properly assessing the situation, fired at the robbers. Two of the robbers fled but Rooney was a bit slower in getting started, so two of the brothers grabbed him and a struggle ensued. The three men fell over an embankment and, as Harold Sweet hurried to his brothers' assistance, Rooney reached around and shot Harold in the back. The two uninjured brothers tackled and held Rooney until he was arrested. Drs. Webber and Darrow of Fargo removed the bullet but Harold Sweet, the oldest brother, lingered for only a day before he died of his wound.

John Rooney was charged with his murder

and it was learned that the prisoner had a criminal record for robbery from ten years earlier. Judge McConnell, in 1892, on account of Rooney's youth, had reduced the charge and sentenced Rooney to a brief jail term. Rooney became a favorite of newsmen and he told them a great many facts about the gang which preyed upon the seasonal harvest workers. From the first moment of capture Rooney insisted that Harold Sweet had been shot by one of the other men, whom he identified only as "Kansas Slim." However, with the evidence of his gun, the matching bullet removed from Harold's back, and the testimony of the two surviving Sweet brothers, Rooney was easily convicted of first degree murder. His case had caught the interest of two prominent Fargo attorneys, W. S. Stambaugh and Burliegh Spalding. They were appointed by the court to defend him and while they lost the case they managed to get the execution delayed three times. Finally every ploy and manipulation of the law was exhausted and the date for the hanging was set for October 17, 1905. The condemned man was brought to the penitentiary at Bismarck where the execution was to take place, the first and only hanging to occur within the prison walls.

A half hour before midnight on October 16, Rooney's last night, the prisoner ordered a variety of delicacies for his last meal. He had maintained a good appetite during his incarceration and it was not diminished by his impending doom. He dressed in a suit of black cloth, a white shirt with collar, tie and cuffs, and he was wearing two carnations when the death warrant was read to him by Warden Boucher at 12:30 A.M. In twenty-four minutes the procession was formed and the prisoner, escorted by guards, followed his religious advisors out of the cell block. He walked across the prison yard and stepped onto the new portable gallows which had been set up inside a building to ensure privacy.

On the platform the condemned man said, when given his chance to speak, "Good evening, Gentlemen. I am sorry to entertain you all here so late tonight, but you know my circumstances and condition." He surveyed his surroundings and then talked of his crime and the subsequent legal events. He complimented his attorney and thanked the warden and guards. He said he was not afraid to die and felt assured of God's forgiveness. Next he sang several verses of a song he said was titled "There is a Lonely Spot on the Missouri Slope," afterward admitting he had made up the verses and apologized for its faulty rendition. He talked for eleven minutes before he concluded with, "Gentlemen, that is all." The prisoner walked up the three steps to the platform and stood on the center of the trapdoor. He said, "Jesus, have mercy on us for Christ's sake."

Straps were applied to his arms and legs and a white robe and hood pulled on to completely cover his body and face. The noose was adjusted and at 1:05 A.M. the trap was sprung. The prison physician recorded his pulse and in twelve minutes pronounced him dead. Rooney had told the warden to dispose of his body as he saw fit and the law required that remains, unclaimed by family or friends, be given to a school within the state for medical research. On Monday afternoon the doctors of Bismarck persisted in their demand for Rooney's remains and quickly established a school there. Assistant Attorney General Stevens had threatened a mandamus proceeding if the law was not followed, but the quick action of Bismarck's doctors had precluded such action and they received the remains of the murderer.

The Settler (Bismarck, ND): October 18–19, 1905.

Oregon

Oregon was a part of the "Oregon Country" when it was acquired from Great Britain. A dispute persisted over the northern boundary of the Oregon Country between the parallels of 42° and 54°40', which at the time was under joint control of the United States and Great Britain, and consisted of the area between the northern border of California and Russia's southern border of Alaska. Although there was a strong movement in America to claim the 54°40' boundary, President James K. Polk surprised everyone when, on June 15, 1846, he agreed to the parallel of 49° to separate the United States from Canada, and his agreement gave the United States sole control over Oregon.

The "Oregon Territory," stretching from the northern border of California to the new Canadian border, and including what would become Washington, Idaho, and Montana, was established in 1848. Oregon was admitted to the Union as the 33rd state on February 14, 1859.

Roe, Charles J.
April 2, 1859

Charles Roe was an old Oregon pioneer. He arrived in the "Oregon Country" when there was hardly a white man in the Pacific Northwest. He had been in the area three years when he married Nancy McKay in 1837. His first wife died so in 1856 he took a second wife, Angelica Carpentier, and the following year she gave birth to a son. There were rumors that Angelica had several "husbands" prior to her marriage, but there were no children by those relationships. Angelica was a young, beautiful woman in a region where women of any appearance were rare. Roe was constantly jealous of his second wife, always suspecting she might be having an affair with one man or another.

On the evening of February 11, 1859, Angelica's niece and her husband were visiting the Roes when Charles once again accused his wife of having an affair. She was sitting with their son on her lap as she denied it, called him a liar, and challenged him to prove it. Roe was in no mood for an argument so he pulled his long bladed pocketknife from his pocket, opened the shorter of two blades, and grabbed his wife's hair. He pulled her head back exposing her neck and then cut her throat from ear to ear. Blood was spurting everywhere, drenching the husband, wife and son, and Angelica was choking on the blood as she jumped up and ran out into the street where she collapsed and bled to death.

A deputy sheriff was called and he found Roe awaiting his arrival. Roe was arrested and lodged in the newly built Marion County jail. The following morning the prisoner was taken before Justice of the Peace Purdy for his examination, and he freely told of the murder. He was held over for action by the grand jury, indicted in mid–February, and his trial commenced in Judge Reuben Boise's courtroom on February 24. Roe's confession was admitted into evidence, including his statement that "I loved my wife as I did my own soul, and I killed her to keep anyone else from enjoying her." The jury had no difficulty in finding the defendant guilty of first degree murder and Judge Boise sentenced him to hang on April 2, 1859. Neither appeal nor application for executive clemency delayed the proceedings.

Roe spent his last weeks showing little concern for his dead wife, his soon-to-be orphaned son, nor for his own fate. He embraced religion, was baptized, and spent a great deal of time with the Reverends William Roberts and A. F. Waller praying and reading the Bible. When the day of his execution arrived the two clergymen walked with him to the scaffold after 11:00 A.M., escorted by Marion County Sheriff Narcisse A. Cornoyer and several deputies. On the scaffold he gave a speech of repentance to the crowd of more than one thousand spectators, which included a large proportion of women and children. He said he expected a "heavenly pardon," then stepped onto the trapdoor.

While a prayer was offered, Roe's arms and legs were pinioned, the noose adjusted, and the black hood was pulled over his head. When the reverend said "Amen!," at 12:12 P.M., the trap was sprung. Roe's neck was broken in the fall and the body showed no sign of movement, but he was allowed to hang until it was certain he could not be revived, and then he was pronounced dead. The body was cut down, lowered into the coffin provided by the county, and buried before sunset.

Oregonian (Portland): February 19, 1859.

Balch, Danforth
October 17, 1859

In 1850 Danforth Balch, sometimes written as Danford, his wife Jane and three children settled on a tract of land a bit larger than a half section located in the Willamette Valley, Oregon. During the next eight years Jane gave birth to five more children. The oldest child was sixteen-year-old Anna. Farming such a large piece of fertile land to its fullest potential was an overwhelming task for one man even with the help of the two older sons — Hosea and Thomas. Balch hired a hand to help them, a young man named Mortimer Stump, who came from a local family. Stump lived at the Balch farm and, in a brief period, made quite an impression on Anna. There were not many young pretty girls nor handsome eligible bachelors in the vicinity, so it should have seemed inevitable that the two would become interested in one another. Anna's father disapproved of their growing fondness, fired the farm hand, and forcibly put the young man off his property. However, Mortimer Stump was not a man to be put off by such meager efforts, so he snuck back onto the property and the two youngsters made plans to elope.

During the first week of November 1858 Balch discovered that his daughter was gone, and the circumstances were such that he knew who had taken her, where they had gone, and their intentions. It was 1858 so there was little alternative to marriage, and the two young lovers welcomed the prospect. They were wed at Vancouver, Washington Territory, and then took up residence with the Stump family. Anna had not contacted her father, knowing that he would be livid, and even more so at her new husband. On November 18 Balch was in Portland, Multnomah County, and had been drinking liquor quite heavily. He encountered the Stumps — his new son-in-law in company with Mortimer's brother and father — and they exchanged fighting words, but the Stumps were determined not to aggravate the relationship between Anna and her father and retired to the dock of the Stark Street ferry to take their wagon of supplies across the river. Balch retrieved his double-barreled shotgun and followed and when he arrived at the ferry he saw that his daughter had been waiting with the wagon, and this only infuriated him further.

He started toward Anna but Mortimer stepped between to protect his bride and Balch's shotgun went off, the heavy load of buckshot from one barrel striking Mortimer's face and neck. The blast killed Mortimer Stump immediately. Balch did not make any effort to avoid arrest; perhaps he was too drunk to even realize the gravity of his situation, and he was lodged in the Multnomah County jail to await action by the grand jury. By April 28, 1859, his situation was clearer to him, so when an opportunity arose he escaped with several other prisoners. He was found at his home on July 23 and arrested by City Marshal J. H. Lappeus without incident.

Balch was returned to jail and in early August he was indicted for murder. The trial of Balch began on August 17 in Judge A. E. Watts' courtroom. On August 21 the attorneys made their final arguments and the case went to the jury, which quickly found him guilty as charged in the indictment. Judge Watts then sentenced Balch to hang on October 17, 1859. There was no delay from appeals nor from an application for executive clemency.

The gallows had been erected in an open field on the corner of Front and Salmon Streets. The hanging was a public affair at a time when it was believed that such a display was a deterrent to other would-be murderers. More than five hundred people gathered at the foot of the scaffold on the fatal day, including the entire Stump family and Mortimer's widow, Anna. Before 10:30 A.M. Sheriff Addison M. Starr went to the cell of the condemned man and read the death warrant. The procession to the gallows then began and Balch emerged from the jail to find the weather overcast and rainy, appropriately a very gloomy day. In ten minutes Balch stood on the scaffold and was asked if he had anything to say, but he said only, "I have written out a detailed confession, as best I could recall the events through the alcoholic haze."

The condemned man was positioned on the center of the trapdoor, his arms and legs were pinioned, and the black hood was pulled over his head. Almost at the same instant that the noose was adjusted to place the knot behind his left ear, the signal was given and the trap was sprung. Balch dropped through and the fall broke his neck. Dr. A. M. Loryea of the Hawthorne Insane Asylum had been designated the attending physician and he waited beneath the scaffold. When Balch's body appeared he monitored vital signs and finally pronounced him dead. After hanging a short while longer, to ensure the condemned man could not be revived, the body was cut down and placed in a wooden box. The remains of Balch were turned over to his family, who took them back to the Balch farm for burial in the family cemetery.

Oregonian (Portland): November 20, 1858; July 2, 1859; July 30, 1859; August 27, 1859; October 15–22, 1859.

Moss, Matthew
March 20, 1860

Twenty-seven-year-old Matthew Moss was a desperate and despicable character. He bragged just enough so that his neighbors knew he had killed a man in Kentucky before fleeing to Oregon. He lived with another bachelor in a cabin eight miles south of The Dalles on the Luckiamute River in Polk County. The cabin was nestled in a cluster of similar cabins, and not far from the home of Mr. and Mrs. George Harper. Perhaps because Mrs. Harper was a beautiful woman, or just because females were so rare in early Oregon, Moss fixed his attention upon her and made repeated, unwelcome advances. When his suggestive comments and actions became intolerable Mrs. Harper left home without telling her husband her reasons. George followed his wife and, upon his promise to put an end to Moss' behavior, she returned.

On January 12, 1860, many people in the small community gathered at the home of Samuel Gothard for a pleasant evening of music and conversation. When Moss appeared Mrs. Harper demanded her husband take action, and with pistol in hand he confronted Moss and warned him to leave Mrs. Harper alone, then ordered him off the property. Moss did not make a fuss and left, but instead of going home he went to the cabin of another neighbor and borrowed a rifle, saying he was going hunting the next day. He returned to the Gothard cabin and, skulking about, finally got a clear view of Mr. Harper through a window. He took careful aim, fired a single bullet, and killed Harper instantly. There was no doubt who had fired the shot, as he was seen.

The next morning, after a warrant was issued, Sheriff James S. Holman organized a small posse of well armed and determined men and they rode to the Moss cabin. They found Moss at home and arrested him without incident. The grand jury convened in early February and Moss was indicted for murder. Three material witnesses were detained but each posted a bond and was released. These three and ten other witnesses would constitute the case for the prosecution. The trial began on February 6 in Judge Reuben Boise's courtroom and lasted a single day. That evening the jury retired and deliberated for only a few minutes before returning a guilty verdict. The prisoner was then sentenced to hang in seven weeks, on March 20, 1860. Neither appeal nor application for executive clemency would delay the execution.

As the condemned man sat in his cell he compiled his autobiography to wile away the hours, and when the fatal day arrived Moss walked to the scaffold with a firm step and took his place on the trapdoor. During these early days executions were public, so nearly twelve hundred people had gathered around the gallows. Among them, and at the forefront, was the coroner's jury of six men who would sign the death certificate.

Moss did not disappoint the crowd, as he confessed to every crime he had ever committed, and perhaps more, and professed Christianity and repentance. He warned everyone not to follow in his footsteps to the gallows, and to look at his body after death as an example. Once his speech concluded his wrists and arms, and knees and ankles were pinioned and a handkerchief was tied over his eyes. The noose was carefully adjusted so that the knot was behind his left ear, and the trap was sprung by Sheriff Holman. Moss fell to his death, breaking his neck. After he was pronounced dead by the attending physician he was cut down and lowered into a cheap pine coffin, which was put on display so that everyone had the opportunity to see the remains of the murderer, and then he was buried in an unmarked grave.

Oregon Argus (Oregon City): January 18, 1860; March 31, 1860. *Statesman* (Salem, OR): January 17, 1860; January 24, 1860; February 14, 1860; March 20, 1860; March 27, 1860. *Oregonian* (Portland): March 23, 1860; March 30, 1860.

Casterlin, William
May 11, 1860

William Casterlin, a barrel maker from Illinois, had come west during the early days of pioneering and settled in Jacksonville, Jackson County, Oregon. On December 3, 1859, he returned home to the house he shared with his partner in the cooper business, Samuel Mooney, a man he had known for years. He was in the company of Dr. George Elliott and Hiram Abbott, and the four men began drinking heavily. Some insignificant remark led to an argument between Casterlin and Mooney, which quickly escalated, and Elliott and Abbott tried to calm the situation. Finally Mooney, wanting an end to a silly dispute that was more the result of whiskey than a real issue, left the house. No sooner had he exited than Casterlin took up his rifle and, through the door, fired a shot at him. Mooney collapsed and the three men ran to him. The bullet had entered Mooney's head right between his eyes and exploded his brain, killing him instantly, and there was nothing Dr. Elliott could do.

There had been a recent rash of murders in Oregon and there was strong feeling that the lawlessness should end by strict adherence to the law. Casterlin was well known and liked though he had a penchant for drinking to excess. In fact, he was best known to the jailors in Jacksonville, where he spent many nights in a jail cell sleeping off a stupor.

When the grand jury met on March 26 they indicted Casterlin for Mooney's murder and the trial began in Judge P. Prim's court two days later. The presentation of evidence and the arguments were brief for a trial of such importance, but the deliberations took a great deal of time before the jurors returned a verdict of "guilty as charged in the indictment," and Casterlin was sentenced to hang on May 11, 1860. There was an application, accompanied by a lengthy petition, requesting Governor John Whiteaker to grant a commutation of sentence to life in prison, but he denied the request.

On the prisoner's final day Sheriff Legrand Duncan read the death warrant to the condemned man in his cell, and at 11:00 A.M. the procession to the gallows formed. The prisoner was accompanied by the sheriff and the Reverend Driver. On the scaffold the Reverend read a short prayer and then led the crowd in a hymn before retiring from the platform. The prisoner was next asked if he had anything to say, and he stepped forward to the railing and warned everyone against evil ways. He confessed to a life of sin but claimed, as he had always done, that he remembered nothing of the evening when he killed Mooney.

Once he had finished his speech he stepped back onto the trapdoor, centered himself, and cooperated when his arms and legs were pinioned. The black hood was pulled on and the noose adjusted just moments before the trap was sprung at 11:20 A.M. Casterlin dropped straight through, but his neck was not broken by the fall and he struggled for several minutes before he strangled to death. It was a horrible affair and the prisoner's misery affected everyone who watched it. Finally he was pronounced dead and the body was cut down and placed in a cheap pine coffin. Casterlin was buried later that evening in the local cemetery.

Oregon Argus (Oregon City): May 12, 1860. *Oregon Statesman* (Salem): March 20, 1860; April 17, 1860; May 1, 1860; May 22, 1860; May 29, 1860. *Weekly Union* (Corvallis, OR): December 12, 1859; May 22, 1860.

George, Phillip
June 22, 1860

In 1860 Philip George and John Clark, both in their 50s, opened the American House in Corvallis, Benton County, Oregon. Corvallis was the center of a large German population and the two German men felt comfortable in their new home, having moved from Jackson County, where they had been in business together for several years. The American House had sleeping quarters, a dining room and complete kitchen, and a livery. Clark worked as the overall proprietor of the concern while George, a much better cook, was primarily responsible for food preparation. The two men continuously argued over every detail of management and George's penchant for alcohol.

On May 10, 1860, George was "sleeping it off" after a Wednesday night drunk, which had extended into the early morning hours, but finally he fell asleep. At 2:00 P.M. a guest woke him to get his horse, and George accompanied him to the stable. George was already in a bad mood so, when they arrived at the stable and found Clark busy selling hay to two teamsters, George objected. Soon the two partners were arguing and this quickly escalated into a fist fight. The two men finished their fight in the barn, out of the sight of the others. After a brief silence Clark staggered out of the barn toward the house and collapsed on the porch, semi-conscious and suffering, though there appeared to be no serious wound. George soon followed and, when encouraged to get the doctor, he declined and said disparaging things toward his partner, expressing his wish that Clark should die. George then went through Clark's pockets. No one objected but George felt obligated to mention that the money was joint property and he was entitled to it.

Clark soon died and coroner Dr. T. J. Right held an inquest, but there was no way to determine the cause of death so, the following day, Drs. J. S. Coombs, J. R. Hayley, and McAfee performed a post-mortem examination. They determined that Clark had died from a blow to the head, consistent with being struck by a thrown rock. The only person who could have thrown a rock at Clark at that time was George. They reported their findings to Dr. Right and George was arrested and charged with the murder of Clark. The prisoner was lodged in the newly built Corvallis jail and at his examination he was held over for the grand jury. On April 1, 1860, he was indicted and on April 4 his trial began in Judge R. E. Stratton's court. Only five witnesses testified for the prosecution, none for the defense, so the case went to the jury in the afternoon and after brief deliberations they returned a verdict of guilty of first degree murder. George was sentenced to hang on May 25, 1860.

On the fatal day all went according to schedule. Two thousand people, including women and children, surrounded the scaffold to watch Philip George die. He was conducted onto the scaffold and stepped onto the trapdoor, where he gave what all thought was his final speech. Just at the moment when he would have been prepared for the drop, Sheriff Sheldon B. Fargo stepped forward and announced that Governor John Whiteaker had rejected a plea for a commutation of sentence, but had granted the condemned man a thirty day respite so that the state Supreme Court could consider the case. However, the form was improper so the sheriff, unwilling to take responsibility, asked for a vote and the popular opinion was to let the legal process play out. George was returned to the jail.

With two days to spare, the Supreme Court affirmed the lower court's decision and George was scheduled to hang at noon on June 22, 1860. The disappointment at the delay of the first hanging kept many away, so when the prisoner mounted the scaffold fewer than one thousand spectators were present, but still included a large number of women and children.

He again made his speech denying guilt and professing Christianity as he stood on the trapdoor, and then his arms and legs were pinioned. A black hood was pulled over his head and the noose was adjusted. George had been accompanied by several lawmen and by the Reverends Rayner and Avery, and the clergy prayed for him as the trap was sprung. He dropped six feet and broke his neck. Drs. Right and McAfee waited beneath the scaffold and as soon as the body appeared they monitored his vital signs and pronounced him dead. He was allowed to hang a total of twenty-five minutes before being cut down and placed in the cheap pine coffin provided by the county. He was buried in the Corvallis cemetery following a brief service.

Oregon Statesman (Salem): March 20, 1860. *Weekly Union* (Corvallis, OR): March 13, 1860; May 22–29, 1860; June 5, 1860; June 26, 1860.

Pate, Andrew J.
May 27, 1862

Andrew J. Pate had been a transient laborer since his twelfth birthday in 1846. He had run away from home and began slowly working his way westward from Nashville, Tennessee, but without any definite destination. He was unskilled and uneducated, so the best work he could find was often chopping wood. This type of work usually only lasted several months at a time, and by the time the season returned Pate had moved on. In 1854 he finally found a destination, California, and headed there with an emigrant mining party. They arrived too late to profit from the big gold rush so after a number of prospecting failures he headed north with three friends — David Owens, John Winship, and George Lamb. In Oregon Pate and Lamb heard of work near Albany in Linn County, so the two men headed north and found employment as rail splitters. They boarded together at the Crow farm not far from the Conn family ranch.

Lamb was doing well and saving most of his small earnings. He met a lovely young lady and was courting her, and he planned to marry her when his financial situation improved. By February 1862 he was nearing his goal, with nearly $500 saved. Unfortunately, Pate also had a yen for the same young lady but had not saved his earnings and was in no better position to ask for her hand than when he first arrived in Albany. He saw that he was about to lose the girl, and this led to a number of arguments between the young men, and the confrontations grew more heated as Lamb's situation improved while Pate's did not. On February 8, 1862, the Conn family heard a shot and ran to investigate. They found George Lamb floating face down in a creek, shot in the back, and his throat had been slit from ear to ear. His pockets were turned out and empty and the murderer had tried to sink the body before fleeing. They summoned Linn County deputy sheriff Looney C. Bond, who made a careful examination of the boot tracks clearly visible in the snow, and followed them into town. They were easy to follow, as each footprint had a different pattern of boot sole.

Because of the previous arguments Pate was immediately suspected and within a few hours he was arrested at an Albany shoe store and lodged in the county jail. They found that he had Lamb's money in his pockets, was wearing one of Lamb's boots and one of his own, and had gone to the shoe shop to buy a new pair of matching boots. The boots he wore, one of his and one of Lamb's, were taken to the scene and matched to the boot prints, then kept as evidence.

Within days an examination was held and the prisoner was held to answer to the grand jury. Pate was indicted in early April and on April 8 he was arraigned and pled not guilty. His trial began in Judge Reuben Boise's courtroom two days later and he claimed self-defense, but was not believed by anyone, especially the jurors. The trial lasted one day and the jurors, after brief deliberations, found Pate guilty of first degree, premeditated murder. Judge Boise sentenced Pate to hang on May 27, 1862.

An enterprising newsman, George N. Spears, convinced Pate to dictate his confession for a crime pamphlet, thereby memorializing all the details. Pate said, for the pamphlet and substantially in testimony: "On the day of the murder I started to Albany with a gun, going by where Lamb was at work; ... a quarrel took place between us, during which Lamb attempted to seize an ax, swearing to take my life; I fired at him while he was stooping, and then started off. Lamb seized a stick and followed, running and swearing he would kill me yet; I knocked him down, when Lamb not being able to rise, requested me to finish him, whereupon I dragged him to the slough, where the body was afterwards found, laid him in the water, cut his throat, and then rolled a log on the body.... The worst act of my life was the killing of George Lamb, and that was done when under a state of excitement and anger, and not through premeditation."

Pate's attorney's filed an appeal but it was denied well before the scheduled date of his execution. An application for executive clemency was also rejected. On the fateful day two thousand people gathered about the scaffold, including many women and children. Before 12:30 P.M. the condemned man was taken out of his cell, put aboard a carriage, and driven to the gallows, which had been erected a distance from the jailhouse near the cemetery. When he dismounted Pate shook hands with all his death watch guards before being escorted through the crowd onto the platform. He did not show any signs of nervousness and climbed the steps with a quick, steady step. He was seated in a chair behind the trapdoor and the death warrant was read by Linn County Sheriff Timothy A. Riggs. As was customary the condemned man was asked if he had anything to say, so he arose, stepped to the rail, and said that everything in his pamphlet was true, but he was prepared to die. Pate shook hands with several men on the platform and then took his position on the trapdoor.

He was prepared by having his wrists tied behind, his arms secured to his body, and his knees and ankles pinioned. As the work was being done he requested several times that the sheriff "be careful to prevent any accident in the execution." The noose was adjusted and the black hood was pulled over his face. In a moment, at 12:54 P.M., the trap was sprung and Pate fell six feet, breaking his neck. He was pronounced dead by the attending physicians almost immediately after the drop. The body hung for twenty-five minutes before being cut down and lowered into the cheap pine coffin provided by the county. His body was taken directly to the cemetery and buried in the pauper's section, without service or ceremony.

Oregonian (Portland): February 12, 1862; May 27, 1862.

Way, Berry
June 4, 1863

On Monday afternoon, May 4, 1863, Berry Way, sometimes spelled Wey, was given an examination before Justice of the Peace Strowbridge and remanded to the custody of the sheriff to await trial on a charge of murder, but the witnesses had not arrived. He was handcuffed and confined in a log house on Canyon Street where he was guarded by deputy sheriff McDaniels and John Kingsbury. At 1:00 A.M. Kingsbury became ill and Mc-

Daniels went for medicine for his relief and found the prisoner safe upon his return, which gave him the confidence to get some sleep. McDaniels had not slept for forty-eight hours so he asked Kingsbury to stand the guard alone while he slept. Kingsbury agreed but when McDaniels awoke at daylight he found that Kingsbury had also fallen asleep and Way had made his escape. There was a great deal of excitement and frustration among the citizens, and some even suggested McDaniels had been bribed. The sheriff offered a two hundred fifty dollar reward, from his own funds, and N. Olney, sheriff of Wasco County, added the same amount to the fund.

No word was heard of Way until May 15 when McDaniels learned that Way had been seen on Burnt River. The lawman started immediately, in company with Charles McNelley, for Auburn and learned that Way had been in town several days earlier and reportedly started for Boise, Idaho Territory. On May 20, McDaniels and McNelley left for the Boise River and at Old's Ferry learned that Way had passed there. They continued on to Placerville, which they reached on Saturday, May 23, and were directed on to Bannock City.

McDaniels continued on to Bannock City but left McNelley at Placerville, and on May 24 McNelley learned that Way had been seen on Grimes' Creek about half a mile below Fort Hogem. McNelley organized a posse consisting of Messrs. Comings, Stocking, and Pomphries, and they were on the trail of the fugitive that evening. They came upon Way's camp at daylight and McNelley went up to where the escaped murderer was sleeping, took from him two revolvers, woke him, and told him he was a prisoner, and Way replied, "All right; I am not going to do anything." Way arose and dressed, then was securely bound and taken to Placerville. The blacksmith ironed the prisoner while one of the posse men went for McDaniels, who arrived that evening. McDaniels then had Way double ironed and on Wednesday afternoon, May 27, the party started for Canyon City, taking a week to make the trip and arriving on Wednesday morning, June 3.

As Way passed through the large crowd that had turned out to see the prisoner, there were cries of "Hang him!" He was jailed on the second floor of the Fashion Saloon under the guard of McDaniels and McNeeley. At 3:00 P.M. a meeting was called and a Mr. Hare was chosen chairman, George Woodman was chosen secretary, and then B. F. McClure put it to the vote, "Should we give Berry Way a further trial, or hang him on the evidence already in our possession." The vote was to give him a further trial, whereupon four hundred sixty men went to the Fashion Saloon and demanded that McDaniels surrender his prisoner. The lawman refused and made a brief speech, stating that he was sworn to protect the prisoner and see that the law was sustained. He begged the crowd to disperse, which it did.

However, as soon as McDaniels' guard was down he was seized by a large group of men and the prisoner was taken to John Fenessey's place. The crowd elected a sheriff and seated a jury of twelve men. George Woodman acted as counsel for the people and a Mr. Grey acted as counsel for the prisoner. A "people's court" was convened and Justice Strowbridge, who had examined Way, stated that all the documents had been sent to the higher court at The Dalles, but he was able to make a statement of facts from memory. Several witnesses were then called and examined, and the prisoner's statement was offered into evidence, and Way's testimony proved the most damning of the evidence offered. The jurors retired just before midnight and in forty-five minutes returned with a guilty verdict.

It was then put to a vote of all present whether they should hang Way immediately or wait until morning, but after much discussion it was finally agreed to set the time for the following day at 2:00 P.M. Twenty-six men were appointed to take the prisoner into custody and prepare him for his execution. As the time approached for the hanging the crowd swelled to over one thousand men who were very excited but remained orderly. At 3:00 P.M. the prisoner was marched to the gallows a half mile from town by an armed guard of thirty-six men. The crowd parted to allow the guards to take the prisoner to the gallows, and Way was accompanied by deputy McDaniels and the Reverend Knight. The minister earnestly requested that he make his confession, but he made only a few remarks insisting he was innocent and, "It is a hard case to be hung for a crime that I am not guilty of." He exonerated McDaniels and Kingsbury of any responsibility for his escape and maintained his composure throughout the ordeal. The reverend then offered a touching prayer and at 4:00 P.M. the prisoner was "launched into eternity."

Oregonian (Portland): June 12, 1863.

Griffin, Zebulon
June 9, 1863

Zebulon Griffin was hanged at Lafayette on Tuesday, June 9, 1863, for the murder of a man named Shane, but there appears no record of the details. The gallows had been constructed on a small prairie a half mile from the jail and the prisoner walked to it with a firm and careless step. He was accompanied by two Catholic priests, whose faith he had embraced during his imprisonment and who had baptized him into that faith days earlier. Fifteen hundred men, women and children surrounded the scaffold and once the condemned man was in place he was allowed to read his statement justifying the killing. He said he hoped everyone had come, not from mere curiosity, but to "be warned against committing crime" and in sympathy for him.

His arms and legs were then pinioned, a blindfold was tied over his eyes, and the noose carefully adjusted behind his left ear. At 12:10 P.M. the trapdoor was sprung and the prisoner dropped to his death. The vertebrae in his neck were dislocated in the fall and it was reported that he died instantly, without a quiver. After hanging a sufficient time to ensure death the body was cut down and deposited in a pine coffin provided by the county. He was buried in the cemetery later that evening, after a period of public viewing.

Oregonian (Portland): June 15, 1863.

Deadmond, Henry
February 17, 1865

In the spring of 1864 Henry Deadmond traveled to Eastern Oregon from Idaho with a prospecting party. The party camped on Bridge Creek on the Canyon City Trail and, shortly after leaving that location, they were attacked by hostile Indians. During the battle that followed Deadmond was shot in the jaw with a large caliber musket ball. The lead missile tore away part of his jaw, but the wound was not fatal, and by August 1864 he had fully recovered. Deadmond was disfigured but not disabled. He was having no luck looking for gold so he took employment with George W. Meeks, a Lane County cattle man, and the two men drove a small herd of cattle over the Canyon City Trail, a route familiar to Deadmond. They took the cattle to the rich mining districts which had sprung up along the Oregon boundary with Idaho. Meeks expected to get a premium price for his cattle, and he was not disappointed.

As the two men prepared to return to Canyon City, with Meeks' saddle bags filled with gold, they met Cranford Isabell, a twenty-eight-year-old miner returning to Yreka, California. The discussion of mining successes did not come up and the two cattle men must have thought Isabell had failed and was returning home broke. They agreed to travel together as protection from the Indians, who were active along the trail. The party left on September 2 and on the second night had reached Willow Creek. They camped near the fresh water and it was Isabell's night to cook, so he lit a fire and began preparing the evening meal. Meeks went up stream to get a bucket of fresh water while Deadmond drove their horses across the creek and put them to pasture, hobbling them for the night so they could not wander off.

Deadmond then hurried up stream and found Meeks preoccupied filling his bucket and several canteens. He snuck up on his employer and shot him in the head, killing him instantly. Isabell was not alarmed by a single shot, as he may have assumed one of the men saw fresh game and he would soon have it for their supper. Isabell had a loaded revolver in his holster belted to his waist, and his rifle lay near at hand, but Deadmond returned to camp while Isabell was busy with the pans and shot Isabell in the chest. It happened so quickly and unexpectedly that Isabell had no time to reach for his weapons. Deadmond then took Meeks' saddle bags and fled to Eugene City.

Deadmond, to build his alibi, wrote a letter to William Pennington, a friend of Meeks, detailing an ambush in which bushwackers had killed Meeks' and Isabell. The letter arrived on September 8 and explained that Deadmond had gone there to recover from the attack, the second he had experienced in the same area. Meeks' brother Samuel organized a small search posse and found the bodies a week later, about September 15. The bodies lay where they were killed and they had not been searched. When the body of Isabell was examined the posse found a large sum of money hidden on his person, and the story of bushwackers killing for money was proven false.

Warrants were issued for the arrest of Deadmond. He was captured at Bridge Creek on October 10 in company with William Eddings, who was later cleared and released. In mid–December the Wasco County grand jury returned two indictments for murder against Deadmond and trial was set for December 21, 1864, in Judge J. G. Wilson's court. The case went to the jurors after two days of testimony and, following brief deliberations, they returned a verdict of guilty as charged in the indictment—first degree murder. The following day, December 24, Deadmond was brought before Judge Wilson, who sentenced him to hang at The Dalles on February 17, 1865. Deadmond was also ordered to pay for the trial, and costs were eventually recovered by the court.

As often happened when a man commits a heinous crime, all sorts of rumors were spread about Deadmond's "desperate character," and after his arrest he was accused of being the leader of a gang of cut-throats. There was concern that his brother, Riley, might assemble the gang members and stage a rescue. Additionally, during those early days in Oregon, there was always concern there would be some disturbance accompanying an execution, so a detachment of ninety Pendleton soldiers bivouacked at The Dalles on February 10, 1865. They were there to prevent a rescue, a lynching, or a disturbance of any kind.

During the week preceding his execution Deadmond received Catholic Father Vermass and embraced the teachings of the Catholic Church. When it came time for his walk to the scaffold Father Vermass promised to be by his side. The weather had been brutal during the previous week and the streets were badly muddied, but a large crowd of men still gathered to catch a glimpse of the prisoner as he emerged from the jail. Deadmond, when he appeared, was attired nattily in a dark coat, dark pants and white gloves provided by Sheriff Charles White. The prisoner boarded a wagon and was driven to the gallows, which had been erected beside the road to the army garrison. This location was beyond the view of those living in town who did not want to witness the hanging. Nearly four hundred men walked along with the wagon, which was surrounded by a company of soldiers.

At the scaffold the crowd of four hundred joined the six hundred men, women and children already at the site, and the prisoner was escorted through the mass of curious onlookers by a contingent of soldiers. At the foot of the scaffold Father Vermass recited a short prayer before the prisoner ascended to the platform. He asked for a drink of water to wet his dry throat before saying to the crowd, "Gentlemen, I am now on the scaffold and am about to die. Let my fate be a warning to all. I expect to see heaven and will pray for you. I forgive all and ask to be forgiven by all."

He was then positioned on the center of the trapdoor and Sheriff White tied his hands behind and tied his knees and ankles. Deadmond then said good-bye again and repeated his expectations of heaven. He turned to the sheriff and asked how far he would have to fall, and White told him a bit over six feet. He next seemed concerned that his feet might touch the ground, causing him to strangle, but the sheriff assured him they would not touch. The black hood was pulled on and the noose adjusted, and at 1:20 P.M. the pin was pulled springing the trap. Dr. A. M. Belt waited beneath the platform for the appearance of Deadmond and the drop, though properly calculated, did not break the prisoner's neck and he struggled for eighteen minutes before he was pronounced dead. The body was cut down, placed in a coffin, and turned over to Father Vermass. The remains of Henry Deadmond, after a brief service, were buried that evening in The Dalles Catholic Cemetery.

Oregonian (Portland): September 26, 1864; February 15, 1865; February 20, 1865. *Oregon State Journal* (Eugene, OR): September 17, 1864; September 24, 1864; February 25, 1865. *Oregon Statesman* (Salem, OR): October 3, 1864; October 10, 1864; December 31, 1864. *Walla Walla Statesman* (WA): January 5, 1866.

Baker, George; Beale, George
May 17, 1865

George Beale had a mining claim near Turner, Marion County, Oregon, and, when he found free time from running his saloon in Salem, he would work his claim. When he was in that area he would stay at the home of Daniel Delaney, a man he had known for two decades who lived only a few miles from Beale's claim. Delaney had a great deal of money and property which Beale coveted. In late 1864 Delaney sold a large herd of cattle for a substantial sum of money and, as was customary in those times, he cached the money in a secret place on his property. Beale had been planning on stealing Delaney's money but believed he would need an accomplice and had been preparing for the crime by allowing George Baker, a man with a penchant for liquor but without funds to support his habit, to drink on credit. When he learned of the cattle money Delaney had just received he decided it was time to act. With Baker deep in debt he proposed that Baker work with him on the robbery and, in addition to clearing his debt, obtain a large stake. Baker felt he had no choice but to agree, if not for himself then for his wife and two children.

On the evening of January 9, 1865, the elderly Delaney was home with a child named Jack DeWolf, his wife being away at their son's house. Beale, armed with a pistol, and Baker, armed with a shotgun, hid in the woods nearby and blackened their faces as they waited for darkness. When the time came they walked to the front gate and one of them called out that they were lost and needed directions. Delaney came to the door and stepped out into the yard, and just then Beale ordered Baker to shoot. The blast knocked Delaney to his knees and Delaney's dog attacked the two men, but Beale wounded the dog with a shot from his pistol. While the two robbers were occupied with the dog Delaney got to his feet and started for the house but Beale jumped the fence and ran to the wounded man. Delaney recognized him so Beale told him, "Dead men tell no tales," as he shot Delaney in the head, killing him instantly. The youngster, DeWolf, grabbed the wounded dog and ran into the house and secured the door but it was easily battered down with a log. Beale then shot at the boy several times, wounding him slightly, and they ransacked the house looking for the money. Beale would later say he had found only $1,900, and he gave Baker $500 as his share in addition to wiping out his bar tab. Delaney, it was believed, had hidden more than $50,000 but it was never found.

Once the two men split the plunder they decided they had enough killing and left without murdering DeWolf. The next morning the boy ran to the house of Delaney's son and reported the murder. Marion County Sheriff Samuel Headrick assembled a small posse and went to investigate. They recovered a hat band, which proved to be Beale's, and then followed the horse tracks right into Salem. Within five days Baker and Beale were lodged in jail charged with murdering Delaney. At their examination the two prisoners were held over for action by the grand jury. They were indicted and on March 21, 1865, their trial began in the court of Judge Reuben Boise.

The jury was quickly seated without exhausting the venire and the opening arguments began. The primary witness, DeWolf, was challenged because he was half black and because he was too young to understand the questions or the obligation of an oath, and these objections were sustained. Still, the prosecution wove together a case of circumstantial evidence so well linked that there could be little doubt the two men on trial were guilty. On March 25, 1865, the jurors found "the prisoners guilty as charged in the indictment." Judge Boise sentenced them to hang at Salem on May 17, 1865.

On May 15 the two condemned men, perhaps hoping to save their souls, wrote out and signed detailed confessions. When the fatal day arrived Beale and Baker were removed from the jail with a large armed escort about them, taken to a stand of oak trees near South Church Street and seated on chairs beside the scaffold. They were allowed to pray and then to speak to the huge crowd that had assembled from miles around, but when it came time to climb the stairs Baker needed help. The two men were positioned on the trapdoor and their arms and legs were pinioned with ropes, the nooses were carefully adjusted, and the black hoods were pulled over their heads.

In the next moment the signal was given and the trap was sprung. The drop neatly broke Baker's neck and there was hardly a quiver noticed, but Beale's neck was not broken, his jugular vein was severed by the rope, and he struggled for a while. Blood spurted out and ran down Beale's clothing, collecting in a pool on the ground beneath, and blood continued to flow until his heart stopped beating. The bodies were allowed to hang for twenty minutes as Dr. McAfee monitored their vital signs and finally pronounced them dead. Baker's family took his body, after it was cut down, and buried it in the local cemetery, but no one claimed Beale's body and most citizens did not want the murderer buried in their city cemetery. A local rancher named Daniel Waldo finally came forward and agreed to take Beale's body and bury it in his private cemetery.

Oregon Statesman (Salem): March 27, 1865; May 17, 1865.

Cain, William
August 3, 1865

Andrew "Andy" Watson had been mining in the area of Canyon City, Grant County, Oregon, since gold was first discovered there in 1862. He had a productive sluice-mining claim, so productive in fact that he found it advantageous to hire help. In 1864 one of the hundreds of failed prospectors named William Cain, sometimes spelled Kane, took work in Watson's mine. He occupied a small cabin nearby and worked throughout the fall and winter. He had been paid about $50, but this represented only a third of what he was owed. He made several demands for payment but Watson assured him that he would be paid in the spring, and he had no choice but to wait. Based upon the promise of payment of $100, and the money he had already deposited with a Canyon City businessman, Cain was able to secure enough credit from merchants to see him through the winter.

In the late spring of 1865 Cain learned that Watson had received a sufficient sum of money to pay what he was owed. During the first days of June he confronted his employer and Watson immediately paid him off, but did so with paper money. There was little confidence in "greenbacks," a form of money introduced after the Civil War backed by bonds rather than gold. The lack of confidence meant that the money had to be discounted when spent, sometimes by as much as two-thirds of its face value. Cain knew that his $100, now worth about $35, was all he had to pay his debts. Cain confronted Watson several times demanding payment with "real money," or gold, which the mine owner must have had available to pay his worker. Watson refused to pay him in the specie requested, as most certainly he had obtained the $100 in greenbacks at the standard discount rate, giving him a substantial savings.

After several demands, and as many refusals, the frustrated Cain returned to his cabin and secured his large caliber revolver. He returned to the mine and made one last demand, accompanied with the threat to shoot Watson if he refused. Watson again refused to pay in gold and Cain shot his employer without further words or hesitation. He fired twice more as the body fell into the water and was washed downstream, finally coming to rest in the Canyon Creek flume. There were several witnesses present as Cain surrendered his pistol and himself to one of them, and ultimately to Sheriff M. P. Berry. When the body was recovered, dead from the first bullet fired, Cain was charged with Watson's murder.

Watson had been popular while Cain, a repulsive eccentric who was somewhat reclusive, was not well-known or well-liked. There was strong talk of lynching the prisoner but the sheriff finally had the last word and the citizens decided to await justice in the courts. Cain was indicted on June 13, 1865, and his trial began immediately. Two days later, after a strenuous defense, he was found guilty of murder in the first degree and sentenced to hang on August 3. Cain resigned himself to his fate and his last days were uneventful. On the day of the execution people from all over the region came into Canyon City and several hundred gathered at the foot of the scaffold, conveniently constructed at the east end of the town cemetery.

When the hour arrived Cain was taken from his cell and placed in the back of a buckboard, where he sat upon the cheap pine coffin provided by the county. As he was being driven some of the children who had waited at the jail to glimpse the condemned man ran alongside, prompting Cain to warn, "Don't be in a hurry. There won't be anything doing until I get there." Cain was already handcuffed behind and his legs were shackled. When he got to the scaffold he was able to walk up the stairs and then the cuffs and shackles were removed and replaced with ropes, which bound his arms to his body and his legs together at the knees and ankles.

He was asked if he had anything to say to the crowd, and he said only that he had been insane when he killed Watson, a defense not proffered at trial. His eyes were covered and the noose adjusted so that the knot was behind his left ear and, in but a moment, the trap was sprung and he fell breaking his neck, and he was pronounced dead in minutes. Once he had hung a sufficient time to ensure he could not be revived he was cut down, placed in the coffin, and deposited in the grave which had been prepared in advance.

Oregon State Journal (Eugene): August 12, 1865.
Mountaineer (Canyon City, OR): July 14, 1865.
Oregonian (Portland): June 5, 1863.

Smith, Thomas
May 10, 1866

Forty-two-year-old Sidney Smith had a fine farm six miles west of Brownsville, Oregon, where he lived with his wife Barbara, his sixteen-year-old daughter Rhoda Ann, his ten-year-old daughter Leora, and two small children — a toddler girl and a baby son. In mid–1865 he left the farm and family under the care of his thirty-five-year-old brother Thomas, who had always been envious of his more successful brother, and went to Placerville, Idaho, to prospect for gold with his other brother Calvin. They did quite well and by mid–January 1866 Sidney was home with a large sack containing $25,000 in gold, which he hid on the property. In December 1865 Barbara had heard rumors that Thomas was having sexual relations with her oldest daughter, confronted him, and threatened to write Sidney. Thomas threatened to kill her if she did, so she did not speak of the rumors for the next month.

In March Barbara told her husband that their oldest daughter confessed to her that Thomas was having incestuous relations with her. On March 8 the brothers had a confrontation at a neighbor's home and Sidney demanded to know about the rumors. When

Thomas would say nothing he confronted his daughter, who again confessed, and Sidney demanded that she confront Thomas in front of the family. When the moment arrived on March 9, 1866, Rhoda Ann refused to repeat her allegations, and would not answer incriminating questions from her father or her mother. Sidney took a buckskin string, tied his daughter's hands, tore off the back of her dress, and said, "You sha'nt lie to me." He was prepared to beat a confession out of Rhoda Ann, who pleaded with Thomas to prevent the whipping. Thomas did not intervene and after two blows were struck Thomas went out saying, "Well, this will not do for me."

Thomas said later that he felt certain his brother had a pistol in his pocket and would kill him if he tried to prevent the whipping. Thomas went to the Kennedy ranch and took his neighbor's pistol without permission. Thomas would later confess that on March 5 he had already determined to kill Sidney because he was certain his brother would kill him, and to kill Barbara because she told Sidney of his relations with Rhoda Ann. He also said he might have been driven off the property without incident if he had been given time to sell his part of the cattle herd.

Sidney failed to extract the confession and was still standing over Rhoda Ann when Thomas returned, pushed open the door, and as Sidney turned to look at him Thomas fired, the bullet striking Sidney in the forehead. Sidney collapsed onto Rhoda Ann's dress, dead. Barbara was sitting near the fireplace holding the baby boy and Thomas fired his pistol at her, and the bullet struck her in the right breast just missing the baby. Barbara carefully laid the infant aside and ran out with Thomas close behind. She was weakening from blood loss, so when Thomas caught her she could only put up a token resistance. Thomas took her by the wrist and dragged her toward the smokehouse as she begged Rhoda Ann, "Don't let Tom hurt me." Rhoda Ann did nothing as Thomas dragged Barbara into the smokehouse and, taking the butcher knife, slashed at her face, cutting her hands as she threw them up in defense. He administered the *coup de grâce* by stabbing her in the neck "as he might butcher a pig." Thomas, blood soaked and weary, came out of the smoke house and threatened the two older children that they would be brutally killed if they did not say their father went crazy, killed their mother, and committed suicide; and that was the story they told when the authorities arrived.

The bodies of Sidney and Barbara were taken into town and examined by the county coroner, and there were immediate discrepancies in the story. Sidney, if he had committed suicide, would have had powder burns around the wound and there were none. Meanwhile lawmen were already suspicious and after repeatedly questioning the two older girls Rhoda Ann finally said, "How could Papa kill Mama when he was dead already?" Thomas was suspected and the motive was thought to be the gold Sidney had brought from Idaho, though the rumors of incest had spread among neighbors.

On March 17 Thomas was arrested and charged with the murder of his brother and sister-in-law, and on the following Monday he had his examination before Justice of the Peace Ellis at Brownsville, and was held to answer to the Linn County grand jury. On May 1, 1866, the grand jury returned an indictment and trial was set for May 29 in Judge Reuben P. Boise's Albany courtroom, the first case being the murder of Barbara Smith. The entire case, from jury selection to verdict, took only two days before he was convicted of first degree murder and sentenced to hang on May 10, 1866. Sheriff O. W. Richardson was not about to take any chances that his prisoner would cheat the hangman, so Smith was heavily shackled and these were riveted on rather than padlocked, and when in his cell the chains were looped through a ring to limit his movement.

As the fatal day approached, and it became clear that he was about to die, Smith confessed to the killings and said his motive was not the money, but the discovery of his relations with his niece. The gallows was built in an open space southwest of town. On May 10 more than five thousand people, including a large number of women and children, gathered and made a picnic of the affair. That morning the Boise, Idaho, *Statesman* related the details of the suicide of the brother Calvin Smith, and Sheriff Richardson let Thomas know that he was the last of the brothers. The prisoner was unshackled, though watched closely, as he bathed, and dressed and then his wrists were tied behind his back and he was escorted to the front of the jail and helped aboard a wagon. He was driven to the gallows and escorted onto the platform where he sat on a bench while the death warrant was read. Several clergy of the Methodist church were present and they prayed and made speeches, but Smith refused to speak further on any matter.

When all the speeches concluded Sheriff Richardson told Smith to step onto the trap-door, and he did so without hesitation. His legs were pinioned and the noose was adjusted, and a moment after the black hood was pulled over his head the trap was sprung. Smith fell seven feet, a very long drop for this small a man, so his neck was broken and he died instantly. After Smith had hung a sufficient period he was pronounced dead, he was cut down, placed in a coffin, and buried.

Rhoda Ann Smith, at sixteen years of age, was considered a woman and capable of raising her siblings and managing their farm. The Smith farm was prosperous and could support hands to do the work. One day, while playing, the two smaller children uncovered a sack of gold hidden near the house. The twenty-five thousand dollars they discovered was deposited in trust for the four orphans, who each got a good education and a stake to start a new life when they reached adulthood.

Oregonian (Portland): March 13, 1866; March 20, 1866; March 28, 1866, April 10, 1866; May 16, 1866. *Puget Sound Semi-Weekly* (WA): April 12, 1866. *Walla Walla Statesman* (WA): May 25, 1866.

Black Jim; Bogus Charley; Kientpoos; Schonchin John
October 3, 1873

In 1852 the Modoc Indians learned a brutal lesson about parley under a white flag. The Indians had killed sixty-five white settlers at "Bloody Point," named for the massacre which occurred there. Later that year the settlers tried to negotiate a peace with the Indians; the white coalition was led by Ben Wright. He invited the Indians to a feast and planned to lace their food with strychnine, a ploy used at various times in the Old West to exterminate large numbers of Indians in a most brutal manner. When the Indians declined to attend Wright convinced them to meet under a white flag of truce, but when the forty-six Indians accepted forty-one were slaughtered in a hail of gunfire. As a result of that betrayal a war between Indians and whites continued for a dozen years. Finally, in 1864, the Modocs signed a peace treaty and agreed to live on a reservation. The Modocs were required to co-exist on the reservation with the Klamath Indian tribe, their bitter enemy for centuries, typical of the U.S. policy of "relocation and concentration."

They broke out in 1865 and, except for a brief period, stayed off the reservation until November 1872, when the military tried to force them back onto the reservation. As the Indians fled they murdered more than a dozen settlers and made it to their "impregnable stronghold," a rugged lava bed of caves, canyons and ridges. Military forces tried to dislodge the Modocs on January 17, 1873, at a cost of thirty-five dead and many wounded, with no casualties reported by the Indians. The leader, known to the whites as Captain Jack or to the Indians as Kintpuash or Kientpoos, was trying to stall hoping that he could move into the mountains when spring came. By April, however, it seemed he had no chance of holding out and several influential Indians convinced him that if they killed the military leader the rest of the military force would retire, as was the custom among the tribes when a chief was killed in battle.

On April 11, 1873, a peace parley was attended by Captain Jack, Schonchin John, Boston Charley, Bogus Charley, Black Jim and Hooker Jim representing the Modocs, and General Edward R. S. Canby, Alfred Meachum, the Reverend E. Thomas and L. S. Dyer representing the United States. Captain Jack was immediately upset over the mobilization of armed forces, as there had been an earlier agreement that neither side would continue their preparations for war. Captain Jack arose from the group and took a few steps away from the meeting, and signaled to Brancho and Slolux to rush forward from their hiding place among the rocks and kill the whites. The first shot from Captain Jack's revolver, hidden in his vest, killed General Canby. They succeeded in killing the Reverend Thomas and seriously wounding Meachum with five shots, and would have finished the work on Meachum if Toby Winerma Riddle, one of the interpreters, had not saved him when she yelled out, "The soldiers are coming." Orders soon came from headquarters to "kill every Modoc man, woman and child so none can boast of the murder of General Canby."

On April 15 the army was prepared to attack and the following day forces cut off the natives from their water supply. The natives fled before the full attack on April 17 and managed to escape from their stronghold, but a series of skirmishes followed, and on June 4 Captain Jack was captured in Langell's Valley. By July 4 the six Modoc leaders who had been responsible for the murders were held at Fort Klamath, where orders arrived preventing their immediate execution and required that they be tried. The trial was held immediately and on July 8, 1873, Captain Jack, Schonchin John, Black Jim and Bogus Charley were sentenced to hang on October 3, while Slolux and Brancho were sentenced to life in prison. The only appeal was to the president, and on September 10 President U.S. Grant refused to intervene.

When the final day arrived the four Indians marched to the gallows showing no fear. All of the Modocs were required to attend, including thirty-nine men, sixty-four women and sixty children. The four condemned men mounted the scaffold which had been built on the parade ground of Fort Klamath, took their places upon the long trapdoor, and refused to say anything to the large number of civilian and military men who had gathered to witness their deaths. Their arms and legs were pinioned with straps and the black hoods were pulled over their heads. The nooses were adjusted and immediately the trap was sprung and all four men fell to their deaths. They were allowed to hang long enough to ensure death, and this was confirmed by the post physician before they were cut down and deposited into coffins; their remains were buried later that day. The remainder of the Modoc tribe was then transported to Oklahoma and delivered to the Quaw Paw Agency, where they remained until 1909.

New York Times (NY): August 24, 1873. *Oregonian* (Portland): July 12, 1873; April 25, 1988. *Yreka Journal* (CA): April 16, 1873; April 26, 1873; May 7, 1873; June 14, 1873.

Neil, William K.
January 26, 1877

In 1871 the town of Halsey, Linn County, Oregon, started with a depot for the Oregon and California Railroad on land donated by Seth and Ebenezer Hayes. The brothers took a personal pride in the town as it grew up around the depot and when Halsey incorporated, the Hayes brothers participated in drawing up the charter, which prohibited the consumption or sale of liquor within town limits. In 1876 William K. Neil moved to Halsey and set up a saloon a block north of the railroad tracks, just outside the boundary of the prohibition town. The saloon drew many of the bad elements into the area and there were constant reports of violence and excessive noise. Seth Hayes was disgusted with the situation and voiced his opinion openly.

On November 1, 1876, Seth was repairing a well not far from Neil's establishment, so the saloon keeper decided to confront the man who had been criticizing him. The confrontation quickly turned ugly, with voices raised and insults becoming more and more personal, until Seth said that Neil was keeping "a low-down doggery," and "engaging in conduct like a surly cur." Neil considered these insults fighting words, drew his knife, and stabbed Seth three times, once in his chest and twice in his stomach. The stomach wounds would have killed Seth in days from a sepsis infection — a horrible, lingering death. However, Seth died in three hours from the chest wound, or from a combination of the three wounds.

George Miller, a friend of Neil, gave him his horse but Neil was thrown and fled on foot. A posse was organized and overtook the fugitive three miles from Halsey on the road to Brownsville. James R. Herren, Linn County's sheriff, arrived and took the prisoner to the county seat at Albany and lodged him in jail. The grand jury was then in session, so Neil was indicted for murder two days later and his trial began in Judge Reuben Boise's courtroom. The taking of testimony and arguments took one day and the jurors needed only an hour of deliberations to find Neil guilty of first degree murder. On November 10, Neil was sentenced to hang on December 22, 1876, but this date was postponed until January 26, 1877, to allow his relatives to travel from California.

As his final day approached five inmates of the county jail, including Neil, put on a concert which was particularly loud and raucous, and Neil was the loudest of all. The noise was so loud and continuous that the sheriff and jailor George Cline decided they should check on the situation and found that the men, under cover of the noise, had been digging a hole through the wall of the outhouse. A search produced the tool they were using, a chisel sharpened to a fine edge, and it was confiscated.

During his weeks in jail Neil had embraced religion and had been comforted by the Reverends Robert L. Steven and S. G. Irvine. As the fatal hour approached a wagon fought its way through the crowd and unloaded Neil's coffin. With all in readiness it was time for the walk to the gallows, and the reverends led the way, with Sheriff Herren and deputy George Humphrey on each arm in case Neil faltered. The scaffold platform was small, but five men were already waiting for the prisoner, three lawmen and two attending physicians. Hundreds of curious onlookers had crowded around the base of the scaffold. As soon as the procession reached the platform Sheriff Herren read the death warrant, and then Neil was asked if he had anything to say. The condemned man stepped to the rail and spoke in a barely audible tone, professing his innocence, and when he concluded he was positioned on the trapdoor, his arms and legs were pinioned, and the black hood was pulled on.

As the rope was being adjusted Neil cried out, "God help me!" In a moment the trap was sprung by Sheriff Herren and Neil dropped through, but his feet touched the ground and he was struggling as he strangled. The doctors, the sheriff, and his deputy quickly ran under the scaffold and, lifting Neil, one of the other lawmen above tied a loop in the rope. Neil was then dropped the short distance, but it was not enough to break his neck and he took some time strangling to death. Drs. O. P. S. Plummer and J. L. Hill monitored Neil's vital signs and they pronounced him dead after many minutes. The body was then cut down, deposited into the coffin that had been provided, and delivered to the house of his aunt, Mrs. McMechan, who lived in Albany. She made arrangements to have the body shipped to his relatives in California for burial.

Oregonian (Portland): November 4, 1876, January 27, 1877. *States Rights Democrat* (Albany, OR): December 22, 1876.

Lewis, Sevier
August 30, 1878

Twenty-five-year-old Zachariah "Zack" Lewis lived with his parents near Coquille City, Coos County, Oregon. In mid–May 1876 Sylvia, the sixteen-year-old daughter of

Sevier Lewis, begged for Zack's help. She said that her fifty-one-year-old father had, for some time, been forcing her to have sex with him and now she was pregnant. Zack was outraged, as incest was considered as disgusting and heinous a crime then as now. Zack warned Sevier that if he continued he would tell the whole family, and then he arranged for Sylvia to move in with his parents, father and stepmother to Sevier. When Sevier inquired about regaining custody of his daughter, Zack told him that if he tried he would kill him.

On May 22 Zack was plowing a field a mile from his parents' house and Sevier knew where to find his half-brother, loaded his pistol, and told his fifteen-year-old son Hiram to bring it along. They went directly to the field where Zack was preoccupied with his plow and team. Sevier took the pistol from his son, snuck up on Zack, and without warning or hesitation fired two shots. One bullet struck Zack in the left side and the second bullet struck him in the stomach as he turned to face his attacker, and either would have been fatal in time, but with the combined wounds Zack lived only a few moments.

Sevier then returned home, packed necessities, and fled. He eluded detection for a month, even though a large reward was offered and his description was widely circulated. However, he was eventually recognized and lawmen were notified, but by the time they arrived Sevier, who had become suspicious of the sudden attention he was being shown, had fled again. This time he went farther north where he was less likely to be recognized and remained free until December 10, 1877, when he was recognized in Seattle, Washington. Sevier was kept occupied while a man went for Sheriff Lewis V. Wycoff, who arrested the fugitive and lodged him in the county jail. A requisition was sent from Oregon and the prisoner was returned to Empire City in Coos County, Oregon.

Sevier had been indicted for murder *in absentia* on May 27, 1876, so on May 27, 1878, exactly two years later, his trial began in Judge J. F. Watson's court. Sevier's attorney tried a variety of maneuvers to cloud the legal issues and prolong the trial, but only managed to extend it to June 13, 1878, when the jurors found him guilty of murdering Zachariah Lewis with malice and premeditation. Sevier was sentenced to hang on August 9, 1878, but again the defense attorney found a way to delay the proceedings by convincing Governor Stephen F. Chadwick to reschedule the execution to August 30 so that the state Supreme Court could consider an appeal. Neither the appeal nor the application for executive clemency would delay the proceedings further, and the date of execution was set for August 30, 1878.

After 2:00 P.M. on the designated day Sheriff Andrew Aiken went to the prisoner's cell and read the death warrant in the presence of the district attorney and defense attorney. At 2:30 P.M. the condemned man mounted the scaffold with a firm step, escorted by district attorney Silas H. Hazard, his defense attorney, the sheriff and a deputy. Throughout the proceedings he had shown a vindictive nature, claiming he was being executed solely because he was poor and his relatives had conspired to have him convicted. When given the opportunity to speak to the crowd of two hundred fifty spectators, he rambled in an excited manner for several minutes and then, when it came time to take his place upon the trapdoor, he "shrunk back," so the sheriff tried to force him into place. He complained, "What in hell are you doing that for? I am not afraid!" He then stood unaided upon the trapdoor while his arms and legs were pinioned. When the black hood was drawn over his head he said, "Don't put that damned thing over my eyes." At 3:00 P.M. the trap was sprung and he fell, breaking his neck. His heart ceased to beat within two minutes but he was allowed to hang ten minutes before Drs. Charles B. Golden and D. L. Steel pronounced him dead. His body was then cut down and placed in a coffin before being given to his family for burial. Few attended the graveside service, and then only family members who felt obligated. Most in the community knew why he had killed his brother and wanted nothing to do with the incestuous murderer.

Coos Bay News (Empire City, OR): May 31, 1876. *Coos Bay News* (Marshfield, OR): December 19, 1877. *Oregonian* (Portland): June 1, 1876; June 26, 1876; August 31, 1878.

Quit-a-tumps; White Owl
January 10, 1879

Aps
January 17, 1879

In 1877 the Bannack Indians broke out of their Idaho reservation and swept through northern Nevada into Oregon. All along the way they left burned ranches and dead settlers, butchered in the most horrible ways imaginable and often mutilated. The "friendly" Yakima Indians on the Umatilla Reservation became emboldened by the successes of the Bannacks and they began to depredate in Oregon, and did so under the guise of remaining peaceful.

On July 12, 1877, the Cayuse Station, twelve miles south of Pendleton in Umatilla County, was burned and seven miles north of the station that same band of natives "inhumanely murdered" George Coggan and seriously wounded Al Bunker. The members of the small raiding party were well known to other Indians on the reservation, but at first the tribe would not divulge their identities. Several Indians were suspected and closely watched for some indication of incriminating behavior but none was forthcoming. Following a council held in August it seemed likely that the murderers would go unpunished, but General Otis Howard took several prominent chiefs hostage and refused to release them until the guilty parties were surrendered.

The first two Indians brought in were Stock Sweet and Pash-cap-nam, but it could not be proved they were responsible so they were released. Next to be lodged in jail were Yuma, White Owl, Quit-a-tumps and his brother Aps. Yuma, seeing his desperate situation, confessed every detail of the murder of Coggan and other depredations by these four Indian men. Yuma was released upon the stipulation that he testify at trial and, after doing so, he was fully discharged.

All three Indians were indicted for murder in early December and the trial of White Owl and Quit-a-tumps followed immediately. They were both found guilty of first degree murder, based mostly on the testimony of Yuma, but before their arrest both White Owl and Quit-a-tumps each bragged to their tribe that it was he who killed Coggan. Finally, White Owl's claim was honored by the tribe and during the trial Quit-a-tumps finally acknowledged that it was White Owl who killed Coggan; his aim had been off though his intention was deadly. White Owl and Quit-a-tumps were sentenced to hang on January 10, 1878.

Next came the trial of Aps, who was charged only as an accessory to the killing. He testified that he had arrived after the killing and saw Coggan's horses running off. He captured the horses but they were taken away by Snake Indians, who were also in the vicinity in larger numbers. The jury did not believe his story, found Aps guilty of first degree murder, and he was sentenced to hang on January 17, 1878.

After their convictions all three Indians were heavily ironed and under constant watch by Sheriff John L. Sperry and deputy Dave Taylor. The only fear the Indians expressed was that their bodies might be turned over to the reservation's Catholic Priest Conridi, and they denied him access to their cells. They wanted their bodies delivered to friends and begged that no holy water be sprinkled on their faces. They were assured their wishes would be honored.

For several days prior to January 10 the three men conducted religious exercises to Smohallie, the dreamer or mischief maker in the "dreamer religion," sometimes with friends participating. The ceremony of "final leave—taking and bidding farewell to their friends on earth" was conducted on Wednesday. The "final leave" ceremony had drawn sixty Indians, so the prisoners were taken out into the scaffold enclosure, under heavy guard, to give them room to practice their religion. The

Indians were gathered in a tight circle in front of the jail door, undaunted by a driving snowstorm, when the prisoners were brought forth and positioned just outside the jail door. The condemned were dressed in the traditional garb provided by their wives for their journey into the afterlife, and they were gaudily painted. Many whites had come to witness the ceremony, and even one class of school children was present.

White Owl spoke first, in English, saying, "I am not afraid to die. The spirit of an Indian friend came to me three days ago and told me we would be all right in the other world. That spirit is now talking to you through me. After I am dead for thirty days my spirit will go to the happy land and there with the spirits of other Indians my spirit will always remain. I want some of my own people to see me die, see that I die right. I want no priest to sprinkle water on my face or take my body. I want to die in my own religion."

The Indians approved with a guttural groan and then came Quit-a-tumps, speaking in the Yakima tongue, "I do not know much of the hereafter. This land is getting too rotten to stand long anyway, and I am ready to leave it. I am ready to die. I will not be the only Indian that will meet his death at the hands of whites. Other Indians will have to die the same as me. I do not know who put me on earth. In the other world perhaps I will see the man who did it, and will ask him why it was done. Do not grieve for me, for my time has come to die. I have accomplished what was intended of me, and I am ready to die. I want no priest to take my body but want to die in my own religion." Then came the same groan of approval.

After a moment of silence White Owl began chanting his death song and all joined in. The Indians swayed in unison and raised their hands skyward, indicating that, "while they may be bound down here on earth, death will raise them up and give them free passage to the spirit world." When the chanting ended the prisoners shook hands with all present, raising the coupled hands upward three times and tilting the head in a certain way. The prisoners were then returned to their cells and the visiting Indians departed. The same ceremony was repeated on Thursday, except that Pash-cap-nam presided and the families of the two condemned men were present for this last ceremony, and the final farewells to their wives and children were heart-rending. Their final night was spent singing their death song, painting their faces and bodies, and dressing in their traditional burial clothes. There had been rumors that the natives would try to rescue the jailed Indians, and there were threats that the town of Pendleton would be burned before the execution, so a large, well armed volunteer force of three hundred men assembled near the jail and two companies of the 1st Cavalry from Fort Walla Walla, under the command of Major James Jackson, was bivouacked nearby.

As the fatal hour neared one hundred guests were admitted to the enclosure, including ten Indians, and the Greasewood militia was assigned to maintain order within. A great crowd had also gathered outside the enclosure but they could see nothing of the gallows built in the southwest corner. As soon as the witnesses were in position the jail door swung open and White Owl and Quit-a-tumps, each escorted by two deputies, walked to the platform.

They took their place beneath the nooses and were asked if they had anything to say. White Owl again went first, saying, "This is the last time I speak; I will never use a gun again; I die today and forever; my body goes to the setting sun; my gun has gone to the south; I will never shoot another white man; my gun did wrong; my children will grow up and I want them to live in peace with the whites." Quit-a-tumps then said, "I have used a gun for the last time against the whites. It is stopped forever. I did wrong and am sorry. I hope my children will be better than I have been." When a newspaper man asked if they were willing to admit the justice of their punishment they refused to answer.

The two Indians then said farewell to the

other natives present and began to chant their death song as their arms and legs were pinioned. The black hoods were pulled over their heads and the nooses adjusted as they continued singing. With a slight movement of Sheriff Sperry's arm the trapdoor was sprung at 2:45 P.M. and the two condemned Indians fell. Quit-a-tumps' noose slipped behind his neck while that of White Owl shifted under his chin, a typical cause for a bungled execution, but both Indians broke their necks and showed no signs of struggling. In six minutes, twenty-three seconds Quit-a-tumps was pronounced dead by the attending physician and in a few seconds more White Owl was pronounced dead. The bodies hung another nine minutes before being cut down and placed in coffins.

The remains of the two men were turned over to the Indians present. The body of White Owl was taken to McKay Creek for burial while that of Quit-a-tumps was taken to the reservation for interment.

Aps, Quit-a-tumps' brother who was scheduled to die in one week, was allowed to watch from inside the grated jail door and seemed rather complacent. After the execution, however, Aps refused to occupy the same cell for fear he might encounter the spirits of the two dead Indians.

The reservation Indians said they had been told by General Howard that they should deliver up one Indian for the murder of one white man, but now two Indians were executed and a third was awaiting death for a single killing, and they expressed displeasure over this perceived injustice. Aps felt certain he would be granted a reprieve or a commutation of sentence, but neither was forthcoming. Competing petitions were drawn up and sent to Governor W. W. Thayer, who refused to intervene. Early on the day of the execution of Aps the prisoner was brought out of the jail into the enclosure and he participated in ceremonies similar to those conducted for White Owl and Quit-a-tumps. He was dressed in his burial clothes and his hands, face and breast were painted a bright yellow hue. He said to the large party of Indians,

> I am glad you have come to see me. This is the last time we meet on earth; my body dies today, but my soul will go to God; I am innocent of any wrong; if I have done wrong at any time I hope the Great Spirit will wash it away. My brother will wait for me, but when the bugle sounds we will all meet again and never be divided. We have all got to die; I hope you will all live so that after death we will meet again; always try and do good; once more I bid you goodby; I am dying for nothing; God is my witness to what I say; my body shall be covered up with the earth; my soul will go to God; my soul is leaving me; I tell you the truth, I have done nothing wrong; in the presence of whites and Indians I assert my innocence; I want all of you to be good, to be friends of the whites; let there be no more trouble, you must keep quiet and have good hearts; if you do right, after death you will see the Great Spirit, [but] if you do wrong you will never see Him.

Cach-cach spoke next affirming the comments of Aps. An old woman, wife of Massey, told Aps to prepare for the Great Spirit, and then Ya-wash spoke to the whites, asking pardon for any wrongs committed and promising peace. Cach-cach then spoke to the whites emphasizing the Indians' desire for peace. Aps spoke again, briefly, saying he wished he had died with his brother, and to die alone "makes my heart feel small." During the speeches there were interludes where death chants were sung.

At noon the enclosure was cleared while Aps was returned to his cell. At 12:30 P.M. the gates were thrown open for the one hundred witnesses to enter, including a party of Indians and a few women and children, and one small child stood upon Aps' coffin near the stairs to improve his view. As soon as all was ready Aps was brought out and placed on the platform. Before he could be asked he said to Sheriff Sperry that he wanted to speak, and proceeded, "Friends, I have but a few words to say. My body is already turning to dust; my soul has gone to the Great Spirit. You put a rope around my neck; it is the same as dirt; but you cannot kill my soul. It will go to where all is clear. My body is afraid, but my soul is not.

It has gone to God. I die innocent. I think I am innocent. That is all."

As soon as he concluded his statement his arms and legs were pinioned, the black hood was pulled over his head, and the noose adjusted. He chanted his death song the entire time of preparation and at 1:06 P.M. the trap was sprung. Aps broke his neck in the fall but the attending physicians did not pronounce him dead for ten minutes. After hanging a while longer the body was cut down, placed in the waiting coffin, and given to the Indians for burial on the reservation.

Oregonian (Portland): January 9, 1879; January 13, 1879; January 18, 1879; January 20–21, 1879.

Cook, James
February 7, 1879

George Craig, the son of a prominent doctor in Wasco County, and James Cook robbed the saloon of Timothy Baldwin and stole a watch. Craig fled to Portland, where he was arrested and returned to the jail at The Dalles, Oregon. He informed on his accomplice, James Cook, and false rumors were spread that the fugitive had fled to Boise, Idaho. Lawmen searched a house Cook shared with an Indian woman, known as "Cloudy's wife," but there seemed no sign of Cook until deputy sheriff Haines became suspicious of a large packing crate and, flipping it over, found Cook hiding beneath it. Cook was arrested and lodged in The Dalles jail with Craig.

At their examination the two men were held over to answer to the grand jury on a charge of robbery and both men were indicted, tried, convicted, and sentenced to serve seven years in the prison in Salem. They were then remanded to the custody of the sheriff and returned to their jail cells to await transfer to the prison. Through out the entire affair Cook insisted he was innocent and that Craig had perjured himself to get him convicted. Cook was angry with Craig for naming him, as no other evidence could have tied him to the crime.

After noon on December 1 the two prisoners were removed from their cell in preparation for their trip west to the prison. Cook, a large and very strong man, suddenly sprang on Craig and, while restraining him with his left arm, used the prisoners' straight razor in his right hand to slash Craig from ear to ear, nearly severing his head from his shoulders, and Craig was dead within seconds. The entire incident happened so quickly that no one had time to react and save Craig, but they managed to restrain and disarm the murderer.

Cook was kept in the jail, heavily ironed, and was quickly indicted, tried in Judge L. L. McArthur's court four weeks later, and convicted of first degree murder. Cook was sentenced to hang on February 7, 1879, and there was no delay in the proceedings.

In early February the gallows was erected in the jail yard. It was of the trapdoor design with a carpet covering the platform and in one corner beneath the carpet was a foot spring to release the trapdoor. The gallows was in an enclosure; none but those invited would be admitted. On the final morning Cook ate a hearty breakfast and seemed anxious to get on with the hanging. Although Cook had not received the usual attention the clergy afforded condemned men, Catholic Father Louis Gaudon of The Dalles arrived shortly after 1:00 P.M. and joined the ten guards escorting the prisoner to the scaffold and onto the trapdoor.

The death warrant was read by Sheriff James B. Crossen and the prisoner was asked if he had anything to say, but he declined. Multnomah County Sheriff Ben Norden and deputy Haines were assisting Crossen, and they pinioned the arms and legs of Cook. The black hood was pulled over his head, the noose positioned, and at 1:17 P.M. Sheriff Crossen sprang the trap. Cook dropped through, separating the vertebrae but not severing the spinal cord, so it took seventeen minutes for him to strangle to death. Five minutes later Drs. Logan, Richardson and Morrison pronounced him dead and then the body was cut down and placed in the cheap pine coffin provided by the county. Cook was buried in a potter's field that evening without a service or mourners.

Evening Telegram (Portland, OR): December 2, 1878. *Oregonian* (Portland): December 31, 1878; February 5–8, 1879.

Brown, Archie; Johnson, James
March 14, 1879

On the morning of August 20, 1878, Archie Brown, an alias for Eugene L. Avery, Joseph Swoards, sometimes spelled Swords, and James Johnson, an alias for Frank Taylor, walked into Walter O'Shea's pawn shop on Washington Street in Portland, Multnomah County, Oregon. O'Shea did not notice that the last man through the door locked it behind him and he thought they were there on legitimate business when they asked to purchase some blankets. They looked through a number of blankets, finally selecting several, and purchased them. They gave payment which would require change and, when O'Shea squatted to open the money drawer of his safe, one of the men struck him a heavy blow on the head with an iron bar. The pawnbroker was knocked unconscious as the three men hurriedly ransacked the shop, taking only the most valuable items and placing them in a valise also stolen from the shop.

The men were discovered in the act and fled through a rear window, scaled a board fence, and calmly walked through the store of Lewis and Straus, exiting on First Street. In the meantime Constable Daniel Sprague had been summoned and as he came on the scene he saw the men and gave chase, keeping a safe distance, as he was unarmed, but he planned to learn their destination and perhaps identify them. He gained on the robbers, keeping them in sight until they reached Alder Street.

One of the men called loudly to the others, "Damn it, let's make a stand right here!" as he turned and fired at the officer. Just at that moment Louis Joseph, a young boy, was crossing the street. His attention was drawn to the remark and he turned just as the pistol was discharged, and the bullet pierced his heart, killing him instantly. A second shot was fired as Sprague ducked behind a tree. The three murderers then jumped into Mr. Weeks' grocery wagon, which was parked in the street, and while one whipped up the team the other two sat in the back with guns drawn. They abandoned the wagon at Fifteenth Street and fled into the heavy timber west of town.

Word of the robbery followed by the murder of a child spread rapidly, and soon a large number of armed men were scouring the country for the three fugitives. Roads were closed, the telegraph was put to good use circulating descriptions, and a reward of $250 was posted. Of course the usual suspects were corralled, but all proved to be the wrong men.

On August 23 Joseph Swoards, a boy of only sixteen years, was arrested near the Terminus Saloon and on examination he admitted to being one of the three fugitives. He claimed that he was innocent of all the criminal behavior and knew nothing of the intentions of the other two men when they entered the pawn shop. He identified Brown and Johnson, and on September 3, Brown was captured at a ranch eleven miles below the city. He had been at the ranch for days, but a young girl who had read the fugitives' descriptions in the newspapers alerted lawmen, who lodged him in the Portland jail that evening. On October 14 Portland lawmen received a telegram that James Johnson had been arrested in Los Angeles, where he was recognized by a former convict who had served time with the murderer. Johnson arrived in Portland on October 31 and was lodged in a cell with the other two prisoners.

On October 24, 1878, even before Johnson arrived, the three men were indicted for murder in the first degree. The trial of Brown began in Judge C. B. Bellinger's court on November 18, 1878, and his defense was that the killing had not occurred during the commission of the robbery, and therefore was only murder in the second degree, but no effort was made to show that Brown was not guilty of the robbery. The law, according to Bellinger's instruction, said, "Murder in the first degree is where ... one while in the commission of, or in the attempt to commit ... robbery, kills another." The prosecution established that Constable Sprague was in "hot pursuit" and therefore the crime was still in progress. Brown was found guilty of first degree murder on November 21 and was sentenced to hang on February 7, 1879.

Johnson's trial started on December 4, 1878, and their defense, after Brown's defense failed, was that Johnson had not fired the fatal bullet and that Brown had already been found guilty of the murder. However, one of the witnesses testified that he heard one of the men say, "Give it to him," (meaning Sprague) which proved the premeditated intent to kill. He also confirmed that Johnson held the valise in one hand and a pistol in the other when the boy was shot, and self-defense could not be proffered since Sprague was unarmed and no one was shooting at the fleeing robbers. The entire trial, arguments, and deliberation were concluded in two days and Johnson was sentenced to hang with Brown.

Swoards, perhaps because of his young age or his cooperation, was only convicted of second degree murder and sentenced to life at hard labor. He died in prison of consumption on February 12, 1883.

The convictions of Brown and Johnson were appealed on January 28, 1879. The appeal caused a brief delay in the proceedings, so Governor W. W. Thayer granted a respite to March 14, 1879, for both men, so that they would not have to be re-sentenced. The state Supreme Court denied the motions for new trials. Next came the application and petitions requesting the governor to grant a commutation of sentence, and these were denied. The two twenty-five-year-old men were lodged in jail to await the fateful day.

The scaffold was erected on the south side of the courthouse and enclosed by a high board fence obstructing the view from the street. For many hours before the execution the crowd swelled until it included over three thousand men, women, and children. At 8:00 A.M. the militias — the Emmet Guard, the City Rifles, the Portland Battery, and the Washington Guards — assembled at their armories in full dress uniform and at noon took up their positions around the courthouse square. They were armed with rifles, bayonets fixed, and cannon were deployed at the corners of the streets near the enclosure.

On their last night the two condemned men had asked for peace and quiet, and few except the death watch guards were allowed to enter the jail corridor. A few friends and reporters were admitted but they stayed only briefly. Brown spent part of the evening writing letters and once asked for scissors to cut a lock of hair for his mother, and told guard James Barry, "God knows I did not mean to kill the boy. I did not even see him." As the night passed Brown began to show nervousness while Johnson displayed the greatest fortitude, smoked cigars, and chatted freely with newspaper reporters. Johnson was critical of some who attributed malicious motives to the killing and insisted he did not have a pistol and did not strike O'Shea in the pawn shop, but Brown said the same. Brown said, "I am sorry for Johnson."

They drew up an order regarding the final disposition of their remains asking that their bodies be given to Thomas Shortell, their friend, or Shortell's father. Shortly after midnight both men lay down and slept for several hours until Johnson awoke and said he was feeling sick. Brown slept until daybreak and then ate a hearty breakfast, but Johnson refused to eat. At an early hour Sisters Theresa and Josephine joined the men and they were soon joined by the Reverend W. C. Chattin for religious services. Johnson refuted the hereafter but Brown listened intently, and then the two men dressed for their deaths: Brown in blue, with a white shirt and collar and English walking shoes; Johnson in brown pants, gray shirt, dark coat, and embroidered slippers. At 10:00 A.M. a dispatch was sent from the Governor W. W. Thayer to Sheriff Ben L. Norden stating simply, "Execute the warrant."

At 1:40 P.M. the doors to the cells were unlocked and the two condemned men stepped into the corridor. They were accompanied by Sheriff Norden, Guard Barry and deputy sheriff William Church, Jr., with the Reverend Chattin following closely behind as far as the scaffold stairs. After the condemned men climbed the stairs they were seated in chairs and Sheriff Norden then read the death warrants and the denial of reprieves. He then said to the prisoners, referring to the death warrant, "It is this, gentlemen, that causes the proceedings today to take place. Have you anything to say now?" Johnson said he had nothing to say but Brown said, "Well, I don't know but what I have a few words to say." He then jumped onto the trapdoor and said, "Gentlemen, you see before you a man that has caused a great deal of excitement in Oregon. In California six months ago I was chief of a gang of robbers and left there to come to Oregon to see what I could spot. I was to return and with the others and was to undertake to rob a bank of McLaughlin, in San Jose. Two Spaniards, a white man and myself were to do this. I will never tell who they are who were with me in this."

He then, at a prompting from Johnson, exonerated him in the bank robbery scheme and began a long, detailed story of his earlier escapades, until Sheriff Norden asked, "Brown, do you wish to recite every incident of your life — it is now a few minutes past two o'clock; will you be through by half past two?" Brown answered "Yes, I guess so. I will simply say I am a noted highwayman, a great robber — I am guilty of every crime. I will say to the young men, listen to your mothers. If you do, you will not meet the doom I am to. I would like to sing a song." He then sang "John Rodgers," the ballad of a convicted highwayman, and when he concluded he said, "I die feeling penitent, I solemnly declare. God bless the young men. Mr. Norden, if you have no objection I would like to sing another song." The sheriff acquiesced and Brown sang "Trials by Jury." He then continued his speech, saying he did not intend to kill the boy, but did intend to kill Sprague, who he thought was armed. He continued for some time before Johnson interrupted and asked him to "speak to the point ... this suspense is terrible to me." After criticizing Johnson for being an "infidel," he spoke of the hereafter and finally concluded.

Johnson then took his turn, stating, "Gentlemen: I have *not* been a desperate man. I crave no notoriety. I want you all to know, and all the world to know, that I die of judicial murder." He then shook hands with all the officers and others on the scaffold, and finally with Brown. The reporters who had been admitted onto the scaffold were then seated. A number of officers were among the witnesses but not allowed onto the crowded platform. As soon as Johnson concluded his brief statement the two men were positioned on the center of the matching trapdoors and their arms and legs were pinioned with straps. The black hoods were pulled over their heads and the knots of the nooses were adjusted precisely behind the left ears of each man. Sheriff Norden was working on Johnson when the prisoner said, "Take your time Ben, don't be impatient," perhaps as a caution to be sure it was done right. Brown then called out he was a Christian and pleaded with Johnson to believe in Christ.

The Reverend Chattin next said a prayer and at "Amen," precisely at 2:22 P.M., the trap was sprung. Both men appeared to break their necks, as there was little movement. Doctors R. G. Rex and W. H. Saylor waited beneath the scaffold and when the bodies appeared each monitored one man's vital signs. Brown's life ended in seven minutes and Johnson's heart stopped in fourteen minutes, and in thirty minutes both men were pronounced dead. The bodies were cut down, lowered into black wooden coffins, and taken to DeLin's undertaking parlor. After the remains were prepared for burial they were given to Thomas Shortell and buried that evening in the cemetery in east Portland.

Oregonian (Portland): January 29, 1879; March 14–15, 1879.

Kat-koo-at
May 5, 1879

Until 1884 capital crimes committed in Alaska were prosecuted in Alaska's U.S. Circuit

Court, which convened at Portland, Multnomah County, Oregon. The first case brought to Oregon involved the murder of Thomas J. Brown. Kat-koo-at, a Chilikat Indian whose name is sometimes spelled Kot-ko-wot, held a grudge against the whites for treatment he and his brother had received when confined in the military guard house at Sitka, Alaska. Kat-koo-at, his wife, Anna, and friend Okh-kho-not paddled their canoe into Whale Bay and beached it near the Hot Springs Hotel of Thomas J. Brown, twelve miles from Sitka. Anna and Okh-kho-not were told to stay with the canoe while Kat-koo-at went to the hotel. In a few minutes Anna and Okh-kho-not, still at the canoe, heard two shots and started for the hotel at a run. They were stopped short when they came face to face with Kat-koo-at and he said, "I have killed Brown." Anna asked, "Why? Where are you going? Do you want to leave us?" Kat-koo-at replied, "For the punishment from the soldiers while I was confined there. The soldiers wounded my brother and they did not pay anything for him. I asked Brown for some matches but he refused to give them to me so I shot him."

Then the party of three Indians went to the house and found Brown on the floor bleeding badly from the wound in his side. Kat-koo-at planned to dispose of the body, and was about to cut him to pieces with an ax when his wife intervened and stopped him. They dragged the dying Brown to their canoe and collected heavy rocks from the shoreline. As they paddled along the rocks were tied to Brown's body by Anna, and when they reached a place where the water was very deep they dropped Brown's body over the side of their canoe. It was not known if he was still alive, but later Kat-koo-at would claim he was alive and his death was by drowning at the hands of all three.

Word of the killing and the identities of the guilty parties were soon known among tribe members but they would not surrender the perpetrators to the whites. The British cutter *Wolcott* was dispatched to Sitka, but this ship had little effect on the Indians. However, when the man-of-war *Osprey* arrived with its many large guns, the Indians did not hesitate to return most of Brown's stolen goods. Now, backed by the war ships, the whites took several Chilikat chiefs hostage and demanded the surrender of the murderers. The Indians were reluctant to cooperate until it was made clear the chiefs would not be released until the guilty parties took their place. Kat-koo-at, Anna, and Okh-kho-not were delivered to the authorities and lodged in the guard house, and chiefs Ah-na-hontz and Stic A. F. Keesh were released. U.S. Marshal A. W. Waters was sent from Portland and within weeks he returned with the prisoners and several witnesses.

Kat-koo-at and Okh-kho-not were indicted for murder and their trial began on April 16, 1879, in Judge Matthew P. Deady's Circuit Court. After all the testimony was in and final arguments presented, it took only one hour of deliberations to acquit Okh-kho-not, while Kat-koo-at was found guilty of first degree murder. The former was released while Kat-koo-at was sentenced to hang on May 5, 1879, but more controversial was Judge Deady's order that, after death, the body of the Indian was to be turned over to the medical school for dissection. While this outraged many at first, it was clearly shown that Judge Deady was complying with the laws of Oregon.

The scaffold, which had been used twice before, was erected near the jail within an enclosure and a limited number of admission tickets were sent. Very little excitement was exhibited for this execution, so no guards or military companies were mobilized. Still, on the fateful morning a small crowd of curious citizens loitered about the fencing and many were rewarded with admission to the enclosure along with the ticket holders. Some spectators were left outside when the enclosure was filled to the capacity of seventy-five and the gates were closed, but they got a view of the scaffold through knot holes and spaces in the fencing.

On his final morning the prisoner ate a hearty breakfast at 6:30 A.M. and then sat calmly smoking his pipe. Kat-koo-at had resigned himself to his fate, but did not understand why his wife and friend were not hanging with him. It was incorrectly believed he had no religious convictions nor a belief in the hereafter, but at 10:00 A.M. the Reverend W. C. Chattin appeared at his cell and was welcomed. Chattin was one of very few Portland men who spoke the Indian's native Chinook tongue, and he asked if Kat-koo-at knew he would die soon. The Indian said he did and asked the time, then noted he had three hours to live. He had learned about Christianity at the mission school in Sitka and had been singing sabbath songs during his confinement. He asked Chattin to stay with him to the end and pray for him, and the reverend promised he would. At 12:30 P.M. Marshal Waters, deputy marshal W. P. Burnes, Sheriff Ben L. Norden, and Constable M. B. Wallace appeared at the cell. Waters asked the prisoner if his wife and friend were equally guilty and he said they were, and then Kat-koo-at was asked if the Chilikat Indians would take revenge for his execution and he said they would not.

The lawmen and the Reverend took the condemned man from his cell at 12:53 A.M. and escorted him out of the jail and into the enclosure. Once upon the trapdoor the condemned man bowed to the spectators and then Marshal Waters read the death warrant, breaking it into short paragraphs so that Constable Wallace could translate. At the end of each paragraph Kat-koo-at nodded that he understood.

The condemned man then declined to speak and his wrists were handcuffed behind while his elbows were strapped to his body and his ankles were bound. The black hood was pulled over his face and the noose adjusted. At 12:58 P.M. the prisoner was prepared for the drop, but the Reverend Chattin stepped forward and offered a prayer in the Chinook language. The saying of "Amen" was the signal and the trap was sprung. No one had noticed that the condemned man had stood to one side of the trap, so when he dropped he struck the side and, rebounding, struck the other side before dropping through. This took up much of the momentum from the five and one half foot drop and Kat-koo-at failed to break his neck in the fall. His chest heaved for two minutes and at 1:02 P.M. his shoulders were drawn up — the last movement discernible. In a half minute Dr. H. R. Littlefield began monitoring vital signs and found the pulse feeble. The pulse stopped after 1:04 P.M. but the heart still beat but diminished steadily until 1:12 P.M., when he was pronounced dead. The body was cut down at 1:18 P.M. and examined, and it was determined that he had strangled to death. The remains of Kat-koo-at were placed in a crude coffin and taken directly to the medical college for dissection.

Oregonian (Portland): March 16, 1879; March 27, 1879; April 16, 1879; April 24–25, 1879; May 5–6, 1879.

Ah Lee
April 20, 1880

Men in the west were often lonely, disillusioned, and frustrated. They saw others, the few lucky ones, strike it rich and return home or find a situation that made life pleasant and productive. When their prayers were not answered they blamed their religion, or their religious leaders, and often took revenge. But when Chin Sue Ying, a Portland Chinese man, became angry and defiled his place of worship, he became a murder victim.

On Wednesday, October 2, 1878, Ying entered one of Portland's Christian temples established by the Chinese population, which also administered to Buddhists, Taoists and Confucians. The following day was a religious holiday and Ying, as an insult to the deity being worshiped, flung a vessel of putrefying blood on the floor. He was subdued and thrown from the church. He returned the following day and, though men had been posted to watch for him, he managed to mingle with a large crowd and once inside he tried to toss a piece of raw meat at the altar. However, Ying was surrounded by Ah Lee, "Charley" Lee Quong, and Lee Jong. Ah Lee pulled a hatchet from his draping sleeve and struck Ying twice on the head, while in that same moment

Quong and Jong pulled pistols and both men shot Ying in the stomach, once each, and the three attackers then fled from the church.

Ying was taken into an adjacent room so that he would not further disturb the celebration and after some delay a doctor and the authorities were summoned. When the police arrived to investigate several witnesses stepped forward and named Ah Lee, Charley Lee Quong, and Lee Jong as the attackers. The following day the police arrested Ah Lee and Charley Lee Quong and took them to the side of the mortally wounded Ying who, in a death bed statement, identified them as two of his attackers before he died at 2:00 A.M. Saturday. The search for Lee Jong continued but the fugitive had learned of the arrests of his fellow countrymen and fled, never to be heard of again.

Ah Lee and Charley Lee Quong were lodged in the Multnomah County jail in Portland and as soon as Ying died they were charged with first degree murder. The grand jury was then in session, so in three weeks, on October 25, they were indicted. They were tried together in late December 1878 and on December 28 were found guilty of premeditated murder. Both defendants were sentenced to hang on February 7, 1879, but the judge had erred in his instructions to the jury regarding their deliberations, telling them that they had only two choices—find the defendants guilty as charged or acquit them. When the appeal reached the state's Supreme Court, the lower court's decision was overturned, and on May 20, 1879, a new trial was ordered.

The defense attorneys this time took a different approach and had the trials separated. Charley Lee Quong was tried first and the jury found him guilty of second degree murder only, and he was sentenced to serve a life term in prison. Ah Lee had struck the victim in the head with a hatchet and possibly the heinous nature of this attack, in comparison to the familiar attack using a firearm, outraged the jurors, and they found him guilty of first degree murder.

Ah Lee was first sentenced to hang on September 29, 1879, but again his attorney filed an appeal. The appeal was denied and Lee was re-sentenced to hang on April 20, 1880. The application for executive clemency or a respite was rejected by Governor W. W. Thayer and Ah Lee finally resigned himself to his fate. There was a great concern that the Chinese community might try to rescue Ah Lee, or that he might commit suicide and cheat the hangman, so six men were hired to stand the death watch and guard the jail.

During his final days Ah Lee had become despondent, but on his final morning he arose and dressed in a new silk Chinese blouse and black pantaloons provided by the Chinese community. He preformed a ritual which required pasting to his body, beneath his clothing, Chinese symbols written on parchment, and he was assisted by his jailor in arranging them in a specific pattern. Meanwhile, outside the jail, the crowd was growing and they were getting out of hand outside the high wooden fence surrounding the scaffold. There was a balcony which gave a view of the gallows, and this was so filled with spectators it creaked under the weight and threatened to collapse at any moment.

Multnomah County Sheriff Ben Norden read the death warrant to the prisoner in his cell after 11:00 A.M. and then led the procession into the enclosure, but as they exited the jail building they found that they had to force their way through the crowd. The number of men to be admitted to the enclosure had been limited by invitation, but as soon as the gates to the enclosure were opened, throngs of citizens pushed their way in, but the procession finally made it to the scaffold and onto the platform. There was no speech given by Ah Lee, and none would have been heard above the yelling and cursing of the crowd.

The condemned man was positioned on the center of the trapdoor where his arms and legs were pinioned. At 11:22 A.M. the black hood was pulled over Ah Lee's head and the noose was adjusted and, in but a moment, the trap was sprung and the body dropped. The distance may have been miscalculated, as Ah Lee struggled for five minutes before strangling to death. His vital signs were monitored by the attending physician and once he was pronounced dead he was allowed to hang a while longer to ensure he could not be revived. The rope was then cut and the body lowered into a coffin. The remains of Ah Lee were turned over to the Chinese community for burial.

Oregonian (Portland): March 3, 1879; May 21, 1879; October 19, 1884; January 31, 1902. *Evening Telegram* (Portland, OR): April 20, 1880.

Murphy, Arthur
January 5, 1881

S. S. Snyder owned a sheep ranch near Heppner in Umatilla County, Oregon. His property was next to the farm of T. D. French, a grain farmer raising ten children. On June 10, 1880, Snyder's sheep broke into French's grain field and were grazing when discovered. French complained to Snyder, who sent his foreman, B. C. Henderson, to chastise sheepherder Arthur "Pat" Murphy, who used the alias Edward. Murphy, a hot-headed Irishman who took the complaint personally, got his Remington revolver and said, "I'll go down and shoot the son of a bitch!" Henderson calmed Murphy and he put away his pistol but Henderson, fearing that Murphy might still go after French, remained at Murphy's camp. The foreman helped Murphy round up the sheep, return them to the flock, and repair the fence.

That evening French rode into the sheep camp. Murphy, seeing him coming, ran to get his revolver and stuck it in his belt. French dismounted and the two men talked for a few minutes, and Henderson kept his distance so long as everything seemed friendly. Suddenly, without any apparent provocation or hesitation, Murphy pulled his revolver and shot French in the head, causing a mortal wound. French lived a few hours but died in an unconscious condition and never revealed what was said that caused Murphy to shoot him. After the shooting Murphy took off at a run and disappeared into the brush. Henderson was too distant to catch him.

Murphy remained at large for three days before he surrendered to Heppner's constable, A. J. Stevenson. Murphy had his preliminary examination at Heppner and was held over for the grand jury. However, while testimony was being given a large crowd gathered, intent on lynching the murderer, so Stevenson snuck his prisoner out of town and took him by a circuitous route to Pendleton, where he was lodged in the county jail. Murphy was indicted for murder in late October and his trial began in Judge L. L. McArthur's courtroom at Pendleton on November 1, 1880.

The trial lasted four days and Murphy's defense was that he was drunk when he and French got into a heated verbal argument followed by a scuffle for the gun, and the shooting was an accident. Of course this was entirely in contradiction to the testimony of Henderson. The jurors disbelieved Murphy, and they deliberated less than one hour before returning a guilty verdict. Judge McArthur sentenced Murphy to hang on January 5, 1881, and his attorneys prepared to file an appeal, but they missed the deadline. Governor W. W. Thayer refused to intervene when the application for a respite or a commutation of sentence was submitted.

Murphy, a Catholic, was repentant and publicly asked forgiveness from the widow French and her ten fatherless children. He received Father Lambert Conrardi in his cell on many occasions for religious consolation, and the priest was with him his final night and day engaging in religious exercises. Murphy called for the *East Oregonian* reporter at daylight and the newsman found Murphy resigned to his fate.

After noon the prisoner dressed in his burial suit of black broadcloth, a white shirt with white silk tie, a black slouch hat, and embroidered slippers. Sheriff William Martin went to the cell and read the death warrant and then the procession formed. The condemned man, accompanied by the priest and the sheriff, exited into the high board enclosure at 3:00 P.M. Murphy climbed the stairs with a firm step, unassisted. As Murphy stood on the platform,

L. B. Cox, editor for the *East Oregonian* newspaper, read the condemned man's prepared statement in which he admitted killing French but again claimed it was an accident. He accused the witnesses — Snyder and Anderson, but especially Henderson — of perjury. He again asked forgiveness, this time from everyone, and when his speech was done he stepped onto the trapdoor without prompting.

The noose was adjusted and he asked Sheriff Martin to cinch it a bit tighter. Before his arms were pinioned he asked to shake hands with the sheriff, and this was done. Then his arms and legs were pinioned and, as the black hood was pulled over his head, Father Conrardi offered a prayer for his soul. When the priest pronounced "Amen!" the trap was sprung. Although Murphy was only five feet eight inches tall he had asked that the drop be a full six feet, and it was. Murphy broke his neck in the fall and hung motionless for several minutes before the attending physicians pronounced him dead. Murphy's remains were then cut down, lowered into a coffin, and given to Father Conrardi for burial in the Catholic cemetery.

East Oregonian (Pendleton): May 15, 1880; November 6, 1880; January 8, 1881. *Oregonian* (Portland): January 7, 1881. *Spokane Times* (WA): November 27, 1880.

Ka-ta-ta
March 28, 1882

On June 5, 1880, James Hollywood started from Sitka, Alaska, on a schooner of ten tons burden for a prospecting tour. With him were his wife and two children, John Gorman, Thomas Maloney and Kerin Canby. They sailed northward one hundred fifty miles until they reached French Harbor. Upon their arrival they were out of wood and water so Gorman and Maloney, with two dogs, went ashore in a skiff to restock the boat. While they were away a canoe with two Indians came to the schooner, which had anchored some distance from shore, and one Indian warned Hollywood not to sail into the bay until high tide, as the harbor was filled with rocks and whirlpools. Meanwhile the two men ashore sensed that the local Indians might be hostile and wanted to start back, though the Indians tried to discourage them. A storm had come up and as they rowed back to the schooner their small craft was capsized. Hollywood sailed the schooner into the bay and rescued Maloney, but they could not find Gorman nor the dogs. They remained at French Harbor for four days looking for Gorman's body but it could not be found, so they set sail for Behring's Bay, leaving word for the Indians to bury Gorman's body if it washed ashore.

They reached Behring's Bay on July 8 where they built a small cabin for the party. Ka-ta-ta, sometimes spelled Kat-at-cha or Ka-ta-tah, a member of the Yakitat tribe, came into camp and they hired him as guide and interpreter. The Indian led the three men — Hollywood, Maloney and Canby — on a twenty-five day prospecting excursion.

Ka-ta-ta devised a plan to extort goods from Mrs. Hollywood, and he also conspired with other tribe members to kill the three prospectors and take all their supplies. At Ka-ta-ta's suggestion his family went to the Hollywood cabin and demanded six sacks of flour for a broken arm received by their son "when Mr. Hollywood threw him down a mountain." It was a ruse, but when they were refused they vowed vengeance, built a cabin near that of the Hollywoods' cabin, and subjected Mrs. Hollywood and the children to various abuses. When the prospecting party returned Hollywood began building a larger cabin to accommodate the entire party through the winter while Maloney and Canby with their Indian guide, Ka-ta-ta, started on another prospect.

Ka-ta-ta returned in two days and reported that Maloney and Canby had drowned. When Mrs. Hollywood insisted that he was lying, he admitted that he had killed them, shooting each man with a single blast from their own double-barreled shotgun. He confessed that the men had beached their canoe and gone ashore, unarmed, to prepare their dinner while Ka-ta-ta was left to bail water from the canoe.

One man was holding a frying pan and the other a slab of bacon, and when the two men came abreast of one another Ka-ta-ta picked up their shotgun and killed them. He said that Maloney was killed by the first blast, but Canby was only badly wounded by the second and he rushed at Ka-ta-ta. They struggled until Canby collapsed from loss of blood; the Indian then bashed out his brains with rocks. He said he weighted the bodies with rocks and sank them in a nearby stream. Later Indian George would find the bodies just as Ka-ta-ta had described them. The Hollywoods had delayed too long and could not leave due to the harsh winter weather. They lived from day to day throughout the season expecting at any moment to be attacked and murdered.

In the spring they sailed south to Sitka and reported the murders to Captain Glass of the U.S. Navy's ship *Jamestown*. He awaited the arrival of the ship *Wachusete*, which was immediately dispatched to Behring's Bay under the guidance of James Hollywood. The sailors captured two Yakitat chiefs who were held hostage while officers went inland twenty-five miles to the place Ka-ta-ta was hiding. They arrested the native on two counts of murder and brought him back to the ship. The prisoner was taken to Sitka and thence to Portland, where the U.S. Circuit Court for Alaska convened.

Ka-ta-ta was indicted by the federal grand jury, tried and convicted. He was sentenced to hang on March 31, 1882, but the ship taking his friends and family back to Sitka had to leave before that date so, at his request, the execution was moved up to Tuesday, March 28. An enclosure was constructed at the courthouse around the gallows, which had a platform seven feet above the ground. U.S. Marshal Kearney sent out seventy invitations. These witnesses, which included those invited by the condemned man, were the only people allowed inside the enclosure. There had been mild excitement regarding the hanging of a native Alaskan, and curious residents gathered in small groups outside to listen and to talk about the event.

On the fatal day Kearney and Sheriff Joseph Beuchtel led the prisoner into the enclosure and right onto the gallows just before 11:00 A.M. and sat him in a chair behind the trapdoor. An interpreter asked if he had anything to say, and he replied he just wanted to say good-bye and shake everyone's hand. Kearney, through the interpreter, told Ka-ta-ta that he could rise and say good-bye, which he did, then made the sign of a cross. He was positioned on the center of the trapdoor and his wrists, arms, knees and ankles were pinioned, which offended him and he complained it made him helpless. The noose was then put about his neck, cinched and adjusted, and next deputy U.S. Marshal Sanford Watson pulled on the black hood. Ka-ta-ta began to chant his death song as the seconds ticked by, and at exactly 11:00 A.M. the trap was sprung by deputy sheriff Charles Brush and Ka-ta-ta fell six feet, breaking his neck. Several physicians waited beneath the scaffold and they monitored the Indian's vital signs for fifteen minutes before pronouncing him dead. His remains were then cut down, lowered into a coffin and, according to law, delivered to the medical college for dissection.

Oregonian (Portland): March 29, 1882.

Andersen, Alfred
July 20, 1883

On October 29, 1882, the body of a man was found on Swan Island, Multnomah County, Oregon, with part of his skull blown away by a shotgun blast. The coroner assembled a jury and they rowed to the island to hold an inquest. The body was in a terrible state, having decomposed for at least two weeks, so it took several days to identify him as Charles Andersen, a visitor from Chicago. He had arrived the end of September with his mistress, Bertha Nelson, and was met by his brother Alfred. A search was made for Alfred but it was learned that he and Bertha had sailed for Astoria on October 11. He was tracked, by a circuitous route, to San Francisco, and the couple was lodged in jail when they arrived on November 17, Alfred charged with murder and Bertha held as a witness.

The circumstantial evidence began to mount as people came forward saying that Alfred had been all but destitute before Charles arrived, but was wealthy after his brother went missing. Alfred and Charles had rented shotguns on October 9 and late the following day Alfred returned the weapons, one with yellow mud like that on Swan Island caked into the barrel. When Alfred was captured his luggage was seized and searched, and it was discovered that he had his brother's clothes, gold watch, and a small caliber silver plated pistol with white grips. Perhaps the most damning evidence, however, was the eyewitness account of steamboat captain William Whitcomb, who was on the river when he saw two men go into the brush of Swan Island. Within minutes he heard two shots and then saw one man with two shotguns emerge from the brush, dropping one weapon into the mud. The man got into a row boat alone and rowed back to the shore, and he identified that man as Alfred Andersen.

Andersen was held for action by the grand jury and indicted for murdering his brother. His trial before Judge Raleigh Scott began on February 6, 1883. The prosecution called fifty-six witnesses, including Bertha Nelson, who said Alfred told her that his brother had returned to Chicago, abandoning her in Portland. She then agreed to travel with Alfred as she had done with Charles. She identified a number of articles belonging to Charles which were found in the possession of Alfred when arrested. The trial lasted a week but deliberations took only one hour before the jurors announced "guilty of murder in the first degree as charged in the indictment." Andersen was sentenced to hang on April 13, 1883, but an appeal resulted in a delay, so when all the appeals were denied the prisoner was re-sentenced to hang on July 20, 1883.

In preparation for the event a high, wooden enclosure was built around the scaffold, which was constructed adjacent to the courthouse. The fence kept the throng of curious citizens away from the gallows structure when it was being built, but on that final morning the crowd surged forward at times and were so determined that only a company of militia kept them from knocking down the fence and rushing the scaffold. Finally the gates were opened and three hundred invited witnesses were admitted.

Sheriff George C. Sears read the death warrant to the condemned man in his cell and at 12:30 P.M. the procession started from the jail. Deputies Ned Dougherty and W. Witherall escorted the prisoner, with the sheriff in the lead. Once upon the platform the sheriff asked if Andersen had anything to say, and he seemed determined to prolong his life as long as he could, so he spoke for more than one hour, well past the time originally planned for his execution.

Finally at a little past 2:00 P.M. he concluded his proclamation of innocence and was positioned on the trapdoor. The sheriff and deputies pinioned his arms and legs with straps, then quickly pulled on the black hood and adjusted the noose. At 2:09 P.M. the sheriff activated the lever with his foot and the prisoner fell six feet, breaking his neck. Dr. L. L. Hope monitored vital signs and when his heart ceased to beat he pronounced him dead. The body hung a bit longer, was then cut down, and deposited in the pine coffin provided by the county. The remains of the murderer were driven to the city morgue in an open wagon and put on display, and many curious citizens filed past to view the remains. The body of Alfred Andersen was laid to rest in a potter's field that evening.

Oregonian (Portland): February 5–11, 1883; February 16, 1883; February 23–24, 1883; April 12, 1883. *Northwest News* (Portland, OR): February 23–24, 1883; April 12–14, 1883; July 20, 1883.

Murray, John W.
February 13, 1885

John W. Murray, a painter by trade, lived in Amsterdam, New York, with his wife and two children. He was a jealous and abusive husband who became known among the bad element by the sobriquet "Amsterdam Jack." In 1878, when it seemed that his abject behavior toward his wife would land him in jail, he abandoned his family and fled to Oregon. In Portland he met a beautiful German woman named Annie Yenke, whom he courted and married in 1879. Annie gave birth to a daughter one year later and then her husband's brutal character began to surface again. Annie put up with his abuses for three more years, for the sake of her daughter, always hoping her husband would change but finally, one week before Christmas 1883, they had a terrible fight and she left him.

On the night of January 5, 1884, Murray attended the Forester's Ball at the Masonic Hall in Portland. After he arrived he saw his wife enter with her twenty-year-old brother Alfred Yenke. Murray asked his wife for a dance but she refused, saying, "As we have decided to separate I do not think we should be seen together. I would prefer not to associate with you any longer." Murray, in true fashion of a husband who believes his wife a chattel, replied, "I'm going to watch you. If you go home with anyone I'll have you both arrested," perhaps suggesting she would be violating the Edmunds Act. She did not acknowledge his threat, turned her back to him, and walked away.

Murray was living at the boarding house of Fannie Anderson where her daughters Jennie and Clara Dougherty also resided. Anderson arrived home from the dance at 11:00 P.M. and Murray stormed in a few minutes later, and told Jennie Dougherty to keep his dog inside, though he usually took the dog everywhere with him. He went to his room and soon returned with a shotgun and told Fannie Anderson and Clara, "Here is the old gun. Do you see it? I've got two shells in it and six or seven more in my pocket. I'm going to shoot any damned man that goes home with Annie. I don't care who he is, and then I'm going to shoot her!" Anderson pleaded with him to put the gun away, saying of Annie, "Why do you want to kill her away from your beautiful little girl?" He replied, "I'll see about it," and rushed out of the boarding house.

Murray found a place to lie in wait along the path his wife would take returning to her family's home, and sometime after midnight Annie and her brother left the dance and started for home. They stopped to chat with friends for a few minutes but then proceeded to the corner of Second and Hooker Streets in South Portland. Murray leaped out and yelled, "Now I've got you!" He fired both barrels and fifty-two lead pellets struck Alfred Yenke, knocking him backwards into the street and killing him instantly. Annie screamed and ran away before Murray could reload, but the sounds awoke everyone in the vicinity and they rushed out to find Alfred Yenke dead (he was buried on January 7). The police were called and at 5:00 A.M. detective S. Simmons arrested Murray in his boarding house room.

At his examination later that day he was held over for action by the Multnomah County grand jury. Murray was indicted in early February and his trial began on February 13, 1884, in Judge Seneca Smith's Circuit Court room. The prosecution called a number of witnesses who showed that Murray had malice toward his wife and toward her brother, and testimony also showed premeditation in committing the murder. The defense tried to show that Murray was insane at the time of the killing, but the prosecution proved that "the planning and carrying out of the murder was inconsistent with the theory of insanity."

The trial concluded on February 22 at 8:00 P.M. and by 11:30 the jurors had reached a verdict of "guilty of first degree murder as charged in the indictment." The defendant was sentenced to hang on May 9, 1884, but Murray's defense attorneys filed an appeal which served as an automatic stay of execution. It took seven months for the case to come before the state Supreme Court and it denied the motion for a new trial. Judge Smith then re-sentenced Murray to hang on February 13, 1885.

A high board fence was erected at the courthouse and within the enclosure a gallows was raised. The enclosure was small so Sheriff Tom

Jordan only invited thirty witnesses. The gallows' drop had a new device to release the trapdoor, an electric switch activated by a button hidden beneath carpeting covering the platform. A large number of curious citizens was expected, and the sheriff was not disappointed when over one thousand gathered and milled about the outside of the enclosure, even though a light drizzle was falling. The sheriff had made arrangements to keep the peace and turned over this duty to several militias under the command of Captain H. Cooke, who deployed his troops at noon.

On his final night Murray dozed off at 8:00 P.M. but awoke at 11:00 P.M. and complained of hunger, so a meal was prepared and he ate heartily. He seemed a bit dazed and rambled on about the Germans hounding him to his death because Yenke was a German. At midnight he fell asleep again but jailor Ned Dougherty reported that the prisoner was restless throughout the night. Murray awoke in a nervous state but braced up as he prepared for his death. The witnesses gathered inside the jailhouse corridor before 1:00 P.M. and, on the hour, filed into the enclosure. The jury, physicians, and newsmen climbed the stairs and took seats while the rest of the men stood below. In a few minutes the procession appeared with Episcopal clergymen Nathan Pearcy and Charles Kaffenden in the lead and Sheriff Jordan and deputy Witherall next, followed closely by the prisoner supported by D. C. Lounsberry and jailor Dougherty.

As the procession entered the enclosure Pearcy read passages from the Episcopal burial service. As soon as Murray appeared he glanced at the noose and faltered for a moment before continuing his steady march. Once Murray was on the platform Sheriff Jordan read the death warrant and then asked Murray if he had anything to say as to why the sentence of the court should not be carried out, and Murray smiled and said, "Well, I don't know as I can say a great deal; I can't help it, I suppose; that is all there is about it." When he stopped the sheriff asked if he had anything further to say, and he replied, "Well, I don't see what I can say: I have got to go, I suppose; I must die." The Reverend Pearcy then spoke for the condemned man saying he had embraced the Episcopal religion, and then the reverend read the entire Episcopal burial service. The Reverend Kaffenden next offered a prayer while Murray shook hands with several men.

With religious proceedings concluded, jailor Dougherty handcuffed Murray's wrists in back to a belt already around the prisoner's waist, and fastened another strap around his ankles while deputy Witherall adjusted the noose and pulled on the black hood. At 1:21 P.M. Sheriff Jordan pressed his foot on the electric switch, springing the trap. Murray broke his neck in the fall and the attending physicians absented themselves from the platform and took their places beneath the scaffold, where they monitored his vital signs. In five minutes they reported his pulse was almost imperceptible and in another minute it had ceased. Murray hung for fourteen minutes before being cut down, was lowered into a coffin, and was taken to the coroner's office. After the body was examined the doors were flung open and for three hours, from 6:00 to 9:00 P.M., and fifteen hundred people filed through to see the remains of Alfred Yenke's murderer. Murray was a Civil War veteran and, though not a member of the Grand Army of the Republic, members of that organization arranged for his burial the following day.

Oregonian (Portland): February 3–6, 1884; February 13–23, 1884; May 3–8, 1884; May 28, 1884; May 14, 1885.

Drake, Joseph
March 27, 1885

In 1884 twenty-five-year-old Joseph Drake lived in Marion County, Oregon, in violation of the state's exclusionary clause, which prohibited blacks from settling in Oregon. The law, passed four decades earlier, allowed for the arrest and public flogging of any black — free or slave, male or female — refusing to leave the state and provided that the punishment could be repeated every six months. Like many old laws it remained on the books but was largely ignored. Drake lived with the Henry family, William and Emma, and the Henry farm was but one mile from the Swarts farm, where David and Mary raised their three children. Mary was good friends with the Henrys, especially Emma, and visited as often as she could. After all, the frontier even in quickly developing Oregon could be a lonely place, especially for a woman seeking the company of another woman.

David Swarts was the opposite of his wife in relations, as he was rude, insulting, contentious, and litigious with neighbors and family. Swarts insisted that Emma Henry was an Indian woman who had given birth to two illegitimate children from two different Indian men, and the Henrys had once unsuccessfully sued David Swarts. In April 1884 David Swarts filed for a divorce from his wife of eighteen years and alleged that she had an adulterous affair with Joseph Drake. In order for an Oregon court to grant a divorce and for a party to gain the advantage in the distribution of property and rights, each party claimed outrageous behavior on the part of the other, and this was David's attempt to malign his wife.

Late on the evening of May 3, David Swarts was shot to death near his farm. During the investigation it was proved that Emma and William Henry had gone into Salem that day, leaving Drake with Emma's mother Delinda. When the two returned they set about chores and later, Mary Swarts, with her oldest son, arrived and ate supper with the Henry family. Drake claimed that after the meal Mary asked him to take some eggs into town on Monday and then she left with her son George, while he (Drake) went right to bed. However, Delinda Henry said the two, Drake and Mary Swarts, had an intimate conversation in the parlor and then Drake went home with Mary. Delinda insisted that the two were having an affair and that Drake had threatened to shoot Mary's husband. Emma Henry said that her husband had saddled two horses, got his gun, and left, and that she and her mother went to bed and heard nothing more until after the killing of David Swarts.

William Henry's story was the most damning, as he admitted to being Drake's accomplice in the killing of David Swarts and said that he met Drake on his way back from the Swarts farm, as they had agreed, and they lay in ambush for David Swarts. He said Drake shot Swarts from his saddle as William ran in front of the horses, but this first shot did not kill Swarts, so Drake grabbed William's pistol from his hand and ran to Swarts, who was struggling to rise, and shot him point-blank in the neck. This shot put him down for good and he quickly bled to death.

With slight variations the same stories were presented to the Marion County grand jury, which returned an indictment against Drake and William Henry on June 12, 1884, and also indicted Mary Swarts as a conspirator. Drake's trial began in Judge Reuben P. Boise's courtroom on June 17 and under oath Drake admitted to carrying a pistol with him at all times, in violation of a recent law prohibiting Oregon's citizens from carrying concealed weapons, but he denied the affair and denied taking any part in the murder of David Swarts. Mary Swarts was not allowed to testify as she had been indicted with Drake, and thus she could not clear their name of the alleged affair and rebut the motive. However, William Henry, though also indicted as a principal, was allowed to testify. The jury believed the testimony and convicted Drake of first degree murder, and nine days after the trial began the defendant stood before Judge Boise and was sentenced to hang on August 13, 1884. Mary Swarts had already been tried and acquitted and William Henry, soon afterward, was convicted and sentenced to serve a life term at the prison in Salem, but served only nine years before being pardoned by Governor Sylvester Pennoyer. The appeals process began for Drake and this stayed the execution. A new trial was denied by the state Supreme Court in late October 1884 and Drake was re-sentenced to hang on March 27, 1885. Applications for executive clemency, a respite or commutation, were denied even though by that time nearly everyone believed him innocent.

As Drake's final day approached the scaffold was erected within a high enclosure on the east side of Marion County's courthouse. On his last night the prisoner was restless, unable to fall asleep until after midnight, and was awake at 7 A.M. when the Methodist Reverend M. C. Wire joined him in his cell after breakfast and spent those final hours praying with Drake. Before 1:30 P.M. Sheriff John W. Minto went to Drake's cell and read the death warrant, and then he and the Reverend Wire took their places on each side of the prisoner and escorted him out of the jail and onto the scaffold, with deputies Ed Croisan, S. R. Foster and W. J. Bennett walking behind in case the condemned man faltered. Once upon the platform Drake spoke to the twenty-seven witnesses, telling them he was being hanged for the company he kept rather than any crime committed, and outside the high wooden fence five hundred curious citizens strained to hear his final words.

Drake was positioned on the trapdoor and his arms and legs were pinioned by the deputy sheriffs. Next the black hood was pulled over his head and the noose was adjusted. At 1:48 P.M. Sheriff Minto touched the release mechanism with his foot and the trap was sprung. The body dropped through, breaking Drake's neck. His vital signs were monitored by Dr. H. R. Holman and in minutes he was pronounced dead, and the body was then cut down and placed into a coffin provided by the county. Drake's remains were turned over to the Reverend Wire, who conducted a brief graveside service when Drake was buried in the private Waldo family cemetery that evening.

Oregonian (Portland): May 1, 1884; May 6–7, 1884.
Oregon Statesman (Salem): March 30, 1885.

O'Neil, Lewis
March 12, 1886

Forty-five-year-old Lewis McDaniel was a well established merchant, operating a grocery store in Ashland, Jackson County, Oregon, when he met and courted a pretty thirty-two-year-old widow named Sarah Amanda Henry, who went by her middle name. Amanda had a seven-year-old boy whom McDaniel liked and the feeling was mutual. They married on October 5, 1881, but after three years of marriage Amanda became restless, possibly because she was married to a man thirteen years her elder who worked long hours every day. They separated amicably in September 1884 and Amanda took up residence in Ashland while her husband stayed in their home on Church Street. In early November Amanda met Lewis O'Neil and, though he was the same age as her husband, he was a particularly handsome rogue. They had a brief fling but by the second week of November Amanda had reconciled with her husband. When O'Neil was seen lurking about the neighborhood, McDaniel warned him to stay away from his home and his wife. However, the affair was the talk of the town.

Lewis O'Neil had abandoned his wife and six children in Colusa, California, in early 1882 and had migrated over the next two years to Ashland, Oregon, arriving in August 1884 and, after two weeks, left for a visit with his seventy-two-year-old brother George. When O'Neil returned to Ashland about October 1 he had with him an old style double-barreled shotgun he stole from his brother. The gun was a muzzleloader with an odd engraving of an alligator on the stock. It was very distinctive and was seen in his possession by many people. On October 7 O'Neil left for a job in Talent, Oregon, but returned on November 2, when he met Amanda McDaniel. Then followed their brief fling and her return to her husband, but O'Neil, whenever her husband was at work, would sneak over to their house and continue their illicit relations. On November 20, 1884, at 7:30 P.M. Lewis McDaniel was walking home from his grocery store. It was dark and rainy so McDaniel was preoccupied with keeping his head down and his hands in his pockets. He was nearly home when someone behind him stepped out from hiding, pointed a shotgun at his head and, firing one barrel, blew off the top and left side of his head, and McDaniel was dead instantly. A neighbor heard the shot and, investigating, found McDaniel's body and summoned night watchman Charles H. Miller. The night watchman identified McDaniel and knew where he lived, so he took a bystander and tried to contact Amanda McDaniel. He knocked and rang the bell with persistence, but there was no answer at the door, so he checked throughout the neighborhood without success, and upon his return to McDaniel's house his wife answered the door. When told her husband had been murdered not seventy-five feet from her door she seemed unconcerned, and after staying with the widow for twenty minutes Miller joined Ashland's city marshal Taylor at the murder scene. They found distinctive boot tracks and made careful note of them and their course, which went from the body to Granite Street, through several muddy vacant lots, over fences, across Ashland Creek, and continued just above the Ashland Flour Mill.

O'Neil's name had come up immediately and by 10:00 P.M. he was located in High and Taylor's Saloon, where he was arrested. His muddy boots were taken and compared to the tracks by the body, and they matched perfectly. He was lodged in the Ashland jail and, when questioned about his shotgun, he said he had sold it. Two days later a coroner's inquest was held and, while O'Neil was busy denying any part in the killing, his shotgun suddenly appeared in parts spread all over the vacant lot near Cooledge's Nursery, which was in the opposite direction the murderer had fled. O'Neil had been in custody since the night of the 20th and that lot had been thoroughly searched several times without results, so now it was clear he had an accomplice. Amanda would later be arrested and charged as an accessory, but acquitted of the charge and released.

On February 27, 1885, O'Neil's trial began in Judge Lionel G. Webster's courtroom. It lasted two weeks. The judge and jury went on an outing to the scene, walked over the route the murderer fled, and examined the lot where the gun was found. On March 12 the case concluded and went to the jury, which deliberated for one hour before finding O'Neil guilty of McDaniel's premeditated murder. The defendant was sentenced to hang on May 21, 1885, but the defense attorney filed an appeal, which acted as an automatic stay of execution. When the appeal was denied he was re-sentenced to hang on March 12, 1886.

O'Neil, as he sat in his cell, began a series of maneuvers to gain his release. First he tried to implicate McDaniel's widow and also her brother-in-law J. J. Fryer, to shift or mitigate his blame, but these efforts failed. By that time Amanda had been tried and acquitted, so he wrote to her asking her to come forward and confess to the murder, as she could not be tried again, but she ignored his plea. In all he wrote to a half dozen people, each time suggesting some plot to gain his release by shifting the blame and sharing in the money he would get from suing the state for false imprisonment. All his pleas were ignored and it is difficult to see how his schemes could have succeeded, as he was illiterate and had the jailor write the letters for him. His final plea was to his brother, playing upon the welfare of his "poor children" whom he had abandoned, and emphasizing that his brother was old and would not live much longer anyway. His final hope came from an unexpected source when the nephew of his abandoned wife went to Governor Z. F. Moody to plead for a commutation of sentence, but was refused.

As the date of execution approached a sixty by forty foot enclosure of sixteen foot boards was constructed between the courthouse and the jail. Sheriff Abraham S. Jacobs armed the Ashland fire department members and deputized them to act as guards to keep peace outside the enclosure. O'Neil was visited by Father Francis Blanchet, who gave him the religious support he needed in those final hours, and the priest was with the condemned man during his last day. At 2:00 P.M. Sheriff Jacobs appeared at the cell, the door was opened, and the procession formed. Father Blanchet led the way with the sheriff and deputy Steadman on each side of the prisoner, in case he weakened. Within the enclosure one hundred twenty invited guests stood at the foot of the scaffold, including several women and children. Outside there was a large crowd but they were orderly and were kept from the fence by the deputized firemen.

When the party reached the platform deputy Steadman went below to spring the trap. The condemned man was placed on the trapdoor and the death warrant was read, and then the sheriff asked O'Neil if he had anything to say to the crowd and Father Blanchet, as he had agreed, answered "No" for the prisoner. The sheriff then fastened the straps to O'Neil's wrists and arms, knees and ankles and then the noose was adjusted and the black hood was pulled on. The signal was given and the trap was sprung. Drs. Aiken, Robinson, Lembert, and DeBar waited below and monitored vital signs until, at 2:30 P.M., they pronounced him dead. O'Neil's remains were cut down, placed in the coffin provided by the county, and later that evening he was buried in the pauper's section of the Jacksonville Cemetery.

Ashland Tidings (OR): November 28, 1884; December 19, 1884; March 6–27, 1885; April 13, 1885; May 8, 1885; November 18–25, 1885; February 19, 1886; March 5, 1886; March 19; 1886. *Oregonian* (Portland): March 12, 1886.

Marple, Richard
November 11, 1887

David J. Corker was a carpenter by trade, but by 1886 he had established a fine hardware store on Third Street in Lafayette, Yamhill County, Oregon, and built comfortable living quarters in the rear. Corker, a six year resident in the new town, stayed in his store most of the time. He was a deaf reclusive who had few friends but he was honest and industrious and therefore well respected.

On November 1, 1886, Corker retired at the usual hour of 9:00 P.M. At 9:00 A.M. the following day a farmer named Macey arrived to make some purchases and the store should have been open, but when he received no response he summoned several neighbors and they forced entry. They found Corker lying naked in bed in a pool of blood, and a bloody ax lay on the floor near his blood soaked clothes. His arms were cut and broken and his face was cut diagonally from his eye to the opposite side of his chin, and above the eye was a fearsome gash in his skull. In all there were at least four blows to the head from the sharp edge of the ax, one cutting off the tongue and part of the jaw, and several teeth were scattered on the floor. There were also blows from the blunt edge, one breaking his shoulder. They summoned Sheriff Thomas J. Harris, who found that the killer had entered by removing a pane of glass from a rear window, placed a table against the eight foot partition to Corker's living quarters and climbed over, stepping on clothing left on a dresser. It was clear that he was familiar with the layout of the store and with his victim's routine. There were no signs of a struggle but the wounds to Corker's arms suggested he had awakened just before being attacked, or just after the first blow, and had just enough time to throw up his arms to try to protect himself. Corker's trunk was broken open and a sack, which according to his ledger contained two hundred six dollars, was empty.

Coroner D. C. Harver of McMinnville took charge of the body and scheduled an inquest for November 3. Once the inquest concluded Corker was buried in the Lafayette cemetery by his Masonic brothers from the local lodge. When the investigation began a crowd of curious residents gathered outside the store and among them was Richard Marple. He was a young man, only twenty-seven years old, but he had already been suspected of a variety of crimes including several unsolved burglaries. Marple, who was rumored to be from a gypsy clan, had loudly voiced the opinion that it would be easy to burglarize Corker's store, and said he didn't care who heard him and even mimicked Corker to his face on one occasion.

Marple was immediately suspected, so the next day detective Singleton and Sheriff Harris went to the Marple home on the edge of town. They noticed blood on Marple's coat and this was deemed sufficient to make an arrest. They then searched his pockets and found a bloody paper and a diary. They searched the house and found burglar's tools, so they also arrested his mother, Anna, as an accessory. Marple was brought from jail to testify at the inquest and, after denying any knowledge of the murder, he made disparaging remarks about the dead man which angered everyone present. He accused Singleton of taking his coat to the store and dipping it in the blood, then said the blood came from a butchered pig. His wife Julia and his mother testified that the blood came from a child's injury. The jury found the conflicting stories conspiratorial and returned a verdict that Corker had died at the hands of Richard and Anna Marple.

The Marples were returned to their jail cells to await action by the grand jury, but Anna was released several weeks later and the charges against her were dropped. Her son, however, was indicted on several charges, including burglary and assault, but the charge of murder was the first to be tried. On April 2, 1887, Marple's trial began in Judge Reuben Boise's courtroom with selection of the jurors, and twelve men from the first venire were sworn in the following day. On the morning of the April 3 the prosecution presented its case, and the defense concluded before the supper hour. The case went to the jurors and after brief deliberations they returned a verdict of guilty of first degree murder. Judge Boise, on April 9, sentenced Richard Marple to hang on May 29, 1887. The judge had erred in setting the date on a Sunday so when told of his error he changed the date to June 29, 1887. The appeal was filed staying the execution and arguments were heard by the state Supreme Court on May 27. They affirmed all but the date set, which had to be between thirty and sixty days after sentencing, so on October 1, 1887, Judge Boise set the new date at November 11, 1887. Neither appeal nor application to Governor William P. Lord pleading for executive clemency delayed the proceedings.

The scaffold, built within a high board enclosure, measured seven by eleven feet, and the trapdoor was three feet square and centered on the platform with a lever release. The beam was eight feet above the platform and the latter was seven feet above the ground, with the drop set for six feet. A flight of stairs ran from the window of the second floor sheriff's office directly onto the platform. The sheriff had sent out thirty invitations, including the twelve men who would act as the coroner's jury, and they crowded into the enclosure after noon on Marple's final day. Sheriff John W. Minto had come from Salem to assist Sheriff Harris. Marple, who had been uncooperative and arrogant, began to break down during his final week, but braced up with opiate-laced whiskey. As the time neared Marple refused to dress for the occasion so he had to be forcibly clothed, and the prisoner remarked that these were the best clothes he had worn in a decade. His elbows and wrists were bound behind him to prevent him from undressing.

The hanging was scheduled for 1:00 P.M. so the procession formed and marched to the scaffold before the appointed hour. Sheriff Harris held a flask to Marple's lips several times as the crowd waited for him to speak. However, even in his final moments of life, Marple would not confess. Instead he recanted his story that the Freemasons had killed Corker and claimed it was Sheriff Harris and four other men who conspired to murder Corker. He also claimed that the sheriff had abused him while in jail. When Marple concluded his well practiced rant, E. B. Collard read the death warrant. The Reverend Father Joseph White prayed for a few minutes while the condemned man's legs were pinioned, the noose adjusted, and the black hood pulled on.

Once the prayer concluded the trap was sprung and Marple shot downward, but he had squirmed at the last moment, moving the noose under his chin. He struggled and strangled for minutes before hanging lifeless, and the county coroner monitored his vital signs and pronounced him dead in eighteen minutes. The body was cut down, lowered into a coffin, and turned over to the Marple family for burial. Throughout the entire affair Marple's mother yelled curses at the crowd, promising that the town would be destroyed by fire.

After the murderer was dead a jail prisoner came forward to tell another version of the crime. He said that his fellow prisoner, Marple, had confided that his mother had gone to see Corker and drugged him so they could steal his money, which amounted to two hundred three dollars and seventy-five cents. Marple's wife was involved in the planning but was not present at the murder. After Corker was unconscious Anna realized she would be a prime suspect when Corker regained consciousness, so they placed their victim in a ritualistic pose and then chopped him with an ax they found in the store. Marple told of killing other people and said, "It is no harder to chop a person to death than to butcher a hog." This tale, however, is about as incredible as any other lie Marple had told, and was refuted by the evidence at the scene of Corker's death.

Journal (Salem, OR): November 6, 1900. *Oregonian* (Portland): November 3, 1886. *Oregon Register* (Lafayette): August 12, 1887; September 9, 1887; November 18, 1887. *West Side Telephone* (Lafayette, OR): April 2, 1887; April 11, 1887; April 30, 1887; November 2, 1887; November 12–13, 1887; November 18, 1887.

Landreth, William
July 6, 1888

William Landreth was an old man, sixty-three years old in 1888, but for his years he was quite strong and very coarse in appearance. In 1873 he married Elizabeth when his first wife died and Elizabeth came to live with him in Independence, Polk County, Oregon, and brought along her three-year-old daughter. Landreth sexually abused his step-daughter — Symmie Ellis Antle — since she was very young.

At 8:00 A.M. on January 29, 1888, when Symmie was eighteen years of age and had just learned she was pregnant with her step-father's child, Landreth took a fourteen inch butcher knife and entered her bedroom. The motive for the attack was to silence Symmie before William's terrible secret was revealed. In addition he was experiencing uncontrollable jealousy and had accused Symmie of having sex with other men. William restrained his victim with his left arm as he struck fourteen blows to her head and body, any one of the blows inflicting a fatal wound. One blow was to her head just in front of the right ear and penetrated more than five inches, almost passing through her skull, while another blow was to her arm, which she had thrown up in defense, and this blow nearly severed her hand. Symmie's piercing screams alerted the entire family and his wife and two sons rushed to her aid. His wife and their oldest son, William "Willis," Jr., struggled with the elder William while the younger boy, Wilbur, got a shotgun and tried to get a clear shot at the murderer. The old man broke free and ran from the house just as Willis wrested the shotgun from Wilbur, a moment before he pulled the trigger. Symmie's mother would later say that after William ran away she cradled her daughter in her lap and tried to stop the bleeding, but Symmie died in minutes.

Willis followed his father and found him trying to drown himself in the slough. The boy caught his father by the coat and pulled him out, and William then ran up the hill with his son close behind shouting for help. F. L. Hartman heard the boy's screams, ran out, and grabbed the old man. They struggled for some time but finally Landreth tired and surrendered, and he was lodged in the jail at Independence. William made several feeble attempts to commit suicide but each time he was thwarted in his efforts. There was also concern of a lynching, as a wife-murderer had been lynched in Independence six months earlier, so following his examination the following day Landreth was moved to Salem and lodged in the Marion County jail.

Landreth denied that he was guilty of incest, admitted he killed Symmie, but said it was not premeditated but rather "a killing on the spur of the moment." In spite of the evidence and his admission to the killing, Landreth pled not guilty at his arraignment. He was indicted in early May and his trial began on May 12, 1888, in Judge Reuben Boise's court at The Dalles. The trial lasted two weeks and on May 26 the jurors returned a verdict of "guilty as charged in the indictment of first degree murder." Landreth was sentenced to hang at The Dalles on July 6, 1888, and returned to the Salem jail. A death watch was assigned to prevent suicide, but the prisoner was allowed to sleep in the corridor and move about freely. On Wednesday, July 4, the Reverend W. Rollins visited Landreth in the jail but the condemned man refused spiritual consolation. On Thursday night he did not retire until midnight but arose before 6:00 A.M. to prepare for his trip to The Dalles.

Sheriff Ira Smith arrived in Salem at 7:30 A.M. in a two seat carriage and, after granting a quick photograph and eating a breakfast of hash and coffee, the prisoner was handcuffed and placed in the carriage. Landreth arrived in The Dalles at 10:00 A.M. and was lodged in the local jail. He weakened and cried as they neared The Dalles, and when placed in his cell he sat on a stool with bowed head until the Reverend T. F. Royal arrived for a prayer session. At 10:30 A.M. his burial clothes were delivered and he again weakened, so Sheriff Smith gave him brandy. This braced him and he was able to eat a little before he dressed. He then returned to his stool and wept bitterly until his dinner arrived at 11:25 A.M., and after he ate, a long-time friend arrived and begged him to tell the truth for his soul's sake, but he again denied any carnal knowledge with his step-daughter and insisted that he killed her because her lies ruined his reputation.

The scaffold had been built on the north side of the jail within a stockade twenty-two feet high enclosing an area twenty feet by sixteen feet. The area just in front of the gallows had been roped off to hold back the witnesses. The trapdoor was in the center with a drop of five feet eight inches, and the steps were on the east. The scaffold had been used once before, successfully, and the rope had hung three men previously. At noon Sheriff Smith called the roll of the coroner's jury and then the twelve men and other witnesses were admitted, including lawmen, reporters, physicians, and several prominent citizens. At 12:20 P.M. the condemned man exited the jail door escorted by Sheriff Edward M. Croisan and ex–Sheriff John Groves with Sheriff Smith leading the procession. Landreth was very weak so the party moved forward at a solemn pace, and a guard followed with a chair. The prisoner managed to climb the stairs with great effort and took a seat on the chair provided. Sheriff Smith then read the death warrant while Landreth sat with closed eyes and fists clenched, his lips moving continuously as if in prayer. When the sheriff concluded he turned to Landreth and asked if he had anything to say, and the prisoner replied, "No, nothing."

At 12:27 P.M. the condemned man was helped to his feet and the chair was removed. His arms were firmly strapped to his body, wrists behind, and his knees and ankles were pinioned. Groves pulled the black hood over his head and the noose was adjusted by the sheriff and drawn tight, and the prisoner began to sway and had to be supported during the preparations. Sheriff Smith then asked, "Are you ready?" but he was answered with silence, so Smith signaled to Croisan, who sprang the trap, and Landreth plunged through breaking his neck. Drs. L. N. Woods and T. J. Lee went below the scaffold and monitored vital signs, which were steady for six minutes and then became intermittent. They pronounced the prisoner dead at 12:50 P.M. and the body was cut down and placed in the plain pine coffin provided by the county. The body was then taken by the undertaker, who put it on display for the large, curious crowd which had gathered outside the enclosure. Afterward the coffin was taken to a potter's field south of town and buried without a service.

Oregonian (Portland): July 7, 1888.

McGinnis, Patrick
April 26, 1889

Patrick McGinnis was accused of "branding horses not his own" and was indicted in late

April so that bond could be set, but the amount of the bond was one thousand dollars, which was beyond his means, so in early May he was arrested and lodged in the county jail. McGinnis was soon joined by Buccaroo Jim, a Piute Indian who was charged with the murder of J. M. Bright in Harney Valley. McGinnis was not considered a desperate man so his bond was reduced to help him gain his release, but he still could not raise the six hundred dollars required. McGinnis was given the run of the sheriff's office during the day and at night his cell door was left unlocked, and he had free access to the jail corridor. Buccaroo Jim, on the other hand, was considered a dangerous man because of his alleged crime and was kept in the most secure cell, the metal cage within the jail, and granted few freedoms.

July 5, 1888, was a hectic day as Grant County's new sheriff took over the office and jail, and Robert Lockwood, a deputy for eight years and jailor on that final day, was being replaced. However, Sheriff William P. Gray had not sworn in his new staff so he asked Lockwood to continue in his position for twenty-four hours. In the jail were the two prisoners who could not be left unattended, so Lockwood agreed and introduced Gray to prisoners Patrick McGinnis and Buccaroo Jim. The prisoners ate supper at 5:00 P.M. and afterwards Buccaroo Jim complained of stomach pains. Lockwood went home at 6:00 P.M. to have supper with his wife but returned at 9:00 P.M. to check on the sick Indian. Lockwood entered the jail through the office and went directly to the Indian's cell. As he stood with his back to McGinnis' cell, his other prisoner stepped up behind him and fired two shots from the "office pistol." It was the revolver kept in a drawer of the sheriff's desk and McGinnis had obtained it during the day and hid it in his cell, and it had not been missed during the hectic change of command. The first bullet struck Lockwood in the back of the head, severing his spinal cord and traveling through his brain, lodging on the inside of the front of his skull a little left of center. Lockwood fell to the floor and was dead in seconds, and the second bullet missed him as he fell. The two shots were heard but no one was concerned, thinking it was just a drunken cowboy on a spree.

When Lockwood had not return home by 1:00 A.M. his wife asked several neighbors to investigate and the men found the door to the office unlocked and the gate to the jail corridor ajar. They lit a lamp and inside was the body of deputy Lockwood, lying in a pool of blood, and both cell doors were open and the prisoners were gone. The men sounded the alarm, formed posses, and went out in every direction, and in the morning the county court convened and issued a reward of five hundred dollars for each man. Sheriff Gray then added another two hundred fifty dollars per man, bringing the total to fifteen hundred dollars. That morning an inquest was held by coroner N. Rulison, the jurors holding both fugitives responsible until the matter could be sorted out. Toward evening of July 6, Joe Combs came into town to reported that McGinnis was hiding near Alex Fisher's ranch. Every man and boy who could shoot a gun, a party about seventy strong, assembled and went to Fisher's place to apprehend the fugitive, arriving at dusk. Fisher said he had fed McGinnis breakfast and was then preparing a meal for him to take along when he fled the region that night. Fisher was persuaded, with a promise of a substantial reward, to divulge the whereabouts of McGinnis and, with Joe Ivey, Hank Workins and Bill Whit, the four men convinced McGinnis to surrender without a fight.

As soon as McGinnis was arrested he said that Lockwood had committed suicide but then changed his story to say the deputy had been killed by Buccaroo Jim, but he could not explain how the Indian got the office pistol or managed to shoot Lockwood from behind. They put their prisoner in a buckboard, took him to town, and turned him over to Sheriff Gray.

Meanwhile, another party was on the trail of the Indian and, thinking he would make for the Indian camps in the Malheur, they went directly there. They surrounded the camps, secured all the horses, and collected all the firearms as they awaited the arrival of Buccaroo Jim. Men were out in the country and six miles from Indian John's camp, about sixteen miles from Drewsey, one party discovered the Indian fugitive. Joe Prewett saw him first and led the six man party after the Indian, and when Jim saw he was badly outnumbered and outgunned, he surrendered without a fight. They took their prisoner to town, arriving late Sunday night, and as soon as Buccaroo Jim was again behind bars he informed on McGinnis, and even acted out the killing for the lawmen so they could see every detail.

The two prisoners had their examination before Judge N. Rulison and by July 19 they were held to answer to the grand jury, Buccaroo Jim for the added charge of escape and McGinnis for first degree murder. In November the grand jury indicted McGinnis for the murder of deputy Lockwood. The defendant was tried in Judge L. B. Ison's court and after hearing all the testimony and evidence, a matter of a single day, the jurors deliberated briefly before returning a verdict of "guilty as charged in the indictment." Judge Ison sentenced McGinnis to hang on January 18, 1889, but his attorneys immediately filed an appeal and he was granted a sixty day respite by Governor Sylvester Pennoyer. The state Supreme Court affirmed the lower court's judgment and sentence and the date for execution was then set for March 19, 1889, but Judge Fee issued an order to hold the condemned until he could be properly re-sentenced. The mandate was issued and the date for execution was then reset for April 26, 1889. All that remained for the prisoner was submission of an application for commutation of sentence to the governor, but this was denied.

The condemned man had maintained an air of indifference during his last weeks in custody though heavily shackled at all times. The scaffold had been erected at the rear of the jail and as the appointed hour of 1:00 P.M. approached the shackles were removed, the death warrant read, and the procession formed with Sheriff Gray and several deputies surrounding the prisoner, and the Reverend Father John Henrich of Baker City close behind. When they arrived at the gallows McGinnis bounded up the stairs and took his place on the trapdoor. The sheriff asked the prisoner if he had anything to say, but he only denied guilt and declared he was not the murderer of Lockwood, once again trying to put blame on Buccaroo Jim. His wrists were fastened to a strap around his waist, his ankles were pinioned, and the noose was adjusted. As the black hood was drawn over the prisoner's face Father Henrich delivered a short prayer for his soul and in the next instant, at 1:15 P.M., the trap was sprung. McGinnis' neck was not broken in the fall and, though there was no sign of a struggle, it took twenty-two minutes before Drs. Fred Horsley and Scott pronounced him dead. The body was cut down at 1:40 P.M. and placed in the pine coffin provided by the county, and he was buried in the Catholic cemetery that evening.

Grant County News (OR): September 12, 1888; July 19, 1888; April 25, 1889; May 2, 1889.

Chee Gong
August 9, 1889

Chinese immigrants represented cheap labor in the early West, so they were imported by the thousands, and many more emigrated looking for an opportunity to live a better life in America. They worked in the mines and on the railroads, but after the mining opportunities and railroad building waned they moved into the cities, where they took work at menial tasks and domestic situations. They naturally congregated into a cohesive community, usually called "Chinatown." Portland's Chinatown was dominated by more than a half dozen gangs called Tongs, and every Chinese man had to belong to one for self-preservation. Twenty-year-old Lee Yik belonged to the Luen Yu Tong. Lee Yik worked at the Saddle Rock Restaurant as second cook under the watchful eye of the first cook, a cousin of Chee Gong, and many members of the family were employed at the restaurant. When Lee Yik had an argument with the first cook he found that the entire family made his life unbearable, and he decided he could no longer work at the Saddle Rock. He quit his job and quickly found work as a cook at the St. Charles Hotel. Chee Gong, who was a member of a rival Tong, saw Lee Yik talking to the owner of the Saddle Rock Restaurant, which angered him and he withdrew his entire family from employment at the restaurant. Domestic service positions were not difficult to fill but good cooks were rare, so the owner of the Saddle Rock hired back Lee Yik as first cook.

On November 6, 1887, Lee Yik was attending an evening performance at Lee Toy's Chinese Theater when suddenly, without warning, five men leaped from the stage and surrounded Lee Yik. Chee Gong, one of the attackers, had a knife and slashed at Lee Yik's head, opening several very deep wounds, and the men then brutally beat Lee Yik. The attackers fled before the police could lock down the theater and the lawmen found few who admitted seeing anything, but they did find the bloody knife where it had been discarded by Chee Gong. Lee Yik, though in a terrible condition, managed to name Chee Gong and Fong Long Dick as two of his assailants.

Lee Yik was rushed to the Good Samaritan Hospital where he died on November 17. Portland's officers Hoxie and Meyers found Fong Long Dick hiding on the roof of a shed behind his boarding house and arrested him. They next searched for Chee Gong and found him resting in his room at the boarding house. Both men were lodged in the Portland jail, charged with murder, and at their examination they were held to answer to the grand jury. In the meantime the investigation had added Ching Ling, Yee Long, and Chee Son to the list of fugitives. Ching Ling was arrested but Yee Long and Chee Son fled and were not heard of again. The five men were indicted by the Multnomah County grand jury, the last two *in absentia*, and on December 13 the three prisoners stood in Judge L. B. Stearns' court where Ching Ling asked for, and was granted, a separate trial.

On December 15 the trial of Gong and Dick began and ended. There were a large number of Chinese witnesses for and against the defendants, but the difficult part in finding justice was that Chinese men might perjure themselves to advance the interests of their Tong, and a note from Chee Gong had been intercepted before the trial asking two men to perjure themselves in his defense. Still, before midnight the jury of twelve whites was able to find both men guilty of first degree murder, and Chee Gong and Fon Long Dick were sentenced to hang on February 17, 1888. On Christmas eve Ching Ling was found guilty of first degree murder and sentenced to hang on February 17. Appeals followed which stayed the executions, and on November 13, 1888, the state Supreme Court agreed to hear the case. The justices found errors and in January 1889 granted Chee Gong, Fong Long Dick and Ching Ling new trials. Ching Ling, this time, was acquitted and Fong Long Dick was convicted of second degree murder and sentenced to life imprisonment. Chee Gong, however, was again convicted of first degree murder and, after the next round of appeals failed, was sentenced to hang on August 9, 1889.

The gallows had been built within an existing large woodshed north of the jail, to save the expense of building a fenced enclosure. Sheriff P. Kelly also had another innovation to test, the use of an electrical connection to spring the trapdoor. Invitations were sent to forty witnesses, mostly lawmen, but no Chinese were invited. Efforts were underway to obtain executive clemency in the form of a respite or a commutation of sentence but the prospects seemed slight, and finally Governor Sylvester Pennoyer rejected all efforts. On the final morning Chee Gong was in his cell with the Baptist Reverends John Gordan, Yueng Chuen, and Nathan Pearcy and became agitated at the prospect of being hanged inside a woodshed, but finally the clergymen calmed him by reciting Bible verses and with prayer.

At 12:25 P.M. Chee Gong was led through a boarded-in walkway, which obstructed the view of any curious onlookers, and he entered the woodshed. He climbed the stairs onto the platform and took his place at the railing, awaiting the question. When Sheriff Kelly asked if he had anything to say he denied killing Lee Yik, said that the real killer had disappeared, and he was being sacrificed in the real killer's place. At the forefront of the forty witness were the twelve men chosen as the coroner's jury, and beneath the platform the attending doctor awaited the appearance of the condemned man. Chee Gong was positioned on the center of the trapdoor, his arms and legs were pinioned with straps, and the black hood was pulled over his head.

The noose was then carefully adjusted and Sheriff Kelly, with the slightest tap on the button, sprang the electrical trapdoor release and Chee Gong fell to his death breaking his neck in a long fall, as he was of rather a light weight. He hanged a sufficient time to ensure death and then was lowered into a coffin, which was loaded into a wagon and driven to the morgue. Following the post mortem examination the body was taken to the DeLin and Holman Mortuary where his remains were prepared for burial. At 4:00 P.M. the doors were flung open for the Christian service and viewing of the remains, and hundreds of men, women and children filed through. That evening Chee Gong was laid to rest in the Lone Fir Cemetery at the expense of a Portland businessman, a final gesture from a good Samaritan.

Oregonian (Portland): November 7, 1887; November 11, 1887; February 3, 1889; February 22, 1889; February 26, 1889; August 10, 1889; August 11, 1889.

Sullivan, Peter
November 15, 1889

Before noon on Monday, April 1, 1889, Peter Sullivan appeared in Canyon City and went directly to the sheriff's office. He said that he had come to surrender because he had killed John Bronkee at his cabin on Pine Creek the previous night, but claimed it was self-defense. Coroner N. Rulison convened a jury and, with lawmen, went to the Bronkee cabin twelve miles east of town to hold an inquest. The examination showed that Bronkee had been lying in his bed on his left side facing the wall when the first bullet from a Winchester rifle entered his back, severing his spine and ranging upward. Bronkee had fallen backwards onto his back when a second bullet entered his left side, pierced his heart and exited his right shoulder, and a third bullet grazed his left breast causing a minor wound. Either of the first two bullets would have proven fatal and Bronkee was dead within seconds.

The coroner's jury decided the killing was murder. In questioning neighbors the lawmen learned that thirty-four-year-old Bronkee had filed a claim on the land and was improving it so he could "prove up" on the claim. Sullivan, who was destitute, was in the neighborhood in the fall and Bronkee allowed him to stay the winter, but with spring approaching Bronkee issued an ultimatum, telling Sullivan that he could either work with him or he could settle up for his board and leave on April 1. Sullivan apparently did not intend to do either and murdered Bronkee on his last night in the cabin. The lawmen also learned that immediately after the killing Sullivan had gone to Dr. Fred Horsley's home at 6:30 A.M. and told them "there's a dead Dutchman up the creek," and Sullivan left his rifle there, which had a broken stock, before he started for town. Horsley went to the cabin and found the body as described later by the coroner, hurried after Sullivan, and returned to the cabin with Coroner Rulison.

Sullivan had his examination before Justice Rulison and was held over for action by the grand jury. In early September he was indicted and his trial began in Judge Ison's courtroom by mid–September. Sullivan abandoned his claim of self-defense and instead adopted a claim of insanity, but this was rejected by the jurors and Sullivan was found "guilty as charged in the indictment." When Judge Ison asked if he had anything to say, he replied, "Life is a misery to me and I prefer to have it over with as soon as possible." Sullivan was then sentenced to hang on November 15, 1889. Neither appeal nor application for executive clemency delayed the execution.

Sullivan had shown little emotion until his final few days, when he weakened and all his bravado evaporated. He asked for religious consolation and the Rev. Eads, with several other clergymen, came to his aid, but by his final day his appetite failed and his food went untouched. Shortly before the final hour he told a *Grant County News* reporter that he had repented and knew that he had been forgiven. After 1:30 P.M. Sheriff William P. Gray went to the cell and read the death warrant, then the cell door was swung open and the procession formed with Sheriff Gray and deputy Eads escorting the prisoner out into the yard at the rear of the jail, into the enclosure, and up the stairs onto the platform.

The witnesses were gathered below the scaffold as the sheriff asked Sullivan if he had anything to say and he replied, "Show respect to my body." Sullivan was positioned on the center of the trapdoor, where his wrists and arms, knees and ankles were pinioned and the noose adjusted. The black hood was pulled over his head at 2:01 P.M. and Sheriff Gray immediately pressed the button, and the trap was sprung. The knot slipped under Sullivan's chin and he struggled with violent contortions for eight minutes, but finally the body hung motionless, and in eleven minutes more he was pronounced dead by Drs. Orr and Pruden. The body was allowed to hang another nine minutes before being cut down and put in the pine coffin provided by the county. Sullivan's remains were conveyed to the hill outside the local cemetery and buried in an unmarked grave, without ceremony or a single mourner.

Grant County News (OR): April 4, 1889; November 11, 1889.

Gilman, John F.
December 13, 1889

Christopher and Elizabeth Eationhover, and their five-year-old son William, moved to Coquille City in Coos County, Oregon, in July 1888. The Eationhovers signed a five year lease on farm land belonging to sixty-year-old John F. Gilman and his wife Fidelia, and the Eationhovers built a small house. During the first year of the lease the Gilmans and the Eationhovers had several disagreements over the lease and use of the land, and the Gilmans wanted the Eationhovers to cancel the lease and move but they refused.

During the second week of July 1889 Christopher had been working on a distant farm but all week he had been looking forward to returning home to spend the weekend with his family. When Christopher reached the river he saw Gilman on the opposite bank and called for him to row over and bring him across to that side of the river. Gilman accommodated his German tenant, who then hurried home. Gilman followed Christopher up the path to the Eationhover house, still carrying his oar, and as soon as they were in the yard he struck Christopher over the head, and then pulled a knife from his pocket and stabbed him several times. Gilman had two knives in his pocket and, in his haste, he pulled the one with a broken blade which could not penetrate deep enough to cause a fatal wound. As the two men struggled Fidelia Gilman arrived and intervened. Christopher stumbled down to the river, fell into the boat, and rowed it across the river, where he sounded the alarm. Gilman's error in grabbing the wrong knife had spared Christopher's life, and after the struggle had ensued Gilman had no chance to correct the error.

The posse which hurried across the river found Gilman in his bed, still dressed in his bloody clothing, and he was arrested. He was questioned but denied any knowledge of the whereabouts of Elizabeth and William. The party investigated the Eationhover house and found the table set and breakfast food on the plates. The party then started a systematic search working outwards from the house in a widening circle until, on the following day, they found a shallow grave in a gulch where the bodies of Elizabeth and William were poorly hidden. Another shallow grave had already been dug and it was assumed this was for Christopher.

The next day Dr. J. A. Simmons, acting as coroner, held an inquest and determined that the two deceased had been strangled to death. Elizabeth also had been bludgeoned and had a bad cut to the back of her head below her left ear; her nose had been broken, both arms and both hips were bruised, and there were fingerprints on her arms, and this proved there was some delay in her death, long enough for Elizabeth's bruises to appear. The delay in administering the *coup de grâce* resulted from William's frantic effort to flee, but the murderer was too fast for the young boy, caught him and wrapped a rope around his neck, then literally hung him. After the boy was dead the murderer put the boy across his knee and, to be certain, broke his neck. He then returned to Elizabeth, who was still alive but completely helpless, and he used the same rope to strangle her to death, and the jurors identified the murderers as the Gilmans.

Elizabeth and William Eationhover were buried at Coquille City while the Gilmans were lodged in the Coquille City jail. They had their examination and were both held over for action by the grand jury, then taken to the jail at the county seat of Empire City. Over the next three months John Gilman confessed every detail of the murders, and said he had decided on July 12 to kill the Eationhovers. He confessed that he used the handle from a hoe to knock Elizabeth semi-conscious before beating her all over her body, and then killing the boy before returning to finish off his mother. He had the two knives in his pocket at the time but did not want to leave bloody evidence in the house. He was confident he could kill the woman and boy without using the knives and held the knives in reserve for Christopher, and planned to kill Christopher outside where the crime scene could be better disguised. He had prepared graves in advance and buried the bodies of the woman and boy before going to the river to wait for Christopher to return home. During this same period Gilman also admitted to the unsolved murder of George Morras, but later recanted that confession. Still, most believed he was responsible for that third killing.

On October 9, 1889, the grand jury indicted John Gilman on two counts of murder. His wife was tried later as an accessory and acquitted. The trial for the murder of William began in Judge R. S. Bean's court in Empire City and the first proceeding was a motion to dismiss, stating that Gilman was insane and should be in the asylum. That motion was overruled, allowing the jury to decide the question of sanity. The trial continued with a parade of witnesses for the prosecution, and several for the defense, which tried to prove the claim of insanity. The case went to the jury on October 16, 1889, and, after brief deliberations, they returned a verdict of "guilty as charged in the indictment—first degree murder." Judge Bean sentenced Gilman to hang on December 13, 1889. Neither appeal nor application for executive clemency intervened.

As the final day approached Sheriff Lintner Harlocker sent out several hundred invitations. The scaffold, a trapdoor model, was built near the jail but it was not enclosed by a high board fence, a practice which had become commonplace in most western states and territories. After 12:30 P.M. on Friday, December 13, 1889, Sheriff Harlocker went to Gilman's cell and read the death warrant. The prisoner was then taken out of his cell and escorted onto the scaffold. All the invited witnesses attended and had crowded around the gallows.

Gilman took his place on the trapdoor and his arms and legs were pinioned. He was asked if he had anything to say but he declined. The black hood was pulled on and the noose adjusted and a moment later the sheriff sprang the trapdoor and Gilman dropped, breaking his neck. Dr. J. A. Simmons assisted by Dr. J. G. Cook monitored Gilman's vital signs and after a brief period pronounced him dead. The body hung long enough to ensure death before it was cut down and placed in the coffin provided by the county. Gilman's wife was still in jail and could not claim his remains, so he was buried in the Empire City cemetery.

Coos Bay Weekly News (Marshfield, OR): July 17–24, 1889; October 16–23, 1889; December 18, 1889. *Coquille City Herald* (OR): October 8, 1889; October 22, 1889; November 5, 1889, December 10, 1889. *Eugene City Guard* (OR): December 21, 1889.

Pellio
June 6, 1890

On May 26, 1889, forty-year-old Pellio and another Umatilla Indian obtained a large quantity of liquor and by evening were very drunk. Pellio decided to ride to the house of sixty-year-old Agnes Taisson, an Umatilla woman living on the reservation. Taisson was rumored to have a large quantity of cash hidden in her house and Pellio was determined to steal it. As they rode along the second Indian fell from his horse and was unable to rise, so Pellio went on alone. Along the way he was seen by Liberty, another Umatilla, who would later testify to Pellio's apparent destination at the time of the murder. At the Taisson house Pellio quietly removed a window and climbed in, but this awoke the elderly woman and she fought hard for her life, tearing at Pellio's clothing and ripping apart the sash he had tied around his waist. Pellio, a large man "often boasted of his prowess in assaulting defenseless women," but he finally had to pull his knife. He slashed and stabbed at the old woman until her body was horribly mutilated, and she bled to death in minutes. Pellio then ransacked the house looking for money or other valuables.

The next day Taisson's grandson arrived, discovered the crime, and notified authorities. Under the body was a piece of bloody sash, and an identical piece of sash was found near the front gate. Outside the space where the window was removed were moccasin tracks, and outside the front yard fence were hoof prints where the murderer had tied his pony. These moccasin and hoof prints were documented and protected from contamination. Suspicion immediately turned to Pellio but he had fled, which further strengthened suspicion. Pellio's pony was found and taken to the Taisson house; the hoofs matched perfectly with the hoof prints of the murderer's animal. A warrant was then issued but Pellio avoided capture for two weeks before he was found, arrested, and lodged in the county jail. His moccasins were taken and compared to the footprints outside the window, and they matched perfectly.

He was indicted on November 27, 1889, and his trial began in mid–January, when ten Indian witnesses and the Umatilla County's coroner, Dr. Donald McKay, sealed his fate with testimony. Although all the evidence was circumstantial, as no one had actually seen him kill Taisson, it was linked carefully until there was no conclusion the jurors could draw but guilty. On February 3, 1890, U.S. Judge Sabin sentenced Pellio to hang on June 6, 1890. It was a federal case so the U.S. Supreme Court and President Benjamin Harrison reviewed the judgment and sentence, and the findings were affirmed so quickly the date of execution was not delayed.

During his final days Pellio was attended by the Reverend Father B. Orth, and the priest was with him his last full day from 11:00 A.M. and returned at the same time on the final day—June 6. U.S. Marshal L. T. Barin had the gallows assembled in the woodshed at the rear of the county jail, the same on which Chee Gong had been hanged, and the trapdoor release was again activated by an electric button. On his final evening the prisoner was visited by a reporter from the *Oregonian* and said,

> To-morrow the world will know me no more. If I have to die I will die like a man and not weaken. I will have to die, I suppose. The great father don't care for an Indian. When Pellio had money he had lots of friends and they wanted to do many favors for him. Now he is poor and has no friends and he will have to die. Nobody cares enough for him to try to save him. A priest was here to-day and told me I could not be saved and would have to die. I told him that if I had killed the woman I would be willing to die at this moment. I don't see what I have to die for. I did not commit murder. I want to be hanged at Pendleton

> where I can see my friends. If I had killed the woman I would not want to face my friends. The blood found on my clothes and which the officers said was from the woman's wounds was from a cut on my foot made with an axe. I am innocent.

Pellio then paused before he concluded, "Pellio is sleepy now. This is his last chance. To-morrow he will go to sleep never to awake."

On June 6 all was tested and in readiness when at 12:15 Pellio finished his dinner meal and was told the time was near. Deputy Mizner informed the prisoner that he would have to be manacled, but he objected saying, "No good hang me. If I be bad, then yes. But me good. Me no kill him this woman. You kill me for nothing. I want you shoot me." At 12:57 P.M. the procession formed in front of Pellio's cell door with sheriffs Kelly and Waltrus escorting the prisoner and jailor James leading the way. In the woodshed were sixty witnesses and Pellio said to them, interpreted by deputy Mizner, "I am an innocent man. I never killed that woman, and I don't want to be hung. Better you shoot me. Now I am going to die. I don't want to be buried here. If I had killed the woman then it would be all right to bury me here. I want to be buried with my wife and children at home. To all of you my friends I have nothing more to say. I die for nothing."

He shook hands with deputy Mizner and then the condemned man repeated the confessional with Father Orth. Jailor James quickly manacled Pellio's wrists and ankles while deputy sheriff Witherell adjusted the noose and pulled on the black hood. The trap was sprung at 1:15 P.M. and Drs. D. H. Rand, Eisen and Booth monitored vital signs until Pellio's heart ceased to beat and they pronounced him dead. Pellio had expressed the desire to be buried with his wife and children but there was no claim for the body. According to Oregon law, Judge Deady had assigned the body to Dr. Canthron or the University of Oregon medical school for dissection.

Oregonian (Portland): June 6–7, 1890.

Ming How
January 8, 1892

On October 1, 1891, Grant County Sheriff Oliver P. Cresap was on his way down river on business when he was hailed by a party of Chinese men near Chinatown just below John Day. They had in custody a fellow Chinaman who had been badly treated, and they reported that their prisoner had murdered a countryman. The prisoner gave his name as Ah Hy as he quickly climbed into the sheriff's buckboard, apparently more afraid he would be lynched by his fellow countrymen than he was afraid of being arrested. Cresap turned around and returned to Canyon City, where the prisoner was lodged in jail, and later his prisoner disclosed that his true name was Ming How. The legal papers were prepared in the name of Ming How and he was given his examination the following day, Saturday. The prisoner was held without bail to answer to the grand jury on a charge of murder.

Testimony at the examination revealed that Ming How and Ah Foo lived with a half dozen fellow miners in a house located three quarters of a mile below Chinatown. On the evening of September 30 all the men had been gambling and when they returned home all went to bed except Ming How and Ah Foo. Whether it was some matter that arose then or from an earlier argument, Ming How suddenly drew his knife and attacked Ah Foo. Ming How cut and slashed at Ah Foo, causing deep cuts and gashes in his arms, chest and face, but Ah Foo, was unarmed and rather than fight off the attacker he tried to crawl under a table for protection. Ming How, however, took this opportunity to slash and stab at Ah Foo's lower extremities, causing such deep wounds that he soon bled to death. Ah Foo managed to pull the knife from Ming How's grip and was holding it tightly when discovered. Ming How stood nearby calmly waiting for Ah Foo to die, but the commotion aroused the other men in the house and they rushed to Ah Foo's rescue, and as the wounded man lay dying he was asked who murdered him. He could not speak but he managed to point to Ming How. Ah Foo then died and Ming How, who was splattered with blood, was taken prisoner by the other Chinese men and held until morning, when they encountered the sheriff on their way to town.

Ming How was indicted for first degree murder in early November and at his arraignment he entered a plea of not guilty. The prisoner had no funds so W. B. Ellis was appointed as his defense attorney. By November 19 the trial had been concluded and Ming How was found "guilty as charged in the indictment." He was sentenced to hang on January 8, 1892, and neither appeal nor application for executive clemency would delay the proceedings.

As Ming How awaited the fatal day all his countrymen deserted him and he had no visitors, so not speaking English, he was unable to converse with anyone for days at a time. The time for the execution had been set for 2:00 P.M. and as the hour approached the death warrant was read to him in the jail and then Ming How was taken from his cell and accompanied up the jail stairs into the enclosure by Sheriff Cresap, deputy Yorgonson, and his interpreter, Lung On. Once on the trapdoor Lung On asked if Ming How had anything to say and the prisoner, in a trembling voice, said, "I kill him, but I got nothing to say."

His arms were pinioned and his knees and ankles were secured with straps, the noose was adjusted, and the black hood was pulled over his head. At that moment Ming How began to collapse and deputy Yorgonson supported the condemned man until Sheriff Cresap pressed the button which sprang the trap. Ming How was a small man so he had been allowed a seven foot drop, but even this was not enough to break his neck. His body convulsed violently and swayed like a pendulum until Drs. Ashford and Fell took hold of a wrist and steadied him, and it took some time before the doctors pronounced him dead. The body was cut down, put into a pine coffin provided by the county, and turned over to Tom Reynolds. The body was then conveyed to a place just outside the walls of the town cemetery and laid to rest in an unmarked grave.

Grant County News (OR): October 7, 1891; November 12–19, 1891; January 14, 1892.

Zorn, Frederick
August 19, 1892

Frederick "Fritz" Zorn, a German, had been drinking heavily for some months as a result of his divorce from his wife in July 1891. The court awarded her their farm while he took eight hundred dollars in the settlement and Mrs. Summers, his ex-wife's mother, then moved in with her daughter. At noon on Saturday, October 3, 1891, Zorn, in a drunken condition, went to the farm house located seven miles south of town, argued with his ex-wife, and threatened her life. He would not leave, continued his heavy drinking, and as his condition worsened he began to flourish a pistol and repeated his threats to shoot his ex-wife. The two women tried to get control of the pistol but Zorn shot his wife in the breast and side and his mother-in-law in the arm. Zorn then lay down on the bed and went to sleep.

Sheriff McFarland and a physician were summoned to the house and when the lawman arrived Zorn shot himself in the mouth, attempting suicide, but he failed. Zorn was arrested and all three wounded parties were taken into town and placed in the hospital under the continuous care of a doctor, but as soon as Zorn's condition permitted he was removed to a jail cell. Mrs. Zorn's wound was deemed mortal so her deathbed statement was recorded by a notary public on October 4. Meanwhile Zorn talked freely of the shooting and did not deny it. Mrs. Zorn lingered for thirty days before succumbing to her wound and Zorn was then charged with her murder. Zorn's mother-in-law, though only having a slight flesh wound, died several months later from old age, the trauma of being wounded, and the depression caused by the loss of her daughter.

There was a delay in taking action against

the murderer because of his medical condition but Zorn was finally indicted, tried for killing his wife, and convicted of first degree murder. He was sentenced to hang on August 19, 1892, and, to prevent a lynching or escape, he was taken to the penitentiary to await the fatal day. The proceedings were neither delayed by appeal nor by application for clemency from Governor William P. Lord.

The condemned man held up well during his days in prison and was visited by many men and women. On the day before the execution Zorn was shaved by J. F. Robinson, who was afraid he might seize the razor to kill himself, but Zorn promised not to interfere and he was not handcuffed. On his final night he played cards with his death watch guards until 1:00 A.M. and then read his Bible before retiring. He arose at 6:00 A.M., got dressed in his new suit of black diagonal provided by the sheriff, and at 8:00 A.M. he ate a hearty breakfast of sausage, eggs, tomatoes, and coffee. At 11:00 A.M. a photographer arrived to take his picture and an hour later everyone without an invitation was evicted and the doors were closed. At 1:30 P.M. Drs. F. E. Smith and R. J. Pilkington visited to check on Zorn's condition and found him in good spirits. A half hour later the Reverends C. T. Whittlesey and T. S Dulin arrived to give religious support. When the prisoner was led out of his cell he was allowed to telephone Mrs. J. H. Stahl of Walla Walla to bid her farewell, and he had earlier said that his written statement was in the hands of George Retzeer of that same town in Washington.

He was handcuffed and led down the basement stairs to the execution chamber. The handcuffs were removed as he was seated on the platform and sheriff William Furnish read the death warrant. Furnish then asked Zorn if he had anything to say and he replied, "No, I bid you all good-bye. I hope we meet sometime in a better place." The officers on the scaffold shook hands with Zorn, who turned to Furnish and said, "I am well satisfied with your treatment." Straps were then applied to pinion his arms to his body; his knees and ankles were also secured by straps. The noose was positioned with the knot behind Zorn's left ear, and the prisoner said, "Well, Billy, this is a pretty tough way to die, isn't it?" The black hood was pulled over his head as he mumbled prayers for Jesus to take his soul.

At 2:11 P.M. Sheriff Furnish said, "Frederick Zorn, prepare to meet your God." The release lever was pulled at the sheriff's signal by the anonymous executioner in the next room, and the body fell six feet breaking Zorn's neck, and there was not a quiver noticeable. Attending physicians Vincent and Guion, assisted by Smith and Pilkington, timed the pulse and pronounced him dead in nineteen minutes. After hanging a while longer the body was cut down and given to the undertakers, who had instructions to ship the remains to Walla Walla, Washington, where friends would see to the burial. The dozen witnesses then signed the death certificate and the execution chamber was cleared.

Oregonian (Portland): August 20, 1892. *Spokane Review* (WA): October 4–5, 1891.

Gallin, F. W.
July 14, 1893

In early March 1893 the dead body of Alfred W. Shaw, a well-to-do Grant County, Oregon, rancher, was reportedly found by hired hand F. W. Gallin in a stall where a stallion was tethered. Shaw's skull had been thoroughly fractured and this was determined to be the cause of his death. The county coroner was summoned and he empanelled a jury for an inquest. After taking testimony from Gallin and Shaw's widow, Lina, it was concluded that the death was accidental and that Shaw had been kicked to death by the horse. However, suspicion of foul play was raised when Gallin immediately took Shaw's place "at his bed and board." The authorities decided to make a more thorough investigation into the matter and, on closer examination, the floor of the barn revealed blood stains in a different area buried beneath a layer of straw. This seemed to prove conclusively that Shaw had been killed at a place other than the stall and his body carried to the spot where it was found, and it suggested that Lina Shaw and Gallin were involved in his death.

On Tuesday, March 11, the couple was arrested on suspicion of murder and lodged in jail. Lina Shaw and the body of her husband were taken to Baker City and by Friday evening, March 14, the widow confessed that she had been intimate with Gallin. She said that the hired hand had killed her husband with a hammer and then carried his body into the barn. The remains were laid down where the blood stains were found while the stall was being prepared, and then the body was deposited in the stall with the stallion. Gallin had then sent a boy to town to report that Shaw had been kicked to death by the horse, and while the youngster was away he burned the handle of the hammer and threw the head of the hammer into a deep snow drift. The head of the hammer was found where described and held for evidence. Gallin and Lina Shaw were indicted for murder and the sensational trial was held at the spring term of the court. Lina was acquitted but Gallin was found guilty of murder in the first degree and sentenced to hang on July 14, 1893, and neither appeal nor application for executive clemency would delay the proceedings.

On Gallin's last night he confessed but his version varied from that of Lina Shaw. He said that the couple were quarreling loudly over her infidelity with Gallin and when the hired hand went into the house Mr. Shaw pulled a revolver and threatened to shoot them both. He said he had a hammer in his hand and struck the single, fatal blow, but then he and Lina beat on Shaw's head, careful to make it look like it was done by a horse's hooves, and he and Lina working together disposed of the body.

The execution was managed by Grant County Sheriff Joseph D. Coombs, who had the scaffold built within an enclosure in the jail yard at Canyon City. When the time arrived the sheriff read the death warrant at the cell door and then the condemned man was escorted out of the jail and onto the scaffold, where his wrists and arms, knees and ankles were pinioned by deputies. He was asked if he had anything to say to the witnesses and he spoke briefly, "imploring the forgiveness of the world." The noose was adjusted and the black hood was pulled on as he prayed loudly, and in mid-sentence the trap was sprung. Gallin dropped straight down, breaking his neck in the fall. The attending physicians rushed forward and began monitoring vital signs, and when his heart ceased to beat they pronounced him dead. The body hung a while longer before it was cut down and placed in the coffin provided by the county, and Gallin was buried that evening.

Daily Citizen (IA): March 20, 1893. *Daily Tribune* (Salt Lake City, UT): July 22, 1893. *Hamilton Daily Democrat* (OH): March 16, 1893. *Reno Weekly Gazette* (NV): March 23, 1893. *Woodland Daily Democrat* (CA): July 18, 1893. *State of Oregon vs. F. W. Gallin*, Grant County Circuit Court Case #1694.

Reiter, John R.
December 1, 1893

Otto Johansen ran a boarding house on his farm near Olney, Clatsop County, Oregon. On August 4, 1893, he inventoried his supplies and decided he needed to restock. He gave his employee, twenty-five-year-old John Victor Snellman, twenty-two dollars in gold to buy the supplies in Olney the following day. That evening John R. Reiter stopped to ask for work but finding none was invited to spend the night and have supper and breakfast before moving on. The next morning Johansen and Gustaf Adolph left at an early hour on another errand, leaving Snellman and Reiter eating breakfast.

For the next week Johansen expected Snellman to return at any time with his supplies, but finally he became suspicious and contacted Sheriff H. A Smith at Astoria. Smith could find no clue to the young man's disappearance until August 19, when John Duncan and Louis Brazee smelled a decomposing body in a remote area near Green Mountain, not far from Olney off the Military Road. It could have been an animal but the men investigated and discovered the remains of Snellman. He had been struck on the right side of his head three times and had three deep gashes in his abdomen, so deep that his intestines were exposed. Dr. William C. Pohl, the county coroner, examined the remains and set the date of death at August 5, the same day Snellman left the farm for town. Suspicion immediately fell on Reiter, as he had been the last man known to see Snellman alive.

Sheriff Smith circulated Reiter's description widely and, to ensure prompt action, offered a reward of two hundred dollars for his capture. Smith traced Reiter to Portland and dispatched two deputies who could recognize the fugitive: Dell Moore and Bill Kohler. They were met by Portland detective Henry Griffin, who had been keeping a close watch on Reiter, and they arrested him while he was washing dishes at the Terminus Restaurant. Griffin had also traced a watch, pawned by Reiter when he first arrived in Portland, and it was identified as belonging to Snellman. Reiter was returned to Astoria and lodged in the county jail and by August 23 he had confessed, twice. First he said he and Snellman started for Olney together and along the way he met "a shipmate who done the killing." In his second confession he admitted that it was he who had "knocked Snellman over the head with a stone and cut him afterwards and took all his money. I cut him with this knife, with the small blade. I was afraid that after I took his money and he was not dead that he would have me arrested for taking his money."

Reiter had his preliminary examination on August 27 and was held over for the grand jury. They met on September 21 and indicted Reiter on a charge of premeditated murder. The trial began on September 30 in Liberty Hall, because interest was running so high the audience was too large for the courtroom. Judge Thomas A. McBride presided over the trial, which lasted one day and resulted, after less than a half hour of deliberations, in a verdict of "guilty as charged in the indictment." The defendant was sentenced to hang on December 1, 1893, and Reiter was supposed to hang with another murderer, but the other man was reprieved while nothing interfered with Reiter's date with the hangman. Another murderer lodged in the Astoria jail, John Hansen, also had his name on the invitations sent to witnesses.

The scaffold was erected in an enclosure in the jail yard and had a wide trapdoor which was designed to accommodate two men, and was five feet nine inches above the ground. The trapdoor release was an electric switch activated by a button beneath the carpeting covering the platform. Early on the morning of the execution Sheriff Smith delivered Reiter's burial suit, and the prisoner washed and dressed after breakfast. At 11:00 A.M. the doors to the enclosure were opened and the huge crowd of witnesses rushed in, vying for the best positions near the scaffold.

Sheriff Smith then went to the cell and read the death warrant, and at 11:52 A.M. the condemned man was escorted out of the jail, into the enclosure, and onto the platform. The prisoner's arms were already tied behind his back as he was positioned on the trapdoor; his legs were then tied together and weights were attached to his ankles. He was not asked if he had anything to say, apparently having declined earlier, so the noose was adjusted and the black hood was pulled on. Sheriff Smith immediately tapped at the switch but missed and tapped again. The trap was sprung and Reiter shot downward breaking his neck. The weights were excessive and stretched the neck two inches, nearly decapitating the prisoner. Dr. William C. Pohl, the county coroner, pronounced him dead after a few minutes and took possession of the body after it was cut down. Reiter was buried in the pauper's cemetery that evening, at county expense.

Astorian (OR): August 20–27, 1893; September 3, 1893; October 3, 1893; December 8, 1893. *Oregonian* (Portland): August 23, 1893; September 30, 1893; December 2, 1893.

Hansen, John
May 18, 1894

Fifty-six-year-old John Hansen was an eccentric, probably due to dissipation from alcohol abuse. He lived with his wife of thirty-one years, Caroline, on a farm twelve miles from Astoria, Oregon, near the mouth of the Columbia River in Clatsop County. Hansen, when he worked, fished the Columbia River and sold his catch in Astoria. Often, when he had money, he went on a spree that could last many days and he would return home penniless. He and his wife constantly argued over money, especially the way he squandered it on liquor rather than paying their bills. On July 9, 1893, Hansen disappeared, as he often did, but by July 23 his wife became worried and asked a neighbor to row to Astoria, which had to be reached by boat, and search for him. The neighbor did not have to look far. Hansen was passed out on his boat, which was tied to the Astoria pier. As soon as Hansen was able the neighbor put him on a course for home, and he got no argument, as Hansen had spent every penny and had no more money for liquor. John Hansen was in a terrible state but by Monday evening, the following day, he was out in his boat again fishing for a stake to continue his spree. On Tuesday morning he was still too sick to eat but managed to down a medicinal portion of whiskey.

On Friday, July 27, Hansen returned home from fishing and was about to sleep when his wife threatened that if he didn't go to work she would kill him, or so he claimed later, but said he had no reason to take her seriously and went to bed. He arose late in the afternoon and went outside to look for Caroline and once again they argued over money, and then she told him to help her pick raspberries. He refused, so she told him to leave, and when he said no she threw a rock at him but missed. Here the fight ended and she returned to her berry picking.

Lying nearby was a heavy stick "to change the calf in the pasture" and Hansen picked up the stick and struck Caroline on the head so hard that she fell to the ground and shortly died of a crushed skull. An hour later Hansen found John Nyland, a boarder at the Hansen farm, and told him Caroline was dead and that a number of men had beaten her to death to get her money. Nyland went to the house and checked on Caroline's cash drawer, which she always kept locked to prevent her husband from taking the money for liquor. The drawer was open and the contents gone, including money Nyland had given Caroline to hold. He complained to Hansen and was told that his money was safe, and the next time he checked the drawer he found his money had been returned plus $5, so Nyland rowed to Astoria to inform the authorities.

Coroner William C. Pohl, with the couple's son Victor Hansen and an inquest jury, went to the Hansen farm and determined that Caroline had died by the hand of her husband. Hansen and his wife's body were taken to Astoria, Caroline to the morgue while Hansen was lodged in jail charged with her murder. When authorities searched Hansen, who had been penniless after his last spree, he had $52.25 in his pockets. Hundreds of people were allowed to view Caroline's remains and on January 28, the day of Caroline's funeral, Hansen was escorted to the cemetery where he tenderly kissed his wife's forehead just before she was lowered into her grave. The prisoner was then returned to his cell to await action by the grand jury.

As Hansen sat brooding over what he had done, he decided he should confess, so on February 1 he gave all the details of the killing. His confession was written down for him and after reading through the document he signed it. Hansen was indicted in mid–September and the trial began in Judge Thomas McBride's courtroom on September 27, 1893. The defendant pled not guilty by reason of insanity and a number of witnesses came forward to describe his bizarre behavior, but odd behavior is not insanity and local doctors Jay Tuttle and W. D. Baker testified he was sane. Perhaps the most difficult evidence to overcome in establishing insanity was that, after murdering his wife, Hansen had the presence of mind to take a key from Caroline's dead body and use it to take the money from her locked cash drawer and, after he was challenged, he returned Nyland's money to the drawer. The judge gave an instruction that it was the duty of the defense to prove insanity, and if they had failed in their duty the jury could find Hansen guilty of premeditated murder, and this was later one basis for an appeal.

The jury retired at 10:30 P.M. and deliberated less than ninety minutes before returning a verdict of "guilty as charged in the indictment—first degree murder." When the defendant was returned to court he was sentenced to hang on December 1, 1893. An appeal gave the condemned man an automatic stay of execution but the state Supreme Court, after hearing arguments, upheld the lower court's decision on February 19, 1894. Hansen was resentenced to hang on May 18, 1894.

The scaffold, the same which had been used twice before, had an ingenious electric release for the trapdoor and was erected within an enclosure near the jail. This enclosure was small and it took some crowding to get the fifty witnesses inside, but there were more than one thousand people crowding the hills and buildings surrounding the enclosure and peeking through knot holes in the fencing. That morning the condemned man had eaten a hearty breakfast and then received the Reverend Short and his son, who gave him religious consolation. At 11:30 A.M. Clatsop County Sheriff H. A. Smith read the death warrant to the prisoner in his cell and then the procession was formed. They walked out of the side door of the jail directly into the enclosure where the condemned man, Sheriff Smith, and the Reverend Short joined several men on the scaffold, and the prisoner took his place on the trapdoor.

There seems to be no record of a speech so he may have declined when asked, which was a standard procedure even when the prisoner had already said he would not speak. His arms and legs were pinioned with straps, the noose was adjusted, and the black hood was pulled on. The party stood quite still and silent for a few moments, until the noon whistle blew, and then Sheriff Smith touched the button and the trapdoor opened. Hansen shot downward, breaking his neck, and in a few minutes the county physician, Dr. William C. Pohl, assisted by several other doctors, began monitoring vital signs and soon pronounced him dead. Hansen's remains were cut down, placed in a coffin, and taken to the morgue for an autopsy. Afterward the body was turned over to his son, Victor Hansen, for burial next to Caroline.

Astorian (OR): August 31, 1893; September 24, 1893; September 28–29, 1893; October 3, 1893, May 18, 1894. *Oregonian* (Portland): September 29, 1893; May 19, 1894.

Montgomery, Lloyd B.
January 31, 1896

Lloyd Bryson Montgomery, sometimes Loyal Montgomery, lived on his father's farm and had never been out of Linn County, Oregon, during his eighteen years. On November 19, 1895, Lloyd's father and mother, and a visitor named Dan McKercher, were murdered at the farm. Lloyd had a heated argument with his father that morning during which his father had slapped the boy's face and ordered him to chop wood. At 4:30 P.M. Lloyd's father was standing by the corner of the corral fence talking with hop buyer Fred Gilkey when Daniel McKercher arrived and joined the elder Montgomery and Gilkey. Gilkey soon concluded his business and left, and about that time Lloyd's mother went into the yard. Lloyd then snuck into the house and got his rifle, took up a position at the front door, and shot his father dead where he stood. His mother tried to run and he shot her dead, as well. McKercher ran for the house and Lloyd shot at him, but missed, then shot a second time, killing him just as he reached the door.

Lloyd was immediately suspected of the crime and arrested. He vigorously denied the killings, but after several days in jail he broke down and confessed. He said he was so angry after having his face slapped that he did not know what he was doing and, after he fired the first shot, could not stop himself until all three people were dead. Lloyd was tried in District Court in December, convicted of first degree murder, and sentenced to hang on January 31, 1896. His attorney filed a motion for a new trial but this was denied, and no appeals were submitted nor petitions filed for a respite or commutation of sentence.

After the youngster was sentenced to die he changed his story to say that Dan McKercher came to visit while his father was busy outside talking with a hops buyer and his mother was in the house. McKercher asked him what kind of guns they had and Lloyd brought his father's rifle for him to examine. He said he went to the woodshed, where the pump was located, to get a drink of water. At that time his mother went to see her husband at the corner of the corral fence while McKercher looked out the front door. Lloyd said he heard a shot and thought it was an accidental discharge, but when he heard a second shot he became concerned, and at that moment his mother ran toward him screaming, "Help, Lloyd, Help! He is killing us!" The boy said he ran into the house through the kitchen door, got his own rifle, and shot McKercher dead to protect his parents. Lloyd held up well during his incarceration and kept to this self-serving version of innocence.

On his last night he at first refused to sleep and talked with his guards and visitors, practicing the well rehearsed alibi of his defense of his parents. He played "Home, Sweet Home" on his violin, then grew sleepy, retired and slept soundly until 4:20 A.M., when he had to be shaken hard to wake up. A half hour before his execution a cell mate named Fox and his neighbor Joseph Hume of Brownsville urged him to confess and he admitted the killings, then wrote out his confession: "I did it. I am guilty. Oh, God have mercy on me. Take me. I am a poor sinner. I am sorry for what I have done. God, do have mercy on my poor soul; for my sake do, and forgive all my sins, each and every one of them, and forgive those who sinned against me. Oh, God, help the precious souls to see the way of life for my sake. Do help them and guide them through this life. Amen. Lloyd Montgomery."

There were several ministers in his cell, and after he confessed they prayed with him fervently, and he was very contrite and wept bitterly. At 7:00 A.M. Sheriff James A. McFeron announced that his time had come and led the prisoner into the corridor where he said, "I want you people to know I am sorry for what I have done. I am ready to die. I deserve it." The death warrant was read by the sheriff and he and three deputies escorted the prisoner onto the scaffold. The prisoner stepped onto the platform and, advancing to the trapdoor, said, "Friends, I am sorry for what I have done and hope you will all forgive me, and I hope the Lord will be with you. I am guilty and I ask God to have mercy on me as a poor sinner, and I ask you to pray for me." An earnest prayer was delivered by the Reverend J. E. Snyder, after which the prisoner's arms and legs were pinioned. He looked up at the sky and then scanned the landscape as he said, "Oh, Christ forgive me, and I hope you will all meet in heaven, and I ask God to take me as I am."

The sheriff adjusted the black hood and rope, then the boy said, through the black cloth, "Oh, God, have mercy on me, a sinner. Take me as I am. My friends, farewell, farewell!" When he stopped talking the sheriff quickly touched the trigger and Montgomery shot downward six feet. There was only one slight tremor, as the drop had broken his neck. The attending physician took a wrist and at fourteen minutes Montgomery's heart ceased to beat, and two minutes later the condemned man was pronounced dead. The body was cut down and placed in the courthouse for a short time before being turned over to the physicians for an autopsy. His relatives refused to take the body or bury it, so it was placed in a plain wooden coffin provided by the county, driven to the local cemetery the following day, and buried in a pauper's grave.

Seattle Times (WA): January 31, 1896. *State's Rights Democrat* (Albany, OR): January 31, 1896.

Albrecht, Carl
June 26, 1896

Carl Albrecht and his wife, living at Marshfield, Oregon, had been having difficulties for years because "as his right as head of household" Albrecht demanded every cent his wife earned by taking in washing, and required her to support him. Albrecht was, at times, very cruel to his wife and when, in early February 1896, Albrecht suspected his wife had withheld some of her earnings, they argued and he beat her. On February 10 she left him and over the next week Albrecht tried by every means to convince his wife to return to their home. He began by gentle coaxing but as the days passed his approach deteriorated to threats of violence and finally threats of murder. On February 17 he declared to others that he would try one last time to get his wife back and, if she refused him again, he would kill her.

On February 18 Mrs. Albrecht spent the day doing the laundry for John Preuss' family in South Marshfield and was returning to her new home with a basket of clothes for her daughter. Albrecht confronted his wife and she asked him to go away and leave her alone, but he would not, so she fled to the home of Judge Watson. When she thought it safe she again started toward her home but her husband had lain in wait and sprang upon her. A Mrs. Cox tried to intercede to protect Mrs. Albrecht but Albrecht placed his hand on his hip pocket as if about to draw a pistol, so Mrs. Cox stepped aside. Albrecht then walked up to his wife, who had turned to leave, drew his pistol and placed it against her back, and fired a single round. Mrs. Albrecht collapsed and lay helpless as her husband emptied his five shot revolver into her body, and she bled to death in seconds.

He then turned the empty pistol on himself as if to commit suicide, but suddenly turned and ran. William Webster followed at a safe distance and pointed out Albrecht's hiding place to Marshal Elrod, and the officer ordered Albrecht to raise his hands. The fugitive raised one hand but pointed his revolver at the officer with the other. Elrod shot at Albrecht three times, one bullet striking his right hip, one bullet striking his right shoulder, and the third bullet missing its mark as Albrecht collapsed and was disarmed. He was lodged in the Marshfield jail where a doctor treated his wounds.

The prisoner was taken to Empire City and tried in early May, convicted of first degree murder on May 8, and sentenced to hang on June 26, 1896. During the next weeks the condemned murderer attempted to commit suicide once and managed to escape once, but he was quickly recaptured. Neither appeal nor petition for executive clemency delayed the execution.

An enclosure was built in the courthouse yard and within it was erected the high gallows. The Reverend Esbjorn of the German Lutheran Church attended to the prisoner during those last weeks. The condemned man was asked if he would "make the words of the penitent thief his own," and he promised he would. He said his greatest concern was whether he would be reunited with his wife in heaven.

At 9:30 A.M. Sheriff Gage, with the coroner's jury and newspaper reporters in attendance, read the death warrant at the cell door. The prisoner was then brought out and escorted onto the scaffold by two jailors and positioned on the trapdoor. While his wrists and arms, knees and ankles were being bound, he told several hundred spectators that he was sorry he murdered his wife and deserved his fate. The noose was adjusted and the black hood was pulled over his head at 9:55 A.M. and in a moment Sheriff Gage sprang the trap. Albrecht dropped eight feet, breaking his neck, but this was followed by slight muscle contractions for several minutes. In thirteen minutes the attending physician pronounced him dead and the body was cut down, deposited in a coffin, and buried.

Oregonian (Portland): June 27, 1896.

Melson, Lemuel W.
July 2, 1897

Fifty-year-old Charles Perry arrived in Oregon in July 1895, leaving his wife and seven children in Connecticut, and took employment with the Waldo Copper Mine. He was hoping to strike it rich before he returned home, but at least he was able to support his family with the wages he was earning and he accrued a small fortune which he carried with him at all times. He met forty-two-year-old Lemuel W. Melson while working at the mine and Melson often talked of a fine prospect he had located between the coast and the Siskiyou Mountains when he had come north from California.

In March 1896 Perry, still hoping for a rich find which would allow him an early return to his family, decided he would go south with Melson and prospect the claim. Melson and Perry left for the mountains but the following day Melson returned, saying that Perry had gone on to the town of Waldo, and then Melson left for Crescent City, California. After months with no sign of Perry his friends began to question the circumstances of his disappearance. On August 25 Perry's friends formed a search party and started for the Siskiyou Mountains. On August 27 they found Perry's remains at the bottom of an abandoned well near a deserted mining claim, just north of the boundary with California. Perry had died from a .41-caliber bullet wound to his right side, which had ripped through his bowels and intestines but may have allowed him to linger for some time. The bullet casing was lying on the ground nearby and was collected for evidence.

The party immediately suspected Melson, went to Crescent City to investigate and learned that in July Melson had sold a .41-caliber Colt revolver to a merchant in Crescent City, and this weapon proved to be the one which killed Perry. They also discovered that Melson, who had been known to have very limited means, began spending freely as soon as he arrived in Crescent City. When Melson was arrested on this evidence it was found that he carried a watch which was identified, by the initials engraved on it, as belonging to Perry. The location of the murder was in Oregon, so, with a requisition from Oregon Governor William P. Lord, Melson was taken to Grant's Pass and lodged in jail. At his examination he was held over for action by the grand jury, and he was indicted during the first week of May 1897.

On May 8 his trial began in Judge H. K. Hanna's courtroom, and testimony began on Monday, May 10, and lasted through Tuesday. Late the second day the jurors began deliberations and quickly returned a verdict of guilty of murder in the first degree. On May 14, 1897, Melson stood before Judge Hanna and heard his sentence of death by hanging. The date set for the execution was July 2, 1897.

As the date for the hanging approached an enclosure was raised near the jail. The gallows had been built for another murderer but the case of Charles Fiester had been delayed by an appeal, so the scaffold was assembled for Melson. An application had been submitted to the state Supreme Court for a stay of execution but it was rejected, and Governor Lord refused to grant a respite or a commutation of sentence. Melson had a wife and three children, but his wife would not visit him in jail, though they exchanged letters regularly.

On the day before the execution Melson's wish to attend the Episcopal Church was granted and he was baptized by the Reverend Isaac Dawson. On his final night he read his Bible and wrote letters before retiring at a late hour. He slept soundly, arose early, and ate a hearty breakfast before the Reverend Dawson, with church members, came to the jail to pray and sing hymns. Melson sat, quietly weeping, and at this moment he confessed to the Reverend Dawson, admitting the murder of Perry but denying other murders which had been rumored.

County Sheriff Joseph G. Hiatt had issued fifty invitations to the hanging but more than five hundred people gathered outside the enclosure. They were permitted to watch the event by removing a number of boards from the fence, defeating the purpose of the enclosure. A few minutes before 10:00 A.M. Sheriff Hiatt went to Melson's jail cell and, with the Reverend Dawson, escorted the condemned man from the jail onto the scaffold. Once Melson was standing on the trapdoor the death warrant was read and then his arms and legs were pinioned and the noose adjusted. The sheriff asked, "Melson, have you anything you wish to say?" and Melson muttered in a low voice, "I killed Perry." The black hood was then pulled over his head and the sheriff stepped back, saying, "Good-bye, Melson." At 10:13 A.M. the trap was sprung and Melson dropped through, breaking his neck. He was pronounced dead in minutes and at 10:25 A.M. the body was cut down and placed in a pine coffin provided by the county. That evening Melson was buried in a potter's field outside Grants Pass at county expense, following a brief service by the Reverend Dawson.

Oregonian (Portland): July 1–3, 1897.

Porter, Kelsey
November 20, 1897

Forty-seven-year-old Kelsey Porter was a reclusive, and perhaps a bit of an eccentric, but he was not unfriendly and was liked by his neighbors. He had lived in the remote Pine Valley of Union County, Oregon, for years. He continually improved his property with a number of buildings, including corrals for his cows, a house, a barn, and a shed. In late 1896 the Mache family—Joseph, wife Mary, and their seventeen-year-old son Benjamin—moved into Pine Valley. There were a number of routes established for them to drive to Pine, the nearest population center, but the most direct route was right through Porter's property passing within a few feet of his barn. The Mache's persisted in taking this route so Porter extended his fence across the trail to block them, but they just tore it down, which let his cows out, and they continued to trespass. Porter contacted the authorities but the local justice of the peace insisted that the law could do nothing.

Ex-convict William "Six Shooter" Rockwood was staying with the Mache family, so he and Joseph went to the Porter farm and fired several shots at Porter as he worked in his field. Ben, who fancied himself a "gunslinger," may have been with them. They could easily have wounded or killed Porter but they did not want to give the law any reason to interfere, so they missed him closely. Porter ran into his house and hid and, according to Porter, he was then afraid for his life so he borrowed a Winchester rifle and kept it close at hand.

On New Year's Day 1896 the Mache family, Joseph and Mary, were returning home in a sleigh pulled by a team of two horses with their son riding his horse behind. Porter said he had left his rifle inside his house while he cleared heavy snow from the roof of a shed next to the barn and as the Mache family passed nearby Porter yelled at them, "Put the fence back up and keep off my land!" Joseph reined in his team and yelled back, "You lie! This is a public highway. If you fence it up again, we will kill you." Porter later said that Benjamin Mache, taking his parents' lead, rode close to the shed and fired several shots at Porter, apparently missing on purpose. Porter climbed down and ran for the house, as he had done when shot at in his field, much to the amusement of the Maches. However, this time, according to Porter, he reappeared with the Winchester rifle and fired wildly, but with sixteen rounds to expend he managed to place several bullets where they would do the most good. Benjamin was mortally wounded, which knocked him from his horse, and Porter also shot Joseph twice and Mary once. He wounded one horse from their team which bolted at the sound of rapid rifle fire and ran a short distance before the wounded horse dropped dead from blood loss. The sudden stopping of the sleigh, four hundred feet from the barn, threw Joseph's body into a creek where he received a fatal skull fracture.

Porter rode into Pine and surrendered to the justice of the peace and then, accompanied by a small party of neighbors, returned to his farm to wait for the authorities.

Deputy sheriff J. H. McLachlin arrived with Dr. E. R. Lang, the county coroner, and after investigating they held an inquest and found that Porter had acted criminally, and seemed to indicate a different scenario than he had related. The evidence showed that Porter had cleared the snow from a small portion of the shed roof and lay in wait. When the Mache family came along he shot Ben, who was over three hundred feet from the barn, much too distant for his pistol fire to be any threat, and it was supposed his pistol fire was probably in self-defense after being shot at. It also appeared that Joseph and Mary tried to flee but Mary and one horse were shot. Porter followed on foot, finding Mary dead from a bullet wound and still in the sleigh, and Joseph lying in the creek with two bullet wounds and a fractured skull.

Porter was arrested and at his examination he was held over for action by the grand jury. On February 4, Porter was indicted on three counts of first degree murder. His neighbors, who disliked the Mache family, subscribed funds to pay for good defense lawyers, but while Porter was awaiting his trial the bodies of the Mache family were exhumed and an autopsy revealed that Joseph Mache had died from having his skull crushed, and that the two bullet wounds came after his death. The wound to his head was determined to have come from the butt of Porter's Winchester rifle, and afterward Porter had shot him twice, perhaps even reloading the sixteen shot rifle to get the work done.

Porter's trial began in Judge Robert Eakins' courtroom on February 12, 1897, and the prosecution decided to try the defendant for the murder of Ben Mache first, and hold the other two indictments in reserve until they knew the outcome of the first trial. The case went to the jurors at 10:00 P.M. Saturday and by 9:30 the next morning they had reached a verdict of "guilty as charged in the indictment—first degree murder." Porter was sentenced to hang on April 10, 1897, but an appeal acted as an automatic stay of execution. When the state Supreme Court denied, the appeal an application to Governor William P. Lord, with a petition signed by five hundred men, was submitted and rejected. The new date for Porter's execution was set at November 19, 1897, and as the date approached the issue of insanity was raised, and the prisoner was examined by three doctors who pronounced him sane.

An enclosure was built in the yard of the Union County jail and the gallows was erected within. At a few minutes before 6:00 A.M. the prisoner was taken from his cell and escorted to the scaffold by Sheriff J. F. Phy and the Presbyterian Reverend Shields. He stood on the trapdoor as the death warrant was read and, when asked if he had anything to say, he declined to speak to the seventy-five witnesses. His wrists were then handcuffed behind his back, his elbows were secured to the strap around his waist, and his knees and ankles were pinioned. Next the noose was adjusted around his neck and the black hood pulled over his head. At the sheriff's signal the trap was sprung and Porter dropped straight down, breaking his neck. In twelve minutes Dr. Lang pronounced him dead and the body was cut down, placed in a coffin, and turned over to Porter's brother, who had come from Scranton, Iowa. Porter was buried in the Union cemetery the following day.

Oregonian (Portland): January 5–7, 1896; February 6, 1896; February 11–19, 1896; November 19–20, 1897.

Wachline, Gus
February 4, 1898

On March 13, 1894, John D. Ledrick, an aged man living three miles south of Cornelius, disappeared. The old man was reclusive so, for nearly a week, his disappearance went unnoticed and aroused no concern, but neighbors began to wonder about the old man, so a friend went to the cabin and found the door bolted from the outside. He called Ledrick's name but got no response, so he summoned several neighbors and the door was forced open. There was no sign of Ledrick within and the floor appeared to have been vigorously scrubbed, which raised further suspicion as Ledrick was not known to be clean in his habits. In addition, Ledrick was known to have a large sum of money hoarded about the place and the men thought he might have been murdered for this plunder. The place was searched without result until a dog alerted on a manure pile. A pitchfork was then thrust into the pile and, when it met an uncommon resistance, the body of Ledrick was dug out and it was discovered that he had a bullet hole in his head.

Finding the body hidden in that condition first led to the suspicion that a churlish neighbor, Robert Buck, was somehow involved in his murder. Buck was arrested but at his preliminary examination he was cleared of the charge. This misdirection delayed the search for the real killer but soon people began to report that they had seen Gus Wachline, an ex-convict and a hard character, loitering in the vicinity for several days before Ledrick went missing. The description of Wachline, who was twenty-three years old, five feet eight inches tall and weighing one hundred seventy pounds, was circulated throughout the region and the search began in earnest.

Wachline was well known to lawmen, as he had been tried and convicted of a larceny in Washington County, and had just been released from prison after serving four months of a six month sentence. The fugitive was soon traced to Portland and it was learned that he had driven Ledrick's team of horses into that city and sold them. Wachline was next traced to a lodging-house in Portland and, though he had moved on, he left behind Ledrick's overcoat. The search for Wachline continued for nearly four years and in September 1897 he was finally discovered in Morrow County and arrested by Sheriff Edward L. Matlock. Wachline had "a revolver and a wicked-looking Bowie knife" when arrested but did not try to use either. He had been working on a farm near Mitchell under the alias Gus Hanson, and then on a ranch at Willow Creek using the alias A. H. Brown. Sheriff Matlock became suspicious when he matched the description that was periodically being circulated, and he sent the particulars to Sheriff Bradford of Washington County. Bradford left immediately and brought his prisoner back to Forest Grove. Wachline claimed that Buck had murdered the old man and that he had been bullied into burying the remains and driving Ledrick's team to Portland.

His trial began on December 8, 1897, and lasted several days, and the circumstantial evidence against him was strong. His defense was disbelieved and the jurors, with little deliberation, returned a verdict of murder in the first degree. The prisoner was sentenced to hang at Hillsboro, the county seat, on February 4, 1898. Wachline's father lived near Cornelius and his mother lived in Minnesota and, though both were well off, neither would put up the money for his defense counsel nor for his appeals. In January 1898 Wachline filed a sworn statement that Buck had committed the murder and attached it to two statements pleading for a commutation of his sentence to life in prison, or at least the granting of a stay of execution, but both applications were denied by Governor William P. Lord.

The night before his execution the condemned man asked for religious counsel and spent the night in prayer with his clergyman. After the clergy left he talked with death watch guards W. H. Bender, William Pointer, and N. A. Barrett until 3:30 A.M. and then retired. The prisoner arose at 8:00 A.M. but had no appetite and refused breakfast. Hillsboro had a holiday atmosphere with "a trio of Negro singers, a peripatetic fiddler patrolling the saloons to pick up a few dollars, and a phonographic outfit on the streets with all the latest songs at a dime a tune." People had come from all over the county, especially from Iowa Hill near where Ledrick lived. The *Independent* and the *Argus* newspapers put out an "Extra" edition.

At 9:00 A.M. the sheriff's office was besieged by a large crowd wanting to be close at hand when the trapdoor was released, and an hour later Captain A. M. Collins stepped through a window onto the raised passageway to the scaffold, built within a thirty by forty foot enclosure west of the jail. Collins attached the rope and tested the mechanism. The sheriff had selected twelve jurors to act as the official witnesses and, at 11:15 A.M. the sheriff went into the jail corridor, ordered the cell door open, and told the prisoner, "Wachline, come out." The prisoner shuffled out and listened to the death warrant read by the sheriff. Meanwhile three hundred men with invitations were admitted to the enclosure, but men, boys and three women crowded every rooftop and window overlooking the scene. With everything in place the condemned man was escorted from the jail at 12:03 P.M., accompanied by the sheriff and deputies C. E. Deichman and J. H. Wescott. Wachline walked onto the scaffold with a steady gait and was positioned upon the trapdoor. He was asked if he had anything to say and after replying yes he said softly, "All I have to say is that the [sworn] statement I have made is true. I am an innocent man. Let Jesus take me as I am." Everyone had anticipated that, finally, the condemned man would confess, but they were disappointed.

His arms and legs were pinioned, the black hood was pulled over his head, and the noose was adjusted. In but a moment, at 12:10 P.M., the trap was sprung and Wachline's neck was broken in the fall. He was attended by Drs. F. A. Bailey, S. T. Linklater, and J. P. Tamasle, who pronounced him dead in fourteen minutes. His body was cut down one minute later, at 12:25 P.M., and he was placed in the waiting coffin. The remains were removed by undertaker G. W. Patterson and the doors of the funeral parlor were opened for public viewing. William Wachline of Portland, the murderer's brother, made arrangements for the burial at Cornelius, where their father lived.

Oregonian (Portland): February 3, 1898; February 4, 1898. *San Francisco Chronicle* (CA): February 5, 1989.

Fiester, Charles
June 10, 1898

Fifty-two-year-old Charles Fiester, an ex-police officer, lived in Merlin, Josephine County, Oregon, where he remained with his older children after his wife, Nancy, left him. Nancy had taken the three youngest of their ten children and set up a household in Grants Pass, Oregon. There had been difficulties in their thirty year marriage because of Charles' brutality toward Nancy, and she had finally had enough. Their arguing and his wife beatings had affected the children as well, though he did not abuse the children physically. On May 19, 1895, Charles went to his wife's house at an early hour and they talked for two hours, seeming to smooth over their difficulties, and Nancy agreed to return to Merlin with her husband. Charles, Nancy and their three youngest children started on foot toward Merlin, following the railroad tracks. When still five miles from Merlin, Charles confronted his wife with rumors that she had been seeing another man and she admitted to seeing, and exchanging letters with, a Mr. Mudd and said they were going to be together after the divorce was finalized.

She became angry at his tone, turned and started back toward Grants Pass. Charles followed, caught her by the hair and dragged her to a nearby pool of water which had collected from a heavy rain overnight and was about three feet deep, and he held Nancy's head under water until she drowned. Samuel, George and Margaret watched their father murder their mother. He then sent them into Merlin to report the killing, while Fiester sat down next to Nancy's body to wait. Soon a crowd of men arrived on the scene and two men were detailed to escort Fiester into Grants Pass to surrender to Sheriff Joseph G. Hiatt. Nancy's body was taken to Merlin, where a coroner's jury found that Nancy Fiester had died from drowning by the hand of Charles Fiester, and Nancy was buried at Merlin several days later.

Charles Fiester had his examination based upon the same testimony heard at the inquest, and he was held over, without bail, to answer to the grand jury. Fiester was indicted in late September; his trial began on September 30, 1895, and concluded in four days. The jurors only deliberated for forty minutes before returning a verdict of murder in the first degree. On October 11 Judge H. K. Hanna sentenced the convicted murderer to hang on November 28. Appeals were filed and their consideration was postponed several times, but finally they were denied.

In December 1895 Fiester began showing signs of insanity, so a physician was called in for an examination, and the prisoner was pronounced insane. Fiester lay in his cot, would not acknowledge the presence of anyone nor respond to them in any way, and he had to be fed and groomed by a deputy. In early May 1897 he was served breakfast by deputy Fallen, who said, "You can eat that or let it alone. I will never again feed you." The deputy then left and when he returned the meal had been eaten. Deputy Fallen then told Fiester, "Old man, you have played your game well," and Fiester replied, "Yes, but it has been hard." The old man had feigned insanity for a year and a half. During the first days of May 1897 Fiester's son was convicted on a charge of larceny and housed in a cell adjoining his father's cell while awaiting transfer to prison. During the nights the old man and his son were heard, by other prisoners, whispering long, coherent conversations, and this was reported to deputy Fallen, who determined he would prove the old man sane by laying the trap. When the court convened for the May term, Fiester, then sixty years old, was brought in and re-sentenced to hang on June 10, 1897. Fiester's attorney, R. G. Smith, continued doing all he could to get a reprieve or commutation, but Governor William P. Lord refused to intervene and the prisoner was told of the decision on the evening of June 9.

On the morning of June 10, deputy Fallen took breakfast to the condemned man and found him in what appeared to be a dying condition. It was at first thought he had somehow obtained poison and a doctor was called, but it was determined that he had simply broken down under the strain of his impending death. The execution, scheduled for the morning hours, was postponed until afternoon so the prisoner could recover. It was considered that the prisoner might again be feigning his condition so, when he showed no sign of recovery by 1:00 P.M., he was strapped to a board and carried onto the scaffold by Sheriff Hiatt, deputy Fallen, sheriff-elect Edward Lister, and Constable Colby. The scaffold, which had been built for him in 1895, had been assembled within a high enclosure erected near the jail. The witnesses had been patiently awaiting the procession and when the prisoner appeared he was carried directly up the stairs and propped up on the trapdoor. The officers supported Fiester as they quickly applied the straps to his arms and legs, adjusted the noose, pulled on the hood and, without any further ceremony, stepped off the trapdoor while still supporting the prisoner; then the trap was sprung. The death warrant was not read nor was the prisoner in any condition to speak to the crowd, which sped up the process considerably. Fiester fell five feet, ten inches at 1:11 P.M., and was pronounced dead at 1:23 P.M. by Drs. Myer and Devore. The body was then cut down, placed in a coffin, and given to the Fiester children for burial next to his wife at Merlin.

Oregonian (Portland): June 11, 1897.

Branton, Claude
May 12, 1899

Claude Branton shared ownership of a herd of seventy horses with John Linn, and Branton hatched a scheme to take the entire herd and the $1,000 Linn was known to carry with him. Unsure if he could handle the work alone, twenty-two-year-old Branton enlisted the help of Courtland Green, who was the same age, and they agreed to share in the plunder. Branton convinced Linn, an old man, that they should drive the horses one hundred miles to the south from Gilliam County into Crook County, with Green along but working for wages, then graze the herd before selling them. Once in Crook County, Branton and Green found that there were too many witnesses about, so they convinced Linn they must drive the horses across the mountains to a valley near

Eugene, Oregon, saying they could get a better price. Linn agreed and they started out on June 11, 1898. After three days on the trail the men and horses were tiring, but they were still making good progress. On June 14 they ate dinner in the saddle and after crossing the summit, about dusk, they settled into camp at Isham's Corral. They ate supper at 9:00 P.M. and Linn immediately rolled into his blankets.

Branton and Green stepped away from camp and Green said he wanted to pull out of the conspiracy. However, Branton was determined to avoid losing his partner, so he pulled his British Bulldog pistol, walked to where Linn was sleeping, and shot him in the chest twice, killing him instantly. When they went through the old man's pockets the found only a few personal belongings, $65.40, and a note for an $800 loan he had made just before departing on the drive. They also took Linn's saddle and branding iron. The two men dragged the body onto the campfire and piled brush and wood on top until the blaze consumed all the flesh. They then separated the calcified bones and smashed the larger ones before throwing them back into the flames, then buried the smaller bones in a hole nearby. Although they had been up all night, at daybreak they drove the herd down the mountain and were seen along the trail by more than a half dozen individuals.

Now confused and frightened, they decided to use whatever money they had to bribe a witness to say they had seen Linn with them after leaving Isham's Corral. After only two days Green was becoming despondent, and at least once threatened suicide. Three days after committing the murder the two young men arrived at Branton's hometown of Walterville, put the herd out to pasture, and began looking for someone corruptible enough to become their alibi. They approached a considerable number of men, but the matter seemed so suspicious that none would take a hand. Now desperate, Branton made a disguise of whiskers from horse tail hair and, in the dark of night on June 19, he tried to convince William Seavey that he was John Linn, but Seavey recognized Branton's voice. They next tried to sell the horses but without a bill of sale no one would take a chance.

Branton and Green separated company and the former drove the horses to eastern Oregon and sold them. He then went east to Arkansas, but by July 5 he was in Kansas. Green went to Eugene in Lane County where he began drinking heavily, and during the early morning hours of July 4 Green confessed the details of the murder to deputy sheriff Henry Day. Sheriff William W. Withers, Dr. W. L. Cheshire, Assistant District Attorney Lawrence T. Harris, and two others, serving as a coroner's jury, left for Isham's Corral later that morning and arrived on July 6. The sheriff was a well-known amateur sleuth and he began to investigate the scene. He carefully raked through the ashes and found a variety of evidence confirming the victim's identity and corroborating Green's confession. Green had been detained and, upon the sheriff's return on July 10, he was arrested and charged with murder. He was taken before Justice C. Wintermiere for his examination and held over for action by the grand jury.

The search for Branton began with a post office alert to watch for letters from Branton to his girlfriend in Waltersville, and it was not long before they learned he was nearly broke and coming home. Branton arrived in Eugene on July 19 and a friend asked him to surrender so he could collect the $250 reward, but Branton refused and was arrested the following day. He claimed he had last seen Linn when they placed the horses in Seavey's pasture, but he was carrying Linn's leather purse in his pocket.

Branton was also held over for the grand jury and the two men were lodged in the Eugene jail until they were indicted on October 26. The two defendants were arraigned on October 31, 1898, and their motion for a continuance, filed two days earlier, was overruled. The trials were separated and the jury in the Branton case was seated that evening. The next morning, as Branton's trial began in the adjacent courtroom, Green pled guilty and sentencing was postponed until after the trial of

Branton. Dr. Cheshire testified about the inquest and described finding in the ashes suspender buttons, clothing, teeth, buckles, and human bones, and all these items were entered into evidence. Green also testified, being very easy on himself and very harsh toward Branton. In hearing Green's testimony Branton broke down, weeping and moaning loudly, sometimes drowning out the testimony. On the second day of testimony Sheriff Withers displayed the saddle, bridle and spurs left with Seavey by Branton, but identified as belonging to Linn. Other items belonging to Linn, and traced through Branton, were also displayed. The prosecution rested their case at noon on November 2 and at 1:00 P.M. Branton was called to the stand. He laid the blame on Green and then a succession of witnesses testified that Branton's mind was weak and he could be easily persuaded to do almost anything. The prosecution gave a detailed summation, followed by the defense, whose main thrust was to discredit Green's testimony and blame the newspapers for fomenting prejudice against their client. Arguments took so long that the trial was extended to November 4.

Judge J. W. Hamilton charged the jury and after only one hour of deliberations they returned a verdict of guilty of first degree murder as charged in the indictment. After hearing the verdict, and upon being returned to jail, Branton made a desperate attempt to escape, saying he would have "killed everyone to gain my freedom," but he was subdued after a terrible struggle. On November 7, Green was convicted of second degree murder, partly because of his cooperation and the belief that he had not fired the fatal bullets. He received a life sentence and arrived at the prison in Salem, Oregon, three days later.

On November 8, Branton was sentenced by Judge Hamilton to hang in the Lane County jail yard on December 23, 1898. Four days before Branton was to hang he received a respite, granted by the state Supreme Court, to allow time to review the case. Meanwhile the condemned man embraced religion and on February 6 was baptized in his prison cell by three clergymen. Six days later his appeal was heard and two weeks later the lower court's judgment and sentence were affirmed. On March 1, Branton tried again to escape but his mock pistol, made from a potato, did not fool the sheriff sufficiently to facilitate his freedom. On April 5, 1899, Branton again faced Judge Hamilton and was re-sentenced to hang on May 12.

Branton finally seemed resigned to his fate and on his final morning he ate a hearty breakfast and then entertained his family, bidding them farewell. He then wrote letters and read his Bible. At 10:00 A.M. the gates to the twelve foot high enclosure that surrounded the scaffold were opened and only the fifty witnesses with invitations were admitted. The walls of the enclosure had been extended from the door of the jail to the enclosure, so none of the curious crowd could see the procession. The Reverends E. M. Patterson and John Handsaker accompanied the condemned man from his cell onto the scaffold where Branton was positioned on the trapdoor and then Sheriff Withers read the death warrant.

At 10:05 A.M. the straps were applied to pinion his wrists and arms, knees and ankles, and Branton was asked if he had anything to say. After thanking the lawmen for their kind treatment he prayed and then said, "I haven't much to say. I hope for God's sake no one will try to run my folks down on account of this. They are innocent. I hope people will learn a lesson from this and tread the right path. I hope to meet you all in the other world. I ask this for Jesus' sake. Amen." The noose was then adjusted and the black hood was pulled over his face. At 10:45 A.M. a lever sprang the trap and Branton dropped seven feet, breaking his neck. Drs. T. W. Harris and L. D. Scarborough monitored vital signs and in sixteen minutes pronounced him dead. After a brief pause the body was cut down and given to R. M. Day and Harry Graham, undertakers, who prepared the body for burial and then delivered it to family members. Branton's remains were driven to the Camp Creek Cemetery and buried.

Eugene Guard (OR): October 27–31, 1898; November 1–7, 1898; November 10, 1898; November 14, 1898; December 17–23, 1898; December 31, 1898; January 21, 1899; February 2, 1899; February 7, 1899; February 11, 1899; February 21, 1899; February 27, 1899; March 1, 1899; March 28, 1899; April 3–5, 1899; May 11–12, 1899.

Magers, William
February 2, 1900

William Magers was born in Gervais, Oregon, on June 24, 1873. He was the apple of his mother's eye and she spoiled him terribly. He had become wild and reckless and felt he was above the law and occasionally committed petty crimes. In 1896, though his mother tried to give him all the money he needed, he broke into a neighbor's house and stole a small sum. He was tried, convicted, and sentenced to serve eighteen months in prison. It was unusual for a young man to serve out his entire first term but Magers served out his term plus six days for bad behavior. He was released on November 28, 1897, and, like many ex-convicts, he could not seem to find employment near his home. Magers went to Sherman County where he was not well known and found employment with Raymond Sink, a man who owned six hundred acres and was planning to buy a commercial property near Salem. He told Magers that he planned to move there once he was married and Magers insisted he could help Sink find a property so, in July, they went to Gervais. Magers and Sink stayed with the Manning family, as Magers' sister had married Sylvester Manning's brother, and they had a home in Gervais. Sink did not find the property he wanted but he liked Gervais, so a month later he returned and learned that Sylvester Manning's livery stable was available. Sink offered $2,400 and Manning counter-offered $3,400. After negotiating for two weeks an agreement could not be reached so Sink decided to let the matter rest and go to Salem.

On September 13, Sink and Magers rented a buggy and team at the Manning livery and arrived in Salem at 10:00 A.M. They took rooms at a boarding house but at 7:30 P.M. they started out again, with Magers driving. They passed several people but most observant was John Spar, who watched the buggy traveling erratically up and down several side roads including that of E. E. Harritt, the occupants apparently looking for something. Finally the buggy pulled onto the main road and headed for Salem and at 11:00 P.M. Magers, now alone, arrived back in Salem. He went to the boarding house, collected Sink's valise, and drove to Gervais. He arrived at 1:00 A.M., met two women and, showing a large sum of money, convinced them to accompany him to Portland. Sink's brother became concerned when he could not locate Raymond but he knew his brother was last seen with Magers in Salem, so he tracked Magers to Portland. Magers said Raymond had gone to Newberg with a lady friend but knew nothing more.

On September 20 two men went fishing on the Williamette River and hooked a dead body. They brought it to shore and summoned Polk County Coroner L. N. Woods. An inquest was held and the jurors found that the man had his forehead bashed in, his carotid artery slashed, and his mouth was bruised with several teeth missing. His arms and legs were tied with rope and iron weights were attached to his ankles to keep the body submerged. It had putrefied sufficiently to float head-up and that was how it had been hooked. The pockets had been turned out so there were no valuables nor identification on the body, but the iron weights were identified as those stolen from E. E. Harritt's gate on September 13. John Spar then identified the body as the man he had seen riding in the buggy, but he did not know the name of the deceased. It was not long before a man named E. Niece from Sherman County identified the body as that of Raymond Sink and Sink's family was notified.

On September 21, Portland detective John Cordano detained, searched, and questioned Magers, who had in his pockets fifty-eight dollars and sixty cents. This was more money than he could explain, and then he made a number of conflicting statements before a firm story evolved: Raymond Sink met an old school friend at 7:00 P.M. on September 13, 1898, and drove to Newberg in the rented buggy. Magers said he had seen Sink in Portland a few days earlier and Sink had also talked with Stephen Hillbauch within the last two days, and these inconsistent statements would haunt him at trial. Apparently it never occurred to him that Sink's body could have been found. Sheriff Joseph G. van Orsdel took Magers back to The Dalles and lodged him in the Polk County jail. At his examination he was held over for action by the grand jury, which indicted him on December 7, 1898, on a charge of murder, and his trial began the following day in Judge George Burnett's courtroom.

The circumstantial evidence was linked so meticulously over the three days of testimony that there could be little doubt of the facts. On December 11 the jurors, who deliberated for twelve hours, returned a verdict of "guilty as charged in the indictment." On December 14 Judge Burnett sentenced Magers to hang on February 3, 1899. An appeal was filed and this acted as an automatic stay of execution, and on April 24 the state Supreme Court found error in the lower court's record. Magers expected to be released but instead a second indictment was returned and he was scheduled for retrial.

Magers then began to plan an escape, and on May 1, 1899, he and another prisoner overpowered Sheriff van Orsdel, but the commotion alerted a woman passing by and by the time the men had secured the sheriff a large party of armed men awaited them outside. The two prisoners thought they were about to be lynched so they untied the sheriff and begged him to protect them from the mob, and he did.

Magers' second trial began on May 23, 1899, and testimony concluded on May 27, and in less than two hours the jurors returned a guilty verdict. Judge Burnett then sentenced Magers to hang on July 21, 1899, but he was not done yet. Affidavits were filed alleging prejudice on the part of one juror, but Judge Burnett refused to issue orders for subpoenas to question the affiants. Another affidavit claimed the crime occurred in another county but this was dismissed. The defense filed another appeal on these and other grounds but it was denied by the state Supreme Court on November 13, 1899. One month later Judge Burnett again set the date of execution, this time February 2, 1900, and nothing further would intervene.

On the day before Magers was to be hanged, his doting mother visited him for the last time and begged him to confess, but he steadfastly denied any part in the killing. February 2, 1900, was appropriately a gloomy day and Magers arose early and ate a hearty breakfast, still confident he would avoid the hangman. At 7:00 A.M. a party of men arrived to report that their efforts throughout the night to obtain executive clemency from Governor T. T. Geer had failed, and Magers resigned himself to his fate. Sheriff van Orsdel called in the twelve men who had last convicted Magers and polled them and each confirmed his guilty verdict, so at 10:00 A.M. the sheriff went to the prisoner's cell and read the death warrant. Magers became agitated and smashed every piece of furniture in his cell, but in ten minutes he was physically and emotionally spent. The cell door was then opened and the procession formed with Elder Barton Riggs leading the way, deputies John T. Ford and W. E. Williams on either side in case the prisoner faltered, and his night death watch guard Charles McDermitt following. The sheriff had secured a coroner's jury of ex-sheriffs, and these twelve men took their place beneath the gallows. The scaffold had been built next to the jail inside a forty by forty foot enclosure of thirty foot boards. Within were the two hundred men invited by the sheriff, and outside five hundred men had gathered.

Once Magers was on the platform Elder Riggs offered a prayer and then Magers said, "Gentlemen, you are looking upon an innocent man. I pray that those who have testified against me will be forgiven and that I will meet them in heaven. I forgive those who have done me wrong." He was positioned on the trapdoor, his arms and legs pinioned, the noose adjusted, and the black hood pulled on, all with utmost efficiency. The lever was pulled and the trap was sprung as Drs. R.E.L. Steiner and Otis D. Butler waited beneath. They monitored Magers' vital signs, pronouncing him dead at 10:18 A.M. Magers had broken his neck in the fall and did not struggle or suffer. After death the body was cut down and given to Eugene Manning for burial in the Old Dalles Cemetery.

Oregonian (Portland): May 2, 1899; May 6, 1899; May 22, 1899, May 24, 1899; February 2–3, 1900. *Polk County Observer* (Dallas, OR): December 10, 1898; December 12, 1898; December 16, 1898; May 5, 1899; May 26, 1899, June 2, 1899.

Gillespie, Coalman
October 5, 1900

Seventy-seven-year-old Christina Edson lived a difficult life, her last sixty years in Oregon. In 1856 Indians raided her home in Curry County and killed her husband and three sons. The natives tied Christina and made her watch the brutal murders and mutilation of the bodies, then held Christina and her two daughters captive for two weeks; one was just a baby. In 1899 Christina lived alone and on September 18 her two daughters pleaded with her to come live with them, but she was determined to remain independent. That same day her first check for $75 arrived from the Indian Depredation Fund. She had twice filed for benefits and it had taken forty-three years for the federal government to grant her claim.

On September 19, 1899, the postal rider was making his usual rounds when he came upon the Edson cabin, burned to the ground. He carefully picked through the smoldering remnants, hoping he would not find Christina inside, but her charred body was sprawled across her bed springs and a coal oil can with a hole in it to help it drain quickly, lay nearby, proving it was arson and that Christina's death was murder. It was immediately presumed that she was killed for her money, but there were no clues to the perpetrator even when a reward of $450 was posted.

Finally the depredation check was cashed at a Roseburg bank by C. O. White. He was questioned and lawmen learned he had bought it, at a discount, from Coalman Gillespie, who was well known. His description was circulated and during the last week of September Gillespie was recognized at Cottage Grove, arrested by Constable Warren McFarland, and lodged in the Roseburg jail. A dispatch was sent to Sheriff Jesse Turner and, with deputy Alf Miller and district attorney George Brown, they went to Roseburg to question the prisoner. They arrived on October 1 and found a very uncooperative Gillespie expecting them. They questioned him at length and he changed his story as he rambled, trying to patch up weak spots or correct conflicting statements, until it became clear even to him that he was lying. He then confessed every detail and named Charles Strahan as his co-conspirator.

The three lawmen took the prisoner to the nearest justice of the peace in Curry County where he had his examination, and he was held over for action by the grand jury. The prisoner was next taken to Coquille, then the Curry County seat, and lodged in the county jail to await the next session of the Circuit Court. As soon as Gillespie was behind bars in Coquille he wrote out his full confession and signed it, and the search for Strahan began in earnest. Strahan had disappeared and it was rumored that he had tried to flee and had drowned in the Rogue River. This was probably partly true, as it seems Strahan, a commercial salmon fisherman, had gone to Port Orford and there had drowned in a fishing accident. Strahan, being deceased, was never indicted and other evidence suggested that Gillespie had acted alone. Perhaps he had heard of the drowning of Strahan and decided to blame the entire affair on a dead man. However, his many admissions and his confession would haunt him at trial.

Gillespie was indicted in mid–August 1900 and on August 21 his trial began in Judge J. W. Hamilton's courtroom. Seventeen witnesses testified, including Sheriff Turner, who also testified that Gillespie admitted to choking to death Christina Edson, throwing her body on the bed, splashing about the coal oil, and setting the cabin afire. These admissions had been left out of the written confession, a statement which was made when Gillespie was still trying to blame the entire matter on Strahan. The following morning the case went to the jury and after very brief deliberations Gillespie was found guilty of first degree murder. Judge Hamilton had the prisoner brought back the next day, August 23, when he sentenced him to hang at Gold Beach on October 5, 1900. Gillespie was a determined lad of twenty-two years, still trying to lay blame on Strahan and not realizing that, even if he made his case, he was still just as guilty. On the day before his execution he again wrote out a confession blaming the entire affair on Strahan, and as time had passed his part in the murder and arson continually diminished. Every effort had been made to get a new trial by appeal to the state Supreme Court, but it denied the appeal, and the condemned man's family and others pleaded with Governor T. T. Geer to grant him a commutation of sentence, but this was also denied.

The task of hanging Gillespie fell to newly elected Sheriff James G. Walker. Walker went to the prisoner's Gold Beach jail cell before 3:00 P.M. on October 5 and read the death warrant. The prisoner was then taken out and escorted to the gallows, which had been erected within a small enclosure which did not admit the witnesses but allowed his head and shoulders to be seen above the fencing when he stood on the platform. The condemned man was positioned upon the trapdoor and his arms and legs were pinioned. When asked, he declined to give a speech, so the noose was adjusted and the black hood was pulled over his head.

Eight men were on the scaffold to assist the sheriff and when the prisoner was ready one signaled and Walker sprang the trap. Gillespie dropped six feet, which should have been sufficient to break his neck, but he slowly strangled to death and after struggling for some time, his body hung lifeless and he was pronounced dead. The coroner's jurymen were then admitted beneath the scaffolding to confirm death, and later they signed the death certificate. Gillespie's body was cut down, placed in a coffin, and given to his mother and sister, who lived in Gold Beach. He was buried the next day following a brief service.

Coos Bay News (OR): October 3, 1899; October 9, 1900. *Coquille City Herald* (OR): October 3, 1899; October 9–10, 1899; October 17, 1899; October 24, 1899; October 9, 1900. *Oregon Sentinel* (Jacksonville): October 6, 1899; October 31, 1899.

Dalton, William; Wade, John
January 31, 1902

James Barkley Morrow, a bartender in Portland, Multnomah County, Oregon, had been sparking his fiancée on the evening of November 21, 1901. The lovesick Morrow was returning home when he encountered John "Jack" Wade, an alias for Joseph Ewing, and William "B. H." Dalton, an alias for Bill Strickland, who had just left a saloon two blocks away. As the men neared one another Dalton whispered to Wade that he knew Morrow, and when they came abreast of one another Dalton drew his .44-caliber Colt revolver and jabbed the barrel into the young man's face. He then commanded, "put your hands up." Dalton, for some reason, passed the gun to Wade, who continued the work of robbery. Morrow made no resistance but struggled to pull his wallet from his inside jacket pocket and as Wade reached out for the wallet the gun fired. The bullet struck Morrow in the face killing him instantly, and the two robbers fled empty-handed.

Dalton lived at a boarding house on First Street, sharing a room with two other men. Mrs. W. T. Whitlock, the landlady, discovered that her belongings had been ransacked and she was missing $60 worth of clothing and jewelry, but she did not report the crime immediately. When she heard of the murder of Morrow, and thought Dalton might be involved, she confronted her tenants and, not receiving a satisfactory answer, telephoned her attorney for legal advice. Following his instructions she contacted district attorney George Chamberlain and asked him to come to her house immediately. Chamberlain contacted police detective Day and the two men went to the boarding house, but Dalton was gone, so they questioned his two roommates, who said they knew nothing.

When Dalton returned he confessed to robbing Morrow but blamed Wade for the shooting. Dalton was arrested, along with his roommate Charles Smith, and they were lodged in jail while Chamberlain and detective Day searched Portland's many saloons for Wade. They had no luck but later cornered Wade in his room at the La Fayette Hotel. The following day, Smith, Wade and Dalton were closely questioned and the two guilty parties confessed to the robbery, each blaming the other for the shooting, and Smith was discharged. Each prisoner then tried to malign the character of the other to lend credence to his own story.

The community was outraged by the killing of Morrow and an unruly crowd gathered outside the jail, so Sheriff William Frazier spirited away his prisoners and they were lodged in different jails. Once the public sentiment calmed the two prisoners were brought back to Portland and arraigned in Judge A. L. Frazer's courtroom on November 25. Wade pled guilty and "threw himself on the mercy of the court," relying on his claim that Dalton had fired the fatal bullet. Dalton pled not guilty and was tried on December 5, was found guilty of first degree murder and, when the two men were brought into court for sentencing, Judge Cleland noted that under Oregon law each was equally guilty of first degree murder and sentenced them to hang on January 31, 1902. Nothing occurred to delay the executions.

A week before the executions Dalton took sick and nearly cheated the hangman, but doctors managed to cure him in six days. A twenty-foot enclosure had been built in the courtyard of the Multnomah County courthouse to keep the hanging private, but Sheriff Frazier over-booked the witnesses, sending out four hundred invitations even though only about two hundred fifty witnesses could fit comfortably inside. Both prisoners arose early on that final day and at 6:15 A.M. they ate hearty breakfasts of chicken, eggs and ham. Following the meal a lively song service was held with two local missionaries, and it continued until the chief deputy sheriff appeared at 7:05 A.M. to read the death warrants. The song service then continued with "Rock of Ages," followed by a prayer led by F. C. Marshall.

At 7:30 A.M. the gates were opened and the witnesses crowded into the enclosure. The twelve man coroner's jury was spirited to the forefront and Drs. H. R. Littlefield and Harold McKay took their places beneath the scaffold. Two ropes hung from the crossbeam, eight feet apart, and at 7:45 A.M. the two condemned men were placed beneath the nooses, escorted by five deputy sheriffs. There was heavy snow piled up outside the enclosure and a light rain began to fall, which made the crowd of one thousand men, women and children restless, but inside all was calm and orderly. Barriers had been erected and manned by a strong police presence under the command of Captain John T. Moore, and they held back the crowd though several times the masses surged forward and almost broke through to the fence.

Once in position on the trapdoors each condemned man was asked if he had anything to say, and Wade replied he had nothing to add to his published confession, and Dalton made the usual warning about avoiding evil doings and repeated his confession, ending with a brief prayer. When Dalton paused Wade pulled a cigar and handkerchief from his pocket and threw it to the crowd, then rubbed his nose with the noose and said, "It's rough!" The interruption, especially with humor at that solemn moment, upset Dalton, so Wade took a step forward and made a brief statement regarding the futility of life in Salem, Oregon, and then stepped back onto the trapdoor.

Straps were produced and the arms and legs of each men were pinioned, the black hoods were pulled over their heads, and the nooses were adjusted. The sheriff raised his hand at 7:58 A.M. to signal for three ropes to be pulled by three different men, two being dummy releases so none knew who actually sprang the two traps. Dalton, the heavier of the two, fell five feet six inches and Wade fell six feet two inches. Dalton's neck was broken in the fall but Wade strangled to death, though the attending physicians assured everyone they were beyond pain after thirty seconds. It was fifteen minutes before the attending physicians pronounced both men dead and at 8:15 A.M. the bodies were cut down. They were placed in the coffins provided by the county and taken to the morgue for a postmortem examination by coroner Dr. D. H. Rand. A large crowd followed the coffins to the morgue and were kept out only by force.

Later that evening, when the crowd had shrunk to a manageable size but still included women and children, the doors were opened and people were allowed to view the remains. The following day the bodies were turned over to the county authorities for burial, side-by-side, at the county's Poor Farm Cemetery. The scaffold was taken down by noon on the day of the hanging and the enclosure was taken down the following day.

Oregonian (Portland): November 25–28, 1901; December 2, 1901; January 2–4, 1902; January 31, 1902; February 1–2, 1902.

Schieve, August
July 2, 1902

Twenty-seven-year-old Joseph Schulkowski boarded with the Schieve family after he was mustered out of the army in mid–1901. He homesteaded a tract of land near Yankton, Columbia County, Oregon, in a predominantly Polish immigrant area and was in the process of improving the land with buildings, which would allow him to "prove up" on the land. Like the other Poles living there he planned to farm and had deposited his entire mustering out pay, two hundred seventy-five dollars, in the bank at St. Helens to finance his dream. He also carried a money belt containing more than one hundred fifty dollars, money to pay for materials used for his planned improvements.

On December 24, 1901, Schulkowski ate breakfast with the Schieves, including his twenty-seven-year-old friend August, and then started on foot for his homestead. After Schulkowski had left, August saddled his white horse, put his Winchester rifle in the scabbard, and rode off toward Bunker Hill Road, the same road Schulkowski had taken. August returned in time for dinner at 12:30 P.M.

On Christmas day miners James McKay and O. D. Garrison were on their way to work at the Bunker Hill Coal Mines when they saw bloody boot prints in the snow. They followed the tracks and found the body of Schulkowski in a sitting position, leaning against a tree, with a bullet hole on the back of his left side and another through his mouth, and his money belt and gold watch were gone. The Schieve family was immediately suspected, as they had been the last to see Schulkowski alive, but suspicion quickly narrowed and on December 28 August Schieve was arrested by Columbia County Sheriff R. S. Hatton. At his examination August Schieve was held over without bail for action by the grand jury, but there was fear of a lynching by the other Poles, so a week later Schieve was taken to Portland and lodged in the Multnomah County jail.

In early May Schieve was indicted and his trial began in Judge Thomas A. McBride's courtroom on May 14. Twenty-two witnesses were called by the prosecution before the defense tried to prove that August Schieve could not have killed Schulkowski. Their contention, as stated in the testimony of August, his two brothers, and his sister, was that he had ridden away on his horse, with his rifle, but had returned for dinner at 12:30 P.M. and this would not have been enough time to commit the murder. However, prosecution witnesses showed that there were boot prints at the scene matching August Schieve's boots, the murder had ridden a white horse based upon horse hair found at the scene, Schulkowski had been killed with August Schieve's rifle, and an empty .32-.20 Winchester shell was found eighteen feet from the body. The prosecution proved that Schulkowski had been shot in the back, the murderer operated the ejector of his rifle to load another round, leaving the expended casing behind, dragged the badly wounded and helpless victim off the road to the tree, put the rifle barrel in his mouth, and blew out his brains. The trial lasted fifteen days but deliberations took only fourteen hours. On Sunday, May 25, the jurors returned a guilty verdict. Six days later the defendant was sentenced to hang on July 2, 1902. This was followed by a strong community effort to have Schieve's sentence commuted to life in prison, but Governor T. T. Geer refused to intervene.

As the day approached a stockade of sixteen foot boards was erected next to the county jail. There was a fir tree growing between the jail and courthouse and it was encircled by the stockade, with the gallows built next to the tree. Several days before his execution Schieve was baptized by the Reverend Lew Davies of the Scappoose Methodist Episcopal Church. On his final morning the condemned man ate a hearty breakfast and then received his pastor, who was accompanied by the Reverends F. H. Lange and C. A. Preissing. They spent the morning praying and reading Bible passages, and Schieve's uncle Carl remained with him in his cell and was by his side until the end. There had been some question of Schieve's sanity but there had been no evidence of insanity. Still, as the crowd of two hundred fifty witnesses waited, Sheriff Hattan mounted the scaffold and made the announcement that, in his opinion, Schieve was guilty but he felt the prisoner was not mentally responsible for his actions. The sheriff retired to Schieve's jail cell at noon and read the death warrant, and then the doors were swung open and the procession formed. The clergymen led the way with Sheriff Hattan and a deputy on each side of the prisoner, to support him if he faltered.

Once on the platform the prisoner was asked if he had anything to say and Schieve had promised Sheriff Hattan he would make a full confession, but he reneged and adamantly professed his innocence. He gave the usual warning to live by the law before saying goodbye and stepping onto the trapdoor. His arms and legs were pinioned as the reverends took turns praying, the black hood was pulled over his head, and as the noose was being adjusted he requested, "Have that knot hard." At 12:05 P.M. the trap was sprung and eleven minutes later Drs. W. K. Haviland, R. J. Pilkington, A. P. McLaren and H. R. Cliff conferred and pronounced him dead. The body was cut down, lowered into the coffin provided by the Schieve family, and taken to the undertaker's parlor to be prepared for burial.

Oregon Mist (St. Helens): June 6, 1902; June 27, 1902. *Oregonian* (Portland): December 29–31, 1901; May 18, 1902; May 23–24, 1902; July 2–3, 1902.

Belding, Alfred L.
March 27, 1903

Twenty-three-year-old Alfred L. Belding married seventeen-year-old Sylvia "Maude" McCroskey at Portland, Multnomah County, Oregon, in early 1895. Relations during the first months seemed normal to all observers as Sylvia began to show her pregnancy, and in September, less than six months after their marriage, Eddie Belding was born. After Eddie's birth the relationship steadily deteriorated until, in early 1902, Sylvia left taking Eddie and moving in with her parents, Lemuel and Deborah McCroskey, in their small house at the corner of Fifth and Flanders Streets. Sylvia, then twenty-five years old, was an industrious woman and was soon back on her feet financially. She had more than a few suitors but one, George Woodward, became favored by her, her parents, and Eddie. There was no secret, especially to Belding, that his wife and Woodward had become serious in their relationship.

He kept a close watch on his wife and son and knew that Sylvia planned to file for divorce and marry Woodward, whom he suspected had become more than just a suitor. His desire to prevent the divorce, which might disclose many embarrassing facts about his treatment of his wife and child, and his jealousy toward Woodward led him to plan a deadly confrontation. His chance came on July 11, 1902, when he learned that Sylvia and their son, with Woodward, were visiting at the McCroskey home. The McCroskeys had not approved of Belding, who had gotten their daughter pregnant out of wedlock, but encouraged Sylvia's relationship with Woodward. Her new love was good to her and to Eddie, and Belding was particularly angry at his in-laws for their interference.

A little after 8:00 P.M. Belding loaded his two pistols, one a large caliber Smith and Wesson and the other a Colt revolver, and an hour later he arrived at the McCroskey home. His son Eddie saw his father coming and ran into the house to give warning, and Woodward was able to cut him off at the door to prevent his entry to the house. Without hesitation or warning Belding raised his Smith and Wesson pistol and fired a single round into Woodward's chest, bursting his heart and killing him instantly. Belding stepped over his first victim's body as Sylvia, hearing the shot, ran into the hallway. Before she could turn he fired one shot from his Colt revolver and again his aim was true. The bullet pierced her heart and killed her where she stood. He walked down the hall past Sylvia's body where he was confronted by Deborah, also coming out to investigate the shots, and at close range he shot her through the heart.

Lemuel, suspecting what was occurring, got his pistol and managed to get off one shot before Belding shot him three times, emptying his Colt revolver. One of the bullets passed through Lemuel's arm, missing the bone, a second bullet nicked Lemuel's neck causing a terrible loss of blood but not inflicting a fatal wound, and the third shot was in Lemuel's side, which would have been a fatal wound to the bowels or kidneys if it had not been deflected by his pocket watch. The placement of Belding's last bullet, and the blood from the neck wound, convinced Belding that Lemuel was dead or dying so he did not bother to administer the *coup de grâce*. Meanwhile, little Eddie cowered in one of the bedrooms, convinced that his father intended to shoot him.

Belding walked to a nearby saloon and telephoned the police, confessed his crime, disclosed his whereabouts, and promised he would await their arrival. When the police arrived Belding surrendered his weapons and was arrested without incident. He was lodged in jail, charged with three counts of murder and one of attempted murder, which was much to his chagrin, as he was certain he had killed his father-in-law. At his examination he pled not guilty by reason of insanity but was held over to answer to the grand jury. Belding was indicted and his trial in Judge M. C. George's court began on September 9, 1902. He was charged only with the murder of his mother-in-law, the prosecution deferring on the other two counts in case they might be needed later.

The most damning testimony came from his son, Eddie, and from Dr. Harry Lane, who found him sane at the time of the murders. The jurors retired for only one hour and on the first ballot found Belding "guilty of murder in the first degree as charged in the indictment." On September 26, 1902, Judge George sentenced Belding to hang on October 31. Belding's attorney filed the usual appeals and this caused some delay in the proceedings. Meanwhile Belding tried to execute a plan to escape, but when discovered he abandoned the plot and claimed it was all in jest. Everyone who might have considered helping him then abandoned the murderer for fear of being implicated in the escape attempt, and he could do nothing but resign himself to his fate. Oregon's state Supreme Court considered the appeals for four months before upholding the lower court's decision on January 29, 1903. He was re-sentenced to hang on February 20 but Governor George Chamberlain granted a thirty day respite to consider the application for a commutation of sentence. The governor denied the application and Belding was re-sentenced to hang on March 27, 1903.

The condemned man had embraced the Catholic religion and was visited by Father Gartland on the morning of his final day. The prisoner waived the reading of the death warrant and said, before leaving his cell, he would say nothing on the scaffold. At 6:25 A.M. the procession to the gallows began. The scaffold was a double trapdoor affair which had been constructed for an earlier execution and the release was arranged with three ropes, including two dummy releases, so no one knew which man actually released the trapdoor, and the drop was set at five feet, so the prisoner's feet would be suspended two feet above the ground. Belding was placed on the right trapdoor facing the crowd. He was asked if he had anything to say to the two hundred fifty witnesses present, but he again declined to speak. His arms and legs were pinioned and the noose was adjusted, and then Father Gartland reached into Belding's pocket and pulled out a crucifix which he had presented to the condemned man on a prior visit, and held it to his lips moments before the black hood was pulled over his head.

As soon as Belding's head was covered Sheriff W. A. Storey gave the signal and the three release ropes were pulled. All had been done with such expeditiousness that it was only 6:30 A.M., five minutes after the procession began, that Belding dropped, striking his head on the platform floor but still breaking his neck in the fall. He hung for seventeen minutes before he was pronounced dead by Drs. H. R. Littlefield, S. Langworthy, and T. D. Perkins. There were a number of medical students among the witnesses and Dr. H. R. Littlefield invited them to come forward to examine the body. Belding's remains were then cut down and lowered into a pine box. By 8:00 A.M. the triple murderer was laid to rest in the Calvary Cemetery.

Oregon Journal (Portland): September 9–12, 1902; September 24, 1902; October 18–20, 1902; October 27–28, 1902; December 31, 1902; March 26–27, 1903. *Oregonian* (Portland): March 27–28, 1903.

Lyons, Edward E.
April 17, 1903

Edward Elliot Lyons was a horse thief, but no petty crime was beneath him. While serving as a deputy sheriff Lyons embezzled a $10 gold eagle from the Lane County, Oregon, tax collection agency and was sent to prison for a year. The governor took pity on the ex-lawman and commuted his sentence to five months. After his release he moved to Medford in Jackson County, where he traveled in bad company, and he and his associates turned their attention to two fine horses belonging to Frank M. Ferguson.

On July 6, 1902, they stole the horses and Lyons was captured and lodged in jail, but in mid–December 1902 Lyons managed to escape through some ruse played on the jailor. He fled north to the home of his parents and wife near Walton in Lane County, thirty miles west of Eugene. A warrant was issued for Lyons on the horse stealing charge and for escape. William W. Withers, the sheriff of Lane County, was notified of the warrant and listened for word that Lyons had arrived at Walton. On February 3, 1903, he was told that Lyons had been seen at his family's home, so he outfitted a two man posse, including himself and Constable Jack Smith, leaving Undersheriff Fred Fisk in charge at Eugene. They got an early start on February 5 and stopped at Elmira for dinner and then, nearing Walton, they stopped at Hale's Stagecoach Station near Noti for supper. At Hale's they met C. William Cornelius, a reliable Walton area rancher, and he was deputized to accompany them to the Lyons' ranch.

Once their horses were rested they started out and at dusk reached their destination. Withers sent his deputies to cover the back, expecting Lyons to bolt as soon as he knocked on the front door, and once the two men were in place Smith whistled a signal and Withers knocked. He could hear sounds of skittering about inside but in a few seconds the front door was opened by Lyons' wife. Withers, a very likeable man, apologized for the late intrusion and showed the arrest warrant, and then made a request for her husband to surrender. Mrs. Lyons backed toward the kitchen where Lyons' mother and father were standing and Withers followed, his revolver still holstered. Lyons appeared suddenly from a bedroom and the two women responded by charging at the sheriff and holding his arms as they pleaded for him to leave Lyons with them. Withers struggled to free himself from the women as he informed Lyons that he was wanted on the warrant and was under arrest. Withers, unable to free his arms, still had not drawn his revolver when Lyons drew his .38-caliber revolver and shot the sheriff in the neck. Withers fell to the floor, mortally wounded, as the fugitive bolted out of the front door and disappeared into the darkness. Smith and Cornelius rushed in by the back door but Lyons was gone and Withers told Smith, "Jack, I guess they have done me."

Smith commandeered the Lyons' buggy and took Withers, along with the Lyons family under arrest, to Hale's Stage Station while Cornelius hurried to Eugene to notify Undersheriff Fisk and summon the doctor. Once everything was under control at the station Smith organized a small posse of Walton residents and they searched for Lyons, but he was not to be found. When the party returned from Eugene it included Withers' wife, who stayed with her husband every moment until his death on February 7.

Meanwhile, in Eugene, Fisk issued a reward of five hundred dollars for the capture of Lyons, and this was increased to one thousand dollars after Withers' death. Eventually the total reward reached fifteen hundred dollars, as the good citizens of Lane County subscribed additional funds to ensure that the murderer would be caught. The loss of their very likeable sheriff, a man destined for much higher political office, and the large reward soon had dozens of armed men looking for Lyons. Two days after Withers' death one of those posses saw a suspicious looking man climbing aboard a boxcar at Creswell, twelve miles south of Eugene, so they surrounded the boxcar, captured the man, and found it was Lyons. He told his captors that when he arrived at his family's ranch he had stated, "Any person attempting to get the drop on me does not value his life," and he intended to shoot the next lawman who tried to capture him. Lyons was indicted for murder on March 2, 1903, and his pregnant wife was also indicted as an accessory, but she was released on bail and later the charges were dropped.

The trial began and ended on March 4 in Judge J. W. Hamilton's courtroom and the jurors deliberated only twenty minutes before returning with a verdict of guilty of murder in the first degree. On March 6 Lyons was brought into court for sentencing and when the judge asked if he had anything to say, the prisoner responded "I don't know why I fired the shot.... I didn't mean to do it." He blamed Smith, saying that if the deputy had come in and covered him he could not have fired. Hamilton then chastised the prisoner for trying to lay blame on another person and sentenced him to "hang by the neck until dead" on April 17, 1903. Neither appeal nor the application to Governor George Chamberlain pleading for executive clemency delayed the execution.

As the fatal day approached Lyons found religion, reading his Bible daily and receiving the Reverends H. A. Green and F. E. Billington for religious consolation. On the final morning the condemned man arose early and ate a hearty breakfast. He took a great deal of time preparing, shaving closely and dressing slowly before the clergymen joined him in his cell. At 9:00 A.M. Sheriff Fisk arrived and read the death warrant, and fifteen minutes later the sheriff unlocked the cell door and the procession formed. The prisoner was escorted to the gallows by Sheriff Fisk, deputy Harry Brown, five Lane County citizens, and the two reverends. The scaffold had been erected in the jail yard within an enclosure and, excepting those in the procession, only twelve witnesses were admitted. Lyons took his place on the scaffold and, though he showed no sign of faltering, he had asked the Reverend Green to speak for him. On Lyons' behalf Green thanked everyone for their kindnesses, said Lyons had confessed his crime, and had professed penitence.

As the reverend spoke the prisoner's arms and legs were pinioned, the noose adjusted and the black hood was pulled over his head, and at the conclusion of the statement the trap was sprung. Beneath the platform Drs. F.M. Day and D.A. Paine awaited the body, and as soon as it appeared they monitored vital signs. Lyons was pronounced dead at 9:31 A.M. and, after hanging a while longer, the body was cut down, placed in a coffin, and given to his wife and brother, Benton Lyons. Later that afternoon he was buried in the I.O.O.F. section of the Eugene Cemetery after a brief graveside service.

Eugene Guard (OR): March 3, 1903; March 6, 1903; March 16, 1903; April 17, 1903; April 18, 1903. *Eugene Morning Register* (OR): February 10, 1903. *Oregonian* (Portland): April 9, 1903. *Oregon Journal* (Portland): April 16–17, 1903.

Smith, George
June 5, 1903

Twenty-nine-year-old George Smith was well known to lawmen in the Portland, Oregon, area. He had served a three year term in the penitentiary at Salem and since his release in 1891 had been in and out of the local jail, but his offenses were usually petty, often resulting in no more than an overnight stay in jail sleeping off a drunk. George Smith met a thirty-year-old woman, a "soiled dove" who went by the name Anna M. Smith, and they kept constant company, and George claimed they had been married in 1900. When George became involved in a legal case as a witness the defendant hired Edward Potella to harass him, and Potella managed to lure Anna away from her paramour and install her in a bordello above the Boston Saloon in north Portland. This, however, did not satisfy Potella, so he ambushed George one evening and pistol-whipped him into unconsciousness.

On August 22, 1902, George Smith was in the Boston Saloon and reportedly threatened to "get some white person." Carl Quall was present and, hearing the threat, later said he noticed that Smith was carrying a pistol. The following evening George went to Anna's room and knocked on her door. They argued, George trying to convince her to come home and Anna refusing repeatedly. Finally, George, frustrated by this rejection, drew his revolver and, without hesitation or warning, shot Anna. She fell to the floor and died within minutes. Smith ran down the stairs and across the street into the Sportsman Saloon. Carl Quall was sitting outside the Boston Saloon, heard the shot, and watched Smith flee. Quall told lawmen where the murderer could be found so he was quickly arrested and taken to the police station. At first Smith claimed that there was someone crouching behind a dresser in Anna's room, and he had been warned that Potella was going to kill him. He said that he shot at the crouching figure but shot Anna by mistake. However, he soon decided to confess and said, "There was nobody in this thing but me. I went up there and talked to Annie and tried to get her to come home and she would not come so I shot her. She had gone away with another man and wouldn't come home with me."

At his examination the prisoner pled not guilty but was held over for action by the Multnomah County grand jury, and in early October he was indicted for Anna's murder. His trial began in Judge M. C. George's courtroom on October 13, 1902. The defendant, reviving his first confession, claimed self-defense and testified that the shooting of Anna was an accident, but the jurors chose to disregard his self-serving testimony and on October 21 they found him guilty of first degree murder. The defendant was sentenced to hang on December 19, 1902, but an appeal was filed and this acted as a stay of execution. The appeal was finally denied and the prisoner was re-sentenced to hang on June 5, 1903.

Executions had been moved to the prison by act of the state legislature but this did not apply to cases where sentencing preceded the date the act was signed into law, so Smith was scheduled to hang in Multnomah County. The county's scaffold was readily available so all Sheriff William A. Storey had to do was buy a new rope and send out the invitations. A petition and application for commutation of sentence was submitted to Governor George Chamberlain but he refused to intervene.

While the condemned man waited out his final days he knitted shawls and blankets for his guards and their families, which helped pass the time. He had received religious consolation from the Reverend C.B.F. Moore and the Reverend promised to be with him at the end. At 6:00 A.M. on June 5, 1903, the witnesses were admitted to the enclosure and then Sheriff Storey went to the prisoner's cell and read the death warrant. The procession formed and at 6:30 A.M. George appeared at the jail door, stepped into the enclosure, and climbed the steps onto the platform. A dozen men were already seated on the platform, including the Reverend Moore, nine lawmen, and two prison officials. The condemned man took his place on the trapdoor and when asked if he had anything to say to the crowd of witnesses, he declined. His wrists were secured behind his back, his arms were then pinioned to his body at the elbows and his ankles and knees were strapped together, the noose was adjusted, and the black hood was pulled on.

Inside the sheriff's office three men stood at ropes, two dummies and one attached to the release pin so no one knew who actually sprang the trapdoor, and on the signal they all pulled simultaneously. The trap was sprung and the prisoner dropped to his death, breaking his neck in the fall. His vital signs were monitored by the attending physicians and after his heart ceased to beat he was pronounced dead, lowered into a coffin, and released to his mother for burial.

Oregonian (Portland): March 31, 1903; April 1, 1903; June 5, 1903.

Armstrong, Pleasant
January 22, 1904

Pleasant Armstrong was born in Columbia County, Washington, in 1877. His parents died when he was a baby and he was raised by a brother and then by a rancher named Patterson. He was a difficult child and was sent to live with a family named Walters. The Walterses attempted to educate the boy but Armstrong chaffed at the schooling and, when nine years old, he ran away and returned to his brother. At the age of eighteen he left home to try his hand at prospecting and mining and ended up in North Powder, Oregon, in 1899. Here he met and became engaged to Minnie Ensminger, a school teacher from a prominent Baker County family. The family objected to her engagement and after twenty-two months they had a falling-out and, in late 1902, the engagement ended. Armstrong tried every way to reconcile with his sweetheart but she would not consider it.

Finally he wrote a note saying she must see him before Christmas day and resolve the matter. In anticipation of being again rejected, Armstrong, who had returned to Baker City, had a friend purchase a .44-caliber Colt revolver for him on December 16. Minnie Ensminger was at the home of her sister and brother-in-law, Joseph Henner, near Haines, Baker County, Oregon, on Christmas eve 1902. The Henners were hosting a dance on Christmas eve with dozens of their friends in attendance and Pleasant Armstrong, an accomplished violinist, was present as a member of the orchestra. Armstrong became quite moody upon seeing his ex-fiancée present and, after playing poorly, declined to play any further. At 9:30 P.M. he retired to another room, threw himself onto a lounge, and refused to talk to anyone. When the dance ended after 1:00 A.M. Armstrong put on his overcoat and left with the rest of the musical company, in advance of the guests.

Once outside he lay in wait near a path through the barnyard of the Henner farm, which led to the sleigh awaiting Minnie and her sister Blanche. When Minnie and her sister entered the barnyard he sprang forward, put the gun to his head and said, "Good-bye Minnie," but then turned the gun on Minnie and shot his ex-sweetheart in the side and back.

He ran a few paces and again put the pistol barrel against his forehead and fired, attempting suicide, but in his haste he aimed too high and the bullet glanced off his skull, inflicting only a slight wound but knocking him senseless. He was carried into the barn where he regained consciousness, and he was restrained until Sheriff Harvey K. Brown from Baker City came and placed him under arrest. Minnie Ensminger lingered near death for forty-seven hours, but finally succumbed to her wounds without reviving sufficiently to comment on any specific reason for the shooting.

Armstrong was lodged in the Baker City jail and, when his victim died, he was charged with her murder. He waived his preliminary examination and was held over for action by the grand jury. On February 26, 1903, he was indicted for murder and was arraigned the following day. He pled not guilty on February 28 but the trial could not begin because the jail was quarantined due to a smallpox outbreak. On March 2 a large lynching party arrived in Baker City from Haines, but Sheriff Brown had been warned and had taken the prisoner out of jail and hidden him, even though he was still under quarantine. The men were allowed to go through the jail to show them the prisoner was absent, and then they dispersed. The following day Judge Robert Eakin issued an order to take Armstrong to Portland for safekeeping. He was lodged in the Multnomah County jail, and on March 20 the defense attorneys filed a motion for a change of venue but it was denied.

Armstrong was returned to Baker City by March 23 when the trial began. The trial lasted five days and on March 28 the defendant was found guilty of murder in the first degree. Three days later Judge Eakin sentenced Armstrong to hang at Baker City on May 8 and the appeals process began. First a motion for a new trial was denied and then the case was appealed to the state's Supreme Court. The court took up the matter on October 6 and affirmed the lower court's judgment and sentence on October 19. After some corrections to the mandate, Armstrong's attorneys argued for his discharge, as the death warrant had a certain date and that date, for execution at Baker City, had passed and the new law required all executions to be conducted at the state's prison in Salem. Judge Eakin did not issue a new death warrant but entered an order directing the sheriff to carry out the existing order on January 22, 1904. The defense attorneys then filed every motion and application they could conjure, and all were denied.

As the condemned man awaited his death he asked to be baptized into the Roman Catholic Church, and Father Peter Ollivotti accommodated him. When the final day arrived Armstrong received his two brothers and bid them farewell, then ate a hearty breakfast before Father Ollivotti arrived. At 6:45 A.M. Sheriff Brown led the procession from the jail to the scaffold where prison superintendent C. W. James, twelve lawmen, and Father Ollivotti waited. Armstrong, upon reaching the platform, stepped forward and, in a clear voice, addressed the crowd of two hundred fifty men. At first his speech was incoherent as he waived a crucifix over his head and occasionally stomped his foot to emphasize some point he was trying to make, but finally he focused and said,

> Love — which I had for a girl now dead; and I will die here for her murder. Now she knows there was nothing wrong in my crime. I will say this to you who have daughters, when a man comes to you loving her truly, even though he wear an old pair of shoes and is in rags, if they love truly you cannot burst that love. Minnie knew I wasn't responsible for her killing, and I hope the people look into the matter. She knows that I was not responsible when I shot. I have prayed day and night for my crime. I will now die here in the faith of Jesus Christ. I am sorry for the things I have done. I have asked God to forgive me, and I now also ask God to forgive you.

When he concluded he stepped back onto the trapdoor and received the last rites on bended knee. As soon as he arose the straps were applied to pinion his arms and legs, the black hood was pulled over his head, and the noose was adjusted. At 6:58 A.M. the signal was given and the trap was sprung, and Armstrong dropped six feet breaking his neck. His pulse did not cease entirely nor did the muscles of the body relax until 7:15, or nine minutes, fifteen seconds after the drop, and then Drs. McDaniel, Dodson and Curry of Baker City; doctors Brock and Anderson of Sumpter; and doctor Francis of Haines each examined the body and pronounced him dead. A coroner's jury of twelve men, from among the witnesses, signed the death certificate as required by law. The body was given to brothers E. and Grant Armstrong, who had it delivered to the undertaking parlor of Fred Eppinger and prepared for burial. The remains of Pleasant Armstrong were buried in the Catholic cemetery at 4:00 P.M. that same day.

Oregonian (Portland): March 6, 1903; January 21–23, 1904.

Egbert, Harry D. January 29, 1904

Harry D. Egbert, alias John or Jack Frost, was born in Audubon County, Iowa, in 1877. He explained that his true name was Frost, but that he had been adopted by an aunt named Egbert while still quite young. He received a good public education and graduated from high school, but soon embarked on a life of crime operating an illegal liquor saloon, a "blind pig," in a prohibition town. In 1900 he moved to Oregon, where he was soon arrested for horse stealing and sentenced to a brief prison term.

Not long after his release from prison a Douglas County warrant was issued for Egbert's arrest, charging him with a burglary in Drain, Oregon. Harney County Sheriff Tom Allen deputized John G. Saxton to make the arrest and on September 26, 1903, the lawman found Egbert on the Mahon Ranch near Burns, after missing him on the road the previous day. On some pretext Egbert was allowed to enter the house to speak to his wife and he escaped through a rear window. Saxton deputized Joseph "Jack" West to help and they continued on Egbert's trail.

On October 4 they again located the fugitive at Fields' Ranch in Wild Horse Valley, one hundred twenty-five miles south of Burns. The lawmen approached at 2:00 P.M. while Egbert was in the kitchen with his wife and Charles Fields. When the fugitive saw the deputies he ran into the front room for a rifle. His wife and Fields asked him not to fire and he promised he wouldn't, but insisted he would not be arrested. Fields then went out and told Saxton and West that their man was inside with a Winchester, and suggested they get more help. However, West said they were going to get him and they tied their horses before starting toward the house, Saxton in the lead and West still outside the fence when Egbert appeared.

West ran for cover as Egbert shot him in the back and Saxton returned fire, which drove Egbert back into the house and into a first floor bedroom. Saxton followed and the two men exchanged shots through the wall. Saxton was struck in the shoulder with a spent bullet which only caused a bruise, and the butt of Egbert's pistol, which was tucked in his belt, was struck by a bullet, but no one was seriously wounded during this gun battle. While the battle raged Fields and Egbert's wife fled two hundred fifty yards to a sod house and when the shooting ceased Saxton joined them. Fields then went to the main ranch house to convince Egbert to surrender, or to overpower him if the opportunity arose, but Egbert stood his ground and would not let Fields approach.

Meanwhile, West, who had been mortally wounded, was begging for water. Fields returned to the sod house and warned Saxton not to go to West, as he would be in plain view from the house. Saxton then asked Egbert's wife to take water to West, but she refused. Saxton, frustrated, poured water into a cup and took it to West. When he returned to the sod house Fields again warned Saxton not to go to his partner, but Saxton ignored the warning and took a blanket to cover him and another to place beneath his head. Egbert, seeing what Saxton was about, had taken up a position at a second floor window with a clear aim at West, a distance of fifty-seven feet.

When Saxton bent over to tend the dying man Egbert shot him, the bullet ranging downward through his breast, piercing his heart, and killing him instantly, and West also soon died of his wounds.

Egbert then ransacked Fields' house and took money from his wife's purse. He went outside and took Saxton's rifle and a cartridge belt from West. Just then Sid Kurtz rode up and Egbert stole his black horse at gunpoint, then fled toward Nevada. Fields took the woman and her small child to Pedro's Ranch while Justice Catlow took a coroner's jury to the ranch and held an inquest. The bodies were then removed, West taken south to Wild Horse for burial and Saxton brought into Burns and buried on October 10. A reward of $500, later increased to $1,000, was offered for the capture of Egbert and his description was widely circulated. Sid Kurtz telegraphed from Winnemucca, Nevada, saying he had followed Egbert and wanted to know if funds were available for him to continue on his trail. Kurtz had been turning up at odd times during the pursuit of Egbert and he refused to help with the arrest, so deputy sheriff Hughet telegraphed the sheriff of Humboldt County to arrest Kurtz.

Tom Murray had also gone to Nevada to pursue Egbert and learned that the fugitive was headed toward Elko. He took the train but when he got there found he was four days behind Egbert. Elko's constable, T. N. McCoy, agreed to take up the trail, as Murray was well known to Egbert and could not get close. Murray gave him an advance of $100 for expenses and McCoy started out. McCoy trailed his man to Rockland, Idaho, with the help of four Indian trackers. He found Egbert's horse stabled at the livery and tried to arrest the fugitive but Egbert bolted. With the aid of a small posse of citizens armed with Winchester rifles, McCoy captured Egbert on October 26 after a running gun battle of three miles. The fugitive had taken refuge in a thicket but when the men came close he had to surrender as he was out of ammunition. He was returned to Oregon on a requisition from Governor George Chamberlain.

Court was scheduled to close but when the capture of Egbert was announced it was held open awaiting his arrival. Once Egbert was captured interest waned in trying Kurtz as an accessory in the escape, and Kurtz was released in late November. While Egbert was on the run he had been indicted *in absentia*, so as soon as he arrived in Burns he was arraigned, pled not guilty, and court was convened on December 1 for the purpose of seating a jury. The trial began on December 7 and concluded the following day, and by 4:00 P.M. Egbert was convicted of first degree murder. On Thursday, December 10, Egbert was sentenced to hang on January 29, 1904. That night he tried to commit suicide by bashing his head against the bars but only succeeded in knocking himself unconscious. He lay in bed until the next afternoon, then revived and complained his head ached. The following day he was taken to the prison to await his execution, the first man in Oregon to be hanged under a new law that required executions to be carried out at state prisons instead of county jails.

Egbert was lodged in the upper tier in the south wing and during his confinement the condemned man found religion and insisted that he had repented his sins. The last few hours of his life were spent smoking cigarettes, writing letters, and talking with death watch guards, P. N. Patterson, J. B. Chenoweth, and W. B. Cyrus. At noon all the prisoners were locked in their cells, which was the custom when feeding them dinner, and then seventy-five witnesses were escorted from the prison's waiting room through the chapel, into the yard, and then into the execution chamber. At noon Superintendent C. W. James and Warden Frank Curtis went to Egbert's cell and offered to read the death warrant, but this ceremony was waived by the prisoner. The cell door was swung open and the prisoner, unshackled, was escorted down the corridor, down the stairs, through the chapel into the yard, and around the east wing. He then climbed the stairs into the execution chamber and up another narrow flight of stairs onto the scaffold.

Though pale and puffing nervously on a

cigarette, he walked with a firm step. He was asked if he had anything to say and after a moment's hesitation he stepped to the railing and said, "My friends, you see me a condemned man. Take me as a mark. If you have any children, keep them off the street at night and keep them out of saloons and bad company. Gentlemen, my heart aches for you and your children. Bad raising and bad company were the cause of my downfall. That's all — my heart is too full to say much — I have repented of my sins." When he concluded he stepped back and centered himself on the trapdoor. His wrists and arms, knees and ankles were pinioned with straps and then the Reverend E. W. St. Pierre read an appropriate Bible verse. The black hood was pulled over Egbert's head and the noose was adjusted. At a signal James and Curtis pulled levers, one a dummy, which sprang the trap at 12:30 P.M. and Egbert fell six feet, breaking his neck. Doctors J. D. Shaw and E. A. Pierce monitored Egbert's vital signs and pronounced him dead after nine minutes and eighteen seconds. The body hung a while longer to ensure he could not be revived, and the body was then lowered into a wooden coffin and covered. The witnesses dispersed while twelve men, chosen as the coroner's jury, signed the death certificate. No relative had come forward to claim the body. According to law, the remains must be turned over to a medical school if requested. The medical department of Willamette University had filed a request and later received Egbert's remains.

Times-Herald (Burns, OR): October 10, 1903; October 16–17, 1903; October 24, 1903; October 31, 1903; November 8, 1903; November 14, 1908; November 28, 1908; December 5, 1903; December 10, 1903; December 26, 1903. *Oregonian* (Portland): January 30, 1904.

Guglielmo, Frank
May 5, 1905

On Christmas day 1902 Frank Guglielmo's father, who owned a saloon in Portland, was murdered by G. Castro. The business passed to his twenty-one-year-old son and he operated it for the next two years. At the time of his father's death Frank was a bridegroom of just three weeks, but a few weeks after the murder Frank's wife filed for divorce, naming the step-mother as the co-respondent.

In early 1904 Guglielmo became acquainted with the Guarascia family residing at 324 Harrison Street and he became hopelessly infatuated with their beautiful sixteen-year-old daughter, Freda. He pursued her relentlessly until they became engaged. Her father, Guisippino, wanted an end to the budding relationship and forbid her to associate with the young saloon keeper, and she acquiesced to her father's wishes. Guglielmo had made secret visits to the home to be with his sweetheart and had been rebuffed, but on June 14, angry at being rejected and determined to give Freda one last chance, he went to her home and found her at work in the kitchen, and engaged her in conversation. Following her father's instructions she rebuffed him once more, so he pulled his six-shooter and shot her once in the head and once in the heart. Neighbors, hearing the shots, rushed to her aid and she tried to speak to them, but she died within minutes without identifying Guglielmo as her murderer. The young saloon-keeper had fled but he was immediately suspected.

Guglielmo ran to his saloon, took his bicycle and peddled toward Linnton, where he was captured later that day. He was brought back to Portland and lodged in the Multnomah County jail. He was indicted and tried, convicted of first degree murder on June 30, and sentenced to hang on August 16. This action of the District Court was appealed to the state Supreme Court, which affirmed the lower court's judgment and sentence on March 20, 1905, and Guglielmo was re-sentenced to hang on Friday, May 5, 1905.

Days before the execution prison clerk Tom Wilson, while at the Perkins Hotel in Salem, gave an interview to an *Oregonian* reporter and said, "Guglielmo is bracing up and some of us are inclined to believe that he will face the gallows like a man. He still has his moody spells, which consist of a big cry, but at times he seems real cheerful and attempts to amuse his guards by telling funny stories. Then at other times he gets desperate and pretends he is not sorry he killed the young girl. He has said since, he regretted that he did not kill the old man, too."

The forty invitations to witnesses had been sent and prison superintendent C. W. James planned the event for 12:30 P.M., when the other prisoners were locked in their cells for the dinner meal. On Wednesday, Guglielmo could not eat and that night he had difficulty sleeping. On Thursday he was able to eat a little but told his guards that he was afraid he would not be able to walk to the scaffold. Warden Frank Curtis had a long talk with the prisoner, pointing out how people would say he was a coward if he broke down, and Guglielmo then said he would exert whatever measure it would take to walk on his own. He told superintendent James that he would need an hour to talk to the crowd of witnesses, but when limited to a few minutes, he agreed.

By Friday morning the condemned man had braced himself for the ordeal. He bathed and "dressed in a perfectly fitting suit of dark blue, white shirt, standing collar, and carefully adjusted tie. His hair well combed and brushed and his shoes highly polished." At 12:30 P.M., in company with Father Dominic Faber of Salem, superintendent James arrived at the cell and read the death warrant. James and Father Faber led the procession with Warden Curtis on one side and Assistant Warden J. N. Smith on the other side of the prisoner, in case he needed support. Guards followed behind. The prisoner, his face deathly pale though whiskey had braced him, kept his eyes to the ground and puffed vigorously on a cigar. The procession passed through the chapel into the yard and into the execution chamber. Guglielmo climbed the narrow stairs with a steady gait and took his position at the railing, ready to address the witnesses. He spoke in a strong voice, but in broken sentences, calling on God several times. He looked down at his victim's father several times stating that the fault was his, and finally concluded, "I am sorry she is dead, and I am willing to die and pay for her life."

As soon as Guglielmo concluded he stepped back onto the trapdoor and centered himself. Father Faber held up a crucifix and prayed as the straps were applied to pinion his arms and legs. The prisoner was allowed to kiss the crucifix twice before the black hood was pulled over his head and the noose was adjusted. In response to a prayer by the father, the condemned man yelled out, "Mercy, God, mercy!" and at that moment the trap was sprung. The body swung about but there was not a twitch nor a quiver of muscle, and in twelve minutes Drs. Bayliss H. Earle of Astoria and F. E. Smith of Salem pronounced him dead. The body was cut down and given to Coroner Clough, who prepared it for shipment by train to Portland, where friends had planned his burial.

The following day the train arrived at the Portland depot at 6:25 P.M. where a band and six empty carriages were supposed to assemble, and several hundred curious people waited, but neither the carriages nor the band appeared. The body, enclosed in a rough pine box, was placed in the casket wagon of Dunning, McEntee and Gilbaugh and taken to their undertaking parlor at 3 North Seventh Street. Only a few friends were admitted but the interest was so strong that the following day the doors were flung open and hundreds filed through to see the body of the executed murderer. The *Oregonian* reported, "The features of Guglielmo are not distorted and do not show any signs of agony or pain in his last moments. The physicians say his death was instantaneous and that he did not suffer any pain. There is a slight abrasion below the chin and the neck is slightly swollen, but hardly enough to be noticeable without close observation."

Oregonian (Portland): May 2, 1905; May 5, 1905; May 6, 1905. *Seattle Daily Times* (WA): May 6, 1905.

Lauth, George W.
July 13, 1905

George W. Lauth, a twenty-four-year-old gambler, lived an "illicit relationship" with

Leonora B. Jones at Oregon City, Clackamas County, Oregon. In June 1904 Jones became disillusioned with the situation and took all of Lauth's money before she left him. By September, Lauth had traced Leonora to her mother's home and on September 6 he entered the home, confronted his paramour in the hallway, and shot her four times inflicting several mortal wounds. He tried to make his escape but Leonora's father captured him and held him for the police. Lauth told the lawmen, when they arrived, that he believed she had left him for another man and claimed that his act was due to insanity induced by jealousy. Leonora was rushed to the local hospital where doctors told her the wounds were fatal. She then made an ante-mortem statement naming Lauth as her murderer and died the following day. Lauth was indicted and tried at the fall term of court, his plea of insanity was rejected by the jury, and he was convicted of first degree murder. He was delivered to the prison at Salem to await his execution and after exhausting all appeals he was re-sentenced to hang on July 13, 1905.

As soon as Lauth was behind prison walls he professed religion and, relying upon this, seemed cheerful and resigned to his fate. Prison Chaplain E. W. St. Pierre visited the condemned man nearly every day and provided religious support. The condemned man said he had no fear of death, showed no sign of fear to the end, and on his final day spent the morning reading the New Testament with St. Pierre. The execution was conducted during the noon hour when all the prisoners were routinely locked in their cells for dinner. Superintendent Calbreath went to Lauth's cell to read the death warrant, and then the prisoner was escorted through the chapel into the yard. He crossed to the execution chamber and climbed the narrow stairs onto the platform. He took his place on the trapdoor, refusing to speak to the thirty-one witnesses present in the chamber.

The process of applying the straps, which pinioned his arms and legs, began as he prayed, "Into thy hands, oh God, I give my spirit." These were the only words spoken and the black hood was pulled over his head and the noose adjusted. Within a few moments the trap was sprung and Lauth dropped six feet, breaking his neck. Several doctors had been invited but none attended so Calbreath, also a doctor, summoned Dr. Griffith of the State Insane Asylum to assist him. In thirteen minutes they pronounced Lauth dead. After hanging a bit longer the body was cut down and placed in a pine coffin provided by the state. Lauth was laid to rest in the Lee Missionary cemetery that evening, with few attending the graveside service conducted by St. Pierre.

Capitol Journal (Salem, OR): July 13, 1905. *Oregonian* (Portland): July 14, 1905. *Salt Lake Tribune* (UT): September 7–8, 1904.

Williams, Norman D. July 21, 1905

Louise J. Nesbitt, sometimes Nesbit, and her thirty-one-year-old daughter Alma lived near Hood River, Oregon, on a tract of land on which Alma had filed a homestead claim. The land was adjacent to a tract of land on which Norman Daniel Williams, sometimes given as Daniel Norman Williams, had filed a homestead claim. Williams and Alma Nesbitt were engaged when they came west to Hood River in May 1899 and they married on July 25, 1899, but, unknown to Alma, Williams already had a wife in Nebraska. They kept their marriage secret, as disclosure would have voided the second land claim under the federal Homestead Act. Williams and the Nesbitts built structures on their land as required to prove up on their claims but, by some error in a survey, Williams built his house on Alma's land.

In February the Nesbitts went to Portland and took up temporary residence in a boarding house where Williams was an infrequent visitor. On March 8, 1900, the Nesbitts and Williams took the train to Hood River and, though it was storming heavily, they rented a buggy and drove to Williams' house. Williams returned to town the following morning and claimed that the women had preceded him and left by train, but the women had not been aboard the only train leaving Hood River on March 9 which left at 5:30 A.M. Williams felt he was under suspicion so, after a year, he relinquished his claim and later that year submitted a letter, dated June 23, 1900, relinquishing Alma Nesbitt's homestead claim.

Alma was a striking young woman and she was remembered by the land office clerk, who found her letter of relinquishment suspicious and brought it to the attention of U.S. Attorney John H. Hall. Hall followed up by comparing the signature on the letter with that on the original claim and found the letter to be a forgery. He brought the matter before the federal grand jury and in November 1903 an investigation into the disappearance of Alma Nesbitt began. Alma's brother George learned of the investigation and decided to investigate on his own. He traveled to Hood River and, with a local livery man, went to the Williams home, which was then vacant. Seven feet beneath the soft earth of a small henhouse they found the remains of two females, including hair attached to bits of skull resembling that of Louise and Alma Nesbitt, and blood soaked gunny sacks. Wasco County district attorney Frank Menefee worked up a case of circumstantial evidence, every piece carefully linked to arrive at only one conclusion — that Williams had murdered the Nesbitt women and forged the letter of relinquishment. Williams had moved to British Columbia but as time passed, and there were no charges filed nor an investigation instituted, he had returned to Bellingham, Washington, and remarried. He was arrested at Bellingham on February 8, 1905, and, on a requisition from Governor George Chamberlain, he was returned to Oregon where the Wasco County grand jury indicted him on April 27, 1904.

Williams' trial began on May 23, 1904, and, though there was no defense offered and Williams did not testify, there was strong cross-examination of prosecution witnesses and objections to nearly everything done by the prosecution. The most damning testimony was by doctor L. Victoria Hampton who proved that the hair and blood were human. Five days later on May 28, 1904, after only three and one half hours of deliberation, the jurors convicted Williams on two counts of first degree murder. This was prior to enactment of the law moving executions to the prison at Salem, so the prisoner was sentenced to hang in the jail yard in The Dalles, Wasco County, Oregon. His appeal delayed the execution but in June 1905 the state Supreme Court rejected his appeal and upheld the lower court's judgment and sentence. On June 10 Williams was re-sentenced to hang on July 21, 1905.

On his final day Williams arose at 3:30 A.M. and, with Father Louis Desmarais of St. Peter's Church, prayed as he made preparations for his execution. He refused breakfast, then bathed and dressed in the suit provided by Sheriff Felix C. Sexton. Minutes before 6:00 A.M. the sheriff arrived and read the death warrant, then admitted newspaper reporters. As soon as the condemned man saw the reporters he announced, "I have nothing to say; my lips are sealed to the world." Then, with the sheriff and priest, they started for the gallows. The prisoner walked unassisted into the enclosure and onto the scaffold, avoiding even a glance toward the one hundred witnesses, and he took his place on the trapdoor. The previous evening Williams had told the sheriff that he would have nothing to say on the scaffold but Sexton felt obliged to ask, "Do you wish to make a statement?" and Williams replied faintly but firmly, "No!"

Deputy sheriff Haight and Marshal Wood applied the straps that pinioned the prisoner's arms and legs and then Sheriff Thomas Linnville of Clatsop County pulled the black hood over the prisoner's head and adjusted the noose. Sexton had taken his place at the lever, and two minutes after the prisoner left his cell the trap was sprung and Williams dropped six feet. His neck was broken and not a twitch of a muscle was noticeable. In fifteen minutes Drs. Reutyer, Ferguson and Doane pronounced him dead and then the body was cut down, placed in a pine coffin, and Coroner Burget delivered the remains to the Catholic Church. Father Desmarais held mass with only a few early-morning attendants present, as the condemned murderer had no friends and no relative had come forward, so following the services the body was buried in the Catholic cemetery at county expense.

Journal (Portland, OR): April 28, 1904. *Oregonian* (Portland): October 29, 1903; February 9, 1904; May 31, 1904; July 21–22, 1905; July 29, 1905.

Barnes, John G.
September 18, 1906

On the evening of April 28, 1905, John G. Barnes and his neighbor, William H. "Six-shooter Bill" Graham, were returning to their diggings in the mining district near Glendale, Douglas County, Oregon. While walking along the railroad tracks Barnes attacked Graham and there was a violent struggle, during which Barnes struck Graham on the skull with a rock. Barnes dragged Graham's limp body a considerable distance down a steep embankment and, near the fence of the long trestle north of Glendale a mile and a half from town, he wedged the body between two logs. Barnes piled railroad ties, bark, sticks and brush on top of the body, creating a funeral pyre, and then set it ablaze. The blow to the head might have killed Graham, or perhaps he was only unconscious and burned alive afterwards. Barnes fled, expecting the fire to consume all evidence of his crime.

On May 1, Ed Holtz, a railroad track-walker, spotted the ashes of the large fire and, investigating, found a body burned to a crisp. Holtz summoned Sheriff H. T. McClallen, who began an investigation, and on searching the ashes McClallen recovered part of a trouser leg which had not been burned and shoe soles with new hobnails, and while searching the vicinity found a hat with parlor matches in the band which had been stuffed into a tree stump. The area around the tracks was examined and blood stains pinpointed where the initial attack had been committed, and the scene was carefully documented. The remains and evidence were taken to the county seat at Roseburg and Justice of the Peace Montgomery convened a coroner's jury for an inquest.

It was first thought that the murdered man was one of two men who had passed through recently and a tramp was arrested on suspicion of being involved, but all these proved false leads. When word of the hat became generally known many suggested that it might be the old miner, William Graham, who lived several miles from Glendale and who had been missing for several days before the remains were found, and this directed suspicion onto his neighbor, John G. Barnes. Barnes, people then remembered, was the last person seen with Graham. Within a week Sheriff McClallen had located Barnes at Glendale and arrested and lodged him in the jail in Roseburg. Barnes' cabin was searched and Graham's knife, gun, belt, another hat and gold nuggets were found, but Barnes claimed he had bought the gun from a man named George Hittman and had acquired the gold nuggets from others who had bought them from Graham. While Barnes sat in his cell the sheriff began gathering evidence and, though circumstantial, each small bit fit nicely into a chain that pointed directly to the prisoner's guilt.

By mid–May a grand jury had been summoned and on May 18 it returned an indictment against Barnes based upon the overwhelming evidence. That same day Barnes was taken into Judge Hamilton's court to plead and he argued that he would represent himself, but the judge appointed attorney J. A. Buchanan to assist him and gave the defendant until the following day to plead. Meanwhile, Sheriff McClallen had gone to The Dalles to get George Hittman and his wife, who had been arrested by Sheriff Felix C. Sexton. Sexton charged Hittman with receiving stolen property because, when arrested, he had one of Graham's gold nuggets in his pocket. Hittman said he had bought the nugget from a man who was then in Idaho, but he and his wife both admitted being in Glendale at the time of the murder. When they arrived at Roseburg,

Hittman was charged as a principal in the murder of Graham. On May 22 J. A. Buchanan, who had taken over the defense of Barnes, moved to have the trial postponed to the October term of the court, and this was granted.

The case of the *State vs. Barnes* was called in Judge Harris' courtroom on October 5 and began on the following Monday. Thirty-six witnesses were called by the prosecution, including George Hittman and his wife, and three witnesses were called by the defense, including Barnes, whose testimony tried to prove that Graham was still alive. After the case went to the jurors they deliberated for some time and at 8:15 P.M. asked for additional instructions as to whether a verdict of guilty of second degree murder was possible. The judge said, "I suppose that such a verdict could be brought in, but I do not expect such a return as no evidence of self-defense had been offered." The jury retired for less than an hour and returned a verdict of "guilty of first degree murder." Before sentence could be imposed Buchanan argued a motion for a new trial, citing errors by the judge and jury. Judge Harris denied the motion and on October 23 sentenced Barnes to hang on December 15, 1905. This was followed by an appeal and on December 18, 1905, the *Umpqua Valley News* reported that the state Supreme Court had granted a new trial and stayed the execution of Barnes.

The defendant was retried at the spring 1906 term of court and he was easily found guilty of murder in the first degree on the same evidence, and sentenced to hang. His attorneys again began an aggressive campaign to appeal the case but this time the judge and prosecution had been careful and deliberate, and the lower court's decision was affirmed. Barnes was sentenced to hang on September 18, 1906, and the application to Governor George Chamberlain for a commutation of sentence to life in prison was denied.

Father Anthony Moore was with the prisoner during the hours of his last morning but the condemned man would not confess. At 12:30 P.M. Barnes was taken out of his cell and escorted to the execution chamber by Superintendent C. W. James and Warden Frank Curtis, followed by a number of prison officials. When they passed through the chapel into the yard Barnes asked that the warden take along a hymn book, and he did. Looking over the small crowd, he said, "Gentlemen, this is not going to be an execution; this is a murder. I expect to die like a man. Although Governor Chamberlain has seen fit not to commute my sentence, I am ready to die; but this is not an execution; it is a murder." He turned to Warden Curtis and asked that hymn number five from the Pentecostal hymn book be sung, but no one present could sing it, so it was dispensed with. Barnes then shook hands with the guards from his death watch and said he was ready to meet death.

He was positioned on the trapdoor where his wrists and arms, knees and ankles were strapped, the noose was adjusted, and the black hood was pulled on. Shortly after 12:30 P.M. the trap was sprung and Barnes dropped, breaking his neck in the fall. Beneath the scaffold stood Drs. J. D. Shaw, Frank E. Smith, and O. B. Miller, who monitored his vital signs and in ten and one half minutes they signaled to Warden Curtis, who announced, "He is dead." After hanging a bit longer, to ensure Barnes could not be revived, the body was cut down and placed in a coffin. His half brothers, William and David Patterson of Portland, were not present but it was supposed they were on their way and would take charge of the remains.

Plaindealer (Roseburg, OR): May 1, 1905; May 4, 1905; May 8, 1905; May 11, 1905; May 15, 1905; May 18, 1905; May 22, 1905; October 5, 1905; October 9, 1905; October 12, 1905; October 16, 1905; October 19, 1905; October 22–23; 1905. *Umpqua Valley News* (Roseburg, OR): December 18, 1905; September 20, 1906.

Shepherd, Fred A.
November 30, 1906

On the morning of September 24, 1906, during the early morning hours, farmhand Fred A. Shepherd shot Benjamin F. Zell, his employer, at Zell's ranch in Crook County, Oregon. He had become obsessed with Mrs. Zell and finally could not control his lustful passions and after committing the brutal, cold-blooded murder he went into the ranch house and raped Zell's wife. He fled but was quickly captured and lodged in jail and at his examination he did not deny the crime, and was easily indicted on his own testimony. His trial began on October 10 and his defense was insanity, but three physicians pronounced him sane and he was convicted of murder in the first degree. Shepherd was sentenced to hang on November 30, 1906, and nothing intervened to delay his appointment with the hangman.

As the hour of his death approached the condemned man dressed in the suit provided, but then tied a gaudy red silk handkerchief around his neck, "to make me look pretty," he explained as he posed for his photograph. He wanted a copy of the picture sent to his mother and this wish was granted. As he posed he "tipped his hat back in a careless fashion and assumed an air of recklessness." He had caused no difficulties during his time of confinement, except to complain that no death watch had been posted, but it seemed none was needed, as his manner reflected a man who did not care for life or death and joked about the gallows. When he was shaved he complained that he was not handcuffed as other condemned men were, and when he asked for the same treatment as the others he was accommodated.

At noon the prisoners were locked in their cells for their dinner, as was the usual routine. The prison superintendent then went to Shepherd's cell and read the death warrant. The prisoner was escorted through the chapel into the yard and into the execution chamber. Shepherd walked to the gallows and climbed the stairs with unfaltering steps, and there he recited the religious rites of the Roman Catholic Church. He stood firmly as his arms and legs were pinioned and the noose was adjusted. He made a brief statement to the fifty witnesses acknowledging the crime, which he had also done before and during his trial. Father Anthony Moore of Salem conducted religious exercises and offered a crucifix for the prisoner to kiss and then the black hood was pulled over Shepherd's head and in another moment, exactly at 12:30 P.M., the trap was sprung. The prisoner's neck was broken in the fall and he died without a struggle. After Shepherd was pronounced dead, and had hung a sufficient time, his body was lowered and placed in a coffin. The witnesses were allowed to examine the remains and the coroner's jury signed the death certificate. Shepherd was taken to the local cemetery and buried that evening.

Oregonian (Portland): December 1, 1906.

Hose, Henry
December 21, 1906

Henry Hose lived with Madge Doyle, alias Madge Wilson, in a cheap lodging-house on Third and Burnside Streets on the north end of Portland, Oregon. Hose, an ex-soldier, had squandered all his money trying to keep the woman content. On the morning of October 19, 1906, they were discussing the condition of their affairs and Doyle made it clear she would leave him if he went broke. At 10:00 A.M. she told him to go out and spend his last twenty-five cents to buy her a quart of beer, but he refused. Hose said Doyle was lying in bed and calling him vile names, and saying she cared nothing for him. She said, "There was once a man who spent everything he had on me and went hungry, and if you cared for me you would do the same. You are no thoroughbred."

Hose said he could take it no longer, "so I decided it was time for her to die. Some terrible feeling took possession of me, but I was not excited. I took the razor in my hand and said, 'Madge, I am going to kill you now.' She begged me not to, but when I said I would die with her she said it was all right — although she did not want me to die." He said that Madge, still lying in bed, leaned back and stretched to expose her neck as she laughed at her lover. "I missed her with the first cut I made," Hose continued, "and killed her next time. The razor broke when I killed her, or I would have killed myself. I was glad when it was over and she was dead. I cared for her and I knew none could take her then, even if my money was gone."

The sharp blade had caused slight cuts to both Madge and Henry as they fought for control of the razor after the first cut, but Madge told him she would not scream out since, as Hose described her mood, "she did not wish me to be caught and punished for what I was doing." Hose overpowered Madge and slashed her throat from ear to ear; but she had kept her promise and never called out for help. After seeing the gory results of his work, and seeing that the razor was broken, he decided he would rather hang. Hose washed his hands and then walked to the police station where he approached Captain Moore. "I wish to give myself up," he said and the captain asked, "Is that so? What have you been doing?" Hose replied, as calmly as if talking about the weather, "I just killed a woman friend down the street here."

As Moore booked the prisoner he got the details of the event and the location and dispatched detective Price to investigate. Price telephoned in a few minutes to confirm the murder. By 10:30 A.M. Hose was in jail and Madge Doyle, well known to police as an opium fiend and a loose woman, was on her way to the city morgue. Doyle's husband, Jack Doyle, was then doing time in the county jail and he was told of his wife's death. Hose was indicted for murder and he pled guilty. He was sentenced to hang on December 21, 1906, only two months after the murder was committed. He did not want to file an appeal nor submit an application for executive clemency, and was anxious and determined to meet his fate.

On the final day Hose walked to the gallows with a firm step and, once upon the platform, was asked if he had anything to say. He stepped forward to the railing and said, "Dear Friends: I committed the crime and never did deny it. I feel awful sorry for it, and all I can do is ask that God will have mercy." The crowd of forty witnesses consisted of a dozen medical students, several newspaper men and lawmen, and the twelve citizens, selected as a coroner's jury, who would sign the death certificate. After the brief statement Hose stepped back onto the trapdoor and centered himself. The straps were applied, pinioning his arms and legs, and the noose was adjusted while a clergyman muttered a prayer. The black hood was pulled on and in the next moment, at 12:30 P.M., the trap was sprung and the entire time spent on the platform, before the trap fell, was less than two minutes. There was a slight muscle twitch but otherwise there was no sign of life and within minutes he was pronounced dead. The remains of Henry Hose were buried at county expense that evening.

Capitol Journal (Salem, OR): October 20, 1906. *Oregonian* (Portland): October 20, 1906; December 22, 1906.

Megorden, Henry O.
June 28, 1907

On March 28, 1905, Henry Oliver Megorden returned home to Nyssa from Vale in Malheur County, Oregon, where he had gone to pay taxes. Supper was not on the table, which resulted in an argument with his wife. Megorden's eighteen-year-old son, Robert, tried to intervene and reportedly struck his father with a pistol when the elder Megorden became violent. The relations between the husband and wife had been deteriorating for some time, and fearing another beating, Mrs. Megorden fled toward a neighbor's house. The elder Megorden wrestled the pistol from his son, ran after his wife, and overtook her in the roadway. With the pistol in his right hand he grabbed her with his left and held her firmly. She pleaded, "Henry, I implore you not to kill me," but her husband paid her no heed, placed the pistol against her breast, and pulled the trigger. She died instantly, the bullet piercing her heart. Two of their five children, the others being away at the time, followed when their father pursued their mother and witnessed the entire affair. Henry, after killing his wife, left her body lying in the road and went to Nyssa, where he surrendered to the authorities. The two children, Robert and Olive Megorden, got a wheelbarrow and took home the body of their mother and she was buried at Nyssa several days later.

The defendant was brought to trial at Vale and it took three days, until Tuesday, to seat a jury. The trial began on Saturday, September 16, 1905, with Robert and Olive Megorden the principal witnesses against their father. The trial concluded on Friday when the argument by the prosecution's attorneys, W. J. McCulloch and E. L. Bryan, moved the audience to tears. Defense attorneys Will R. King and Frank Harris then tried in vain to influence the jury to find a verdict of not guilty, but the jurors were out only forty-five minutes before convicting the defendant of murder in the first degree. Megorden was sentenced to hang and was taken to the prison in Salem. The case was appealed to the state Supreme Court, which affirmed the lower court's judgment and sentence and on January 12, 1907, Megorden was sentenced to hang on June 28.

Throughout his time in prison Megorden showed no dread of his impending death, asserting that he did not care for life in prison. On his final night he rested peacefully, fully resigned to his fate, and arose at an early hour to eat his usual breakfast. At noon the death warrant was read to him in his cell and then he was taken out and escorted into the death chamber. He walked between Warden Frank H. Curtis and deputy Warden J. N. Smith, with superintendent C. W. James leading the way. Once in the death chamber he climbed the stairs of the gallows with a firm step. On the platform he was asked if he had anything to say but he only shook his head. The attendants then began to pinion his limbs, and a sudden metamorphosis took place.

He had seemed weakened but emotionless to that moment, but suddenly he began to tremble from head to foot and threw his hands over his eyes. The attendants had slight difficulty pulling his hands to his sides and worked quickly with the straps to prevent a complete collapse, and one attendant immediately pulled the black hood over his head and positioned the noose. At exactly 12:30 P.M. the trap was sprung and the prisoner fell six feet to his death, breaking his neck in the fall. There was not a quiver as Dr. J. D. Shaw, the prison physician, monitored his pulse. The doctor was called away for a few minutes when juror Charles McCarter fainted, but he returned and pronounced Megorden dead in ten minutes. After hanging a while longer, to ensure Megorden would not revive, the body was cut down and placed in a coffin and he was buried next to his wife at Nyssa.

Oregon Statesman (Salem): June 29, 1907. *Oregonian* (Portland): September 23, 1905.

Johnson, Walter M.
February 5, 1909

Walter Montgomery Johnson, a man who had been raised and lived in Washington County, Oregon, and was well known, lured Elmer Purdue to a lonely cabin twenty miles northeast of Hillsboro and six miles northeast of Buxton. Johnson had convinced Purdue that he would provide him with a claim, but this was a ruse to get the man to an isolated place where he could be murdered. The men were tired from their journey and soon went to bed, but at 3:00 A.M., while Purdue slept soundly, Johnson arose and went outside with his rifle. He raised a window to get a better angle for a shot and killed the sleeping Purdue with one bullet to his head. Johnson then returned to the cabin and rifled through Purdue's belongings, stealing the $140 he knew his victim had with him.

The murder of Purdue was discovered and Johnson, the last man seen in his company, was soon captured and taken to Hillsboro. At his examination he was held over for the grand jury, though he claimed that the two men had quarreled and he had killed Purdue in self-defense. The evidence of murder for robbery against Johnson was strong and on December 14, 1908, he was convicted of murder in the first degree. Judge T. A. McBride pronounced sentence on December 14, stating, "Johnson shall be remanded to the Washington County Jail for a period not longer than 20 days, when he will be conveyed to Salem, where, on Friday, February 5, he shall be hanged," and he was soon taken to the prison to await his execution. He persisted in his claim of self-defense, hoping for a retrial or at least a commutation of his sentence to life in prison. All efforts failed, but he had been weakened and sickened by his situation, so he was moved from his death row cell to the prison hospital.

After noon on his final day Johnson collapsed and had to be carried down the stairs from the hospital ward, accompanied by the Rev. W. H. Selleck. At the foot of the stairs he was met by prison superintendent C. W. James, who asked if he wished to hear the death warrant read. The condemned man was, at first, unable to speak but finally managed to mumble "I don't care." It was apparent that he was not interested in hearing the death warrant, or at least too preoccupied with his impending death, so Selleck waived the reading on Johnson's behalf. The prisoner was then led into the execution chamber, where the largest crowd ever to witness an execution in the prison had assembled, and Johnson managed to climb the stairs onto the scaffold with a firm step.

He was asked if he had anything to say and he told the witnesses, "Whiskey has led me to this crime. If it had not been for whisky, I would never have done what I did. I drank so much and so long it took my mind away, and I pray to God that from this day on none of you will ever touch a drop of whisky again." He then called Sheriff H. G. Hancock of Washington County to the scaffold and confessed, "I killed a man for his money. I've said all along, during the trial and during my time in prison, that I killed him in self-defense, but I killed him for his money. I got up at 3 or 4 o'clock in the morning, took my rifle, went around the cabin, pulled up the window, and as he lay there sleeping I shot him through the head. I robbed him. I pray if the Almighty God can ever help anyone that he will help me now." He also called out to Sheriff Robert L. Stevens of Portland, Multnomah County, "Forgive me, Sheriff, I lied to you," referring to his persistence in claiming self-defense.

The preparations then began and Johnson was positioned upon the trapdoor. As his arms and legs were being pinioned with straps he repeated his warning concerning whisky, saying, "Everyone be careful what you do." The black hood was pulled over his head and the noose was carefully positioned behind his left ear. Seconds before the trapdoor was sprung he called out, "Be sure and break my neck," and in the next instant he dropped to his death. His neck was broken in the fall and there was barely a quiver. He hung for fifteen minutes before the prison doctor pronounced him dead, and he hung a while longer to be sure he would not revive. The body was taken to Cornelius, Oregon, and buried.

Oregonian (Portland): December 15, 1908; February 5, 1909; February 6, 1909.

Timmons, C. Y.
February 26, 1909

C. Y. Timmons and his wife Estella S. Timmons resided in an apartment in the basement of Mrs. Hayball's boarding house in Salem, Marion County, Oregon, and in another apartment lived John and Eva Sekavec. During the early morning hours of October 21, 1908, Timmons seemed restless and paced about the room, the sound of his heavy boots disturbing the Sekavecs and Mrs. Hayball, who also had rooms on the basement floor. At one point Mrs. Hayball arose and went to the door of the Timmons' apartment. Estella answered and the two women had a whispered conversation, possibly Estella was complaining about her husband's unreasonable jealousy, and the conversation ended with Mrs. Hayball saying, "Stella, now Stella."

Mrs. Hayball then returned to her apartment and in a little while the Sekavecs reported hearing "a loud thud as if a body had fallen to the floor and then heard the sound of a blunt instrument as if an ax were striking." The next morning Timmons came to the door of the living room with his clothes drenched in blood and a gaping wound to his neck. The gash had missed the veins and arteries but had severed the trachea, but it had sealed and prevented him from drowning on his own blood. The authorities were summoned and they found Estella on the floor of the Timmons' apartment, her throat cut from ear to ear, and there was a deep gash in the back of her head from an ax. A bloody straight razor was found and the bloody ax was discovered hidden under the mattress, and these were taken as evidence.

Timmons was rushed to the hospital, where it was determined that the wound to his throat, though serious, was not fatal and by then Timmons was able to speak. He said that he was asleep on the bed and was awakened suddenly as his throat was being cut by Estella. He said he wrestled the razor from her grasp, cut her throat in self-defense, and then administered the *coup de grâce* to the back of her head with the ax. He then lay down and waited for daybreak before asking for help. His story was given a modicum of credibility at first, as the cut to his throat could only have been self-inflicted if he was left-handed. Timmons must have been at least somewhat ambidextrous, as all the time he was under observation by the authorities he exclusively used his right hand, but the police asked the nurses to watch and document any variance, and they determined that at all other times he favored his left hand. Timmons' motive, too, was in question until it was learned that he believed his wife was having an affair with Robert Hornbuckle.

At his trial in mid–January 1909, Timmons took the stand and testified, "Hornbuckle was familiar with my wife and stood between us, alienating her affections." While the defendant may have hoped the jurors would be outraged by Estella's infidelity, the testimony only served to enforce his motive for killing his wife. Worse for Timmons, testimony proved that the "affair" was entirely imaginary. On January 13, 1909, testimony and arguments were concluded and the case went to the jurors at 11:30 P.M. They deliberated only thirty-five minutes before returning a verdict of guilty of murder in the first degree. Timmons had remained composed throughout the ordeal of his trial, though nervous and sometimes seemingly irrational, except for the few moments when his ax was admitted into evidence and he nearly collapsed. However, as he was being taken from the courtroom following his conviction he completely broke down and sobbed convulsively. Several days later he was returned to court and Judge George Burnett sentenced him to hang on February 26, 1909. There had been no transcript made during the trial and there seemed no valid grounds for an appeal, so none was made. The obligatory application for a respite, reprieve or commutation of sentence was submitted to Governor George Chamberlain and quickly denied.

Timmons was delivered to the prison at Salem on January 19 to await his execution, and over the next week he became increasingly silent and sullen. On February 7 the *Oregon Statesman* article "Timmons May Cheat (the) Gallows" said he was suffering from "acute troubles of the heart super-influenced by loss of blood as the result of the cut sustained in his throat on the night of the murder." The loss of blood coupled with anxiety for his impending doom had caused him to weaken considerably and he was moved to the hospital floor. By February 24, however, he had "regained his failing nerve" and it was proposed "he will possibly go to the gallows without showing the yellow streak that was expected."

The next day Timmons visited with several friends, his brother, and a pastor and they noted that the prisoner's fits of trembling had ceased and he seemed resigned to his fate. He had adopted an outlook of religious fervor and said he wanted to "straighten out some of the tangle" of his case. It was believed he meant to make a full confession but he still clung to his claim that he awoke with his throat cut before killing his wife in self-defense. Before 12:30 P.M. on February 26, Timmons, who seemed unable or unwilling to walk, was carried down the stairs from the hospital. At the foot of the stairs he waived the reading of the death warrant and was taken directly to the execution chamber. He nearly collapsed while climbing the stairs but was supported until he stood upon the trapdoor. He was asked if he had anything to say, but he was sobbing so violently that he only mumbled, "I tried to be good and am ready to die."

The straps were quickly applied to his wrists and arms, knees and ankles, the noose was adjusted, and the black hood was pulled on. In a moment, at 12:31 P.M., the trap was sprung and Timmons dropped six feet, one inch. The force of the drop caused the neck wound to open and for some time the hanging figure breathed through the gaping wound beneath the rope, and the body was drenched with blood. The attending physicians differed on whether Timmons' neck was broken in the fall, but later examination proved that the vertebrae had been dislocated. This complication, breathing through the open wound, prevented pronouncement of death until 12:54 P.M., and the body was allowed to hang another seven minutes to ensure he was dead. Within two hours Timmons' remains were buried in the Lee Mission Cemetery, the Reverend H. A. Green of Woodburn officiating. The funeral was attended by a few friends and relatives.

Oregon Statesman (Salem): January 10, 1909; January 13–15, 1909; January 27, 1909; February 7, 1909; February 24, 1909; February 26–27, 1909.

Nordstrom, Adolph N.
June 18, 1909

On Sunday, February 28, 1909, twenty-five-year-old Adolph Nicholas Nordstrom, Fred Hagglund and E. Larsen quit the railroad, received their final paychecks, and went into the town of Tillamook, Tillamook County, Oregon, where they went on a spree with their fifty-year-old rail crew foreman John Peterson. The three young men had agreed to leave the county together and returned to their camp, but Nordstrom went into town again that night and again early on Monday morning. On Monday, Hagglund and Larsen looked for Peterson but could not find a sign of him and went into town to make inquiries. By late evening they had become convinced that there might have been foul play and contacted Sheriff H. Crenshaw, saying that if anything had happened to Peterson he should arrest Nordstrom. The sheriff made inquiries and learned that after noon Monday Nordstrom had left town for Sheridan in a buggy driven by Drew Dawson. Crenshaw could not contact Drew Dawson by telephone so he deputized Drew's brother Henry and told him to bring back his brother and capture Nordstrom "dead or alive." The deputy started after his brother and the fugitive, and he caught up with the pair at Albert Mason's store late that evening. Henry made no arrest and the two brothers spent Monday night with the fugitive, making plans and telephoning Crenshaw. In the morning Nordstrom went to the barn to continue his trip but the brothers got the drop on him and made the arrest without resistance.

In Tillamook, Sheriff Crenshaw formed a search party and went to Kodad Hill, where Peterson had a small house on the left side of the road. After some time, and with nothing to indicate foul play, the party was about to give up the search when the sheriff stepped up onto a log for a better view and saw the body of a man lying in a pool of water, face down with coat and vest pulled over his head.

Crenshaw summoned the search party and, now knowing there was foul play, they made a more careful examination of the house and found where Peterson had been killed in the small rear room, and they found blood splattered on a wall and window. They followed the trail where Peterson's body had been dragged to the pool of water and also found several pieces broken from the butt of a revolver and several spent shell casings. The party returned to town to await the arrival of Nordstrom and meanwhile assembled a coroner's jury. When Nordstrom arrived his possessions and clothing were searched and blood was found on his coat sleeves. The prisoner was taken to Peterson's house and Crenshaw encouraged Nordstrom to confess. The prisoner then agreed to show where he had hidden the murder weapon, the revolver, and agreed to confess. Crenshaw, with Coroner W. C. Hawk and District Attorney W. H. Cooper, took the prisoner into the small back room where the murder was committed and Nordstrom confessed that on Sunday night he had rented a horse to go to Bay City and learn about getting a boat ride, but stopped at Peterson's house intending to steal two dollars. He crept up to the house but heard Peterson talking and, knowing then that he was still awake, moved his horse some distance away. Nordstrom then went into Peterson's house and the two men talked for a while, Peterson saying that he thought Hall had been in his house, as he had heard a horse. Nordstrom said he decided to knock the old man senseless and took his revolver from his pocket. He clubbed Peterson with the pistol butt and the old man's head struck the wall, splattering blood. He clubbed him several more times and then dragged the body outside. Nordstrom was shown the pieces of the pistol butt and he identified them as coming from his revolver.

Nordstrom then said he dragged Peterson's body through the woodshed, through the barbed wire fence and left him in the meadow, as he was too heavy to drag further. He searched the body and took two hundred dollars. He said there was no water in the meadow when he left the body there, and said Peterson was not dead when he dragged him down the hill as he struggled a little. Crenshaw asked if Nordstrom thought Peterson would die and Nordstrom said, "Yes, I thought he would die as he was making a gurgling sound and his mouth was full of blood."

Nordstrom said he then got his horse and, as he came back to the house, pulled the revolver from his pocket and threw it as far as he could into the brush. Nordstrom was asked if he had shot Peterson and he replied, "No, I did not shoot him with the revolver. I beat him to death. If I had fired a shot someone would have heard it." Nordstrom said he returned to the livery and, when he found no one there, put the horse in a stall and left a dollar on the counter. He went to Stephen's Saloon and had a couple of drinks. Over the next few hours he tried to get a boat ride to Bay City but, failing, finally went to Charley Lundquist's and spent the night. On Monday morning he went into town for drinks, then went to Dawson's livery to ask about the stagecoach, but it did not leave until 4:00 P.M. He then made arrangements for a buggy to take him to Sheridan at noon. They got underway at 12:30 P.M. and went as far as Mason's store, where he was arrested.

He was then asked if Peterson had fought back and he said, "Yes, he tried to fight me. I did not hit him very hard the first time." He was asked if he had hit Peterson after they were outside the house and he replied that he had. Nordstrom then guided the party along the path he had dragged the body and showed them where he had thrown the revolver. It was dark but Crenshaw sent W. R. Catterlin and Will Harris to search, and they returned with the murder weapon, which Nordstrom identified, and there was blood and hair on the pistol butt. Nordstrom identified the body, which had been left where found pending the inquest. Peterson's remains were then taken to the front of the house where someone remarked that Nordstrom had done a good job on Peterson, and the prisoner replied, "I was pretty well loaded up when I was at the livery stable."

At the inquest Dr. R. T. Boals said the cause of death was by skull fracture, ending the speculation he had drowned in the pool after being left face down but alive. Nordstrom was examined and held over for the grand jury, indicted in early April, and his trial immediately began in Judge W. Galloway's courtroom. The prosecution, feeling they had a sure conviction, did not put on a strong case and the first jury was not able to convict him on the evidence, but did not acquit him either. He was then remanded to the sheriff to be tried again and this time the prosecution "cured" their case. The second trial stretched into the following month, and on May 5, 1909, the defendant was found guilty of first degree murder after only one hour of deliberations. On Wednesday Nordstrom was sentenced to hang on June 18, 1909, and ten hours later he was in his cell at the state prison in Salem. Neither appeal nor application for executive clemency would delay the execution.

On his final day the condemned man was prepared for his execution, and before 11:00 A.M. the death warrant was read to him in his cell. The procession formed and he was escorted to the execution chamber where he climbed the stairs with a firm step and took his place at the railing. When given his chance to speak to the witnesses he said, "Well people, do you know why I am standing here? Can any of you answer? I am to be hanged for the murder of a man. Keep away from the booze; keep away from liquor; I am taking my punishment and don't deny the crime. I am just as good as any of you. If any of you have hard feelings against me, forgive me as I have you." He then turned toward Sheriff Crenshaw and said, "You may think I have something against you, but I haven't. I forgive you all that you have done. I know that you have only done your duty." When the sheriff replied, "Thank you," Nordstrom continued, "Keep liquor down, people, if you can. I am not the first man to be hanged on account of it. I am sorry for what I have done and wish God will save my soul. God bless all of you — good-bye."

He then stepped back onto the trapdoor and the straps were applied to his wrists and arms, knees and ankles, the noose was adjusted, and the black hood was pulled on. The trap was sprung at exactly 11:27 A.M. and in sixteen minutes he was pronounced dead. He had dropped six feet and, though he had a peculiarly thick neck, it was broken in the fall. After hanging long enough to ensure that he could not be revived the body was cut down and deposited in the coffin provided by the state. Nordstrom was buried that afternoon.

Tillamook Headlight (OR): March 4, 1909; April 29, 1909; May 6, 1909; June 24, 1909.

Anderson, Joseph
July 2, 1909

Forty-year-old Harry M. Logan, a railroad engineer from Pocatello, Idaho, moved to Portland in Multnomah County, Oregon, and resided at 565 Third Street with his wife and two children. On Wednesday evening, October 23, 1907, he was celebrating his employment that afternoon by the Terminal Company. He arrived at the Bridge Saloon at 643 First Street sometime after 5:00 P.M. and early the following morning he started for home. It was 12:50 A.M. when he got to the Fourth Street bridge and was accosted by a masked footpad (highwayman), who brandished a revolver and demanded that Logan raise his hands. The engineer swung at the robber with his right fist, knocking him to the ground, and the robber shot Logan twice. The first bullet struck Logan in the left elbow, splintering the bones and ligaments, and the second bullet struck him in the chest just above the heart, severing the large arteries. Logan, bleeding profusely, staggered to D. Ragnon's Saloon, which was nearby at Fourth and Sheridan Streets, and collapsed through the door crying out, "I'm shot."

Patrolman Anderson was only one hundred feet away when he saw the flash of the revolver, and ran to the scene. He first started after the robber but when the robber disappeared over the rail, dropping twenty feet to the soft ground below and fleeing into Marquam Gulch, the patrolman returned to Logan. When he saw the seriousness of the chest wound he decided to stay with Logan rather than pursue the shooter. The patrol wagon was summoned and the officers rushed Logan to the Good Samaritan Hospital where Dr. L. C. Ross immediately put him on the operating table. Despite the excellent work by Dr. Ross, the chest wound and the great loss of blood proved fatal at 5:00 A.M.

Coroner Finley took charge of the body and scheduled an inquest for the afternoon of the following day. Patrol Sergeant John Wendorf then went to the scene and took up the search.

He had no luck and all officers were alerted to watch for a suspect, and it was supposed that this was the same footpad who had been working the city for some time. Logan's wife expressed the opinion that the shooting was motivated by someone who wanted to prevent her husband from getting employment in Portland as an engineer, as this would prevent a fireman from promotion. However, chief of police Gritzmacher dismissed the notion, saying that he felt a dying man would not have concocted the story of an armed robber at that moment. The chief assigned three men to investigate and, though they claimed to have no leads, they were working hard on the case, as it mirrored a number of similar unsolved Portland cases.

On October 26 "Carl" Anderson was arrested at his room behind a candy store on the east side. He was, at that time, charged with vagrancy but detectives had been keeping a close watch on Anderson after he arrived in Portland, knowing he had previously served two terms in the Oregon penitentiary and was rumored to have just been released recently from the Montana penitentiary serving a term for stagecoach robbery. Once he was in jail detectives began questioning him about the Logan murder. Anderson, whose real name was Joseph Anderson but who also used the alias Joe Betz, was "a notorious stick-up man." He admitted to being in the area of Fourth and Sheridan Streets after midnight on the day of the shooting but could not account for his whereabouts thereafter. Detectives were led to suspect Anderson by a raincoat, sometimes described as an overcoat, which had been discarded beneath the Fourth Street bridge and found by *Telegram* reporter W. P. Strandborg, who investigated the scene immediately following the shooting. Anderson became nervous when shown the coat and remained in an agitated state for some time afterwards. He was questioned closely by the police and by District Attorney Manning, who later told the press, "I cannot give you any details, but you can say this for me: I am positive that the police have the murderer of Harry Logan in this man Anderson. I have never had, since my tenure in office as District Attorney, a more complete or better line of circumstantial evidence laid before me in a murder case.... I am satisfied the prisoner is Logan's murderer and that is all I can say on the subject at present."

The coat was soon identified by members of the Salvation Army as one from the Industrial Home which had been sold to Anderson days before the murder. Anderson was baldheaded and had shaved off his beard, but during his examination he was easily recognized by the Salvation Army workers and positively identified as the owner of the coat, so Anderson was held over for action by the grand jury. He was indicted and tried during the late 1907 session of the Circuit Court at Portland and, though the evidence was entirely circumstantial, the prosecution linked it together so carefully that he was easily found guilty of murdering Logan. He took the stand in his own behalf even though he claimed insanity as his defense. As soon as he was sentenced the appeals process began in earnest and his defense attorneys were able to delay imposition of the death sentence for more than a year. Finally all efforts failed and the date for his execution was set for July 2, 1909.

As the final day approached Anderson's death watch guard began to keep a closer eye on him. They suspected he was about something untoward and on his final night they made a surprise search of his cell. There they found a sharp pointed knife, fashioned from sheet iron, hidden in the top of a shoe box. It was clear that he was awaiting the final word on a reprieve or commutation before taking his own life, but was prevented by the alert guards. He had been nervous for several days previous but Anderson slept well his last night in spite of the officers foiling his plan to cheat the hangman.

On Friday, July 2, the prisoner arose at an early hour and ate a hearty breakfast. He showed little agitation after hearing that his application for commutation had been denied by Governor Frank W. Benson. The death warrant was read to him in his cell at noon,

Father Anthony Moore by his side. He was then taken from his cell and marched through the prison chapel, accompanied by the warden, superintendent and Father Moore. The chapel opened into the yard and led to the entrance of the execution chamber. He walked up the narrow flight of stairs onto the scaffold and stepped to the railing where he leaned forward and, in a strong voice, proclaimed his innocence. He insisted he had no knowledge of the killing of Harry Logan and begged that everyone forgive him, while he forgave everyone.

He then took his place upon the trapdoor and the straps were applied to his wrists and arms, knees and ankles, the noose was adjusted, and the black hood pulled over his head. At 12:32 P.M. the trap was sprung and the condemned man dropped six feet, and in six minutes his pulse stopped and in another eight minutes prison doctor J. N. Smith pronounced him dead. After hanging a while longer, to ensure Anderson would not revive, the remains were lowered into a coffin and later taken to Portland on the afternoon train for burial there.

Oregonian (Portland): October 24–25, 1907; October 29, 1907; June 30, 1909; July 3, 1909.

Jancigaj, Matthias
October 22, 1909

When Matthias Jancigaj, twenty-four-year-old Austrian, arrived in Oregon City, Clackamas County, Oregon, in 1906 he naturally gravitated to the "Austrian Colony." He boarded with the John Schmrekar family, who had arrived from Michigan the previous year and lived on Fifteenth and Water Streets. He found work at the Willamette Pulp and Paper Company and lived with the Schmrekars until February 1908, when he moved in with Matt Poloni in a house at the rear of the post office building. The Schmrekars had several full grown sons, none living at home, and daughters sixteen-year-old Mary and her younger sister Anna. Mary was a strikingly beautiful girl and Jancigaj became obsessed with marrying her. He showed her much attention, which she accepted graciously, but she had no feelings for Jancigaj so, when her father told her to end the relationship she readily acquiesced. Jancigaj was persistent so, thereafter, he was not welcome at the Schmrekar home.

There were other suitors for Mary's hand but Charles Koman was favored. On the evening of July 11, 1908, Jancigaj and Koman were drinking together and Jancigaj told his rival that he was going to give up Mary and step aside, but after they parted Jancigaj went to an isolated location and was seen test firing his six-shooter. He then went down Water Street to the Schmrekar home and found a ladder propped against a cherry tree. He used the ladder to climb into Mary's second floor bedroom window and found her sleeping with Anna. The younger girl awoke and woke her sister, and Mary demanded to know the reason for the intrusion, ordered Jancigaj to leave, and threatened to call her father. Jancigaj started for the window when Mary ran for the door, but Jancigaj grabbed her, placed the muzzle of his revolver against her breast, and fired twice, killing her. The shots awoke the family and, as the father pursued Jancigaj, the murderer fired at Schmrekar three times, emptying his revolver.

Jancigaj fled to the home of Antone Perni at Fifth Street and Railroad Avenue, confessed the shooting, and asked him to hide the revolver. By morning Perni convinced Jancigaj to surrender and, when the fugitive agreed, Perni started for the courthouse but he met Koman on the way and sent him ahead to make the report. Koman returned with jailor Peter Nehren and Constable F. A. Miles, and Jancigaj had climbed up the bluff at the rear of the house but seemed to be waiting for the officers. Nehren ordered, "Up with your hands, come down" and Jancigaj slid down the embankment. Nehren demanded, "Where is that gun?" and the prisoner replied, "Mister, I have no gun. I threw it in the river." A crowd of over three hundred men, hearing of the imminent arrest of Jancigaj, had followed the lawmen and called for a lynching, but the mob had no leader no one took action, and in five minutes the lawmen had their prisoner safely behind bars.

Later that morning Coroner Holman held an inquest over the remains of Mary Schmrekar and the six man jury was taken to the jail, where Jancigaj confessed and then the jurors found that Mary's death was at his hand. At his examination the prisoner was held over to answer to the grand jury. The prisoner was indicted in early November and the trial began in Judge Thomas McBride's courtroom in mid–November. The defense tried to show that the defendant was insane but the effort was futile, as Jancigaj had been living and doing business in Oregon City for several years and there were many who could testify to his sanity, and only a few Austrian friends tried to raise any suspicion of insanity. In addition there were eye witnesses to various aspects of the case, such as Anna, who was present at the shooting, and Dr. Hoeye, a neighbor of the Schmrekars who heard the shots which killed Mary and saw Jancigaj fleeing, and shooting at Mary's father. The defense failed and the defendant was found guilty of first degree murder.

On November 20 Judge McBride sentenced Jancigaj to hang on January 8, 1909, and on the following Monday, November 23, he was taken to the prison at Salem by Sheriff R. B. Beattie. The defense attorneys filed an appeal which automatically stayed the execution while the state Supreme Court considered the case, but finally the appeal was denied. The prisoner was then re-sentenced by Judge Robert Eakin to hang on October 22, 1909, and next an application was sent to Governor Frank W. Benson for a respite or commutation of sentence, but it was rejected.

For nearly a year the condemned man was housed in the death row cells located at the far end of the second tier of the cell block, furthest from the chapel. As the final day approached Jancigaj's death watch guard began to keep a closer eye on him, but he caused no difficulties. Father A. A. Hildebrand administered to his religious needs and the condemned man had resigned himself to his fate. Jancigaj was administered the last rites in his cell on the final morning and he prayed continually from that time until the trap fell.

On Friday, October 22, the prisoner had arisen at an early hour and ate a hearty breakfast. As the noon hour approached the prisoners were locked in their cells for the dinner meal, as was standard routine at the prison. The death warrant was read to Jancigaj in his cell a little before noon and then he was taken from his cell and marched to the execution chamber. However, before the procession proceeded far a fire broke out in cell number 23, located on the second tier nearest the chapel. The two prisoners in that cell desired to get out and had poured kerosene into the cell cuspidor and set it afire. The guards rushed to the scene but, seeing that there was no threat of the fire spreading, they let it burn out. The cells were fire proofed and there was little material in any cell which could burn. The two prisoners "were compelled to remain inside and receive a good smoking."

As soon as the emergency was evaluated and dismissed the march continued down the stairs and through the prison chapel, and the condemned man was accompanied by the warden, superintendent and Father Hildebrand. The chapel opened into the yard and led to the entrance of the execution chamber, where Jancigaj walked up the narrow flight of stairs onto the scaffold. He had declined to speak to the witnesses so he immediately took his place upon the trapdoor and the straps were applied to his wrists and arms, knees and ankles, the noose was adjusted, and the black hood was pulled over his head. At 12:32 P.M. the trap was sprung and Jancigaj dropped six feet, and in six minutes his pulse stopped, and in another eight minutes prison doctor J. N. Smith pronounced him dead. After hanging a while longer, to ensure he would not revive, the remains were lowered into a coffin and later buried in the Catholic cemetery.

Oregon City Courier (OR): July 17, 1908; November 20–27, 1908; October 29, 1909. *Oregon Statesman* (Salem): October 23, 1909.

Finch, James A.
November 12, 1909

James A. Finch started out as a newspaper man in Polk County, Oregon, but he studied law and after he passed the bar he moved to Salem. He became involved in politics and was a valued supporter, as he had a faculty for anticipating the moves of his opponents. As a reward for his political support he was made calendar clerk for the 1903 and 1905 legislatures, and in the latter year moved to Portland, Multnomah County, Oregon, where he practiced law for three years. In 1908 Finch was suspended from practicing law because of excessive use of liquor and other improprieties, and Ralph B. Fisher, a lawyer and prosecutor for the Oregon State Bar Association, prosecuted the case before the state Supreme Court. Finch tried to get Fisher to assist him in being reinstated but Fisher refused to assist his disbarred associate.

During the late hours of November 28, 1908, Finch went to the law offices of Fisher and called out "Hello, Ralph" as he pulled his revolver and sent three bullets into Fisher's head, killing him instantly. Finch tried to escape but other tenants, hearing the shots, captured him at the elevator door. He was taken to the police station, where he said he remembered nothing of the incident, but later said he would prove an alibi. The next day he returned to his first statement, that he remembered nothing, and maintained that defense to the end. He was brought to trial in an unusually short time and his defense, directed mostly by himself, consisted of a multitude of technical objections to the evidence. He was convicted of murder in the first degree; he appealed to the state Supreme Court and when the lower court's decision was affirmed, the prisoner appealed to the U.S. Supreme Court, but this failed. The only course of action remaining was to petition Governor Frank W. Benson for a commutation of his sentence to life in prison, or at least to grant a respite so he could continue to fight for his life. The governor had two petitions on his desk which occupied a great deal of his time but finally, on November 11, Finch's petition was denied while the death sentence of convicted murder Harry Daley was commuted, and these results were withheld from Finch until the morning of his execution.

On Friday, November 12, Finch arose at an early hour and ate a hearty breakfast. However, he showed great agitation after hearing that his application for a commutation had been denied by the governor. He was taken from his cell at 12:20 P.M. and marched through the prison chapel, which opened into the yard and led to the entrance of the execution chamber. He walked up the narrow flight of stairs to the scaffold and stepped to the railing. He leaned forward and in a firm voice said,

> Gentlemen, I can imagine no sadder predicament than this in the life of any man. The humiliation of this moment is very real to me, but I wish to say a few words before I must bid you all good-bye. In a few minutes I expect to stand face to face with my God, and, realizing this as I do, and as I know you do, I wish all to believe that I am speaking the truth and the whole truth in what I am saying now. I did not assassinate Ralph B. Fisher as he was sitting in his chair in his office with his back toward me. I shot in self-defense. I want Dr. [J. N.] Smith and the other physicians to make a postmortem examination and they will find upon my head the marks where the notary seal thrown by Ralph Fisher hit me. This is the truth as my last statement, and this deed today will rank [as] injustice under the law. I want to forgive Mr. Kay and the newspapers who have misrepresented my actions. I want to thank Dr. Smith and the officers of the prison and of the jail for the fair treatment I have always received at their hands. Gentlemen, I wish to thank you; good-bye.

Finch then took his place upon the trapdoor where the straps were applied to his arms and legs, the noose was adjusted, and the black hood was pulled over his head. At 12:28 P.M. the trap was sprung and the condemned man dropped six feet, and in four minutes prison doctor J. N. Smith pronounced him dead. After hanging a while longer, to ensure he would not revive, the body was lowered into a coffin and later given to Mrs. Finch, who arranged to take the remains to Portland on the afternoon train for burial there.

Oregon Statesman (Salem): August 11–12, 1909. *Oregonian* (Portland): November 11, 1909; November 12, 1909; November 13, 1909. *Seattle Daily Times* (WA): November 13, 1909.

Roselair, John D.
September 8, 1910

John D. Roselair murdered his wife in Hillsboro, Washington County, Oregon. She had been beaten badly but Roselair claimed that she had first attacked him. He did not claim self-defense but, rather, alleged that he had struck at a pan of milk thrown at him, and it had rebounded, striking his wife and killing her — thus demonstrating that her death was an accident. He was lodged in jail and held over for the grand jury. He was indicted before Christmas and his trial began on December 26, 1909; the following day he was convicted of first degree murder and sentenced to hang. Appeals stayed the execution but finally he was re-sentenced to hang on Thursday, September 8, 1910, and the condemned man was taken to the prison in Salem to await the fatal day. A number of individuals had been involved in the appeals process, trying to get a new trial or to get his sentence commuted to life in prison, but by the Wednesday before his execution all had given up hope except the Reverend W. H. Selleck of the First Methodist Church in Salem. Selleck's efforts were in vain, however, as Acting Governor Jay Bowerman would not grant any concession for Roselair, nor for Isaac N. Harrell, who was to be hanged the following day.

Roselair was not changed by his imprisonment but as the moment of his death approach he became anxious and talked incessantly all morning. Superintendent C. W. James and Father Francis of Grant's Pass escorted the condemned man to the execution chamber and as soon as he was on the scaffold he stepped forward and began to speak to the witnesses: "It has never before been allowed me to speak in public and it is hard for me to say anything here. But I am very, very sorry. I have not deserved this, and I could go down on my knees with tears in my eyes." Here his voice broke and he started to sob, but gaining control of himself he continued, "God says, 'Your thoughts are not my thoughts,' and God knows whether I am innocent or guilty. I wish to advise wives against attacking their husbands. If the woman I killed were here now she would advise the same thing. I did not strike at her when she threw a pan of milk on me, but I struck at the pan and accidentally hit her. A woman should never attack a man. It is all wrong, and this woman was the cause of her own accidental death. There was no murder committed."

Roselair, after lamenting over his inability to speak in public, managed to engage the crowd for a full fifteen minutes. Finally, he could find no more words to prolong his life so he was positioned at the center of the trapdoor where his arms and legs were pinioned with straps, the noose was positioned, and the black hood was pulled on. Sheriff H. G. Hancock of Washington County then gave the signal to an anonymous person in the next room who pulled the lever that sprang the trap at 12:45 P.M., and Roselair dropped six feet breaking his neck. His vital signs were monitored for nine and one half minutes before he was pronounced dead. The body was allowed to hang a while longer and then was cut down and placed in the pine coffin provided by the state, and he was buried that evening.

Oregonian (Portland): September 6–9, 1910.

Harrell, Isaac N.
September 9, 1910

Isaac N. Harrell, his name sometimes given as Harrell I. Newton, was born on Gales Creek above Forrest Grove, Oregon, in 1862. In the 1880s his family moved to Hillsboro and Isaac maintained a good reputation as he worked about the area at various jobs. In June 1910, Harrell was working as a sheep herder for Walter and Herbert Newell near Lakeview in Lake

County. The Newells accused him of being careless in performing his duties and he quarreled with the brothers. Harrell then carefully planned and prepared before he shot the two men in cold blood. One of the Newell brothers survived for a brief period, during which he was able to write a letter in which he described all the details of the shooting, and this letter led to the arrest of Harrell who, upon being captured and jailed, confessed to the killings.

He was to be tried in July but, when brought into court, he pled guilty and Circuit Court Judge George Noland of Klamath Falls sentenced him to hang on Friday, September 9, 1910, the day following the hanging of John D. Roselair. Neither appeal nor application for executive clemency would delay the proceedings. Harrell was taken to the prison to await his doom and his incarceration was uneventful. During his final few days he refused to talk further of the crime or make any statements regarding his impending death.

Although Harrell pled guilty and related the horrific details of the murders, certain parties were active in trying to influence Acting Governor Jay Bowerman to commute Harrell's death sentence to life in prison, or at least grant a stay of execution. Among them was his brother D. H. Harrell of Portland and the Reverend W. H. Selleck of the First Methodist Church in Salem. Bowerman communicated with practically everyone who had an interest in the proceedings and in every case the decision went against Harrell. Judge Noland wrote that the "sentence of death pronounced by me should be executed" and County Judge B. Daly observed, "There probably never has been a murder in the state with more deliberation and without a single extenuating circumstance than the cruel murder of Herbert and Walter Newell."

The time set for the execution of Harrell was noon. Just before the hour superintendent C. W. James, Father Francis of Grant's Pass, and Father Anthony Moore of Salem went to the cell for the reading of the death warrant. The prisoner was escorted through the yard into the execution chamber and up the narrow flight of stairs onto the scaffold. He was asked if he had anything to say to the witnesses but he was either unable or unwilling to speak, so Father Francis spoke for him, saying that Harrell was sorry for his crime and had thoroughly repented. The prisoner had taken his place on the trapdoor and as soon as Father Francis concluded his arms and legs were pinioned with straps, the noose was adjusted, and the black hood was pulled over his head. A signal was given and the anonymous person in the next room activated the lever which sprang the trapdoor, and Harrell dropped.

The *Oregonian* noted that "the spectacle was especially horrifying, as Harrell's jugular vein on the right side was severed by the drop of five feet eight inches and great quantities of blood spurted from his neck to the floor and drenched a portion of his clothing." The attending physician stepped forward at three and one half minutes and pronounced him dead, but it was presumed he had died a minute earlier, as his heart had stopped beating as evidenced by blood merely oozing out of the neck wound. After hanging a brief period longer the body was cut down and placed in a coffin, and he was buried in the Salem cemetery later that day.

Oregonian (Portland): September 7, 1910, September 10, 1910.

Fauldner, Noble; Garrison, Frank; Morgan, Michael; Roberts, H. E.
December 13, 1912

In the first days of August 1911, Noble Fauldner's dog became ill and showed signs of being poisoned. Within days his dog became sick again and he suspected the camp cook, Louis Gebhart, of intentionally giving the dog tainted food or possibly even putting a light dose of poison in the dog's food, but he did not single out Gebhart when he warned everyone to leave his dog alone. Gebhart openly showed his dislike for the dog because the animal was always begging for food or hanging about the chuck wagon when food was being cooked or served. Fauldner kept a close eye on the cook but saw nothing incriminating before his dog again became sick on August 6. He confronted Gebhart, made accusations, and they argued until suddenly Fauldner pulled his pistol and shot Gebhart dead. Fauldner was arrested and at his examination he was held over for the Klamath County grand jury. He was indicted, tried at the fall term of the court, and found guilty of first degree murder when it was proved Gebhart was unarmed when killed. Fauldner was sentenced to hang but his court appointed attorney filed an appeal and the matter dragged on for a year before the state Supreme Court affirmed the lower court's judgment and sentence. The date for execution was set at December 13, 1912.

On September 1, 1912, Frank Garrison murdered Roy Perkins at Eastside near Marshfield in Coos County, Oregon. After he murdered Perkins he threw the body into Coos Bay, but after he was arrested he confessed to the murder and disposal of the body. He was indicted, tried, convicted, and sentenced to hang but on appeal the state Supreme Court found that the confession, which had been repudiated, had been extorted and the justices granted Garrison a new trial. Garrison was once again tried, convicted, and sentenced to hang on December 13, 1912.

Michael Morgan deserted from Company A, Fifth Infantry, at Fort Douglas, Utah, and fled to Douglas County, Oregon, where, using the name Hallie Wilkes, he found work on the ranch of John Yorke. On July 12, 1912, he snuck up on his sleeping employer and clubbed him to death. He then hitched up Yorke's team to the wagon, put the body in the wagon bed and wrapped it in a log chain, and drove to the Rogue River. He threw Yorke's body into the river and then continued on to Glendale. He sold the team and wagon but when he was arrested he was nearly broke. On July 24 he confessed but claimed that he had killed Yorke in self-defense, though the evidence clearly showed otherwise. Morgan was charged with Yorke's murder, indicted, tried, convicted at the August term of the court, and sentenced to hang on December 13, 1912.

At 10:30 P.M. on March 29, 1912, Bruce D. Stewart was driving his car on White House Road near Riverdale in Multnomah County, Oregon, when he saw H. E. "Jack" Roberts standing in the middle of the road hailing them to stop, and the masked robber aimed an automatic shotgun. In the car with Bruce Stewart were Donald M. Stewart in the front passenger seat and in the rear seat was Irving Lupton on the right with George Hastings in the center and H. L. Tubb on the left. The driver, instead of complying, accelerated and, after the car sped past, the highwayman fired four shotgun blasts at the fleeing car. At the first shot Tubb and Donald Stewart fell forward, Tubb uninjured but Stewart mortally wounded with buckshot riddling his back. The second shot of heavy buckshot pellets struck Hastings in the back of the head, killing him instantly. Pellets from the third blast struck Lupton in his right arm, wounding him slightly. The last blast blew out a tire but Bruce Stewart continued driving the party out of shotgun range. Posses were soon combing the area and Roberts, an ex-convict, was arrested and lodged in jail. He was identified by the surviving victims of the attempted robbery, charged with two counts of murder, indicted, tried, convicted in August, and sentenced to hang December 13, 1912.

A week before the executions the gallows was taken from storage in the little room just north of the state prison's dining room and dragged across the prison yard into the old pillow and mattress factory. Prisoners then hammered and bolted the various parts into place and the entire apparatus was carefully tested. On the day before the execution a fifth murderer had his sentence commuted to a life term, but there was no relief from Governor Oswald West for the other four condemned men. During their final hours Fauldner spent a quiet night and was the most composed of the four prisoners. Garrison spent his last night toiling over the statement he planned to make on the gallows, and in the morning he told the guard, "I did not kill Perkins, and I am not afraid to die." Morgan spent his last night in prayer and consultation with Father A. A. Moore. The gallows could only accommodate two men so Fauldner and Garrison were chosen to go first. The death warrants were read to the two men in their cells on the second tier of the north wing of the Salem, Oregon, penitentiary, and then they were escorted down the stairs, across the prison yard and into the death chamber.

They took their places on the trapdoors, where Garrison decided not to give his speech to the one hundred witnesses. Instead he said, "I want to say that I did not commit the crime of which I was convicted. False witnesses were...." and here his voice broke and after a moment he composed himself and continued, "Gentlemen, I have prepared a statement which will be given to the press. Good bye everybody, good bye!" Fauldner then gave a brief speech on the causes of crime and concluded, "Hanging will never cure crime. You will have to get at the root of the evil to cure it."

While the men spoke their wrists and arms, knees and ankles were bound and the nooses were adjusted, and Garrison complained of the noose, "My God, not so tight." As soon as Fauldner concluded his statement the black hoods were pulled over their heads and at 11:40 A.M. the trap was sprung by Warden Bengen and Guard Snodgrass. Both men broke their necks in the fall and the three attending physicians monitored their vital signs until Garrison was pronounced dead at 11:54 A.M. and Fauldner was pronounced dead two minutes later, when the prison doctor turned to the warden and announced, "They are dead." The bodies were cut down and deposited in the wooden coffins provided by the state, and it took some effort to close the lid on Fauldner's coffin as his feet were too large.

Meanwhile Warden Bengen and Guard Snodgrass returned to the death row cells and read the death warrants to Morgan and Roberts. When they reached the prison yard Roberts hailed the guards, "So long fellows!" They were then taken into the death chamber, where Father A. A. Moore, Morgan's religious adviser, made his speech for him, and claimed that he had shot in self-defense. Roberts, in a rambling statement, claimed that the officers had "hounded me while I was suffering from an accident. I did not get a square deal." The men were prepared as had been Fauldner and Garrison, and Warden Bengen and Guard Snodgrass sprang the traps at 12:25 P.M. Roberts was pronounced dead at 12:45 and Morgan at 12:47 P.M. and then the bodies were cut down and deposited in the wooden coffins provided by the state. All four men were buried the next day in the prison cemetery, as no one had made a claim for the remains of any of the murderers.

Centralia Chronicle (WA): March 30, 1912; December 13, 1912. *Oakland Tribune* (CA): April 4, 1912; December 13, 1912. *Anaconda Standard* (MT): December 13, 1912. *Lima News* (OH): December 13–14, 1912.

Humphreys, Charles; Humphreys, George
March 22, 1913

Between 1907 and 1911 there were several mysterious deaths in the vicinity of Corvallis, Oregon, but there was not enough evidence to make an arrest, though brothers Charles and George Humphreys were suspected. In May 1911 the widow Eliza Griffith sold her farm for one thousand dollars and Dr. Edward N. North, an itinerant dentist, planned with the Humphreys boys to rob her. Griffith withdrew the money on the morning of June 2 and Dr. North sent the two boys to the Griffith farmhouse near Philomath, where they bludgeoned Griffith to death, stole her money, and then hid her body in the heavy brush near an abandoned mill pond. Her unexplained absence, coupled with the withdrawal of the money, raised suspicions of robbery and murder, so a search was made and on June 5 her body was found.

The Humphreys were immediately suspected, traced to Portland, separately arrested, and neither could explain their sudden newfound wealth. Charles confessed and when George was told he replied, "Well, its all up with me then," and he then confessed all the details of the murder and robbery to Detective W. J. Mitchell. Charles' written confession differed from George's confession only in that Charles said George participated in the murder and robbery while George claimed that he had acted alone. On July 15, Dr. North, who was living at the home of a Philomath reverend, learned that he was under suspicion and that night he was heard pacing the floor and moaning to himself, "Oh, why did I do it?" He left for Portland but was followed and arrested on July 17, but a case could not be worked up against Dr. North and he was released.

Charles and George Humphreys were tried at Corvallis during the latter part of April 1912 and on April 27 the defense presented four witnesses who testified that both defendants "were good boys, but of low mentality." Nevertheless, the jurors found them guilty of first degree murder on May 2 and they were sentenced to hang in June, but their attorneys filed an appeal which stayed the execution for nearly a year. In early 1913 the state Supreme Court affirmed the lower court's judgment and sentence, and the prisoners were returned to Corvallis. Their execution was set for March 21, 1913, but this turned out to be Good Friday so, at the urging of the boys' spiritual advisor, Episcopal minister Barr G. Lee, Governor Oswald West moved the hanging to the following day.

On their final night the two prisoners were interviewed by Sheriff Gellatly and District Attorney Wilson of Corvallis to determine if there was any change in their claims that Dr. North was the instigator of the murder and robbery, but all they would say was that they were innocent and he was guilty. They spent their last hours with the Reverend Lee and before 8:00 A.M. the Reverend accompanied the two condemned brothers to the gallows as they were guided into the death chamber with a guard on each arm. Once the prisoners were in position prison officials prepared to read the death warrants. George waived the proceeding while Charles insisted on hearing it read.

They then took their places on the trapdoor where their wrists and arms, knees and ankles were bound, the nooses were adjusted, and the black hoods were pulled over their heads. While they were being prepared the Reverend Lee read their statement of innocence to the witnesses, then prayed for their souls. At 8:07 A.M. the trap was sprung and both men broke their necks in the fall. Prison physician Dr. R. D. Byrd monitored their vital signs and at 8:20 he pronounced Charles dead, and two minutes later he pronounced George dead. The bodies were cut down and deposited into their coffins, when it was discovered that Charles' feet were too large for the cheap pine coffin provided by the state. With some effort his feet were made to fit and the lids were fastened. The Reverend Lee then took charge of the remains and saw to their burial.

Oakland Tribune (CA): July 17, 1911; March 15, 1913. *Oregonian* (Portland): March 22, 1913. *Billings Gazette* (MT): April 28, 1912. *Logansport Pharos* (IN): May 3, 1912.

Seymour, Frank; Spanos, Mike
October 21, 1913

On September 22, 1912, eighteen-year-old Frank Seymour, alias Frank Parker, and twenty-year-old Mike Spanos murdered fellow Greek George Dedaskiou during a robbery at Medford, Oregon. Spanos was arrested first and he quickly confessed, naming Seymour as his partner in the crime. Seymour was then arrested, and when he learned that Spanos had informed on him he confessed on October 28 and laid all the blame for the murder on Spanos. The two were indicted at the fall term of the court at Medford and at their trial each defendant insisted he was innocent of the charge and insisted that the murder was done by another Greek named Tom Fricas. However, Fricas testified and proved an alibi so, with their confessions and other direct and circumstantial evidence against them, both defendants were convicted of first degree murder and sentenced to hang in early 1913.

Their court appointed attorneys filed appeals with the state Supreme Court, but these were disposed of within months and the judgment and sentence of the lower court was affirmed. The two prisoners were then sentenced to hang on October 21, 1913. Petitions for executive clemency sent to Governor Oswald West, praying for a commutation of sentence, were denied.

The two condemned men were attended by Fathers Moore and Victor during their final days and, as neither man had family to claim their remains, the priests agreed to see to their burial in the Catholic section of the cemetery. After 8:00 A.M. the guards appeared at their cell doors and escorted them into the death chamber, where the death warrants were read. They were then conducted onto the scaffold where they took their places on the trapdoor. While the priests prayed for their souls their wrists and arms, knees and ankles were bound and the nooses were adjusted. The two were then given an opportunity to speak to the witnesses and each claimed his innocence of the crime for which they were being executed and again accused Tom Fricas of the murder.

Each man kissed the crucifix pressed to his lips and the black hoods were pulled over their heads. The trap was sprung at 8:35 A.M. and the two men broke their necks in the fall. Prison physician Dr. R. D. Byrd monitored their vital signs and pronounced Seymour dead in two minutes, but it was not until 8:45 A.M. that Spanos was pronounced dead. The bodies were then cut down, lowered into the pine coffins provided by the state, and turned over to their priests for burial.

Centralia Chronicle (WA): October 31, 1913. *Oakland Tribune* (CA): October 31, 1913. *Anaconda Standard* (MT): October 29–30, 1913; November 1, 1913.

Hansel, Oswald C.
November 14, 1913

Oswald C. Hansel and his wife, living at Astoria, Oregon, had been having marital difficulties for years and argued every day of their marriage. Finally Mrs. Hansel left her husband and hired ex-judge Frank J. Taylor as her lawyer to prepare the paperwork to file for a divorce. The application cited a number of charges against her husband to justify the request for a divorce decree, and Hansel blamed the former judge for instigating the divorce and believed that Taylor "should have endeavored to effect a reconciliation." On September 14, 1913, Hansel went looking for Taylor and found him standing on the platform at the train depot waiting for the train to take him to his summer house, where his wife and two daughters awaited his arrival. Hansel, without comment or hesitation, emptied his six-shooter into Taylor, killing him instantly. Hansel then calmly walked to the Columbia River, threw in the revolver, and was arrested without resistance.

Hansel was indicted and his trial began on September 24, and he was represented by the firm of Norblad and Mullins. He was convicted of murder and sentenced to hang November 14, 1913, but his attorneys filed an appeal, and on November 11 the state Supreme Court denied the stay of execution. On the day before the execution, attorney George Arthur Brown appealed to Governor Oswald West to grant a reprieve until a property matter could be resolved. It was alleged that Hansel on the day before his trial deeded all his property to his attorneys, and Hansel's daughter had brought a civil action to recover the property. Brown wanted Hansel alive to testify at the trial, but Norblad and Mullins proved they did not have the deed, so Governor West denied the request. Late that same evening the governor also denied a petition for a commutation of sentence.

Shortly before the execution the gallows was taken from storage in the little room just north of the state prison's dining room and dragged across the prison yard into the old pillow and mattress factory. Prisoners then hammered and bolted the various parts into place and the entire apparatus was tested. After Hansel was told he would have to die the following day,

November 14, he was baptized into the Lutheran faith by the Reverend George Koehler. He seemed to resign himself to his fate but a close watch was placed over him to prevent suicide, and the officers removed from his cell everything which they thought could be used as a weapon, leaving only his pipe and a tin of tobacco. At 3:00 A.M. Hansel tore the tin lid of his tobacco can leaving a sharp edge, and he sawed through his throat and the artery in his left wrist. After he weakened from blood loss he called to the guard, saying he had reconsidered suicide because of his recent religious conversion, and prison physician Dr. R. D. Byrd was summoned.

After the wounds were dressed Hansel slept, and when he was awakened he was given an injection which left him semi-conscious on his bed. When the guards arrived to escort him to the execution chamber he refused to rise until the Reverend Koehler pleaded for him to cooperate. He then arose and dressed, the death warrant was read to him by the warden, and he was taken from the cell. He kept his eyes closed and his head thrown back, and he muttered a prayer as he walked down the corridor of the second tier of the north wing of the Salem, Oregon, penitentiary, but at the top of the stairs he collapsed. The guards grabbed his arms before he fell and carried him down the stairs, across the prison yard into the death chamber, and onto the scaffold.

Once on the trapdoor Hansel had to be supported while his wrist and arms, knees and ankles were bound, and the noose was adjusted. The black hood was immediately pulled over his head as he was in no condition to make a statement. At 8:37 A.M. the trap was sprung and Hansel broke his neck in the fall. His vital signs were monitored by Dr. R. D. Byrd, who pronounced him dead at 8:56 A.M. The body was then cut down, deposited into the coffin provided, and turned over to his daughter for burial.

Fairbanks Daily Times (AK): November 15, 1913. *Nevada State Journal* (Reno): September 15, 1913. *Oregonian* (Portland): November 13–14, 1913. *Anaconda Standard* (MT): November 12, 1913.

Bancroft, Emmett
November 5, 1920

Kirby, Elvie D.; Rathie, John L.
July 7, 1922

On July 13, 1920, Emmett Bancroft, alias Neil Hart, and Elvie D. Kirby, alias James Owens, Indians, fired a fusillade of shots at Eugene Lyman, a concession operator at the Cayuse Indian celebration, as he was driving back to Pendleton, Oregon. Lyman stopped his automobile and the two Indians escorted him off the road, bound him, piled his car full of property stolen from the Cayuse tribe, and drove off. Lyman managed to free himself and he hurried into Pendleton to summon help from Sheriff Til D. Taylor. The following morning the sheriff and deputies Jake Marin and Glen Bushee found Bancroft and Kirby in the hills behind Reith, three miles west of Pendleton, and after a running gun battle that lasted four hours they captured the fugitives and lodged them in the Umatilla County jail at Pendleton. On July 25 deputy Marin was preparing to feed seven prisoners when six of the prisoners broke jail and Robert Jeffries, the prisoner who refused to participate, said that "immediately before the jailbreak the men gathered in one cell and whispered earnestly together for a moment." He then told of the jail break:

> It all happened when deputy sheriff Marin came into the corridor to feed us. First he let the two trusties out to build the fire and go after the food. Then he locked us all in the cell where we eat and when the food basket arrived he unlocked the cell door to give us the food.
>
> Just then the trusties who had gone to light the fire came up and started to talk to Marin. While he was thus engaged, with his back to the rest of us, the big Indian, Owens, who was arrested by Sheriff Taylor last week after a running fight in the hills southeast of Reith, jumped onto Marin's back and bore him to the floor. Hart, the other Indian, and Owens' partner, closed in and hit Marin with the jail key ring, knocking him out.

> They bound and gagged him and threw him into the cell where I was and locked it. One of the trusties locked himself in with us. I started to help Marin but a man covered me and shouted, "Stay right where you are; don't move."
>
> Marin worked himself loose, however, and a fight started between the trusty and the deputy. In the meantime we heard two shots ring out and Marin groaned: "My God! Somebody's killed!" The men had gone out into the sheriff's office and had obtained Winchesters and heavy ammunition. After the shots the last I heard of them was retreating footsteps. Owens had returned and let the trusty out of the cell where we were, saying to me, "You keep your head out of this." Then they ran out.
>
> After about 10 minutes somebody came in and unlocked the cell and Marin went out. I thought they had been acting strangely but never took me into their confidence and I didn't want anything to do with them anyway. They are a tough lot. Owens and Hart, the two Indians, kept saying, "Well, they got us now, but will they hold us?"

While deputy Marin, Jeffries and the trusty were locked in a cell the escaping prisoners went into the sheriff's office to search for guns and ammunition. Bancroft found a rifle, loaded it, and with John Rathie and Irvin L. Stoop returned to the cell area while Kirby and Floyd Henderson rummaged for more ammunition. Just then Sheriff Taylor and Guy Wyrick entered the office, and when they saw the two prisoners Taylor grabbed Kirby and Wyrick grabbed Henderson and they wrestled them to the floor. Bancroft, hearing the commotion, returned to the office and shot Taylor in the neck and then threatened to shoot Wyrick if he did not release his hold on Henderson. Taylor was lifted onto a couch and Bancroft would not allow the sheriff to be attended until he was told where the ammunition was hidden. Once all the prisoners were armed and supplied with ammunition they fled to the tracks of the OWR&N Railroad, boarded the eastbound train, rode it to Mission, and then fled into the heavy timber where they separated.

Back in Pendleton the doctor and Taylor's family were summoned to the jail and Taylor said, "Well, this is a corker. I could have shot the dirty cur (meaning Kirby) but he got me all right." Taylor was given morphine to ease the pain but he never rallied, as the bullet had severed the jugular vein and arteries in his neck and he bled to death at 6:10 P.M. The bullet had ranged downward and was found just under the skin on the right side between his hip and shoulder. As soon as the jail break was broadcast to the community a large posse was organized and they pursued the fugitives toward Mission, acting on information brought to Pendleton from the crew of a westbound train. That night bloodhounds were brought from the penitentiary at Walla Walla and they joined in searching the mountains near Mission.

Rathie, Stoop and Henderson were captured on July 30 after Rathie demanded food at gunpoint from a woman at a farm. Bancroft and Kirby were captured on July 31 at Kamela, nineteen miles northwest of La Grande when they were discovered asleep in an abandoned cabin, disarmed, and handcuffed before they awoke. On the evening of July 31 a large mob assembled in front of the Pendleton jail intent on lynching the prisoners, but the mob was convinced to let the law take its course. All the prisoners were indicted for murder but Bancroft pled guilty and was sentenced to hang on November 5, 1920. The other defendants were tried in Judge Gilbert W. Phelps' Pendleton courtroom at the fall term and convicted of first degree murder, with Bancroft testifying against them. Kirby and Rathie were sentenced to hang on December 3 and Stoop and Henderson were sentenced to serve life terms in the penitentiary. There was no relief for Bancroft and his date for execution remained November 5, 1920, but appeals were filed for Kirby and Rathie and their cases were considered by the state Supreme Court until March 1922, when the lower court's judgment and sentence were affirmed.

During his early days on death row Bancroft decided to become a Protestant and the Reverend H. N. Aldrich baptized him. On the day before his execution, as he awaited word from Governor Ben W. Olcott, Bancroft said, "If I am hanged I will walk to the gallows unassisted." Meanwhile the governor heard from Bancroft's aged father and brother but found no reason to intervene, and the prisoner was advised he would be executed in the morning. He went to sleep at 11:00 P.M. and arose after 6:00 A.M. when breakfast was served. At 8:20 A.M. he was taken from his cell and conducted into the prison chapel, where Warden Compton read the death warrant, and then he was escorted across the yard into the death chamber and onto the scaffold by an ensign from the Salvation Army and the Reverend Aldrich.

He took his place on the trapdoor and while his wrists and arms, knees and ankles were being bound he told the forty witnesses, "I know I made a mistake, but the Lord is on my side and I am ready to go when he calls me." The noose was then adjusted, the black hood was pulled over his head, and below the gallows three men stood by three electric switches, including two dummies. At a signal all three switches were pressed and at 8:31 A.M. the trap was sprung. Prison Physician Dr. W. C. Smith, assisted by Drs. R. D. Byrd and M. B. Marcellus, monitored vital signs and pronounced him dead in twelve minutes. This was the first execution since capital punishment had been restored the previous May, so when the trap was sprung the convicts staged a ten minute demonstration. After Bancroft was pronounced dead his body was lowered into a coffin and turned over to the Salvation Army, which would conduct a service before sending the remains to the state crematorium.

After their appeal was denied by the state Supreme Court, Rathie and Kirby were taken to Pendleton and resentenced to hang on July 7, 1922. An application was then submitted to Governor Ben W. Olcott praying for executive clemency, but this was denied. It had been decided to hang Rathie and Kirby separately and twenty-four-year-old Rathie was elected to go first. On their final night both men insisted they were innocent of the murder of Sheriff Taylor. They slept peacefully that night and were awakened at daybreak when breakfast was served. After 8:00 A.M. the death warrant was read to Rathie in his cell and then he was escorted down the stairs from the second tier of the cell block, across the prison yard, and he entered the death chamber at 8:28 A.M. He took his place on the trapdoor and declined to make a statement, so his wrists and arms, knees and ankles were bound, the noose was adjusted, and the black hood was pulled over his head. The trap was sprung at 8:30 and he broke his neck in the fall. He was pronounced dead by the prison physician at 8:44 A.M. and the warden then returned to death row to read the warrant to Kirby. He was conducted into the death chamber at 8:53 A.M. where he declined to make a statement, he was prepared, and in one minute the trap was sprung. He also broke his neck in the fall and was pronounced dead at 9:06 A.M.

Oakland Tribune (CA): July 31, 1920. *Oregonian* (Portland): July 25, 1920; November 4–5, 1920. *Reno Evening Gazette* (NV): July 30, 1920; July 7, 1922. *Ogden Standard-Examiner* (UT): July 26, 1920; November 5, 1920; July 7, 1922; July 12, 1922.

Howard, George
September 8, 1922

George R. Sweeney, a salesman in Malheur County, Oregon, owned a fine automobile and twenty-year-old George Howard was determined to have it. On September 14, 1920, Howard murdered Sweeney, weighted the body with chains, and dropped the body into the Deschutes River. Later he became concerned that the body would work itself free and be discovered if left in the water, so he dredged it up and buried it in a shallow grave. The body was soon discovered by the authorities and Howard was arrested driving Sweeney's automobile, and he was lodged in the Malheur County jail. Once he was behind bars Howard confessed to the crime.

At his trial at the end of the year he was

convicted of first degree murder and sentenced to hang in early 1921, but his attorney filed an appeal resulting in a stay of execution. The case was reviewed by the state Supreme Court for many months before the justices affirmed the lower court ruling and set the date for Howard's execution at September 8, 1922. The sentencing was followed by a strong campaign to convince Governor Ben W. Olcott to grant a commutation of sentence, but he refused to intervene even after he received a petition with thirteen hundred signatures. Father Buck and Howard's attorneys, during the last hours, appeared before the governor and made one last plea to spare the life of Howard, but the governor would not be swayed by mere sentiment or opposition to the death penalty.

Howard was attended by Father Rubis while Father Buck was appearing before the governor, and when all hope was lost Father Buck delivered the news, and the two priests helped the condemned man brace up. They remained in his cell throughout that last night and in the morning Warden James E. Lewis appeared at the cell door after 8:00 A.M. and read the death warrant. Two guards and Father Rubis then escorted Howard into the death chamber, up the thirteen stairs, and onto the platform. When the warden asked if he had anything to say he stepped forward and said, "I am sorry for what I done. I forgive everyone, heartily. Goodbye to you all."

He then took his place on the center of the trapdoor where his wrist and arms, knees and ankles were bound, the noose was adjusted, and the black hood was pulled over his head. At 8:31 A.M. the trap was sprung and Howard broke his neck in the fall. Prison physician Dr. W. Carlton Smith and Multnomah County Coroner Dr. Earl Smith monitored his vital signs and pronounced him dead at 8:41 A.M. Howard's parents, who lived at Rockville, Oregon had not made a claim for his remains so it was presumed that Fathers Buck and Rubis would take charge and see to the burial in the Catholic portion of the Salem cemetery.

Oregonian (Portland): September 8–9, 1922.

Walters, Husted A.
March 9, 1923

On Wednesday evening, November 17, 1920, there was a string of armed robberies in Portland, Oregon. Police patrolman Jerome Palmer observed two men whose description matched the robbers and, with other officers, tried to make an arrest, but one of the men drew his pistol and shot Palmer dead. The other officers overpowered and disarmed twenty-four-year-old Husted A. Walters, a soldier from Camp Lewis, and they arrested his seventeen-year-old accomplice, John A. Tillman, without resistance. The two men were lodged in the Portland jail and Husted was charged with murder while Tillman was charged with highway robbery. Tillman insisted he was an unwilling participant in the robberies and, when deputy Richard Diech brought in one of the robbery victims, Tillman was identified as the second robber. The prisoner then told the victim to check his overcoat pockets and he found that his purse, and all the contents, had been returned and Tillman explained that he had put the purse back when Walters had been distracted.

At his examination Walters was held over for the grand jury, indicted in early 1921, and tried at the spring term of the Multnomah County court. Tillman testified against Walters and in consideration of his cooperation he was released, and Walters was found guilty of first degree murder and sentenced to hang. Walters' court appointed attorneys filed an appeal which stayed the execution and they persisted for two years in their fight to save their client's life. Finally in December 1922 the state Supreme Court affirmed the lower court ruling, denied the request for a new trial, and the date for Walters' execution was set for March 9, 1923. His application to Governor Walter M. Pierce, praying for a commutation of sentence, was denied.

During his final weeks the condemned man turned to religion and this helped him brace up for his death. On that final morning only prison officials and newsmen were permitted into the death chamber. The death warrant was read to the prisoner in his cell after 8:00 A.M. and then he was conducted down the stairs from the second tier of the cell block, through the chapel, and across the prison yard. He entered the death chamber at 8:33 A.M. and climbed the thirteen stairs, where he took his place on the trapdoor. While his wrists and arms, knees and ankles were being bound he said, "I'd like to tell you I am guilty of the crime, but I cannot. I was full of moonshine at the time. The Lord has blessed me and I am saved. You can kill the body, but you can't kill the soul."

While his religious advisor prayed the noose was adjusted the black hood was pulled over his head, and at 8:38 A.M. the trap was sprung. Walters dropped, breaking his neck in the fall, and the attending physician pronounced him dead at 8:47 A.M. The body was then cut down, deposited into the coffin provided by the state, and later that day he was buried in the prison cemetery, as there had been no claim for his remains.

Billings Gazette (MT): November 19, 1920. *Oakland Tribune* (CA): March 9, 1923. *Reno Evening Gazette* (NV): March 9, 1923.

Casey, Dan
August 24, 1923

During the early morning hours of June 14, 1921, Union Pacific's special agent J. Harold "Buck" Phillips discovered two men trying to break open a boxcar in the Portland, Oregon, rail yard. They fled and he pursued them but, during a running gun battle, Phillips was mortally wounded and bled to death in two hours. One of the men, forty-four-year-old Dan Casey, was captured three days after the killing in possession of a .38-caliber revolver which proved to be the murder weapon, but his accomplice escaped and Casey would never confirm his identity, though it was thought to be John L. Burns. Casey had been found hiding under a bed in Burns' room and he had a wound on his right wrist from one of Phillips' bullets. Casey was tried in Judge Kavanaugh's Multnomah County Circuit Court in November 1921, convicted of first degree murder on November 23 and sentenced to hang, but his attorney filed an appeal which stayed the execution. He was sent to the prison in Salem on December 10, 1921, but he was returned to the Multnomah County jail on April 17, 1922, pending the outcome of his appeal. The state Supreme Court considered the matter and the justices finally affirmed the judgment and sentence of the lower court, so on January 21, 1923, Casey was resentenced to hang on August 24. There was then a strong campaign to have Casey's death sentence commuted to life imprisonment, but after Governor Walter M. Pierce heard the arguments he declined to interfere.

During his time on death row Casey bore up well under the strain, and on the day before his death Casey was baptized into the Catholic faith by Fathers Rubis and Keenan. He slept peacefully that last night and arose at an early hour for breakfast, but ate sparingly. Warden Johnson Smith, deputy warden Lilly and other officials appeared at his cell door for the reading of the death warrant, but Casey said, "Oh, don't read that. I know what it is." The prisoner then shook hands with everyone present, praised the warden and guards for his treatment while at the prison, and then his wrists and arms were bound.

He started his walk to the death chamber and entered at 8:33 A.M. He took his place on the trapdoor accompanied by his two priests and they prayed for him as his knees and ankles were bound and the noose was adjusted. When asked if he wanted to make a statement he declined, saying, "Come on. Make it fast." After he kissed the crucifix pressed to his lips, the black hood was pulled over his head and at 8:35 the trap was sprung. Casey broke his neck in the fall and the prison physician pronounced him dead at 8:45 A.M. The body was then cut down, deposited into the coffin provided by the state, and turned over to the priests for burial in the Catholic section of the prison cemetery.

Oakland Tribune (CA): November 23, 1921. *Ore-*

gonian (Portland): August 23–25, 1923. *Oxnard Courier* (CA): August 24, 1923.

Parker, George
January 4, 1924

During the late night hours of May 20, 1923, Linn County Sheriff William J. Dunlap and traffic officer J. E. Lillard spotted two automobile thieves at work in Albany, Oregon, and a running gun battle followed, during which twenty shots were exchanged. Dunlap was seriously wounded by George Parker, and he and the other thief were each wounded by the officers. Dunlap collapsed but Lillard kept up the chase and captured the two thieves, who gave their names as Art Beckley and George Parker. Parker, Beckley and Sheriff Dunlap were rushed to the hospital but it was found that Parker had been firing soft nosed bullets, which had mushroomed through the sheriff's body destroying several vital organs. He died the following day.

As soon as word was spread that the sheriff had died there was talk of lynching, so the two prisoners were removed to the jail on May 22 and kept under heavy guard. Both men were indicted on May 31 and their trial was concluded in early June, with both men convicted of first degree murder. Beckley, who had not fired the fatal shot, was sentenced to serve a life term at the state prison in Salem, but Parker was sentenced to hang in the autumn, and he was lodged in the death row cells at the state prison. However, Parker's court appointed attorneys filed an appeal which stayed the execution for several months. The state Supreme Court acted expeditiously and affirmed the lower court's judgment and sentence in October and Parker's date for execution was set for January 4, 1924; and the application for executive clemency sent to Governor Walter M. Pierce was denied.

On the final morning the warden read the death warrant to the prisoner in his cell after 8:00 A.M. and then he was escorted down the stairs from the second tier of the north cell block, through the chapel, across the prison yard, and into the death chamber. He climbed the thirteen stairs and took his place on the trapdoor where he declined to speak to the witnesses, consisting of prison officials and newsmen. His wrists and arms, knees and ankles were bound, the noose was adjusted, and the black hood was pulled over his head. The trap was sprung at 8:33 A.M. and Parker broke his neck in the fall. The prison physician monitored his vital signs for fifteen minutes and pronounced Parker dead at 8:48 A.M. The body was then cut down, deposited into the coffin provided by the state, and buried in the prison cemetery later that afternoon.

Billings Gazette (MT): January 5, 1924. *Logansport Pharos-Tribune* (IN): January 4, 1924. *Oakland Tribune* (CA): May 21–22, 1923

Peare, Lew W.; Covell, Arthur
May 22, 1925

On December 27, 1922, sixty-seven-year-old Lew W. Peare, who lived with his wife on a ranch in the Kitchen Canyon District nineteen miles southwest of Myrtle Point in Coos County, Oregon, had been drinking heavily of moonshine. He became crazed and during a heated argument with his forty-seven-year-old wife he attacked her, and her screams for help brought neighbor James R. Culver. Peare then murdered Culver and after he was dead he choked his wife to death. Peare next killed his three dogs and his cats and hurried to the nearby ranch of Sam Stevens, where he confessed the murders. The authorities were called and they found Mrs. Peare dead in the ranch house, but Culver's body was missing and Lew Peare could not remember what he had done with it, or at least he would not tell. A search was made and Culver's remains were finally found, and Peare was charged with two counts of murder.

Peare confessed the murders to the authorities but at his arraignment he pled not guilty. He was tried, convicted, and sentenced to hang in late 1922 but his attorneys filed an appeal, which stayed the execution, and the matter dragged on for several years. Finally in

March 1925 all forms of judicial relief were exhausted and Peare's date of execution was set for May 22, 1925.

Forty-six-year-old Arthur Covell, a mystic and student of the occult, decided that several people must die "when the stars are favorable." The first of those he targeted was his sister-in-law Ebba Covell. Arthur, crippled from the waist down, enlisted the help of his fifteen-year-old nephew Alton Covell and his younger sister Lucille. Arthur had chosen Ebba to be first because "she never came upstairs to see me and she fussed because I ate too much." Arthur designated 11:00 A.M., September 3, 1923, as the "Venus hour," and at exactly that moment nephew Alton placed an ammonia-soaked rag over his mother's mouth as she worked in the kitchen. She collapsed and within a few minutes she was dead. Alton and Lucille then carried the body to the sofa and washed her face to remove any traces of ammonia. At her inquest there was no sign of foul play, so it was determined she had died of natural causes. However, at her funeral the coffin lid, which had been fastened, was removed so a close friend could deposit a keepsake. It was then that the mysterious death took on a new significance, as there was a suspicious discoloration of her face. A new examination was made of the corpse and the cause of death was determined to be ammonia poisoning.

Ebba's husband, Dr. Fred Covell, was arrested on suspicion of being the murderer. However, continued investigation soon attached suspicion on Arthur and Alton Covell. Arthur's room was searched and authorities found a notation, "This is the day. Will Alton carry out the plan?" Fourteen-year-old Lucille, Ebba's daughter, then told the authorities that her uncle had planned the murder for several months, and as soon as Arthur and Alton were confronted with the evidence they confessed to the killing.

Arthur had a typewriter with astrological signs instead of letters and he had written out dozens of murder, kidnapping and robbery plots in code, but criminologist Luke S. May managed to decipher many of the plots in time for the trial at Coquille, Oregon. Arthur and Alton were indicted in early October and by the end of the month they had been found guilty of the first degree murder of Ebba Covell. Alton, because of his age, was sentenced to serve a life term at the state prison in Salem, but Arthur was sentenced to hang in early 1924. Appeals followed which stayed the execution, but the state Supreme Court affirmed the lower court's judgment and sentence in early 1925, and Covell was sentenced to hang on May 22, with Lew Peare.

Both condemned men applied for executive clemency from Governor Walter M. Pierce, but he denied both requests. Covell relied upon the stars to determine his fate in the hereafter, but there is no mention of religious consolation for Peare. It had been decided to hang the prisoners separately and Lew Peare was chosen to go first. Both men were awakened at an early hour and served breakfast and then, before 8:00 A.M., the warden read the death warrant to Peare in his cell. He was then taken out and escorted down the stairs from the second tier of the cell block, through the chapel, across the prison yard, and into the death chamber. He climbed the thirteen stairs and took his place on the trapdoor where his wrists and arms, knees and ankles were bound and the noose was adjusted. When asked if he had anything to say he declined, so the black hood was pulled on and at 8:00 A.M. the trap was sprung. Peare broke his neck in the fall and the prison physician pronounced him dead in eleven minutes.

While Peare's body was being taken down and placed in its coffin, the warden returned to Covell's cell and read the death warrant, and then he was carried to the first floor corridor and placed in a wheelchair. He was wheeled into the death chamber and carried onto the platform, where he was strapped to a collapse board. He was propped up as the noose was adjusted and then he was given the opportunity to say goodbye to the small group of witnesses. The black hood was pulled over his head and at 8:32 A.M. the trap was sprung, but the drop failed to break his neck and it took until 8:58 for him to strangle to death, and then the prison physician pronounced him dead. The body was cut down and placed in the coffin provided, and both coffins were returned to Coos County for burial.

Albuquerque Morning Journal (NM): May 23, 1925. *Nevada State Journal* (Reno): October 16, 1923. *San Antonio Evening News* (TX): December 29, 1922. *Ada Weekly News* (OK): May 28, 1925. *Capital Times* (Madison, WI): December 30, 1922. *News Standard* (Uniontown, PA): May 20, 1925. *Ogden Standard-Examiner* (UT): December 29, 1922. *Titusville Herald* (PA): May 23, 1925.

Lloyd, W. R.
November 30, 1925

On April 26, 1925, twenty-six-year-old W. R. Lloyd was released from Oregon's state prison, where he had just completed a four year sentence for forgery. By the end of August he was already wanted for another major crime so he hired thirty-four-year-old Clinton I. Baun, owner of an automobile taxi service at Independence, Oregon, to drive him to another town. Lloyd planned to murder Baun and steal his automobile so he could escape from Oregon before he was arrested. As soon as they were in an isolated area Lloyd pulled a pistol, ordered Baun to pull to the side of the road and get out, and there he shot Baun to death, rifled his pockets for all his valuables, and stole his car. Lloyd was arrested a few hours later near The Dalles, Oregon, still driving the stolen car and he confessed to the killing, saying, "I don't know why I did it. I was full of moonshine at the time." At his arraignment he pled not guilty, was indicted and tried, and on October 7 he was convicted of first degree murder after the jurors deliberated only four hours. Lloyd was sentenced to hang on November 30 and there would be no delays from appeals nor petitions for executive clemency.

Executions at the prison in Salem had typically been conducted about 8:00 A.M., but Lloyd was still in his cell after 9:30 when the warden appeared and read the death warrant. The condemned man was then escorted to the stairs from the second floor corridor, down to the first floor and through the chapel, across the prison yard and into the death chamber. He climbed the thirteen stairs and took his place on the trapdoor where his wrists and arms, knees and ankles were bound and the noose was adjusted. There is no record of a statement before the black hood was pulled over his head, and the trap was sprung at 10:04 A.M. The prison physician waited beneath the gallows and he monitored Lloyd's vital signs until 10:17 A.M. when he pronounced him dead, and confirmed that his neck was broken in the fall. The body was then taken down and deposited in the coffin provided by the state. He was buried in the prison cemetery that evening.

Hayward Review (CA): November 30, 1925. *Reno Evening Gazette* (NV): November 30, 1925. *Indiana Progress* (PA): October 28, 1925. *Sioux City Journal* (IA): December 1, 1925.

Cody, Archie
April 16, 1926

Archie Cody, alias Fred Yardlow, of Elko, Nevada, had been uttering bad checks to pay for horses he bought in Malheur County, Oregon. On August 27, 1924, Malheur County Sheriff W. Austin Goodman appeared at the ranch where Cody was tending his horses, one and one half miles from the border with Harney County. The sheriff told Cody his business and the young man agreed to go with him but asked to be allowed to get his coat from his horse. The sheriff agreed but Cody, instead of getting a coat, pulled out a pistol and shot the sheriff through the leg. Cody then mounted his horse and fled into the hills while the sheriff was taken to the ranch house for treatment, but the bullet had severed an artery and he bled to death within an hour.

F. Goodman, the sheriff's son, and deputy Renshaw organized a posse and went after Cody and they overtook him at the head of Deep Creek, seventy miles from the scene of the murder. The fugitive tried to escape but his horse was shot from under him and he had to surrender without a fight when he was outnumbered and outgunned by the large posse. He was returned to Vale on August 30, and on Tuesday, September 2, he was indicted for murder. The court did not convene until December, and on December 9 the defendant was convicted of first degree murder and sentenced to hang in January 1925. However, his attorneys filed an appeal and the case was before the state Supreme Court until late February 1926, when the justices affirmed the lower court's judgment and sentence, and on March 8, Cody was resentenced to hang on April 16. Neither appeal nor application for executive clemency, sent to Governor Walter M. Pierce, would delay the proceedings.

On Thursday, April 15, Cody's parents were in his cell with him all day, and they would return to the prison the following morning but would not attend the hanging. Just before 8:30 A.M. the warden appeared at Cody's cell and read the death warrant, and then the prisoner was escorted from the second tier of the cell block, down the stairs into the chapel, across the prison yard, entering the death chamber at 8:40 A.M.

He climbed the thirteen stairs and took his place on the trapdoor where he declined to make a statement, so his wrists and arms, knees and ankles were quickly bound, the noose was adjusted, and the black hood was pulled over his head. At 8:41 the trap was sprung and the prison physician monitored his vital signs until his heart ceased to beat, and then he pronounced Cody dead, and an examination showed his neck had been broken in the fall. His remains were taken down, deposited in the coffin provided by Barney Cody, his father, and turned over to his parents for burial at Elko, Nevada.

Nevada State Journal (Reno): August 29, 1924. *Reno Evening Gazette* (NV): April 16, 1926. *Ogden Standard-Examiner* (UT): August 30, 1924. *Waterloo Evening Courier* (IA): April 16, 1926.

Brownlee, Albert
May 17, 1927

On February 27, 1927, Albert Brownlee and Dewey Russell robbed the pool hall belonging to John Maddaugh in Veneta, Oregon, and Brownlee shot the owner, causing a serious but not fatal wound. The robbers were pursued by a Lane County posse which included Easton Hooker, a local postman deputized for the pursuit, and during a running gun battle Brownlee shot Hooker to death. The pair of robbers was then captured and lodged in the Lane County jail. They were indicted, tried at the spring session of the county Circuit Court, and convicted. Dewey, who was convicted only of the "assault and robbery" against Maddaugh was given a long prison term, but Brownlee was convicted of the first degree murder of Hooker and sentenced to hang on May 17, 1927. Nothing would arise to delay the execution, but on May 13 two of Brownlee's sisters and a brother-in-law appeared before Governor I. L. Patterson and argued for a commutation of sentence, claiming he suffered mentally from shell shock during his wartime years fighting in France. The governor refused to grant the request but said that there was still a possibility of new developments in the case which could halt the execution, but these new developments did not materialize.

After sentencing Brownlee had been delivered to the prison at Salem and lodged in the death row cells on the second tier of the cell block. On his final morning he was awakened at an early hour and served breakfast, and after 8:00 A.M. the warden appeared at his cell door and read the death warrant. The prisoner was then escorted from his cell, down the stairs into the chapel, across the prison yard and into the death chamber. He took his place on the trapdoor where his wrists and arms, knees and ankles were bound and the noose was adjusted. He was asked if he had anything to say and he insisted that he was innocent and told the newspaper reporters and other witnesses, "the state has framed me."

The black hood was pulled over his head at 8:29 and the trap was sprung immediately. Brownlee broke his neck in the fall and the prison physician monitored his vital signs until he pronounced him dead at 8:45 A.M. The body was then cut down and deposited into the coffin provided by his family, then taken to a local undertaker to be prepared for shipment to Libby, Montana, for burial.

Oregonian (Portland): May 17, 1927. *Salt Lake Tribune* (UT): May 14, 1927; May 18, 1927.

Butchek, John
June 10, 1927

Forty-six-year-old John Butchek and his wife of twenty-five years had been living with two of their four adult children at 440 Benton Street in Portland, Oregon, for two years. They had been quarreling constantly for six months as John insisted his wife had been unfaithful, and sometimes spied on her when he should have been at work. On January 14, 1926, the couple again began arguing over Mrs. Butchek's infidelity, and her denials merely infuriated John further. John suddenly grabbed a hatchet, chased his wife into the hallway, and bludgeoned and hacked her to death. He then walked to a barber shop for a shave and a haircut, so he would be presentable when he surrendered, and when the barber finished he walked into the police station and said, "I've killed my wife with a hatchet. I've come to give myself up." He told the officers where they could find the body and then dictated his confession of the murder to two deputy district attorneys. He said he killed her

> because she was going out with another man. I never caught her but I knew she was doing it. I wanted to build up a home but she spent all the money and then went out with other men while I was at work. I couldn't stand it any longer.... After the children had all gone my wife and I started to quarrel. She took after me with a broom. I grabbed it away from her and told her to get packed up and get out. She grabbed a hatchet which she had hidden under some paper and struck at me. We fought over the hatchet and I got it. I struck her I don't know how many times before I realized what I was doing. When I saw she was dead I got dressed and left the house.

Officers found the murder scene exactly as described by Butchek, and the deputy coroner who removed the body reported that Mrs. Butchek's skull had been fractured in twelve places, she was bruised on the shoulders, and her face and hands were cut. Their four children told the police that their father had started acting strangely in June 1925 and making accusations of infidelity, and in July their father had beaten their mother, but they insisted their mother had been faithful to their father. In the fall Butchek thought his wife was plotting to kill him and called the police to search for a gun, but there was none.

County coroner Dr. Earl Smith convened an inquest and recommended that Butchek be held over for the grand jury. The prisoner was indicted, tried in the Multnomah County Circuit Court, and convicted of first degree murder. After he was sentenced to hang his attorney filed an appeal but the state Supreme Court affirmed the judgment and sentence in early 1927. Two weeks before his execution the condemned man was examined by doctors from the state hospital, who reported that the prisoner was insane but was able to tell right from wrong. Then came the petition to the governor praying for a commutation of sentence, but this was denied and the date for Butchek's execution remained at June 10, 1927.

On the day before Butchek's execution two sons and a daughter visited with their father for two hours. After they left he seemed resigned to his fate and that night he slept soundly. He was aroused at an early hour for breakfast and just after 8:00 A.M. the warden appeared at his cell door and read the death warrant. The prisoner was escorted from the second tier of the cell block by three guards and Father Rubis, down the stairs into the chapel, across the prison yard, entering the death chamber at 8:29 A.M. He climbed the thirteen stairs and took his place on the trapdoor. He declined to make a statement, so his wrists and arms, knees and ankles were quickly bound, the noose was adjusted, and after he kissed the crucifix pressed to his lips the black hood was pulled over his head. At 8:30 A.M. the trap was sprung and the prison physician monitored his vital signs until his heart ceased to beat, and he pronounced Butchek dead at 8:45 A.M. The body was cut down and deposited in the coffin provided by his children, and they arranged for his burial the following day.

Oregonian (Portland): January 15, 1926; June 11, 1927. *Oxnard Courier* (CA): January 14, 1926. *Salt Lake Tribune* (UT): June 11, 1927.

Kelley, Ellsworth; Willos, James
April 20, 1928

On August 12, 1925, "Oregon" Bert Jones, Ellsworth Kelley, James Willos and Tom Murray, convicts serving long terms at the state prison in Salem, Oregon, returned to their cells after their exercise period but when the dinner bell rang they fell out of line and hid in their cells. After the other prisoners had left the cell block the four men climbed to the top tier of the north wing and cut a hole through six boards and the tin roof using jailmade knives. Then, using a rope which they had made by tying together pieces of material, they lowered themselves into the prison yard. At 5:55 P.M. they made a desperate dash for the prison armory, attacked a turnkey, and then armed themselves with four rifles and several revolvers. Warden A. M. Dalerymple discovered the prisoners in the armory and sounded the alarm, and guards John L. Sweeney and J. M. Holman took positions on the walls. The prisoners used their weapons to murder the two tower guards and wounded guard Lute Savage with a stray bullet. The four prisoners then climbed over the wall, but as they were dropping to the ground, guard John Davidson shot down Jones, and rather than be captured Jones committed suicide using one of the revolvers. Murray then took command of the group and they made for the state hospital, kidnapped a hospital attendant as a shield, and made their escape in a taxi cab commandeered from in front of the hospital.

Posses were quickly organized and began searching for the three escaped convicts, and Governor Walter M. Pierce returned from Portland and mobilized the Oregon National Guard. The three convicts made their way to New Era, Oregon, and took over a house, holding the family captive and making them cook and care for them. When they felt it safe to resume their flight they separated with Murray heading for Centralia, Washington, while Willos and Kelley struck out for Goldendale, Washington. At Vancouver, Murray met an old friend named Carson and then continued on to Centralia, but Carson betrayed his friend and he was captured without a fight before midnight Friday, August 21, and by 1:00 A.M. Saturday he was back in the penitentiary at Salem. On Saturday afternoon Willos and Kelley were tracked by a Portland posse to Goldendale, where they were captured while eating lunch, and by Sunday, August 23, they were in the Multnomah County jail awaiting return to the prison in Salem to stand trial for two murders.

The Marion County grand jury called for a special session to indict the three murderers and they convened on Wednesday, August 26, for that purpose. The three defendants were tried in early May 1926, convicted of first degree murder, sentenced to hang, and by May 9 they were back in their cells at Salem. As soon as Murray was locked down he wrote a confession exonerating Kelley and Willos, then fashioned a rope from his bed sheet, tied it over a steam pipe while standing on the end of his bunk, tied the other about his neck, and stepped off. He was dead when discovered, and then his note written in chalk was found on the back of an oil painting by Willos given to Murray, which read, "Before going south, with what money I have on the books, please pay the paper man what I owe him. Mail two letters, if you want to, one to the folks and the other to Attorney Johnson of the *Portland News*. I killed Sweeney, Jones killed Holman. Kelley and Willos shot no one or at anyone." This left only Kelley and Willos to face the hangman, but appeals to the state Supreme Court stayed their executions and when the lower court was affirmed the case was appealed to the U.S. Supreme Court, but the state courts were affirmed and the date for their executions was set for April 20, 1928. Petitions for a commutation of sentence sent to Governor Walter M. Pierce were denied.

It had been decided to hang the men separately and Kelley was chosen to go first. The warden appeared at his cell door after 8:00 A.M. and read the death warrant. He was then escorted from his death row cell, down the second tier corridor of the north wing, down the stairs into the chapel, and across the prison yard into the death chamber. He climbed the thirteen stairs and took his place on the trapdoor, where he declined to speak to the small crowd of witnesses. His wrists and arms, knees and ankles were bound, the noose was adjusted, and the black hood was pulled over his head. At 8:31 A.M. the trap was sprung and thirty-two-year-old Kelley dropped breaking his neck in the fall. The prison physician in attendance monitored vital signs until 8:43, when he pronounced Kelley dead. While the body was being cut down and deposited in the coffin provided by the state, the warden returned to the death row cells and the same procedures were followed for Willos. The trap was sprung at 8:52 A.M. and thirty-year-old Willos dropped, breaking his neck, and he was pronounced dead at 9:05 A.M. His body was then placed in its coffin and later that day both coffins were taken to the prison cemetery and buried.

Nevada State Journal (Reno): August 19, 1925; August 23, 1925. *Oakland Tribune* (CA): March 4, 1928. *Bismarck Tribune* (ND): April 11, 1928. *Chehalis Bee-Nugget* (WA): August 29, 1925. *Lowell Sun* (MI): August 13, 1923. *Ogden Standard-Examiner* (UT): April 20, 1928. *Salt Lake Tribune* (UT): May 11, 1926.

Kingsley, James E.
October 30, 1928

In October 1930 twenty-four-year-old James E. Kingsley escaped from the state prison at Canon City, Colorado. He made his way to Salt Lake City, Utah, where he stole an automobile and drove to the West Coast, where he remained for several months taking part in a number of armed robberies. On January 6 he held up a drug store in Seattle and when two policemen stopped him for questioning he got the drop on them and took their pistols, but when a third patrolman began firing at him he fled. On January 24, Kingsley, with one passenger, was driving in Ashland, Oregon, when he was stopped by traffic officer Sam Prescott, who demanded to see his automobile ownership papers and driver's license. Kingsley shot the officer once in the back as he turned. Prescott collapsed to the ground, and then Kingsley exited his car and at point-blank range shot the officer three more times, killing him instantly. Within an hour Kingsley, who gave the name J. C. Adams, was captured and lodged in jail at Ashland, but there was strong talk of lynching, so he was moved to the jail at Medford. His passenger proved he had been picked up the previous day while hitchhiking at Eugene, Oregon, and knew nothing of Kingsley, so he was released but ordered to be available to testify.

As soon as Kingsley was identified he confessed, admitted to a number of armed robberies, and bragged that the gun he used to kill Prescott was one of two taken from Seattle policemen. On January 27 he told district attorney George A. Codding he shot Prescott "because I didn't want to go to the police station and get turned up for the stolen car." He concluded his confession with, "I'm not bellyaching, I am going to get my neck stretched and I don't care." He signed his confession and then waived his preliminary examination and was held over for the grand jury. Kingsley was indicted by a Jackson County grand jury in early February and his trial started immediately. He was convicted of first degree murder, sentenced to hang April 3, 1931, and on February 11 he was delivered to a death row cell in the north wing of the cell block at the state prison in Salem, and a constant guard was placed over him to ensure he did not commit suicide. His court appointed attorneys filed an appeal and on March 28 he was informed that his execution had been stayed until the state Supreme Court heard the arguments. Up to that time, according to Warden J. W. Lewis, "He has been a model prisoner but he has not smiled until told of the stay. He sleeps by day and plays cards all night. We granted him every request possible, and served him with the best of food." The justices affirmed the judgment and sentence of the lower court and Kingsley was sentenced to hang on October 30, 1931. Nothing further would occur to delay the proceedings.

On the morning of Kingsley's execution more than sixty-five witnesses were conducted into the execution chamber, most of whom were police officers from all parts of the state. After 8:00 A.M. Warden Lewis appeared at Kingsley's cell door to read the death warrant. The prisoner's arms and wrists were then bound and he was escorted from his death row cell to the death chamber. He took his place on the trapdoor where he declined to speak, so his knees and ankles were bound, the noose was adjusted, and the black hood was pulled over his head. At 8:30 A.M. the trap was sprung and Kingsley dropped, breaking his neck in the fall. The prison physician in attendance monitored his vital signs until 8:43 A.M., when he pronounced him dead. The body was cut down and deposited in the coffin provided by the state and was buried in the prison cemetery later that day.

Oregonian (Portland): October 31, 1931. *Billings Gazette* (MT): March 29, 1931; October 31, 1931. *Inter Lake* (Kalispell, MT): January 24, 1931. *Independent* (Helena, MT): January 25, 1931. *Ogden Standard-Examiner* (UT): February 11, 1931.

McCarthy, Leroy H.
June 20, 1939

On August 10, 1937, twenty-four-year-old Leroy Hershel McCarthy tried to rob a gas station in Portland, Oregon. The manager, thirty-year-old Floyd Fuelner, handed over $26 and McCarthy fled, but Fuelner chased the robber and overtook him after two blocks. In the struggle that followed McCarthy shot Fuelner in the abdomen. A motorcycle patrolman was nearby and he disarmed and arrested McCarthy, and Fuelner was rushed to a hospital where he soon died of his wound.

McCarthy was charged with Fuelner's murder, tried at the fall term of the Multnomah County court, found guilty on October 6 without a recommendation for mercy, and the following day he was sentenced to die at the state prison in Salem. He arrived at the death house on October 19. The legislature had replaced the hangman's noose with lethal gas and McCarthy would be the first to die by this new method. The matter of intervention was presented to Governor Charles A. Sprague and he said he would only interfere at the recommendation of both houses of the legislature, but both houses declined make that recommendation even though one bill was pending to abolish the death penalty and another to repeal the gas chamber law. The judicial appeal which had originally stayed the execution for more than a year was resolved when the state Supreme Court justices affirmed the lower court's judgment and sentence, so McCarthy's date with the executioner was set for Friday, June 20, 1939.

On Friday morning the death warrant was read to McCarthy in his cell and then he was led into the steel gas chamber. He was seated in a steel chair and his chest, waist, wrists and ankles were strapped securely. He was asked if he had anything to say to the small number of witnesses present, but there is no record of a statement. The chamber was vacated and sealed and at 8:37 A.M. and the cyanide pellets were dropped into the crock of sulphuric acid. In a few minutes white fumes enveloped the condemned man and, as he had been instructed, he took a deep breath, and in fifteen seconds he was unconscious. In three minutes all signs of life were absent and then the chamber was flushed with anhydrous ammonia and cleared of the poisonous fumes by fans which directed the poison through "scrubbers" using water as a neutralizer. The process took about twenty minutes and then the two doctors in attendance entered and pronounced that McCarthy had died painlessly at 8:40 A.M. The body was then removed and cleansed with a chlorine solution before it was released to a funeral home.

Albuquerque Journal (NM): January 21, 1939. *Billings Gazette* (MT): January 21, 1939. *Centralia Chronicle* (WA): August 11, 1937. *Nevada State Journal* (Reno): October 7, 1937.

Cline, Claude E.
July 26, 1940

Forty-six-year-old Claude E. Cline and thirty-five-year-old George W. Chetty were prospecting partners near Fossil, Oregon, but Cline preferred to murder his partner for his money rather than dig in the ground. In early May 1940, Chetty's body was discovered in a shallow grave in Spanish Gulch, Wheeler County, Oregon, and Cline's absence made him an immediate suspect in the murder. Cline was arrested and lodged in jail on May 13 and then he led the police to the shallow grave of his previous prospecting partner, Eugene Rosenstiel. Sheriff E. J. Kelsay announced that Cline had confessed to the murders of Chetty and Rosenstiel. Cline was tried for Chetty's murder, convicted on June 15, and sentenced to die in the gas chamber at the state prison in Salem on July 26, 1940. There was no appeal nor other delay in the proceedings.

On June 18 Cline was removed from his solitary cell and moved to a death row cell near the gas chamber. When interviewed Cline told reporters, "I have no grudge against anybody. I feel that I am paying my debt. I am ready to meet my God." The Reverend P. W. Erikson was with him from Thursday night through Friday morning and said he only slept three hours. Early on his final morning the prisoner was stripped to his shorts and his head was shaved, and while that was being done Warden George Alexander read the death warrant.

Cline, with the eye mask in place, was guided into the gas chamber where he took a seat in the steel chair at 8:30 A.M. His chest, waist, wrists and ankles were strapped securely and a stethoscope was taped to his chest so his heart beat could be monitored from outside the chamber. Everyone then retired and the chamber was sealed. There was only a brief delay before the pellets of potassium cyanide were dropped into the crock of sulphuric acid beneath the chair and the room quickly filled with a cloud of white fumes. Cline inhaled deeply thirteen times and his head drooped forward, then slumped onto his chest, and his body thrust convulsively against the straps. One minute forty seconds after the fumes were first inhaled, 8:34 A.M., his heart ceased to beat. The chamber was then flushed with anhydrous ammonia and the fumes were evacuated by fans which directed the poisonous gas through "scrubbers" which used water as a neutralizer. The body was removed and cleansed with a chlorine solution and when the remains were safe to touch the doctor examined the body before it was released to a funeral home.

Centralia Chronicle (WA): July 25, 1940. *Hamilton Journal* (OH): May 13, 1940. *Montana Standard* (Butte): July 27, 1940. *Oregonian* (Portland): July 27, 1940.

Thomas, James H.
October 30, 1941

Nineteen-year-old James Harvey Thomas joined the Navy but by early June 1941 he deserted. On June 11 he was hitchhiking his way from Oregon to Washington State when he was picked up by twenty-six-year-old Douglas Smith, a Seattle, Washington, salesman. They had only gone a short distance, and were near Condon, when Thomas pulled out a concealed pistol and shot Smith in the head killing him instantly. He threw Smith's body into a roadside ditch near Arlington and went through his pockets, taking his gasoline credit card and money, then continued on with Smith's automobile. Thomas stopped to fill the gas tank using Smith's credit card and forged Smith's signature, which put the police on his trail. Thomas was arrested on a farm near Nespelem, Washington, still in possession of Smith's automobile and credit card, and he confessed that he shot Smith because he thought Smith figured out that he was a deserter and would turn him in.

At the same time Thomas was arrested the body of Smith was discovered and taken to Portland, where Dr. Joseph Beeman determined death was caused by a single gunshot wound to his head. On June 26, Sheriff Frank E. Bennett filed a first degree murder charge against Thomas in Judge C. O. Portwood's Condon courtroom. Thomas waived his preliminary hearing and was held over for the grand jury, indicted, tried, convicted of first degree murder without a recommendation for mercy, and sentenced to die on October 30, 1941. There was no delay in the proceeding, though two sets of petitions praying for clemency were sent to Governor Charles A. Sprague and denied.

At 8:00 A.M. Thomas was stripped to his shorts and his head was shaved, and then he was guided to the gas chamber by two guards and the Reverend Robert N. Hutchinson. At the door he told newsmen, "I'm sorry, and all that, and I wish to thank everybody who tried to help me." The newsmen then joined the other witnesses, making fifty in all, while Thomas was seated in the steel chair and his chest, waist, wrists, and ankles were strapped securely. A stethoscope was taped to his chest so his heart could be monitored from outside the chamber, and the eye mask was pulled on. Everyone stepped out and the chamber was sealed. On the signal of the warden the potassium cyanide pellets were dropped into the crock of sulphuric acid at 8:36 A.M. and a white cloud of poisonous gas enveloped the condemned man. He breathed deeply as instructed and in one minute his heart ceased to beat, and he died without a visible struggle. The chamber was then flushed with anhydrous ammonia and evacuated of the poisonous fumes by fans which directed the gas through "scrubbers" which used water as a neutralizer. The body was removed and cleansed with a chlorine solution, and then examined by the doctor in attendance before being released to his parents, who planned to bury their son at Holyoke, Colorado.

Centralia Chronicle (WA): June 28, 1941. *Oregonian* (Portland): October 31, 1941.

Soto, John A.
March 20, 1942

In September 1941 twenty-five-year-old John Anthony Soto had been boarding at the Gorsuch farm in Hermiston, Oregon, for several days while he worked on a construction job nearby. At noon on September 25 Soto took his pistol and shot sixty-eight-year-old Cora Tobin in the back of the head killing her instantly. He then waited five hours for the twenty-five-year-old nephew Marvin Adams to return and he shot him in the back of the head, also killing him instantly. Three hours later Kenneth L. Gorsuch, Tobin's son, returned home and Soto shot him in the back of the head, but he did not think Gorsuch dead, so he shot him six more times, using all his ammunition. After he killed Tobin he had ransacked the house for valuables and after he murdered Adams and Gorsuch he went through their pockets and took all they had. He also took some items from the house, loaded them into their 1929 automobile, and fled to Kennewick, Washington, where he rented a room at a hotel. The following morning a neighbor stopped at the Gorsuch farm to borrow eggs and when he got no response he investigated, found the grisly murder scene, and called authorities.

A broadcast described Soto and the automobile, and the murderer was quickly captured at Kennewick by Sheriff A. M. Richter. He gave no resistance though he carried his loaded pistol in a shoulder holster, and by September 27 he had confessed to Yakima, Washington, police chief M. H. Kershaw, who had the confession transcribed. Soto signed it. He said that his motive, in addition to the robbery, was that "they had found out who I was," and he said he would have also shot two neighbors if he had not run out of ammunition. Soto would not elaborate on his history nor explain his concern over his identity being discovered, but it was later learned that he had escaped from "an institution for the feeble-minded" in Sonoma, California, and did not want to be sent back. He was tried at the next term of the court in Pendleton, found guilty of first degree murder, and sentenced to die in the gas chamber at Salem. Over the next eighteen months every effort was made to save his life, but to no avail.

On the morning of March 20, 1942, Soto, smoking a cigar but dressed only in his shorts, was escorted into the gas chamber, where he said, as he was being strapped to the steel chair, "Remember me to my folks." A stethoscope was taped to his chest before the door was sealed shut, and then the potassium cyanide pellets were dropped into the crock of sulphuric acid. As the white fumes enveloped his body the prisoner took one deep breath and his head fell forward, and it was estimated that he had died in five seconds. After the doctor in attendance pronounced him dead the chamber was flushed with anhydrous ammonia and then fans evacuated the poisonous fumes, directing the gases through "scrubbers" using water as a neutralizer. Soto's body was then removed and cleansed with a chlorine solution before being sent to a funeral home to be prepared for shipment to Niles, California, where his family lived.

Fairbanks Daily News-Miner (AK): March 21, 1942. *Lowell Sun and Citizen-Leader* (MA): September 27, 1941. *Ogden Standard-Examiner* (UT): March 21, 1942. *Tucson Daily Citizen* (AZ): September 27, 1941.

Wallace, William H.
February 26, 1943

At 6:30 P.M. on August 8, 1941, thirty-two-year-old Benjamin H. Finkell was sitting in his car with his fiancée, Patricia Martin, on S. W. Park Avenue at Yamhill Street. Fifty-four-year-old William H. Wallace, in a drunken condition, staggered up to the car shouting vile and profane language. Finkell ordered Wallace to "shut up." Wallace stopped next to the car and a sharp exchange of words followed, and then Wallace drew a .38-caliber automatic pistol from a shoulder holster with his right hand (he had no left hand) and shot Finkell once in the left side. Wallace holstered the pistol and continued north to Morrison and then east to Broadway. Woodrow Wilson, a large man, saw the argument and shooting and followed Wallace, and when Wallace reached Broadway, Wilson grabbed him. A struggle followed as bystanders came to help Wilson, and James C. Winslow took away Wallace's pistol. Meanwhile Finkell, after being shot, got out of his car and staggered a few feet before he collapsed against a wall. He was rushed to St. Vincent's hospital by ambulance where he died at 7:20 P.M.

Wallace was lodged in the city jail and he said, "I was drunk. I don't know why I did it. I never saw the man before." Wallace was tried in the Circuit Court in November and on November 28 he was found guilty of first degree murder. Within days Judge Alfred P. Dobson sentenced Wallace to die in the gas chamber at the prison in Salem. It took over a year for all the appeals and petitions to be handled, but finally the date of execution was set for February 26, 1943.

When the moment arrived an eye mask was pulled over Wallace's eyes and he was guided from his cell to the gas chamber by two guards, dressed only in his shorts. The prison superintendent helped him into the steel chair where his chest and waist, wrists and ankles were firmly strapped. A stethoscope was taped to his chest and then everyone retired and the chamber was sealed tight. In a moment the potassium cyanide pellets were dropped into the crock of sulphuric acid and a white plume of poisonous vapor filled the chamber. Wallace breathed deeply and in a few minutes his heart ceased to beat, and he died without a tremor. The chamber was flushed with anhydrous ammonia and then it was evacuated of poisonous fumes by fans which directed the gases through "scrubbers" which used water as a neutralizer. The body was removed and then the prison physician officially pronounced Wallace dead. The body was cleansed with a chlorine solution before it was turned over to an undertaker for final disposition.

Inter Lake (Kalispell, MT): August 9, 1941. *Independent* (Helena, MT): November 30, 1941. *Ogden*

Standard-Examiner (UT): February 26, 1943. *Oregonian* (Portland): August 9, 1941.

Cunningham, Henry
March 6, 1944

During a street altercation on August 29, 1942, Henry "Harvey" Cunningham murdered Richard Kerr in Portland, Oregon. On January 29, 1944, Cunningham confessed to two previous killings, "a seventeen-year-old boy and a thirty-seven-year-old man in Kansas City, Kansas." He later recanted his confession claiming he was only trying to be extradited to Kansas where he might get a life sentence, but Oklahoma officers cleared the murders of eighteen-year-old David Middleton and sixty-two-year-old Lawrence Johnson, and there was no doubt Cunningham was responsible for both killings. Cunningham was tried in the Multnomah County Circuit Court at the fall session, convicted of first degree murder and sentenced to die, but his case was appealed to the state Supreme Court. After many months the justices affirmed the judgment and sentence of the lower court and Cunningham was sentenced to die by lethal gas on Tuesday, March 6, 1944, the first black man to die by that method in Oregon.

Cunningham slept well his last night and arose early to eat a hearty breakfast. As the time neared Cunningham waived the reading of the death warrant and declined to make a statement. He was escorted into the gas chamber at 8:32 A.M. dressed only in his shorts, and his chest, waist, wrists and ankles were strapped to the steel chair. After a stethoscope was taped to his chest the chamber door was sealed. The potassium cyanide pellets were dropped into a crock of sulphuric acid at 8:35 A.M. and the white fumes quickly enveloped the condemned man. Cunningham breathed deeply and in minutes all signs of life ceased. The chamber was then flushed with anhydrous ammonia and evacuated of the poisonous gas with fans, which directed the fumes through a "scrubber" which used water as a neutralizer. The guards removed the body and as soon as the doctor could gain access he examined the body and officially pronounced that Cunningham had died at 8:45 A.M. The body was then cleansed with a chlorine solution and released to an undertaker for final disposition.

Nevada State Journal (Reno): March 7, 1944. *Ogden Standard-Examiner* (UT): March 8, 1944.

Layton, Richard H.
December 8, 1944

Thirty-six-year-old Richard H. Layton, an ex–law enforcement officer, assaulted a Portland woman on about June 30, 1943. The woman identified Layton and his automobile, and during the investigation that followed officers found clues regarding the disappearance of seventeen-year-old Ruth Hildebrand of The Dalles, Oregon. The pretty high school senior had bought a bus ticket from Rickreall to Camp Adair on June 7 but missed the bus, so she accepted a ride in Layton's automobile. On June 20, Hildebrand's nude, battered body was pulled from the river near Buena Vista and she had been raped, but there was no clue to the murderer until Layton was arrested. On July 7, Layton was returned to Hillsboro and charged with Hildebrand's murder, and he confessed that after he convinced the girl to get into his car he drove to an isolated "lover's lane" where he raped her. He said Hildebrand then tried to flee so he struck her and she fell into the river.

He was arraigned on a charge of first degree murder on July 22, tried in mid–August, and on August 18 he was found guilty as charged in the indictments. On August 30 Circuit Judge Arlie G. Walker asked the prisoner if he had anything to say before judgment was pronounced and he replied, "I still say I am innocent." The death sentence was mandatory when the jury found a defendant guilty of first degree murder without a recommendation for leniency, so Layton was sentenced to die in the gas chamber on October 8, 1943. An appeal followed which stayed the execution for fifteen months but the state Supreme Court justices affirmed the judgment and sentence of the lower court and the date of execution was set for December 8, 1944. Executive clemency was also denied.

Layton slept soundly his last night and showed no signs of nervousness as the time neared. The execution had been scheduled for 8:30 A.M. but there was a delay of a half-hour when the electro-cardiograph machine malfunctioned. At 9:05 Layton, dressed only in his shorts, was escorted into the gas chamber by two guards, and his chest and waist, wrists and ankles were securely strapped to the steel chair. The electrodes were attached to monitor his heartbeat and then the door was sealed. The potassium cyanide pellets were dropped into the sulphuric acid at 9:09 A.M. and as the white fumes enveloped the prisoner he gasped once, then took a deep breath, and in thirty seconds his head dropped forward. In thirty seconds more, at 9:10 A.M. his heart ceased to beat and he was pronounced dead. The chamber was flushed with anhydrous ammonia and then fans directed the poisonous fumes through "scrubbers" which used water as a neutralizer. The body was then removed from the chamber, cleansed with a chlorine solution, and released to a funeral home.

Nevada State Journal (Reno): July 9, 1943; July 22, 1943; August 19, 1943; August 31, 1943; December 10, 1944.

Folkes, Robert E. L.
January 5, 1945

Twenty-year-old Robert E. Lee Folkes was a dining car cook on a train heading southbound from Tangent, Oregon, to Los Angeles, California, on Friday, January 22, 1943. After the passengers retired to their Pullman bunks the workers gathered to drink beer and whiskey and "discuss the attractiveness of the women passengers." After midnight, when the train was in Linn County, Oregon, Folkes donned an overcoat to cover his white work clothes and went into the Pullman car, where twenty-one-year-old Martha V. James was sleeping in lower 13. He pushed aside the curtain and climbed in, straddling James, and she awoke while he was trying to fasten the curtain closed. She said, "Who are you, get out." Folkes put the point of a boning knife to her chin and with his other hand continued to fumble with the curtain snaps. Folkes warned her "keep still," but she screamed out and tried to throw him out of her bunk. As the scream awakened the other passengers he cut her throat, and James cried out, "My God! He's killing me." A marine in an upper bunk stuck his head out and saw Folkes fleeing, and then James tumbled out into the aisle with her nightgown soaked in blood, and she bled to death in minutes.

Folkes went to the baggage car and hid the knife and overcoat in his baggage. When the train reached Los Angeles the crew was questioned and Folkes made "innumerable contradictions as to his movements immediately before and after the murder," and finally said, "I know the slayer's identity but feel obligated to protect him because he has a wife and children." When questioning continued he confessed to being the murderer, saying, "You'll never find the knife I used to cut the woman with," then recanted his confession. He said that if he was allowed to see his wife he could provide an important clue, and after seeing his wife on January 27 he confessed the murder to Captain Vernon Rasmussen. He then repudiated the confession, but the following morning he confessed again and gave many facts that only the killer could have known.

Folkes was taken to Albany, Oregon, the Linn County seat, tried and convicted of first degree murder, and sentenced to die in the gas chamber. An appeal followed but the state Supreme Court affirmed the judgment and sentence of the Circuit Court and Folkes' date with the executioner was set for January 5, 1945, nearly two years after the murder. Executive clemency was denied so nothing further would delay the proceedings.

On his final night Folkes spent time with his mother and the Reverend C. H. Steinmann of Salem, and this helped him brace up. When the moment arrived at 9:00 A.M. Folkes seemed anxious to end the ordeal and, dressed only in his shorts, he walked quickly to the chamber. He took his seat in the steel chair and his chest and waist, wrists and ankles were strapped and the electrodes of the electrocardiograph machine were attached. Newsmen were present and he protested his innocence, claiming that he was framed by the Los Angeles police captain who told him, "Someone has to pay for this crime and its easier to convict a Negro than a white man." As the chamber was being cleared of witnesses he cheerfully cried out, "So long, everybody." He then shook hands with the Reverend Steinmann and a mask was pulled over his eyes. At 9:07 A.M. the potassium cyanide pellets were dropped into the crock of sulphuric acid and the white fumes enveloped him in seconds. He gasped, jerked back, and breathed deeply and heavily for several minutes and in six minutes, at 9:13 A.M., he was pronounced dead. The chamber was flushed with anhydrous ammonia and then the poisonous fumes were directed by fans through "scrubbers" which used water as a neutralizer. The body was removed and cleansed with a chlorine solution before being released to a funeral home.

Billings Gazette (MT): January 6, 1945. *Burlington Times-News* (NC): January 30, 1943. *Piqua Call* (OH): January 28, 1943.

Merten, Henry W.; Wilson, Walter L.
January 15, 1945

During the early morning hours of July 22, 1943, thirty-year-old Henry William Merten and thirty-three-year-old Walter Lorne Wilson held up a tavern at Milwaukie, Oregon. During the robbery they fatally wounded twenty-seven-year-old Ralph Dahlen of Oak Grove. The two murderers were soon captured and lodged in jail. They were tried at the fall term of the Circuit Court, convicted of first degree murder, and sentenced to die on March 10, 1944, but an appeal stayed the execution. After the justices of the state Supreme Court affirmed the sentence and judgment of the lower court, the two prisoners were sentenced to die in the prison gas chamber at Salem on January 15, 1945, and neither man asked for a rehearing on the case or other relief.

On his final morning Merten walked to the gas chamber unaided, dressed only in his shorts, and declined to speak to the newsmen present. His chest and waist, wrists and ankles were strapped to the steel chair, the eye mask was pulled on, and the electrodes of the electrocardiograph machine were attached. The door was sealed at 9:00 A.M. and in seconds the potassium cyanide pellets were dropped into the crock of sulphuric acid. A white plume of poisonous fumes reached Merten's face in three and one half minutes, but he failed to breathe deeply, so it took until 9:07 before he was pronounced dead. The chamber was flushed with anhydrous ammonia and the gases were cleared from the chamber by fans which fed the poisonous fumes through "scrubbers" which used water as a neutralizer. The body was then removed and everything was made ready for the second execution.

Wilson entered the chamber at 10:00 A.M. and declined to speak to the newsmen. He was strapped into the steel chair, the eye mask was pulled on, and then the chamber was cleared of witnesses. The same process was followed and the fumes reached Wilson's face at 10:06 A.M., and he breathed deeply as instructed. Wilson was pronounced dead in one minute and, after the chamber was cleaned, Wilson's body was removed. Both remains were then cleansed with a chlorine solution before being released to a funeral home.

Ogden Standard-Examiner (UT): January 15, 1945.

Dennis, Andrew W.
February 2, 1946

On January 29, 1944, fifty-eight-year-old Anna Belle McNallen was found in her Portland, Oregon, apartment with her head bashed in, and with bruising and fingerprints about her neck. Forty-three-year-old Andrew W. Dennis, her son-in-law, was suspected and, though he insisted he was innocent and was home in bed when she was killed, four neighbors picked him from a line-up as the man they saw using the entrance telephone and wandering in the hallway at the time of the murder. They also said they heard screams but did not call police when the noises quieted. McNallen's body had not been found until January 31 when a neighbor, Mrs. J. D. Burnside, entered the apartment to give McNallen a newspaper. The police then interviewed fifteen-year-old neighbor Betty Lou Lloyd, who said she saw Dennis in front of the apartment door, saw him enter, and in a short time she heard a woman scream, "Don't, don't!" followed by the thud of a blow, a moan, and the woman cried out, "I'm dying!" She said she had been afraid to tell anyone until asked.

Dennis was lodged in jail while an autopsy was being performed and the finding was that McNallen had been strangled to death. On February 1 a first degree murder complaint was filed and Dennis was tried at the spring term, and he continued to insist that he had not returned to the apartment after Wednesday when he visited his ex-wife, who then left for San Francisco. He was found guilty and sentenced to die at the prison in Salem, Oregon, but his case was appealed, which stayed his execution for two years. In late 1945 the state Supreme Court affirmed the judgment and sentence of the lower court and Dennis' date with the executioner was set for February 2, 1946.

Dennis showed no nervousness and at 8:30 A.M. he entered the gas chamber unaided, dressed only in his shorts, and without the customary eye mask. His chest and waist, wrists and ankles were strapped into the steel chair and the electrodes of the electrocardiograph machine were attached. He told the newspaper reporters, "This is an awful miscarriage of justice. Some day the state will find they have done the wrong thing sticking me in the gas chamber. I did not commit this crime, and never committed any crime in my life." The witnesses were removed from the chamber and the door was sealed. The potassium cyanide pellets were immediately dropped into the crock of sulphuric acid and in a few minutes the white fumes rose to envelope the condemned man. He breathed deeply, as instructed, and at 8:49 A.M. he was pronounced dead. The chamber was flushed with anhydrous ammonia and the fumes were then evacuated by fans, which directed the poisonous gas through "scrubbers" which used water as a neutralizer. The body was removed and cleansed with a chlorine solution before being released to a funeral home.

Nevada State journal (Reno): February 2, 1944. *Santa Fe New Mexican*: February 2, 1946.

Bailey, Kenneth W.
September 13, 1946

On April 28, 1945, twenty-six-year-old Kenneth William Bailey and twenty-two-year-old William Ronald Duffey were stealing gasoline from a Nampa, Idaho, gas station when they were confronted by officers Arthur O'Keefe and George Jordan. Bailey and Duffey pulled pistols and covered the two officers, took their pistols, and fled. Later that evening they were seen on the Oregon side of the Snake River practicing shooting with the revolvers taken from the Nampa officers. Oregon officers approached them and they fled, but they were tracked overnight by patrolman Max Smith, Sheriff Art Caviness, Weiser's chief of police Clarence Saunders, and deputy sheriff Al Walters. The trail led to a Malheur County, Oregon, school annex building just across the Snake River from Weiser, Idaho, and sergeant Ted Chambers and officer Ted O'Brien of Ontario, Oregon, deputy sheriff Walters, and chief of police Saunders went into the basement to search for the fugitives. The two men were hiding in a barricaded coal bin and opened fire without warning, killing Chambers and wounding O'Brien and Saunders. The two men then captured Saunders and forced him to walk between them as a shield as they made their way out of the building into an open field, where Duffey was killed and Bailey wounded by rifle fire.

Bailey and Saunders were taken to the Weiser hospital and Bailey was charged with murder. When questioned Bailey said, "It was the damndest fool thing I ever heard of. We were armed to the teeth and all we had to do was start shooting. If they had thrown a tear gas bomb we would have come out without shooting." Bailey was tried at the fall term of the Circuit Court and he was found guilty of murdering Chambers. He was sentenced to die in Oregon's gas chamber and his efforts at appeal were brief, and his date for execution was set for September 13, 1946.

Early on the morning of his execution Bailey wrote to Warden George Alexander, "I am going upstairs in five hours. Maybe I'll break down and cry like any little child who stole a cough drop, but I hope you'll find a way to keep other kids from becoming convicts," and his letter gave a brief reminisce of his early life leading him into crime. When the moment arrived a mask was pulled over Bailey's eyes and then he was guided from his cell to the gas chamber by two guards, accompanied by Warden Alexander. The prisoner was seated in the steel chair where his chest and waist, wrists and ankles were firmly strapped and the electrodes of the electrocardiograph machine were attached. Everyone retired and the chamber was sealed tight. In a moment the potassium cyanide pellets were dropped into the crock of sulphuric acid and a white plume of poisonous vapor filled the chamber. Bailey breathed deeply and in a few minutes his heart ceased to beat. The chamber was flushed with anhydrous ammonia and then evacuated of poisonous fumes with fans which directed the gases through "scrubbers" using water as a neutralizer. Guards then removed the body and the prison physician officially pronounced Bailey dead. The body was cleansed with a chlorine solution before it was turned over to an undertaker for final disposition.

Altoona Mirror (PA): September 18, 1946. *Ogden Standard-Examiner* (UT): April 30, 1945.

Henderson, Wardell H.
January 29, 1948

Aaron T. Robinson of Vanport, Oregon, enlisted in the army under the alias Wardell H. Henderson. He deserted in March 1945 and, still using the name Henderson, made his way back to Vanport where he rented an apartment. Early on the evening of December 24 Henderson tried to rob twenty-seven-year-old Jerry Taylor, who resisted and was shot at twice before Henderson fled to his apartment. Taylor was wounded but recovered. After hiding out until after midnight Henderson went out again looking for a mark and saw thirty-nine-year-old Walter Howard Poole leaving a Jantzen Beach store where he had worked late. As Poole approached his car Henderson took him prisoner at gunpoint and forced him to drive to a remote location in Vanport, where he struck Poole over the head three times using his pistol. On the third blow the gun discharged, shooting Poole in the head. Henderson then threw Poole's body out of the car and dragged it into a vacant lot near the housing project, where he shot Poole in the back to be sure he was dead. Henderson went through his pockets, taking everything of value, and then started east in Poole's automobile. However, he had to stop at a Portland garage for repairs before continuing to Philadelphia, so he was seen driving Poole's automobile right after the murder. In Philadelphia, Henderson visited with his mother and the following day he surrendered to military authorities as a deserter, confessed to the killing of Poole, and by January 10, 1946, the extradition proceeding began.

Henderson was returned to Rose City where he was tried at the spring term of the Circuit Court, convicted of first degree murder, and sentenced to die on June 28, 1946. An appeal followed and it was not until late the following year that the state Supreme Court affirmed the judgment and sentence of the lower court and set the date of execution at January 23, 1948. The Portland Council of Churches, on January 8, asked Governor Hall to grant a stay of execution to reconsider the matter because of "concern over what appears to be an excessive penalty.... Comparing the sentence inflicted on Mr. Henderson with sentences meted out in other cases of murder in this state, one would be inclined to ask whether the matter of race was an influence in arriving at the verdict." The governor granted a one week respite while he considered the matter but could find no reason to intervene, so the date for Henderson's execution was finally set at January 29, 1948.

The prison chaplain was with Henderson until just before the eye mask was pulled on and he was guided from his cell to the gas chamber by two guards, accompanied by the prison superintendent. He was seated in the steel chair where his chest and waist, wrists and ankles were firmly strapped and the electrodes for the electrocardiograph machine were attached. Everyone retired and the chamber was sealed tight. In a moment the potassium cyanide pellets were dropped into the crock of sulphuric acid and the white plume of poisonous vapor filled the chamber. Henderson breathed deeply, as instructed earlier, and he died without a tremor. In two minutes his heart ceased to beat and then the chamber was flushed with anhydrous ammonia and evacuated of the poisonous fumes by fans which directed the gases through scrubbers using water as a neutralizer. Guards removed the body and then the prison physician officially pronounced Henderson dead. The body was cleansed with a chlorine solution before it was turned over to an undertaker for final disposition.

Union-Bulletin (Walla Walla, WA): January 9, 1948.

Long, Wayne L.
August 8, 1952

On Wednesday, June 13, 1950, twenty-six-year-old Wayne Leroy Long was released from the Oregon State Prison in Salem after serving eight years for assault with intent to rob. He was under constant surveillance by agents of the Federal Bureau of Investigation (FBI) because of his association with August Omar Pinson, who was on its "ten most wanted" list. Shortly before noon on June 15, 1950, Long entered the Powell district branch of the First National Bank in Portland carrying a submachine gun. He fired several rounds in the air, terrorized the customers and employees with threats, and said to Donna Fraisheim, "I want some money, and I want it quick." He put his shopping bag on the counter as Fraisheim glanced toward bank manager Lewis Wilshire, and he nodded for her to cooperate. Long then told Wilshire, as the robber brandished his machine gun, "Tell her to hurry up. I mean it." Fraisheim grabbed a handful of currency from a drawer and handed it to Long, and he threw the $9,716 into the shopping bag and ran for the door. He had not gone far when he was confronted by eight FBI agents and they exchanged gunfire during a running gun battle, until Long was shot down in front of a nearby grocery store. In the exchange thirty-year-old agent Leonard Frank was wounded in the arm. Long was trying to make it to his getaway vehicle, a pickup truck, which was later determined to belong to Walter Rucker, whose bullet-riddled body had been found on June 14. Agents saw Rucker when he went with Long but it appeared he went of his own volition, and Long slipped surveillance long enough to drive to an isolated location near Eagle Fern Park, and when next seen Long was alone.

Long was tried in federal court for bank robbery, convicted, and sentenced to serve a life term. He was then tried in the Clackamas County Circuit Court on a charge of murdering Walter Rucker, convicted, and sentenced to die. He was taken to the prison at Salem and lodged in a large cell block housing two hundred seventy-five prisoners. After the usual delays for appeals in a death penalty case, the justices affirmed the lower court and Long was sentenced to die on Friday, August 8, 1952. On August 7, Long's attorney, Dale Jacobs, saw Governor Douglas McKay in a last minute attempt to obtain a reprieve or commutation, but the governor declined, saying Long had a fair trial and there was no new evidence.

On August 4 the prisoners in Long's cell block staged a boisterous protest, claiming it resulted from denial of medical attention to convict Sampson. It was thought, however, that it was a diversion to allow an escape attempt by Long, John Pinson, and Dupree Poe. Sampson was treated in his cell and it was found his illness was feigned, and any thought of escape was abandoned. On Friday, August

8, Long arose at an early hour and was joined by prison Chaplain Father William McClory. McClory was with him until just before 7:00 A.M. when Long was escorted from his cell to the gas chamber by two guards, accompanied by prison superintendent George Alexander. He chewed gum vigorously as his chest and waist, wrists and ankles were strapped to the steel chair and the electrodes for the electrocardiograph machine were attached. Alexander spoke with him briefly and then retired, leaving the priest to give the prisoner his last words of encouragement, and Long smiled. The prisoner's eyes were not masked as the chamber was sealed tight and at 7:04 A.M. the potassium cyanide pellets were dropped into the crock of sulphuric acid, and the white plume of poisonous vapor filled the chamber. Long breathed deeply, died without a quiver, and in two minutes his heart ceased to beat. The chamber was then flushed with anhydrous ammonia and evacuated of poisonous fumes before guards removed the body, and then the prison physician officially pronounced Long dead. The body was then cleansed with a chlorine solution before being turned over to an undertaker for disposition.

Independent (Long Beach, CA): June 17, 1950.
Pharos-Tribune (Logansport, IN): June 16, 1950.
Union-Bulletin (Walla Walla, WA): August 4, 1952; August 7–8, 1952.

Leland, Morris; Payne, Frank O. January 9, 1953

On Saturday, August 6, 1949, twenty-two-year-old Morris Leland lured fifteen-year-old Thelma Taylor, a farm laborer's daughter, to a secluded spot beneath the St. Johns Bridge on the bank of the Willamette River near Portland, Oregon. He kept her a prisoner for twenty-four hours and made sexual advances toward her, but she would not cooperate so he beat her and then stabbed her to death and hid her body beneath a pile of logs. When she did not return home Saturday evening her parents reported her missing but there was no evidence of foul play, so the case was handled as a missing person. On Thursday, August 11, Leland was arrested on suspicion of driving a stolen automobile and while being driven to the police station he said he wanted to talk with homicide detectives. When detectives Noel Eck and Dan Mitola appeared, Leland blurted out his confession that he murdered Thelma Taylor. He led the detectives to her body and told them he had killed her "because she was a good girl and would make trouble with the police," and then explained his confession, saying, "It has been on my mind ever since it happened." He was tried and pled not guilty by reason of insanity, but he was convicted of first degree murder and sentenced to die in the gas chamber in the state prison at Salem. All efforts for judicial relief were exhausted and executive clemency was declined, so the date for his execution was finally set for Friday, January 9, 1953.

At closing time on the evening of January 9, 1951, forty-seven-year-old Frank Oliver Payne entered the grocery and meat market of Nathan Butler in downtown Portland, Oregon. Payne displayed his pistol and demanded the day's receipts but Butler refused. Payne shot Butler five times before fleeing with several thousand dollars. Butler died on the way to the hospital but not before he had given a good description of his killer. The following day Payne was arrested four blocks from the market and he was lodged in the Multnomah County jail. He was tried on a charge of first degree murder, pled not guilty by reason of insanity, was convicted, and sentenced to die in the gas chamber of the state prison in Salem. All his efforts at judicial relief were exhausted and Governor Paul L. Patterson refused to intervene, saying, "The law must take its course," so Payne's date with the executioner was set for Friday, January 9, 1953, the first double gas chamber execution in Oregon.

Warden Virgil O'Malley said that on Wednesday the two men spent a quiet night and slept well, though Leland seemed nervous and excited. Leland had broken down on Monday but had recovered his composure over the following two days. Payne, on the other hand, had been entirely calm, possibly because he had been given sleeping pills for some time and feigned swallowing them so he could accumulate a small stockpile. On Thursday night he swallowed all the pills in an attempt to commit suicide but when guards could not awaken him a doctor was summoned. He was aroused by injections, which delayed the executions for a half hour, and Leland had to go first while Payne was recovering, as the chamber could accommodate only one man.

Leland, dressed only in his shorts, entered the chamber at 12:07 A.M. where his chest and waist, wrists and ankles were strapped to the steel chair and the electrodes for the electrocardiograph machine were attached. There is no record of a statement to the seventy-five witnesses, but as soon as the airtight chamber was sealed the potassium cyanide pellets were dropped into the crock of sulphuric acid and the white cloud of poisonous fumes enveloped the prisoner. He breathed deeply and was pronounced dead at 12:33 A.M., and then the chamber was flushed with anhydrous ammonia and the fumes were evacuated with fans before the body was removed. Payne was still too groggy to walk so at 1:50 A.M. two guards carried him into the chamber and the same preparations were completed. Payne was in no condition to make a statement but witnesses said "he appeared aware of what was going on." Payne was pronounced dead at 2:12 A.M. and after the fumes were evacuated from the chamber his body was removed. Both bodies were cleansed with a chlorine solution before being released to a funeral parlor.

Charleston Gazette (NC): August 12, 1949. *Hawk-Eye Gazette* (Burlington, IA): August 12, 1949. *Stillwell Democrat-Journal* (OK): January 19, 1951. *Union-Bulletin* (Walla Walla, WA): January 8–9, 1953.

Karnes, Albert W.
January 30, 1953

Twenty-four-year-old Albert William Karnes had rented a room from the eighty-one-year-old widow Susan Litchfield in Salem, Oregon, but he had recently moved. On June 7, 1952, Karnes returned to the Litchfield home, dragged his former landlady to the woodshed behind the house and hacked her to death. He then ransacked the home and stole $30. Karnes fled to The Dalles where, on June 10, he attacked Mrs. Benjamin Callaway with a hammer for the purpose of robbery. Karnes was captured, and at his trial on June 18 he was found guilty and Circuit Court Judge Malcolm Wilkinson sentenced him to serve fifteen years in the state prison at Salem. However, while Karnes was in jail he confessed to killing Litchfield, so he was returned to Salem and tried for first degree murder. Karnes was found guilty and sentenced to die in the state's gas chamber on January 30, 1953, and nothing would delay his date with the executioner.

Karnes was described by the warden as "one of the calmest [condemned] men I have ever seen." At ten minutes past midnight on January 30, Karnes, with his eye mask in place and dressed only in his shorts, was guided to the gas chamber and seated in the steel chair. His chest and waist, wrists and ankles were strapped to the chair, and the electrodes for the electrocardiograph machine were attached before he declined to speak to the twenty-three witnesses, mostly guards and newsmen. The chamber was sealed and at 12:17 A.M. the potassium cyanide pellets were dropped into the crock of sulphuric acid and the white cloud of poisonous fumes rose to envelope the prisoner. He breathed deeply, did not struggle, and was pronounced dead at 12:30 A.M. The chamber was then flushed with anhydrous ammonia and the fumes were purged using fans which directed the poisonous gases through scrubbers using water as a neutralizer. The body was then removed, cleansed with a chlorine solution, and released to a funeral parlor.

Union-Bulletin (Walla Walla, WA): January 19, 1952; January 30, 1953.

McGahuey, Leroy S.
August 20, 1962

In February 1961 forty-two-year-old Leroy Sanford McGahuey took a hammer and beat to death thirty-two-year-old Mrs. Charles T. Holt and her twenty-three-month-old son Rod Cameron Holt at their home in Central Point, Oregon. McGahuey was captured and lodged in jail, where he confessed to the murders. The police tried to get him to talk about the 1957 murder of thirty-one-year-old Eleanor Bolinger, a teacher at Mineral Wash, but he insisted that he knew nothing of that killing. Even though he had confessed to murdering the Holts he pled not guilty when tried for murdering the toddler. He was convicted and sentenced to die in the gas chamber, but McGahuey's case was appealed and it took until mid–1962 before the state Supreme Court justices affirmed the judgment and sentence of the lower court, and McGahuey was sentenced to die on August 20, 1962. Nothing further would delay the execution.

On Monday morning, McGahuey, dressed only in his shorts, was escorted into the gas chamber at 1:00 A.M. where his chest and waist, wrists and ankles were strapped to the steel chair and the electrodes for the electrocardiograph machine were attached. He did not make a speech but as the black eye mask was about to be put in place he turned to the deputy warden and said, "That's it." The chamber was sealed and at 1:15 A.M. the potassium cyanide pellets were dropped into the crock of sulphuric acid and a white cloud of poisonous fumes arose to envelope the prisoner. He breathed deeply as instructed and did not struggle, and at 1:23 A.M. he was pronounced dead. The chamber was then flushed with anhydrous ammonia and purged of fumes by fans directed into scrubbers using water as a neutralizer. The body was removed, cleansed with a chlorine solution, and release to a funeral parlor.

Courier (Connellsville, PA): August 21, 1962. *Humboldt Standard* (Eureka, CA): August 20, 1962.

Wright, Douglas F.
September 6, 1996

In 1991 fifty-one-year-old Douglas Franklin Wright promised work to three homeless men if they would accompany him onto the Warm Springs Indian Reservation in Wasco County, Oregon, but he took them to a remote area and murdered them. The case was investigated for months before Wright was arrested, he was tried at the fall 1993 term of the court, found guilty, and sentenced to die by lethal injection, the first use of that method in Oregon. He had also been charged with killing Anthony Nelson, a Makah Indian, on reservation land but he was never tried for that killing. Wright was taken to the prison at Salem while his case was being appealed, but in early 1996 he demanded that the appeal be withdrawn and that he be allowed to die, perhaps to avoid a federal trial for killing an Indian (Nelson) on reservation land.

As his date with the executioner neared Wright confessed to the abduction and murder of ten-year-old Luke Tredway in May 1984. Luke's mother had dropped her son at a friend's house the afternoon he disappeared and when he had not returned home by 5:30 P.M. she telephoned and was told her son had left fifteen minutes earlier, but he never arrived. Wright said, "I was hunting for boys between the ages of fourteen and eighteen years old and Luke was just in the wrong place at the wrong time." Wright said he grabbed Tredway off a Portland street and kept him prisoner for thirty-six hours, molesting him repeatedly before shooting him to death and burying his body in a remote location on the side of a mountain east of Portland. Kathleen Tredway, Luke's mother, was determined to attend the execution and said, "I want the bastard to die—slowly. Getting killed is the easy way out. He should be made to suffer."

Oregon established a meticulous protocol for executions by lethal injection. As soon as the death warrant was delivered to the prison the protocol was implemented and no less than four days before the execution Wright was moved to a secure cell and placed under a constant death watch guard. Two days before the execution the staff received a refresher course in procedures and all the necessary forms were checked for accuracy and completeness, to ensure a clerical error did not result in a delay. One day prior to Wright's execution all the medical equipment and solutions were checked and the proper medical staff was scheduled, and all prison personnel were given their assignments. One such duty was to check all the equipment, especially the telephones and camera monitoring system, and the telephones would be checked again every half hour beginning at 9 o'clock on the night before the execution. A radio system was also put into operation and checked regularly as a back-up to the phone system.

As witnesses began to arrive they were conducted to a staging area and kept under guard, while media representatives were taken to the Media Center where those few who would actually witness the execution were chosen, and they would afterward share their information with the other news persons. A half hour before the execution the camera monitor was activated and then the condemned, in security restraints, was escorted into the execution chamber where he was strapped to a gurney. Medically trained personnel next attached to the condemned the skin electrodes for the electrocardiograph machine and inserted two intravenous catheters (IVs), the second IV a back-up in case the primary IV failed. The executioner was conducted into the control, or execution, room to maintain his anonymity and then the witnesses and selected media persons were escorted into the witnessing room and the curtains covering the windows were drawn open. As near after 12:01 A.M. as feasible, the superintendent signaled for the flow of drugs to commence, beginning with sodium pentothal to induce sleep, pancuronium bromide to stop respiration, and finally potassium chloride to stop Wright's heart. The executioner signaled to the superintendent when the drugs were administered and as soon as Wright's heart ceased to beat, in seven minutes, a medical professional certified death. The camera monitoring system was then turned off and the media witnesses were conducted back to the Media Center. The body was later removed to a funeral home, as previously arranged.

Sitka Sentinel (AK): September 3, 1996.

Moore, Harry C.
May 16, 1997

Fifty-one-year-old Harry Charles Moore had married two of his nieces, but was estranged from second wife, Cindy. In 1992 there was some discussion that she, with one or both of her parents, would take their infant daughter Jennifer and move to Las Vegas, Nevada. Moore took a 9 mm handgun and went looking for Cindy's parents and when he found his wife's father, sixty-year-old Thomas Lauri, parked in front of a Salem post office, he shot him four times in the face killing him instantly. He next drove to the home of Lauri's ex-wife, Moore's half-sister fifty-three-year-old Barbara Cunningham-Lauri, and he shot her in the stomach. When she collapsed and lay helpless he shot her three times in the head, killing her instantly. He was soon arrested and explained that he had to kill them to prevent them from moving his wife and daughter to Las Vegas and "exposing them to a life of prostitution and drugs." Moore was tried at the July 1993 term of the court and on July 20 he was sentenced to die by lethal injection. He fought the appeal and finally threatened to sue anyone who tried to stop his execution, and petitioned the Oregon state Supreme Court to drop the automatic appeal of his death sentence. All judicial relief was finally exhausted and Moore was sentenced to die on May 16, 1997, and nothing further would delay the proceedings.

As soon as the death warrant was delivered to the prison Oregon's protocol was implemented and no less than four days before the execution the prisoner was moved to a secure cell and placed under a constant death watch guard. Two days before the execution the staff received a refresher course in procedures and all the forms were checked for accuracy and completeness, to be sure a clerical error did not result in a delay. One day prior to the execution all the medical equipment and solutions were inspected and the proper medical staff was scheduled, and all prison personnel were given their assignments. One such duty was to check all the equipment, especially the telephones and camera monitoring system, and the telephones would be checked again every half hour beginning at 9 o'clock on the night before the execution. A radio system was also tested regularly as a back-up to the phone system.

As witnesses began to arrive on the night of the execution they were conducted to a staging area and kept under guard. The media representatives were taken to the Media Center and those few who would actually witness the execution were chosen, and they would afterward share their information with the others. A half hour before the execution the camera monitor system was activated, and then the condemned, in security restraints, was escorted into the execution chamber where he was strapped to a gurney. Medical personnel then attached to the condemned the skin electrodes for the electrocardiograph machine and inserted an intravenous cannulas (IVs) in each arm, the second being a back-up in case the primary IV failed. The executioner was conducted into the control, or execution, room so he would remain anonymous and then the witnesses and selected media were escorted into the witnessing room and the curtains covering the windows were drawn open. At 12:15 A.M. the superintendent signaled for the flow of drugs to commence, beginning with sodium pentothal to induce sleep, then pancuronium bromide to stop respiration, and finally potassium chloride to stop the prisoner's heart. The executioner signaled to the superintendent when the drugs had been administered and as Moore lay dying he whispered, "I want the last word I say to be Jennifer, J-e-n-n-i-f-e-r," his daughter's name. A medical professional certified at 12:23 A.M. that Moore was dead and then the camera monitoring system was turned off and the media witnesses were conducted back to the Media Center. After the witnessing room was cleared the body was removed to a funeral home, as previously arranged.

Sitka Sentinel (AK): May 16, 1997. *New York Times* (NY): May 17, 1997.

SOUTH DAKOTA

The region that would become South Dakota was acquired from France in 1803 as part of the Louisiana purchase, excepting a small portion in the northwest corner acquired from Great Britain in 1818. The territory had been explored in 1742 and the land was claimed by France, but in 1762 it was ceded to Spain, then returned to France in 1800. The first permanent European settlement was established at Yankton in 1859 and this became the capital of the Dakota Territory established in 1862. On November 2, 1889, the Dakota Territory was divided into the states of North and South Dakota and South Dakota became the 40th state.

Lehman, John B.
February 19, 1892

John B. Lehman owned land near Custer in South Dakota that adjoined the Fuhrmann property. Fuhrmann owned cattle which occasionally trespassed onto Lehman's land and the two men quarreled, and Lehman assaulted his neighbor. Fuhrmann swore out a warrant in Fairburn so Lehman was arrested and held in the Custer County jail to await the next grand jury. Soon after he was jailed he gave a bond for his appearance and was released. When it was discovered that Lehman's bond was worthless another warrant was issued and given to Constable John Burns for service. Burns and John Siebert left Fairburn for Lehman's home on the afternoon of July 11, 1889, and as they neared Lehman's ranch house Lehman saw them and suspected their purpose. He armed himself and went out to meet the lawmen and after parleying for a brief time Lehman drew his six-shooter, aimed it at Siebert and pulled the trigger, but the gun clicked as the round misfired. Siebert jumped down from the wagon and ran a short distance, then turned just in time to see Burns getting down from the wagon and Lehman shooting him. The constable fell to the ground but Siebert continued into town to raise the alarm, and a party returned to the Lehman property where they found Burns shot through the body. The wounded man was taken to Fairburn where he lingered for five hours before he died at 11:30 P.M.

A posse was formed but the members waited until Burns was dead before starting for Lehman's to arrest the murderer. Lehman stood off the posse, so they returned to town the next morning and sent word to Sheriff Wood at Custer. The sheriff went to Fairburn and organized another posse, but again they failed to arrest Lehman when the fugitive made his escape into the hills. Lehman fled southwesterly until hunger forced him to stop at the cabin of C. C. Chambers on Cascade Creek in Fall River County. That evening he arrived at the residence of a man named Lindsey on the Cheyenne River and he remained there three weeks.

It was during that time that Governor Arthur C. Mellette issued a reward of $500 for Lehman's arrest, and it had the desired effect of raising interest in the fugitive. Sheriff Gifford of Fall River County began a search for Lehman and the fugitive joined in the search for himself. When Gifford obtained one of the circulars which had been broadcast over the country, and included a description of Lehman, the fugitive believed he was about to be discovered so he fled from the territory. Lehman worked his way into Nebraska and found work haymaking for a rancher near Rushville. His employer, while in town on business, read one of the circulars and recognized his newest employee as the fugitive. He told Sheriff Rosencrans of Sheridan County and the lawman formed a posse. On September 9, 1889, they arrested Lehman without incident and notified the authorities in Custer County. Lehman was returned to South Dakota and indicted in November 1889. That same month he was tried before Judge Nowlin and convicted, but a motion for a new trial was filed and granted. The second trial was held before Judge Nowlin in September 1890 and the defendant was again convicted of first degree murder. He was sentenced to hang and the case was appealed to the Supreme Court. After considerable delay they finally affirmed the lower court's decision and the sentence of death was passed by Judge Thomas. In the meantime, however, Governor Arthur C. Mellette granted a sixty day reprieve so the case could be presented to the Board of Pardons on the grounds that the prisoner was insane. In January 1892 a sheriff's jury was summoned for a hearing before Judge Gardner, to pass upon the matter of the prisoner's sanity, and they found him sane. Judge Gardner, for the fourth and final time, sentenced Lehman to hang, this time on February 19, 1892.

The prisoner arose at an early hour his final morning, dressed in a neat blue suit, and spent the day with his religious advisor. A large crowd began to assemble outside the fenced enclosure and blocked the way from the jail door to the scaffold. The sheriff had instructed the witnesses to be inside the enclosure by 2:00 P.M., and they made their way through the crowd well in advance of the fatal hour. At 1:55 P.M. Sheriff Wood read the death warrant to the prisoner in his cell and at 2:30 the prisoner was handcuffed and the procession formed. They left the jail at 2:40 P.M. and, after a path was forcibly cleared through the crowd, reached the gallows five minutes later. The scaffold had been erected twenty feet from the courthouse and was surrounded by a high board fence and, though it was rough in appearance, it was quite sturdy in construction.

The prisoner was seated on a chair next to the trapdoor and his wrists and arms, knees and ankles were pinioned with straps. Sheriff Wood told Lehman to stand but he could not do so without help, and needed to be supported as he moved onto the trapdoor. The noose was positioned but before the sheriff pulled on the black hood he asked if the prisoner had anything to say. Lehman spoke loudly, "I wish to tell the audience and the inspectors here that Sheriff Wood and his brother are very cruel men," and turning to the sheriff said, "You are murdering me for wages." The black hood was pulled on at 2:55 P.M. and Sheriff Wood immediately threw the lever, and the body dropped breaking Lehman's neck. After the body hung ten minutes Dr. Taylor pronounced Lehman dead and the body was cut down and placed on a table. The gates to the enclosure were opened and the crowd was allowed to file through and view Lehman's remains. His body was then removed and a post-mortem examination made. Lehman was buried at Custer the following day.

Rapid City Journal (SD): February 20, 1892.

Thompson, Nathaniel K.
October 20, 1893

Nathaniel K. Thompson's wife had gotten a divorce and moved to the home of Electra J. Bliton, a friend in Arlington, South Dakota. Thompson went to the Bliton home to talk with his ex-wife, and Bliton remained nearby during the conversation. Thompson suddenly drew a knife and tried to stab his former wife but Bliton threw her arms around the attacker in an attempt to restrain him and received the knife thrust. She soon died of the wound and Thompson was arrested and charged with her murder. The murder outraged the citizens of Kingsbury County, where DeSmet was the county seat, but Arlington was a major town and there was strong talk of lynching. Wise counsel prevailed, however, and the law was allowed to take its course. Thompson was indicted, tried and convicted of first degree murder and sentenced to hang on October 20, 1893.

Thompson caused no disturbance during his confinement and had fully resigned himself to his fate when his final day arrived. The witnesses, physicians and ministers were summoned to the jail at 1:00 P.M. and when they arrived the sheriff and deputies went to Thompson's cell and read the death warrant. The cell door was unlocked and handcuffs were presented, which the prisoner took and put on his own wrists, saying, "I want you to be quick about this." He was taken out and placed in a closed carriage under guard and driven the short distance to the scaffold, with one hundred men following the carriage to the site of the execution. Once at the gallows the witnesses were admitted while the sheriff, guards and two ministers accompanied the prisoner onto the platform.

Thompson's legs were strapped while the ministers said good-bye and shook his hand. Next his arms were bound at his sides and he was asked if he had anything to say to the small crowd. The prisoner replied, "No, I have nothing to say, nor anything against anybody. Be as quick as you can." While the noose was being adjusted a short prayer was offered, at the prisoner's request, and the black hood was pulled over his head. At 1:25 P.M. the minister said "Amen!" and the trap was immediately sprung by the sheriff. The condemned man never moved a muscle after the drop, indicating that his neck had been broken in the fall. He hung twenty minutes before the attending physician pronounced him dead and then the body was cut down, placed in a plain wooden coffin and sent to Hetland for burial.

Yankton Press and Dakotan (SD): October 21, 1893.

Hicks, Jay
November 15, 1894

In November 1893, Jay Hicks and his brother Bob were at William C. Walker's place playing cards all night. In the morning they discussed hard times and the possibility of robbing someone when Jay Hicks spoke about "going to make a raise." Walker said, "Yes, if we knew where to go and make the raise?" and

Jay answered, "I know where there is a good place to make a raise; that is over to old man Meyers." Jay had mentioned Meyers to his brother previously but nothing more had been said until that morning. Jay described how much money he thought old man Meyers had with him and Walker agreed it would be the place to go, and asked Jay if he would go along, and Jay agreed. Jay then invited his brother and Bob agreed to go as well. On the way home they stopped above Walker's house to discuss how they could get a gun and Walker said he thought they could borrow one from a cowboy named Bragam. Instead Walker sent his brother-in-law to Morgan's on Bad River with $5 but he returned without a gun. A short time later they were playing cards at Holcomb's when the three men agreed to "put up" for a gun. Walker and Jay contributed $7 each and Bob gave $1. Jay had previously gone to Cottle's Store and selected a .44-caliber revolver with black rubber grips, so Walker and Bob Hicks went into town and bought that revolver and two boxes of cartridges, and when they returned they gave the pistol to Jay.

The morning after they purchased the six-shooter, December 14, 1893, they met at Walker's place and decided to go immediately, taking along a six foot length of rope to tie the old man. The twenty-five mile trip took all day and when they got to the cabin they were not sure it was Meyers' place, so they went in to check. Meyers was busy feeding his cattle so the boys asked if he had a fire in the house as it was very cold. Meyers said he did not so the boys asked for food, and Meyers said they should go on to Elk Creek where there was a woman who could fix them a meal. Meyers was dressed so poorly that Bob Hicks said, "I don't believe the old man has any money; we had better leave him alone," but Jay told him, "Yes he has. You can't tell by the looks of him." Jay asked again for, "any little thing to take away the hunger," so Meyers told them to wait until he fed his cattle and then he would fix something for the four of them. Soon they went into the house where Meyers built a fire and cooked a meal. The boys ate first and when they were done Meyers sat at the table to eat. The boys moved about the cabin and went outside several times, but finally they were all settled in the cabin — Bob by the stove, Jay in the corner on a stool, Walker on the bed, and Meyers still at the table eating.

The old man finally finished and started to clean his plate with a butcher knife when Jay tried to pull his revolver from his waistband, but the gun was stuck between his drawers and his pants. Finally he got it out and pointed it at Meyers saying, "Ha! Old Man!" Meyers had his back to Jay and didn't hear him so he called to him twice more without any response. Finally Jay whistled at Meyers and the old man turned and saw the gun for the first time. He dropped the plate but held onto the knife and Jay yelled, "hands up!" Jay did not hesitate a moment and fired once, and the old man fell on the floor causing the lamp to go out. The boys rushed through the darkness for the door and when they got there Jay accidentally put the gun against Walker and fired a second round, but the ball only passed through his clothes, setting them afire and burning his skin. Outside they put out the flames and then Jay said, "Come on back. We have to finish the job," so they went in and Jay lit the lamp. Meyers was seated on the floor leaning against the bed and Jay kept his gun on the old man as Meyers asked, "Oh! My God! What does this mean?" and Walker said, "You old son of a bitch, why didn't you throw up your hands; you came pretty near getting me shot."

Jay interrupted and asked where his money was and the old man said it was in his pocket. Bob then took out a leather purse from one pocket and a tobacco bag and some change from the other. There was $1 in the tobacco bag and $35 in the pocketbook. The boys did everything they could to find out where the rest of his money was but he insisted he had no more money, having just loaned $300 to Jim Baird. Jay threatened, "If you don't tell me where the money is I'll blow your brains out." Will took out his pocket knife and threatened to cut Meyers' throat and when that didn't work he poured coal oil around the bed and floor, stacked wood, and threatened to burn the cabin with Meyers inside. Still the old man insisted he had no more money while Jay pleaded with him to give up the money. There were numerous other threats but nothing worked on the old man. Finally Jay started to count to three and Bob said, "Don't kill him," and Meyers pleaded, "No! Don't kill me!" Walker took out a match and lit the cabin on fire, then told Jay "give it to him." Jay shot Meyers and followed Bob out of the cabin, Walker coming out last. Walker said, "That's good," as they got their horses and started for home. It was dark and they got lost so they camped on Elk Creek and started again at daybreak. The three riders were seen by several people but were too distant to be recognized, though one woman accurately described their horses later. The three murderers rode to Martha Hicks' place on the Belle Fourche where Bob Hicks lived with his mother. They told her they had been playing cards at Holcomb's all night and hunted wolves on the way home.

On Saturday the body of Meyers was discovered and James K. Baird rode into Rapid City that night to report the crime to the sheriff. The next morning Sheriff V. M. Beaver, Coroner William G. Smith assisted by Dr. Ira L. Sanderson and the state's attorney, with a coroner's jury, went to the scene and held an inquest. The time of the murder was set as Thursday night because on Monday he had received a bottle of medicine with instruction to take a dose three times a day and sixteen doses had been taken, and Meyers had been seen on Tuesday but not after. The investigators found two meal settings on the table and one in the dishpan, suggesting that at least two men had done the work. There were two wounds on the body, one bullet entering one inch above the right nipple and ranging down to exit by the left hip bone and coming to rest between the skin and clothing; the second bullet entered the right part of Meyers' forehead, passed through the brain and came to rest at the back of his skull. The second wound had been fired at such close range that there were powder burns on the face of the dead man. The first wound would have been fatal in a short time but the second wound caused instantaneous death.

The fire had not destroyed the cabin, which was a dugout. The investigators found firewood burned on the dirt floor but the upper part of the cabin, made of logs, had not caught fire. There was no money found though he had several hundred dollars on Monday, but on the floor was found a promissory note for $300 made out to J. K. Baird, and a draft for $1,000 from the sale of cattle was waiting for Meyers at the post office. Meyers was buried at Sturgis on Wednesday and Baird was appointed administrator, so he began efforts to locate Meyers' nephew at Yankton. By December 27 the boys heard that they were suspected but they went about their business as if nothing had happened. At the inquest Robert A. Walker, William's brother, testified that the three men had been at his home playing cards on the night of the murder. On January 14, 1894, Sheriff Beaver went to John Dunn's place and arrested Jay Hicks and soon Bob Hicks and Walker joined him in jail. At their preliminary examination on February 2, R. A. Walker gave the same testimony and Maggie Walker, William's wife, corroborated the testimony of R. A. Walker, but both recanted their testimony at the trial in late May and admitted they had committed perjury. Maggie said at the trial that when she asked Jay about the murder he said, "The damned old son of a bitch, if I had him here under my thumb I could eat him without salt."

Between the time of the preliminary examination and the trial the Hicks boys escaped from jail. On April 24 deputy sheriff Henry W. Conklin sent jailor Rupe home, and when he went to lock up Jay Hicks the prisoner hit him with a club. They struggled for some time when Jay called to Bob Hicks to come help. Bob hit Conklin on the head so the deputy pulled his revolver and shot at Jay, but missed. Bob grabbed the hammer so that the pistol could not fire again and the two prisoners continued to beat the deputy on the head until it appeared they might kill him, so Conklin put his head under a bunk, groaned, and feigned death. After the prisoners left their cell Conklin ran into another room and locked the door. He was later treated at the Sheridan House for painful, but not serious, wounds. The Hicks boys broke down the door to the kitchen and, with Conklin's pistol in hand, escaped. Walker was not with the Hicks boys because he had turned state's evidence, confessed, and was being held in Custer in solitary confinement.

A $500 reward was offered and many men watched for the two fugitives, and they were finally captured almost by accident. On May 4 a party of ten men were riding together on Dry Creek at about 4:00 P.M. with only three guns among them. They were returning from the round-up at Belle Fourche but knew of the escape and ongoing search for the escaped prisoners. The fugitives were hiding in an old house on the bank of the creek and when they saw the large party they thought they were after them, so they ran from the house and jumped over the creek bank. Elmo Bitney said, "Boys, I believe there are the Hicks!" The cowboys went after the two fugitives, covered them with the few weapons they had, and made the arrest without resistance. The trial began in late May and all three defendants were found guilty of first degree murder, and on May 25 Bob Hicks was sentenced to life imprisonment, William Walker was sentenced to ten years in prison, and Jay Hicks was sentenced to hang. A petition was filed with Governor C. H. Sheldon on behalf of Jay Hicks asking for a reprieve, but this was denied and work began on the gallows.

Joel Seward and George Gilbert were erecting the structure in the jail yard in mid–July when word came from the state Supreme Court granting a stay to August 15, when the case would be heard, and on September 12, 1894, the justices affirmed the judgment of the lower court. On October 9, Judge Plowman sentenced Jay Hicks to hang at Sturgis on November 15, 1894. The prisoner threw a tantrum, refused to put on his coat, verbally abused the judge and generally ranted and raved, causing quite a disturbance. From that moment he was placed under a close watch to prevent escape or suicide. By then the scaffold had stood for several months but it was still ready for use. On his final morning Hicks arose early and dressed in a new black suit, but he refused to shave a month's growth of beard. The Reverend J. B. Carns had spent time with the prisoner over his final days and on Hicks' last morning the Reverend arrived early and encouraged the prisoner to confess, but to no avail. The time for the hanging had been set for 10:15 A.M. but the reverend asked for, and was granted, an additional hour. He used the time to pray for the condemned man but Hicks said,

> I don't pray; never pray and don't want to. You ask me if I am guilty, but I won't say. People have me sized up for a worse man than I am. I regret that I broke out of jail, and am sorry for the break on Conklin. The jailors have been very good to me, and my lawyers did the best they could. If I don't confess my wrongs, then what? See mother if you can, and tell her good-bye for me. If I had my life to live over again I would make some changes. My soul must look after itself. You can't help me. I may say something on the scaffold, but don't know.

The reverend, optimistically, insisted that the condemned man refused to confess to spare his mother.

At 11:00 A.M. the coroner's jury of twelve men were polled and admitted to the anteroom, and twenty-seven minutes later they filed into the cell to identify the condemned man, and then were escorted to the scaffold. At 11:40 Sheriff Beaver read the death warrant to Hicks in his cell and the procession formed. At 11:57 A.M. the prisoner mounted the stairs accompanied by the Reverend Carns, Sheriff Beaver, deputy Conklin, jailor Carney and Sheriff Remer of Lawrence County. Sheriff Remer bound the prisoner's wrists and arms, legs and ankles, and then Sheriff Beaver asked if he had anything to say to the witnesses. Hicks replied, "I guess not," then called for Conklin and apologized for his escape. The noose was adjusted, the black hood pulled on, and at 12:01 P.M. the trap was sprung. The condemned man dropped six feet but his neck was not broken and he strangled to death. Drs. Smith, Sanderson and Sadler recorded Hicks' pulse and pronounced him dead at 12:20 P.M. The body was allowed to hang another eleven minutes before being cut down and deposited in its coffin. Jay Hicks was buried the following day in the Sturgis cemetery.

Sturgis Weekly Record (MT): December 15, 1893; February 2, 1894; April 27, 1894; May 4, 1894; May 25, 1894; September 21, 1894; November 16, 1894.

Cha-nopa-uhah
December 28, 1894

The Indians at the Pine Ridge Reservation were well fed and properly clothed, according to Indian Agent Brown, but among them were two hundred Brule bucks who were inclined to make trouble. This band was supposed to have arms and plenty of ammunition and had been engaged in ghost dancing, which was intended to drive the whites from Indian lands. Among the two hundred were Cha-nopa-uhah, whose English name was Chief-two-sticks, his two sons Work and First-eagle, and also White-faced-horse, Two-two, Fights-with and Mars. On Wednesday February 1, 1893, four of these Indians were arrested for stealing cattle from the Stringer and Humphreys Cattle Ranch near the mouth of Battle Creek in the badlands. They believed that four cowboys at a remote camp had identified them, but there was not enough evidence to hold the rustlers, so on Friday, February 3, they were released. The four cattle thieves returned to their camp and danced in the sweat house until the Great Spirit told them to go and kill white men "because the whites killed the buffalo and took our possessions." They told another Indian named Crow that their hearts were bad toward the four cowboys and that they would kill them first.

That evening Cha-nopa-uhah, Work, First-eagle, and White-faced-horse went to the camp of the cowboys, which was located twenty miles from Wounded Knee on White Clay Creek. The camp consisted of corrals, stables, and a dugout and the Indians waited until the four cowboys bedded down for the night in the dugout, and then crept up on each side. They riddled the sleeping men with bullets. George Hadaway, Joe Bennett, Rodney Royce and Edward Cochran died instantly, but the Indians continued their rampage and mutilated the bodies by slashing them with knives and beating them with clubs, breaking several arm bones.

The bodies were discovered on Saturday afternoon and word was sent to the agency. Captain Brown ordered out his Indian Police, under command of Sergeant Joe Bath, to bring in the bodies and the murderers. The Indian Police went to the dugout but friends of the murdered cowboys refused to give up the bodies, as they were going to send them to Hermosa for burial. Sergeant Bath acquiesced but also learned that the murderers had gone to the camp of Chief No-waters, so he proceeded to that place and ordered Cha-nopa-uhah and the other murderers to surrender. The fugitives refused and a pitched battle ensued during which three of the four murderers and another Indian named Mars and one policeman were killed. Chief Cha-nopa-uhah received a serious wound through his right lung and was captured, but he was expected to die. Two-two and Fights-with were thought to have had something to do with the murders but they fled, and it was decided the law was satisfied so they were not pursued.

The band of No-waters witnessed the fight and the chief called upon his people to avenge the deaths of the three Indians, and would have killed all the policemen if Young-man-afraid-of-his-horses had not arrived with his band of Indians and intervened. He made a speech to all present and said that the dead were bad Indians and that the police had acted correctly in killing them. Still, word of the battle spread through the Indian camps and it was feared there might be a general uprising.

At Fort Meade, Troop L, a company of full-blooded Sioux soldiers, was outfitted and sent to the Pine Ridge agency, where they were expected to arrive in three days. Meanwhile other troops at Fort Meade were made ready to march as soon as notified of trouble, while four troops from Fort Robinson and two from Niobrara were ordered out to quell any disturbances which might occur. However, it was the freezing temperatures and harsh weather that kept the Indians restrained and it was believed that trouble, if it was to come, would wait until spring. Agent Brown held a consultation with sixty chiefs to assure them that, as far as the agency and military were concerned, the matter was closed. The bodies of the dead murderers, the dead policeman, and the wounded chief were brought to the agency where the bodies were buried the next day and the chief received medical attention. Chief Cha-nopa-uhah surprised everyone, recovered and was tried in the Circuit Court in the spring, convicted of first degree murder, and sentenced to hang. W. L. McGlaughlin, his defense attorney, made every effort to save the life of his client and his final appeal was to President Grover Cleveland.

Shortly after breakfast on the Indian's final day McGlaughlin visited his client to report that the president had refused to interfere. Cha-nopa-uhah was given religious comfort and counsel by Father Digmann during his final weeks and they talked freely and entered into prayer and religious exercises with the greatest fervor. The chief, it was believed, was of a race which did not fear death and it was expected he would go to the gallows without a tremor. That morning he had been moved from inside the steel cages to the top of the cages, where he had an unobstructed view of the gallows' enclosure, and either John Skelly or W. S. Harding, his death watch guards, were with him constantly in his new quarters. As he stood at the window watching contractor J. M. Taplin erect the gallows, he showed no emotion. The scaffold was erected in the jail yard east of the jail and enclosed within a forty by sixty foot area between the jail and the stable, and it was enclosed with a board fence sixteen feet high.

Friday, December 28 was a bright, warm day so people began to gather at the jail before 8:00 A.M., but Cha-nopa-uhah remained unconcerned. He had slept well during the night, though he arose several times to pace his cell and sing his death song. In the morning he ate a hearty breakfast and then met with Father Digmann. At 9:30 A.M., U.S. Marshal Peemiller and deputies Beiglemeir and Bray, accompanied by interpreter Frank Young, entered the corridor. Two sheriffs and members of the press followed as the chief was seated in a chair, but he immediately arose to shake everyone's hand. When he took his seat again, with Father Digmann at his shoulder, the death warrant was read and slowly interpreted. He was asked if he had any reason to give why the sentence should not be carried out and he replied,

> My heart is not bad; I did not kill the cowboys, the Indian boys killed them. I have killed many Indians but never killed a white man; I never pulled a gun on a white man. The great father and the men under him should talk to me and I would show them I was innocent. The white men are going to kill me for something I haven't done. I am a great chief myself. I have always been a friend of the white man. The white men will find out some day that I am innocent and then they will be sorry they killed me. The great father will be sorry, too, and he will be ashamed. My people will be ashamed, too. My heart is straight and I like everybody. God made all hearts the same. My heart is the same as a white man's. If I had not been innocent I would not have come up here so good when they wanted me. They know I am innocent or they would not let me go around here. My heart knows I am not guilty and I am happy. I am not afraid to die. I was taught that if I raised my hands to God and told a lie that God would kill me that day. I never told a lie in my life.

When the chief finished his statement, and it was translated, he raised his hands and sang his death song, which was "not very musical, but fervent and impressive." The meaning of the song, according to Young, was that the chief's heart was good toward God and everybody, and that God must take him when he died. He was allowed to continue for several minutes and became so enthusiastic that the priest had to calm him. The chief began shaking hands and thanking certain people for their kindnesses, and then was told to prepare for his march to the gallows. He removed the old red handkerchief from his neck and put on his coat.

Deputy Beiglemeir tried to bind his wrists behind him but found this impossible because the shoulder, wounded when he was captured, had stiffened. The deputy left the straps on a chair and went to look for a long piece of rope but as soon as Marshal Peemiller was distracted by a visitor the chief grabbed and buckled a strap, put it around his neck, and gave it several hard jerks to cinch it tight. This failing he passed the loose end through the bars to Eagle-louse, telling him to pull it tight. But his attempt at suicide was quickly discovered, he was restrained, and the strap removed. Father Digmann told the condemned man that he had done wrong and God would not like him for that. The priest told him to have a good heart and be resigned to his fate, and Cha-nopa-uhah replied that he would prefer to be hanged by his people but not by the whites. He said his heart got bad for a minute and he was sorry. Thereafter he was composed and displayed a happy mood. Deputy Beiglemeir then tied the chief's wrists behind him and the death march began. Marshal Peemiller led, with the condemned man directly behind escorted by a deputy on each arm. Father Digmann followed directly behind the prisoner and the others followed him. When they entered the enclosure, and the chief saw the gallows up close, he said, "Washta [good], you bet!" The prisoner walked up the stairs at a quick pace and stood on the trapdoor. While the straps were being applied to the prisoner's knees and ankles Father Digmann read a prayer. The chief bowed his head and when the priest announced "Amen," the prisoner nodded his approval. He sang his death song again as the noose was being placed around his neck and cinched in place.

When the song concluded the black hood was pulled over his head and at 10:38 A.M. the trap was sprung. The condemned man dropped seven feet, four inches breaking his neck, and the weight of the Indian and sudden jerk stretched the rope from three-quarters inch to one half inch diameter. After several minutes there were three muscular contractions which drew up the Indian's legs and shoulders. Drs. Wedelstaadt, Rogers, Freeman, and Howe monitored the dying man's pulse and reported it had ceased in five minutes, but did not pronounce him dead until 10:53 A.M. The rope was loosened from above and the body was lowered into a coffin. Twelve jurors retired to the sheriff's office and signed the certificate of execution. The body of Chief Cha-nopa-uhah was taken to the undertaking establishment of H. R. Smith where curious citizens were allowed to file through and view the remains. At 2:30 P.M. the body was taken to the Catholic cemetery where it was buried, following services by Fathers Digmann and Traynor.

Black Hills Daily Times (Deadwood, SD): February 6–8, 1894; December 27–29, 1894.

Brown, Charles
July 14, 1897

Charles Brown had been born into slavery on March 1, 1843, at Colonel Halliday's farm located between Paris and Macon City, Missouri. His mother died when he was nine years old and his ownership passed to another slave owner at Shelbino, where he was under the constant supervision of a strict overseer. When he was twenty years old, and the Civil War was raging, he was taken to St. Louis and transferred to a man named Cavanaugh, who took him to St. Joseph, and in April 1863 they started for California, Brown already having been freed to some extent. Once on the Pacific Coast he was freed entirely and he left for Oregon by stagecoach. At Portland he purchased passage on a ship to New York City, then traveled to Chicago, New Orleans, and then to Gonzales, Texas. He traveled around the southwestern states and worked on seven cattle drives, the last in 1869 when he was on a crew that brought three thousand six hundred head of cattle to Fort Randall near the Yankton Agency. He spent the winter at Fort Randall and then went to Nebraska, where he was married in 1872. He and his wife moved about Wyoming for some years before moving to Denver and then in August 1879 he moved to the Black Hills.

Brown had lost his wife sometime after 1879 and by 1897 he had been living with a woman for several years, whom he said he always intended to marry. In the mid–1890s Brown worked as a cook for Colonel L. P. Stone, living in a room in the quarters above the restaurant in Deadwood, South Dakota. On the evening of May 15, 1897, Brown and a boy named Ralph Walker went to Deadwood by wagon and, in the evening, Brown went to the restaurant to ask if he could use the room he had occupied when he worked there, and Emma Francis Stone granted permission. Brown and the boy went to the room and the older man told the boy to retire. The boy went to sleep but Brown soon woke him and told him to go out. The boy arose and began to dress but Brown gathered up his clothes, pushed him out, and told him to dress outside. In a few minutes Brown appeared with his shoes wet, as if just washed. The boy said they should leave and started toward Lee Street, but Brown stopped him and told the boy if they went that way they would be hanged. When the boy asked what he meant Brown said that Stone had been murdered, and then explained that he had been listening while the crime was committed.

The next morning at 6:00 A.M. Maggie Hudson, a domestic, entered Stone's room and discovered her body in bed. The bed clothes had been thrown over her face but she was clearly dead. A male boarder who took his meals at the restaurant was called. He examined the body and saw that her head had been split in two, as if by a broad axe, and the room had been thoroughly ransacked. Suspicion immediately attached to Brown, as it was known he had been at the house during the night, was familiar with the home, and had left at an early hour. It was learned that he had started for Whitewood in a lumber wagon. Brown was overtaken at the Walker Ranch and he and Ralph Walker were arrested. While the prisoners were being brought back to Deadwood on the passenger train, a search was being made for the murder weapon. The Red Creek channel was changed so it would drain and a heavy meat cleaver and butcher knife were found in the mud. At the moment the weapons were found the train from Elkhorn arrived at the depot, but the sheriff had taken his prisoner off before reaching town and tried to bring him in by a circuitous route to avoid a lynching. However the sheriff's party was seen and a large crowd started for them with cries of "Hang him!" The officers, with prisoners cuffed and pinioned, drew their revolvers and held off the crowd until the mob decided to let the law take its course.

On May 20 a special grand jury was summoned to convene in two days. Brown, Walker, and two other witnesses were called and after the jury was out one hour they returned an indictment against Brown. The defendant was then arraigned by Judge Plowman and given until Monday, May 24, to plead. J. P. Laffey was appointed to represent Brown and it had been rumored that he would plead guilty, but when the court convened he was called to his feet and announced that he was "not guilty!" and the trial was set for Thursday, June 10. On the designated day Brown entered through the south door, went to the table, and made a show of kneeling for prayer. It had been anticipated that the empanelling of the jury would be a long battle but there were only two men removed and the jury was seated in a half hour, and the trial began. Two witnesses, John Roberts and Julius Simmons, testified that Brown had told them on Friday evening that Stone had a considerable amount of money hidden between her mattresses. Brown had suggested that they steal the money while he stood guard on the ground floor. Roberts said they wanted no part of the affair but afterwards Brown sold him a watch, a stolen item, for $1.75.

A few days before the trial Brown had summoned deputy sheriff Thomas J. Sparks and, with Sheriff Plunkett and jailor Bertrand present, made a full confession exonerating all others under suspicion. Brown said that he was trying to pry open a trunk with the meat cleaver when a little dog, which was sleeping with Stone, growled at him and he struck it several times with the cleaver. He said the blow to Stone was accidental and had been aimed at the dog. Deputy sheriff Sparks testified that Brown had confessed and told him where he had buried some stolen jewelry at Crook City. He searched but could not find it so he had Brown draw a map and then, searching as indicated on the drawing, found the jewelry buried in an old barn. When the prosecution rested the defense attorney arose. He had only cross-examined four witnesses and made but one objection. Mr. Harvey then said,

> Your honor and gentlemen of the jury, the defense in this case has no evidence to offer. Soon after being appointed by this court to defend the accused the true nature of this case came to us so forcibly that we have no theories of a defense, but allow the case to be submitted upon the evidence adduced by the prosecution. The defendant rests, admitting the statement of Mr. Sparks and corroborated by Sheriff Plunkett and Mr. Bertrand, which are the facts. That we admit, and we are now ready to submit this case to the jury, and say to your honor and the jury that on your verdict and the judgment that your honor may pronounce, if any, upon that verdict we rely. We bend to no other law, we will submit to no other law than upon that of the verdict of this jury and the judgment of this court.

He then thanked the judge, jury and officers and sat down. The jury spent little time in returning a verdict of guilty of first degree murder. When Brown returned to court several days later Judge Plowman sentenced him to hang on July 14, 1897. As promised, neither appeals nor petitions delayed the execution of Charles Brown.

The prisoner spent the early part of his last night smoking cigars and conversing with his death watch guard, Richard Hickey. He retired at midnight and slept until 6:00 A.M. He was eating his last breakfast at 8:00 when a reporter from the *Pioneer-Times* called and was admitted. In his last statement to the newspaper reporter he admitted the killing of Stone and expressed confidence that he had been forgiven his sins. He thanked all the Christians and forgave everyone and hoped they would forgive him. At 9:00 Sheriff Plunkett, accompanied by deputy Harris and Brown's attorney, entered the cell for the reading of the death warrant. The prisoner said he was glad of it and was ready to die. When the sheriff concluded, Brown asked at what hour he would be required, and was told he could have any reasonable amount of time to prepare. Brown replied he was ready at any time, but after a few minutes he requested to be allowed to pace the corridor and his cell. He smoked his pipe until Father Burke, his religious advisor over the past several weeks, arrived at 9:45 A.M.

When the final moment was near, the sheriff, deputy, attorney and newsmen gathered in the corridor and knocked on the cell door for admission, but Brown and the priest were engaged in prayer and there was a delay of five minutes. The procession was formed then, with the prisoner leaning on the arm of the sheriff and priest, a crucifix clutched tightly in his left hand. As they proceeded he bid farewell to the prisoners on the second floor jail, then descended into the jail yard where the gallows had been erected. He ignored the large crowd, keeping his eyes fixed on his crucifix while he mumbled prayers. He climbed the stairs at 10:22 A.M. and, upon reaching the platform, removed his hat and bowed. He stepped aside and laid his hat down, then took his place on the trapdoor facing north, with the door opening on the east and the lever release on the west. Father Burke offered a lengthy prayer as Brown stood motionless with his right hand raised. When the priest said "Amen," Sheriff Plunkett asked the prisoner if he had anything to say. Brown half-turned to face the largest group of spectators, confessed his crime, expressed his belief in the hereafter, and thanked all who had shown him kindness. He concluded with "Good-bye to the world!" and then centered himself on the trapdoor.

The prisoner's arms and legs were quickly pinioned, the black hood was pulled over his head, and the noose was adjusted and cinched. Everyone on the scaffold stepped back and there was a delay of a few seconds as Sheriff Plunkett surveyed the situation to be sure everything was in order. During that brief delay the only sound heard were the muffled prayers of Brown from under the hood. At 10:29 Sheriff Plunkett sprang the trap and the condemned man dropped eight and one half feet. His neck was not broken by the substantial fall, but there were only a few convulsive movements. In twenty-three and one half minutes he was pronounced dead and the rope was cut. Brown's remains were placed in the coffin provided and given to county undertaker Robinson for burial.

Pioneer-Times Extra (Deadwood, SD): July 14–15, 1897.

Asaaupila
September 19, 1902

Asaaupila, whose name in English was Earnest-loves-war, resided at the Pine Ridge Agency. During the winter of 1900 he ran away with two Indian girls from the Pierre Indian School and "cohabitated with them as they traveled across the reservation, and the usual result followed." He was a camp follower of the round-ups and was suspected of being involved in a number of shady horse transactions on the ranges, consequently he was afraid of the Indian police and usually went armed with his .38-caliber six-shooter. In the spring of 1902 Asaaupila was interested in a girl who lived at Whitewood and she was interested in him, which led him to believe she would marry him. But George Ostrander was also interested in the girl and Asaaupila told him the girl would not have him, which led to three quarrels prior to June 10, 1902. During their fourth, and last, quarrel Ostrander threw Asaaupila to the ground and choked him, but Ostrander's cabin mate, George Puck, pulled Ostrander off and told them not to quarrel. Asaaupila challenged Ostrander to fight with guns or knives but not with fists. The Indian said he would kill Ostrander, or be killed, but he would not give up the girl and he insisted she was not interested in Ostrander.

Asaaupila did not have his pistol with him at that moment so the matter rested and Puck invited Asaaupila to spend the night in their cabin on Red Owl Creek. Asaaupila retired at the same time as his hosts but did not sleep. As soon as the two white men were sleeping soundly he arose, took out his .38-caliber revolver and Puck's .41-caliber revolver and, pointing his at Ostrander and Puck's at its owner, fired simultaneously. Ostrander was killed instantly, but Puck rose up so the Indian finished him with a blow from an axe. He claimed later that he felt terrible over killing Puck as he had nothing against him, but could not get Ostrander alone after trying several times. The Indian said he did not search the cabin or take anything but fled immediately.

On the evening of June 11 William Horlocker found the bodies of Puck and Ostrander on their beds covered with bed clothes and a tarpaulin. Horlocker and John Timmons rode into Sturgis, making the trip of eighty miles overnight, and reported the crime. A party went to the ranch and held an inquest, after which the bodies were sent to Sioux City. Meanwhile, word of the crime had spread and Asaaupila was arrested when he cashed a check at Whitewood which was dated April 23 and endorsed by Puck. The prisoner soon made two confessions, first saying that the two white men got into a fight and killed each other but, when it was shown that the circumstances did not support that version, the prisoner said that Puck and Ostrander had refused to advance him money on a horse transaction so he killed them. The defendant was brought to trial in July and convicted of first degree murder on August 1, and Judge Rice sentenced him to hang on September 19. Neither appeal nor petition for clemency delayed the execution.

While in custody at the Lawrence County

jail the prisoner caused no trouble except when he tried to get a gun to escape or to commit suicide, it was never clear which from the evidence. He wrote to John-eagle-dog, a jail trusty, asking him to get the pistol while the trusty was out of his cell tending the horses, but John-eagle-dog turned the letter over to the authorities. Asaaupila also wrote a letter to his brother in which he said, "I shot them and they will hang me up soon.... I got one squaw coming after me, for these two white men going to take my squaw out, and I don't like to let my squaw out and I kill these two white men, be sure. I was a man, but these two white men take my woman, that's the reason I killed them, these two white men."

The prisoner spent his last days playing solitaire. He generally answered questions with "yes" or "no" but once when the Reverend Wyllie spoke with him he said, "I still have another game to play," and, still hoping for a pardon or reprieve, stated he knew nothing of the murders. The doomed man was a member of the Episcopal Church so the reverend attended to his religious needs over his final days and administered the last sacrament several times. The prisoner became so resigned to his fate, thanks to the efforts of the reverend, that several days before his execution he asked his night death watch guard, H. E. Gibboney, to listen to his confession of the crime. He gave a factual account, denying he struck Puck with an axe but said he struck Ostrander, which was not in accord with the condition of the bodies and suggests he might have been quite agitated and confused after the killings. The following day he wrote out his confession and the only new information was that the girl in question, whom no one would name, had feared some trouble and warned Asaaupila not to take any action against Ostrander.

The scaffold had been erected at the northwest corner of the courthouse by W. E. Jones within an enclosure twenty by thirty feet. It was the same scaffold used to hang Jay Hicks. V. M. Beaver, who had officiated at that execution, gave Sheriff Smith the same rope to use for this prisoner. The rope was hung with a heavy sack of sand for forty-eight hours to be sure the fibers were stretched tight, and the trapdoor release was tested several times. Only those with invitations would be admitted so there was quite a demand for tickets, and the sheriff had to reject most requests, including one from two Indians intent on seeing that everything was done correctly. He limited the witnesses to seventy-five, including the twelve man sheriff's jury who would sign the death certificate. The condemned man spent his last evening entertaining a number of women and writing autographs before retiring at 11:10 P.M. He slept soundly and arose at 5:40 A.M., dressed for the occasion, and ate a hearty breakfast at 6:20, the largest meal he had eaten in two weeks. He told Sheriff Smith that he wouldn't need any help getting to the scaffold and was "ready to die like a brave man."

At 9:00 the sheriff read the death warrant at the cell door with the Reverend Wyllie at the prisoner's side and deputy Brown standing nearby. The prisoner had spent the morning with the reverend and at noon he ate a hearty dinner. Just before the prisoner left his cell he asked for a drink and was given a large dose of whiskey. He had been given a small but steady supply of liquor during his final week to help him brace up, which ensured that he would sleep well. At 1:37 P.M. the sheriff's jury was called to the cell of Asaaupila. They identified the prisoner as the candidate for execution and the procession was formed. The Reverend Wyllie led the way, with the prisoner next bracketed by guards, and then came the jury. On the platform awaited Sheriff Smith, Jesse Brown and Coroner Dr. McSloy, the attending physician. Asaaupila arrived on the scaffold at 1:50 P.M. and was asked if he had anything to say and he replied, almost in a whisper, that he was satisfied and hoped that "all you fellows will die as I do."

The straps were applied to his wrists and arms, knees and ankles and the noose was adjusted while the condemned man smiled at the small crowd. At 1:56 P.M. the black hood was pulled over his head and the trapdoor was immediately sprung by the sheriff. The knot in the rope, which had been so carefully attended, slipped and the prisoner's feet barely touched the ground. He was allowed to hang five minutes while a new rope was prepared, and then the unconscious body was brought up onto the platform and dropped again, and this time the prisoner's neck was broken. Dr. McSloy recorded the dying man's pulse and at 2:14 P.M. he pronounced him dead. The body was then cut down and given to the undertaker. After the body was prepared for burial it was delivered, at the request of the deceased, to a certain high hill in back of Pete Culbertson's house on Pine Creek, where the Belle Fourche emptied into the Cheyenne River southeast of Red Owl, and buried.

Sturgis Weekly Record (SD): September 12, 1902; September 19, 1902.

Kahacanda Mani
October 21, 1902

Kahacanda Mani, whose English name was Allen Walking Shield, was enamored of Mabel, the daughter of a widowed woman named Ghost-faced Bear. The two women lived in a two room frame house on the Rosebud Reservation. On May 8, 1902, Mani was working under the direction of government farmer Robinson cutting willows at a point four miles from the home of the Indian women. He had dinner with Red Elk, his brother-in-law, and afterward Red Elk left his teepee, and Mani left within minutes of his brother-in-law's departure. When Red Elk returned he suspected that Mani had taken some of his possessions, searched, and found that his gun of Zulu pattern and two cartridges were missing.

Mani rode his horse to the home of Ghost-faced Bear, loitering along the way so that he would not arrive until 10:00 P.M. He knocked at the door but the women ignored him, as they had retired, one to each room, and they did not expect anyone. In a while they heard a gunshot and became alarmed, but still would not venture outside to investigate. After another brief period a shot was fired through a window at Ghost-faced Bear. The bullet struck the woman a little back of and below the right ear at the base of her skull and completely passed through her head, tearing out her left eye as it exited and she died instantly. Mani broke down the front door, stepped over the body of Ghost-faced Bear and went to the room of Mabel. He had a white sheet wrapped around him with the rifle resting upon his arm as he demanded that the terrified girl run away with him, but she refused. He attacked her but she fought him off until daylight. Mabel, who had not been allowed to go into the other room, asked about her mother and was told that Ghost-faced Bear had gone to a nearby school. Mabel found the opportunity during the night to investigate and, upon seeing her mother's dead body, was told by Mani that he had killed her. At daybreak Mabel escaped from the house with Mani in close pursuit, and he swung his lariat around her body, mounted his horse, and told her she must go with him. Frightened into obedience, she trudged along on foot beside his horse but, after traveling three miles, she had gathered her senses sufficiently to watch for a chance to escape.

When they came near the home of Mrs. Turning Bear she slipped the loop and ran into the house. Mabel told Mrs. Turning Bear and Eagle Crow the story of her mother's death and her abduction and, after they had quieted and fed Mabel, Mrs. Bear and another Indian woman hitched a team of horses to a wagon and drove to the murder scene. Mani, as soon as the girl made good her escape, rode as fast as he could from that part of the reservation. Six Indian policemen and several whites were soon on his trail but he managed to elude capture for eight days, and during his flight his horse played out so he had to steal another. Finally at 5:00 P.M. on May 16 Kills-two and Little-day, two Indian policemen, captured the fugitive. Mani was exhausted when his pursuers took him by surprise so he had no opportunity to resist. They took their prisoner to the Rosebud Agency and lodged him in jail.

U.S. Marshal John R. Petrie took charge of the prisoner and transferred him to Chamberlain, and there the prisoner had his preliminary hearing before U.S. Commissioner Tidrick, who ordered him held over for trial at Deadwood in September. After his arrest Mani made several confessions, and in one he said only that he had trouble with the widow but later confessed that the trouble was Ghost-faced Bear would not allow Mabel to run away with him. Mani was tried, convicted of first degree murder, and Judge John E. Carland of the Circuit Court imposed the death penalty, so Mani was removed to the jail at Sioux Falls. While being brought from Deadwood to Sioux Falls the prisoner threatened suicide, saying he would never hang, and his brother had recently committed suicide while in the Deadwood jail, so his threat was taken seriously. A death watch of two special deputies was assigned to be with him every minute, but the prisoner surprised his guards by acting a model prisoner who spent his time at a small window staring at the sky. During his last days Mani prepared a will in which he bequeathed a substantial amount of property to relatives.

Between 7 and 8 o'clock on Mani's last night the Salvation Army visited and spent a half hour singing and praying with the prisoner. Once they left Mani spent several hours talking to George Bear, another Indian murderer. They retired at 11:15 P.M. and Mani did not awaken until 6:00 A.M. He arose, dressed, and with a smile told his death watch that he was ready. He ate a hearty breakfast and then the Reverend N. Boe of St. Olaf's Lutheran Norwegian Church visited the condemned man in place of the Reverend John Babcock, whose feeble condition prevented his participation. They prayed and then Mani smoked a cigar, and again announced he was ready and handed the butt of his cigar to George Bear. By 8:00 A.M. men, women, and children had gathered around the jail and many Indians were among them. At 9:00 A.M. people began to appear on the tops of nearby buildings and in windows overlooking the scene of the execution. Several hundred people without tickets of admission had crowded in around the jail yard and they had to be pushed back.

Shortly before 9 o'clock on October 21, 1902, the death warrant was read to the prisoner, his arms were pinioned and then the procession formed, and Mani said, "You think I die a brave man? I am a brave man." His finger was twitching but he said it was because of sickness, and then he said, "You may think I am a squaw. I am brave." He said he was going to sing his death song on the gallows, but was reminded that he had promised not to sing and was warned that "singing will hurt your neck," so he agreed not to sing. The procession moved quickly out of the jail and as he passed several Indians he said to them, "See, me good!" The prisoner climbed onto the platform, which was within an enclosure at the rear of the county courthouse, and he took his place on the trapdoor.

The deputies hurriedly pinioned his knees and ankles and positioned the noose. His knees trembled as the straps were being applied and the prisoner said, in his native tongue, "Hurry up, hurry up!" The black hood was pulled on and at 9:04 A.M. the trap was sprung. For a few minutes there was a heaving of Mani's chest and twitching of his legs, but in four minutes the body hung motionless. In eighteen minutes the attending physicians pronounced him dead and stated that the condemned man had broken his neck in the drop. At 9:35 A.M. the body was cut down, placed in a coffin and turned over to C. H. Bennett, the farmer at the Rosebud Agency. Bennett accompanied the body back to the reservation and saw that Kahacanda Mani was buried at the Lost Nation Camp, in accordance with his last request.

Argus-Leader (Sioux Falls, SD): October 21, 1902.

Bear, George
December 5, 1902

C. Edward Tayloe was born in Virginia in 1858 and came west when he was still a young man. He settled in South Dakota and in 1887 married Maud Robertson of Smolek. Six years later he entered the Indian service at the Cheyenne River Station. The couple was stationed at Ouray, Utah, for a time and then at Whirlwind Soldier, but in April 1902 the Tayloes moved to the Ponca sub-agency on the Rosebud Reservation. He was assigned there as the school teacher and additionally as a government farmer, but often organized religious services and preached to the Indians under his charge. One of the Indians under Tayloe was George Bear, who was considered as peaceful an Indian as there was on the Rosebud Reservation. George Bear, his Indian name is not recorded, married an Indian widow named Shaw whose husband had died some time previously. Shaw had a son named John who was twenty-seven years old and had been well educated at the Indian School in Genoa, Nebraska. John Shaw's deceased father had owned a valuable allotment of land situated on a creek and with a considerable stand of timber, and this was bequeathed to his son. Bear also owned an allotment of land but it was some distance from the creek and barren of timber, so it was considered ordinary hay land of much less value.

When Bear married Shaw he took up residence at her home and John Shaw soon afterward married an Indian girl and, so that they would not crowd his parents, John took up residence on Bear's allotment. So, in effect, they had traded allotments as far as the places they lived, with Bear getting the far better of the deal. Bear freely cut and sold the timber on Shaw's land but never offered him any part of the proceeds, and Shaw did not object, as his mother benefited from the income. During the fall Shaw and an uncle named Shorty Thighs, because of his unusually short legs, planted a crop of hay on Bear's land. They did all the work of planting and harvesting and sold one small load of hay for $2. Bear heard of it and demanded a share of the $2, but Shaw refused and the feeling between them became bitter. Shaw's mother sided with her son and because of this disagreement George Bear and his wife separated.

Bear next took the matter to Tayloe for adjudication, who in turn forwarded the matter to Charles E. McChesney, the United States Indian agent at the Rosebud Agency. While the matter of hay money was under consideration Bear purchased a quantity of goods in Bonesteel and agreed to pay for them with a load of wood from the Shaw property. However, during the previous summer a special agent of the Indian Bureau visited the Rosebud Reservation and noted that the supply of timber would soon be exhausted if the Indians were allowed to continue cutting wood at the current rate. An order was issued to discontinue granting permits to sell the reservation wood, permits which had to be obtained from Tayloe. When Bear applied for his permit he was denied and this caused bitterness toward Tayloe.

Bear had heard nothing on his hay money case by October 3 so he went to John Kelly, who lived in Bonesteel, and borrowed a double-barreled shotgun saying he was going to hunt prairie chickens. Bear had no shells so he purchased some, and also a quantity of double B shot. He extracted the larger shot from the shells and reloaded them with the smaller shot. At 3:00 on the afternoon of October 8 Bear started in a buggy toward the sub-agency. On the road he passed within view of the place where Shaw lived and saw his stepson and Shorty Thighs in the field loading hay, Shaw on the wagon and his uncle throwing bales up to him. He drove up to them and demanded money, which was refused, and after talking briefly Bear shot Shaw, who was unarmed. Shaw fell off the opposite side of the wagon, so seriously wounded that he was unable to rise. The horses started to bolt so Bear quieted them, which distracted him for a few moments, then walked up to Shaw and point-blank shot him dead with a load of buckshot. He turned to look for Shorty Thighs to kill him but the Indian was running away at surprising speed, and was out of range for the shotgun. Bear then reloaded his weapon and started for the Ponca sub-agency. He drove his buggy into the yard, dismounted with his shotgun in hand, and asked Miss Kleckner, a cousin of the Tayloes, "Where is the teacher?" She said he was away but a servant girl quickly corrected her and said he was in the school house. One corner of the school house had been made into an office and Ed and Maud Tayloe were busy counseling two Indian boys. When Bear entered the room with a weapon no one was alarmed and Maud Tayloe, seeing the shotgun, asked in the Sioux language, "Why, George, where are your chickens?" Bear replied, "I have already got one and I will have another in a minute." Edward Tayloe turned and extended his hand toward Bear, but the Indian raised the gun and fired both loads into Tayloe's right shoulder. The heavy double charge of birdshot entered near the arm pit and tore a hole about four inches long and two inches wide, and Tayloe bled to death within minutes. The body of C. Edward Tayloe was later sent to Virginia for burial and his wife accompanied his remains, and was so affected that she had been under the close care of a physician since she saw her husband murdered.

After killing Tayloe Bear walked to his buggy and drove away. He traveled two miles from the sub-agency when he met his wife on horseback, who heard of her son's death and was searching for Bear with a large butcher knife. Bear stopped the buggy, dismounted with the shotgun and handed it to his wife, saying she should shoot him to avenge her son's death. She returned the weapon and said, "No. I guess I'll let the government kill you." Bear's wife rode off and Bear continued on to Bonesteel, where he intended to kill a liveryman named Slaughter because he had purchased the disputed hay from Shaw. Slaughter was out of town so Bear drove his buggy at a dangerous pace up and down the street while singing his death song. The town's marshal, believing he had a drunken Indian on his hands, grabbed the reins of the buggy and arrested Bear. Only after the Indian was lodged in jail did the marshal learn he had arrested a murderer when one of the Indian boys, who had been in the office when Tayloe was killed, brought in a telegram to be sent to the Indian agent at the Rosebud Agency. George Bear was indicted, tried, convicted of murder in the first degree, and sentenced to hang. During the time he was a prisoner in the county jail he caused little trouble.

Two days before his execution the Indian said to an official, "When I am gone I want you to tell the newspapers what a good prisoner I have been and how I have kept up my courage." On his final night the Reverend William Holmes, a native Episcopal minister from the Santee Agency in Nebraska, remained with Bear for some time. The prisoner retired at 11:30 P.M. and slept soundly until 6:10 A.M. During the morning the Reverend returned for prayer and provided support when the death warrant was read. He accompanied Bear onto the scaffold at 9:00 and the condemned man took his place on the trapdoor, appearing entirely unconcerned. The reverend repeated, in low tones, an appropriate portion of the Episcopal service while the prisoner's arms and legs were being bound, the noose adjusted, and the black hood pulled over Bear's face. The trap was sprung at 9:16 A.M. and the fall broke his neck, and he was pronounced dead in thirteen minutes. Bear's remains were cut down, placed in a coffin, and at noon the body was driven to the Ponca Creek Cemetery and buried.

Argus-Leader (Sioux Falls, SD): December 5, 1902.

Victor, Emil
November 16, 1909

On July 5, 1909, John F. Ronayne and his fourteen-year-old son, Michael, were hoeing potatoes near J. W. Christie's farm near Rudolph. Christie had rented the farm and his family lived in the small, ugly cottage while their home was being built in town. Mrs. Christie and her thirteen-year-old daughter, Mildred, lived there and Michael Ronayne had spent the previous winter with the Christie family so he could attend school in the country. John Ronayne usually put up his horses at the Christie place while working in his potato field. When it was time to go home Ronayne was hitching his team when Christie suggested that Michael and his father spend the night so they could be fresh for work the next morning, but John could not stay and returned to town. In the morning John drove his wagon and team into the fenced yard at the Christie farm and expected to be met by Christie or his son, but the place was quiet. He later said that he supposed the two men had gone to the elevator in Rudolph and that the women were still asleep in the house.

It was about 7:00 A.M. when John went to the house and found Mrs. Christie lying in a pool of blood in the doorway between the small porch and the kitchen, shot through the body and dead. Mildred was lying on her bed, her bed clothes ripped from her body and a bullet hole in her forehead, but there were no marks to suggest a further violation. John hurried to the barn and from the door he could see his son lying on his face in the dirt of an empty stall. He went to him and found that he had been shot and his head had been crushed with a hammer, which lay nearby. He looked further and in the next stall, just behind the cow, he found Christie, who had been shot through the head and his hat, with a bullet hole through it, lay beside the body. The murderer had apparently used the same hammer he later used on Michael to crush Christie's head. The scene showed that Christie had been milking the cow when murdered and the sequence of events suggested that Michael must have come at the sound of the shot and been killed next. Mrs. Christie, upon hearing two pistol shots, rushed out with the stove lifter in her hand and met the murderer, who placed the muzzle of his six-shooter against her body and fired. Mildred, who put up a struggle, was the last to die. When the investigation began it was clear that the house had been carefully ransacked with every bureau drawer, box, and purse gone through and the mattresses and rugs pulled apart. Still, in his haste, the murderer had left a $5 bill in one purse and a gold watch in a drawer.

The authorities were summoned and while at the farm investigating the sheriff heard of Emil Victor, who had worked for John Morrow and was now at Northville, and he was suspected. The sheriff started for Mansfield in Ford Zetlow's automobile and from there the sheriff telephoned Marshal Alden Wilson at Northville. When Emil Victor came into town the marshal arrested him. He was searched and on his person was found a watch, three knives, three gold brooches, two books of stamps, a pocketbook filled with change, and $13 in small bills and, from the moment of his arrest, he told several conflicting stories. Victor was a middle-aged man of medium height and weight, sandy complexion, light hair and blue eyes. Two strangers had also been seen in the area but they were cleared of involvement, and Victor insisted he could provide an alibi. He said he ate breakfast at Conde on Saturday morning and took the train to Northville, talking with the conductor about work at Northville. He said his father was a successful dry goods merchant in Buffalo, New York, and he was well known there. However, all he professed proved to be lies when investigated. Emil Victor had come to South Dakota from East Aurora, New York, where he left behind his father, mother and a younger sister.

The bodies of the murder victims were taken to Wilson's undertaking parlor and an inquest was held by Coroner George Countryman. The sheriff was the second witness, after John Ronayne, and he told how a watch had been torn out of the trouser button hole when the two men were searched by the murderer. He produced three bullet casings and one cartridge recovered from the floor in Mildred's bedroom, where the murderer had dropped them as he reloaded his pistol. The watch and the pearl-handled knife found with Victor were identified as Christie's. Morrow, who had been Victor's employer, said his men told him that the prisoner had boasted how easy it would be to rob Christie, but he had not heard the boast. D. G. Gallett, a jeweler, had sold the watch to Christie, kept a record by number, and later confirmed that the watch found on Victor was the one owned by Christie. On June 24 Emil Victor had gone to the office of the *American* newspaper and expressed an interest in having his name in print.

He was so anxious that it be printed by a certain date that he paid the advertising rate in advance and the following story, believed to be an effort to establish an alibi, was printed on June 25:

EMIL VICTOR GOES EAST
Eastern Man Here for a Year
Returning Home to Gather
Material for Airship

Emil Victor who has been working on the 2300 acre farm of John Morrow at Rudolph arrived here Wednesday and remained until Friday, the guest of Aberdeen friends, leaving for Northville yesterday, where he will spend a week. From Northville Mr. Victor will go to Chicago for a visit with his brother, and from there to Buffalo N. Y. where his parents reside, his father being a proprietor of one of the leading dry goods stores in that city.

Mr. Victor came west about a year ago and is delighted with the country. He will spend the summer months in the east and will return next fall. He has been inspecting considerable land in this vicinity, and will make some purchases upon his return. He also intends registering for the Cheyenne reservation opening that will take place in the fall.

Mr. Victor has invented a flying machine and has plans drawn up for its construction. He will busy himself this summer in the east gathering materials and will complete building of the flyer here upon his return so that the trial flights will be made upon the Dakota prairies. Mr. Victor has a host of friends in South Dakota who are hopeful for the success of his invention.

Victor was held on a charge of murder and indicted by the grand jury. At his trial in the fall term of the District Court he was convicted of murder in the first degree and sentenced to hang on November 16, 1909. His family could not be present on his final day but had made arrangements for his burial. A few days before his execution Victor received a letter from his family bidding him farewell, and his mother sent a $5 money order to his attorney asking him to make one last appeal to Governor Robert S. Vessey for a stay of execution. She apologized that it was all she had since her garden had been neglected while she tried to save her son. He returned the money and explained that no effort would be successful at that late hour and assured her that every effort had already been made, but in vain.

On his last night the condemned man spent his time writing letters to his relatives and to some acquaintances he had made in Rudolph, then he retired. He spent a restless night but finally fell asleep after midnight. At an early hour Sheriff John Anderson called him awake to hear the death warrant read. He arose to find deputies Reese Price and Art Wagner on duty as his death watch, Dick Cameron and Vilas Quinn having been relieved while he slept. A small crowd of a dozen curious men gathered in front of the jail at midnight and remained through the cold, snowy night because they had heard a rumor that the execution might occur at 2:00 A.M., and they were still there when the sun appeared. After the death warrant was read, the Reverend F. J. Graeber, pastor of the German Lutheran Church, spent time with the prisoner consoling him and praying. The reverend had been attending to Victor's religious needs from his first day in jail, taking over the duty from another clergyman who had become ill.

The prisoner was brought forth after 7:30 A.M. wearing a black shroud over his entire body, hiding the straps which tightly bound his arms and wrists, but were loosely applied to his legs so he could walk. He bid farewell to his death watch guards as he was led into the jail yard, the knee straps making his progress difficult. First came the sheriff, then the prisoner between deputies Price and Cameron, and behind him were deputies Henry Moulton and Art Walker. Deputy Jerry Castleton of Sioux Falls and a Reverend stood nearby in case they were needed. The scaffold had been erected on the north side of the jail yard within an enclosure and twenty-five witnesses, including lawmen, officials, clergy, doctors, and newsmen, wore heavy overcoats and shuffled about to keep warm as they stood in the snow. The prisoner was halted at the foot of the stairs and allowed to make his speech. He said nothing of significance, but when halfway up the stairs he suddenly turned to the crowd and called out, "God forgive me for my sins and bless you all!"

He then walked onto the platform and positioned himself in the center of the trapdoor. The straps were quickly tightened about his knees and ankles and the noose was placed over his head. The black hood was drawn on and then the noose was positioned and cinched tight to hold it in place. At 8:09 A.M., the trap was sprung by the sheriff and Victor dropped, breaking his neck in the fall. Coroner Dr. Countryman, assisted by Drs. R. D. Adams and R. L. Murdy, recorded the dying man's pulse and in sixteen minutes pronounced him dead. After hanging a few minutes more the body was cut down, placed in a coffin, and given to the undertaker, who saw that the family's funeral arrangements were fulfilled.

Aberdeen American News (SD): June 25, 1909; July 6, 1909; November 16, 1909.

Rickman, Joseph
December 3, 1913

Twenty-two-year-old Joseph Rickman moved from Bryant to the Bixby area in Perkins County, South Dakota, in 1910 and filed on a plot of land six miles south of Bixby. Rickman's land was a half mile north of the home of forty-five-year-old Ellen Fox, where the widow lived with her fourteen-year-old daughter, Mildred. At 8:00 P.M. on Saturday evening, September 27, 1913, the Fox women went to the shack of Rickman for a pail of water and the following evening Rickman returned the visit, taking along paper to kindle a fire. When he arrived he did not knock but took the ax Ellen Fox kept by her back door, entered quietly, and brutally murdered the unsuspecting mother and then murdered the daughter, and neither woman even had the opportunity to scream. Rickman mutilated the bodies with a knife and this work took until after midnight, then he placed the paper around the outside of the house and lit it, hoping to burn down the house and conceal the murders.

On Monday Guy Montgomery and George Bierlieu were looking for stray horses and stopped at the Fox home, where they found the structure burned down but still smoldering. They inquired about the residents and it soon became clear that the bodies would probably be found among the ashes, and then part of one of the bodies was noticed on a iron bed, so foul play was suspected and they sent for the coroner. The state's attorney, Justice P. H. Woll, deputy sheriff Ellefson, and Dr. J. F. Walker drove to the scene on Tuesday, recovered the remains, and Dr. Walker found that the skulls of both women had been crushed. Ellen Fox's skull was crushed over the eyes and the back of her head had been nearly cut off; a hole one inch in diameter was found in the left breast and the right breast had been severed from the body; and a cut on her back near the shoulder blade was clearly from a knife. Mildred's skull was crushed at the base of her neck, as if lying face down when struck, and there was a deep gash on her leg, but a complete analysis of wounds was impossible as much of the remains were cremated.

Dr. Walker summoned a coroner's jury and testimony revealed that Rickman had been infatuated with Mildred but Ellen Fox was opposed to his attentions. Several witnesses testified that Rickman said he would have the girl, regardless of her mother's objections, and they testified that Ellen Fox "lived in mortal fear" of Rickman. One of the witnesses was with Rickman when Bierlieu arrived at his shack and said that the house had been burned, but made no mention of the women, and Rickman had responded, "Oh My God! They were burned up!" Then when the party returned to the burned home Rickman suggested that some of the roof poles might have collapsed and crushed their skulls but Rickman, an incessant talker, grew silent when the authorities arrived. The coroner's jury indicted Rickman on September 30, he waived his preliminary examination, was arraigned and pled not guilty, and he was lodged in jail that evening.

He continued to protest his innocence and

tried to implicate others, so on October 9 deputy Ellefson went to Bixby to investigate and he determined no other persons were involved. The deputy also learned that after Rickman was arrested a party of neighbors went to his shack and found that the clothing, hat and shoes which he wore habitually had been burned and all that remained were buttons, bits of cloth, and the leather hat band. The hat band, which he had hung on the wall, had blood streaks and they found part of a door panel spotted with blood hidden under the wood pile. They could not find the murder weapon, the ax, nor Rickman's .32-caliber revolver. When Ellefson returned Rickman saw that he could not shift the blame so he confessed every detail of the murders to Sheriff Anderson and his deputy. However, he insisted that he had not molested either woman nor had he taken the money which Ellen Fox reportedly kept at her house, and the only motive he could give was that he had an irresistible impulse to kill. On Wednesday, October 22, 1913, Rickman was brought into the Circuit Court where he pled guilty to the charge of first degree murder, and Judge Dilman sentenced him to hang on December 3. There would be no delays from appeals nor from applications for executive clemency.

As the day of execution approached, Rickman, who had refused to talk of his crime since his confession, began to fill in the details and finally admitted that he had raped both women before he killed them. He said that he was not certain they were dead when he set the house afire and had fled to his home in case someone heard their screams. During his entire time behind bars he had not lost his appetite nor spent a restless night. On his final morning he had to be aroused from sleep at 4:00 A.M., and he dressed quickly while demanding his breakfast. He was then led into the corridor of the jail where his wrists were cuffed behind, the death warrant was read and then, with the Reverend Hyink of Lemmon leading, he was escorted into the stockade built on the north side of the jail by Sheriff Anderson and deputy Ellefson.

He mounted the scaffold, took his place on the trapdoor, and glanced down at the small crowd of witnesses. The area was lighted with gasoline torches, which gave the scene an eerie character, but Rickman had nothing to say, so the black hood was pulled over his head and the noose was adjusted, and then his arms were strapped to his body and his ankles were pinioned, and immediately Sheriff Anderson pulled a lever which sprang the trap. Rickman dropped through and broke his neck, and in four minutes Dr. Walker pronounced him dead. After the body hung a while longer it was cut down and given to undertaker Kruse to prepare for shipment to Lemmon. The Vermillion medical school had made requisition for the remains for use in their dissecting room so the Perkins County authorities, according to law, delivered the remains.

Lincoln Daily News (NE): December 3, 1913. *Bison Courier* (SD): October 2, 1913; October 9, 1913; October 23, 1913; December 4, 1913.

Sitts, George
August 8, 1947

On December 12, 1945, George Sitts attempted to hold up a convenience store in Minneapolis, Minnesota, but clerk Erik Johannson engaged him in a gun fight and was shot to death. Sitts fled empty-handed but was arrested the following day at Glencoe. He was returned to Minneapolis where he pled guilty in January and was sentenced to serve a life sentence at the prison in Stillwater. Early on January 24, as he awaited transfer to prison, he and three other prisoners sawed through two bars of their cell, slipped through the opening, knocked the police dispatcher unconscious, and escaped. Sitts stole a black sedan, license number 109-106, and fled west. A broadcast alerted law enforcement officers; Butte County Sheriff Dave Malcolm and special agent Tom Matthews set up a roadblock two miles south of Spearfish in South Dakota. After sunset a third car approached the roadblock from the east while a truck approached from the west, and the officers stopped the automobile. As the truck passed the three automobiles, driver Earl Cook saw the man from the third car get out and immediately heard a loud report "like an explosion." He had gone about one hundred fifty yards when he stopped to look back and heard a second explosion. He saw something lying in the road and the man walked to it, bent over and picked up something, and then Cook heard a third explosion and saw a "spurt of flame shoot down." The man returned to his automobile and drove west at a high rate of speed. Cook turned around and drove to the place where the original two vehicles were still parked, Matthews' car engine was still running with the lights on, and Cook saw that the object was a body lying in the road, and another body lay nearby, so he drove into Spearfish and reported to the police. Officers responded to the scene and found the bodies of Sheriff Malcolm and agent Matthews lying in the center of the road. Malcolm had been shot in the heart and he clutched a slip of paper in one hand, on it written the license plate number of the vehicle driven by Sitts. Matthews had been shot in the back and in the head and his wallet and service pistol, a 9mm Luger, was missing. They found in the roadway four bullet casings from a .45-caliber automatic pistol. A broadcast was sent throughout the West and truck drivers were notified by Citizen's Band radio, and officers began looking for a cop killer. The following day Sitts was spotted near Newcastle, Wyoming, by another truck driver, G. W. Donely, who refused to stop when Sitts tried to flag him down. The fugitive was soon arrested.

Sitts was taken to Deadwood, South Dakota, and tried in March 1946 on two counts of murder. On March 21 defense attorney John Heffron stressed that malice was lacking for a first degree murder conviction, "as it had been done in the heat of passion." The jury disagreed and Sitts was found guilty of first degree murder and sentenced to die in the prison at Sioux Falls. Over the next year Sitts sat in his cell while motions, appeals and petitions were submitted and denied, and he never showed any emotion or remorse. He was finally sentenced to die in the electric chair on April 8, 1947, the first and only execution by that method in South Dakota.

On the Saturday before his execution, April 5, Sitts attacked assistant warden P. H. Plymate but was quickly subdued, and the officers then found two hooks he had fashioned and with which he may have planned to commit suicide, so the death watch was increased to prevent the prisoner from cheating the executioner. In his last hours Sitts bequeathed his cornea to anonymous persons to help restore their sight, and two New Yorkers benefited. Forty witnesses were in place on Monday night when the death warrant was read to Sitts in his cell, and at midnight he was guided from his cell to the "home-spun electric chair" in the execution chamber with the "death hood" already in place. His head had already been shaved, as had the place on his leg where an electrode would be attached, and he was seated and strapped in, raising his arms to aid the officers. After the electrodes were attached everyone stepped away and Warden G. Norton Jameson leaned over and asked, "Have you any last words?" and Sitts replied, "In my experience this is the first time the authorities ever helped me to escape prison." In a few moments the warden gave the signal and there followed four jolts of electricity, and then a doctor checked for a heartbeat and pronounced Sitts dead at 12:15 A.M.

Charleston Mail (SC): April 9, 1947. *Huronite* (Huron, SD): January 25, 1946. *Plainsman* (Huron, SD): June 6, 1947. *Evening Tribune* (Albert Lea, MN): March 21, 1946. *Globe Gazette* (Mason City, IA): April 7, 1947. *Oakland Tribune* (CA): April 8, 1947. *Wisconsin State Journal* (Madison): April 10, 1947.

Page, Elijah
July 11, 2007

On March 13, 2000, eighteen-year-old Elijah Page, nineteen-year-old Briley Piper and twenty-year-old Darrell Hoadley decided to rob nineteen-year-old Chester Allan Poage. They kidnapped Poage from his Spearfish, South Dakota, home and took him to Higgins

Gulch where, over the next two hours, they tortured him mercilessly. They stripped him of most of his clothing and made him stand in snow and icy water and at one point forced him to drink hydrochloric acid. Piper stabbed Poage in the head and neck three times and Page kicked him in the head thirty to forty times and tore off his ears. Finally all three bashed in Poage's skull with large rocks and left the dead body where it lay. They returned to the Poage home and stole a Chevrolet Blazer, loading it with the television, stereo system, video games, a coin collection and other items.

Poage's body was discovered on August 22 and the three murderers immediately came under suspicion, were arrested, and lodged in jail. Hoadley confessed and told the police that he participated only at the end, when Poage was already dead or dying, because he was afraid the other two would kill him if he refused. Page and Piper pled guilty but were tried at Deadwood to make a record for the inevitable appeal, while Hoadley pled not guilty and was convicted and sentenced to serve a life term when the jury split on sentencing. Hoadley testified against Page and Piper and they were both sentenced to die by Circuit Judge Warren Johnson, but both condemned men filed appeals which stayed the executions. In early August 2006, Page withdrew his appeal and demanded to die, and the date for his execution was set for the week of August 28. However, Governor Mike Rounds became concerned that the three drug combination, which was then the standard for lethal injection executions, violated the 1984 South Dakota law which called for a two drug combination. He stayed the execution until the legislature could act, and then the date for Page's execution was set for Wednesday, July 11, 2007.

Page had been living in the newer wing of the South Dakota State Penitentiary in Sioux Falls but as the date for his execution neared he was moved into the older part of the prison where the death chamber was located. He was remorseful, and complained that he thought of Poage and saw him in his dreams every day, and some argued that the withdrawal of his appeal was his way to commit suicide. Page spent his last day preparing for his death and before 10:00 P.M. the death warrant was read to him in his cell. He was then escorted to the death chamber and strapped to a gurney where medically trained personnel inserted two intravenous cannulas (IVs), one in each arm with the second IV as a back-up in case the primary IV failed. Electrodes were then attached so that his heart could be monitored on an electrocardiograph machine. The executioner was conducted into the control room where he would activate the mechanism which administered the three drugs: first sodium thiopental to induce sleep; second pancuronium bromide to restrict respiration, which in time would cause death by asphyxiation; and finally potassium chloride to stop Page's heart. The curtain on the viewing window was pulled back for the witnesses and Page was asked if he had any last words, but he declined to speak. The signal was then given and the drugs were administered. At 10:11 P.M. all signs of life left the prisoner and the attending physician pronounced him dead.

Piper, #37433, continued his appeal and as of December 2010 he was still living on death row with two other condemned men.

Aiken Standard (SC): August 30, 2006. *Sitka Sentinel* (AK): February 20, 2008. *Post-Standard* (Syracuse, NY): July 12, 2007. *Salina Journal* (KS): August 27, 2006.

WASHINGTON

Washington was a part of the "Oregon Country" when it was acquired from Great Britain in 1846. In March 1853 a proposal for a "Columbia Territory," to be created from the northern half of the Oregon Territory, was passed by Congress but by amendment the name was changed to the Washington Territory. Washington was admitted to the union as the 42nd state on November 11, 1889.

Gallagher, Edward D. July 11, 1890

In November 1889, Edward D. Gallagher murdered Louis Mar, sometimes given as Moran, an aged farmer who lived near the Lower Cascade Locks in Clark County, Washington. Gallagher was quickly suspected and captured, but claimed he was innocent and laid blame for the shooting upon a man known only as "Snowball." However Snowball, a character well-known in that region, had disappeared. Snowball was never found nor heard of and his absence was under circumstances which suggested that Gallagher may have murdered him also and hidden the body.

Gallagher's trial began at the spring term of the court and though the evidence against the defendant was entirely circumstantial, the prosecution linked every piece together into a chain that left no reasonable doubt as to his guilt. The jurors deliberated only briefly before returning a verdict of guilty as charged in the indictment, and Gallagher was sentenced to hang on July 11, 1890. Neither appeal nor pleas for executive clemency delayed the execution.

By noon Friday, July 11, a large crowd had gathered outside the gate to the temporary courtyard in Vancouver. Two hundred ticket holders were admitted and took positions near the gallows, and then the gates were thrown open and three hundred more men crowded into the enclosure. A thousand more people crowded against the fence or climbed atop the roof of the shed on one side of the enclosure or onto the windmill on the other. In the crowd outside were many women and children. Gallagher believed until the last minute that he would be saved by some intervention, and even suggested that the soldiers of the barracks with whom he was well acquainted might mount a rescue attempt. He had refused any religious consolation and said, "The soldiers will keep me."

At 12:56 P.M. Sheriff M. J. Flemming, assisted by several deputies, marched his prisoner out of the jail. When Gallagher reached the stairs he resisted, but was taken up onto the platform. He walked with a steady gait though he seemed dazed by the large crowd. Once on the scaffold he sat in a chair and Father Schram tried to get him to make his peace with the world, but he refused and insisted he did not care about eternity. Gallagher told the sheriff he could say a few words to the crowd and he made a short, stammering, nearly inaudible speech of no significance, apologizing for having to appear in that condition. The prisoner was escorted to the trapdoor where the deputies tried to pinion his arms and legs, but Gallagher fought like a madman. He knocked down the sheriff and several deputies, and it took seven men nearly three minutes to restrain him and bind his knees and ankles, his arms and wrists as he struggled against every effort.

Once secured the noose was positioned and cinched tight and the sheriff told him, "Be a man. Tell me whether you killed Mar," and the condemned man spat back, "None of your damned business!" The sheriff pulled on the black hood and prepared to spring the trap. Through the dark cloth the prisoner hissed, "I don't give a damn," as the trapdoor fell at 1:04 P.M. Gallagher dropped seven feet, breaking his neck and in eleven minutes the attending physicians pronounced him dead. After the body hung several more minutes it was cut down, placed in a plain coffin, and buried in a pauper's grave without ceremony.

Oregonian (Portland): July 12, 1890. *Seattle Post-Intelligencer* (WA): July 12, 1890.

Day, Robert T.
June 3, 1892

Robert Thompson Day, an old man, had built up his farm near the logging camp not far from Woodland in Cowlitz County, Washington. Several times the cattle of twenty-four-year-old Thomas Clinton Beebe had broken down the fence and trespassed into Day's field, destroying a portion of his crops. On Friday morning, October 9, 1891, Day found Beebe's cattle in his field again and, taking his Winchester rifle, found Beebe and ordered him to remove his stock. The two men began to argue, Day becoming more agitated until he suddenly, without provocation or hesitation, raised his rifle and shot Beebe dead. Beebe was liked by the loggers, so Day immediately fled into the mountains to avoid a lynching. The authorities were notified and Sheriff Ben Holmes went in pursuit. It did not take long to run down the aged fugitive and soon the old man was in custody and then Day begged not to be taken to Woodland, where he seemed certain the loggers would lynch him. The sheriff took his prisoner directly to Kalama and he was lodged in the county jail.

At his examination he pled not guilty but was held over to answer to the grand jury. Day was indicted in early April and immediately tried. The trial was brief and the jurors required little deliberations before returning a verdict of guilty of first degree murder. Day was sentenced to hang on June 3, 1892, and neither appeal nor application for executive clemency delayed the hanging.

During the first days of June the gallows was erected in the courthouse yard in Kalama and during the early morning hours of June 3 two hundred people gathered to watch the execution. Before 11:00 A.M. Day walked the short distance to the scaffold, unsupported and with a firm step. Once he was upon the platform the death warrant was read by Sheriff Holmes. Day was then asked if he had anything to say to the crowd and he talked for ten minutes, reviewing his life and denying that he was a vicious and desperate character. He said that Beebe had abused him and his family, and when he spoke of his wife he was visibly affected but quickly composed himself. He concluded by saying he had no regrets for killing Beebe. The prisoner's wrists and ankles were then pinioned, the noose was adjusted, the black hood was pulled over his eyes at 11:10 A.M., and in a moment the trap was sprung. The condemned man dropped six feet, breaking his neck, which killed him instantly. The body was suspended for thirteen minutes before it was cut down and given to his family for burial.

Seattle Daily Times (WA): June 4, 1892. *Spokane Review* (WA): October 13, 1891; June 4, 1892.

Brooks, Charles
September 6, 1892

Charles Brooks was born in Baltimore, Maryland, on July 26, 1820. His parents were natives of Africa and he was born five months after their arrival in America. His childhood was spent in the place of his birth, where Brooks' father was employed as an expert horse-trainer. It was natural that Charles would apprentice in the same business, and he became a capable horseman and jockey. He was employed for years by John Ahardt, a well known turfman, who paid him well. After seven years on the race track Brooks grew tired of the business and accepted a position with the firm of Steward and Company in Virginia, where he remained for five years, but things started to get warm along the Mason-Dixon line. The laws of the country at that time were such that if three colored men were caught talking they were taken directly to the whipping posts and given thirty-nine lashes on their bare backs. Brooks said, of this situation, "The only difference between me and a dog is that a dog carries his tag on his neck while I carry mine in my pocket to prove I am free."

When the Civil War broke out Brooks joined the Eighth Tennessee Cavalry, and while resisting a charge received a severe saber wound, which put him in a Nashville hospital for months. When discharged he went to Virginia, where he married. He and his wife Jane had a child which died in its infancy, and after that tragedy they moved to Raytown where Brooks worked as a coachman. They next moved to Chattanooga where Brooks worked on the railroad as a cook, and during one trip away from home his wife died. In 1876 he became restless and tried the Southwest, but soon returned to the South where he met George Turner and Paul Strobach at Pullard, Alabama. Brooks worked in Conecuh County, Alabama, for a period where he met his second wife, and soon they were on their way to Spokane, Washington, working as domestics for Paul Strobach. They arrived on August 1, 1882, and his second wife died soon afterward.

In late 1890 Brooks was employed as a janitor in the Webster block where he met Christine Dohlman, a white woman. A relationship developed and by late January 1891 they were living together as man and wife. After two and one half months Christine Dohlman left Brooks. Dohlman complained that he had moved her from a house into a shanty, that Brooks was a heavy drinker, and he abused her. However, Brooks denied all of these allegations and said the reason she left him was that a man named Williams and his wife and a man named Lewis Berg and his wife talked against him and were instrumental in convincing Dohlman to leave. Brooks tried everything he could, and made every plea, to get Dohlman to renew their relationship but she resisted. On July 5, 1891, Brooks made one final plea and when he was again rebuffed he shot Dohlman four times, killing her instantly. He had planned to kill Williams and Berg and then himself but he was cornered by deputy sheriff Smith. When one of the men in the crowd yelled out, "Kill the damned Negro," Brooks changed his plans to resist arrest and surrendered. He was lodged in jail and at his examination he was held to answer to the grand jury. Brooks was indicted, tried, convicted of first degree murder, and sentenced to hang. Every effort was made to obtain a new trial but the appeals, which delayed the execution for months, all failed. At 8:40 P.M. on Brooks' last evening his defense attorney, Judge George Turner who had been tireless on Brooks' behalf, sent a wire of two hundred ninety words to Governor Elisha P. Ferry suggesting several issues he thought the governor might have overlooked or failed to consider. Two hours later the governor, outraged, replied, "A respite for Brooks can not be granted. Your statement that I had not fully considered the question of commutation is both insulting and false." When Brooks was informed that his last hope had vanished, he said, "I did not expect anything else," and changed the subject.

Ever since the death sentence was passed the visitors at the jail always asked to see Brooks particularly, and many of them went to the jail with no other purpose than to see the condemned man. During Brooks' final week Sheriff Francis McKay Pugh was kept busy answering questions and turning away those who could not state a valid purpose for a visit with Brooks. The sheriff also had to sort through the many requests for tickets to the execution, as the number would have filled the jail yard several times over. Several women applied, with the stated reason that they were as entitled as any man to witness the execution, but they were denied admittance. The sheriff limited the number of invitations to one hundred fifty, and one hundred thirty-five men were expected to attend. Some of the morbidly curious even tried to buy tickets, offering from $5 to $20 for an invitation card, but none could be bought and several cards were returned to the sheriff to end pressure on the holder to sell his ticket.

On Brooks' final day there was an unusually large number of visitors at the jail but he spent the day, as he had the previous week, sitting quietly in his cell. The near approach of the hour of his execution caused but little change in his demeanor. Several women spent most of Sunday afternoon with him singing hymns and reading the Bible, and he listened earnestly to all they had to say and then told them how happy he was. In stating to them the great love he bore for his wife he broke down for the first time and cried like a child for several minutes. Afterwards he asked his visitors to pardon him for what was evidence of weakness, but his apology was unnecessary, as several of his visitors were also in tears. Members of the Salvation Army had been particularly zealous in their efforts to make Brooks' last hours pleasant, and they had always been welcome visitors at the jail.

The prisoner was much fatigued after a hard day's work entertaining his visitors and he lay down at 8:00 P.M. for a nap, but was too nervous to sleep, so by 10 o'clock he arose and talked with his guards for two hours and it was after midnight before he retired and slept soundly. He awoke at 5:00 A.M. and smoked a cigar while lying in bed and at 6:15 A.M. he arose and dressed in his new black Prince Albert suit. He ate a light breakfast and a few minutes later received the Reverends Brown and Taylor. They prayed and sang hymns, in which Brooks joined. Next the Reverends read scripture followed by the hymn, "Ask the Savior to Help You," sung at Brooks' request. At 7:40 A.M. Sheriff Pugh entered the cell and read the death warrant and when he concluded he told the prisoner that his time had come.

The scaffold had been erected in the courtyard of the county jail not far from the cell where the prisoner had lived for nearly fifteen months. Brooks walked from his cell to the scaffold smoking his cigar, a smile on his face, and he nodded to everyone he knew. Once upon the platform he threw away the cigar and began talking in a subdued tone to those near him. As he proceeded his voice became gradually higher pitched until it reached a shriek, so the Reverend Brown interrupted and asked him to join in singing "When I Can Read My Title Clear." At 8:04 A.M. Brooks was moved onto the trapdoor where deputies pinioned his wrists and ankles with stout leather straps, adjusted the noose, and pulled the black hood over his head. Two minutes later Sheriff Pugh touched the button that released the trapdoor and the prisoner shot downward, breaking his neck. He died almost instantly, and without a tremor. Once his heartbeat ceased he was pronounced dead by the attending physician and then the body was cut down. Brooks' remains were placed in a coffin, which had been stored nearby, and conveyed to the undertaking establishment of Webster and Sullivan in the auditorium. Brooks was buried that afternoon following a brief graveside service by the Reverend Brown.

Seattle Daily Times (WA): September 7, 1892.
Spokane Review (WA): September 6, 1892.

Myers, Charles E.
September 30, 1895

By 1893 forty-eight-year-old Charles Myers, sometimes spelled Meyers, had lived in the town of Asotin in Asotin County, Washington, for many years. He was a stock raiser and farmer and had been married, but he was a very difficult man to live with so his wife divorced him and remarried. His ex-wife and her new husband made a ritual of passing by Myers' ranch house, fifteen miles south of town, and insulting him with taunts and jeers until, one day, he responded by shooting the man dead. He was arrested without incident, tried and acquitted. Myers remarried but his behavior did not change, so his new wife soon left him. A year later she was managing the City Hotel in Asotin and the hotel was next to Shafer's Saloon, and Shafer was another enemy of Myers.

On March 13, 1893, Wesley Steele, a stock buyer from Asotin, rode with Myers to his ranch and on the way Myers said, "I am settling my business affairs in order and just as soon as I am done I will settle family affairs and then somebody will bite the dust." Myers was riding his favorite animal, an unshod black mare with one peculiar hoof that made a mark like a shod hoof. At the house Steele saw a red half-gallon syrup can on a kitchen shelf with a number of oddly speckled beans scattered about, and in the front room was a pile of barley sacks. The next day they were joined by A. J. Steele, who made similar observations, except the nearly empty syrup can was now on the table with a paper stopper in it, and in the shed was a five gallon can of coal oil. After the Steeles left Elmer Mosier stopped by Myers' ranch and found him rinsing out the syrup can.

Washington Woodruff lived with Myers and he noticed that on the evening of March 15 his landlord went to bed fully clothed. At 11:00 P.M. on March 15 the City Hotel caught fire and though the point of origin was in the rear, the flames quickly spread. The people lodged on the first floor escaped easily but the stairs were quickly engulfed and the people on the second floor were trapped. R. W. Newman threw himself out a window and was saved. Frank Sherry burst open the door of George Gibson's room and fell over a spare cot stretched across the middle of the floor. Gibson, though horribly burned, threw himself out the window and survived. Sherry crawled to the window but could go no further and was burned to death. Everyone on the first floor, and those who quickly responded, smelled the distinct odor of coal oil. As soon as the alarm was sounded people rushed out of their houses, and those on the edge of town heard hoof beats heading south over the graveled street, then across the Asotin bridge, and continuing south toward Asotin Creek, directly toward Myers' ranch.

In the morning, after the blaze had been extinguished, lawmen found an empty, red, half-gallon syrup can behind the hotel. It had flecks of paper in the spout where a paper stopper had been inserted and it had been filled with coal oil. There was a barley sack nearby and it contained barley and some oddly speckled beans. They found hoof prints going to and from the rear of the hotel, one with a rather peculiar track, and the hoof prints were followed right to Myers' ranch. The horse had been ridden over a short-cut to the ranch, one known to be favored by Myers, and in the barn they found Myers' favorite mare, her rough hair crusted with sweat. That afternoon Myers accompanied the sheriff into town, but on the way he refused to take his favorite shortcut, saying, "The road is too rough and there are too many barbed wire fences to go through." The sheriff took that opportunity to examine the mare's tracks and noted they were identical to the tracks he had followed that morning.

Though the evidence against Myers was all circumstantial, it was carefully linked and in July he was indicted, tried and convicted of the first degree murder of Frank Sherry. However, Myers did not testify and the judge failed to instruct the jury that they could draw no inference of guilt from that fact. This was found by the state Supreme Court to be an error, and the court ordered a new trial. Myers' attorney, trying to better the chances for an acquittal, filed a motion for a change of venue and it was granted. The trial was moved to Pomeroy in Garfield County and was held in June, but Myers was again found guilty and sentenced to hang on September 30, 1895. The case was appealed but this time the state Supreme Court affirmed the lower court's judgment and sentence, and the application to Governor John McGraw praying for clemency was denied. Myers had been lodged in the jail at Dayton but on Friday night, September 27, Myers was brought from Dayton to Pomeroy and J. H. Davidson was assigned as his death watch guard.

On his final day Myers arose at 5:30 A.M. after a sound sleep and ate a hearty breakfast. He refused to shave or don new clothes and instructed deputy sheriff Baldwin to have Sheriff S. S. Russell dispose of his body as he chose. The prisoner refused to see anyone during his last hours, except the Reverend Buzzell, who had been his religious advisor. The gallows had been constructed and thoroughly tested by September 29 so that a view could be had from only two sides, and every available point of view was crowded with one thousand spectators that morning. Of the five hundred invited witnesses only one hundred fifty were admitted into the enclosure. At 10:40 A.M. the condemned man walked the short distance to the scaffold between deputy Baldwin of

Garfield County and Sheriff John L. Wormell of Asotin County and he positioned himself facing the crowd. On the scaffold, awaiting his arrival, were the sheriffs of King, Whitman, Snohomish and Nez Perce Counties, along with members of the press. Deputy Baldwin announced that Myers would speak, and the prisoner stepped forward and declared that he died as he lived, an innocent man.

When he concluded his remarks he stepped back and centered himself on the trapdoor. The Reverend Buzzell delivered an eloquent prayer for Myers' soul as the straps were being applied to his wrists and arms, knees and ankles, but when his hat was removed he said he wanted to speak again. This was granted and he said, "May the Lord save my soul as He will save yours, Amen!" The noose was then positioned and the black hood pulled on. At exactly 11:00 A.M. the trap was sprung and the noose slipped from behind Myers' left ear so that his neck did not break and he strangled to death. Ten times his chest heaved and his fingers twitched nervously, but at 11:08 the attending physicians pronounced him dead. After hanging a few more minutes the body was cut down and sealed in a coffin, the black hood left on to hide Myers' features. No friend or relative stepped forward so the prisoner's remains were given to deputy Baldwin, and Myers was buried in a pauper's grave that afternoon.

Spokesman-Review (Pomeroy, WA): September 29–30, 1895; October 1, 1895.

Asimus, Charles F.
January 31, 1896

Charles F. Asimus was a hunchback who was thirty-eight years of age in 1896. He had been born in Germany where he lived until reaching the age of majority, then emigrated to America and settled in Nebraska. When he was sixteen years old he was carrying a heavy sack of potatoes up stone steps when he fell in such a manner that he injured his spine, but his father refused to have the injury properly cared for, saying his son was only a trifling boy and not worth the expense, and this lack of attention caused the deformity. The condition caused him nervous spells and much embarrassment, which embittered him greatly. When he first went to the Pacific Coast he found employment with a nurseryman in Woodburn, Oregon, and while working there he met John Greenwood and later moved to Washington to work on Greenwood's farm. Asimus had worked for three months when he and Greenwood had a disagreement, which resulted in the discharge of Asimus and a refusal to pay the wages he had earned. Asimus sued Greenwood and won a judgment for the wages, but could not give the bond necessary to execute it. This angered the hunchback so he took a revolver, which he later said was to scare Greenwood into paying the money owed, and went looking for his former employer.

On September 21, 1895, they met at Fowler's ranch near Kelso in Cowlitz County and Asimus demanded payment. When Greenwood said he had no money a quarrel ensued, during which Asimus became increasingly angry. Finally, without further provocation or hesitation, he pulled his pistol and shot Greenwood, killing him instantly. Asimus was arrested and lodged in jail and he was in a deplorable physical and mental condition, and said, "I am nothing but a hunchback and everyone is against me." During his confinement he tried to kill himself by using the metal aglets of his shoelaces to open the arteries in his arms, but he was discovered while unconscious from the loss of blood and saved by physicians. He was tried and convicted of first degree murder at the fall term of the District Court and sentenced to hang on January 31, 1896, and neither appeal nor petition for clemency delayed the date of his execution.

When asked if he could walk to the gallows he said he was much relieved by the sentence to die, as life in prison would have been unbearable. The condemned man had been raised a Lutheran and he believed that his sins had been forgiven, but refused religious consolation, as he also believed "every man must do his own praying." As the days passed the prisoner became increasingly nervous and could not sleep without the assistance of drugs. On his last night he spoke of his brother, who lived in Utah, saying he was "a big man but had a small heart" because he had not come to his aid. The prisoner, as he retired, said he wanted to rise early so he could prepare for the gallows. Asimus slept soundly but awoke several times to ask the guard for the time, then arose at 7 o'clock. His usually hearty appetite failed him but he managed to eat a light breakfast, and he was more pleasant and composed than he had been for some time.

The death warrant was read to him after breakfast and just before 9:30 A.M. the prisoner exited his cell, walking between two deputies. He walked up the stairs onto the platform without assistance and as soon as he was on the trapdoor he began talking, in a disconnected manner, to the thirty spectators saying, "I must die. I am all right. The sheriff, he good man; I one bad man. I must die; I am all right." As he spoke the straps were being applied to his wrists and arms, knees and ankles and the noose was adjusted. The black hood was pulled over his head as he spoke his last words and at 9:32 A.M. the trap was sprung. The prisoner dropped nine feet, breaking his neck, and after three minutes his pulse could not be detected and he was pronounced dead four minutes later. His body was allowed to hang until 9:47 before being cut down and placed in a plain wooden coffin provided by the county, and he was buried in a pauper's grave before noon.

Seattle Daily Times (WA): January 31, 1896.

Straub, Richard H.
April 23, 1897

A feud developed between Richard H. Straub and Leo Lanterman over school matters on Blakeley Island, San Juan County, Washington. Straub lived with Irving Tarberry on a farm adjoining the farm of Mrs. J. C. Burns, who lived there with Lanterman, and a brother and a half-brother named R. H. Blythe.

On August 30, 1895, Straub and Tarberry found Lanterman, Burns and her brothers in their field digging potatoes. Straub approached them and a quarrel soon developed. Suddenly, without warning or provocation, Straub pulled his six-shooter and shot Lanterman in the stomach, and he soon died of the wound. Straub next shot at Blythe but missed, and then shot several times at Burns, one bullet striking her in the shoulder. Straub fled into the woods and a posse spent several days trying to find him. The fugitive swore he would not be taken alive and the citizens of the island were equally committed to lynching him if captured alive. The fugitive was captured without resistance and he was quickly moved to New Whatcom by steam launch, to prevent the lynching. Straub was indicted, tried and convicted of first degree murder at the fall term of the District Court, and he was sentenced to hang. An appeal and petitions delayed the execution for more than a year, but finally the date for his execution was set for April 23, 1897. Nothing further would delay the proceedings.

The scaffold was erected near the jail at Friday Harbor and it was surrounded by a board fence twenty feet high. Only forty people were invited to witness the execution, including officials, doctors, and representatives of the press. Straub had hoped, to the last, that he would be reprieved but, when the last boat arrived without a commutation or respite from Governor John Rogers, Sheriff Steven Boyce and deputy sheriff Jones proceeded with the execution as required by law. The sheriff told Straub, "There is nothing from the governor. You must get ready to bid your friends goodbye," and the prisoner buried his head in his hands and groaned, "My God! My God!" while heavy sobs shook his whole body. Straub quickly regained his composure and put on his coat before he marched to the scaffold, where everything was in readiness. As he stood on the trapdoor he seemed dazed, barely able to stand alone, and he declined to speak to the small assembly. His wrists and arms, knees and ankles were bound, the noose was adjusted, and the black hood was pulled over his head, and in a moment the trap was sprung. The condemned man broke his neck in the fall and the doctor in attendance pronounced him dead in a few minutes, but the body hung for fourteen minutes before being cut down and turned over to relatives for burial.

Seattle Daily Times (WA): April 24, 1897.

Gin Pon
April 30, 1897

Gin Pon and Lee Tong lived in adjacent apartments on First Avenue in the Chinese quarter of Spokane, Washington, east of the Hotel Spokane. They were separately sentenced by the municipal court judge to serve jail terms for petty crimes and were released together on March 1, 1896. They hurried to their homes and Lee Tong, who was afraid of Gin Pon, stayed inside his apartment for several hours. Finally, in need of water, Lee Tong went outside with a bucket. Gin Pon had been lying in wait the entire time and set upon his victim with a club. Lee Tong fought off his assailant during a long scuffle, but Gin Pon suddenly ran into his apartment and returned with a hatchet in each hand and he nearly decapitated Lee Tong, but did not stop his attack and hacked his victim to pieces.

Gin Pon was arrested at once and on April 1, 1896, prosecuting attorney Feighan filed an information charging him with first degree murder. Alexander M. Winston was appointed to defend the accused when the trial began four weeks later, and on April 30, Gin Pon was found guilty as charged. Judge Jessie Arthur denied the motion for a new trial and set the date for execution at August 20, 1896, but an appeal was filed so Judge Buck set aside the order for execution and granted a stay. On March 22, 1897, the state Supreme Court affirmed the lower court's judgment and sentence and denied the petition for a rehearing. Judge Prather then sentenced Gin Pon to hang on Friday, April 30, 1897. The prisoner's attorney then questioned his sanity as Gin Pon had a hideous laugh, which escaped regularly and without reason, and this was proposed to be evidence of insanity. A jury convened to examine the matter and found the prisoner sane after the Reverend Lee To explained that it was a peculiarity of some Chinese tribes to laugh in that strange manner when in jeopardy or excited. All that remained to save Gin Pon was a petition to Governor John Rogers for a commutation of the death sentence to life imprisonment. On April 27 Attorney Winston wired the governor asking for a respite of ten days so he could file the petition for a commutation, but the governor was not at the capitol. Winston said he would not chase the governor about the state and insisted that he had fulfilled his obligation on behalf of his client. Others, including the Reverend N. McInturff, continued the effort and on April 29 Attorney J. E. Fenton found Governor Rogers and presented the petition, but the governor declined to intervene.

During his last week Gin Pon was visited by throngs of curious citizens, two-thirds of whom were ladies "well dressed and refined." The scaffold was being constructed on Saturday, April 24, and at that time the condemned man was allowed the freedom of the corridor, where he paced, smoked, and watched the carpenters at work. The prisoner maintained a hearty appetite throughout his incarceration but refused anything different from the regular jailhouse fare, excepting some fruit. He would not drink or smoke anything intoxicating, went to bed early each night, and slept soundly. He bathed every morning and seemed to enjoy it. The prisoner spent part of his time talking to or playing poker with his death watch guards, James McKirk and M. McCabe, or with cook Nathan Burke. One day Burke asked him if he liked women and Gin Pon said, "Yes, ketchum one soon — Melican [Mexican] girl." When asked where he would find her he replied, "Heaven, up in the sky!"

On Tuesday, April 27, Sheriff C. C. Dempsey sent out the last of over four hundred invitations. He was confounded by the cost to make the affair private until he hit upon the idea of using a large tent, which was on hand from the Republicans' recent presidential campaign.

It was brought out of storage, inspected, and scheduled to be pitched over the scaffold on Thursday. Dr. P. S. Byrne and coroner Dr. Edwin L. Kimball were notified that they would be responsible for monitoring the vital signs of the prisoner and pronouncing him dead. On Thursday the scaffold was completed and hundreds of people, including many Chinese, filed past to see it before it was enclosed beneath the tent. The prisoner was photographed by Spear and Washington and each attendee was promised a copy of the photo. The sheriff decided to use the same rope used to hang another man, which was of solid hemp and cost the county $16. The sheriff and deputy Ferguson removed one thread and, though both men were powerful, they were unable to break it. Colonel Wilder, the clerk in Judge Richardson's court, knew how to tie a hangman's knot with seven coils, and was given that task.

That evening Gin Pon ate an unusually hearty supper and during the evening F. J. Pierce, a fine tenor, visited the prisoner and sang an imitation of an Oriental classic. Gin Pon laughed so hard he fell off his chair and, upon rising, began to dance around his cell. He later played poker with the evening cook and won all the beans used to bet, which seemed to please him greatly. After the game he became concerned about his clothes and asked guard McKirk if his shirt was ready, and was assured it was. He remained restless until 1:00 A.M., then slept. Early Friday morning, after a hearty breakfast, Gin Pon adopted a merry mood as hundreds of curious visitors filed through. He had the freedom of the jail corridor but as soon as he entered his cell he threw himself on his cot and pulled the blankets over his head. When aroused by deputy McCabe it was noticed that he had been crying. The Chinese Baptist clergymen then arrived and they were with him for an hour of prayer. He confessed and through the clergy said he was deeply penitent.

People began to gather outside the tent as early as 9:00 A.M. The jail yard was almost entirely enclosed by the courthouse building, the exception being the barred carriage gate on the north side. The jail door from which the doomed man would exit was in the center of the jail and visible from that gate so the crowd had assembled there, mostly boys eager to see Gin Pon alive for the last time. In the sheriff's office were visiting lawmen and news reporters, but the ticket holders began to assemble at the Mallon Avenue entrance to the jail at 11:15 A.M. and soon more than five hundred people were crowded inside the tent. At 11:39 A.M. deputy Ferguson took the straps onto the platform and twenty minutes later the prisoner emerged from the jail. The crowd parted voluntarily, making a clear passage to the scaffold stairs. First came Gin Pon with Chinese Baptist Minister Lee To on one arm and interpreter Charley Lam on the other. The prisoner seemed rather apologetic but laughed that curious, nervous laugh as he saw the size of the crowd. Next came Sheriff Dempsey and deputies Rutherford, Ferguson, and J. M. Rose, and behind them was Dr. Byrne and two news reporters, the only parties allowed on the scaffold. The two Chinese were there to assist Gin Pon up the stairs, but he needed no support. He went directly to the center of the trapdoor, bowed his head, and put his hands in his pockets. A slight breeze blew the rope so it lightly tapped the prisoner's forehead and again caused his peculiar laugh, which had become more guttural and sounded like the snarl of a wild animal. Sheriff Dempsey asked the prisoner if he had anything to say but Gin Pon did not reply at first, then said, "I have nothing to say. I can not say anything at this time. I am ready to die." He raised his head, inflated his chest, and visibly braced himself. The Reverend To, Chinese Bible in hand, grasped the prisoner's hand, spoke to him for a few moments, and then the two prayed together. When the Reverend concluded the prisoner looked up at the rope and beam and smiled.

The sheriff and his deputies applied the straps and placed the noose around the prisoner's neck, but it had to be removed and replaced under his queue. The sheriff pulled on the black hood, but then realizing he had not offered Gin Pon a last opportunity to speak, removed the cap. When the prisoner declined to speak the cap was pulled on once more and the sheriff stepped to the side rail, where the lever was tied in place. He loosened the cord, moved the lever, and the trap was sprung thirty seconds after 12:03 P.M. Drs. Byrne and Kimball, assisted by Dr. D. C. Newman, stepped beneath the scaffold into a pit a foot deep, which had been dug as a precaution, and the condemned's toes dangled three inches off the ground. As the body swung around Gin Pon's toes brushed small clumps of dirt and rock left on the floor of the pit. There was a slight tremor of the dying man's feet, a jerk of the left leg, and a slight movement of his arms but as soon as the body was motionless the doctors, pocket watches in hand, began recording Gin Pon's pulse. At twelve minutes the pulse ceased and a minute later the doctors examined the heart and found no beat. Four minutes later Dr. Kimball said, "I pronounce him dead. Doctors?" Dr. Byrne responded, "So say I, Doctors," and Dr. Newman replied, "I concur, Doctors." The body was lifted up by undertaker Gilman and deputy sheriff Ferguson while the rope was cut a few inches above the knot by deputy sheriff Rutherford. The body was then lowered into a black coffin, the lid attached, and Gin Pon's remains were taken out the east gate where an ambulance waited. The body was driven to Gilman and Walborn's undertaking establishment on East Riverside Avenue. In the evening the attending physicians performed an autopsy and determined that the condemned man's neck had been broken, the vertebrae separating an inch just below the base of the brain, so that death had been instantaneous. They also found that consumption of the bowels had set in and Gin Pon's remaining days were very few, in any case. Funeral services were conducted for Gin Pon the following day by the Reverend Lee To, followed immediately by his burial paid for by the Chinese population.

Seattle Daily Times (WA): April 30, 1897. *Spokesman Review* (Spokane, WA): April 24, 1897, April 27–28, 1897, April 30, 1897, May 1, 1897.

Leonard, John
March 25, 1898

On July 5, 1896, thirty-five-year-old John Leonard, alias John Dillon or James Lawrence, was released from the penitentiary at Walla Walla, Washington, where he had completed two years of a three year sentence for burglary. He was given a new suit of clothes, a ticket to Lewiston, and $10 to start him off on his return into society. Leonard reached Riparia too late to catch the boat to Lewiston and had to wait overnight. He took the Texas Ferry across the Snake River into Whitman County and went to the saloon of Jacob Malquist, an eighty-six-year-old Swede who had worked the steamboats on the upper Columbia and Snake Rivers for thirty years before retiring to become a saloon owner.

Leonard was in the company of the telegraph operator and some men employed in the ship yards and the party, with the saloon keeper, played cards for drinks. The stakes increased until Leonard was down fifty cents, when the other men went back to Riparia and left him alone with Malquist, and the two men continued playing cards. Later that evening two men went to the saloon for drinks and found Malquist lying dead on the floor, his head crushed in by a piece of firewood. The saloon keeper's watch, revolver, and pants with seven dollars in the pockets were missing. Leonard had been the only customer during the afternoon and a search was organized. At 7:00 P.M. Leonard was found a mile from the saloon, lying off the trail asleep on the sand behind a sagebrush. The watch was never found but the revolver was found lying near Leonard, and the fugitive wore the dead man's pants with Malquist's seven dollars still in the pockets.

Leonard was arrested and confined in a boat house until a deputy sheriff from Colfax took him there and lodged him in jail. Leonard claimed he had killed Malquist in self-defense and said the other men "put up a hand on him" and won fifty cents. He said that after they left he, being an expert card player, was determined to get his money back. He said he had won back one dollar from Malquist when he showed his winning cards from the next hand, and Malquist accused him of cheating and reached for the money. Leonard said he was quicker and grabbed the money from the table and Malquist reached for his revolver. He said that he grabbed a stick of stove wood and struck the old man on the arm, knocking the gun down, then struck him on the head once killing him. He could not, or would not, explain why Malquist had been badly beaten on the head from behind, nor why there was no evidence of an injury to the dead man's arm or hand, nor why he had stolen the items found in his possession.

Leonard was tried in mid–August and the prosecution's theory was that the old man was sleeping at a table in the saloon when Leonard struck the fatal blows from behind for the purpose of robbery. The state prevailed and Leonard was convicted of first degree murder on May 17. Judge E. H. Sullivan sentenced the defendant to hang on September 25 but his appointed attorneys, John Pattison and U. L. Ettinger, served notice of an appeal to the state Supreme Court, so a stay of execution was granted. The appeal was never perfected so on May 18, 1897, it was dismissed. On May 24 Leonard appeared before Judge William McDonald, who re-sentenced him to hang on July 2. In June Leonard had secured the services of Attorneys Del C. Smith and J. E. Fenton of Spokane, using seventy-five dollars sent by his sister, and they carried the case to the federal court asking Judge C. H. Hanford for a writ of habeas corpus. The application was denied but permission was granted to appeal to the U.S. Supreme Court. The execution was again delayed and Sheriff Robert A. Sims, who had good reason to believe the people of Colfax might lynch Leonard out of frustration with the legal system, moved his prisoner to the jail in Spokane. The appeal to the U.S. Supreme Court was never perfected so, on December 4, 1897, the case was remanded back to the federal appellate court from which the appeal had been taken, and in due course this order reached the Superior Court. On February 21, 1898, the prisoner was taken before Judge McDonald and for the third time he was sentenced to hang, the date set for Friday, March 25, 1898.

Leonard held up well during his confinement, but once all hope was lost and that fatal moment neared he began to break down. On March 24 he prepared a written statement but was too nervous to read it, so it was handed to the press. He repeated his claim of self-defense, his inability to get a fair trial, and his charges of perjury, and he insisted he had been hounded to death by prejudice. The *Spokesman-Review* said of the statement, "Every line of the letter betrays the extreme nervousness of the writer. His mental condition is judged by the incoherency of his sentences." During the last evening David Drizzell, a family friend from Sunset, visited the prisoner but Leonard would not allow him to speak of family affairs, and Drizzell left after an hour. The prisoner spent a sleepless night, arising several times to pace his cell, and when the guard changed at midnight Leonard asked deputy sheriff Robert Matlock to forgive harsh words spoken the previous evening. He said, "Bob, I hate to die knowing that you believe I am a thief and murderer," and Matlock reminded the prisoner that it was a jury of twelve men who had found him guilty, and this seemed to hurt Leonard.

At 8:00 A.M. Father Kearns was admitted for religious consultation and at 9:00 A.M. Leonard confessed and received holy communion. He whispered to the priest, "I don't know how I can bear up." The priest then left and a large and varied breakfast was served, but Leonard could eat only sparingly, and at 9:30 the barber arrived. The prisoner was taken into the jail corridor where the barber's chair had been placed and he was handcuffed to it by jailor Treff while guards Payne and Coffman stood close by. While he was being shaved he said to barber L. E. Taggart that he still held out hope for some intervention. Next, Lucy Hogan, daughter of Colonel Hogan of Colfax, visited and asked to speak privately with the prisoner, but this request was denied. She then asked to be allowed on the scaffold, but this request was also denied. At 11:00 A.M. Father Kearns returned, dressed in his sacerdotal robes, and prayed with the condemned man until 1:20 P.M. when the prisoner was told to prepare for the gallows.

At noon people began to gather in front of the courthouse and on the hill to the east, and by 1:00 P.M. more than one thousand people were in attendance. Inside the jail the death warrant was read as Leonard noticeably weakened, so three doses of morphine were administered. He exited the jail and walked quickly up the stairs with Father Kearns on one arm and death watch guard G. B. Payne on the other. Leonard handed a paper to the priest who read his final, brief statement and when finished Father Kearns whispered directions to Leonard, and he took his place on the trapdoor facing the jail where the prisoners were crowded at the windows. He shook hands with those on the platform and then his wrists and ankles were bound, the noose was adjusted, and the black hood was pulled on. Father Kearns stepped forward and lifted the hood so Leonard could kiss the crucifix and repeat with the priest, "Into they hands, oh Lord, I place my soul. Accept my soul, Lord Jesus." The crucifix was placed in the prisoner's right hand and he said, "Good-bye, brothers and sisters. Good-bye all. I am an innocent man."

The priest then pulled the hood down again and stepped back as Sheriff Sims untied the cord securing the release lever. Charles Bass, editor of the *People's Advocate*, started down the stairs and said, "Good-bye, Jack," and Leonard replied, "Good-bye, Charley." In that moment, at 1:29 P.M., the trap was sprung and the prisoner dropped seven feet. The knot, which had been so carefully positioned behind the left ear, slipped behind but still dislocated Leonard's vertebrae at the base of the brain. Drs. J. Cooper of Farmington, D. Clark of Garfield, John S. Powell of Pullman, and R. C. Coffee, Albert E. Stuht and W. A. Mitchell of Colfax surrounded the body and recorded the pulse of the dying man, and in ten minutes pronounced him dead. At 1:43 P.M. the body was cut down and a prayer was offered as Leonard's remains were deposited into his coffin, and then removed to the courthouse basement, where the physicians made a thorough examination. From the basement the coffin was carried out and placed in a hearse in the charge of undertaker Hail and driven directly to the Colfax cemetery. A brief funeral service was conducted by Father Kearns and Father Dwyer of the DeSmet Mission, and then Leonard was buried at the expense of the Catholic church.

Seattle Daily Times (WA): March 25, 1898. *Spokesman-Review* (Spokane, WA): March 25–26, 1898.

Webster, George
March 30, 1900

George Webster arrived in Cheney, Spokane County, Washington, on May 2, 1897. He was a farmhand, and made a pretense of looking for work, but spent his time in the company of saloon patrons, particularly a man named Arnold, and on May 5 they were labeled undesirables and ordered to leave town. Webster had worked on the Aspland farm in 1896 so he went there and asked to spend the night. He had with him a flask of whiskey and shared it with Mr. Aspland, and after the flask was empty the family retired. Mr. Aspland, his young son and Webster shared the bedroom off the kitchen while Lize Aspland bedded down in the kitchen with her two daughters.

During the night Webster arose three times and went into the kitchen under the pretense that he wanted a drink of water, and by the third trip he had built up his confidence to make improper proposals to Lize Aspland. She flew into a rage and drove Webster from the house, and locked the door behind him. Webster went around to the kitchen window and said he would not leave the farm until he got his hat and coat, which were hanging on a nail in the kitchen, so Mrs. Aspland lowered the top sash of the window and passed them out.

She had just stepped back from the window when Webster drew a revolver and fired once at her through the open sash, and the bullet struck Mrs. Aspland's left side three inches below her navel. Mr. Aspland arose at the sound of the shot and thought the wound was not serious, so Webster was allowed to re-enter the house and go directly into the back bedroom while Mrs. Aspland returned to her daughters on the kitchen bed.

During the night the wound festered so in the morning Mr. Aspland went to Cheney for the doctor and the authorities. When they returned they found Mrs. Aspland writhing in pain and groaning on the kitchen bed while Webster still slept in the next room. Webster was arrested and, at the direction of the doctor, Mrs. Aspland was taken to Cheney where it was found that the bullet had caused serious injury to internal organs. Mrs. Aspland lingered for several days, during which time she made an ante-mortem statement naming Webster as her assailant, and she died on May 8.

Webster had been lodged in jail and on May 13 an information was filed charging him with murder. He was tried at the fall term of the District Court and on September 25, 1897, he was found guilty of first degree murder. An appeal was taken to the state Supreme Court and the judgment and sentence was affirmed after nearly twenty months' delay. Webster was then re-sentenced to hang on July 28, 1899, but a few hours before the execution Judge L. H. Prather revoked the death warrant because an appeal had been filed with the U.S. Supreme Court. This appeal was never perfected so it was dismissed and Judge Prather then set the date of execution for March 30, 1900.

On the day before the execution Sheriff C. A. Cole had all the windows of the jail and courthouse covered with canvas so that no unauthorized spectators could find a vantage point, and he assigned a force of eight men to keep the area clear of spectators. Those who had invitations were instructed to be at the Mallon Avenue entrance to the jail before 11:00 A.M., as the jail would be locked at that time, and thereafter there would be no admittance. Drs. H. M. Martin and D. L. Smith were notified that they would have the duty of pronouncing death. The scaffold was in readiness and fully tested and the high fence enclosing the scaffold was installed and had been thoroughly inspected for gaps or knot holes.

Webster assumed a pleasant attitude on his final day and spent much of his time conversing with his death watch guard, John Dimmick, with fellow prisoner William Freundt, or with his religious advisors, Dean Perine and Captain McClelland. A representative of the *Spokesman-Review* visited and Webster said he wanted to thank everyone who had showed him kindness, declared he was innocent, insisted he would die game, and said he believed in the hereafter as preached by the Episcopal Church. He ate a hearty supper at 5:30 P.M. The sheriff visited and, after he left, Webster talked with his evening death watch guard, J. W. Webdell, as he smoked several cigars and ate candy and nuts. He retired at 10:30 P.M. but talked to his death watch for half an hour before falling asleep, then slept soundly throughout the night. The prisoner awoke at 6:45 A.M. and had a warm greeting for his guard, then dressed in his dark suit, white shirt with lay-down collar and white four-in-hand tie, into which he carefully inserted a scarf pin. He ordered the lightest breakfast he had eaten since his incarceration, but he ate it with relish. While eating he talked with Webdell until 7:00, when Dimmick relieved the night guard. He told Dimmick he would see no one but the sheriff and his religious advisors, and McClelland arrived shortly and spent several hours with the prisoner, praying and discussing religious matters. When defense attorneys Del Carey Smith and James Crotty arrived he said he would see them.

At 9:00 A.M. Sheriff Cole entered the cell and read the death warrant and, after the sheriff concluded, Dean Perine was admitted and the door was closed so that the two men could be in religious seclusion until the time for the execution. The last sacrament was administered during that time and Webster braced-up. He requested that his body not be put on display and Perine promised he would see to it. A large crowd began to assemble at an early hour trying to find some viewpoint, but there was no place from which to view the execution, so the people began to mass on Madison Street and Mallon Avenue. Many men crowded around the Mallon Avenue entrance to the jail asking for tickets and besieging the doorkeepers for some way to gain entrance, but only officers were allowed access until 10:30 A.M., when the doors were swung open and the jail yard quickly filled with two hundred fifty men. There was a roped in area around the scaffold with separate areas reserved for the doctors and for the visiting sheriffs and deputies. There was an awning covering the scaffold to protect it from the slight mist that fell that morning, but the sun broke through the cloud cover before 11:00. The scaffold, on the south side of the jail, was in the shade of the building with the rope and nine coils of the hangman's knot dangling.

At 11:00 A.M. the jail doors were locked and Webster's cell door was opened and the prisoner walked out with Dean Perine, and the procession formed. Sheriff Cole led the way and as he appeared in the courtyard he bared his head, and all present followed his example. Dean Perine came next with the prisoner close behind his religious advisor; deputies Henry Desgranges and F. K. Pugh came next with Captain McClelland and Drs. Benjamin R. Freeman, H. M. Martin and D. L. Smith in the rear. The prisoner mounted the scaffold and was told to turn around when he paused facing the wrong direction. The sheriff asked if he had anything to say and Webster replied, "No, I don't believe I do." Sheriff Cole nodded to Dean Perine and he read the commendatory prayer, and when this first prayer ended deputies Desgranges and Pugh arranged the upper body straps and then Perine shook hands with the prisoner and bid him goodbye, followed by Captain McClelland who whispered words of encouragement.

Webster was led onto the trapdoor where the leg straps were applied by the deputies and the black hood was pulled on by Desgranges, and the noose was adjusted by Pugh. Perine offered a last prayer commending the spirit of the condemned man to the mercy of God and at the conclusion of the prayer, at 11:07 A.M., the lever was thrown and Webster's body dropped. There followed a gurgling and gasping sound but the condemned man's neck had been broken in the fall. The attending physicians stepped forward beneath the scaffold and reported that the pulse ceased at eleven and one half minutes and the heart stopped beating two minutes later, and Webster was pronounced dead. The body hung twenty-one minutes more before it was cut down and given to undertaker Gilman. The black hood was removed and there was a slight bluish tinge to his lips and a small abrasion under the chin. A burial plot had been provided by friends and he was buried the following day, after a brief graveside service by Dean Perine.

Seattle Daily Times (WA): March 30, 1900. *Spokesman-Review* (Spokane, WA): March 30, 1900.

Michaud, Albert
April 6, 1900

Albert Michaud married Julia Murat in Wisconsin in 1887, and soon afterward revealed himself to be a drunkard and wife-abuser, squandering his money and beating his wife whenever he was intoxicated. Two years after the marriage, Rosalie Murat, Julia's mother, moved to Tacoma, Washington, and in 1890 she sent funds for her daughter to bring her granddaughter Annie and move to Tacoma. Michaud stayed in Wisconsin for two years, with little word of his family and providing no support, but in 1892 he moved to Tacoma and promised to reform. They reconciled but soon he had degenerated to his former condition so Julia left him again and found employment as a nurse at the Fannie Paddock Hospital.

In 1896 Michaud went to the hospital, called his wife to the door, and as soon as she appeared he began to shoot at her. One bullet passed through her cheek and ranged upward, taking out her left eye, and part of the bullet lodged in her brain. The wound was so horrible that Michaud was certain he had killed her, so he turned the gun on himself and fired through his own cheek, the bullet ranging upward and taking out his right eye. However, they both recovered and Michaud was tried for assault, convicted, and sent to the penitentiary for four years. After a deduction of six months for good behavior he was released during the summer of 1899 and he went directly to Oregon, where he again intended to reform.

In the meantime Julia Michaud had divorced Albert and married John Ambler. Ambler was a respected citizen of Tacoma and had made a home at South Tenth and Q Streets for his new wife, his step-daughter Annie, and his mother-in-law Rosalie Murat. Michaud was back in Tacoma within a month and drinking as heavily as ever, and his friends encouraged him to leave Tacoma and stay out of the lives of Julia and his daughter. However, he insisted that Julia was still his wife and that the divorce was nugatory and void. He went to the Ambler neighborhood several times to visit his daughter, which was accomplished at the house of a friend of Julia Ambler. One day he went to the Ambler house and tried to call out Julia but she refused to meet him at the gate and refused him admittance. He later admitted he would have killed her then if she had come out to talk.

On September 27, 1899, at 6:00 P.M. Michaud went to the Ambler home and forced entry. Julia Ambler dashed out of the back door screaming for help but Michaud was close behind and fired his revolver at her. The first bullet passed through her body, but she continued to run around the outside of the house, ran through the front gate, and collapsed in the street fifty yards from her front door. Michaud, who had fired at her several times, walked up to the wounded woman and shot her twice at close range, killing her instantly. He then tried to shoot himself but he was out of ammunition so the firing pin snapped on an expended casing. Two neighbors captured Michaud and he was lodged in jail and charged with murdering his ex-wife. Michaud was tried at the fall term of the District Court, convicted of first degree murder and sentenced to hang. Motions for a new trial, appeals and petitions delayed the execution for several months but finally the date was set for April 6, 1900. While he was in jail he asked that his daughter visit him, and he blamed Sheriff A. U. Mills when she refused to come; but his daughter had seen her father shoot down her mother and said he was a brute and she would not visit him.

On his final morning the prisoner arose early and dressed in a neat black coat, vest, gray trousers, white shirt with standing collar, and white tie. Sheriff Mills read the death warrant at 5:00 A.M. while Father Peter Hylebos provided support. It was supposed that Michaud would have attempted self-destruction had it not been for the priest's constant attention and support over the final weeks. The execution was to be held within a room thirty feet by fifty feet divided by a railing around the gallows. All doors to the second story were locked and access was only possible by elevator. The scaffold was twenty feet high and twelve feet square with the four by four foot trapdoor in the center, and the platform was reached by thirteen steps. The release was a spring trigger activated by the foot of the sheriff, and the drop was set at six feet.

One hundred fifty witnesses were assembled in the room before 7:00 A.M. and at 7:05 the condemned man entered with Sheriff Mills leading, deputy sheriffs Ben Davis and Thomas Maloney escorting the prisoner, and Father Hylebos close behind. The sheriff waved his hand, a pre-arranged signal, and all hats were removed. The condemned man was so cool that many of those who did not know him were not sure who was about to be hanged, but after he was on the platform he stepped forward and said, "I am face to face with death, and after murder the best thing is capital punishment. My errors are many," then he spoke incoherently about his ex-wife before he concluded, "That's all, good-bye to all." As he spoke his confidence abandoned him so by the time he stepped back onto the trapdoor his knees were shaking noticeably. Father Hylebos stood close by his side in support and the two men prayed together in whispers, which seemed to give the prisoner strength. The priest offered a crucifix, which the condemned man kissed, but he seemed almost oblivious to everything about him.

Deputy Maloney bound his wrists and ankles, adjusted the noose, and pulled on the black hood. The priest said loudly, "Are you satisfied?" but the reply could not be heard through the cloth of the cap. Sheriff Mills sprang the trap at 7:12 A.M. and the prisoner fell six feet, breaking his neck. Drs. F. Schug, H. Smith, M. Harrison and S. P. Brown later said that all body sensation was instantly gone, but there were several slight convulsions during the first four minutes. The doctors recorded the pulse and at fifteen minutes they pronounced him dead. The body hung until 7:47 A.M. when it was cut down and placed in a coffin. He was buried later that day.

Seattle Daily Times (WA): April 6, 1900.

Stickles, Martin
January 25, 1901

William B. Shanklin lived alone on a farm near Kelso in Cowlitz County. In November 1899 he was sitting at his table having supper when he was shot through a window and killed instantly. His house was ransacked, everything of value stolen, and the house burned to the ground with the body inside. The crime remained a mystery for over a year until, on November 28, 1900, Cornelius Knapp and his wife, an aged couple living near Castle Rock, were shot through the window of their home while at their table having supper and the house was set afire. Similarities in the crimes led authorities to believe that they were committed by the same person.

Martin Stickles lived on a scow at the mouth of the Cowlitz River and shortly after the Knapp murders his movements became noticeably suspicious. Sheriff A. F. Kirby of Cowlitz County and detective Samuel Simmons of Portland arrested him on suspicion and found Shanklin's watch and keys in his pockets. Stickles maintained his innocence for a time but finally made a partial confession implicating his neighbor, Edward Pierce. He admitted being present at both crimes but denied shooting the victims. After it became known that he had made the admissions of involvement there were threats of lynching, so Stickles was moved to the jail at Tacoma. He joined the Salvation Army and soon afterward made a full confession to being the sole killer of all three people and admitted his motive was robbery.

At his trial Stickles pled not guilty and his defense was that he had inherited a criminal disposition and was helpless to resist committing heinous crimes, so therefore he was not accountable for his actions. His mother testified that before her son's birth she was of a surly and morose disposition and that her child was born sick and was always an unnatural child. The trial took only one day and the jurors deliberated one hour before finding Stickles guilty of first degree murder, and he was sentenced to die on January 25, 1901. Neither appeal nor application for executive clemency intervened.

The prisoner slept soundly his final night but was only able to eat a moderate breakfast. At 9:30 A.M. on Friday, January 25, Sheriff Elmer Huntington, with ex–Sheriff A. L. Watson, read the death warrant to the condemned man in his cell. At 9:40 the two sheriffs took the prisoner from his cell and marched him to the scaffold, which had been erected in the jail yard. Once on the platform he said to the crowd, "Gentlemen, I bid you good-bye. God help me and bless you all." While he talked the two lawmen were busy pinioning his wrists and ankles and when that was concluded J. M. Bush adjusted the noose and pulled on the black hood.

The prisoner, through the dark cloth, began singing "Jesus, Lover of My Soul," but when Watson gave the signal Huntington sprang the trap and Stickles, mid-song, dropped six and one half feet. The force of the fall not only broke his neck, it partially severed his head from his shoulders, and blood flowed over his garments in streams. Still, it took four minutes for his pulse to cease and for Drs. McLaren, Levering, and R. E. Darnell to pronounce him dead. After hanging a few minutes longer the body was cut down and turned over to relatives for burial at Catlin on Saturday.

Seattle Daily Times (WA): January 25, 1901.

Boyce, Eben
August 9, 1901

Eben Boyce was thirty-six years old and thought to be a musical prodigy. He could play the coronet and trombone with amazing dexterity and the town's bandmaster, Julius Adler, said he had never met a man during his career who was Boyce's equal on those instruments. Boyce had adroit methods of manipulation which even astonished expert musicians. He was a member of the Tacoma Military Band, but he suffered from terrible stage fright and when facing an audience his music was barely mediocre. When he was alone, however, he could play with such inspiration that those who heard him said it was nearly supernatural. Boyce had a weakness for intoxicants and during his life he had used opium and other narcotics, drank absinthe and liquor, and while a soldier in the Philippines drank a native drink which caused the rapid deterioration of a man's health and morals.

Boyce married and he and his wife had trouble for several months at the end of 1899, and as a consequence she left him and tried to make her own way by taking a job as cashier at the Domestic Bakery on the corner of A and Tenth Streets. In early January, Boyce went to Victoria using money he obtained by pawning his trombone. He wrote to his wife and friends several times asking them to take the instrument out of hock and send it to him, but no one would even write back. Boyce, in a nervous frenzy, returned to Tacoma from Victoria on the evening of February 10, 1900, and went straight from the Victoria boat to the Domestic Bakery and as soon as he opened the door to the restaurant he began to fire a pistol at his wife, who was standing at the cashier's counter a few feet from the door. She was desperately wounded but turned and ran into the dining room reserved for women. Boyce followed and when she collapsed onto the floor from loss of blood, writhing in pain and groaning, he walked up to her, placed the muzzle of his pistol against her side, and shot her through the body, and she died instantly. There was pandemonium in the restaurant and Boyce saw his opportunity to escape, but the police had already been called and they arrested him without incident as soon as he came out the front door. They took him to the city jail and, on the way, he reviled his dead wife and attributed his situation to her actions.

When his trial began at the spring term his attorneys pled insanity, but the evidence was deemed inconclusive and he was found guilty of first degree murder and on April 26, 1900, he was sentenced to hang. The case was appealed to the state Supreme Court, which stayed the execution, but the justices later upheld the lower court's judgment and sentence. However, in the meantime, the Republican Legislature so muddled the capital punishment law by passing the Rand Act that Judge William H. Snell refused to issue the death warrant. The matter was again taken to the state Supreme Court and on June 10, 1901, it issued a mandate commanding Judge Snell to "fix and appoint a day for the execution," and he set August 9, 1901. The legislature met again on June 11, and so tampered with the law that Boyce's attorneys found new grounds for an appeal; but every effort, among the many other appeals submitted, was denied.

Boyce's last night was restless and he arose the next morning determined to join the Catholic Church, and Father Peter Hylebos came at 5:00 A.M. to baptize him and administer the sacrament to the new convert. The death warrant was read to him in his cell before 7:00 A.M. and the procession to the gallows started with Sheriff John Hartman leading.

The scaffold had been erected in the attic of the courthouse on the west side and two hundred witnesses were in place at an early hour, as they had expected the hanging to occur at 6:30 A.M. As Boyce entered the room he leaned heavily on Father Hylebos and when he climbed the thirteen steps his hands clutched convulsively at the railing, more pulling himself up then climbing. Awaiting his arrival on the platform were six lawmen and Father George A. Oswald. Once upon the platform he showed no interest in the crowd and concentrated on the directions of Sheriff Hartman and, when prompted, said, "I have nothing to say. I came here to be murdered, not to make a speech. Hartman will take care of my body and Father Hylebos will take care of the rest of me. I was a soldier in the Philippines and I am a soldier still."

After he concluded he took a step backward and centered himself on the trapdoor, as if to say he was ready, but swayed so noticeably that he required support to keep standing. He kept up a running monologue of jerky sentences while his wrists and ankles were bound, then said, "Ain't that a dirty way to treat a soldier?" and when one of the spectators laughed he said, "To the rubbernecks I have nothing to say." Next came the black hood and Boyce said, "Where is the rest of it?" Father Hylebos then whispered a few words to the prisoner and he responded, "Yes, I will, to please you," and kissed the crucifix. The noose was then placed around his neck, positioned and cinched, and he complained, "Don't choke me to death before I'm dead."

Boyce was still making jests from under the hood when the trap was sprung at 7:03 A.M., and after the body fell there was one convulsive spasm before hanging motionless. In fourteen minutes his heart ceased to beat and Dr. E. M. Brown pronounced him dead, in concurrence with Drs. F. J. Stuart, A. J. Parker, F. R. Hill, Eigholz, and Hoff. The body was cut down, placed in a coffin, and released to Sheriff Hartman, and Boyce was buried in the Catholic cemetery later that day following a brief service by Fathers Hylebos and Oswald.

Seattle Daily Times (WA): August 9, 1901.

Nordstrom, Charles W.
August 23, 1901

On November 21, 1891, Charles W. Nordstrom, a Swedish immigrant who spoke no English, applied for work at the farm of Thomas Mason near Cedar Mountain. Thomas was then cultivating two large tracts of land with the help of his two sons and several farmhands. He needed a ditch dug so he had his eldest son, twenty-year-old Willie, hire Nordstrom for the job. Nordstrom finished the job on November 25 but when he was paid by Willie he felt the amount insufficient, and voiced his displeasure. Willie said he would speak to his father and left and while he was gone Nordstrom told another farmhand that, should the Masons fail to pay him what he felt he deserved, he would kill the boy. Nordstrom then, apparently anticipating a refusal, left for Seattle. In a short while Willie returned with additional money but Nordstrom was nowhere to be found. Nordstrom went first to Renton where he bought a supply of whiskey, which he drank all the way to Seattle. As soon as he was in the city he went straight to the gun shop of Hardy and Hall and bought a Winchester rifle and cartridges before continuing his drinking spree. He arose late the next morning and started back to the Mason farm, but in his hung-over condition he forgot his cartridges. When he got to Renton he stopped to buy more cartridges but could only find cartridges for a Springfield rifle, but he found these could work in his Winchester. He bought several cartridges and continued on to the Mason farm, arriving during the evening hours of November 27, the day before Thanksgiving.

He snuck up to the house and peered in the window where he found the Mason family and friends gathered around the supper table. Nordstrom took careful aim and fired one shot, the bullet striking Willie Mason in his heart killing him instantly. Nordstrom took off at a run for the woods, leaving a clear trail of foot prints from his rubber boots in the soft earth. Soon the murderer realized that it would be too easy to follow him so he took off the boots, carried them along, and continued in his stocking feet. This trail of foot prints was as easy to follow as the boot tracks, and a party in pursuit followed them right to the door of Ismay's cabin. Ismay had been away so the men entered and found the rubber boots, and realized that the murderer had exchanged them for a pair of leather soled boots, one of which had a peculiar patch in the sole and was also easy to follow. The trail then led the posse to Gilman, where Nordstrom had stocked up on ham, cheese and crackers, then continued out of town a short distance to the abandoned Lindsey cabin. The fugitive had made that place his headquarters but he did not take up residence in the cabin but rather in the woods nearby. He would return to the cabin only when hungry, and in this way he was captured when he returned for food. He was still wearing the leather boots with the queer patch on one sole, and later would claim that the rubber boots were not his, and proved they could be worn by a man with a larger foot size.

He was lodged in jail to await his examination and was held over for the grand jury. He was indicted, tried, convicted, and sentenced to hang, all within two weeks of the murder, and then began the lengthy appeals process. On August 20, 1901, Colonel James H. Lewis, Nordstrom's attorney, argued before the state Supreme Court trying to overturn the decision of Judge Hanford's denial of a writ of habeas corpus. When that failed he argued that Nordstrom was insane, but when prosecuting attorney Fulton arose to address the court Judge Bell said he did not need to hear from him, as he had decided, based upon his own observations, that the prisoner was sane. Bell said the court would not issue a stay of execution and declined to interfere in any way with the execution of Nordstrom. Lewis had been tireless in his efforts to obtain a new trial for Nordstrom, or at least have the sentence commuted to life in prison. He had the case before the state Supreme Court three times, before the U.S. Circuit Court three times, appeared at three hearings in the King County Superior Court, and argued three times before the U.S. Supreme Court. In all, his "pettifogging tactics" had delayed justice for ten years and outraged many in the press and the public.

After the prisoner was notified of the decision he was visited by several friends, and for the first time he broke down and wept. That evening he was visited by two Swedish ministers who left at 6:00 P.M., and during the remainder of the evening he was sullen and morose. He lay down at 8:00 P.M. and slept restlessly for an hour, then paced his cell for two hours before retiring for a restless night. He arose at 6:00 A.M., when the *Star* reporter arrived to interview him, and fifteen minutes later a breakfast of beefsteak, potatoes, toast and coffee was served. He then began to dress in his burial clothes and at 7:15 he was taken from his cell and told the judge was waiting above to see him, and the death watch guards escorted him up to the courthouse floor. He turned to enter the courtroom as he had done so many times before, but he was told to go up the narrow staircase into the garret. He found a cot positioned in an alcove and he was ordered to sit and rest, and in broken English he asked, "This is not the courtroom. Where is the judge?" One of the guards responded, "He'll be here pretty soon, Charley," and this seemed to satisfy him. However, he soon became restless and began to pace and, when Catholic Father Neata arrived, he declined his services. Nordstrom was asked who he would like to see and he said, "The Salvation Army girls," and he was soon joined by Captain Agnes Peterson and Lieutenant Louisa Peterson. He then requested a package of candy he had left in his cell and it was brought, but by the time of its arrival he was sobbing uncontrollably and being comforted by the women. He had sensed that the gallows was nearby, and he was right, as it was just behind him and screened by a thin board partition, and he asked to see it but this request was denied. Swedish minister Larsen and Baptist minister Johnson then joined Nordstrom in his alcove in preparation for reading the death warrant.

At 8:00 A.M. Sheriff Edward Cudihee

arrived and asked Nordstrom if he thought he could understand as he read the warrant, and Nordstrom said he could not, but the sheriff took a seat and slowly and deliberately read the warrant to the condemned man. As soon as the sheriff began to read Nordstrom took off his coat and the sheriff coaxed him to keep his coat on, but he complained it was too hot, and then took off his tie and collar as well. At 8:20 A.M. the reading was complete and the sheriff retired from the alcove. The ministers were joined by the Reverend E. O. Falk of the Swedish M and E Church and they knelt and prayed, and when they arose a newspaper man asked regarding a confession. The Reverend Larsen said, "Nordstrom confesses nothing. He still insists, as he has insisted to me time and again through all these years, that he has committed no crime. 'Why,' he asks, 'do they want to kill me when I never killed anyone.'" As they talked the Salvation Army women were joined by two Salvation Army soldiers with instruments and the quartet then played and sang hymns, beginning with "There is a Home in Heaven."

At 9:20 A.M. the order was given and deputy Clark began to admit the one hundred witnesses, who filed in quietly and took their places. The moment had arrived and the deputy sheriffs entered the alcove and told Nordstrom to rise. Instead he lay back and grabbed onto the cot, refusing to let go, and began sobbing and begging piteously to be saved. Three times the officers got him to his feet and tried to put on his coat, only to have him sink back and struggle against their efforts. Finally they got his coat on but he threw himself on the floor and cried out for God to save him from his fate. One of the Salvation Army women told him, "Bear up, Nordstrom," but he ignored her. It was then suggested that another song might calm him, but the hour set for the execution had already passed so it was decided to carry him onto the scaffold. It took four strong men to restrain the prisoner and carry him into the death chamber, up the stairs and onto the platform. Sheriff Cudihee had anticipated that Nordstrom might break down completely and had a "collapse board" laid out with straps attached. The prisoner was laid down on the board on his back and the straps were applied to his chest, arms, knees and ankles. He was then raised up and stood on the trapdoor where the noose was quickly adjusted about his neck and the black hood pulled on, and all the while the prisoner sobbed and pleaded to be saved, interspersed with curses for those about to do their duty. His last words were, "Are they going to kill me? Oh, my God, help me! Lord Jesus help!"

At 9:50 A.M. the trap was sprung and Nordstrom dropped five feet, five inches to his death, breaking his neck in the fall. Coroner B. E. Hoye assisted by Dr. G. M. Horton monitored vital signs and in ten minutes pronounced Nordstrom dead. Five other doctors were in attendance as observers: Drs. Bortes, Hoffman, Hinkle, Richter, and Laurie. They saw that the noose had slipped during the drop and slipped further as he hung lifeless, but Dr. Hoye was certain that, with the added weight of the board, his neck had been broken at the head of the spinal column, and the autopsy conducted at 9:00 A.M. the following day confirmed this. Nordstrom's funeral was paid for by the Swedish population in Seattle and the service was set for 3:00 P.M. Sunday, to be conducted by the Swedish clergy assisted by the Salvation Army. Following the service the remains of Nordstrom were driven to Lakeview Cemetery and buried.

Seattle Daily Times (WA): August 21, 1901. *Seattle Star* (WA): August 23, 1901. *Bulletin* (Seattle, WA): August 24, 1901.

Green, James C.
December 6, 1901

Edson V. Benjamin was born in Ohio in 1864. He lived in Indiana, married in Nebraska, and found work in Oregon. He first worked in a distillery in Troutdale until it burned down, then he took a position at a distillery in Grants, Oregon. When it closed he moved to The Dalles and then to Hood River, where he bought a farm. He left his wife on the farm and went to Underwoods, Skamania County, Washington, where he was logging for Nickolai and Cameron. In March it was decided to move the logging operation upriver several miles, and the people of Underwoods on Saturday night, March 23, threw a going away party for Benjamin and for the two ladies who cooked for the loggers. At midnight the third group of six went into the house of William Wendorf to eat, the table being too small to accommodate everyone at once, while the remainder of the people danced in the barn. The group of six had eaten and talked for forty-five minutes when a contest was proposed over which cake was better, the white or the brown, and Benjamin was elected to choose.

Benjamin had not yet sampled the white cake and a piece was served. As he lifted his coffee to his lips to clear his palate a shot was fired through the window. The bullet struck the left side of Benjamin's head, passed entirely through and came out on the right side, then struck Mrs. Brown on the shoulder, and Benjamin died instantly. The room was filled with gun smoke and the people were paralyzed for an instant, but then Mrs. Brown sprang up and blew out the lantern. In a few minutes Billy Jones was sent to the barn to notify Constable Billy Woods and justice of the peace A. J. Haynes of the murder of Benjamin. Haynes believed he would be a witness in the case so he sent for the sheriff, prosecuting attorney and justice of the peace from the county seat at Stevenson. The authorities were delayed because no boats ran on Sunday, so they took the train and arrived just before dusk.

A four person coroner's jury was appointed and they listened to the evidence, after which they found: "We, the jury empanelled [*sic*] to enquire into the cause of death of E. V. Benjamin, find that the said E. V. Benjamin came to his death on the morning of March 24, 1901, from a gunshot wound committed by someone unknown to the jury, but all evidences given before the jury points to James Green as the guilty party."

After the verdict was read the acting coroner made out a warrant for the arrest of James Green. The evidence upon which the warrant was based was that Green was the only known enemy of Benjamin, and he had recently made several threats against Benjamin's life. In early February, Green had gone to the logging camp armed with a rifle and marched Benjamin down the hill to the river at gunpoint. Abraham Ames and Ed Thornton followed and, when Green saw there were witnesses, released his prisoner and allowed him to return to camp. Benjamin, afterwards, said he was certain he was about to be killed. On February 14 Green and Benjamin were at a dance and Green made several threats against Benjamin to other people, but not to Benjamin. Green said Benjamin had talked about him, and that "I am going out of this world, but someone will go ahead of me." James C. Green, according to the *Skamania County Pioneer*, was "a man of great strength, six feet tall and about 200 pounds.... He was a queer mixture of generosity, jealousy, and general cussedness. He would give his last dollar to a friend in need one day and threaten his life for a fancied wrong the next. He once, no doubt, had many good qualities, but he has allowed the bad ones to predominate and this has given his countenance a hang-dog appearance, which is repulsive when in repose."

Green had been staying at the house of B. F. Beals so Sheriff John Totton went there, but Beals said Green had packed his bed and supplies and left and a search proved him right. The sheriff returned the following day, finding that Green had returned to exchange clothes and leave his bed. Beals was arrested as an accessory but he was cleared and released. The search continued for Green, a man who "was thoroughly acquainted with every bridle path and cow trail in that whole country." Several parties went out to search for Green and others took positions to prevent him from leaving the area. On Tuesday Sheriff Totton, George Tyrrell, William Underwood and Abe Ames started for Beals' cabin, hoping to find Green had returned once again. En route one of the men spotted Green hiding behind a tree along the trail and, with four guns pointed at him, the fugitive surrendered without a struggle even though armed with a fully loaded revolver and a vicious hunting knife.

The prisoner was taken before a justice of the peace but he waived an examination and was remanded to the sheriff to await action by the grand jury. Green was indicted and his trial began in Judge Abraham L. Miller's courtroom on April 11, 1901. The defense introduced several motions, including a request for a change of venue and a request for a continuance, but these were denied and the jury was empanelled in two hours, and by 3:00 P.M. the first witness was called. One witness told how Green had gone to her home an hour after the killing and said, "I fixed him. I looked through the window and saw them having a hell of a good time and I shot him." After the court adjourned Green was returned to his cell, where he confessed the crime to the sheriff and asked to talk to the judge, so Judge Miller went to the jail and heard the confession. The next morning Sheriff Totton testified to the capture and then the prosecution rested.

The defense tried to prove that Green had been too intoxicated to premeditate the murder, and called several character witnesses. Mrs. Benjamin was present throughout the trial but when Green took the stand she was required to leave the courtroom. Green admitted to the shooting but claimed he was too drunk to premeditate the crime. He said he saw Benjamin seated near the woman he loved and shot him out of drunken jealousy. The defense was only trying to save the life of their client, never expecting to get an acquittal. The case was submitted to the jurors, who were out less than one hour before returning a verdict of guilty of first degree murder, and Green was sentenced to hang. Appeals followed but the state Supreme Court affirmed the lower court's judgment and sentence. Green's attorneys then submitted an application to Governor John Rogers for executive clemency, but it was denied on October 7, 1901. Even as the governor was rejecting their plea Green's attorneys were claiming they would surely get a new trial, as they had not been given enough time to prepare a defense, but this tactic failed, and nothing further would interfere with the proceedings.

Green, on November 24, had his first look at the gallows when he was placed in the doorway of the jail to provide the barber with sunlight for his last shave. Green had shown no emotion previously and this did not change when he saw the hanging apparatus. On November 26, 1901, the carpenters began work on the enclosure which would surround the gallows, hiding it from public view, and it took up nearly all the space between the jail and the office of the *Skamania County Pioneer* in Stevenson. Green passed his final night peacefully, the only stimulant a cup of tea. He had found religion during his imprisonment and was resigned to his fate, confident in his salvation as he prayed with his religious advisor, the Reverend E. H. Todd of Vancouver.

In the morning the prisoner dressed in his new suit of clothes provided by the county before he ate heartily of the large breakfast served. At 7:45 A.M. he was joined by Sheriff Totton and several witnesses for the reading of the death warrant. Eight minutes later Green stepped from his cell with the sheriff on one side and deputy sheriff Marsh of Vancouver on the other, with the Reverend Todd following close behind. Green mounted the scaffold with a firm step and looked over the crowd before he took his place on the trapdoor. His wrists, arms, and ankles were bound with three straps and then Sheriff Totton asked, "Have you anything to say?" and Green replied "Yes!" The sheriff, with black hood in hand, said, "Then speak," and Green said, "All I have to say is that I stand here not by my own strength, but by the strength of the Lord. He keeps me up. I advise all to change their way of living and be saved, as I have been saved." As Sheriff Totton stepped forward Green said, "Goodbye to everybody," and the hood was pulled over his head.

Totton stepped back at 7:58 A.M., placed his hand on the lever, and in a moment the trap was sprung. Green dropped six feet, breaking his neck, and Drs. August Schroeder and S. A. Locke waited beneath the gallows and monitored his vital signs until they pronounced him dead in eight minutes. Three minutes later Green's body was cut down and deposited in the coffin provided by the county, put into a wagon and driven away. Mrs. Benjamin had come to Stevenson to witness the execution, but she was not allowed to attend.

Immediately after the wagon left the crowd rushed forward in search of souvenirs and the rope was cut into pieces and distributed. The knot was taken by deputy Marsh, who was offered $20 by a collector of hangman's knots, but the money was refused. Meanwhile, the body of Green was taken to the Stevenson Cemetery and buried in an obscure corner, following a brief service by the Reverend Todd.

Skamania County Pioneer (Stevenson, WA): March 28, 1901; April 18, 1901; October 10, 1901; November 28, 1901; December 12, 1901.

Seaton, William A.
January 3, 1902

On December 6, 1900, at 4:00 P.M. William Alden Seaton, who had been in a depressed condition for some time, was chopping wood in the back yard of his home. He said he was suddenly overcome by the desire to kill his sister, Mrs. Roy Clarke, but as he started for the house with axe in hand he saw five-year-old Hazel Hapwood and seven-year-old Myrtle Hapwood playing in the barn. He rushed at them and struck each child one blow to the head. He threw their limp bodies into a manger and again started for the house. His sister was engaged in household duties but when she heard the screams of the children she went out and met her brother, who struck her a terrible blow to the head, and as she fell he struck her another blow to her back. He continued into the house where his uncle, Daniel Richards, was sleeping. He struck him on the head, exposing part of his brain, but his second blow nearly decapitated his uncle. While the murderer was engaged in this deadly act his sister recovered her senses and ran to the neighbor's house to get help.

Word spread quickly and a large party of angry men went to the house and surrounded it, but Seaton had locked and barred the doors. Three men tried to break in but Seaton fired his revolver at them, and neighbor John Kennedy received a minor wound in his back. The party then withdrew, but within a half hour Seaton left the house and started for the sheriff's station, confessing to several friends along the way. As he neared the station he met deputy sheriff Mike Kelly and the deputy ordered him to surrender, but he turned and ran a short distance. He suddenly turned to face his pursuer and fired his pistol at the deputy, who returned fire and wounded Seaton in his neck and he collapsed on the car trestle. Kelly rushed in, disarmed his prisoner, and carried him to the station. He was then taken to Seattle and lodged in jail, where his minor wound was treated by Dr. Emil Borles. The two little girls were treated and then taken to the hospital, where they lingered between life and death before taking a turn for the better; both fully recovered. His sister was also taken to the hospital, where it was found her wounds were not as serious as they first appeared, and she recovered as well.

The body of Richards was taken by Coroner George H. Sparling for the inquest and the coroner's jury brought in a verdict of the willful murder of Daniel Richards by Seaton. The remains of Richards were then delivered to the funeral parlor of Bonney and Stewart. At his examination Seaton was held over for action by the grand jury, he was indicted, tried and convicted of murdering Dan Richards in cold blood. After he was sentenced to hang the appeals process began, and this delayed his execution for a year and a half, but finally the date was set for January 3, 1902. It seemed that all legal maneuvers were exhausted when Seaton's legal counsel, A. G. Speckert, appeared before the state Supreme Court at 10:00 A.M. on January 2, 1902. He presented a petition for a stay of execution, citing California's Mc-

Nulty case, but the court decided not to interfere, referencing Washington's Charles W. Nordstrom case, which experienced a seemingly endless series of delays before his execution on August 23, 1901. Meanwhile, in Olympia, A. N. Mougin carried a petition and affidavits to Governor Henry McBride asking for a respite, but by 2:00 P.M. the governor had decided not to intervene. That evening the *Seattle Star* announced "No Reprieve for Seaton," but this information was kept from the prisoner until the late evening hours.

Sheriff Edward Cudihee, anticipating there would be no interference, had everything in readiness for the execution. The rope was stretched for the last time and the electricians had finished their labors on the new electric release buttons. During the afternoon of January 2 the gallows was tested and worked perfectly. Seaton had remained cheerful most of the time and his mother and sister were allowed to stay with him throughout Thursday late into the evening, but when it came time for their final farewell they all broke down. A photographer had called at the jail several times to take photographs, the last time during the afternoon when he took a keepsake photograph of Seaton with his sister, and she begged him to give her a copy of the photo before her brother's death. The prisoner had given a statement to reporters in the late afternoon hours, professing his innocence. Seaton's mother, Mrs. Larkin, would not surrender and after taking tearful leave of her son boarded the night train to plead with the governor to relent and grant a reprieve or a commutation of the death sentence. The prisoner's brother Lewis and sister Annie were allowed to stay with the prisoner throughout the night, under the watchful eye of the final death watch of James Mullen, James Lambert, and James Lilly. The Reverend P. H. Nelson stayed late and sang hymns and prayed for the condemned man. As the night passed Seaton sent for Ralph Ross, an accomplished violinist, and his music helped pass the time and ease the tension, and those late hours were spent quietly in subdued conversation between family members and guards. Seaton did not retire during the night and his brother and sister finally had to be told to leave at 5:30 A.M.

As daybreak approached Seaton became agitated and every effort was made to calm the prisoner. Once he had braced up he was shaved by Ralph Ross and his last meal was then brought in. As he ate with Jim Mullen he had Jim Lambert write to his friend Ed "Skagway Kid" Roberts, and as soon as the breakfast plates were cleared Sheriff Cudihee appeared and read the death warrant. Several more letters were written and then the Reverend B. H. Lingenfelter arrived and they talked and prayed. Seaton dressed in his new suit, lit a cigar, and at 7:10 A.M. the march to the scaffold room began, with deputy Mullen on one arm and the Rev. Lingenfelter on the other. Seaton made his way through the jail corridor to the stairway into the death chamber and mounted the stairs with no show of emotion. He paused for a moment when he saw the scaffold but then climbed the narrow flight of stairs and took his place on the platform, directly behind the trapdoor. Those on the platform had been limited to the sheriff, four deputies and the reverend, and the sheriff then commanded complete silence from the witnesses, and summoned Seaton to step forward and speak. The condemned man said, "Gentlemen, you all know what I am here for. I am here for something I knew nothing about. I pray God that he will forgive those who have trespassed against me. And I pray that God will forgive me if I have trespassed against anyone. I hope God will forgive Mr. Cudihee. He and his deputies are doing that which they know not. I am thankful for the kindness shown me while in the King County jail. I am satisfied and happy to go and meet my uncle and friends who have gone before. Good-bye all."

Seaton was then positioned on the center of the trapdoor and his wrists and arms, knees and ankles were pinioned, the black hood was pulled on, and the noose adjusted, all of which only took a few moments. At exactly 8:00 A.M. the trap was sprung and Seaton dropped, and his neck was broken in the fall. Drs. David Buckley and Wilbur W. Mckenzie monitored his vital signs and in seven minutes pronounced him dead. After hanging a few minutes more the body was cut down and placed in a receiving basket. He was taken to Bonney and Stewart's undertaking parlor where he was prepared for a 10:00 A.M. funeral the following day.

Seattle Daily Times (WA): January 1–3, 1902. *Seattle Star* (WA): January 2–3, 1902.

Lum You
January 31, 1902

Lum You fancied himself above the other Chinese in Bay Center, Pacific County, Washington. He walked with a touch of arrogance, not quite a swagger, and was a natty dresser. While the other Chinese had back-breaking jobs in the cranberry bogs or canneries, fished or gathered oysters, Lum You worked as a "negotiator" communicating between the Chinese workers and their white employers. Lum You had given a gun to Joe Ging to sell for him, but when Ging gave You the one dollar fifty cents he received, You felt he had been swindled. He went to the sheriff but the law would not interfere in Chinese matters. At the end of June 1894, You snuck into Ging's cabin and struck him on the head with an ax, careful not to cause death but severe enough to cause a three inch scar over his left eye and, as far as You was concerned, marked him as a swindler. Two men saw You flee from the cabin and he was tracked to South Bend. He was arrested, tried for assault, convicted, and sentenced to serve six months in jail and pay a $500 fine. Upon his release he had to take employment next to the other Chinese, in the cranberry bogs and on the oyster farms.

On August 6, 1901, Oscar Bloom, a "good natured bully," had been drinking in the saloons of Bay Center, located a few miles from South Bend, Washington. During the day he had seen Lum You on the street and went out of his way to bump into him. Lum You let the matter drop, though he was annoyed, because he knew that Sheriff Chester Egbert would take no action if he complained. That evening Lum You went to the local saloon and was playing cards when Bloom came up behind him and bumped him so hard he dropped his cards. Bloom then grabbed You around the neck and took his valuables, including forty dollars and seventy-five cents. Lum You started for his house to retrieve a pistol while Bloom started for his house a few minutes later. Bloom had just arrived on his porch, fumbled for his keys and unlocked the door when You came up from behind. Bloom turned to face his adversary and You shot him in the stomach. You ran away while Bloom staggered into his house and fell onto his bed. The shot was heard by many but no one went to investigate.

Bloom, a man of general habit, did not appear as usual the following day so several men, including Sheriff Egbert, went to his home to look for him. They found Bloom collapsed upon his bed with a mortal wound to his stomach. On examination Dr. Wilson Gruwell determined that the bullet had passed through his bladder and intestines and lodged in his spine. He was still alive, though in excruciating pain, and he gave an ante-mortem statement to notary public L. L. Bush. He said that Lum You had broken into his house, though there were no signs of forced entry, and had lain in wait to shoot him. Bloom died during the evening hours of August 7, 1901.

Lum You was arrested in South Bend and he never denied the crime, but neither would he confess to it. In early October he was indicted by the grand jury and on October 8, 1901, his trial began in Judge A. E. Rice's South Bend courtroom, and his defense was that he was provoked into shooting Bloom. When the case went to the jurors they took only two hours to convict You of first degree murder and the prisoner was sentenced to hang on January 31, 1902. On January 14, 1902, Lum You made a desperate escape from jail but there was no evidence of how he gained his freedom, though his tracks in the snow showed clearly that he had fled toward the river. A reward of two hundred dollars was posted and two days later at 8:00 A.M. the fugitive was captured and returned to his cell. Neither appeal nor application to Governor Henry McBride, pleading for executive clemency, delayed the execution.

The scaffold was erected inside the courthouse at South Bend and the trapdoor was built over a ventilator opening in the floor. The release was a pulley contraption which led to another room where four ropes dangled, three dummies and one release, so the men would not know who had sprung the trap. Five hundred people gathered inside the courthouse to witness the hanging. Lum You walked to the scaffold with a firm step, accompanied by Sheriff Thomas Roney and W. H. Cornelius. He said farewell to his friends and then asked that he be killed quickly. He was prepared with all due haste, his limbs bound, the noose adjusted, and the black hood pulled on, and at 9:15 A.M. Roney gave the signal, three taps on a gong, and the trap was sprung. You's neck was broken in the fall so there was barely a tremor before the attending physician pronounced him dead. His body was cut down, placed in a pine coffin provided by the county, and that afternoon Lum You was buried on a plot of land donated by sheriff's deputy Z. B. Brown.

Seattle Times (WA): January 31, 1902. *South Bend Journal* (WA): July 6–13, 1894; August 9, 1901; October 18–25, 1901; November 15, 1901; January 17, 1902; January 31, 1902.

Hamilton, Alfred
May 23, 1902

Alfred Hamilton, alias Alfred Hawkins, was a fisherman, but was believed to be at the head of a desperate gang of Puget Sound pirates. Many fish traps in the lower Sound had been raided by these pirates and two watchmen had disappeared without a trace. He admitted to knowing something of the murder of a fisherman in Deception Pass but would not admit to being the murderer, nor name one. He confessed to killing Mike Whalen with a knife eight years previously when the two men quarreled during a drunken row, but insisted that it was self-defense, and he was also suspected of killing a Seattle policeman. There was never sufficient incriminating evidence against Hamilton and he would never confess to any crimes. On September 6, 1899, Hamilton arrived at Anacortes and disposed of his catch of fish for $1,000. He then went on a spree, drinking heavily, gambling, and threatening one man after another with his revolver.

Early on the morning of September 7 his companion convinced him to take his revolver to the boat and leave it there. They then returned to the saloons and soon Hamilton became ugly again and, believing that certain people were trying to rob him, returned to the boat and got his pistol. His companion found City Marshal Charles Becker at his blacksmith shop and asked the lawman to get hold of Hamilton before he got into serious trouble. Meanwhile, Hamilton had returned to town and found one of the suspected robbers being shaved at McHales' Barbershop. He drew his pistol to shoot the man but the intended victim talked him out of the killing. Marshal Becker found Hamilton at the barbershop and no sooner had he opened the door then Hamilton got the drop on him and told him to throw up his hands. The marshal tried to calm the situation but finally had to back out of the shop. Becker walked up the street and into a stairway closely following Hamilton, who still had his pistol in hand. Becker first went to the second floor office of the justice of the peace but he was not in. He next went to an adjoining office and asked where the justice had gone, but just then Hamilton ordered the marshal to stand still and raise his hands, which Becker did.

Douglas Almond, editor of the *Anacortes American*, heard the commotion, opened his office door and, stepping into the corridor, inquired, "what is the matter?" Hamilton then commanded him to raise his hands as well, and he did. D. M. Woodbury, a leading attorney in Skagit County, also heard the commotion in the hallway and he stepped from his office and asked, "Why, what's the matter here?" Hamilton told him to throw up his hands and Woodbury, who was a peace loving person, said, "Young man, do you know what you are doing?" and as he backed into his office Woodbury said, as soothingly as possible, "You had better put up that pistol and stop this thing." In response Hamilton said, "You won't throw up your hands?" and he shot Woodbury once, the bullet crashing through his stomach and severing his spinal cord. Woodbury collapsed to the floor and called to the others for help, but Hamilton crossed over the hallway to where his victim lay and, pointing his pistol at the prostrate form, said, "Lie still, you son of a bitch." As soon as Hamilton was distracted by his victim Almond ran into his office and called for help from his window. A crowd started for the scene but Hamilton fled into them, clearing his way by brandishing his revolver. The crowd parted, but one venturesome man tripped Hamilton on the stairs and after he landed at the bottom a policeman pounced on him. After a desperate struggle Hamilton was disarmed and lodged in jail. Woodbury was rushed to a doctor's care, but after three days of excruciating agony he died, and Hamilton was charged with murder.

Hamilton was tried at Mount Vernon, Skagit County, Washington, and his defense was that he was crazy from knock-out drops which, he claimed, had been given to him to make the robbery more easily accomplished. He was found guilty of first degree murder and sentenced to hang, but his case was appealed to the state Supreme Court and the justices reversed the decision because of certain erroneous insanity instructions given by the trial judge. A change of venue to Whatcom County was then granted for the second trial, where Hamilton was again convicted of first degree murder and sentenced to hang. The case was again appealed to the state Supreme Court and one objection was that the chief prosecutor at both trials was Henry G. McBride, then Lieutenant governor, who might later become the governor and have to decide on the question of clemency. This objection was overruled, and in due course McBride did become governor. As the date of execution neared a petition for clemency was submitted to Governor McBride, purely as a matter of form, and promptly denied. Hamilton had been born in Bristol, England, and admitted that he still had a family there, but he insisted they knew nothing of him and thought he was in Alaska. He would not give his true name to prevent his relatives from being informed of his ignominious end.

On his last night the prisoner slept soundly, retiring shortly after 10:00 P.M. and arising at 4:00 A.M. After breakfast was served he talked with his guards until Whatcom County's Sheriff William I. Brisbin came at 5:45 A.M. to read the death warrant. Hamilton had to be quieted to listen to the reading, as he was swearing loudly and complaining that his coffee was served cold. Dr. T. J. Kirkpatrick administered a grain of morphine and a twentieth grain of strychnine to calm his raving. He then paced in his cell and the next dozen minutes must have seemed much longer, as the prisoner complained several times, "Won't they ever come." At a few minutes before 6:00 A.M. Sheriff Brisbin took the prisoner from his cell and led the march to the scaffold. Hamilton came next with ex–Sheriff Edwin Wells of Skagit County on one side and deputy Land on the other. The attending physicians, Drs. Kirkpatrick, S. Kelly and A. B. McKinnon, came next and Dr. Smith of Anacortes, at the request of Woodbury's family, was among the one hundred spectators.

The prisoner took the steps to the platform two at a time and took his place on the trapdoor, where he refused to make a speech, saying, "No, I am here to die." He noticed jailor McLeod in the crowd and said "Good-bye, Mac." Wells and Land were applying the straps and one of them pinched the prisoner's hand, to which he said, "Christ, you are cinching that hard," then looked for McLeod again and called out, "Remember me to the boys in Seattle, Mac." There was no delay for religious services, as the condemned man had refused to have any clergy attend him. Deputy Land positioned the knot but it was in the wrong place, and Sheriff Brisbin called that to his attention. Hamilton said, "Yes, that is wrong. Get it under the left ear." The preparations had only taken a minute and a half and as Hamilton finished his final criticism the trap was sprung and he dropped, breaking his neck. He hung motionless for three minutes, then there were two slight tremors. He was pronounced dead at 6:13 A.M. and his body was cut down, placed in a coffin, and taken to undertaker Noice's establishment for preparation before being hurried to a potter's field for burial, as no one had claimed the remains.

Seattle Daily Times (WA): May 23, 1902.

Champoux, Zenon
May 6, 1904

Zenon "James" Champoux, a twenty-six-year-old French-Canadian prospector, met Lottie Brace in Alaska. Lottie was an eighteen-year-old "variety actress" in a local saloon and many men found her extremely attractive, but it was Champoux who won her heart. They courted and soon became engaged as Champoux spent lavishly on his betrothed but, when it came time to marry, Champoux was nearly penniless, so Lottie fled to Seattle where she was sure she could elude Champoux and marriage. In Seattle, Lottie joined her sister Ella and they found work in her chosen profession, as a "soiled dove" in a local brothel south of Yesler Way.

Champoux followed and, after searching the city, found Lottie and Ella at the Arcade Variety Theater. He confronted his ex-fiancée and demanded she keep her promise, but Champoux was soundly rebuffed. In an instant he pulled his hunting knife and, with a single blow to the young girl's temple, administered a mortal wound to her brain. There were many witnesses present and they restrained Champoux to await the authorities, and the outcome of Lottie's medical condition. Lottie died the next day, never regaining consciousness. Champoux was lodged in the King County jail, charged with Lottie's murder and, at his examination, first presented his defense of insanity. He was held over to answer to the grand jury and was indicted. He continued the "insanity dodge" while in jail, eating only uncooked meat and vegetables and acting in a bizarre fashion, and he spoke only with a strange broken French-English accent. However, at his trial the jurors refused to accept his insanity defense and found him guilty of first degree murder. He was delivered to the prison in Walla Walla and lodged in the east wing of the cell block.

As the fatal day approached the condemned man, with the help of his priest, resigned himself to his fate and told his fellow prisoners, "If Lottie will not love me in this world, I will force her to love me in the next." On the night before the execution, after the prisoners were locked in their cells, the parts of the gallows were brought from storage and erected in the prison yard using carriage bolts and screws, so no sound of a hammer was heard. Champoux showed no sign of nervousness and ate a hearty supper. He read his Bible and leafed through some of the religious works provided by Father Flohr. He would not speak of the efforts being made by his attorney to obtain a commutation or respite, and did not seem to expect one. At 9:00 P.M. he began to prepare for bed and retired a half hour later, sleeping soundly throughout the night, so at 4:00 A.M. the guards had to shake him awake.

He did not talk of the woman he had once loved, and murdered, but his thoughts turned to his hometown in Eastern Canada as he wrote a letter to his brother. While he dressed in his new black suit he said he would "be with mother soon." He refused breakfast and stimulants when they were offered, and he knelt for prayer with Father Flohr. They continued their religious activities until the gallows was ready and at 5:00 A.M. the death warrant was read at the cell door by Warden F. W. Payne, and then the procession began from the hospital building, fifty yards from the gallows. When the condemned man came in sight of the gallows he hurried forward, as if anxious to meet his end, and his guards had to hasten to keep up. He climbed the thirteen stairs with a quick step and immediately positioned himself on the trapdoor as he grasped the crucifix offered by the priest. He kissed it and only then did tears stream down his cheeks, but he brushed them away and said loudly, to the thirty witnesses present, "God bless you all!"

When it was clear he had nothing more to say the executioner began to prepare him. Champoux's wrists and arms, knees and ankles were bound, the black hood was pulled over his head, and when the noose was being adjusted he lifted his chin to aid in the process. In a moment, at 5:11 A.M., the lever was pulled and the condemned man's body fell five and one half feet, breaking his neck. The body "hung as motionless as a side of beef from a butcher's hook." The attending physicians monitored his vital signs and pronounced him dead in a few minutes, though his heart beat for seventeen minutes, then waited for the signal to cut the rope and lower the body. This finally came five minutes later and the body was lowered into a pine coffin which had been laid aside for that purpose. Champoux's body was give to Father Flohr and buried in the Catholic cemetery later that day.

Seattle Daily Times (WA): May 6, 1904. *Seattle Post-Intelligencer* (WA): May 6, 1904. *Seattle Star* (WA): May 3, 1904; May 6, 1904. *Lima Times-Democrat* (OH): May 6, 1904. *Salt Lake Tribune* (UT): May 7, 1904.

Clark, Charles C.
September 2, 1904

Charles C. Clark, sometimes spelled Clarke, had been raised properly but when he came of age he developed a penchant for liquor and gambling. In the pursuit of these pastimes he became attracted to Leila Page, a "woman of the half-world" who worked in a brothel known as "The Jewel" in Olympia, Washington's red light district. For some time Clark had been favored by Page but in the winter of 1902 an old flame of Page's returned to Olympia and Clark found he had to share her attentions, and he felt he had been practically cast aside. He became insanely jealous and pleaded with Page to give up her mode of life and marry him, but she refused. Clark began to drink more heavily and threatened vengeance, and even threatened to murder Page. Still, on the rare occasions when Clark had money, he was admitted to Page's crib. He had been there on the morning of January 17 and Page complained to other the women — Cleo Reynolds, Florence Hall and Lee Huntington — that she was missing two hundred dollars and some jewelry and she believed Clark had stolen it.

That evening Clark found Page at a boarding house up-town and tried to cut her throat with a pen knife, but the wound was very slight and they made up. They returned to The Jewel and a seemingly remorseful Clark then plied Page with large quantities of wine, and at 5:00 A.M. they retired to Page's room. Cleo Reynolds was the only woman sleeping at The Jewel that night and at 9:00 A.M. she heard, through the thin board partition, feeble cries for help from Page's room and she went to investigate. She knocked on the door and asked Clark if he was ill, and then asked him to open the door but he said he could not. She kept up her demand that the door be opened and after a while Clark managed to slip the bolt and open the door, and he fell into the hallway striking his head on the door. He had several knife wounds to his throat and his lips were burned by carbolic acid and inside the room was Page, sprawled on the blood-soaked bed.

Reynolds telephoned the police and officer Charles Mort arrived first. Mort found Clark still lying on the hallway floor and Page inside the room, and she appeared to be lying in a natural position, suggesting she had been asleep when her throat was cut. The officer discovered Clark's bloody pen knife on the dresser and under a pile of clothes he found a bloody poll-ax belonging to the house. He later found a carving knife under a cushion of the settee, but it had not been used in the murder though its presence showed premeditation and preparation. Clark was examined and his neck wounds were found to be superficial, and the acid had been diluted by the great amount of alcohol he had consumed earlier in the evening. He was searched and none of the missing money nor jewelry was found.

A coroner's jury was convened at the courthouse that morning and Billy Leybold testified that Clark had left one hundred twenty-five dollars, his and Page's watch and Page's diamond ring in his care, and the jurors then returned a finding that Clark had murdered Page. The prisoner was held over for action by the grand jury, indicted, tried at the spring session of the District Court and found guilty of premeditated murder, even though all the evidence was circumstantial. He was sentenced to hang and his attorney, George C. Israel, began an aggressive appeal campaign. The execution of Clark was delayed until, finally, the date was set for September 2, 1904. On June 13, 1904, the condemned man was taken to the prison in Walla Walla, registered as prisoner number 3408, and lodged in the east wing of the cell block. During the last days of August, Attorney Israel, with four friends and Clark's family, went before Governor Henry McBride to plead for a respite or commutation of sentence, but the governor refused to intervene.

On September 1, after learning that all efforts to save his life had failed, Clark appeared near total collapse and "trembled like an aspen leaf," so he was moved to the prison hospital. He was attended by Father Flohr and after great effort he managed to brace up. During the evening hours, after the prisoners were locked in their cells, the parts of the gallows were brought from storage and erected in the prison yard, using carriage bolts and screws so that no sound of a hammer was heard. On the fatal morning the prisoner was awakened by his death watch guard at an early hour and he dressed in his burial suit. He then sat with his priest to await the designated hour of 5:00 A.M.

After 4:30 A.M., Warden F. W. Payne arrived and read the death warrant and a half hour later the procession formed outside the cell door, including the warden and Captain of the Guard J. D. Smith. They marched to the gallows with a slow, solemn gait, the prisoner calm with head erect. Clark climbed the thirteen stairs and faced the fifty witnesses with composure, if not defiance. He refused to make a speech but said had left a message for his mother, which was not made public. He was positioned on the trapdoor and the straps were applied to his wrists and arms, knees and ankles while Father Flohr prayed for the salvation of his soul. The noose was adjusted and, after he kissed the crucifix, the black hood was pulled over his head, and at 5:20 A.M. the lever was pulled and the trap was sprung. Prison physician Dr. Howard R. Keylor declared that Clark's neck had been broken in the fall, but he did not pronounce him dead for twenty minutes. Clark's body was then cut down, placed in the coffin provided, and turned over to his family for burial.

Morning Olympian (WA): January 21, 1903; September 2, 1904. *Seattle Daily Times* (WA): September 2, 1904.

Arao, Henry
June 3, 1905

Henry Arao came to America from Japan in 1901 and worked around Puget Sound before moving to the city of Spokane in Spokane County, Washington. During the fall of 1904 Arao was employed by Chinese tailor Sam Chong in his Spokane shop. After a brief period as an employee Arao was made a partner in Chong's business, but Arao was dissatisfied with the partnership arrangement so he left Chong's shop and opened his own shop in the same neighborhood. Business was slow coming to Arao and he soon became convinced that Chong was keeping away customers by telling them that the Japanese tailor had left the country. Arao developed a bitter hatred for his former employer and became determined to kill him.

On December 29, Arao called at the shop of Chong, but the Chinese tailor was asleep in his quarters at the rear of the shop. Chong's wife was busy in the shop and she met Arao at the door and, when he explained that he was there to look for a $5 gold piece he claimed he had lost while working there, she let him into the rear to search. Mrs. Chong returned to her labors but in a few minutes she heard her husband's screams. As she ran to him Arao sprang out of the door and ran down the street, and Mrs. Chong found her husband in bed, covered with blood flowing from a dozen knife wounds, and already dead. Arao disappeared from Spokane for several weeks but was finally captured in a little town west of Spokane.

He was returned to the city, jailed, indicted and tried at the spring term of the District Court. He was convicted of first degree murder and sentenced to hang on March 26, 1905. Arao was taken to the prison at Walla Walla on March 16, placed on murderer's row in the east wing of the cell block, and a death watch was placed with him. He was at first awed by his situation, but soon became accustomed to prison life and was one of the jolliest convicts. He spent a great deal of time following the war between Japan and Russia. To his great pleasure, his country had won a great naval victory weeks before his fatal date and when he learned of it he smiled and said he was now ready to die. Efforts to have Arao's sentence commuted failed, but delayed the execution for two months until June 3.

The prisoner spent his last day and night in relative quiet, writing a long letter to his mother in Japan. In the evening he was visited by four countrymen who had been Christianized and they tried without success to convert the condemned man. That evening, after the prisoners were locked in their cells, the parts of the gallows were brought from storage and erected in the prison yard, using carriage bolts and screws so no sound of a hammer was heard. Arao retired at 10:30 P.M. and was sound asleep when his death watch awoke him at 3:30 A.M. He hopped out of bed and greeted Warden A. F. Kees, who was already there to read the death warrant. He refused to eat breakfast but drank a cup of coffee, and then he was ready for his walk to the gallows.

The procession was led by the warden and Captain of the Guard Wood. The prisoner climbed the thirteen steps with a firm step and at 4:27 A.M. Arao stepped onto the trapdoor of the gallows and smiled at the spectators standing on the prison walls above him. It took but a minute to apply the straps to his wrists and arms, knees and ankles and then he was asked if he had anything to say. He vigorously shook his head as he said "No!" Captain of the Guard Wood adjusted the black hood and noose and a moment later the lever was pulled and the trap was sprung. Arao dropped to a slow death as his light weight failed to break his neck, and he strangled to death. Attending physicians Dr. Y. G. Blalock and Dr. W. E. Russel recorded his pulse and pronounced him dead in twenty-two minutes. Arao's remains were then cut down and turned over to his countrymen for burial.

Seattle Daily Times (WA): June 3, 1905.

Pasquale, Frank
September 15, 1905

In May 1904, Charles Gray was working as an insurance agent in Tacoma, Pierce County, Washington, and Frank Pasquale had a policy with his company. Pasquale had an accident which was covered by the policy, and Gray arranged for a settlement. Pasquale believed that Gray had not given him all that was due, but the insurance man assured his client that the settlement was paid in full. Pasquale convinced Gray to accompany him to the south part of the city where he said there were Italians who were familiar with the full facts of the case, and could help him explain his point. Going to that part of the city required that they cross through the railroad yards. Pasquale was walking ahead of Gray when he suddenly turned, his pistol already in his hand, and he shot Gray dead. He planned to conceal his crime by placing the body on the tracks so that the next fast freight train would grind it to pieces, However, as the murderer lifted Gray's body onto his shoulder he was discovered by employees in the yard. He dropped the body and fled toward Puyallup and a small posse of railroad men, reinforced by several clerks from the freight office, pursued the fugitive until night fell and he managed to slip away in the dark. Pasquale eluded capture for several days but while making his way to Seattle at midnight he was discovered, arrested, and lodged in jail.

At his examination he was held over for action by the grand jury, indicted, and tried at the fall term of the District Court. He was convicted of first degree murder and sentenced to hang. As soon as he arrived at the prison he asked to see a priest and one visited him twice a week thereafter. During one visit the prisoner asked the priest to send a petition to Governor Albert E. Mead pleading for a commutation of sentence, and this was done. Strong pressure was brought to bear by the Italian consul and by influential Italians throughout the state, and it was presumed by most that the sentence would be commuted to life imprisonment, but several days before the date set for execution the governor declined to interfere.

Pasquale had a difficult last day, pacing his cell and denouncing his enemies. He calmed down when his religious advisor arrived and, when a newspaper reporter asked for an interview, the prisoner related the full details of his crime but accused his defense attorneys of dereliction of duty in failing to free a guilty man. After the prisoners were locked in their cells for the night the parts of the gallows were brought from storage and erected in the prison yard, using carriage bolts and screws so that no sound of a hammer was heard. Some friends of the condemned man had mounted the prison wall to watch the execution and they were allowed to remain.

The prisoner arose at an early hour, ate breakfast, then heard the death warrant read after 5:00 A.M. Just as the sun appeared over the mountains Warden A. F. Kees, Deputy Warden J. D. Smith and several prison officials emerged from the east wing of the prison and escorted the prisoner to the scaffold. Before he mounted the thirteen stairs Pasquale waved to the spectators on the wall and yelled out, "Good-bye, boys." When he was on the platform he dropped to his knees and silently prayed for a minute, while the prison officials stood to one side. When the prisoner arose he took his place on the center of the trapdoor and his wrists and arms, knees and ankles were pinioned. The noose was drawn tight and the black hood drawn over Pasquale's face, and then the signal was given to Warden Kees. The lever was pulled and the trap was sprung at 5:29 A.M., and the condemned man broke his neck in the fall. There were several convulsive struggles before the body hung motionless, and he was pronounced dead by Prison Dr. J. L. Lane at 6:09 A.M. The body was then cut down and placed in the waiting coffin. The following morning, at 7:30 A.M., the remains of Frank Pasquale were buried in the Catholic cemetery.

Oregon Statesman (Oregon City): September 16, 1905. *Seattle Times* (WA): September 15, 1905.

McPhail, Angus J.
December 8, 1905

In 1901 forty-eight-year-old Angus J. McPhail operated a tent saloon of an unsavory reputation in Trafton, Washington, and earned a "hard reputation" after being involved in several shooting scrapes, and after one such affray he was arrested for attempted murder. However, the complaining witness failed to appear at his examination and the charges were dropped. McPhail soon afterward moved his tent operation to Oso, where he operated his saloon for a year before, in 1902, he had accumulated enough money to move his saloon business into a permanent structure in Darrington. In Darrington there was already a saloon owned and operated for over a year by Fred Alderson, a man of quiet disposition, well-liked and respected by the reputable citizens of Darrington. McPhail, who was then living with Esther Veach, soon ran his business into the ground and blamed Alderson for his failure, and held him responsible for the recent denial of a license to continue in business. To further complicate the matter Alderson had ordered McPhail's paramour, Veach, to stay out of his saloon, implying by this action that she was an "unsavory character."

McPhail and Veach were preparing to leave Darrington but at 6:30 on Saturday evening, May 9, 1903, McPhail walked into Alderson's saloon and stepped up to the bar. He had just ordered his second drink and, while Alderson was busy wiping the bar and turned slightly away from his antagonist, McPhail pulled his .32-caliber revolver. Without hesitation or warning he leveled his pistol at Alderson and fired one shot. The bullet entered just behind and below the left arm, ranged downward through the body, and lodged near the front part of the abdomen so near the skin it could be felt. Although Alderson died instantly from this terrible wound, McPhail walked around the end of the bar and fired a second bullet into the prostrate body. Dr. Adams was summoned but he could do nothing more than preserve the remains for an autopsy and an inquest by Coroner Charles H. Bakeman.

The coroner's jury found "the deceased, Fred Alderson, came to his death from a pistol shot at the hands of A. J. McPhail." Coroner Bakeman then issued a warrant for the arrest of McPhail and groups of men began to search for the fugitive. Immediately after the killing McPhail had fled into the heavily wooded area near town and managed to elude capture for several hours, but carefully slipped into town and hid in a room until morning where he was captured and held for the authorities. The county sheriff was notified of the killing and capture, and the following day he dispatched deputy Edwin Stanyar from Everett to bring the prisoner by train back to the county seat. Following his capture, while awaiting arrival of the deputy sheriff, McPhail told Coroner Bakeman that he could not remember anything of the killing, and that it had all seemed like a dream. He could not even remember what he had done with his revolver, and suggested he might have dropped it as he stumbled about the woods in a daze, and this was his first effort at establishing his defense. The train to Everett, with McPhail aboard, was halted by a landslide which lodged several logs against the train and held it firmly in place, so the passengers disembarked and walked to Arlington, where deputy Stanyar hired a livery rig and continued on to Everett and lodged McPhail in the county jail.

At his examination McPhail was held over for action by the grand jury and in late October he was indicted for Alderson's murder. McPhail's trial began in Everett on November 3, 1903, and he claimed in his defense that he had been hypnotized by a stranger and given a suggestion to kill Alderson, and therefore he was not responsible for his actions. The jurors rejected his defense and he was found guilty of first degree murder. The prisoner was sentenced to hang on December 26, 1903, and delivered to the prison at Walla Walla on October 8, where he was lodged in the east wing of the cell block. He carried forward his ruse of insanity and was so effective that his attorneys were able to obtain a stay of execution while he was examined, but numerous experts found him perfectly sane. Seeing that his dodge would be of no further value to him, McPhail confessed to his jailor that he was only shamming, but said he hoped he had not hurt his chances for a commutation. Up to the last week he held out hope that Governor Albert E. Mead would act favorably on his behalf.

As the day neared the condemned man told his guards that his only fear was that terrible drop and sudden jerk, but the thought of dying did not concern him. Prison Chaplain John LeCornu was a frequent visitor and this was a great help to the prisoner. McPhail took quite a liking to the chaplain and on Monday he grasped the chaplain's hand firmly and said, "I am not afraid to die. I am willing to go." He then laid down on his bunk and cried like a child, the only time he showed emotion during his confinement. On Thursday evening he confessed that he had killed Anderson but said he was so deranged by liquor and from a blow to his head received several months prior that he was not responsible for his actions. After the prisoners were locked in their cells the parts of the gallows were brought from storage and erected in the prison yard, using carriage bolts and screws so that no sound of a hammer was heard. The prisoner spent an easy final night, but awoke at 12:30 A.M. and chatted with his death watch guard, then slept again until 5:00 A.M. when he was awakened. He ate a hearty breakfast and talked with his guards and the ministers as they waited for daybreak. The death warrant was read to him in his cell and as soon as the sun appeared the prisoner was escorted to the scaffold by two guards, Warden A. F. Kees, Chaplain LeCornu, the Reverend Morton Gregory and several prison officials. He climbed the thirteen stairs "never showing a white feather," positioned himself on the trapdoor, examined the noose hanging above his head, and then glanced at the spectators on the wall. He declined to speak so the guards quickly adjusted the straps, noose, and black hood, and at 6:46 A.M. Warden Kees pulled the lever which sprang the trap. The drop broke the prisoner's neck but it took twenty-four minutes for his heartbeat to cease, and then prison Dr. J. L. Lane pronounced him dead. The body was cut down, placed in a coffin provided by the state, and that afternoon he was buried in the prison cemetery after a brief service by Chaplain LeCornu.

Everett Herald (WA): May 10, 1903. *Seattle Times* (WA): December 8, 1905. *Snohomish County Tribune* (WA): May 15, 1903. *Monroe Monitor* (WA): May 14, 1903.

White, William
March 2, 1906

William White, alias Whiting or John White, was born in 1884 to a dysfunctional family in Lowell, Michigan. His father was a drunk and his mother died while he was still quite young, so he was never sure of his birth date. As soon as he was old enough he left home and went to San Francisco where he periodically signed on as a sailor aboard different ships, and between voyages he made his way as a third rate boxer using the sobriquet "Kid" White, taking any preliminary bout he could find. In September 1904 White joined with John Hildebrand in a plan to rob Conway's Saloon in Seattle. White was a braggart but most of his bravado was pure bluster. During the robbery White, who had no previous criminal experience, shot Matthew Murphy "in a fit of nervousness" and Murphy died of his wound. The two robbers were identified and Hildebrand was soon arrested in a Seattle dive. As soon as he was in jail Hildebrand confessed and named White as the shooter.

Two days later White was arrested in Tacoma, Washington, where he was staying with friends. White also confessed every detail of the crime and admitted to firing the shot which killed Murphy. However, later he would try to recant his confession and claim he had confessed only to shield Hildebrand. The two men were indicted for murder and robbery and tried in late 1904. Both men were found guilty with Hildebrand receiving a sentence of life in prison and White was sentenced to hang. An appeal was filed for White and this resulted in an automatic stay of execution. The appeal was denied and a new date for the execution was set at January 26, 1906. Once the new execution date was set every effort was made to have Governor Albert E. Mead grant a respite or a commutation of sentence to life in prison, and the governor granted a reprieve to March 2, 1906, to review the matter. However, after careful consideration, he refused to intervene further and denied the application.

White was delivered to the prison at Walla Walla, registered as prisoner number 4000, and lodged in the east wing of the cell block. He had embraced the Catholic religion and spent many hours of his final days with his priest in silent prayer. On his final night the condemned man was escorted through the prison, where he bid farewell to each prisoner. He was placed in the death row cell and put under a close death watch guard, to be sure he would not commit suicide and cheat the hangman. On the evening before the execution, after the prisoners were locked in their cells, the parts of the gallows were brought from storage and erected in the prison yard, using carriage bolts and screws so no sound of a hammer was heard. Usually condemned men were hanged at an early hour but Warden A. F. Kees was informed that White's attorney was then at the state capital where he would make one last appeal to the state's Supreme Court, so the warden informed all concerned that the execution would be delayed until 3:00 P.M. The Supreme Court convened *in bank* at 11:30 A.M. and the justices listened to an application for a writ of habeas corpus, then denied the application and denied an additional application for a stay of execution to allow an appeal to the U.S. Supreme Court.

As soon as Warden Kees was informed of the denials he relayed the information to the prisoner, who began his final preparations, and then the death warrant was read to White in his cell. The prisoner took that opportunity to ask Warden Kees, "I have one last favor to ask of you. It's all I've asked, and I hope you will grant it." The warden asked what he wanted and White replied, "I want you to take Jack King out of solitary confinement. He's in here for life. He can't get away. He's been punished enough in that dark cell." The warden wanted to know why White was interested in King, who was a notorious highwayman, safe cracker and burglar, and to the warden's surprise White replied, "King is my own uncle." The warden considered this last request for a few moments, as White had been surly and uncommunicative whenever his family was mentioned, but then the warden granted White's wishes. The officials knew that King, if given any chance, would try to escape, so it was decided a close watch would be kept on him at all times. In an hour King was out among the other prisoners and put to work.

White was taken from his cell and the procession was formed, led by the warden and Captain of the Guard J. D. Smith. The condemned man marched to the gallows with a firm step and mounted the scaffold without assistance. He took his place on the trapdoor and declined to speak to the witnesses gathered beneath the platform so he was quickly prepared, with his wrists and arms, knees and ankles strapped tightly. The noose was adjusted and the black hood was pulled on as the priest prayed for his soul. In a moment the lever was pulled and the trap was sprung, and White dropped to his death, breaking his neck in the fall. Hardly a quiver or tremble could be seen and in minutes prison Dr. J. L. Lane pronounced him dead. White was then cut down and deposited in the coffin provided by the state. He was buried in the Catholic cemetery the following morning after a brief service.

Seattle Times (WA): March 2, 1906. *Seattle Star* (WA): March 2, 1906.

Brooks, Simon
April 13, 1906

Simon Brooks had been employed as a wood hauler near Ridgefield, Clark County, Washington. His foreman at the logging camp, which was about a half mile from town, was Adolph Miller. In February 1905 a small party of women was visiting the logging camp when Brooks launched into a tirade of vile and disgusting profanity, and he ignored warnings, and then orders, to cease. After the women left Miller fired Brooks, so the disgruntled employee obtained a gun and took a shot at Miller, but missed and then fled for the Big Bend country. Brooks tried for several months to get employment at another logging camp but no one would hire him. He returned to Ridgefield in November, after he became convinced that Miller had black listed him and "tried to do me up with the unions."

Brooks was determined to take his revenge on Miller so at 2:00 P.M. on November 20, 1905, Brooks went to the logging camp where he found Miller in his cabin and shot him dead. He then went into Ridgefield, where he was met by a posse, which had been formed quickly by camp foreman C. T. Egge. The foreman got the drop on Brooks with a double-barreled shotgun and the murderer had no choice but to surrender. The posse sent for Sheriff E. S. Biesecker who, with prosecuting attorney W. W. Sparks and Coroner Smith rushed to the logging camp to investigate and hold an inquest. Sparks questioned Brooks, who confessed he had come to Ridgefield to kill Miller, "and I am glad I done it."

Brooks was taken to the county seat at Vancouver and lodged in jail. He was indicted and tried, and the evidence was so strong that he was easily convicted of first degree murder, the jurors deliberating only briefly. Several days after being convicted Brooks was sentenced to hang on Friday, April 13, 1906. The condemned man was taken to the penitentiary and registered as prisoner number 4053 to await his execution, and lodged in the east wing of the cell block. Brooks refused to have his case appealed, and no request was made for a commutation of sentence.

The night before the execution, after the prisoners were locked in their cells, the parts of the gallows were brought from storage and erected in the prison yard, using carriage bolts and screws so that no sound of a hammer was heard. On the fatal morning at 5:00 A.M. prison Warden A. F. Kees went to Brooks' cell and read the death warrant. The prisoner had been silent and sullen during his imprisonment, refusing to discuss the crime, and declined to say anything on the gallows nor to confess to the prison's chaplain. He had been composed and resigned to his fate until, as he was being escorted by the superintendent and warden, the procession rounded the corner of the hospital building and he hesitated for a moment when he saw the gallows for the first time. He quickly braced up and continued to the scaffold, where he again hesitated as he looked at the thirteen stairs, but then climbed them with a firm step after the slightest encouragement.

Once upon the platform a priest and the warden took his arms and asked him to step forward onto the trapdoor, and once again he had to be prodded as he held back when he saw the noose dangling above his head. According to the reporter from the *Morning Oregonian*, Brooks at this point began to "waver and quiver like an aspen leaf" as the straps were fastened to his wrists and arms, knees and ankles. The officers were ready to catch him, but he did not collapse when the noose was adjusted and the black hood was pulled over his head. At 5:13 A.M. the lever was pulled springing the trap, and Brooks broke his neck in the fall. Prison physician Dr. J. L. Lane was in attendance and in eleven minutes he pronounced Brooks dead, and then the body was cut down and placed in the coffin provided by the state. He was later buried in the prison cemetery.

Oregonian (Portland): November 21, 1905; April 14, 1906.

Armstrong, A. A.
June 8, 1906

A. A. Armstrong, who was sixty years old, lived on a ranch adjoining the ranch of Robert Patton on the Wynoochee River in Lewis County, Washington. Ownership of the land between the two ranches came into question and led to a number of quarrels, and several times Armstrong was arrested for assaulting Patton. In early 1904 Patton was on the disputed land chopping wood when Armstrong, on the opposite bank of the river, discovered Patton and ordered him off the property. Patton ignored the order, even after Armstrong fired two warning shots with his rifle. Armstrong fired the third shot at Patton and the bullet struck him in the breast, the wound proving fatal in a short time.

Armstrong was arrested and lodged in jail at Aberdeen to await action by the grand jury. The prisoner was indicted in the spring and his trial began immediately in Judge Mason Irwin's District Court, he was convicted of first degree murder and sentenced to hang. Armstrong was delivered to the penitentiary on April 20, 1904, with his execution set for July 1, but his attorneys obtained a stay of execution by pleading trial error, and the state Supreme Court ordered Armstrong to appear in the Superior Court at Aberdeen to testify on the appeal. He arrived in Aberdeen on May 22, 1905, where his attorneys tried to have the sentence reduced to life in prison, but they failed when the justices ruled against them on February 11, 1906. Armstrong was re-sentenced to hang on June 8 and returned to the penitentiary on April 26, 1906, where he was lodged in the east wing of the cell block. The prison officials had told the prisoner repeatedly that they believed Governor Albert E. Mead would commute his sentence, or at least grant a stay of execution, so when prison Chaplain John LeCornu told him all hope was lost he was quite agitated. He said, "It is not right. It is not justice."

On the night prior to the hanging, after the prisoners were locked in their cells, the parts of the gallows were brought from storage and erected in the yard, using carriage bolts and screws so no sound of a hammer was heard. Armstrong did not give up hope and on his final night he had difficulty sleeping until 2:00 A.M., then awoke at 4:00 to ask if any word had come from the governor, but there was none. He could not sleep again and an hour later ate his breakfast while asking repeatedly if word had been received. The death warrant was read to him in his cell and the march to the scaffold began at 5:24 A.M., and the condemned man had finally resigned himself to his fate and told Warden A. F. Kees he was ready to die.

The prisoner, escorted by the warden and Captain of the Guard J. D. Smith, walked firmly into the prison yard and as he passed the newspaper reporters he returned their salutations. He required no assistance in climbing the stairs and took his place on the trapdoor. His wrists and arms, knees and ankles were quickly pinioned and the noose was adjusted. He was not offered an opportunity to speak so after the black hood was pulled on he began a speech, which was so muffled by the cloth that he was not understood. At 5:26 A.M. the lever was pulled and the trap was sprung, even as the prisoner was speaking, and he broke his neck in the fall. In thirteen minutes Armstrong was pronounced dead by prison Dr. J. L. Lane and in a few minutes more his body was cut down. The remains were placed in a coffin and prepared for shipment to Aberdeen, where he was to be buried by his family.

Seattle Times (WA): June 8, 1906.

Miller, Frederick
March 22, 1907

Frederick Miller and a man named Fred Dlerks worked together at the logging camp near Castle Rock and on the night of October 15, 1906, they were making the rounds of the saloons at Castle Rock. At a late hour Dlerks was running low on funds and cashed a check for one hundred twenty-seven dollars. Miller suggested that the two men go to his room, as it was too late to walk back to the camp. It was just before midnight when Miller suggested they go out one last time, and he lured his friend to a lonely spot on the edge of town. The suggestion to return to his room was a ruse so he could get his revolver and once he had his man in an isolated location he shot him and then beat him into unconsciousness with the pistol barrel. Miller picked his pockets clean and immediately headed for the train station. Dlerks regained consciousness and dragged himself to the nearest house and knocked on the door, asked for help, and told the man that Miller was responsible. Dlerks was taken in and his wound was dressed, and he was cared for until he could be sent to Portland by train. In Portland he was taken to the hospital where everything possible was done for him, but he died in two days.

Miller was captured while waiting for the train and he was lodged in jail. At his examination he was held over for action by the grand jury and in mid–December he was indicted; his trial began immediately at Kalama, Washington, and on December 17, 1906, he was found guilty of murder in the first degree. His defense throughout the proceedings was simply a denial that he had committed the crime, but he could not overcome the death bed statements made by Dlerks and the evidence that he had Dlerks' money in his pocket when arrested. The jurors were at first deadlocked at eleven to one for conviction but finally arrived at a guilty verdict. A few days after the verdict was announced Miller was sentenced to hang on March 22, 1907. He was taken to the prison at Walla Walla, registered as prisoner number 4397, and lodged in the east wing of the cell block. Neither appeal nor application for executive clemency delayed the fatal day.

The evening before his death, after the prisoners were locked in their cells, the parts of the gallows were brought from storage and erected in the prison yard, using carriage bolts and screws so no sound of a hammer could be heard. On the fatal morning the prisoner was awakened at an early hour and he ate a light breakfast before dressing in his black burial suit. Before 5:00 A.M. Superintendent M. F. Kincaid arrived at Miller's cell and read the death warrant, and then the procession formed and started for the gallows. As the procession rounded the corner of the hospital building Miller saw the gallows for the first time and he suddenly faltered, fainted, and could not be revived. In an unconscious condition he was carried up the thirteen stairs and onto the platform. There was a delay as the officers again tried to revive the condemned man, but finally he was propped-up and supported on the trapdoor while his wrists and arms, knees and ankles were strapped, the black hood was pulled on, and the noose was adjusted. Miller still had not regained consciousness when the lever was pulled and the trap was sprung. Miller dropped, breaking his neck, and prison Dr. J. L. Lane later announced that death was instantaneous, though he monitored vital signs for a brief period before pronouncing him dead. The body was then cut down, deposited in the coffin provided, and buried later that day.

Bellingham Herald (WA)*:* March 22, 1907. *Oregonian* (Portland): December 20, 1906.

Niculas, Jose
April 16, 1909

Twenty-year-old Jose "Joe" Niculas, sometimes spelled Nicolos or Nocolos, worked at the Blakely Mill in Port Blakely, Kitsap County, Washington, with thirty-five-year-old Jose Santos, a Filipino. Santos lived near the mill with his family, which included his wife, four-year-old son Ramon and a baby girl. Niculas, also a Filipino, boarded with the Santos family. Niculas had lost his job just before Christmas and he held Santos responsible, or at least felt Santos had not done enough to save his job. On December 26, 1908, he and Santos had a violent quarrel and Santos ordered Niculas to leave his home and not return, so Niculas stormed out while vowing vengeance. Over the next few days Niculas repeatedly threatened the life of Santos but he was not taken seriously.

Niculas went to Seattle and bought two revolvers and on Tuesday evening, December 29, Niculas lay in wait at a place along the route Santos usually took from the mill to his home. George A. Brown, a blacksmith at the mill, and his wife passed in a buggy and Niculas asked him the time. When Brown answered, "It is 6:15 o'clock," Niculas seemed agitated at the late hour, apparently thinking he had missed Santos. Brown continued on a short distance when Niculas shot Brown in the back, and he fell from his buggy. Niculas, in a murderous rage, rushed past Brown and dove through a window into the Santos home where he blew out the light and then began firing wildly. One bullet pierced the kidneys of four-year-old Ramon Santos, killing him in a few minutes, while another bullet caused a serious but not fatal wound to the baby's neck. Jose Santos was not yet home but he was not far behind Niculas, so when he heard the gunfire, and being unarmed, he did not enter but sounded the alarm. Deputy sheriff McKay rushed to the scene and found that the murderer had fled. He summoned the coroner and immediately organized a posse, and meanwhile, Brown was rushed to a hospital in Seattle where he lingered until December 31 before succumbing to his wound.

The posse was soon on the trail of Niculas and they tracked him to Pleasure Bay at the north end of Bainbridge Island. They had little luck finding the fugitive until, on January 8, he surrendered suffering from exposure and hunger. The prisoner was taken to Port Orchard for the night and the following day he was taken by boat to Seattle and lodged in the county jail, charged with two counts of murder. He was indicted and tried at the early spring session of the court, convicted of first degree murder, and sentenced to hang. Niculas was delivered to the prison at Walla Walla, registered as prisoner number 5266, and lodged in the east wing of the cell block. Neither appeal nor application for executive clemency delayed the fatal day.

The evening before his death, after the prisoners were locked in their cells, the parts of the gallows were brought from storage and erected in the prison yard, using carriage bolts and screws so no sound of a hammer could be heard. The prisoner was scheduled to hang at sunrise, so on the fatal morning the prisoner was awakened at an early hour and he ate a hearty breakfast before dressing in his black burial suit. Before 5:00 A.M. Superintendent C. S. Reed and Captain of the Guard J. D. Smith arrived at the prisoner's cell and read the death warrant, and then the procession formed. The condemned man was escorted to the gallows where he climbed the thirteen stairs with a steady gait and, once upon the platform, in a smiling and cheerful mood, bade farewell to his spiritual adviser.

He stepped onto the trapdoor, where his wrists and arms, knees and ankles were strapped, the black hood was pulled on, and the noose was adjusted. In but a moment the lever was pulled and the trap was sprung. The prisoner broke his neck in the fall and prison Dr. L. R. Quilliam later announced that death was instantaneous, though he monitored vital signs for a brief period before pronouncing him dead. The body was then cut down, deposited in the coffin provided, and Niculas was buried that evening.

Bellingham Herald (WA): April 16, 1910. *Bremerton News* (WA): April 17, 1909.

Gauvette, Joseph
August 27, 1909

Joseph Gauvette, a saloon man who had moved to the city of Spokane from Canada, was having serious marital difficulties with his wife. She left him, taking their little girl, and rented rooms at a boarding house on College Avenue. Joseph tried everything he could think of to convince his wife to return to their home, including threats of murder, but she was determined to end the marriage. On the night of June 27, 1908, Gauvette lay in wait along the route that he knew his wife and daughter would take in returning to their boarding house, and when the two reached the corner of College Avenue and Maple Street he jumped out with pistol in hand and, without warning or hesitation, shot his wife dead. Joseph was arrested for her murder and their daughter was sent to live with his relatives in Canada. Joseph was held over at his examination to await action by the Spokane County grand jury, and in the autumn he was indicted and tried. His defense of insanity was rejected by the jurors and he was convicted of first degree murder. The defendant was sentenced to hang but an appeal resulted in an automatic stay of execution. Finally the appeal was denied and the application for a respite or commutation of sentence was rejected by Governor Marion E. Hay. The new date for Gauvette's execution was set for August 27, 1909, and he was taken to the prison and lodged in the east wing of the cell block. During his final days the condemned man showed no signs of nervousness and embraced the Catholic religion, and was attended by Father Jones of the Walla Walla Catholic Church.

On the evening before the execution, after the prisoners were locked in their cells, the parts of the gallows were brought from storage and erected in the prison yard, using carriage bolts and screws so no hammering was heard. During his final evening the prisoner slept only two hours, spending the remainder of the time writing to his family in Canada, and especially a very touching letter to his daughter. He also spent some time talking with his death watch guards and praying, and thanked Superintendent C. S. Reed for the kind treatment he had received since arriving at the prison. At an early hour he ate breakfast, dressed in his burial clothes, and was then ready for the execution, and Father Jones arrived in time to be at his side for the reading of the death warrant. The prisoner only became emotional for a brief moment after taking a last look at a picture of his daughter, and then just after 5:00 A.M. the procession formed, led by Superintendent Reed and Captain of the Guard J. D. Smith.

On the gallows the condemned man stepped forward to the railing and told the witnesses, "I have no hard feelings against anyone. My punishment is just, and I feel that my peace is made with my Maker." He stepped back and was positioned on the trapdoor, where his wrists and arms, knees and ankles were strapped while Father Jones prayed for the salvation of his soul. Next came the noose and the black hood, and as the latter was pulled over his head he said, "Good-bye, Father, good-bye!" As soon as the black hood was in place, at 5:30 A.M., the lever was pulled and the trap was sprung. The prisoner dropped, breaking his neck in the fall. He died without a struggle and within minutes prison physician Dr. L. R. Quilliam pronounced him dead. The body was cut down and deposited in the coffin provided by the state, and he was buried the following day.

Spokane Chronicle (WA): August 27, 1909.

Barnes, Hezekiah
November 12, 1909

Hezekiah "Bud" Barnes, a twenty-five-year-old man with a wife and child, was employed by Anna Aldrich, a seventy-year-old woman who owned several properties in the Dixie area. Barnes told Aldrich he was interested in renting the Kenney Ranch in Coppel Canyon and convinced her to go there with him to examine the property. He hitched up the buggy and they started out, stopping in Dixie where Barnes bought a pick handle, remarking that it was "worm-eaten but good enough for my purpose." When they reached the canyon, an isolated spot along Coppel Creek, he urged Aldrich to get out of the buggy. He then broke her skull with his pick handle and dumped her body into a hole caused by the uprooting of a tree. Barnes had been seen leaving with Aldrich and returning without her, so he was arrested on suspicion of foul play, and a search party was organized. He told conflicting stories, saying that he had rented the Kenney place and then Aldrich had gone away, but her body was found four days later and Barnes was charged with her murder.

He was indicted and tried in the District Court, offering as his defense a plea of insanity. The first jury disagreed, but when he was retried on the same charge he was convicted of first degree murder, all the evidence pointing to premeditation and malice. The case was appealed to the state Supreme Court, which affirmed the lower court's judgment and sentence. He was taken to the penitentiary to await his new date with the executioner, November 12, 1909, and he was lodged in the east wing of the cell block. Petitions to Governor Marion E. Hay for a commutation or a respite were denied.

Barnes, throughout his time behind bars, refused to confess. During that final night, after the prisoners were locked in their cells, the parts of the gallows were brought out of storage and erected in the prison yard, using carriage bolts and screws so that no sound of a hammer disturbed the peace. The condemned prisoner awoke at an early hour on his final morning, dressed in his burial clothes, and ate a hearty breakfast. The death warrant was read to him in his cell after 6:00 and afterward he started his walk to the scaffold, escorted by Superintendent C. S. Reed and Captain of the Guard J. D. Smith. His gait was unsteady and he stumbled twice while ascending the thirteen stairs. He refused to speak to the witnesses, which included only lawmen, newspaper reporters, and clergymen. He was prepared by five guards, one of them pulling the lever which sprung the trap at 6:30 A.M., and Barnes was pronounced dead by prison physician Dr. L. R. Quilliam in thirteen and one half minutes. His body was cut down, placed in the coffin provided, and delivered to his family for burial.

Seattle Times (WA): November 12, 1909.

Quinn, Richard
May 13, 1910

Twenty-eight-year-old Richard Quinn and his wife, Margaret, had domestic difficulties long before they left Michigan for North Dakota in 1904, and then started for Washington in 1907. However, it seemed the difficulties had all been resolved when, in 1908, they settled at Everett, the Snohomish County seat. Quinn found work as a fireman at the Ferry-Baker Mill but lost that position, and in September was working in the woods sawing shingle bolts. These setbacks led to more arguments and Margaret complained to friends that Richard drank too much, abused her, and often threatened to shoot her. Finally, on about August 1, Margaret left her husband for the second time since arriving in Washington and moved into the "Purdy House" run by Sadie Bond at 2920 Norton Avenue. She found work as a domestic for a widower with three children, but on September 15 she found a more permanent position at a restaurant and was determined to make her own way. Richard was just as determined to disgrace his wife, and he made disparaging remarks to anyone who would listen.

On September 17 Richard was seen riding his horse back and forth near the intersection of Summit Avenue and Twentieth Street, near the Quinn home, as if he expected his wife to make an appearance. That evening he was in the Rainier Saloon and strangely, for those modern times, he was carrying his rifle and threatened to shoot his wife. However, no one took him seriously as he had made similar threats on previous occasions and nothing happened. On September 18, Richard Quinn telephoned Margaret and told her to come for her trunk, threatening to throw it out if she did not come immediately. Margaret started for their home near the Ferry-Baker Mill but, when she reached the intersection of Twentieth Street and Summit Avenue, Quinn appeared on horseback. He rode up and dismounted with rifle in hand, said, "Good-bye, Maggie," then shot her at such close range that the blast set her clothes afire. The bullet passed entirely through her body, entering near the center of her breasts and ranging downward until it pierced her abdomen and came out her back between the tenth and eleventh ribs. Later, at the autopsy, Coroner Challacombe determined that the bullet had pierced the pericardium, the membrane which encloses the heart, and passed through the liver and diaphragm, shattering the spleen before exiting. William Watts, a neighbor of the Quinns, heard the shot and a woman's scream so he ran out and saw Richard standing with bridle in hand, watching his wife stagger along the sidewalk toward James C. Devery's home at 2006 Summit Avenue. Margaret went through the gate to Devery's porch and collapsed in a sitting position. Watts yelled at Richard so he mounted and rode off, and Watts returned to his home to get his rifle. When Watts returned to the scene of the shooting he found that Richard, still mounted, had also returned and was trying to take aim at Margaret. Watts pointed his rifle at Richard and threatened to shoot if he fired again, so Richard galloped down Twentieth Street.

Immediately after the shooting a report reached the police station that Quinn had barricaded himself in his house and would defy the officers but within an hour, before a force of officers could be dispatched, he arrived at police headquarters with brother-in-law Bert Mason and surrendered. Quinn was placed in a patrol wagon and taken to the county jail at Everett, and he begged the patrolman to sit close to him so he would not be shot while in transit. Richard's friends and relatives then came forward and said that Margaret Quinn had a gun and had threatened to shoot her husband and, though Richard claimed the shooting was accidental, they said it may have been in self-defense. Margaret's room and belongings were searched and it was proved she had no gun, and others testified that she had never threatened her husband and was afraid of him.

As Margaret sat on Devery's porch doctors and an ambulance were summoned, but the physicians decided that their patient would bleed to death if driven to the hospital so she was taken to a nearby house and given opiates to ease the terrible pain. It first appeared that she would die within hours, but by that evening she had rallied and it was briefly thought she might survive. However, she continued to weaken and, after careful examination, the doctors determined that the wound was a mortal one and it was just a matter of time until Margaret died. She was conscious and, though she gave an ante-mortem statement naming her husband as her murderer, she could not comment on any particular reason for the shooting. Margaret lingered until September 23 when, a few minutes before 1:00 A.M., she died.

Richard was asleep at the jail and was not aroused but when he awoke he was told of her death and he showed no emotion, asking only if he could see the body before burial. Margaret Quinn was buried the following day, but Richard was not permitted to attend. Quinn was indicted in early December and his trial began in Judge W. W. Black's courtroom on December 14, 1908. His defense, that the shooting was accidental, was rejected by the jurors and in two days he was convicted of first degree murder. The prisoner was sentenced to hang but appeals automatically stayed the execution until the state Supreme Court could hear the case. They finally denied the appeal and Quinn was resentenced to hang on April 15, 1910. Efforts were then made to gain a commutation of the death sentence, or at least a reprieve, and Quinn's sister, Mrs. Bert Mason, who lived in Everett, managed to get a twenty-eight day reprieve from Governor M. E. Hay while the case was taken under consideration. Quinn's sister worked night and day until, at 7:00 on the evening of May 12, the governor denied the application, even though she had submitted petitions signed by five hundred residents of Everett including eleven of the twelve jurors who found her brother guilty.

Quinn was delivered to the prison at Walla Walla to await the date of his execution, registered as prisoner number 5661, and lodged in the east wing of the cell block. During the days he was at the prison he was encouraged to confess and repent by Fathers John LeCornu, the prison chaplain, and Father Jones of the Walla Walla Catholic Church, but he resisted all efforts at religious counseling. The prisoner had, at one time, been a Baptist and a number of clergymen tried to gain access to give religious advice, but he refused them admittance and was rude and insulting to any clergyman who came near. After word was received that the commutation had been denied it fell upon Captain of the Guard J. D. Smith to tell him the news, and he advised the condemned man to "prepare for death with the break of day," and Quinn paled at the news and seemed nervous. After Father LeCornu made his final plea the priest reported, "That man will go to his death this morning refusing to embrace any salvation. When I talked with him he thinks he will 'die game.'" Quinn seemed to have resigned himself to his fate but still had great difficulty sleeping that last night. After the prisoners were locked in their cells the parts of the gallows were brought from storage and erected in the prison yard, using carriage bolts and screws so no sound of a hammer could be heard.

On the final day the prisoner was awakened at an early hour and he ate a hearty breakfast before dressing in his black burial suit. Before 5:00 A.M. Superintendent C. S. Reed arrived at his cell and read the death warrant, and then the procession formed. Quinn was escorted to the gallows by prison guards and persistent clergymen, and faltered only slightly as he rounded the corner of the hospital building and saw the gallows for the first time. He climbed the thirteen stairs with a steady gait and, once upon the platform, stepped to the forward railing. He looked over the small crowd of witnesses, mostly physicians, prison officials, and newspaper reporters, and made a brief speech in which he protested his innocence, still claiming that the shooting of his wife was an accident. When he concluded he stepped backward onto the trapdoor where his wrists and arms, knees and ankles were strapped, the black hood was pulled on, and the noose was adjusted. In but a moment the lever was pulled and the trap was sprung, but Quinn's neck failed to break in the fall because the cords in the back of his neck were abnormally large. He was slowly choking to death and his legs were twitching, and he managed to loosen the straps on his arms and dropped them to the ground. Still gasping for breath he begged the officials "This is awful, boys. For God's sake, take me up and drop me again, boys." Quinn struggled for some time as his speech became increasingly garbled and inarticulate, and finally he hung lifeless. Prison physician Dr. L. R. Quilliam monitored vital signs for twenty-two and one half minutes before allowing the body to be cut down and placed in a coffin, and then the remains were turned over to his sister for burial.

Prison officials warned the newspaper reporters that publication of the horrible details would result in prosecution of the public morals law. Newspapers which "printed the sickening details of the execution" violated a section of Oregon's criminal code which expressly forbid the publication of such matters, and the offense was punishable by "a fine of not more than $100." On May 19, 1910, the *Spokane Daily Chronicle* announced that W. D. Dodd, the editor of the *Bellingham Herald*, had been arrested on an information filed directly with the Superior Court charging a violation of the public morals statute forbidding the publication of the story of Richard Quinn's execution. Dodd asked for a speedy trial and was scheduled to appear on May 21. The article in the *Walla Walla Union* had been censored, leaving out all the gruesome details of the botched execution, and even showed a space in the text where the word "not" had been removed regarding Quinn's neck failing to break.

Everett Herald (WA): September 23–24, 1908. *Everett Tribune* (WA): September 19, 1908; September 23, 1908; May 13–14, 1910. *Morning Union* (Walla Walla, WA): May 13, 1910. *Spokane Chronicle* (WA): May 19, 1910.

Barkar, Frank
June 20, 1910

In 1908 Frank Barkar, a twenty-three-year-old soldier from the Third Infantry at Fort George Wright, and Civil War veteran Ira Messinger became embroiled in a heated argument at Medical Lake in Spokane County, Washington. The argument escalated into a physical assault and Barkar murdered the old soldier. He was tried and convicted of first degree murder when the jury refused to believe his claim of "self-defense during mutual combat." He was sentenced to hang in early 1909 but appeals delayed the execution until early 1910. After the state Supreme Court denied his last appeal an application was sent to Governor Marion E. Hay asking for a commutation of sentence, but the governor refused to intervene.

The condemned man was delivered to the prison, registered as prisoner number 5720, and lodged in the east wing of the cell block. While he awaited his date with the hangman he refused all offers of religious advice and displayed not the slightest concern for his fate. On the evening of June 19, after the prisoners were locked in their cells, the parts of the gallows were brought from storage and erected in the prison yard, using carriage bolts and screws so that no sound of a hammer was heard. On his final night the prisoner retired at an early hour and slept so soundly that he had to be jostled awake at 4:00 A.M. The prisoner ate a hearty breakfast and followed that with a chaw of tobacco, which he savored until he reached the scaffold. As he awaited the arrival of Superintendent C. S. Reed in his cell he dressed in his black burial suit, and before 5:00 A.M. the superintendent arrived to read the death warrant, and afterward Barkar told Reed that he would not speak to the witnesses. As the prisoner was escorted to the gallows the condemned man smiled and joked with the guards escorting him until he reached the foot of the stairway, and then refused to utter another word. He climbed the thirteen stairs and took his place on the center of the trapdoor where his wrists and arms, knees and ankles were strapped, the noose was adjusted, and the black hood was pulled on. There was a slight delay as the designated moment of sunrise was determined, and then the lever was pulled and the trap was sprung. Barkar's neck broke in the fall, and prison physician Dr. L. R. Quilliam monitored Barkar's vital signs and when his heart ceased to beat the doctor pronounced him dead. The body was lowered into the coffin provided by the state and he was buried in the prison cemetery, without a service, later that afternoon.

Bellingham Herald (WA): June 20, 1910. *Spokane Chronicle* (WA): June 20. 1910.

Jahns, William F.
April 21, 1911

In 1909 the widow Agnes Jansen migrated from Germany to America, arriving in Spokane, Washington, in May where she took a room at the boarding house of Margaret Aherns. Three months later she met sixty-three-year-old James Logan, an alias, as his real name was William Frederick Jahns, who had come to the city to hire a housekeeper. Jansen took the job and went with Logan to his Cedonia farm, where Logan employed George Hilton and Jack Tisth as hired hands. In mid–October Logan went to Spokane and stopped by Aherns' boarding house to pick up Jansen's mail. She had one letter written in German and, though Logan was German, he could not read the language. He had the letter translated and learned his housekeeper had just received $3,500 in American money, which was to be transferred from a German bank to an American bank account in her name. He immediately planned her murder, returned to his farm, and began laying the groundwork.

He went to the abandoned Hergesheimer ranch and stacked a large pile of logs, six feet square and six feet high, to serve as a funeral pyre, and some logs were so large they could only be hauled by a horse. He then convinced Jansen to accompany him on a business trip to Chicago, saying he was going to recruit other Germans to settle on his extensive land holdings. On October 27, 1909, at midnight the couple left the Logan farm, but instead of turning toward Blue Creek where the train depot was located, Logan turned the opposite direction toward the Hergesheimer ranch and Jansen, who was unfamiliar with the area, did not realize they were heading in the wrong direction. Three hours later they arrived at the Hergesheimer ranch and Logan convinced Jansen they should wait until daylight. She agreed and Logan opened the gate for Jansen to drive the team through. When Jansen came abreast of Logan he pulled his pistol and, without hesitation, shot her in the head twice. He dragged the body from the wagon, threw it onto the pyre of logs, and ignited them and within hours Jansen's remains were almost entirely consumed by the flames.

Logan had not expected anyone to be in the vicinity at that hour but he was seen by Al Stayt as they pulled their wagon up to the Hergesheimer gate. The Giffords — Elmer, Ira and uncle Charles — were hunting in the area and saw the fire, much too large for a mere campfire. The fire raised concern from other neighbors as well and soon "Swede" Johnson came to investigate. Johnson did not have any reason to suspect foul play and, after a brief conversation with Logan, he left. At 6:00 A.M. O. D. Taylor, a farmer living two miles from the Hergesheimer ranch, noticed the fire and he went to investigate. Logan was found asleep in his wagon and, when aroused, said that he had a sick horse so he had waited there while his housekeeper continued on to Blue Creek, riding with a man who had passed during the night. As soon as the fire burned down to a safe level Logan continued on his way to Blue Creek, arriving the next day, but meeting people all along his route. He paid Johnny Cline to take his team and wagon back to Cedonia and he went by train to Davenport. There he went to the bank, identified himself as Jansen's husband, and tried to withdraw her money but he was refused. He took a room at the hotel while he pondered how to get his hands on Jansen's fortune.

After hunting throughout the night the Giffords decided to investigate that huge fire, and went to the Hergesheimer ranch. They picked through the ashes and found the remains of a human hand, and hurried to Taylor's farm house to summon Stevens County Sheriff W. H. Graham from Colville. The sheriff arrived with Coroner Cook and the district attorney, and they found a box of .32-caliber shells, a hat pin, wires from a woman's hat, a woman's belt buckle, corset stays, and a bit of bridge work. The ashes were carefully searched and they also found a small piece of a vertebrae, a piece of a skull, and a leg bone. These were gathered for evidence and investigators next documented the blood stain at the gate and the wagon tracks in the muddy yard. The sheriff backtracked the wagon to the Logan farm and while Graham was questioning the hired hands Johnny Cline arrived with Logan's wagon, and told the lawman that Logan was heading to Davenport. Graham called Davenport's Sheriff Gardiner to be on the lookout for Logan, and he soon had the culprit behind bars, and Logan gave up his .32-caliber Navy revolver without resistance. Gardiner then searched Logan's room and found many incriminating items, including letters and checks belonging to a David R. Shively, who had been reported missing, and the letter addressed to Jansen. He also found a number of notary seals, stamps, and perforators used on railroads.

Sheriff Graham went to Davenport and collected his prisoner and evidence, and he believed he could solve a number of cases with this one arrest. He soon found out that Logan was not his prisoner's real name, so he sent photos around the region and had the picture published in the *Seattle Times*. From Bellingham's deputy DeHaven he learned Logan had previously used the name of Romandorf and had disappeared from Maple Falls at the same time as James Logan, and then presumably assumed his name to steal his property and money. However, there was no direct evidence he had murdered Logan, but it was learned that while he was using the name Logan he had lured Shively, a landowner from Addy, to Spokane and poisoned him. He put the body in a trunk and shipped it to his Cedonia farm where George Hilton buried it without questioning the order. George Hilton, it was discovered, was Logan's son Edward and the photos circulated revealed he had been known in Maple Falls as Edward Romandorf.

During his early days in jail, and as the story of his background unfolded, Logan speculated, "I suppose that when you start trailing me back and find out I was once in South Africa, you will accuse me of doing things like that down there, too." This alerted Graham that Logan, alias Romandorf, might have other aliases so he sent photos to South Africa and found that Logan's true identity was William Frederick Jahns, sometimes misspelled Johns, a man wanted for murdering eight men during diamond robberies. South African lawmen had tracked Jahns to New Orleans before losing his trail.

Jahns was indicted for the murder of Jansen and his trial began in Judge Daniel H. Carey's Colville courtroom on January 4, 1910. It took several days just to seat the jury before the prosecution presented a large number of witnesses, and linked together a trail of evidence which seemed impossible to refute. The defense had elected not to plead insanity, but as the case against their client strengthened they decided to try that legal ploy. Unfortunately for the defense there were many reputable witnesses who were able and ready to refute their claim of insanity, and Drs. L. B. Harvey and M. F. Setter examined the defendant and pronounced him sane. When the jurors retired to consider the evidence they were out just one hour, long enough for two votes, before bringing in a unanimous verdict of guilty of first degree murder. Judge Carey sentenced Jahns to hang at the prison in Walla Walla on April 21, 1911. He was delivered to the prison, registered as prisoner number 5998, and lodged in the east wing of the cell block. Neither appeal nor application for executive clemency delayed the fatal day.

Jahns was scheduled to hang at sunrise, so

on the evening before his death, after the prisoners were locked in their cells, the parts of the gallows were brought from storage and erected in the prison yard quietly using carriage bolts and screws. During his final days in prison Jahns spent his time reading everything he could acquire. Officials were hopeful that Jahns would eventually confess and give the location of the remains of the missing Logan and also details related to the murder of Bellingham butcher Frederick L. Dames, but the prisoner would not speak of them. On his final morning the prisoner was awakened at an early hour and he ate a hearty breakfast before dressing in his black burial suit. Before 5:00 A.M. Superintendent C. S. Reed arrived at Jahns' cell and read the death warrant, and then the procession formed. Jahns was escorted to the gallows, where he climbed the thirteen stairs and stepped to the railing, looked over the small crowd of witnesses consisting of mostly lawmen and newspaper reporters, and made a brief speech in which he protested his innocence. When he concluded he stepped backward onto the trapdoor where his wrists and arms, knees and ankles were strapped, the black hood was pulled on, and the noose was adjusted. In but a moment the lever was pulled and the trap was sprung. Jahns dropped, breaking his neck in the fall, and prison Dr. L. R. Quilliam announced that death was instantaneous, though he monitored vital signs for a brief period before pronouncing him dead. The body was then cut down, deposited in the coffin provided, and delivered to the dead man's son for burial.

Bellingham Herald (WA): April 21, 1911. *Idaho Statesman* (Boise): April 22, 1911. *Spokane Review* (WA): October 30–31, 1909; November 4–7, 1909; January 2–4, 1910; January 9, 1910; January 12–22, 1910; April 21–22, 1911.

Mayberry, Edward
April 19, 1917

Thirty-seven-year-old Edward Mayberry, a one-quarter Cherokee Indian, and Alice Vivian, half Colville Indian, lived together as man and wife on the Colville Indian Reservation. Mixed-blood Indians were not allowed to wed but the law was about to change and Mayberry and Vivian planned to be married in December. On August 14, 1916, Mayberry and Vivian were at home when they had a heated argument and Mayberry shot Vivian to death with his revolver, and a careful examination of the scene showed the killing was murder. Mayberry fled but never went far from their home and, even though hundreds of Indians bent on revenge and dozens of lawmen were scouring the area, Mayberry managed to avoid detection until Wednesday night when he surrendered to Thomas Dennen at Keller. Dennen warned, "If you surrender to me I will kill you if you try to get away," and Mayberry handed over his rifle and revolver and said, "Take these and kill me." He insisted that the shooting was accidental and he begged to be taken to the grave of his wife, and also admitted he had watched the funeral the previous day from a hill not far from the cemetery. When he arrived at the grave he collapsed onto it and cried.

He was then taken to the home of B. D. Dixon and the three started for Spokane the next morning, but Dennen and Dixon sent word ahead and were met by a small force of deputies. Deputy marshal David L. Hiatt was in charge of the deputies and during the trip to the Spokane jail Mayberry confessed the killing, and the circumstances supported the conclusion it was murder. Washington State had abolished the death penalty but the murder had occurred on an Indian reservation so it was a federal matter, and the death penalty was still available. Mayberry was tried in the U.S. Circuit Court in mid–November and on November 23 he was found guilty of first degree murder. Judge Rudkin then sentenced the prisoner to hang on January 29, 1917, but an appeal delayed the execution.

Once the judgment and sentence were reviewed and affirmed by the U.S. Supreme Court the case was postponed to March 20 while a place was found to conduct the hanging. The roof of the federal building was considered first but on March 15 the treasury department denied U.S. Marshal J. E. McGovern use of the structure for that purpose. Meanwhile President Woodrow Wilson granted a respite to Tuesday, April 10, to review the request for a commutation or pardon, and it was believed by most that Mayberry would never hang. However, President Wilson surprised everyone when he declined to intervene, and then Marshal McGovern was allowed nine days, to April 19, to make his arrangements at Fort George Wright. Mayberry, meanwhile, was lodged in the Spokane jail while the gallows was being built behind a stand of pine trees at the base of a hill not far from the fort's guardhouse.

On his last night Mayberry slept soundly, arose at 4:30 A.M., and ate a hearty breakfast. It was still dark when an automobile drove up to the jail and Mayberry was brought out by Marshal McGovern and a deputy. They drove onto the military reservation, but there McGovern stopped his automobile and turned back the seven vehicles following them. They then continued to the guardhouse and from there walked directly to the gallows, where the small number of authorized witnesses had already gathered. Mayberry climbed the stairs and took his position behind the trapdoor, where he waived the reading of the death warrant. He was asked if he had anything to say and he spent five minutes proclaiming his innocence, thanking everyone for his treatment while in jail, and concluded by saying he held no malice toward anyone.

He took his place on the trapdoor and did all he could to help the deputy marshals bind his wrists and arms, knees and ankles. Marshal McGovern then pulled the black hood over his head to his shoulders and adjusted the noose. As McGovern stepped back he signaled and deputy marshals Thorp, Dennison and Sunday each pulled a rope, two being dummies, and the trap was sprung just as the first rays of sunlight appeared. Mayberry dropped five feet, breaking his neck, and Drs. H. H. McCarthy and E. P. Condon monitored his vital signs until his heart ceased to beat and then they pronounced him dead. Marshal McGovern cut the rope and lowered the body into the arms of jailor William Nelson, who turned the remains over to undertaker Hazen and Jaeger to be held for relatives.

Ogden Examiner (UT): April 20, 1917. *Ogden Standard* (UT): November 23, 1916. *Press* (Piqua, OH): April 2, 1917. *Spokesman-Review* (Spokane, WA): August 22, 1916; April 24, 1917.

Schmidt, John
April 1, 1921

On Monday evening, December 22, 1919, a lone bandit held up a store in Olympia, Washington, and as he fled he was chased by E. H. Schultz, a garage man in Olympia. The two men exchanged gun fire and Schultz was shot dead. The next night the same bandit, after moving his operation to Seattle, tried to rob a stationery store but the streets were filled with Christmas shoppers and when the bandit failed in his attempt he fled into the streets. He held a crowd of over a hundred people at bay with his automatic pistol by wounding two men, but finally escaped by blending into the crowd, and over the next year the same bandit committed a number of armed robberies throughout Washington state.

At 9:00 P.M. on January 21, 1921, Seattle patrolmen William T. Angle and Neil C. McMillan were walking their beat in the Capitol Hill section of town and at Second Avenue and Cherry Street they stopped a suspicious person and began frisking him for weapons. The suspect suddenly pulled a handgun and shot Angle twice, then turned his pistol on McMillan and shot him several times. Angle had been incapacitated by his wounds and officer McMillan fired several shots at the fleeing suspect but missed his target, and McMillan died where he collapsed. Angle was rushed to the hospital where he died in two hours, as the bullets had destroyed vital organs. At 10:00 P.M. officers throughout Seattle were searching for the murderer of McMillan when patrolmen James O'Brien and C. G. Montgomery stopped a likely suspect, Dean Carman, at Second Avenue and Columbia Street. While they were preoccupied with Carman the murderer walked up to them and without warning shot O'Brien. O'Brien returned fire as he fell, wounded the murderer in the leg, and died in seconds. Montgomery continued the gunfight but soon the wounded murderer surrendered. On January 24, John Schmidt, an alias, confessed to killing the patrolmen, saying to Sheriff Matt Starwich, "Anything to escape arrest." He said that after he killed officers Angle and McMillan he reloaded his automatic pistol, kept his finger on the trigger, and walked down Second Avenue toward downtown, where he encountered patrolmen O'Brien and Montgomery.

On January 27 he pled guilty to a charge of first degree murder in the killing of O'Brien, and then the jurors at a formal hearing affirmed the verdict and fixed the sentence at death, and Schmidt was scheduled to hang on April 1, 1921. After sentencing the prisoner turned to Sheriff Starwich and said anxiously, "Let's go, sheriff," and once back in his cell he confessed to the murder of E. H. Schultz. There was no delay in the proceedings from appeal nor from a plea for executive clemency, and Schmidt scolded his attorneys for delaying the proceedings with motions and demanded, "I want to get it over with." Schmidt would not divulge anything from his earlier life, though he gave quite a detailed account of the many robberies he had committed during the previous two years. He was not interested in religion and was anxious to end his life on the gallows.

Just before midnight March 31 the warden appeared at Schmidt's cell door and read the death warrant. The prisoner was conducted into the death chamber where he took his place on the trapdoor and his wrists and arms, knees and ankles were bound and the noose was adjusted. When asked if he had anything to say he shook his head, so the black hood was pulled on and the trap was sprung. Schmidt dropped but the fall did not break his neck so he struggled as he strangled to death, and the prison physician pronounced him dead in twelve minutes. The body was then cut down, deposited in the coffin provided by the state, and buried on prison grounds that afternoon.

Las Vegas Optic (NM): April 2, 1921. *Reno Gazette* (NV): December 24, 1919. *Fairbanks News-Miner* (AK): January 28, 1921. *Ogden Standard-Examiner* (UT): April 1, 1921.

Mahoney, James E.
December 1, 1922

In early April 1921 thirty-seven-year-old James E. Mahoney married seventy-two-year-old Kate Mooers at Seattle, Washington. On April 16, as the newly-wed couple prepared to go east for their honeymoon, Mahoney bludgeoned his bride to death and stuffed her body in a trunk. He took the makeshift coffin to Lake Union and weighted it with rocks, put it in a row boat, rowed it to a deep spot and dumped it overboard. The next day Mahoney left for the east, being careful that no one saw him leave alone, and over the next several months he forged a power of attorney to gain control of his dead wife's $200,000 fortune, sent forged letters back to Seattle to show Kate was still alive, and conducted several transactions including a visit to a notary public while bringing along a woman he introduced as his wife. When Mahoney returned to Seattle he was arrested on several counts of forgery and he was still in jail when Kate's body was discovered on August 8. He was charged with her murder and the following day he was subjected to "four hours of grilling," but the prisoner said he would sleep on the proposal to confess, then refused to discuss the matter with the authorities.

He was indicted in September and his trial in Judge J. T. Ronald's Seattle courtroom was in progress when, on September 26, Kate's nieces testified to identification of the remains by articles of clothing and to the forged signatures on several documents. The defense fought hard to keep out the testimony about the forgeries which were uttered to gain control over Kate's money, as this was presented as the motive for the murder, but they failed. All the evidence against Mahoney was circumstantial but was so well linked that the jurors deliberated only briefly before finding him guilty of first degree murder and fixing the penalty at death. After the prisoner was sentenced to hang his attorneys filed an appeal which stayed the execution, but in late 1922 the Supreme Court justices affirmed the judgment of the King County Superior Court and Mahoney's date with the hangman was set for December 1, 1922. The application for a commutation of sentence was denied. As a final effort to save her brother, Dolores Johnson, in late November, sent a written confession to acting–Governor W. J. Coyle saying she killed Kate Mooers-Mahoney in self-defense following an argument over money. However, Johnson, who was thought to be the woman who appeared as Mrs. Mahoney during business transactions, was shown at trial to be, at most, an accessory after-the-fact. On November 29 the condemned man, to prevent his sister from being implicated, finally confessed all the details of the murder of his aged wife, and the following day the acting governor denied the final plea for a respite or commutation of sentence.

During Mahoney's last month he slept little and showed such nervousness that a death watch was posted throughout the entire month of November. On his final night he asked for food but could eat only a cookie with a cup of coffee before receiving the last sacrament from Father Stephen Buckley. He spent a sleepless night with his priest in attendance and arose from his bunk when breakfast was served. Warden John W. Pace appeared at his cell door at 6:30 A.M. and read the death warrant, and then he was conducted into the death chamber a few minutes before 7:00 A.M. He took his place on the trapdoor where his wrists and arms, knees and ankles were bound and the noose was adjusted. When asked if he had anything to say to the small party of witnesses he declined.

Father Buckley then pressed a crucifix to his lips and as he stepped back, praying for the soul of the condemned man, the black hood was pulled over his head. At 7:02 A.M. the trap was sprung and Mahoney broke his neck in the fall. Prison physician Dr. J. W. Ingram, assisted by another doctor, monitored his vital signs until he pronounced him dead at 7:08. The body was then cut down, deposited in the coffin provided by his sister, and he was taken to a local undertaking parlor. Mahoney's remains were prepared for shipment to Snohomish, Washington, to be buried in the family plot.

Cumberland Times (MD): December 1, 1922. *Anaconda Standard* (MT): September 27, 1921. *Cedar Rapids Gazette* (IA): August 10, 1921. *Lincoln Star* (NE): December 1, 1922. *Salt Lake Tribune* (UT): December 2, 1922.

Whitfield, George E.
June 13, 1924

On the afternoon of March 8, 1923, eleven-year-old Anna Nosko was on her way home from the Battle Ground, Washington, public school and her usual path took her across the farm of John Tuke, not far from the farm house. Suddenly she was attacked, beaten and raped, her head crushed and her throat cut, and then the body was dragged some distance into a patch of thick underbrush and hidden. When Anna did not return home at the usual time her parents became concerned and organized a party of neighbors to search for her. The search party found the trail where a body had been dragged through two barbed wire fences, they found hair and clothing on the barbs, and then they found Anna's dead body where it had been hidden. Twenty-year-old George Edward Whitfield, a nephew of John Tuke, was arrested and lodged in the Clarke County jail when blood was found on his clothes, but he refused to answer any questions. The feeling was intense in Battle Ground, even among the jail prisoners, so Whitfield had to be confined in the solitary cell for his own protection.

On March 11 an information was filed charging Whitfield with the second degree murder of Anna Nosko but the prosecuting attorney said he expected that the charge would be increased to first degree murder, and it was. On March 13, John Tuke's farmhouse was burned to the ground and two men had been seen skulking away before the flames were discovered, but it seems no neighbors were available to lend a hand saving the house. In May 1923 Whitfield was tried for the murder of Anna Nosko and on May 5 he was convicted of first degree murder. The evidence against Whitfield was circumstantial but included: the human blood on his clothing; the murder weapon, a knife that was proved to belong to Whitfield; and his confession to a fellow jail inmate. Whitfield was sentenced to hang on July 12 but his attorneys filed an appeal which stayed the execution, and this resulted in a second trial. He was again convicted of first degree murder and sentenced to hang on June 13, 1924, but on appeal this time the state Supreme Court affirmed the judgment and sentence of the Superior Court. A petition praying for a commutation of sentence was sent to the governor but he declined to intervene.

After Whitfield's second conviction he was baptized into the Catholic religion by Father Stephen A. Buckley, who helped him resign himself to his fate. On his last night he was transferred to the trusty building where the gallows stood. Father Buckley was with him until a late hour and then he retired, but the condemned man slept fitfully, awaking several times. He arose at 3:30 A.M. and ate a light breakfast and he was conducted onto the gallows at 4:15 A.M. He took his place on the trapdoor where his wrists and arms, knees and ankles were bound and the noose was adjusted. After the death warrant was read by Warden Clarence E. Long, Whitfield was asked if he had anything to say but he declined, saying he had written out his statement and this was read to the prison officials and five witnesses:

> As I go to meet my God in whose mercy and goodness I trust, I wish to express the following feelings in my heart. I firmly trust that the good God will forgive me my sins. I forgive all who have injured me and I hope that all whom I have injured will pardon me. There is no bitterness in my heart toward a single one of my fellow beings. I absolve from blame all who took part in my trial because I feel that they did what they thought was right. I am very grateful to my attorney, Mr. Lane, who has stood by me through all my troubles and to all others who have befriended me and also to all the officers of this prison for they have all treated me very kindly. I wish no one ill luck, but to the contrary, I wish one and all good luck, prosperity, a long life on this earth and a happy home in Heaven hereafter.

He had also previously stated that he specifically forgave Sheriff Thompson and the district attorney, saying that the sheriff "spoke the truth all the way through."

After the reading was concluded Father Buckley pressed a crucifix to Whitfield's lips and then stepped back as the black hood was pulled over the prisoner's head. The trap was sprung at 4:38 A.M. and prison physician Dr. J. W. Ingram and Dr. J. P. Kane waited beneath the gallows to monitor vital signs. There was no pulse at three minutes, and in six minutes, at 4:44 A.M., the doctors pronounced Whitfield dead. The body was cut down and turned over to Father Buckley, who had the remains driven to the Calloway and Hennessey funeral parlor to be prepared for burial in the Catholic section of the cemetery in Walla Walla.

Oakland Tribune (CA): March 9, 1923. *Reno Gazette* (NV): March 9, 1923. *Independent* (Helena, MT): August 2, 1923. *Lincoln Star* (NE): June 13, 1924. *Lincoln State Journal* (NE): March 12, 1923. *Ogden Standard-Examiner* (UT): March 10, 1923; March 13, 1923. *Walla Walla Bulletin* (WA): June 12–14, 1924.

Waller, Ralph L.
June 27, 1924

On Sunday, March 23, 1924, Alfred Waldman and his new wife, Ida, were married at Pomeroy, Washington. Ralph L. Waller, a miner at Butte, Montana, believed that Ida would marry him as soon as Waller could get a divorce from his current wife, so he became insanely jealous when she married Waldman.

On the night of April 3 he took his pistol and went from Butte to the Waldman home in Pomeroy, Washington, where, without warning or hesitation, he shot the newlyweds to death and seriously wounded Waldman's mother, Barbara Waldman.

Waller fled to Lewiston, Montana, where he was arrested on the morning of April 4. He confessed to the murders and was on his way to Pomeroy when the officers learned that the community was so outraged it was likely he would be lynched as soon as he appeared there, so he was lodged in the county jail at Walla Walla, Washington. He was tried at Walla Walla and on May 13 the jurors found him guilty of first degree murder and recommended the death penalty, and he was sentenced to hang on June 27, 1924. Neither appeal nor petition praying for executive clemency would delay the proceedings.

Waller was delivered to the death row cells at the state prison in Walla Walla. During his final weeks Waller was visited by two priests from Pomeroy, and at 8:00 P.M. on June 26, 1924, the condemned man told Warden Clarence E. Long that he was "ready to pay the death penalty." Waller handed the warden a letter in which he wrote, "I am praying for forgiveness of my sin for I know I have sinned and sinned deeply, and I am mighty sorry. I am also praying for Ida and Alfred and I shall until my last day."

On the morning of June 27 after 4:30 A.M. Warden Long appeared at Waller's cell to read the death warrant, and then he was conducted from his cell into the death chamber where he stood at the foot of the stairs, and was asked if he had anything to say to the witnesses. He confessed the crime and asked forgiveness saying,

> I want to tell you that one of the worst crimes in the United States today is divorce; men, do all you can to avoid it; it sends men and women to hell. After trouble with my wife, I went to California, back to Oregon, Washington, Idaho, and Montana to try to get away from the feeling I had. One time in Montana I sat on a keg of powder intending to blow myself up but I did not have the nerve. When I heard that the woman I loved was married I came back to this section and could not resist killing her. I deserve everything I have got, and deserve to be hanged. I want to tell you, Warden Long, that you have a model penitentiary; in the time I have been here I have never heard a curse word. I have been treated as a man far better than I deserved. I have made my peace with God Almighty and hope he has pardoned me. I hope to meet you all in Heaven.

He then greeted a group of veterans and talked of his time fighting in France, and shook hands with everyone present. He climbed the stairs and took his place on the trapdoor where his wrists and arms, knees and ankles were bound, the noose was adjusted, and the black hood was pulled over his head. The trap was sprung at 4:45 A.M. and Walton broke his neck in the fall. Prison physician Dr. J. W. Ingram waited below and monitored his vital signs until he pronounced him dead at 4:56 A.M. The body was then cut down, placed in the coffin provided by the state, and the remains were taken to the funeral parlor of Calloway and Hennessey. Funeral services were conducted by the Reverend Father Fredericks, and Waller was buried in the Catholic section of the cemetery at 8:30 A.M.

Oakland Tribune (CA): June 27, 1924. *Billings Gazette* (MT): April 5, 1924. *Independent* (Helena, MT): May 14, 1924. *Walla Walla Union-Bulletin* (WA): June 27–28, 1924.

Walton, Thomas
December 12, 1924

On the evening of May 7, 1919, night watchman David Moorehouse discovered two men inside a Paso Robles, San Luis Obispo County, California, store after closing hours. During a running gun battle Moorehouse was killed and by May 28 the two murderers were behind bars. The two prisoners identified themselves as twenty-three-year-old Edwin Langdon and nineteen-year-old Hugh Moore, and they confessed to the killing. However, by July 30 Langdon had been identified as Seth P. Burt, an expert automobile thief who claimed credit for the theft of over three hundred fifty automobiles. Burt was sentenced to serve a life term at San Quentin Prison for killing Moorehouse and he shared a cell with Thomas Walton.

In 1915 Walton and George Hill, fellow workers at a box factory in Bray, Siskiyou County, California, argued in the cook house over the Thanksgiving day feast. Walton left but soon returned with a rifle and without warning or hesitation shot Hill twice, killing him. He then called the authorities at Weed, surrendered, was tried and convicted of first degree murder in January 1916, and sentenced to serve a life term at San Quentin Prison.

On January 25, 1922, a small prison automobile was parked in the prison yard and Burt and Walton, waiters in the prison dining room, snuck out of their work assignment and drove the car through the gates at 7:30 A.M. They were not missed until the inmate count at 11:00 A.M. and a subsequent search showed they were missing from the prison grounds. On April 16, 1923, Burt and Walton were giving an automobile ride to Gladys Homer, an eighteen-year-old waitress in Spokane, Washington, when Burt made certain proposals which caused the girl to leap from the speeding car. Deputy sheriff J. R "Dick" Cashatt, a motorcycle officer, saw the girl jump out and went in pursuit of the automobile. He stopped the car and was in the process of arresting Walton when he was shot through the right lung, but he survived. The girl had a fractured skull and it was thought she might die but she also recovered, and both victims gave a detailed description of the two men and their automobile. Posses were combing the area around Spokane for the two men or their automobile but Burt and Walton had driven east out of the area right after the shooting, and there was no clue to their destination.

One month later the automobile was observed by officers in Des Moines, Iowa, and after a harrowing chase the two men were captured and, though they gave the names Fred Fletcher and Jack Haines, they were known to be the two fugitives. They were extradited to Spokane, Washington, tried, convicted of shooting Cashatt, and sentenced to serve terms at the prison in Walla Walla: Burt was sentenced to serve five years to life and Walton was sentenced to serve eight to twenty years. They were not housed together and Burt's new cell mate was twenty-seven-year-old George MacDonald, who was serving a term of two to five years for burglary. Walton and Burt had a falling out because Walton was convinced Burt was telling MacDonald about his former cell mate.

At 11:00 A.M. on the morning of October 7, 1923, as a line of convicts was emerging from the chapel and passing another line entering, Walton suddenly leaped out of his line and rushed toward the other line of convicts, and he drove his prison-made knife into Burt's heart killing him instantly. He then turned on MacDonald and stabbed him several times before guard E. P. Gregory knocked him down and disarmed him. MacDonald was taken to the prison hospital where he died that night and Walton was charged with two counts of first degree murder.

Walton was tried before the end of the year, convicted of first degree murder, and sentenced to hang in February 1924. His court appointed attorneys filed an appeal with the state Supreme Court which stayed the execution, but in October the justices affirmed the judgment and sentence of the Superior Court and the date for Walton's execution was set for December 12, 1924. Neither appeal nor petition for executive clemency would delay the proceedings further.

On the morning of December 12 after 5:00 A.M. the warden appeared at Walton's cell to read the death warrant, but the condemned man waived the reading and seemed anxious to proceed. He was conducted from his cell into the death chamber and took his place on the trapdoor where his wrists and arms, knees and ankles were bound, the noose was adjusted, and the black hood was pulled over his head. The trap was sprung at 5:30 A.M. and Walton broke his neck in the fall, and the prison physician pronounced him dead within a few minutes. The body was then cut down, placed in the coffin provided by the state, and he was buried on the prison grounds later that day.

Lincoln State Journal (NE): May 17, 1923; December 13, 1924. *Nevada State Journal* (Reno): October 8, 1923. *Oakland Tribune* (CA): July 30, 1919. *Reno Gazette* (NV): May 28, 1919. *Woodland Daily Democrat* (CA): January 25, 1923. *Independent* (Helena, MT): October 8, 1923. *Ogden Standard-Examiner* (UT): April 17, 1923.

Moseley, L. E.
February 19, 1926

During the late evening hours of July 4, 1924, Seattle police officer Amos J. Comer responded to a disturbance at a businessmen's club at 614 Jackson Street and was told that a man had brandished a revolver and threatened, "I will shoot the first guy who bothers me." Comer searched inside the club but could not find the man, but when he returned to the front door the man was waiting for him. Comer was patting him down for the weapon when he pulled the revolver and shot Comer twice, and the officer collapsed. The man then tried to attack the wounded officer using the pistol as a club but bystanders restrained him, and then the attacker managed to break free and flee. Comer was rushed to the hospital but the two bullets had caused severe damage to several vital organs and he died after midnight, but he named L. E. Moseley as his murderer before succumbing to his wounds.

Officers began a systematic search for the murderer of their fellow officer and soon they had Moseley, a former convict from California's Folsom Prison, behind bars. Moseley had served a term for second degree murder and moved to Seattle, Washington, after he was released, and was well-known to the police. He was tried at the fall term of the King County Superior Court and on October 24, 1924, he was convicted of first degree murder. He was sentenced to hang in December but his attorney filed an appeal which stayed the execution. The state Supreme Court justices affirmed the judgment and sentence of the lower court on December 7, 1925, and Moseley was sentenced to hang on February 19, 1926. His attorney then petitioned Governor Roland H. Hartley for executive clemency, but the governor refused to intervene.

Moseley was described as one of the most composed condemned men ever to await his death at the prison in Walla Walla, but he had refused all religious consolation saying he did not believe in a life after death. On his last night he ate heartily of a steak dinner and then wrote four letters, and in each he proclaimed his innocence. After being awakened at 5:00 A.M. he ate a large breakfast and then Warden Clarence E. Long appeared at the cell door at 5:45 to conduct him to the gallows. When they arrived Moseley bounded up the stairs and his guards had to hurry after him, and he quickly took his place on the trapdoor without prompting. He glanced down at the witnesses, comprised of several physicians, police officials, and newspaper reporters, as his wrists and arms, knees and ankles were bound and the noose was adjusted. Warden Long asked if he wanted to hear the death warrant read and he declined, saying, "I know the contents of the warrant and there is no point in repeating it." The warden then asked if he had anything to say, and he replied, "That would be a joke. What I have already said still stands."

The black hood was pulled over his head at 5:56 A.M. and the trap was sprung immediately. Beneath the gallows Dr. J. W. Ingram waited and monitored vital signs until he pronounced Moseley dead at 6:03 A.M., but the body hung until 6:11 and then was cut down and deposited in the coffin provided by the state. Moseley was buried in the prison cemetery that afternoon, without any service according to his last request.

Seattle Times (WA): February 19, 1926. *Salt Lake Tribune* (UT): February 20, 1926. *Walla Walla Bulletin* (WA): February 19, 1926.

Winters, Alfred
May 27, 1927

Twenty-five-year-old Alfred Winters, alias Williams, and twenty-five-year-old Minnie

Scott had lived together as husband and wife at Aberdeen, Washington, since 1920 but in June 1925 Scott moved to Longview where her sister Louise Kelly lived. Winters soon followed Scott to Longview and the couple again lived together. Kelly would later say Scott had left Winters at Aberdeen because she did not want to live with him any longer, but Winters claimed Scott sent for him. On December 21 the police told Scott that she was an undesirable character and ordered her to leave Longview, so the following day Winters gave her $25 to go to Portland, where the rest of her family lived. At 11:00 A.M. on December 23, 1925, Winters, Scott and Kelly were walking in the corridor between the colored section and the business district in Longview, discussing what they had done the previous Christmas. Scott intended to leave Longview later that afternoon and Winters believed he would not see her again. He suddenly grabbed Scott's arm and spun her about as he pulled a .38-caliber automatic German Luger pistol from his belt and fired two shots point-blank. One bullet struck Scott in the breast but the second bullet missed its mark as she collapsed, and she bled to death in seconds. Winters then turned to Kelly and said, "Don't you say anything or I'll kill you too," and then he started walking toward Commerce Street.

Kelly called the authorities and Coroner W. D. van Note arrived to take charge of Scott's body, while the officers went to the Rainier Building on Commerce Street. Winters worked as a janitor at the Rainier Building and at 11:30 A.M. the police arrested him without resistance. As soon as he was in jail he confessed the murder to chief H. W. Jackson and said that he and Scott had been "arguing off and on for five years over money, and I was tired of her nagging." At 2:00 P.M. an information was filed charging Winters with Scott's murder; Judge Homer Kirby then gave him until the next morning to plead. He pled not guilty and attorney E. D. Germain was appointed to defend him. Winters was tried at Kelso in January 1926 and sentenced to hang in March. His attorney filed an appeal which stayed the execution and he remained in the jail at Kelso until the state Supreme Court affirmed the judgment and sentence of the Superior Court, and on April 27, 1927, he was delivered to the prison at Walla Walla with his execution scheduled for May 27. Nothing further would arise to delay the proceedings.

During Winters' time on death row he was attended by Catholic chaplain Michael Hessian, and the priest helped him resign himself to his fate. Father Hessian was with Winters his last night and they remained awake praying and reading scripture. After breakfast was served Warden Clarence E. Long appeared at the cell door and read the death warrant, and then the warden and Captain of the Guard S. E. Bunker, with father Hessian, conducted Winters to the gallows. As soon as he was on the trapdoor his wrists and arms, knees and ankles were bound and the noose was adjusted. Warden Long asked Winters if he had anything to say to the members of the state parole board who were acting as witnesses and he replied, "Not a word." Father Hessian pressed a cross to the prisoner's lips and when he stepped back the black hood was pulled over Winters' head, and at 5:06 A.M. the trap was sprung. Prison physician Dr. J. W. Ingram waited beneath the gallows and he pronounced Winters dead at 5:20 A.M., and the body was then cut down and deposited in the coffin provided by the state. Winters was buried in the Catholic section of the cemetery later that afternoon.

Longview News (WA): December 23–24, 1925. *San Mateo Times* (CA): May 27, 1927. *Walla Walla Bulletin* (WA): May 27, 1927.

Lopez, Manuel
February 15, 1928

In 1926 Manuel Lopez worked for the Union Pacific Railroad at Riparia, Washington, but he had not been doing his work to the satisfaction of his supervisors. On October 26 section foreman Charles Markham fired Lopez, who vowed revenge. Lopez got a pistol, found Markham, and shot him to death. He was quickly captured, lodged in the jail at Colfax, and charged with murder. He was tried in December and on December 16, after brief deliberations, the jurors convicted him of first degree murder and he was sentenced to hang in February 1927. His court appointed attorney filed an appeal which stayed the execution for a year, until the state Supreme Court justices affirmed the judgment and sentence of the lower court and Lopez was resentenced to hang on February 15, 1928. Governor Roland H. Hartley, when petitioned for a commutation of sentence, refused to intervene.

During his final days on death row the condemned man was attended by the prison's Catholic chaplain and on the morning of February 15 he was awakened at an early hour and served breakfast. His priest then administered the last rites and the warden appeared after 5:00 A.M. to read the death warrant. Lopez was then conducted onto the gallows where he took his place on the trapdoor and his wrists and arms, knees and ankles were bound. He was asked if he had anything to say to the witnesses but the condemned man declined to make a statement.

The noose was quickly adjusted, the black hood was pulled over his head, and at 5:36 A.M. the trap was sprung. Dr. J. W. Ingram, the prison physician, waited beneath the gallows and monitored Lopez' vital signs until he pronounced him dead at 5:45 A.M., and the doctor announced that the prisoner's neck had been broken in the fall. The body was then cut down, deposited into the coffin provided by the state, and he was buried in the Catholic section of the prison cemetery later that day.

Seattle Times (WA): February 16, 1928.

Bailey, Emmett
August 10, 1928

Forty-two-year-old Emmett Bailey and his wife, Erma, who lived at Centralia, Washington, had serious marital difficulties and finally she divorce him and reclaimed her maiden name of Skinner. On the night of January 29, 1927, Bailey attended a dance and drank liquor to excess and when he left the dance after midnight he decided to stop at the home of his estranged wife, but when he arrived he found three men had arrived ahead of him. He became inflamed with jealousy, pulled and brandished his revolver, and when his wife appeared he shot her. Skinner lingered for two days before she died of her wound and then Bailey, who was lodged in the Lewis County jail, was charged with her murder.

Bailey was indicted and tried in Judge H. E. McKenney's Cowlitz courtroom in early March and in his defense he claimed the fatal shot was an accidental discharge of his weapon. The jurors, on March 12, found the defendant guilty of first degree murder and recommended the death penalty. After he was sentenced to hang an appeal was filed with the state Supreme Court. Baily was kept in the Lewis County jail while the appeal was pending and he tried twice to escape, and when that failed he attempted suicide by swallowing bichloride of mercury tablets, but he was saved by prompt medical attention. Fifteen months after being sentenced the Supreme Court justices affirmed the judgment and sentence of the Superior Court and the date for Bailey's execution was set for August 10, 1928, and he was delivered to the death row cells at the state prison in Walla Walla. The family of the condemned man then became active and collected five thousand signatures on a petition to have the sentence commuted to life imprisonment, but when it was submitted to Governor Roland H. Hartley he refused to intervene.

On Wednesday, August 8, as the sound of hammers and saws echoed off the prison walls from construction of the gallows, Bailey's mother and sisters arrived for their final visit. The condemned man was attended by the prison chaplain Reverend E. T. Allen and the reverend was with him when the warden appeared at his cell door at 4:30 A.M. to read the death warrant.

Bailey was then conducted onto the gallows where he took his place on the trapdoor. His wrists and arms, knees and ankles were strapped and then he was asked if he had anything to say to the dozen witnesses, but the condemned man replied only, "Reverend Allen has all I have to say." The noose was quickly adjusted, the black hood was pulled over his head, and at 5:06 A.M. the trap was sprung. Dr. J. W. Ingram, the prison physician, waited beneath the gallows and monitored Bailey's vital signs until he pronounced him dead at 5:14 A.M., and the doctor announced that his neck had been broken in the fall. The body was then cut down, deposited into the coffin provided by his mother, and shipped to the Sticklin Mortuary in Centralia where he would be prepared for burial.

Centralia Chronicle (WA): August 8, 1928; August 10, 1928. *Billings Gazette* (MT): August 11, 1928.

Gaines, Wallace C.
August 31, 1928

Twenty-two-year-old Sylvia Howard Gaines, after she graduated from Smith College in Massachusetts, located her estranged father and traveled to Seattle, Washington, to visit Wallace C. "Bob" Gaines and her stepmother Bessie, who had been in California for several months. On Wednesday evening, June 16, 1926, Sylvia and her father argued and at 8:00 P.M. she left the house to walk around Green Lake. Suddenly at 9:00 P.M. a roughly dressed man leaped from the bushes and seized Sylvia, and when she screamed he put his hands about her throat to quiet her, and her dead body was found on Thursday morning at 9:00 A.M. The first clue to the murderer came from F. S. Stokes and his wife who were walking on a path when they saw "a horrible looking man" making his way through the brush several yards from the path. After they had walked a short distance they passed Gaines walking in the opposite direction, but when they heard screams several minutes later it sounded more like children at play and they dismissed the incident. They reported to the police and their description of the roughly dressed man was very detailed.

Detectives processing the scene recreated the crime: the man seized Gaines without warning but she screamed; he choked her and dragged her, and her hat and slippers fell off; she broke away and waded through the shallow edge of the lake for several yards while her attacker pursued her; as they emerged from the water he again strangled her and then murdered her with five blows to the head with a large rock. Odessa and Dwight Gaskill, after hearing of the murder, came forward and said they may have seen the murder:

> We were returning home from the Green Lake library Wednesday evening just about dark, between 9:00 and 9:15 o'clock I should say, and took a shortcut along a path that skirts the lake. I noticed what I thought was a boy of slender build cross the path a short distance in front of us, walking from a pile of refuse on the right where a fill was being made. He was walking hurriedly and seemed slightly stooped, as if he was carrying something heavy. He crossed to the lake shore or almost, and seemed to kneel down. Maybe he stepped down a little bank at the edge of the water. We heard a moaning sound and Dwight called, "Hey, kid, what's the matter there?" The fellow answered, "Oh, just a drunken guy here." And then he cried — at the time we thought it was to the drunken companion — "Shut up or the cops will get you." The moaning sound was like a gurgle. We saw the fellow raise a rock. I thought then he threw it into the lake for there was a sort of splashing sound. This was repeated several times. I guess we walked on thinking it was only a couple of boys who were drunk.

The investigation continued and on June 29, after the inquest, the victim's father was arrested when evidence pointed to a "strange and unnatural relationship" between the father and daughter, and showed that the quarrel on the night of her death was over her desire to end the relationship. Sheriff Matt Starwich announced that Louis Stern, a friend of Gaines, had said that Gaines confessed to killing his daughter. Gaines was charged with murder and he was tried in mid–August. On August 12 his neighbors, George and Olive Memmers, testified and George said, "Gaines told me that he and Sylvia intended getting an apartment downtown when his wife returned from California." Olive then testified that she saw "Gaines peek out the front window and not answer the door when visitors called. I can't recall whether he wore a bathrobe or not. Sylvia, wearing a silk nightgown, peeked too. Sylvia rearranged the covers and messed pillows on the living room couch. The following day he told me 'I am not sleeping with Bessie. I am sleeping with Sylvia.'" Patrolman Davis then testified that he had arrested Gaines and his daughter sitting in an unlighted automobile in a Seattle Park at 1:00 A.M. Fred Neindorff testified that Gaines told him he had driven around the lake looking for Sylvia on the night she was killed.

The evidence, though circumstantial, was strong and well linked and the jurors found Gaines guilty of murder in the first degree. Gaines was sentenced to hang but his attorneys filed an appeal with the state Supreme Court and, when that failed, they filed an appeal with the U.S. Supreme Court, but that was also to no avail. The date for his execution was finally set for August 31, 1928, two years after his conviction. His attorneys then filed an application praying for a commutation of sentence, but Governor Roland H. Hartley declined to intervene.

Gaines prepared a statement and gave it to his wife to publish, and it said, "I do not forgive the friends who are the cause of taking an innocent man's life, and I know that they will be made to suffer for the unjust punishment they have inflicted upon my family. They will pay dearly for this outrage on earth and in the hereafter, for their sins will find them out." Frank Novak, the prison evangelist, arrived at Gaines' cell on Thursday at 7:00 P.M. and remained with him until the warden appeared shortly before 4:00 A.M. to read the death warrant. Novak accompanied the condemned man as he was conducted from his cell into the death chamber. He took his place on the trapdoor and said to Novak, "I am sorry, I was drinking that night," perhaps as a sort of last minute confession to save his soul. He then turned to the warden and said, "Get it over with as quick as possible."

He had nothing further to say to the small group of witnesses, made up of prison officials and newsmen, so his wrists and arms, knees and ankles were bound, the noose was adjusted, and the black hood was pulled over his head at 4:07 A.M. The trap was sprung immediately and Gaines dropped, breaking his neck in the fall, and Dr. J. W. Ingram monitored his vital signs until he pronounced him dead eight minutes later. The body was then cut down, deposited in the coffin provided, and released to his wife for burial. Bessie Gaines had stood by her husband throughout the ordeal and had testified that the relationship with his daughter was not unnatural, even though she had been absent from their home the entire time the daughter was living there.

Fairbanks News-Miner (AK): August 12, 1926. *Olean Times* (NY): August 31, 1928. *Reno Gazette* (NV): June 18, 1926. *Santa Fe New Mexican*: August 31, 1928. *Morning Herald* (Hagerstown, MD): September 1, 1928. *Salt Lake Tribune* (UT): June 30, 1926.

Baker, Luther
March 29, 1929

On Sunday morning, May 22, 1927, Clarke County deputies Kemp, Johnson and Jones were investigating reports of a moonshine still hidden in the woods in Dole Valley, thirty miles northwest of Vancouver, Washington. As they approached the area where the still was supposed to be operating they were confronted by a man armed with a rifle who ordered them to turn back. Deputies Kemp and Jones worked their way through the woods until they found the still hidden inside a tent, and meanwhile Johnson telephoned Sheriff Lester M. Wood.

Later that afternoon the sheriff arrived and started for the still with deputies Johnson and Ben Miller. They were nearing the tent when someone fired on the party from ambush and Sheriff Woods collapsed and died within minutes. Deputies Johnson and Miller returned fire but failed to hit their target, and the murderer fled to a house a mile away. The lawmen surrounded the house and soon captured sixty-year-old Ellis Baker, father of Ted Baker, who it was believed ran from the place of the ambush; Luther and Edwin Baker, uncles to Ted; Lester Hunting; and Norma Campbell, who was held only as a material witness. Hugh Miller, a soldier on furlough, was later arrested for having dealings with the Bakers, and on May 23 Ted Baker was arrested in Vancouver.

The investigation which followed showed that it was Luther Baker who had fired the fatal shot and he was assisted by Ellis Baker, but Ted Baker had not been at the scene of the killing. The two men were tried at the fall term of the Clarke County Superior Court in Vancouver and found guilty of first degree murder. Ellis Baker was sentenced to serve a life term in the prison at Walla Walla and was delivered to the prison, but Luther Baker was sentenced to hang and he was kept in the county jail pending his appeal. The state Supreme Court had the case before them for eighteen months before they affirmed the judgment and sentence of the lower court in January 1929, and then the date for Baker's execution was set for March 29. Baker was delivered to the prison on January 29 and Baker's attorneys filed an application with Governor Roland H. Hartley praying for a commutation of sentence, and Baker held out hope to the end, saying, "He's a busy man, but he'll take time to sign for me." Baker told prison chaplain J. Morgan Lewis that if Hartley refused to save him, "I'll take it as it comes." The governor declined to intervene so Baker had to resign himself to his fate, and did so with the help of the Reverend Lewis.

On Thursday afternoon his brother Ellis was brought from his cell to the death row cells and allowed to visit, but no other relatives came to the prison. The condemned man spent a last, quiet evening with the Reverend Lewis but would not speak of the shooting, retired at a late hour and slept soundly until awakened for breakfast. The Reverend Lewis remained nearby all night and was with the condemned man when the warden arrived to read the death warrant after 4:00 A.M. Baker was then conducted to the death chamber, where he took his place on the trapdoor and thanked the officials for his treatment since he was brought to the prison.

His wrists and arms, knees and ankles were then bound, the noose was adjusted, and the black hood was pulled over his head. The trap was sprung at 4:34 A.M. and Baker broke his neck in the fall. Prison physician Dr. J. W. Ingram waited beneath the gallows and monitored vital signs until he pronounced Baker dead eleven minutes after the drop. The body was then cut down and placed in the coffin provided by the state, as no relatives had made a request for the remains. The body was held for a day before the family notified the officials they wanted the body shipped to Dole Valley for burial, and they made the arrangements.

Centralia Chronicle (WA): March 29, 1929. *Independent* (Helena, MT): May 24, 1927. *Salt Lake Tribune* (UT): May 23, 1927.

Clark, Preston R.
July 11, 1930

In 1927 forty-year-old Bessie Mae Bidwell had been married to forty-nine-year-old Alpheus L. Bidwell for twenty years but she was being pursued by thirty-six-year-old Preston Rae "Slim" Clark, a boarder in their home, and she responded favorably to his attention. Clark became convinced that the only way the two could be together was to kill Bessie's husband, so in late December he bought poison. On December 30 he laced Bidwell's breakfast with the poison and he died, but it appeared he had a heart attack. Neighbors then reported that Bessie Bidwell had been intimate with Clark and her husband had told them he was worried he would lose his wife to the interloper. When the officers searched the back yard of the Bidwell home they found the empty poison bottle, which Clark admitted he had thrown away. He told Sheriff McInroe he had been given medication by Dr. J. E. Vanderpool, but the doctor denied there was any poison in the medicine he had given Clark. This raised the suspicion of foul play so on Saturday, the day after Bidwell died, county attorney W. G. Coleman and Sheriff McInroe arrested Clark and Bidwell on suspicion of murder, and they were lodged in the jail at Walla Walla.

The widow Bidwell was questioned for several hours and after making a number of conflicting statements she weakened and said, "Slim did it, and he told me so. I'll make a confession. You write it and I'll sign it." It was dictated by the widow and then, with five witnesses present, she signed it. The confession stated, "Slim admitted he put some poison in some hog brains we had for breakfast. When I accused him of it he turned red. I gave him another jolt in the front room when Bidwell was on the couch, before Slim went for a doctor. He admitted putting the poison in the brains. He did not tell me when he put it in."

On January 6 officers took Clark to the morgue where he viewed the body of Alpheus Bidwell, and he broke down and confessed that he had bought the poison but said it was for Mrs. Bidwell. He said she asked him to buy the poison to kill rats, but then she poisoned her husband with it. In March, Clark was tried for first degree murder and Bessie Bidwell for second degree murder in Judge John L. Sharpstein's courtroom and on March 13 both were found guilty. Bidwell was sentenced to serve ten years and was delivered to the prison but soon afterward she went insane and was transferred to the state asylum. Clark was sentenced to hang and his attorneys filed an appeal with the state Supreme Court, which stayed the execution for fifteen months. The justices affirmed the judgment and sentence of the Superior Court and then the attorneys submitted an application for a commutation of sentence to Governor Roland H. Hartley, and also requested a one week reprieve to have the sanity of Clark examined. The governor denied the request for a commutation of sentence and refused to grant a reprieve of a week for a hearing, so Judge Sharpstein appointed a commission of doctors which examined Clark on July 10 and found that he was "low grade, mentally defective and irresponsible, but not insane." Meanwhile Warden Clarence Long had not heard from the governor, so on June 9 he ordered the men to work erecting the gallows, as it took two days to construct and test.

Elder W. W. Stewart of the Seventh Day Adventist Church stayed with Clark throughout his entire last night, and the condemned man continued to insist that he was innocent of the murder of Bidwell. At 3:00 A.M. he was offered food and stimulants but he refused everything but a cup of coffee. At 4:00 A.M. the warden appeared at the cell door and read the death warrant. Clark was then conducted from the cell block to the gallows and at the foot of the stairs he said, "If I can't make it up these stairs without a shot, nobody can." He ascended and took his place on the trapdoor where his wrists and arms, knees and ankles were bound and the noose was adjusted. Clark was then asked if he had anything to say to the dozen witnesses, and he gave a brief speech reiterating all the reasons he was innocent.

When he concluded the noose was adjusted and the black hood was pulled over his head at 4:11 A.M. The trap was sprung immediately and Clark broke his neck in the fall. The prison physician monitored his vital signs until he pronounced him dead in twelve minutes, and the body was cut down three minutes later. The body was deposited into the coffin provided by the state and turned over to an undertaker from Milton and Freewater, Oregon, who delivered it there for burial by Clark's aged parents.

Centralia Chronicle (WA): July 9, 1930; July 11, 1930. *Oakland Tribune* (CA): January 2, 1928. *Ogden Standard-Examiner* (UT): January 6, 1928.

Wilkins, Robert L.
August 15, 1930

On the evening of December 9, 1928, John W. Brooks, who lived in Walla Walla, Washington, was playing cards with his housekeeper Gertrude Burshaw when there was a knock at the door and Brooks answered. Burshaw said that Brooks backed away from the door as a masked man entered, pistol in hand. She said the masked man demanded money and when Brooks took a step toward the robber he fired two shots into Brooks' chest, and then fled empty-handed. Brooks crumpled to the floor and died in minutes.

Officers tried to solve the mystery of the murderer for several months until, on February 10, 1929, the young son of Robert Lee Wilkins confessed that they had gone to Brooks' home and while he waited outside his father went in to rob Brooks. He said he heard two shots and his father rushed out. Wilkins, when confronted by his son's statement, confessed the killing but claimed self-defense and mental irresponsibility, and would use that as his defense at trial in March. He was convicted of first degree murder and sentenced to hang May 17, 1929, but his attorneys appealed to the state Supreme Court and it was not until the spring of the following year that the justices affirmed the judgment and sentence of the lower court. While the case was pending Wilkins was kept in the Walla Walla County jail, where he adopted religion and was baptized in a small pool of water. Once his rehearing was denied in mid–July his date of execution was set at August 15, 1930, and he was delivered to a death row cell at the prison in Walla Walla. The day before the execution his application praying for executive clemency was denied by the governor.

During his wait at the state penitentiary he was attended by the prison chaplain J. Morgan Lewis. The chaplain was not with him during his last night but arrived at an early hour, just after breakfast was served, and Warden Clarence Long appeared at the cell door at 4:00 A.M. to read the death warrant. As Wilkins was conducted from his cell, which was next to condemned murderer Archie F. Moock, he handed a letter to Chaplain Lewis. The letter, dated July 25, was a confession to the murder of Catherine Clark in Spokane in September 1928. Though the letter contained many details of the murder it was believed that it was a "put up job" by Moock, as Wilkins' cell had been searched several times over the previous several weeks and the letter was not there. In any case, it was forwarded to the Spokane County attorney for his consideration.

Wilkins was escorted to the gallows and he took his place on the trapdoor. His wrists and arms, knees and ankles were bound, the noose was adjusted, and when he declined to speak to the dozen witnesses the black hood was pulled over his head. The trap was sprung at 4:16 A.M. and in three minutes the prison physician pronounced him dead. After hanging a while longer the body was cut down, deposited into the coffin provided by the state, and give to the Reverend Lewis for burial on the prison grounds later that day.

Centralia Chronicle (WA): August 15, 1930. *Charleston Mail* (WV): December 10, 1928.

Schaffer, Arthur
August 29, 1930

Twenty-two-year-old Joe Kirk and his pretty young wife, with their three small children, returned home from a dance after midnight Monday morning, September 17, 1928. The Kirk family lived at their isolated ranch home near Dayton, nine miles west of Shelton, Washington, and after the children were in bed Joe lit a light. Just then a shot rang out and Joe dropped to the floor, but when there were no other shots fired he went to the door to look out and from the window behind him he was shot through the back of the head and the bullet exited through his mouth. He collapsed and died almost instantly and then twenty-five-year-old Arthur Schaffer rushed into the house, tore away all of Mrs. Kirk's clothing and raped her, and during the struggle his revolver discharged twice seriously wounding her. Schaffer then dragged Mrs. Kirk's limp body into the brush, left her for dead, and fled. Mrs. Kirk was found by neighbors after daylight and she was taken to the hospital in Shelton, where she was able to give a clear description of Schaffer: light complected, five feet eight inches, one hundred eighty pounds, and now driving the Kirks' Star touring car—

Washington license 98-972. Her husband was already at the morgue when she died that afternoon.

Schaffer was known to the authorities, as he had been committed to the insane asylum from Grays Harbor County and had been released three months previously after being diagnosed as cured. On September 18 Schaffer was arrested at Snoqualmie and lodged in jail, where he managed to get his hands on a razor and cut his throat. He was rushed to the King County Hospital where he was manacled to his cot under constant guard. On September 25, when he was able to speak, he told the authorities of King and Mason Counties that he was suffering from a guilty conscience and wanted to confess, but said he wanted to be electrocuted rather than hanged.

He then told the details of the murders to Mason County Sheriff W. A. Tucker and later repeated the confession for King County Sheriff Claude G. Bannick, deputy O. K. Bodia, and a transcriber. He said that he had appeared at the Kirk ranch house about September 9 and over the next two days was given work and food, but when he returned on the third day he was accused of stealing a revolver and ordered off the property. He said he went to an abandoned shack nearby where he brooded and planned revenge for three days. He said that on Sunday night he crept through the brush and lay in wait for the Kirk family to return. He watched through the window, shot Joe dead, and then assaulted Mrs. Kirk. He said he took their automobile and drove about back roads aimlessly until he abandoned the car near Puyallup Monday night, and then hitched a ride to Snoqualmie, where he was arrested. He said he had two guns but left them in the car. Authorities found the automobile and the two guns, but most important to the prosecution was the revolver used to murder Joe Kirk and his wife.

Schaffer was tried in Grays Harbor County at Montesano, he presented a defense of insanity, was convicted of first degree murder, and he was kept in the local jail while his appeal was under review. The state Supreme Court justices affirmed the lower court's judgment and sentence and Schaffer was delivered to the death row cells at the prison in Walla Walla on March 29, 1929, sentenced to hang April 5. His attorney then used every "pettifogging legal maneuver" he could conjure to delay his client's execution until June 1930, when all avenues of judicial relief were exhausted and Schaffer was sentenced to hang on August 29, 1930. His attorney then petitioned to the governor for executive clemency, but the governor refused to intervene.

During his time at the state penitentiary Schaffer was attended by prison chaplain J. Morgan Lewis. On the Monday before his hanging Schaffer showed his Bible to the chaplain and pointed to where he had written on the inside cover, "I am innocent." Schaffer told the chaplain that he had dreamt that another man did the killing and fled to the East, and he could not have written it in the Bible unless it was true. The chaplain, in explanation, said that Schaffer was "illiterate and of the moron type." The chaplain did stay not with him during his last night but arrived at an early hour, just after breakfast was served, and Warden Clarence Long appeared at the cell door after 3:30 A.M. to read the death warrant. Schaffer was conducted from his cell to the gallows where he took his place on the trapdoor without prompting, seemingly anxious to make his speech. His wrists and arms, knees and ankles were bound, the noose was adjusted and when asked if he had anything to say he cried out, "Mother, I am innocent. My liberty and life is being taken while a guilty man goes free." He seemed very agitated until the black hood was pulled over his head at 4:07 A.M., and the trap was sprung immediately. The prison physician waited below the gallows and monitored Schaffer's vital signs until he pronounced him dead in fourteen minutes. The body was then cut down, deposited into the coffin provided by the state, and given to the Reverend Lewis for burial in the prison cemetery later that day.

Centralia Chronicle (WA): September 17, 1928; September 25, 1928; March 29, 1929; August 29, 1930.

Oakland Tribune (CA): August 29, 1930. *Daily Mail* (MD): August 29, 1930.

Moock, Archie F.
September 12, 1930

In September 1928 thirty-six-year-old Catherine Clark, who owned and operated a rug repair business in Boston, Massachusetts, left for Spokane, Washington, with the intention of marrying a man named "Murphy." She had been exchanging letters with Murphy for several months and he claimed he lived at Cour D'Alene, Idaho. In his letters Murphy arranged for her to stay with mill worker Archie F. Moock at Spokane, and Moock would drive her to her betrothed in Idaho. Clark arrived in Spokane on Friday, September 21, and stayed at the Moock home and the following day Moock borrowed an automobile from Grover C. Tyree and then he and Clark started for Cour D'Alene. Moock returned the car Sunday morning under circumstances that raised the suspicions of Tyree, as the odometer showed they had traveled only thirty miles. Tyree enlisted the help of F. C. Winkleblock and they drove until they saw signs along the highway fifteen miles east of Spokane. They stopped and found blood stains and a trail where a body had been dragged into the old Davis orchard. They followed the trail and near a spring they found the dead, mutilated body of Catherine Clark. She had been brutally bludgeoned to death and nearby was a shingler's hatchet stained with blood, and Tyree identified it as one he had loaned to Moock.

Tyree contacted the authorities, who collected the body and other evidence and found that Clark still wore her wrist watch, rings and necklace, so at first robbery was discounted as the motive. Moock was arrested and charged with the murder of Clark and when the police searched Moock's home they found money, letters, and clothing belonging to Clark. Moock, as soon as he was behind bars, began trying to build an alibi but over time he made so many inconsistent and conflicting statements that they only served to incriminate him further.

At his trial he insisted that Murphy actually existed, though he was never able to show any proof, suggested that Murphy might have killed Clark, and claimed that he was the victim of circumstances. At trial in the fall session of the court he was found guilty of first degree murder and sentenced to hang in January 1929, but his attorney filed an appeal with the state Supreme Court and it was not until June 1930 that the justices affirmed the judgment and sentence of the lower court and set the date for Moock's execution at September 12, 1930. The governor, when petitioned, refused to intervene.

In July 1930 Robert L. Wilkins arrived on death row and was placed in the cell next to Moock. The two condemned men conceived of the idea that the first of them to exhaust all possible judicial and executive relief would confess to the other's murder, and they shared enough details to make the confession seem plausible. It turned out that Wilkins was to be executed first and he left a confession to the murder of Clark, but all the circumstances of the confession made it appear a mere ploy so it was dismissed.

During his final days Moock was visited by his wife Tenna and she brought letters from the oldest of his five children, but on his last night she left early and went directly to the office of the governor to beg for a commutation of sentence. The warden appeared at Moock's cell door before 4:00 A.M. and read the death warrant, and then the condemned man was escorted to the gallows. He took his place on the trapdoor where his wrists and arms, knees and ankles were bound and then he was asked if he wanted to make a statement to the small group of witnesses. When he declined the noose was quickly adjusted and the black hood was pulled over his head at 4:07 A.M. The trap was sprung immediately and Moock broke his neck in the fall. The prison physician monitored his vital signs until he pronounced him dead at 4:27 A.M., and then the body was cut down and placed in the coffin provided by his wife. Moock's remains were delivered to a local undertaker where Tenna Moock had made arrangements for his burial.

Las Vegas Optic (NM): September 12, 1930. *Oakland Tribune* (CA): September 24, 1928. *Inter Lake* (Kalispell, MT): September 12, 1930. *Olewein Register* (IA): September 24, 1928.

Miller, George
December 18, 1931

On the evening of October 30, 1929, George Miller, armed with a .45-caliber automatic pistol, and Frank Bojarski bustled into the office of the Railway Express Agency with a package addressed to a fictitious person. It was closing time and messenger John Ivester was checking the day's receipts as the two robbers, seeing the office empty of customers, took clerk W. H. Johnson prisoner. When Ivester heard the commotion he glanced through the bars of his cashier's cage and Miller shot him twice, one bullet striking him in the forehead killing him instantly. Bojarski bound Johnson with shoe laces while Miller looted the cash register of $600, leaving behind a clear set of fingerprints. Bojarski, who was not armed, threw down the package and the two men ran outside, climbed into an old touring car, and fled.

The police gathered the evidence including the package, two bullet casings, and two slugs removed from Ivester's body, sent out circulars with fingerprints and descriptions, and waited for a break in the case. In April 1930 Miller failed to stop at a red light in Detroit, Michigan, and when the patrolman pulled him over he found a .45-caliber automatic pistol in the car. The patrolman took Miller to the station for questioning, took his fingerprints, and circulated them to police departments nationwide. From Miller's description it was believed he was wanted at Bryan, Ohio, on a charge of robbery, but the real break came when an alert Florida police officer noticed a similarity to a circular of fingerprints he had received six months earlier, and matched them to the Spokane murder case.

Once back in Spokane, Miller bragged of his criminal career, said he was a member of Al Capone's mob, and confessed to the Railway Express Agency robbery but said his partner had fired the fatal shot. This was, of course, refuted by the statement of clerk Johnson. However, Bojarski was not present to defend himself until August, when he was arrested in Long Beach, California, on a charge of forgery. When he learned he had been named by Miller as the murderer he confessed to the robbery, but said only Miller was armed. He told the police he prepared and carried the package so it would appear they were on legitimate business, and the writing on the package was matched to his handwriting. Both men were tried at the fall 1930 term of the Superior Court, convicted of first degree murder, and Bojarski was sentenced to serve a life term in the state prison while Miller was sentenced to hang. Miller's court-appointed attorney filed an appeal which stayed the execution. The state Supreme Court affirmed the judgment and sentence of the lower court in October 1931 and Miller was re-sentenced to hang on December 18. The petition filed with the governor, praying for a commutation of sentence, was denied.

During his final days Miller was attended by the prison's Catholic chaplain and the priest helped him resign himself to his fate. As the date of his execution neared he recanted the confession of most of his criminal activities and his affiliation with Al Capone. On his final day the warden appeared at the door of Miller's death row cell just after midnight to read the death warrant. The prisoner was then conducted to the gallows by the warden and his priest. He took his place on the trapdoor where his wrists and arms, knees and ankles were bound and then he was asked if he wanted to make a statement. Miller said only, "I wish to thank everyone for the treatment I have received while at the prison," and then the noose was adjusted.

The priest stepped forward and pressed a crucifix to Miller's lips and as he stepped back praying, the black hood was pulled over

Miller's head at 12:15 A.M. and the trap was sprung immediately. Miller broke his neck in the fall and the prison physician, waiting beneath the gallows, monitored his vital signs until he pronounced him dead at 12:28. The body was then cut down, deposited in the coffin provided by the state, and the remains were turned over to the priest for burial in the Catholic cemetery.

Reno Gazette (NV): December 18, 1931. *Ogden Standard-Examiner* (UT): October 31, 1929.

Carpenter, Harold; Dubuc, Walter
April 15, 1932

On Friday, July 10, 1931, eighty-four-year-old Peter Jacobson, a farmer living on Chamber's Prairie near Olympia, Washington, withdrew $700 from the Olympia Building and Loan Association before returning home. On Saturday night twenty-six-year-old Ethel Willis drove thirty-year-old Harold Carpenter, her lover, and sixteen-year-old Walter Dubuc to Jacobson's farmhouse to rob him. She waited in the car while the two men lured Jacobson into his front yard and then they beat him to death, Carpenter swinging a rifle as a club and Dubuc using his fists and feet. Carpenter broke the rifle and threw it into the brush before the two went into the house, ransacked all the rooms, and later claimed they found only $2, a $1 watch, and a pocket knife, but an open tin box with an empty money pouch was found in the house. Later Jacobson's daughter would say her father had $3,000 in currency and $650 in gold coins in the house and it was never found.

The following day Jacobson's son-in-law, Al Murphy, stopped by to check on the old man and found his battered, dead body in the front yard. He called the authorities and it was not long before suspicion settled on Carpenter, when the broken rifle was traced to him. Carpenter was arrested at Yakima on July 19 and he had Jacobson's watch and pocket knife in his pocket and, after he was behind bars, he informed on Dubuc and the youngster soon joined Carpenter in jail. Willis was also arrested and at first she was held as a material witness, but soon she was also charged with murder. Dubuc was the first to weaken and he confessed to his part in Jacobson's beating death. Carpenter, confronted with Dubuc's statement, confessed next, and then Willis quickly told what she knew. Carpenter and Dubuc were arraigned on July 23 and they both pled not guilty, and Carpenter's attorney also pled "mental irresponsibility." Two days later Willis was arraigned and she pled not guilty. An effort was then made to call a special session of the Thurston County Superior Court but the state's attorney general advised against it and the matter was left to the regular fall session. All three defendants were tried in September and found guilty of first degree murder, and the jury fixed the penalty at death for Carpenter and Dubuc and at life imprisonment for Willis. The death sentences were appealed and it was not until early 1932 that the state Supreme Court affirmed the judgment and sentence of the lower court, and the date for the double execution was set at April 15, 1932. Applications for executive clemency were sent to Governor Roland H. Hartley, and a number of organizations campaigned on behalf of Dubuc because of his youth. A petition with more than six thousand signatures was delivered to the governor on April 14 but nothing new was offered to justify clemency so the governor declined to intervene.

During their last days both prisoners were attended by the prison chaplain Reverend E. T. Allen and he was with them on their final evening, praying and reading Bible passages. The two condemned men wrote a statement, which they gave to the Reverend Allen, stating that in the excitement of the robbery they did not realize what they were doing and that it had been "all a mistake." The statement concluded, "We are willing to die if by so doing we will pay for the crime." The warden appeared at the door to the death row cells at midnight and read the death warrants to both prisoners. They were then conducted to the specially built gallows with a single trapdoor which could accommodate both men. Carpenter was composed during the march but Dubuc's spirit was completely broken and he cried out, "Jesus, save me!" several times. As Dubuc stood on the trapdoor he began crying and pleaded, "I don't want to be hung, Jesus, save me!" The Reverend Allen did all he could to help the youngster brace up as his wrists and arms, knees and ankles were bound and his noose was adjusted.

Neither man made a statement so the black hoods were pulled over their heads at 12:27 A.M. and the trap was sprung immediately. Both men broke their necks in the fall and prison physician Dr. J. W. Ingram pronounced Carpenter dead at 12:29 and Dubuc was pronounced dead two minutes later. The bodies were cut down at 12:43 A.M. and deposited into the coffins provided by the state. There had been no requisition for the remains of either man so plans were made to bury them in the prison cemetery later that day.

Centralia Chronicle (WA): July 23, 1931; April 15, 1932. *Oakland Tribune* (CA): July 26, 1931. *Salt Lake Tribune* (UT): July 20, 1931.

Stratton, Arthur
July 28, 1933

On August 26, 1931, twenty-one-year-old Arthur "Ollie" Stratton shot to death his army buddy, retired sergeant William Frawley, at Port Townsend, Washington. The two men had served together at Fort Casey on Whidby Island, Washington, before Frawley retired. Stratton took Frawley's body to the trash dump on Whidby Island and buried it in a shallow grave. Foul play was presumed when Frawley was missed but there was no clue until Stratton attempted to transfer one of Frawley's accounts to a Seattle bank and withdraw funds. After Stratton was arrested his quarters were searched and a number of Frawley's possessions were recovered and, when confronted with the discovery, the prisoner confessed and led officers to the body.

At his trial at Port Townsend in late October the defendant claimed self-defense, saying he killed Frawley during a quarrel when his friend refused to take him and his fiancée, Norma Solid, on an automobile trip. He claimed Frawley attacked him, and his attorney also pled "mental irresponsibility." On October 28 the jurors, after seven and one half hours of deliberating, found Stratton guilty of first degree murder and fixed the penalty at death, and he was sentenced to hang. His attorney filed an appeal which stayed the execution and over the next eighteen months the attorney tried every legal maneuver to save the life of his client. Finally in late April all avenues of judicial relief were exhausted and Stratton's date with the hangman was set for July 28, 1933. An application was then sent to the governor praying for a commutation of sentence, but it was denied.

The prison at Walla Walla finally had opened its new execution chamber and Stratton would be the first man to be hanged there. The warden appeared at Stratton's cell door before midnight and read the death warrant.

The prisoner was then conducted into the death chamber and onto the trapdoor, where his wrists and arms, knees and ankles were strapped, the noose was adjusted, and the black hood was pulled over his head. He was not asked to make a statement, as he had said earlier he would not speak on the gallows. The trap was sprung a few minutes after midnight and Stratton broke his neck in the fall. The prison physician waited below and monitored his vital signs, and when his heart ceased to beat after several minutes he was pronounced dead. The body was then cut down and deposited into the coffin provided by his mother, Nancy Stratton, and conveyed to a local undertaker where the remains would be prepared for shipment to Port Townsend for burial.

Centralia Chronicle (WA): October 29, 1931. *Ogden Standard-Examiner* (UT): July 28, 1933.

Bradley, Ted
May 11, 1934

The Seattle grocery store of George Ikeda had been robbed three times by the same man before Wednesday, March 16, 1932. On that day the robber tried again but was scared off without gaining access to the cash register because Ikeda slipped out and called the police. Fellow businessmen reported to detectives that the man had been loitering and begging in the area for two weeks, posing as a deaf mute carrying a pad and pencil. Detective Lieutenants W. D. Rehmke and F. G. Sands hid in the back room of the store on the following evening and just before closing time the robber appeared, and they tried to make an arrest. A gun battle followed during which Ikeda was mortally wounded with several bullets in his abdomen and detective Rehmke was shot in the wrist, and Rehmke was also shot in the chest but the bullet was deflected by an object in a vest pocket. During the close range exchange of bullets the bandit was shot in the abdomen and arm but he escaped. Ikeda was rushed to the hospital where he died after midnight, but by then his murderer was in custody.

Soon after the shooting, a woman who identified herself as Mrs. Bradley summoned the police to a rooming house and reported that her husband had been shot during a drunken brawl. The wounded man was immediately identified as the robber and he claimed to be Ted Bradley, but after some questioning he admitted he was George Everett Slate of Tacoma, Washington, a former inmate of the state prison at Walla Walla. Mrs. Bradley was then identified as the wife of Slate's fellow inmate at the prison, still serving his sentence, and the woman told the detective they had been together three months. Slate was rushed to the hospital where doctors performed emergency surgery and gave their patient little chance of recovery; but he surprised the doctors when he fully recovered.

He was moved to the King County jail and charged with the murder of Ikeda. He was tried as Ted Bradley in the Superior Court at Seattle, convicted of first degree murder, and sentenced to hang. His court-appointed attorney filed an appeal which stayed the execution until early 1934, when the state Supreme Court affirmed the lower court's judgment and sentence. Bradley's date of execution was set for May 11 and nothing would delay his date with the hangman, as the application to the governor praying for a commutation of sentence was denied.

During his stay at the prison Bradley refused any special treatment, except a special choice of meat for his last meal. He refused all attempts by clergy to attend to his religious needs and said he wanted no minister on the gallows with him. He was bitter toward all the guards and on his last afternoon said, "I'd like to get one more bull before I drop through the trap." Bradley was the second man to hang in the new execution chamber. The warden appeared at the door to his death row cell just before midnight to read the death warrant. As the condemned man exited the cell he handed the warden three letters: one to his mother and one each to his sister and sweetheart, both in Seattle. He was conducted into the death chamber and took his place on the trapdoor where his wrists and arms, knees and ankles were bound. He was asked if he had anything to say to the sixty witnesses and he replied, "I'd like to say goodbye to all my friends and to Hell with the ___ bulls." The noose was adjusted, the black hood was pulled over his head, and at 12:05 A.M. the trap was sprung. The prison doctor waited below, monitored his vital signs, and at 12:20 he pronounced Bradley dead. The body was then cut down and deposited in the coffin provided by the state. There had been no requisition for the remains so arrangements were made to bury Bradley on the prison grounds later that day, without a service or sermon.

Centralia Chronicle (WA): March 18, 1932; May 11, 1934. *Reno Gazette* (NV): May 11, 1934.

Miller, Byron
October 3, 1934

On the evening of May 26, 1931, Byron Miller returned to his home in Mabton. He was drunk and he began to create a loud, raucous disturbance. Town marshal George Warring was called to quell the disturbance and arrest Miller, and he was accompanied by several deputy sheriffs. It was Warring's responsibility to arrest Miller but as he approached the house Miller fired one barrel of a double-barreled shotgun through a glass door, and the heavy buckshot seriously wounded Warring in the left shoulder. Miller called out, "Did I kill you George?" and when Warring replied, "No!" Miller responded, "Well, you will be." Miller then fired the second barrel and the buckshot struck Warring in the side, and the marshal bled to death within minutes from the second wound. The deputies, as soon as the shooting ceased, rushed in, disarmed, and arrested Miller. The prisoner was lodged in the county jail at Yakima and charged with murdering Warring. The body of the marshal was shipped to Chehalis, where he had lived for many years, for burial.

Miller was tried at the next term of the Superior Court in Yakima County, found guilty of first degree murder, and sentenced to hang. His attorney filed an appeal which stayed the execution for two years, but in early 1934 the state Supreme Court affirmed the judgment and sentence of the lower court and Miller's date with the hangman was set for July 20. Miller's attorney then asked Governor Clarence D. Martin for a hearing into his client's sanity, and the governor granted a reprieve until the matter could be resolved. A commission of doctors was appointed to examine Miller and they pronounced him sane, so he was returned in August to Yakima, where his date of execution was set for October 3, 1934. An appeal to the U.S. Supreme Court was then disposed of expeditiously and nothing further would occur to delay the proceedings.

During his stay at the prison Miller seemed indifferent to his fate and played his violin during every spare moment, including nights when he had trouble sleeping. On his last evening Miller penned three notes, one a will dividing his property among his wife and his four children ranging in ages from three to twelve years. The warden appeared at the door to his death row cell at midnight and read the death warrant, and then the prisoner was conducted into the death chamber.

He appeared calm to the small party of witnesses as he took his place on the trapdoor, where his wrists and arms, knees and ankles were bound, and the noose was adjusted. He was asked if he had anything to say and in a weak voice he said, "God bless and have mercy on my soul. To my wife and babies I bid you all goodbye." The black hood was pulled over his head at 12:10 A.M. and the trap was sprung immediately, and Miller broke his neck in the fall. The prison doctor waited below to monitor his vital signs and he pronounced Miller dead at 12:23 A.M., and then the body was cut down and deposited in the coffin provided by his family. His remains were delivered to a local undertaker where he was prepared for shipment to Mabton for burial.

Centralia Chronicle (WA): October 3, 1934. *Chehalis Bee-Nugget* (WA): May 29, 1931.

Hong Yick
July 19, 1935

In early December 1934 twenty-five-year-old Lee Wing Quen, a member of the Chinese Hop Sing tong in Seattle, Washington, stole a membership roster of the rival Suey Sing tong. Several days after the theft forty-four-year-old Hong Yick, watchman for the Suey Sing tong, bludgeoned Quen with a heavy hammer, crushing his skull, and Quen died on December 11, but Yick had recovered the membership roster. An investigation followed and after three months Yick was arrested on a charge of first degree murder, and on March 27, 1935, he confessed to killing Quen but said, "I feared that with the names of all our members in possession of another tong, there might be a tong war if I did not kill him." He was tried in April, found guilty of first degree murder, and sentenced to hang on July 19, 1935. Neither appeal nor application for executive clemency would delay the proceedings.

Yick was the first Chinese to hang at the state prison at Walla Walla and he was a model prisoner during the few weeks he was housed on death row. On his final night Warden James M. McCauley appeared at his cell door at midnight and read the death warrant and the prisoner was then conducted into the death chamber where he took his place on the trapdoor. His wrists and arms, knees and ankles were bound, the noose was adjusted, and then he declined to speak to the witnesses. The black hood was pulled over his head at 12:11 A.M. and the trap was sprung immediately. The prison doctor waited beneath the gallows to monitor vital signs and he pronounced Yick dead at 12:24. The body was cut down, deposited into the coffin provided by the state, and given to his friends for burial in the Chinese portion of the Seattle cemetery.

Centralia Chronicle (WA): March 27, 1935. *Ogden Standard-Examiner* (UT): July 19, 1935.

Fleming, Barney
April 3, 1936

Twenty-eight-year-old Barney Fleming, a junkman, and thirty-year-old La Bella Butler had been living together as husband and wife for some time in their Seattle, Washington, apartment when Fleming began to suspect infidelity. On October 15, 1935, after drinking liquor for hours, he flew into a jealous rage, accused her of seeing other men, and when she denied the accusations Fleming murdered Butler.

He was tried and on November 15 he was convicted of first degree murder, and the jurors recommended the penalty of death. Judge Malcolm Douglas then sentenced Fleming to hang but the case was appealed to the state Supreme Court which resulted in a stay of execution. In February, Fleming withdrew his appeal and instead appealed to the high court for a speedy date of execution, as he wanted to be hanged before his spiritual advisor, the Reverend Arvid Ohrnell, left for Europe. On March 4 he appeared before Judge Douglas, who said, "Your spiritual advisor informs the court it is your wish to be executed early in April," and Fleming responded, "Yes, your honor." The date was then set for April 3, 1936.

The Reverend Arvid Ohrnell attended to Fleming during his time on death row and on the morning of his hanging the prisoner confessed his crime and asked the reverend to "warn all youngsters to avoid drink, women, and jealousy." Warden James M. McCauley appeared at his cell door after 9:00 A.M. and read the death warrant and the prisoner was then conducted into the death chamber, where he took his place on the trapdoor without prompting. His wrists and arms, knees and ankles were strapped, the noose was adjusted, and when asked he declined to speak to the seventy-five witnesses. The black hood was pulled over his head at 9:50 A.M. and the trap was sprung immediately. The prison doctor waited beneath the gallows to monitor vital signs and he pronounced the prisoner dead fifteen minutes later. The body was cut down, deposited into the coffin provided by the state, and buried in the prison cemetery by the Reverend Ohrnell later that afternoon.

Centralia Chronicle (WA): November 16, 1935; April 4, 1936. *Ogden Standard-Examiner* (UT): March 4, 1936. *Vidette-Messenger* (Valparaiso, IN): April 6, 1936.

Stringer, Glenn
May 29, 1936

On the afternoon of March 10, 1934, two young men, masked and armed, confronted Herbert Lee Caples in his back yard in Vancouver, Washington, intent upon robbing him. Caples struggled with the robbers, was shot to death, and the two murderers shared $560 in loot before fleeing. There were no leads to the murderers for two years but one of the men, Glenn Stringer, while serving a sentence at the prison in Salem, Oregon, for a burglary at Medford, confessed to killing Caples and named Ralph T. Tremaine as his accomplice. The revolver taken from Stringer when arrested in Oregon proved, through ballistics testing, to be the murder weapon.

As soon as Stringer completed his sentence in Oregon he was brought to Vancouver, where he pled not guilty and recanted his confession, and his trial began in Judge George B. Simpson's courtroom on March 23, 1936. Two days later at 8:30 P.M. the jurors returned a verdict of guilty of first degree murder and recommended the death penalty, and Stringer was sentenced to hang on May 29. The condemned man was taken to the prison at Walla Walla and lodged in a death row cell. Neither appeal nor application for executive clemency would delay the proceedings.

On Stringer's final night Warden J. M. McCauley appeared at his cell door to read the death warrant and then he was conducted to the gallows. He climbed the thirteen stairs and took his place on the trapdoor where his wrists and arms, knees and ankles were bound and he was asked if he had anything to say to the small group of witnesses, but there is no record of a statement. The noose was adjusted and the black hood was pulled over his head at 12:08 A.M. and the trap was sprung immediately. Stringer broke his neck in the fall and he was pronounced dead at 12:23 A.M. The body was then cut down, deposited in the coffin provided by the state, and buried on the prison grounds later that day.

On March 21, 1960, forty-nine-year-old Jerome P. Young was arrested for assault and battery in Anderson, Indiana. By May 20 Young was committed to the Logansport State Hospital undergoing treatment for a serious mental disorder. His fingerprints were forwarded to Washington, D.C., and it was determined that he was Ralph T. Tremaine, and that Young was only one of many aliases on record over the past twenty-five years. When Washington State authorities were contacted they declined to prosecute, as all the witnesses were either dead or could not be found, and Tremaine was then insane.

Centralia Chronicle (WA): March 23, 1936; March 26, 1936. *Anderson Herald* (IN): May 20, 1960.

Hall, Leo
September 11, 1936

In 1933 Oregon Governor Julius L. Meier suspected irregularities in the affairs of Portland's port management and appointed accountant W. Frank Akin to investigate. As a result J. H. Paulhemus, the port's general manager, and a number of lower level employees were forced to resign. On the morning of November 20 Leo Hartoin, manager of Akin's apartment building, opened the door to Akin's apartment to admit a domestic and discovered Akin's dead body lying on the bed fully clothed. Akin's head had been bashed in and he had been shot through the right eye, the bullet lodging against the back of his skull. The investigation focused on those who had resigned from port management, as that was the only controversial matter in which Akin was involved which might explain the execution-style murder, but the preoccupation with this line of investigation left the crime unsolved for several years.

In late March 1934 Peggy Peterson-Paulos, working as a waitress in a Bremerton, Washington, café, overheard Anna Flieder discussing her wealth with friends. The Fleiders, Anna and Frank, were well known for their lavish parties at their beach house at Erland's Point and they often invited many interesting persons to join them there. In Seattle, Peggy told Leo Hall about the conversation and he insisted that she accompany him to Erland's Point for the purpose of robbery. Hall retrieved his .32-caliber nickle-plated revolver from a bank safety deposit box and on March 28 they took the ferry from Seattle to Bremerton, then hitched a ride to Erland's Point.

They arrived at the Flieder house at 11:30 P.M. and, after putting on masks and gloves, Hall knocked at the door. Forty-five-year-old Frank Flieder answered and Hall pointed his pistol at him, demanded entry and took him to the sitting room where Hall and Paulos found Frank's fifty-one-year-old wife, Anna, forty-eight-year-old Margaret Chenevert, and fifty-six-year-old Ezra M. Bolcom. They had been engaged in a card game and it was clear there were seats for six players. Hall covered his four prisoners with his revolver while Peggy bound them with adhesive tape and laces removed from ice skates. In a short while,

Margaret's husband, fifty-one-year-old Eugene A. Chenevert, and sixty-two-year-old Magnus Jorden returned from a trip to buy beer and they were captured and tied with strips torn from bed sheets. Anna Flieder felt faint and asked if she could lie down so Hall escorted her into the bedroom, and he stabbed her to death with a carving knife he took from the kitchen. Paulos protested the killing but Hall next took Bolcom to the bedroom and bashed in his head with a stove poker. Paulos then tried to leave but Hall called her back and fired a warning shot, but she fled and lost a heel from her shoe in the back yard, and then she made her way to Bremerton. After Paulos left, Hall continued the killing by slashing, bashing and shooting his victims, but Eugene Chenevert worked free from his bonds and the two men engaged in a terrible fight until Chenevert was killed, and Hall received a cut from a broken beer bottle on his head which took twenty-eight stitches to close. Paulos saw Hall in Seattle three days later and asked him, "Why did you kill them?" and he replied, "I had to. One of them recognized you."

On March 31 two neighbors investigated three poodles locked in a car, barking incessantly, and after they freed the dogs and gave them water and food they looked into a window of the house and saw two dead bodies. They summoned Sheriff Rush Blankenship who, after surveying the scene, assigned a deputy to guard the house and sent for Luke S. May, a noted criminologist, to process the murder scene. The deputy allowed many people to contaminate the scene but May was still able to collect a great deal of forensic and physical evidence when he arrived on April 1. A year and a half passed without a break but then Peggy's husband, Larry Paulos, was arrested in Yakima and he informed on the murderers of W. Frank Akin — Leo Hall and Jack Justice. A manhunt then began for Leo Hall but Peggy Paulos, once she learned that her husband had informed to the police, was afraid Hall would blame her and exact revenge, so she went to a renowned attorney and gave him the details of the "Erland's Point massacre." The information was forwarded to the authorities on October 19, 1935, and four days later Hall was found in Portland, Oregon, and arrested for possession of a loaded gun. Hall was taken to Seattle for questioning and then Jack Justice and Peggy Paulos were arrested, and she gave the police an official statement on October 24.

On October 29 Kitsap County Superior Court Judge H. G. Sutton charged Hall with the first degree murder of Eugene Chenevert, and Peggy Paulos was charged as an accessory to his murder. Both defendants were arraigned within a week and they pled not guilty, and then the judge entertained a motion for separate trials which he denied, and set the trial date for December 9, 1935. Hall and Paulos were tried at Port Orchard and after sixty-one witnesses testified over a ten day period Hall took the stand on December 17, and the following day Hall's entire family was called to testify to his "flawless" character. The case went to the jurors before 5:00 P.M. on December 18 and before noon on December 19 they found Hall guilty of first degree murder and fixed the penalty at death, but Peggy Paulos was acquitted and freed. Meanwhile in Oregon, Jack Justice was tried for the murder of Akin, convicted, and sentenced to serve a life term at the prison in Salem.

Appeals were filed on behalf of Hall asking for a new trial based upon new evidence, but the evidence never materialized so the appeal was denied and the judgment and sentence of the lower court was affirmed. After months of delay the date for Hall's execution was set for September 11, 1936. Governor Clarence D. Martin had already denied the application for a commutation of sentence submitted by Hall's attorney when, on the day before the execution, Hall's mother and brother made their final appeal. The governor declined to intervene but granted a delay to 2:00 P.M. so Hall's mother could return to Walla Walla. Hall's attorney, who had been diligent in his legal maneuvering to save his client's life, tried to obtain a federal injunction but Judge J. Stanley Webster determined his court had no jurisdiction. Warden J. M. McCauley then granted another delay to 11:00 P.M. so Hall's attorney could also return to Walla Walla. Hall asked the messenger to thank the warden.

After 10:30 P.M. Warden McCauley appeared at Hall's death row cell door and read the death warrant. Hall was then conducted to the gallows where he took his place on the trapdoor and his wrists and arms, knees and ankles were bound. He was asked if he had anything to say to the one hundred twenty-five witnesses and he said, "I would like to say that the Justice they convicted in the Akin case is an entirely innocent man. Jack Justice never hired me or, as far as I know, anybody else to kill Frank Akin. The charge they convicted him on was a bum charge."

When he concluded the noose was adjusted and the black hood was pulled over his head. There as a momentary delay as the executioner, poised over the electric release button, counted down the seconds to exactly 11:00 P.M. and then sprang the trap. Hall broke his neck in the fall and the prison physician monitored his vital signs until he pronounced him dead at 11:16 P.M. The body was then cut down and delivered to a local undertaker to be prepared for burial, the arrangements made by Hall's mother, Elizabeth.

Muscatine Journal and News-Tribune (IA): September 11, 1936. *Seattle Star* (WA): December 12–20, 1935; September 11–12, 1936. *Syracuse Herald* (NY): September 12, 1936. *Inter Lake* (Kalispell, MT): October 26, 1933. *Ogden Standard Examiner* (UT): November 20, 1933. *Seattle Times* (WA): December 8–19, 1935; September 11–12, 1936.

Hawkins, Clifford
February 23, 1938

In 1936 twenty-five-year-old Tolvo Hautaneimi, a Finnish farmhand using the name Clifford Hawkins, worked for the Grimm brothers, Ernest and Floyd, on their farm near Mount Vernon in Skagit County, Washington. Hawkins developed an unnatural attraction for twelve-year-old Edith Grimm and the brothers objected to his attention to the very young girl. In December 1936 Hawkins seized upon an opportunity to murder Ernest under circumstances which suggested the farmer had left home and would not return. He buried the body in an isolated place on the farm and when Floyd persisted in his objection to Hawkins' intimacies with Edith Hawkins, he murdered Floyd in March 1937 and buried the body next to his brother. Hawkins then had his way with Edith until June, when he was arrested on a statutory charge of "criminally assaulting Edith Grimm," and he was lodged in the county jail at Mount Vernon.

The continued absence of the two Grimm brothers raised the suspicion of foul play and Hawkins was questioned until early November, but would divulge nothing. On November 12 the bodies of the Grimm brothers were found and brought to Mount Vernon for an autopsy and on the following day Hawkins, who was already facing a life sentence, confessed to the murders. Hawkins was arraigned on November 24, pled not guilty, and Superior Court Judge W. L. Brickley set the trial date for December 14. The trial lasted four days and on December 18 the jurors found the defendant guilty of first degree murder, fixed the penalty at death, and Hawkins was sentenced to hang on February 23, 1938. Neither appeal nor application for a commutation of sentence would delay the proceedings, and Hawkins was delivered to a death row cell at the prison in Walla Walla.

During Hawkins' final weeks he was attended by the Reverend Arvid Ohrnell and on his last evening he gave his final written statement to the reverend. Warden James M. McCauley appeared at Hawkins' cell door before midnight to read the death warrant and then the condemned man was conducted into the death chamber by the warden and the Reverend Ohrnell. He took his place on the trapdoor where his wrists and arms, knees and ankles were bound and then Warden McCauley asked if he had anything to say to the one hundred three witnesses, mostly lawmen. Hawkins replied, "My written statement is with Reverend Ohrnell. As for myself, all I have to say is: Goodbye, Edith!"

The noose was adjusted and the black hood was pulled over his head at 12:03 A.M. and the trap was sprung immediately. Hawkins broke his neck in the fall and he was pronounced dead in fourteen minutes. The body was then cut down and deposited into the coffin provided by the state, but Hawkins had no one to requisition his remains so arrangements were made to bury him on the prison grounds that afternoon, following a brief graveside service by the Reverend Ohrnell.

Centralia Chronicle (WA): November 24, 1937. *New Castle News* (PA): November 13, 1937. *Reno Gazette* (NV): November 13, 1937. *Billings Gazette* (MT): February 24, 1938. *Chillicothe Constitution-Tribune* (MO): February 23. 1938.

Ryan, Claude H.
February 25, 1938

Early on Wednesday morning, April 7, 1937, two men broke into the house of Emma Cartier of South Bend, taped her mouth and bound her, then searched until they found all her money and other valuables before they fled. She worked herself free and called the police. Fifty-four-year-old deputy sheriff S. R. "Riv" Jackson of Chehalis received a telephone call from South Bend saying that the two hold-up men were driving in his direction in a 1928 Nash coupe. With deputy J. D. Compton driving his 1937 Chevrolet, the two officers started toward Meskill Hill where they intercepted the Nash on Ocean Beach Highway. Freeland Miller was following the Nash and he reported on the gun battle which followed:

> I was traveling directly behind the bandit's Nash coupe when it was halted by the deputies. One of the bandits opened fire. Jackson, on the right side of the officer's car, stepped out. He didn't have time to pull his revolver. He just walked over to the other machine and the bandits shot and he fell to the pavement.
>
> J. D. Compton, the other deputy, got out of the deputies' automobile. He didn't have any weapon at the time. The bandits opened fire, one bullet hitting Compton and knocking him down. Compton went back to his car and came back with a revolver in one hand and a shotgun in the other.
>
> He emptied the shot gun at the bandits as they got out of their machine. One bandit fell in the roadway between the two machines. He had been hit by Compton's fire.
>
> The uninjured bandit came round the front of the deputies' car to get Compton. He blazed away; some of the shots whizzed by my truck. Compton returned fire but was too badly injured to aim. He kept backing away, shouting, "Give yourself up!" I found out later he had only two bullets in his revolver.
>
> The bandit kept coming on, firing all the time. Meanwhile the wounded bandit was on the ground, trying to reload his revolver. Just as his pal took a final shot at Compton, he crawled into the deputies' machine. His pal opened the door, got in and they drove away.
>
> I got out and helped Compton. Compton told me to leave him and hurry for help. I went up the road about two miles and telephoned the jail at Chehalis.
>
> The wounded bandit was hit below the right arm, and was injured seriously. Compton was a brave man. Frankly, I was frightened. When Compton began backing toward me I thought the bandit was going to fire on me, too. I had just started to back my truck when the bandits fled. I hope they get them. They're deadly killers.

The two men continued their flight in Compton's Chevrolet and when they crashed the car into a telephone pole on the dirt road near the Claquato Cemetery they abandoned it. Sheriff J. A. Blankenship rushed to the scene of the shooting and ordered road blocks on all roads leading out of the area, and when Compton's car was found later that day the trail of the fleeing murderers was clearer. The sheriff organized a posse of over one hundred armed men who began searching the nearby woods, and bloodhounds were brought in. The trail finally led back to the Ocean Beach Highway and it was thought the two men were picked up at Adna by ex-convict Claude H. Ryan. When William S. Erckenbrack reported seeing Ryan's gray automobile near Winlock the search shifted to that area. Meanwhile, deputy Jackson's body was taken to the Newell and Hoerling funeral parlor at Centralia for burial on April 9, and by that time the fugitives had been identified from letters they left in the Nash automobile they abandoned at the murder scene: Claude H. Ryan and Walter Seelert, the latter wounded by buckshot, and both men were on parole from the Washington state prison.

On April 14 Ryan stumbled into a beer tavern in Tacoma and surrendered "unarmed and weeping." He was suffering from severe hunger and exposure and said that he and Seelert had been kept on the constant move through rain soaked timberland by the relentless pursuit of posses. He said Seelert and he had separated days earlier and he did not know where his partner had gone, but he blamed him for the shooting. Ryan was taken to Chehalis and lodged in jail and on April 27 he was arraigned by Judge George B. Simpson. The judge denied a motion for a change of venue and Ryan was tried in Lewis County, convicted on July 23, 1937, of the first degree murder of deputy Jackson, and sentenced to hang. Ryan's attorney then filed an appeal which stayed the execution and Ryan was taken to the prison in Walla Walla.

On June 24, 1937, detectives in Denver located Walter Seelert. He had taken a job at a local iron foundry and he was soon supposed to leave for his shift, so the detectives surrounded the boarding house and waited for him to appear. When Seelert did not come out four detectives went in after him, and when they entered Seelert's room they found Seelert with roommate C. B. Wilson. The two men immediately opened fire and the detectives shot back, and two bullets struck Wilson and four struck Seelert, killing both, but none of the detectives were injured.

Meanwhile in Washington, the state Supreme Court labored over the Ryan case until November 8 when the justices affirmed the judgment and sentence of the lower court and Judge J. E. Stone of Kelso rescheduled the date of execution for January 13, 1938. On December 30 the Supreme Court concluded the possibility of judicial relief when they denied a rehearing on the matter, and then the application praying for a commutation of sentence was submitted to Governor Clarence D. Martin and denied.

Although Ryan was attended by the Reverend D. Arvid Ohrnell during his final days, he refused all religious service on his final night, and was so nervous he could not eat his supper. He spent his last hours scribbling a final farewell to his father and another to his sweetheart in Drewsey, Oregon. Shortly before midnight Warden J. M. McCauley appeared at the door to Ryan's death row cell and read the death warrant. Ryan was then conducted to the gallows, his face pale, his hands twitching, and his knees wobbling as he appeared before the one hundred forty witnesses, mostly law enforcement officers in town for a convention.

He took his place on the trapdoor where his wrists and arms, knees and ankles were bound and he was asked if he had anything to say. "I believe not, your honor," he told the warden, so the noose was adjusted and the black hood was pulled over his head at 12:05 A.M. The trap was sprung immediately and he broke his neck in the fall, and the prison physician waited below to monitor Ryan's vital signs until he pronounced him dead at 12:16 A.M. The body was then cut down, deposited in the coffin provided by the state, and funeral services were scheduled at the prison later that day.

Centralia Chronicle (WA): April 9, 1937; April 21, 1937; January 13, 1938; February 24–25, 1938. *Billings Gazette* (MT): June 26, 1937. *Chehalis Bee-Nugget* (WA): April 9, 1937. *Inter Lake* (Kalispell, MT): February 25, 1938.

Knapp, Stanley
August 5, 1938

On the afternoon of February 15, 1937, three armed, masked robbers suddenly burst into the Security State Bank in Spokane, Washington, and one of them shouted, "Stick 'em up — this is a stick-up." Six bank employees and seven customers were herded into the open vault at gunpoint when one of the robbers said, "Here comes another customer," and his partner replied, "I'll take care of him." As soon as restaurant owner William E. Walker stepped inside the bank the last robber to speak shot him once, the bullet piercing his right lung. Walker collapsed and then the three robbers took the $4,000 they had collected, ran to a stolen car they had parked outside with the engine running, and fled. Walker was rushed to the hospital and given a blood transfusion but the bullet had caused severe internal injuries and he died that evening. Four hours after the robbery the stolen car was found abandoned at the outskirts of the city and turned over to fingerprint experts for dusting.

By March 6 the three robbers had been identified. Nineteen-year-old Stanley Knapp was already in the jail at Sacramento, California, and warrants were issued for Leroy Knapp, the twenty-one-year-old brother of Stanley, and twenty-year-old Herbert Allen. Leroy was soon captured and he joined his brother in the Sacramento jail and they were returned to Spokane. Both prisoners were arraigned, pled not guilty, and they were tried in the Superior Court in Spokane for the first degree murder of Walker. On June 14 they were convicted and the jurors recommended the death penalty, and when told of the verdict Stanley Knapp said, "Tell them [the jurors] we're soaking our necks in brine to get ready for the rope." The brothers were sentenced to hang together in late 1937 but their court appointed attorneys filed appeals which stayed the executions, and they were kept in the jail at Spokane while the appeal was pending.

Allen eluded capture until July 30, 1937, when he was arrested at Williston, North Dakota, and then Spokane detective August Bettinger went to Williston, got a signed confession from Allen, and returned him to the Spokane jail. Allen was tried and convicted of first degree murder and sentenced to hang after the Knapp brothers, but his attorney also filed an appeal which stayed the execution and he remained in the Spokane jail. By May 1938 the state Supreme Court justices had affirmed the judgment and sentence of the lower court and denied the request for a rehearing for the Knapps, and the brothers were sentenced to hang together on August 5 while Allen was sentenced to hang on August 16.

The three desperate men then hatched a plan of escape and on June 10, as their noon meal was being served, they slugged jailer Al Coldeen with cans of condensed milk, knocking him unconscious, and then they tried to get out a side door of the jail. An alarm had been sounded so deputy sheriff William Deeler posted himself at the side door and when the three men appeared he was surprised to find that Allen was in possession of a pistol. The two men exchanged gunfire, Leroy Knapp was shot in the stomach and collapsed, and then Allen threw down his gun and he and Stanley surrendered. They were returned to their cells while the elder Knapp was rushed to the hospital where he died on July 8. Meanwhile the other two men were taken to the prison at Walla Walla and housed in adjoining death row cells. Though all avenues of judicial relief were exhausted their attorneys continued their efforts to save the lives of their clients and filed petitions with Governor Clarence D. Martin requesting a commutation of sentence, but the petition for Knapp and appeals by his parents were rejected.

During his last hours Stanley Knapp pleaded with the authorities, in a written statement, to spare the life of Allen because he had not fired the fatal shot. Just before midnight the warden appeared at Knapp's cell door and read the death warrant and then he was conducted to the death chamber. He took his place on the trapdoor where his wrists and arms, knees and ankles were bound and the noose was adjusted. He was asked if he had anything to say to the small group of witnesses but there is no record of a speech.

The black hood was pulled over his head at 12:06 A.M. and the trap was sprung immediately. Knapp dropped breaking his neck in the fall and the prison physician pronounced him dead at 12:30. The body was cut down, placed in the coffin provided by the state, and conveyed to a local undertaker where he would be transferred to another coffin and prepared for burial, the arrangements made by his parents. Governor Martin then took into consideration the written statement of Knapp and granted Allen a ninety day reprieve. When the new date for his execution neared, the governor, on November 17, 1938, granted Allen a commutation of sentence to life imprisonment.

Centralia Chronicle (WA): August 3, 1938. *Capital News* (Jefferson City, MO): August 6, 1938. *Lincoln Sunday Journal and Star* (NE): August 8, 1937. *Montana Standard* (Butte): June 11, 1938; August 6, 1938. *Billings Gazette* (MT): February 16, 1937. *Independent* (Helena, MT): March 6, 1937.

O'Donell, Joseph R.
November 21, 1938

At 4:30 A.M. on November 26, 1935, Fred Winkler, who lived in north Seattle, called the police station to report that burglars had broken into the tavern at 8904 Roosevelt Way Northeast. The area was four blocks outside the city limits but officers Trent A. Sickles and Theodore E. Stevens, intending to back up the responding deputies, drove to the scene and first noticed a suspicious automobile parked nearby, then they found that the front door had been jimmied. It was 4:55 A.M. when they decided to contain the building for the deputies, so Sickles took up a position at the front door and Stevens went to the back of the building to watch the back door. Within seconds the three burglars shot Sickles to death and as he fell his shotgun discharged, wounding one burglar and shattering a wall clock inside. As soon as Stevens heard the gunfire he ran to his partner's aid, and he was shot down, but he got off one shot from his revolver which struck a table top in the tavern. The three burglars then ran to their automobile and one called out, "My God, Mac. I'm hit. Help me!" One of the men then helped the wounded man to the car and they drove off.

Deputies arrived moments later and Stevens was rushed to the hospital, but he died a short time afterward. Sheriff William B. Severyns and his chief criminal deputy O. K. Bodia processed the murder scene and found that the cash register and a pinball machine had been rifled, and the tools left behind indicated that the burglars planned to cut through the walls into a butcher shop on one side and a drug store on the other side of the tavern. At 7:30 A.M. a dairy truck driver found two pistols a hundred yards from the tavern and pointed them out to detective Bodia. Winkler, who had seen the entire affair, provided a detailed description of the men and their automobile.

The investigation continued for five months but by April 4, 1936, thirty-seven-year-old Joseph O'Donell was in jail at Los Angeles, California, his forty-one-year-old brother John J. O'Donell and twenty-four-year-old Lester A. Rorick were in jail at Seattle, and the three were charged with the murders of officers Sickles and Stevens. Joseph O'Donnel was extradited to Seattle and tried in the Superior Court in November 1936. Joseph confessed to his part in the burglary and shooting, but his brother claimed he was nursing a sick cat and attending a dance with another man's wife, whom he would not name. On November 25 the jurors found both O'Donells and Rorick guilty of first degree murder and fixed the penalty at life imprisonment for John and Rorick, and death for Joseph.

Appeals were filed for the O'Donells and on September 17, 1937, the state Supreme Court, split five to four, granted them a new trial. They were retried at Seattle with the same outcome and sentence, and John was returned to the prison at Walla Walla to serve out his life term. On September 27 Sheriff W. B. Severyns and jail superintendent Matt Starwich drove Joseph O'Donell to the prison at Walla Walla and lodged him in a death row cell. All that remained for Joseph was the application to Governor Clarence D. Martin praying for a commutation of sentence, but the governor refused to intervene.

During his final weeks Joseph O'Donell was attended by prison chaplain Father John J. Callanan and the priest helped the condemned man resign himself to his fate. On his final night O'Donell ate a hearty supper and then spent the evening hours praying and reading Bible passages with the priest. The warden appeared at the cell door at midnight and read the death warrant and then O'Donell was conducted into the death chamber by Father Callanan and the warden, who had to support him to make the walk. He took his place on the trapdoor and his wrists and arms, knees and ankles were bound before he was asked if he had anything to say to the fifty witnesses. O'Donell talked for three minutes, beginning, "I have information which says that my brother Jack wrote a letter saying he did the shooting. I want to say he did not. I am looking for Claude Fortner [Seattle captain of detectives]. Knowing he was going to frame me I intended to kill him but my brother talked me out of it. I don't see Ernie Yoris [chief of detectives]. My opinion of him is very bad."

He rambled on and throughout his speech he had to be supported so he would not collapse, and when he concluded the noose was quickly adjusted and then he kissed the crucifix when it was offered. The black hood was pulled over his head at 12:14 A.M. and the trap was sprung immediately. O'Donell dropped breaking his neck in the fall and the prison physician waiting below the gallows pronounced him dead at 12:26 A.M. The body was then cut down and deposited in the coffin provided by the state and he was buried on prison grounds later that day.

Centralia Chronicle (WA): November 26, 1935; April 4, 1936; November 25, 1936; September 17, 1937; September 27, 1938; November 21, 1938. *Reno Gazette* (NV): November 21, 1938.

Leuch, Bernhard R.
August 4, 1939

In 1938 fifty-two-year-old Bernhard R. Leuch had been having an affair with a young usher at an Olympia, Washington, movie house and, when she became pregnant, Leuch was determined to rid himself of his thirty-seven-year-old wife, Lena. On June 1, 1938, Leuch, who had been a police officer in Minnesota, went home unexpectedly and after a heated argument he shot his wife to death. He left by the back walk thinking he would not be seen, but his fifteen-year-old daughter, Dorothy, was returning home from school early and saw him leaving, then she found her dead mother and called the authorities. Leuch returned later by the front door and was "surprised to find that his wife had committed suicide." He was arrested and lodged in the Mason County jail at Shelton on an open charge. Noted Seattle criminologist Luke S. May was called in and after he concluded his investigation Leuch was charged with murdering his wife, and his seven children were distributed among relatives in three states.

Leuch was indicted and his trial began at Shelton on July 16, and on July 21 the jurors returned a verdict of guilty of first degree murder and fixed the penalty at death. After he was sentenced to hang his attorney filed an appeal but while the case was still pending Leuch escaped from the Mason County jail. On August 7, 1938, the condemned man overpowered the jailor and a matron and fled. He remained free for three days but on August 10 at 10:00 A.M. a tired, hungry, and nervous Leuch was discovered at the home of Hugo Seipold and he surrendered, saying, "I'm all through boys." He was returned to the jail and he gave a detailed account of his whereabouts over the previous seventy-two hours. The state Supreme Court finally affirmed the judgment and sentence of the Mason County Superior Court and Leuch was sentenced to hang on August 4, 1939, the request for a rehearing was denied, and he was delivered to the prison at Walla Walla. An application praying for executive clemency was delivered to Governor Clarence D. Martin but he declined to intervene.

Warden James M. McCauley described Leuch's time on death row as "pretty good and rather quiet." The prisoner was attended by the prison chaplain Reverend E. T. Allen and the Reverend Arvid Ohrnell, and the Reverend Allen spent the final day with the condemned man praying and reading Bible passages. The clergymen said that Leuch refused to ask for God's forgiveness until the last minute because "he felt his sins were too great." At 9:00 P.M. the prisoner began writing letters and completed four before Warden McCauley appeared at his cell door at midnight. The warden read the death warrant and then Leuch was conducted into the death chamber by the warden and the Reverend Allen.

He appeared before the fifteen witnesses at 12:08 A.M. and took his place on the trapdoor where his wrists and arms, knees and ankles were bound. He was asked if he had anything to say and he replied, "I am an innocent man. I feel in my heart I am innocent." The noose was then adjusted and as the hood was about to be pulled over his head he shouted, "I know I am innocent." The trap was sprung at 12:09 A.M. and Leuch broke his neck in the fall. The prison physician waited below the gallows and at 12:23 A.M. Leuch was pronounced dead. There had been no claim for the remains so the body was cut down, deposited into the coffin provided by the state, and he was buried on the prison grounds later that day.

Centralia Chronicle (WA): June 2, 1938; August 10, 1938; August 4, 1939. *Lincoln State Journal* (NE): July 16, 1938. *Billings Gazette* (MT): August 4, 1939.

Buttry, Paul
September 15, 1939

On the evening of June 8, 1938, thirty-eight-year-old Paul Buttry and thirty-seven-year-old William Hugh Warren, life-long friends from Arkansas who had come west together in 1922, were in Chitwood's Tavern at Hoquiam, Washington, but the men stayed at opposite ends of the bar, would not talk, and neither man took a drink. Buttry was living in the attic of Warren's ex-wife Catherine, and Warren tried to encourage Buttry to marry her and this led to a heated argument as Buttry resisted the notion. During the argument both men made death threats, according to witnesses, and Warren finally had enough of the tension and left the tavern. However, Buttry followed closely behind and as soon as they were outside Buttry pulled a revolver and shot Warren in the face five times, killing him instantly. The murderer then walked to the police station, laid the revolver on the counter, and confessed to killing Warren "over family trouble."

Buttry was charged with murder and his trial began in November before Montesano Superior Court Judge W. E. Campbell. The defendant was found guilty of first degree murder and sentenced to hang on January 19, 1939. He was to be held at the county jail pending appeal but on November 19, at the request of Judge Campbell, he was taken to Walla Walla and lodged in a cell on death row. His attorney filed the appeal which stayed the execution, but the state Supreme Court heard the case on May 9, 1939, and affirmed the judgment and sentence of the Superior Court, and Buttry was resentenced to hang on September 15, 1939. The application to Governor Clarence D. Martin praying for a commutation of sentence was denied late on his final day.

Buttry had remained calm and hopeful up to the last moment as he was attended by prison doctor E. T. Allen, who had previously been a reverend, and the Reverend Arvid Ohrnell. In the early afternoon he said goodbye to Earl Talbott, another condemned man in a nearby cell, and then he wrote out his final statement for the Reverend Ohrnell to read on the gallows. He ate a hearty last supper and then spent the evening with the clergymen. The warden appeared at his cell door before midnight and read the death warrant, and then the warden and the Reverend Ohrnell escorted him into the death chamber. He took his place on the trap door at 12:05 A.M. and while his wrists and arms, knees and ankles were being bound the Reverend Ohrnell read his statement:

> I highly appreciate the attitude of the captain, the chief turnkey, and all the officers of this institution. They have all been very kind, fair, and square. I also appreciate all the help I have received from my relatives and friends and my spiritual advisors Dr. Allen and the Rev. Arvid Ohrnell. When I now depart from this world everything is alright between me and my Cre-

ator. And there is no condemnation in my soul. And my last greetings and love are to my sisters and dear mother.

When the reverend concluded, the noose was adjusted, the black hood was pulled over Buttry's head at 12:07 A.M., and the trap was sprung immediately. Prison physician Dr. Allen waited beneath the gallows and he pronounced Buttry dead at 12:12 A.M. The body was cut down and deposited into the coffin provided by his family, and his remains were driven to a local undertaker to prepare for burial in the Mountain View cemetery later that morning.

Centralia Chronicle (WA): June 9, 1938; November 19, 1938; September 15, 1939.

Talbott, Earl
September 18, 1939

On August 9, 1938, eighteen-year-old Earl Talbott was hunting squirrels along the Touchet River near Waitsburg, Washington, and at noon he met seventy-year-old W. E. McKinney, a local farmer. They argued over a proposed horse deal and suddenly Talbott turned the gun on McKinney and shot him dead. He put the body into an old four-wheeled trailer parked near the machine shed and towed it through the gate toward the river. However, the tongue of the trailer caught, it overturned and spilled out the body, so Talbott covered McKinney with old automobile fenders, slabwood, and other debris. He took McKinney's automobile and drove to Freewater, Oregon, where he let a girl drive the car. Meanwhile McKinney's body was discovered and the description of his missing automobile was broadcast. Oregon police officers spotted the car in Milton, pulled it over, and the girl told them where she had gotten it, and the officers captured Talbott.

The prisoner was returned to Walla Walla that night and the following day he had confessed to the killing and showed the officers how he had hidden the body. He was tried at the fall term of the Walla Walla County Superior Court and pled not guilty by reason of insanity, but he was convicted of first degree murder and sentenced to hang. His court appointed attorney filed an appeal which stayed the execution but the state Supreme Court affirmed the judgment and sentence of the lower court on June 30, 1939, and he was rescheduled to die on September 18. His petition for a commutation of sentence, sent to Governor Clarence D. Martin, was denied.

During his time on death row Talbott was attended by prison chaplain the Reverend Eli T. Allen, who said the prisoner "has been one of the most docile of men who in recent years have met his fate. He has not flinched his fate nor refused it. He has expressed regret, but with the regret he has consistently said he had no reason for the deed." The condemned man, who had recently turned nineteen years of age, wrote out his last statement and gave it to the reverend to read. He ate sparingly of his supper and then spent the evening in prayer with the chaplain. The warden appeared at his cell door before midnight and read the death warrant, and then Talbott was conducted into the death chamber. He took his place on the trap door at 12:05 A.M. and merely shook his head when asked if he wanted to speak to the witnesses.

While his wrists and arms, knees and ankles were being bound the Reverend Allen read his statement, saying Talbott "wants me to express his gratitude to the officers and his friends for their kindness to him and to send his love to his mother." When the reverend concluded the noose was adjusted, the black hood was pulled over his head, and the trap was sprung immediately. The prison physician waited beneath the gallows to monitor Talbott's vital signs and he pronounced him dead as soon as his heart ceased to beat. The body was cut down and deposited into the coffin provided by his family, and his remains were driven to a local undertaker to prepare for the burial arranged by his mother.

Centralia Chronicle (WA): August 10, 1938; June 30, 1939; September 18, 1939.

Wright, Roy
October 6, 1939

On November 7, 1938, eighteen-year-old Roy Wright visited a Yakima, Washington, automobile dealership and arranged for a demonstration drive. Sixty-year-old John Dee Moore, salesman, rode in the passenger seat and after the two men reached an isolated spot Wright pulled to the side of the road, pulled out a .38-caliber revolver, and ordered Moore out of the car. Moore reached for the keys to the car with his left hand and tried to push away the revolver with his right hand but Wright fired twice, and Moore crumpled forward against the gear shift. Moore's dead body was in such a position that Wright had to drive thirty miles in second gear and when he reached the lonely Salus Creek area he parked. Wright then dragged the body three hundred feet to an embankment, but at one point Wright fell and the body rolled on top of him. Struggling to free himself he lost papers from his pocket and, in his haste to be rid of the body, did not notice the papers on the ground.

On November 9 Moore's body was found, and back-tracking the trail over which he was dragged officers found the papers identifying Wright. A description of Wright and the automobile was broadcast and on November 15 Wright was arrested for auto theft near San Jose, California. On November 24 Wright was brought back to Yakima and along the way he showed officers where he had disposed of Moore's body, but in talking of the murder he showed no remorse. On November 28 H. A. Budlong of Salem called the police to report that he had found the murder weapon hidden in a wood pile. It was carefully hidden with a flashlight, but Wright said he had thrown the gun along the railroad tracks near Salem so it appeared someone had found it and moved it to the wood pile.

When it came time for his trial Wright asked that no attorney be appointed for him, as he wanted to plead guilty, but the judge refused the plea and appointed Eugene Ivy as his attorney. Wright was tried, convicted of first degree murder, and sentenced to hang but an appeal stayed the execution. The appeal was quickly disposed of by the state Supreme Court and Wright's date of execution was then set for October 6, 1939, only eleven months after the murder of Moore. The petition to the governor praying for a commutation of sentence was denied.

On Wright's last evening he dictated a full confession of his crime spree over the year previous to the murder of Moore, and it included the theft of many automobiles. Just before midnight the warden appeared at the cell door and read the death warrant and then the prisoner was conducted to the gallows. He took his place on the trapdoor where his wrists and arms, knees and ankles were bound and he was asked if he had anything to say to the witnesses, and he said that he hoped that all boys and girls would benefit from his experience. He prayed audibly as the noose was adjusted about his neck, but he showed no sign of nervousness. The black hood was pulled over his head at 12:05 A.M. and the trap was sprung immediately. The prison physician monitored Wright's vital signs until he pronounced him dead at 12:19 A.M. The body was cut down, placed in the coffin provided, and buried on the prison grounds pending a requisition from his family at Watsonville, California.

Oakland Tribune (CA): November 24, 1938; November 30, 1938; October 6, 1939. *Centralia Chronicle* (WA): November 28, 1938. *Times and Daily News Leader* (San Mateo, CA): October 6, 1939.

Carson, Ralph
December 8, 1939

In early 1937 fifty-three-year-old Ralph Carson, alias Allen Sears, began paying particular attention the seventeen-year-old granddaughter of Lynwood Sproul, his employer at Mora in Clallam County, Washington. He began having intimate relations with Alma and was afraid he would be arrested if Sproul filed a complaint so, on October 4, 1937, Carson shot Sproul to death with a single shot to his breast. Carson, who was also believed to be an army deserter, was arrested for murder but he claimed that he had shot Sproul by accident while cleaning a rifle. The evidence did not support his story but when all the facts surfaced Carson was also held on "statutory charges," tried for his relations with Alma, convicted, and sentenced to serve twenty years in prison.

There seemed no hurry to try Carson for the murder, as the prisoner was safely tucked away at the prison at Walla Walla, but Sproul's friends were convinced that his death was a murder and pushed for a trial, so in April 1939 Carson was tried in Judge John R. Ralson's Superior Court at Port Angeles. He persisted in his defense of an accidental shooting but after six hours deliberation the jurors, on April 21, found him guilty of first degree murder and fixed the penalty at death. He was sentenced to die the week of December 4, 1939, and the warden chose December 8. On December 7 acting Governor Victor A. Meyers considered the petition for a commutation of sentence and declined to intervene, but called the prison at 11:45 P.M. to be sure everything was in order.

The Prison chaplain Reverend Eli T. Allen and the Reverend Arvid Ohrnell attended to Carson's spiritual needs during his months on death row and the Reverend Ohrnell reported, "He was in his usual good spirits, living a normal life ... and is calmly awaiting the outcome of his suspense." Prison officials described the prisoner as "a very unimaginative man having no visions of the future and no dreams of the past." On his last evening Carson wrote out a statement for the Reverend Ohrnell to read on the scaffold, and then the two spent those last hours in prayer. The death warrant was read to Carson late that evening and the warden reappeared at Carson's cell door at midnight and conducted the prisoner onto the gallows.

The prisoner took his place on the trapdoor and was asked if he had anything to say, but he just shook his head. While his wrists and arms, knees and ankles were being bound the Reverend Ohrnell read his statement: "The testimony I gave on the witness stand was the whole truth. I am thankful to my spiritual advisers, the Reverend Ohrnell and Dr. Allen. I depart from this world with peace in my soul to meet my Creator through my Lord and Savior." The noose was adjusted and the black hood was pulled over his head at 12:05 A.M. and the trap was sprung immediately. Carson dropped, breaking his neck in the fall, and the prison physician monitored his vital signs until his heart ceased to beat and then he pronounced Carson dead. The body was cut down, deposited into the coffin provided by the state, and the Reverend Ohrnell and Dr. Allen arranged the details for Carson's funeral in the prison cemetery that afternoon.

Albuquerque Journal (NM): April 22, 1939. *Centralia Chronicle* (WA): April 22, 1939; September 18, 1939; December 7, 1939. *Seattle Times* (WA): December 9, 1939.

Bouchard, Edward L.
September 6, 1940

In October 1939 twenty-eight-year-old Cyril Ables of Van Nuys, California, and thirty-two-year-old Ralph Allinson of Reseda, California, were in Portland, Oregon, looking for work when they met forty-two-year-old Edward L. Bouchard. Bouchard, an automobile salesman, convinced the two men to accompany him in their car to a wilderness location near Arlington, Washington. Once they were in an isolated location Bouchard bludgeoned the two men with an ax and then garroted them until they were dead. He stole their automobile and all the property they had stored in the car trunk and drove back to Portland.

The bodies, in an advanced state of decomposition and mutilation from the attack and from wild animals, were found on March 21, 1940, and they were soon identified from items in their pockets. Following up on the investigation officers began looking for their automobile and on March 28 Bouchard was arrested in Portland driving the stolen car. He admitted driving with them to the lonely wooded spot in Snohomish County, Washington, but denied killing them. He said they had continued on to Seattle where they gave him the car and other property in payment of a bill, and he left them in Seattle and drove back to Portland.

Bouchard was booked for investigation, but after only one day he was charged with two counts of murder. On April 4 Bouchard was taken to Seattle where he was questioned for hours by detective chief Ernest W. Yoris, who would only say that there were some clues and ties to Seattle that had to be explained. On May 19 Bouchard was indicted by the Snohomish County grand jury and arraigned at Everett, Washington, and his trial was set for June 24. His trial lasted one week and on July 2 the jurors, after three hours of deliberations, found him guilty of two counts of murder and fixed the penalty at death. Defense counsel William Johnson filed a notice of appeal but the case was disposed of by the state Supreme Court so expeditiously that his original date of execution, September 6, 1940, was not delayed. His application to the governor praying for a commutation of sentence was also quickly denied.

As the time neared Bouchard told the warden he would make no statement on the gallows. Just before midnight the warden appeared at the door to Bouchard's death row cell and read the death warrant. The prisoner was conducted to the gallows where he took his place on the trapdoor. His wrists and arms, knees and ankles were bound, the noose was adjusted and the black hood was pulled over his head. At 12:05 A.M., a half minute after he appeared before the witnesses, the trap was sprung and he broke his neck in the fall. The prison physician waited below and at 12:17 he pronounced Bouchard dead. The body was cut down and deposited in the coffin provided by the state, and he was buried that day on the prison grounds.

Montana Standard (Butte): March 29, 1940. *Nevada State Journal* (Reno): May 20, 1940; July 5, 1940. *Oakland Tribune* (CA): July 2, 1940. *Reno Gazette* (NV): September 6, 1940. *San Antonio Express* (TX): September 7, 1940. *Billings Gazette* (MT): March 30, 1940. *Centralia Chronicle* (WA): April 4, 1940.

Marable, Jack
October 4, 1940

On January 28, 1939, seven desperate convicts sawed through their prison cell bars at the Draper Prison in Speigner, Alabama, and escaped. Soon six of the escaped convicts were either dead or behind bars awaiting prosecution and additional prison time, but forty-two-year-old Jack Marable, who was serving fifteen to twenty-three years for burglary, avoided capture and made his way as far from Alabama as he could.

On the evening of October 3, 1939, Marable, with his sixteen-year-old accomplice, Robert Kimmich, kidnapped at the point of a knife Geraldine Roloff from the steps of the post office in Olympia, Washington. They forced her to drive them to an isolated shack near Tenino and then they took turns raping the young mother repeatedly. When they were through with their victim they drove off, leaving her to find her way to some inhabited dwelling to ask for help. The two rapists were soon captured based upon the excellent description Roloff gave the authorities of the men and the automobile, and by October 6 both prisoners had confessed. On October 14 they were arraigned under Washington's "little Lindbergh kidnapping law" in the Thurston County Superior Court and Judge John M. Wilson appointed defense attorneys, then gave them until October 16 to plead. The defendants pled not guilty and the trial was set for the first week of November.

Marable, as soon as he was arrested, insisted that he was so drunk that he could remember nothing and used that as his defense at trial, but on November 10, 1939, the jurors found both defendants guilty and fixed the penalty at death for Marable and life imprisonment for Kimmich. Appeals were filed which stayed Marable's execution and the state Supreme Court considered the matter for ten months before they affirmed the judgment and sentence imposed by the lower court, and the justices set the date for Marable's execution for October 4, 1940. Governor Clarence D. Martin, when petitioned, refused to intervene.

Marable never reconciled himself to his fate and believed to the last moment that he would be saved, so he never accepted religious support. On Thursday night, October 3, the warden appeared at Marable's death row cell door just before midnight, exactly one year after the crime, and read the death warrant. The prisoner was then conducted into the death chamber and he took his place on the trapdoor where his wrists and arms, knees and ankles were bound. He was asked if he had anything to say and he denied the kidnapping and assault of Roloff, a change from his persistent claim that he was too drunk to remember anything, and then said he was "the victim of a bloodthirsty politician."

When he concluded the noose was adjusted, the black hood was pulled over his head, and at 12:06 A.M. the trap was sprung. The prison physician waited beneath the gallows and monitored Marable's vital signs until he pronounced him dead at 12:19 A.M. The body was then cut down and deposited in the coffin provided by the state. Marable had claimed to be from Riverdale, Georgia, but no one from there requisitioned the remains, so he was buried on the prison grounds that evening.

Centralia Chronicle (WA): October 7, 1939; October 14, 1939. *Montana Standard* (Butte): October 5, 1940. *Oakland Tribune* (CA): November 1, 1939; October 4, 1940. *Sunday Journal and Star* (Lincoln, NE): November 12, 1939.

Lewis, Arley
January 30, 1941

On September 13, 1940, Arley Lewis, at gunpoint, robbed twenty-one-year-old Jack Avent on a public street in Vancouver, Washington. When Avent resisted Lewis shot him dead. He next kidnapped Betty McIlvain but released her when she gave him $5, all she had. On September 20 Lewis burglarized a grocery store in Bucoda, and this was one of three burglaries attributed to him between September 13 and 20. The following day he kidnapped fifty-five-year-old Charles Null, a Centralia automobile salesman, and forced him to drive to Little Hanover Valley. He then struck Null over the head with his pistol, took $3 from his pockets, and when Null started to run away he shot him through the stomach. Null was rushed to the hospital and by September 28 he had recovered and was released from the hospital. Null's description of his attacker, and indications that he had fled the state to avoid prosecution, brought in Federal Bureau of Investigation agents and within sixteen hours they had identified Arley Lewis, an ex-convict from Missouri.

On the same day that Null was released from the hospital Lewis was captured by Oregon State Patrol officers near Newburg, and he was held for the Washington authorities. He was returned to Centralia and charged with the shooting of Null, but on October 3 he confessed to the murder of Avent and a count of first degree murder was added to the long list of criminal charges filed. He was tried at the fall term of the Superior Court in Vancouver and found guilty of the first degree murder of Jack Avent, and the jury fixed the penalty at death. Lewis was sentenced to hang on January 30, 1941, and at his insistence neither appeal nor petition for executive clemency was submitted.

During his final days, according to Warden P. E. Mahoney, Lewis became "pretty jittery." He denied that he was guilty of the murder of Avent and claimed he had been double-crossed because "the prosecution promised to spare me the death penalty if I would confess to killing Jack Avent." However, Warden Mahoney said, "Lewis made no bones to me about killing Avent. He just felt he didn't have execution coming for it."

On Lewis' final night the warden appeared at his cell door before midnight and read the death warrant, and then he was conducted to the gallows. He took his place on the trapdoor where his wrists and arms, knees and ankles were bound and he was asked if he had anything to say to the thirty witnesses. He warned that "all boys and girls should follow the straight road." When it was clear he had no more to say the noose was adjusted and the black hood was pulled over his head at 12:05 A.M. The trap was immediately sprung and Lewis broke his neck in the fall. The prison physician waited beneath the gallows and monitored vital signs until he pronounced Lewis dead at 12:19. The body was cut down, deposited in the coffin provided by the state, and he was buried later that day on the prison grounds.

Centralia Chronicle (WA): September 26, 1940; January 30, 1941; October 3, 1955. *Oakland Tribune* (CA): September 25, 1940; January 30, 1941.

Davis, Denzel
March 24, 1941

Twenty-three-year-old Denzel Davis had been married to twenty-year-old June Davis for several years and they had one child, but as the 1939 holiday season approached marital difficulties worsened and they separated. Davis' forty-five-year-old mother, Harriet R. Arnold, did not like June and was pleased when the couple separated. Early on Monday, March 18, Davis told his mother that he was going to meet June at a local motel the following day and try to reconcile. Davis and his mother were in the kitchen when the argument began and Arnold said some very hateful things about June. Davis suddenly grabbed a heavy object and struck his mother on the head, crushing her skull and knocking her senseless but not killing her. He then took electrical cords and tied her wrists and ankles and used a dog chain to strangle her, but still she would not die. Davis next took an ice pick from the utensil drawer and stabbed his mother repeatedly until she was dead. He stuffed her body into the cabinet beneath the kitchen sink and nailed the doors shut, mopped up the blood with a rag, took the ice pick, and fled.

On Tuesday, Davis met his wife and baby at the motel and that evening, tormented by guilt, he confessed the murder to June. After Davis left the next morning June alerted the police but an independent investigation had already begun because Harriet Arnold, a very dependable employee at a downtown department store, had failed to report to work for two days and had not called to explain her absence. The police went to the Arnold home and found the bloody rag in a box in a closet and a blood stain on the kitchen floor. Next they found that the cabinet beneath the sink was nailed shut and when they pried it open they found Arnold's body. Dr. Gale Wilson, county autopsy surgeon, took charge of the remains and determined the cause of death was from eighteen stab wounds to the upper torso of the deceased. The police also searched the motel room rented by Davis on March 19 and found the murder weapon rolled up in the window shade. An arrest warrant was issued and every route out of Seattle was watched, while every place Davis might hide was searched.

On Saturday, March 23, police checked the apartment of one of Davis' friends, found that the occupant had been out of town for some time, entered and discovered Davis curled up on the top shelf of a closet. He was arrested and questioned by detective O. K. Bodia and he readily confessed, "Yes, I killed her. I'm glad its over."

Davis was lodged in the King County jail and within months he was tried, convicted of first degree murder, and sentenced to hang. His attorney filed an appeal which stayed the execution and the state Supreme Court heard arguments in late 1940. The justices affirmed the judgment and sentence of the lower court and Davis' date of execution was set at March 23, 1941. The prisoner was taken from the Seattle jail to the prison at Walla Walla and placed in a cell on death row. Efforts to obtain a commutation of sentence from Governor Arthur B. Langlie failed during Davis' final hours and there was nothing further he could do but resign himself to his fate.

Davis had been calm throughout his days on death row and when he learned all avenues of relief had been exhausted he did not lose his composure. On his final night the warden appeared at this cell door just before midnight and read the death warrant, and he was then conducted into the death chamber. He took his place on the trapdoor where his wrists and arms, knees and ankles were bound and he was asked if he wanted to make a statement. Davis replied, "I ask forgiveness of all, my wife and baby." The noose was then adjusted and the black hood was pulled over his head at 12:06 A.M., and the trap was sprung immediately. The prison physician waited below the gallows and at 12:17 A.M. Davis was pronounced dead. The body was cut down and deposited into the coffin provided by the state. Davis had murdered the only person who would have seen to his burial, so arrangements were made to bury him on the prison grounds later that day.

Inter Lake (Kalispell, MT): March 24, 1941. *Independent* (Helena, MT): March 24, 1940. *Lowell Sun* (MA): March 20, 1940. *Tyrone Herald* (PA): March 27, 1940.

Anderson, John
November 14, 1941

In May 1940 Spokane Valley farmer David Johnson noticed that his hens were not producing eggs at their usual rate, and there appeared nothing wrong with the chickens. He began keeping a close watch on the hen house and one night he discovered his neighbor, John Anderson, stealing the eggs. When he confronted the thief Anderson killed Johnson in cold blood, rather than face prosecution on a minor criminal charge. He drove the body across the state line into Idaho to an abandoned barn and then set the barn afire. The body was nearly consumed but when found later that year there were sufficient remains to identify Johnson. Anderson was suspected but he denied being the murderer and named another person, but the other person had a solid alibi. Circumstantial evidence accrued in the "hen house murder case" until there was a strong case against Anderson.

He was indicted and tried in December, and he was convicted of murdering Johnson. On January 4, 1941, Judge Louis Bunge sentenced him to hang in March but the case was appealed and this stayed the execution. The state Supreme Court affirmed the judgment and sentence of the Superior Court in September 1941 and the date for Anderson's execution was set for November 14, 1941. A petition to the governor asking for a commutation of sentence was denied.

On his final night Anderson wrote out his dying statement insisting he was innocent and again naming another as the murderer. The warden appeared at his cell door before midnight and read the death warrant, and then he was conducted onto the gallows. He took his place on the trapdoor where his wrists and arms, knees and ankles were bound and when asked if he had anything to say he declined. The noose was adjusted and the black hood was pulled over his head at 12:08 A.M., and the trap was sprung immediately. The prison physician stood beneath the gallows and monitored his vital signs until his heart ceased to beat and then Anderson was pronounced dead. The body was cut down, deposited in the coffin provided by the state, and he was buried on the prison grounds later that day.

Montana Standard (Butte): November 15, 1941. *Greeley Daily Tribune* (CO): November 15, 1941. *Ogden Standard-Examiner* (UT): January 5, 1941.

Montgomery, Chester
March 19, 1943

Forty-eight-year-old Jessie Sellers operated a beauty parlor in Spokane, Washington. Sellers and a friend looked into the possibility of opening a parlor in the basement of the Victoria Hotel and as they looked over the property she caught the eye of twenty-seven-year-old hotel porter Chester Montgomery. On June 9, 1940, Montgomery lured, or forced, Sellers to an unoccupied upper floor of the hotel and there he stripped her, beat her, and raped her repeatedly. When he was finished with his victim he dragged her nude body to an elevator shaft and after the elevator had ascended above his floor he threw her into the shaft. The body was discovered two days later but was in such a poor condition that county coroner Dr. L. S. Collins could not identify the remains.

On June 15 a friend of Sellers, who had not seen her for days, read of the slaying in the newspapers and contacted the sheriff's office. That evening she viewed the remains and identified the body. During the investigation the untimely absence of Chester Montgomery focused suspicion on him and the Federal Bureau of Investigation became involved when it was clear he had crossed state lines to avoid prosecution. On February 13, 1942, after searching for Montgomery for two years, FBI agents announced they had captured Montgomery in Battle Creek, Michigan. The prisoner was returned to Spokane, Washington, and his murder trial began in early June; then on June 7, 1942, the jurors, after brief deliberations, found him guilty of first degree murder and fixed the penalty at death. His defense at trial was that he had seen the rape and murder of Sellers but the guilty party was Willie Thomas. Thomas had testified that he knew nothing of the murder, and he was believed. Montgomery was sentenced to hang in August but his court appointed attorney filed an appeal with the state Supreme Court which stayed the execution. In late 1942 the Supreme Court justices affirmed the judgment and sentence of the Spokane County Superior Court and Montgomery was re-sentenced to hang on March 19, 1943. Neither appeal nor application for executive clemency would delay the proceedings further.

At midnight of the fatal day the warden appeared at Montgomery's death row cell door and read the death warrant. Montgomery was then escorted into the death chamber where he mounted the gallows and took his place on the trapdoor. His wrists and arms, knees and ankles were bound and the noose was adjusted. There is no record that he spoke to the witnesses but after the black hood was pulled over his head at 12:15 A.M. the trap was immediately sprung, and he broke his neck in the fall. The prison physician waited beneath the gallows to monitor his vital signs and he pronounced Montgomery dead at 12:26 A.M. The body was cut down, deposited into the coffin provided by the state, and later that day he was buried on the prison grounds.

Albuquerque Journal (NM): February 14, 1942. *Mansfield News-Journal* (OH): March 19, 1943. *Independent* (Helena, MT): June 8, 1942. *Ogden Standard-Examiner* (UT): June 15, 1940. *Sandusky Register-Star-News* (OH): March 19, 1943.

Jacobs, Roy W.
April 6, 1943

On July 15, 1935, shortly before noon an unmasked robber armed with a revolver entered the State Bank in Orling, Washington, stuck his gun in the face of teller Leslie Stone and said, "Hand it over." He got $500 and fled northwest toward Seattle in a car he had stolen earlier that morning. Orling officers telephoned Puyallup's Chief of Police Frank Chadwick and asked him to watch for the robber, and gave him a good description of the robber's automobile, so Chadwick with forty-two-year-old officer Harry Storem drove toward Alderton. Near the farm of John Urdea the officers drew alongside the robber's automobile and pulled him to the side of the road. The robber quickly got out of his car and walked around to the officers' car and immediately opened fire. Urdea said, "There were no shots from the police car. Then the man jumped into his car and raced toward Buckley. I ran to the police car and found that Chief Chadwick had opened the door of the car and fallen out. He couldn't talk. Storem was in the front seat and he was unconscious." Chadwick had been shot just below the collar bone and the bullet had deflected downward piercing vital organs. Storem had been shot in the right wrist and dropped his revolver without getting off a shot and then, as he struggled to pick up the pistol with his left hand, he was shot in the head. Both officers died within a few minutes and the search for the robber-turned-cop killer intensified, and his car was found abandoned near Sumner and dusted for fingerprints. The description of the murderer fit closely "scar-faced" William Dainard, alias Mahan, who was already the subject of a nationwide manhunt for his part in the George Weyerhaeuser kidnapping and four bank robberies in northwest Washington. The focus on Dainard prevented a more thorough investigation into other possible suspects, but after Dainard was sentenced to serve a sixty year prison term beginning May 9, 1936, he was questioned and proved an alibi.

Detectives began searching for another suspect and in late January 1937 suspicion focused on bank bandit Chester William Clark, who was serving a life term at Folsom Prison in California. His pistol and bullets, taken from him when captured, were tested for a ballistics match but were not the murder weapon. In early 1942 detectives found another likely suspect in Roy W. Jacobs but he seemed to have an airtight alibi that he was in Kelso, Washington, one hundred miles away when the Orting bank was robbed. It took several months before Jacobs' alibi was disproved and then the circumstantial evidence began to fall into place and accumulate.

In the fall of 1942 Jacobs was tried on two counts of murder, convicted, and sentenced to hang. His attorney filed an appeal which stayed the execution for several months but in January 1943 the justices of the state Supreme Court affirmed the judgment and sentence of the lower court, and the date of execution was set at April 6, 1943. The application to Governor Arthur B. Langlie, praying for a commutation of sentence, was denied and nothing further would delay the proceedings.

Just before midnight on Jacobs' final day prison superintendent Bert O. Webb appeared at the door to his death row cell door and read the death warrant. The prisoner was then conducted into the death chamber and at 12:07 A.M. he took his place on the trapdoor, where his wrists and arms, knees and ankles were strapped and he was asked if he had anything to say. Jacobs, who continued to insist he was innocent, replied, "I hope you will live to see the day that my name will be exonerated." The noose was then adjusted, the black hood was pulled over his head at 12:09 A.M., and the trap was sprung immediately. Jacobs broke his neck in the fall and the prison physician waited beneath the gallows and monitored vital signs until he pronounced Jacobs dead at 12:20 A.M. The body was then cut down, deposited into the coffin provided by the state, and he was buried on the prison grounds later that day.

Mason City Globe-Gazette (IA): April 6, 1943. *Reno Gazette* (NV): April 6, 1943. *Herald* (Provo, UT): July 17, 1935. *Ogden Standard-Examiner* (UT): July 16, 1935; May 9, 1936; January 24, 1937. *Titusville Herald* (PA): July 16, 1935.

Williams, Persia
September 8, 1944

On Saturday evening, December 11, 1943, three men, one armed with a pistol, tried to rob a man at 12th and East Alder Streets in Seattle, Washington, but the man resisted and was wounded, and the robbers fled empty-handed. Late on Wednesday evening, December 15, 1943, sixty-eight-year-old Joseph Romagnoli and his fifty-two-year-old wife, Marie, were closing their neighborhood grocery store at 801 Dearborn Street in Seattle, Washington, when suddenly three men burst into the store, one holding a nickle-plated six shot .32-caliber revolver. One of the unarmed men started for the cash register and Joseph began to struggle with him so the armed robber fired four shots, two bullets striking Joseph in the chest and the other two striking Marie, one in her neck and the other in her chest. Joseph collapsed and while the unarmed robber rifled the register the armed robber went into the living quarters in the rear of the store. There he encountered Frank Nesci, a seventy-year-old boarder, and shot him in the abdomen twice. The armed robber then returned to the store area and followed his two companions as they fled, but Marie had recovered from the shock of being shot and grabbed the armed robber at the door. His pistol was empty so they wrestled and Marie managed to tear off a piece of his overcoat sleeve, tear off a belt strap and several coat buttons, and the robber dropped his hat.

Two neighborhood high school boys, Jack and Frank Kerrigan, heard the shots and started for the grocery store but when they were just ten paces away the robber tore free of Marie's grasp and ran off. The authorities were called, three ambulances were summoned, and the wounded were rushed to Harborview (King) County Hospital. Joseph died nineteen minutes after he arrived at the hospital but Maria and Nesci recovered from their wounds over the following weeks. Maria Romagnoli and the Kerrigan boys gave a good description of the murderers and on December 16 Romagnoli viewed a photo line-up and immediately identified Persia Williams as the armed robber and James Wilson as the man who had rifled the cash register.

Both were ex-convicts and the following day Williams was found in his hotel room and arrested, and the brown overcoat was found in his room. He denied owning the coat, and the hat found at the scene, but his hotel manager said he had seen him wearing both before the murder. On December 21 the two men confessed to being the robbers but each blamed the other for the shooting. Meanwhile they also named the third man and soon James Howard Keener joined them behind bars. The day after they confessed Lucille Val La Pierre surrendered the murder weapon to the police, saying Mrs. Wilson asked her to hide or dispose of it. With evidence building Williams was now faced with the confessions of both Wilson and Keener, as well as the statements of Romagnoli saying he was the shooter, so on Christmas eve he confessed to shooting Joseph Romagnoli. The three men were tried in the King County Superior Court in April 1944 and all three were convicted of murder in the first degree. Keener and Wilson were sentenced to serve life terms while Williams was sentenced to hang on June 9, but his attorney filed an appeal which delayed the execution for several months. As soon as the state Supreme Court affirmed the judgment and sentence Williams was sentenced to hang on September 8, 1944, and nothing further would delay the proceedings.

On the evening of September 7 Warden Bert O. Webb appeared at Williams' death row cell door to read the death warrant and the condemned man told him, "I am sorry for what I have done." The warden appeared again at midnight and at 12:10 A.M. he conducted Williams into the death chamber where the prisoner took his place on the trapdoor and had his wrists and arms, knees and ankles strapped. Warden Webb then asked if he wanted to make a statement and he replied, "I meant no crime. I have embraced the Lord and hope he will receive me."

The noose was quickly adjusted and the black hood was pulled over his head and at 12:11 A.M. the trap was sprung. Williams dropped six feet, breaking his neck in the fall. The prison physician, with stethoscope in hand, steadied the body and monitored his vital signs until he pronounced him dead at 12:33 A.M. The body was then cut down and deposited into the coffin provided by the state, and Williams was buried in the prison cemetery later that day.

On August 31, 1955, Keener was working on a prison crew picking tomatoes when he just walked away. He remained free for ten years but on October 15, 1965, he was captured at Stockton, California, and returned to the prison, and he marveled at all the changes to the prison during the decade he was gone. Meanwhile Wilson, in 1958, was paroled to Oklahoma.

Centralia Chronicle (WA): September 1, 1955 *Seattle Times* (WA): December 16–17, 1943; December 24, 1943. *Seattle Post-Intelligencer* (WA): December 16–17, 1943; December 19, 1943; December 21, 1943; December 23–24, 1943. *Walla Walla Union-Bulletin* (WA): September 8, 1944 October 15, 1965; October 26, 1965.

Heberling, Edward
December 8, 1944

In 1944 the Lindstrom family moved from Miami, Florida, to Seattle, Washington, where Carl R. Lindstrom found work at the Boeing aircraft plant. The Lindstroms had a pretty fourteen-year-old daughter, Harriet Louise, and she caught the eye of thirty-one-year-old ship yard worker Edward Heberling who lived next door. On the night of July 10, 1944, Heberling snuck into Harriet's bedroom, bound the young girl and gagged her with a wad of paper tied in place with a rayon blouse, and then he raped her repeatedly. It was all accomplished with such stealth that her parents never heard a noise. When Heberling was finished with his victim he beat her to death with an iron stove shaker, and to be sure she was dead drove the longest blade from his pocket knife through the paper wad, through the top of her mouth, and into her brain.

In the morning Carl Lindstrom left for work and then Harriet's mother went to her room to check on her, and discovered her daughter's dead body. She called the police and they soon had Heberling in custody, his arms and wrists slashed when he tried to commit suicide, and he was taken to the hospital and kept under heavy guard. Heberling could hardly wait to confess, and had done so as soon as the police appeared at his house. By September Heberling had recovered sufficiently to stand trial and on Monday, September 11, the jury was seated and the first witnesses were called. The defendant's court appointed attorney, Louis T. Silvain, presented a defense of "mental irresponsibility," but the jurors found Heberling guilty of first degree murder on September 16. Heberling was sentenced to hang on December 8, 1944, and nothing would delay the proceedings.

Shortly after midnight on the fatal day the condemned man was taken from his death row cell and escorted into the death chamber where he took his place on the trapdoor. He told the prison chaplain Reverend E. T. Allen, "If I had been a religious man I wouldn't be here now." It was the only comment he would make as his wrists and arms, knees and ankles were strapped, the noose was adjusted, and the black hood was pulled over his head. Within a few minutes after Heberling entered the chamber the trap was sprung and he broke his neck in the fall. The prison physician monitored Heberling's vital signs and as soon as his heart stopped beating he was pronounced dead. The body was then cut down, deposited in its coffin, and prepared for shipment to Seattle where his wife had arranged for the burial.

Capital News (Jefferson City, MO): December 9, 1944. *San Antonio Express* (TX): September 17, 1944; December 9, 1944. *Billings Gazette* (MT): September 11, 1944. *Emporia Gazette* (KS): July 11, 1944. *Port Arthur News* (WA): July 11, 1944.

Bill, Joe
September 7, 1945

On April 12, 1945, thirty-three-year-old Joe Bill, an Alaskan living in Seattle, Washington, sexually assaulted five-year-old Irma Irene McGough and the attack was so brutal the child died. Bill then stuffed the body into a storage bin and fled. As soon as the child was missed a search was conducted and her dead, battered body was found. Five days after the killing Bill surrendered to the Seattle police and though he did not confess he never claimed innocence. Bill was examined by a panel of psychiatrists and declared sane before his trial began in early June. On June 7, Bill was convicted of first degree murder and on June 26 Superior Court Judge Clay Allen sentenced him to hang on September 7, 1945. Neither appeal or application for executive clemency would delay the proceedings.

For several days before his execution Bill spent most of his time reading his Bible and consulting with the Reverend John J. Callanan, and the prison chaplain helped him through moments of nervousness. His wife visited regularly and made her last call at the prison Thursday morning, then spent the remainder of the day pleading with Governor Monrad C. Wallgren for a commutation of sentence, but to no avail. Before 1:00 A.M. Friday the warden appeared at Bill's cell door and read the death warrant. The prisoner was then conducted into the death chamber where he took his place on the trapdoor at 1:06 A.M. His wrists and arms, knees and ankles were bound, the noose was adjusted, and he was asked if he wanted to make a statement. Bill replied, "Yes sir. All I wish is that most of the young men I am leaving behind will benefit by my mistakes that I made all through my life and especially this one. I hope to God that He forgives me and don't want to bear no grudge against no one." Father Callanan then stepped forward and pressed a crucifix to Bill's lips and when he stepped back the black hood was pulled over the prisoner's head.

The trap was sprung at 1:08 A.M. and as Bill was dying Father Callanan administered last rites. The prison physician positioned himself beneath the gallows and monitored Bill's vital signs until he pronounced him dead at 1:25 A.M. The body was cut down, deposited in the coffin provided by Mrs. Bill, and taken to a local undertaker to be prepared for the journey to Seattle where he would be buried on Saturday.

Nevada State Journal (Reno): June 27, 1945. *Walla Walla Union-Bulletin* (WA): September 7, 1945.

Wessel, Joseph B.
January 18, 1946

In 1945 forty-three-year-old Joseph Wessel and his thirty-five-year-old wife Evelyn were having marital difficulties because Evelyn "had big ideas about money." Joseph maintained he could do nothing to satisfy her and finally they separated. On September 17 Joseph crept into the Tacoma, Washington, home where his wife lived with their four children, including five-year-old daughter Mary Ann. He found his wife and Mary Ann asleep on the bed and attacked them with a claw hammer. Mary Ann died of a crushed skull but Evelyn recovered to testify against her husband when he was tried in late October. On November 3, 1945, the jurors found the defendant guilty of the first degree murder of Mary Ann and of first degree assault against Evelyn. He was sentenced to hang for the murder and his attorney filed an appeal, but it was disposed of so expeditiously that his date with the hangman on January 18, 1946, was not delayed.

During Wessel's last week his wife and sister visited him at the prison and then they went to see Governor Monrad C. Wallgren to ask for a commutation of sentence or at least a reprieve, but he declined to intervene. In his last twenty-four hours Wessel became increasingly nervous but as the fatal moment neared he braced up with the help of the prison chaplain. In his final statement to the chaplain he "whispered his sorrow for having killed his daughter and was solicitous of his wife and family's welfare."

The warden appeared at his cell door before midnight and read the death warrant. The prisoner was supported by the warden and chaplain as they made their way into the death chamber where he took his place on the trapdoor, but he was able to stand unaided. His wrists and arms, knees and ankles were strapped and he was asked if he had anything to say, and he expressed his assurance that the good Lord would receive him. The noose was adjusted and the black hood was pulled over his head at 12:06 A.M. and the trap was sprung immediately. Wessel broke his neck in the fall and the prison physician pronounced him dead at 12:19. The body was then cut down, deposited into the coffin provided, and taken to a local undertaker to prepare for shipment to Tacoma where his family would see to his burial.

Nevada State Journal (Reno): November 9, 1945. *Walla Walla Union-Bulletin* (WA): January 18, 1946.

Clark, Woodrow
February 5, 1946

T. P. Dillon and his wife operated a sign painting shop in Spokane, Washington, and on the evening of January 15, 1944, they threw a party in their living quarters at the rear of the shop. An employee, Arthur D. Brown, became upset at the drinking, quit and left. The party became loud and the police were called and they found the Dillons, twenty-eight-year-old Jane Staples, and thirty-one-year-old Frank S. Winnett in the quarters and quieted their celebrating, but after the officers left twenty-seven-year-old Woodrow Clark joined them. After several hours of drinking and boisterous behavior Clark became determined to have sexual relations with Staples and, when he was rejected, he took a hatchet and attacked four people. T. P. Dillon was killed instantly; the sharp edge of the hatchet had been buried into Mrs. Dillon's head but she was still alive when she was rushed to the hospital, though she died five days later without regaining consciousness; and Winnett had been struck eleven blows but miraculously survived. Staples was then brutally raped before she was bludgeoned and hacked to death, and was so badly mutilated that it took hours to identify her remains.

The bodies were discovered on blood-soaked beds when Brown returned later that night to collect a pair of overalls he had left behind when he quit his job. He called the police, and he was held for questioning. Staples fifty-six-year-old husband, J. C. Staples, a packing employee, was held as a material witness and questioned but he proved he was at home, and insisted he did not even know where his wife was when she was murdered.

On January 20 Woodrow Clark was arrested and held as a material witness and he quickly confessed, and confessed again several times over the next weeks, but when he was brought to trial in March he repudiated the confessions. Winnett was called as a witness but he could recall nothing of the night's events. Still, on March 19, 1944, the jury was able to find Clark guilty on two counts of first degree murder for the deaths of the Dillons and fixed the penalty at death. Clark's attorney filed an appeal which stayed the execution, and over the next two years he tried every legal maneuver to spare the life of his client, but the lower court's judgment and sentence was affirmed by the state Supreme Court and Governor Monrad C. Wallgren refused to interfere with the February 5, 1946, execution date.

The Reverends Arvid Ohrnell and Eli T. Allen were with Clark periodically during his final days and both clergymen were with him all day Monday, February 4. They prayed with Clark and read Bible passages to him, but they did not have to encourage him to confess as he never denied the murders after he was convicted. As midnight drew near the prisoner became increasingly nervous but he had regained his composure by midnight when the warden appeared at his cell door to read the death warrant. The two clergymen then escorted him into the death chamber and onto the trapdoor where his wrists and arms, knees and ankles were strapped while the Rev. Ohrnell read his final statement: "I am thankful to my friends for what they did for me and my last greetings for my mother."

The noose was then adjusted and the black hood was pulled over his head at 12:06 A.M., and the trap was sprung immediately. Prison physician Dr. Elmer Hill waited beneath the gallows and monitored Clark's vital signs until he pronounced him dead at 12:20 A.M. The body was then cut down, deposited into its coffin, and given to the Reverends Ohrnell and Allen for burial.

Lincoln Journal (NE): March 20, 1944. *Journal-Gazette* (Mattoon, IL): January 20, 1944. *Galveston News* (TX): January 18, 1944. *Walla Walla Union-Bulletin* (WA): February 5, 1946.

Clark, John H.
January 7, 1947

On the evening of October 25, 1945, Annie Clark went to the second-hand clothing store of seventy-six-year-old Sam Katz located on skid row in Seattle, Washington, and spoke with him for some time. Clark then summoned her twenty-five-year-old husband, John Henry Clark, for the express purpose of robbing Katz. The couple went to the mezzanine of the store where the door to Katz' living quarters was located and John attacked the partially clothed man with a double-bitted ax. He struck two blows and then stabbed Katz in the throat several times with a long-bladed knife, and Katz bled to death in seconds. The couple searched the store and living quarters and stole all the money they could find. Katz never locked the doors to his store so when a customer entered the next morning he was not suspicious until he saw blood dripping from the ceiling, and then he called the police.

The search for the murderers continued for three weeks and finally on November 14 both suspects were behind bars. John Clark confessed to striking the fatal blows with a double-bitted ax and his wife confessed to distracting Katz and then bringing her husband into the store for the purpose of robbery. Two other men were also arrested so John Clark tried to implicate them, perhaps hoping to spread or deflect the blame, but they proved alibis. The Clarks were tried at the spring 1946 session of the King County Superior Court and found guilty of first degree murder. Annie Clark was sentenced to serve a life term and John was sentenced to hang, but John's attorney filed an appeal which stayed the execution. The state Supreme Court affirmed the judgment and sentence of the Superior Court later that year and John Clark was sentenced to hang on January 7, 1947, and the application for executive clemency submitted to Governor Monrad C. Wallgren was quickly denied.

During Clark's final days he was attended by the prison chaplain Reverend Eli T. Allen and the clergyman helped him brace up for his death. During his last week he was allowed a visit with his wife, who was serving time in the women's section of the same prison at Walla Walla, and they had an emotional farewell when it came time to part. Just before midnight on the final day the warden appeared at Clark's cell door and read the death warrant, and then the warden and the Reverend Allen conducted him into the death chamber. He took his place on the trapdoor where his wrists and arms, knees and ankles were strapped and he was asked if he had anything to say. The condemned man asked to be forgiven for what he had done and then sent his "last remembrances and love to my mother." The noose was adjusted and the black hood was pulled over his head at 12:06 A.M. and the trap was sprung immediately. Clark broke his neck in the fall and prison physician Dr. Elmer Hill pronounced him dead at 12:21 A.M. The body was then cut down, deposited into the coffin provided, and turned over to the Reverend Allen for burial on the prison grounds later that day.

Reno Gazette (NV): October 27, 1945. *Walla Walla Union-Bulletin* (WA): November 14, 1945; January 7, 1947.

Bird, Jake
July 15, 1949

Forty-five-year-old Jake Bird, a transient, quit an "extra gang" job at Pocatello, Idaho, on October 20, 1947, made his way west on freight trains, and stopped at Spokane and Seattle before going to Tacoma, Washington. At 2:20 A.M. on the morning of October 30 Bird broke into the house of fifty-three-year-old Bertha Kludt and took along an ax "to bluff off anyone who tries to bother me." Bertha's bedroom was on the first floor and when she awakened Bird attacked her in her bed, possibly intending to rape her, though Bird later insisted he was only there to steal. Kludt struggled with her assailant and screamed for help so Bird hacked her with the ax, and she collapsed next to her bed and bled to death in minutes. Kludt's seventeen-year-old daughter, Beverly, who had her bedroom on the second floor, awoke and rushed to her mother's aid. Bird caught her in the kitchen and hacked her to death as well. He then rushed from the house right into the arms of police officers and after an intense struggle during which both officers were injured, Bird was subdued, arrested, and lodged in the county jail.

When he was questioned the following day he confessed to killing the two women and said "after they were knocked down I just kept on swinging with the ax." John Pinnock came from Utah to question Bird and he admitted murdering sixty-two-year-old Lee Kay Walker at Ogden on October 4, 1947, and bragged that he had committed twenty-nine murders and knew about fifteen others, most unsolved. He was eventually linked through evidence to eleven of the murders he described.

In December, Bird was tried and convicted of the first degree murder of Bertha Kludt and he was sentenced to hang in early 1948, but his court-appointed attorney filed an appeal which stayed the execution for fifteen months: first the state Supreme Court affirmed the judgment and sentence of the lower court and denied a motion for a rehearing; the case was appealed to the U.S. Supreme Court three times on different grounds and rejected each time, the last time on Bird's final day; and while the last appeal was pending the State Board of Prison Terms and Paroles vetoed any further recommendation for clemency from Governor Arthur B. Langlie. Bird's only recourse was to place a hex on the officials involved in his conviction and execution, but this did not seem an idle threat, as six officials had previously been hexed and died under mysterious circumstances.

Bird was attended by the Reverend Arvid Ohrnell as he awaited his execution and on his last afternoon he wrote out his statement for the reverend to read on the gallows. After he was served supper Warden Tom Smith removed him from his death row cell to the small cell adjacent to the death chamber and then he read the death warrant. Bird thanked the warden "for all the courtesies you have given me during my stay in prison," and then he shook the warden's hand and said, "I guess this is it."

At midnight the prisoner was taken from his cell and conducted the short distance into the death chamber where one hundred witnesses awaited his appearance. He was placed on the trapdoor where his wrists and arms, knees and ankles were strapped, the noose was adjusted, and the black hood was pulled over his head. All the time he was being prepared the Reverend Ohrnell was reading his statement: "Jesus Christ is my Savior. I feel that all my appeals have been successful because the student in the future will ask why the questions were not answered." The reverend paused for a moment at 12:06 A.M. and the trap was sprung, but he was only half way through the statement so he continued, "There is no hatred in my heart. I hope you all who witness my death have no malice in your heart toward me because I feel none toward you." After the reverend concluded the statement he said a prayer for Bird's soul and retired. Prison physician Dr. Elmer Hill had been monitoring Bird's vital signs and at 12:20 A.M. he pronounced him dead, and later confirmed that the prisoner's neck had been broken in the fall. The body was cut down, deposited into the coffin provided by the state, and given to the Reverend Ohrnell for burial on prison grounds later that day.

Council Bluffs Nonpariel (IA): July 17, 1949. *Billings Gazette* (MT): October 31, 1947. *News-Palladium* (Benton Harbor, MI): December 23, 1952. *Ogden Standard-Examiner* (UT): July 15, 1949. *Tucson Daily Citizen* (AZ): July 15, 1949.

Perkins, Arthur B.
November 4, 1949

In 1947 sixty-five-year-old Lee Jessup and his forty-five-year-old wife, Geneva, lived in a rear house three blocks from the capitol building in Olympia, Washington. At 7:00 A.M. on December 16 the resident in the front house, Charles Steele, heard the door of Jessup's car slam shut, but this was the time Geneva usually left for work so he thought nothing of it. Lee was retired but quite active and should have been seen during the day, but by 4:30 P.M. when Lee had not been seen, Steele called neighbor Arley Jones and asked him to check on Lee's welfare. Arley found the front door unlocked and when he entered he found the dead body of Geneva, wearing her night clothes and sprawled on the living room davenport, her face and hair matted with blood from stab wounds. Arley then checked the bedroom for Lee and found him also dressed in his night clothes lying in a pool of blood next to the bed, his head bashed in, and the only sign of a struggle was an overturned rocking chair. Arley called the police and they determined that the only thing missing was the Jessup's automobile. They sent out a broadcast to watch for the car and the following day twenty-two-year-old Arthur Bruce Perkins was arrested at Centralia driving the stolen automobile.

Once behind bars Perkins said the Jessups had been murdered by his twenty-year-old fiancée, Shirley Phelps. He claimed that he had met Phelps at a café the evening of the murders and they quarreled over Geneva Jessup's objection to their marriage. He said that Phelps stormed out and he followed her to the Jessup home, but kept his distance until he heard a scream and then rushed to the house but found the door locked. He said, "I called Shirley by name. She opened the door and screamed as I stepped in. I saw that Shirley had a knife in her hand. Mrs. Jessup was on the floor in the living room. I told Shirley to wipe her hands and I went to see if Mrs. Jessup was still living. I picked her up and put her on the couch. At that moment I didn't realize the extent of the tragedy. I washed Shirley's hands and the knife. Then I went to see Mr. Jessup." He said that he took the Jessup automobile to drive Phelps to a downtown intersection and then he continued to Centralia, where he was arrested.

On March 22, 1948, Perkins took the witnesses stand in his defense and repeated the story he had told the police, but Phelps also testified and rebutted his testimony, and prosecutor Smith Troy then put a number of witnesses on the stand who disproved Perkins' defense. In his closing argument Troy characterized Perkins' defense as "the most preposterous fabrication ever told in any courtroom." Just before 3:30 P.M. the following day the case went to the jury and after deliberating only one hour they returned a verdict of guilty of first degree murder and fixed the penalty at death. Perkins' attorney filed an appeal which stayed his execution and the last avenue for judicial relief was not exhausted until mid–1949, and then Perkins' date with the hangman was set for Friday, November 4. His attorney petitioned Governor Arthur B. Langlie for a commutation of sentence or reprieve and the governor was still considering the matter late on November 3 when he finally decided he could not intervene.

During Perkins' weeks on death row he was attended by Father John J. Callanan. On Thursday, the day before his execution, he was baptized into the Catholic faith by Father Callanan, assisted by another priest, and then Perkins had a brief final visit with his brother. Father Callanan was with him when his supper was served and afterward they moved to the small cell adjacent to the death chamber, where Warden John Cranor read the death warrant. Perkins responded, "Now I know it by heart," and later told Father Callanan, "Some time perhaps the truth of this whole affair will be known." However, even at the urging of his priest, Perkins would neither confess nor deny his part in the killings. Perkins had resigned himself to his fate and did not lose his composure when told the governor had refused to grant his petition.

At midnight Warden Cranor appeared at the cell door and, with Father Callanan, conducted the prisoner the short distance into the death chamber and onto the gallows. Perkins took his place on the trapdoor where his wrists and arms, knees and ankles were strapped and when asked he declined to speak to the small group of police officers witnessing his execution. The noose was adjusted, Father Callanan pressed a crucifix to his lips, and at 12:06 A.M. the black hood was pulled over his head and the trap was sprung immediately. Perkins broke his neck in the fall and the prison physician pronounced him dead at 12:18. The body was cut down, deposited into the coffin provided by the state, and Perkins' remains were given to Father Callanan for burial in the Catholic cemetery.

Walla Walla Union-Bulletin (WA): December 17, 1947; March 22, 1948; March 24, 1948; November 4, 1949.

Williams, Wayne L.
November 18, 1949

On June 10, 1948, thirty-one-year-old Wayne L. Williams, his twenty-seven-year-old wife Hattie Lucille, and their four children arrived at Everett, Washington, where Wayne's mother lived. Wayne had been a farmer and an aircraft worker in Tulsa, Oklahoma, and hoped to start a new life in Everett. On June 17 Wayne and Hattie took their four-year-old daughter, Mary Bernice, on a sightseeing trip to a sixty foot cliff overlooking Puget Sound but the couple began to argue over health and finances, and then Hattie insisted on returning to Tulsa while Wayne countered that he wanted a divorce. Suddenly Wayne picked up a rock and beat Hattie unconscious, then threw her body over the cliff. Mary Bernice had returned to the car but when she saw her mother being beaten she rushed to her aid, screaming, "Quit, daddy! Quit, daddy!" Wayne then used the same rock to knock her unconscious and he threw her over the cliff as well.

That evening, when the absence of Hattie and Mary Bernice could not be explained, Wayne was arrested on suspicion of foul play and the next day he confessed the killings to Sheriff Tom Warnock, and then led him to the place on the edge of the cliff where he had thrown the bodies over. A search party walked to the cliff's edge, seven miles southwest of Everett near Mukilteo, and called for Hattie and Mary Bernice. Mary Bernice answered with weak cries for help and she was rescued from a ledge halfway down the cliff's face. She was rushed to the hospital suffering from a deep gash on her head, a broken collar bone, and exposure, but she recovered. The dead body of Hattie was discovered at the foot of the cliff and Wayne was charged with her murder, and later that day he dictated and signed a detailed confession.

He was tried at the fall term of the Superior Court, found guilty of first degree murder and sentenced to hang, but his attorney filed an appeal which stayed the execution. The state Supreme Court affirmed the judgment and sentence of the lower court in mid–1949 and Williams' date with the hangman was set for November 18. His attorney then petitioned Governor Arthur B. Langlie for a commutation of sentence and on the day before the execution Williams' mother pled for her son's life, but the governor refused to intervene.

Williams had been moody during his final days but on Thursday afternoon when he was told the governor would not grant him relief he became agitated and belligerent. After supper he was moved from his death row cell to the small cell adjacent to the death chamber and his attitude and demeanor suggested that the officials should prepare the collapse board. At midnight Warden John Cranor appeared at the cell door and read the death warrant, but then Williams refused to step out of the cell. Guards rushed in, overpowered the condemned man, and strapped him to the collapse board. They carried him the short distance into the death chamber and propped him up on the trapdoor. They did not ask if he had anything to say, but when they tried to pull on the black hood he "pulled in his neck." They managed to get the hood over his head and then the noose was quickly adjusted, and at 12:06 A.M. the trap was sprung. The preparations made prior to midnight had made it possible to keep the execution on schedule. Drs. Myles H. Robinson and Ralph Keyes waited beneath the gallows and monitored Williams' vital signs until they pronounced him dead at 12:16 A.M., and the extra weight of the board ensured he broke his neck in the fall. The body was cut down, deposited in the coffin provided by his mother, and sent to a local undertaker to be prepared for shipment to Everett, Washington, that afternoon for burial.

Freeport Journal-Standard (IL): November 18, 1949. *Logansport Press* (IN): June 19, 1948. *Reno Gazette* (NV): November 18, 1949. *Lowell Sun* (MA): November 18, 1949.

Odell, Wayne
June 18, 1951

Twenty-one-year-old Wayne Odell and eighteen-year-old Cora Jean Rogers had been dating but as the 1949 holiday season neared they quarreled and separated. On Friday night, December 23, Cora Jean, a student at the Washington State University, attended a hometown dance at Winona, Washington, with a new male friend. Odell watched them closely but he did not make a scene. At 4:30 A.M. Christmas eve morning Cora Jean awoke to find a man standing at the foot of her bed holding a shotgun. She screamed and her father, forty-seven-year-old Harold Rogers, rushed to her aid but as soon as he came through the door the man whirled and shot him. The entire load of heavy buckshot, at such close range, struck Rogers in the heart and killed him instantly. The murderer then dropped the empty shotgun and fled on foot into the snow covered Palouse Hills. Sheriff Clarence Davis was called and he organized a posse to search for the murderer, who he identified as Wayne Odell from the registration of the car parked in front of the Rogers' house.

Odell was quickly captured, jailed at Colfax, and tried in the Whitman County Superior Court in early 1950. He was convicted of first degree murder and sentenced to hang but his attorney filed an appeal, which stayed the execution. It took a year before the state Supreme Court justices affirmed the lower court's judgment and sentence and the date for Odell's execution was then set for June 18, 1951. His attorney petitioned Governor Arthur B. Langlie for a commutation of sentence but it was denied on June 14, and Odell's last hope was an appeal to the governor made by his parents on Sunday morning, but the governor remained unmoved by their pleas and declined to interfere.

After Odell's parents made their appeal in Olympia they hurried to Walla Walla for their final visit with their son, and he asked them to pray for him before they departed at noon. After he was served his supper the death warrant was read to him and he was moved from his death row cell to the small cell adjacent to the death chamber. He was attended by Father John J. Callanan during those final hours and the priest was with him when Warden John Cranor appeared at his cell door at midnight. He was conducted from the cell the short distance to the gallows and he took his place on the trapdoor without prompting.

His wrist and arms, knees and ankles were strapped while Father Callanan prayed for his soul, and then he declined to make a statement. The priest presented a crucifix for him to kiss and then the noose was quickly adjusted and the black hood was pulled over his head. The trap was sprung at 12:05 A.M. and Odell broke his neck in the fall, and the prison physician monitored his vital signs until he pronounced him dead at 12:17 A.M. The body was then cut down and deposited in the coffin provided by his parents, taken to a local undertaker and prepared for shipment to Steptoe, Washington, for burial.

Billings Gazette (MT): December 25, 1949. *Post-Register* (Idaho Falls, ID): June 18, 1951. *Walla Walla Union-Bulletin* (WA): June 15, 1951; June 18, 1951.

Rio, Grant E.
December 10, 1951

Early on December 31, 1950, thirty-nine-year-old Joseph Roberge, a farmhand, was blasted to death with a shotgun while asleep at the Riparia, Washington, farmhouse of his employer, twenty-year-old James Beckner. After Roberge was killed Beckner's young wife Della Mae, shoeless and in night clothes walked three miles in freezing temperatures to get help from a neighbor. When she arrived she was suffering from exposure and shock and was hysterical because she did not know what had happened to her husband. Whitman County Sheriff Clarence Davis was called while Della Mae was rushed to the hospital in Colfax. The sheriff hurried to the farmhouse and found that James Beckner had been shot to death with a shotgun as well, and the house had been ransacked. Suspicion immediately focused on an ex-employee of the Beckner and seven hours later twenty-seven-year-old Grant E. Rio was arrested at Washtuena fifty miles west of Colfax. Sheriff Davis had sent out a broadcast and Rio was captured when he drove his truck into a ditch, and the prisoner was returned to Colfax and lodged in the county jail. As soon as Della Mae was well enough to be released she returned home, inventoried the contents and reported that he wallet containing $360 was missing, which supported the theory of murder during a burglary.

Rio was indicted, his trial began in late March, and he pled insanity. On March 29 Rio's sister, three brothers and a life-long friend attributed the defendant's insanity to war nerves and alcohol. They claimed that Rio had blackouts and his sister testified that on the day after the murders the defendant told her, "I've been lying awake all night trying to remember what happened but I don't seem to be able to." The jury disregarded Rio's "insanity dodge" and found him guilty of first degree murder, and they fixed the penalty at death. Rio's attorney filed an appeal which stayed the execution for a year and a half, but the state Supreme Court finally affirmed the judgment and sentence of the lower court and the date for Rio's execution was set for September 19, 1951. Rio's attorney, H. Earl Davis, then appealed to the U.S. Supreme Court, which caused a further delay. That appeal was turned down on November 5 and on November 27 Colfax Judge John D. Evans sentenced Rio to hang on December 10, 1951. His attorney's last effort was to petition Governor Arthur B. Langlie for a commutation of sentence, but it was denied.

During Rio's weeks on death row he refused every effort to provide him spiritual aid, though on his final day, Sunday, he spent some time with the assistant prison chaplain. On Sunday morning his brothers and sister had visited for the last time and after they left he spent most of the day playing cards with the Wilson brothers, also condemned to death. On his final afternoon he wrote out several letters and asked Warden John Cranor to post them, and then asked to remain in his death row cell until after he heard the Jack Benny show. At 10:15 P.M. he was moved to the small cell adjacent to the death chamber and he was served supper.

Warden Cranor appeared at midnight and conducted the prisoner into the death chamber where he took his place on the trapdoor without direction. His wrists and arms, knees and ankles were strapped and he was asked if he had anything to say, but he declined. The noose was adjusted, the black hood was pulled over his head at 12:06 A.M., and the trap was sprung immediately. Prison physician Dr. A. R. Kincaid waited beneath the gallows and monitored vital signs until he pronounced Rio dead at 12:25 A.M. The body was then cut down, deposited in the coffin provided by his family, and transported to a local undertaker where his brothers and sister would arrange for his burial.

Inter Lake (Kalispell, MT): January 1, 1950. *Idaho State Journal* (Pocatello, ID): December 10, 1951. *Walla Walla Union-Bulletin* (WA): March 26, 1950; March 29, 1950; November 27, 1951; December 10, 1951.

Wilson, Turman; Wilson, Utah E.
January 3, 1953

On the evening of March 19, 1950, pretty Joann Dewey, an eighteen-year-old hospital worker, left St. Joseph's Hospital in Vancouver, Washington, and started walking home. Suddenly a black Buick sedan pulled up, two men got out, wrestled Dewey into their car and drove off. V. F. Andrews saw the abduction and he gave the authorities all the details, and the police back-tracked the automobile to the place the car had been parked while the two men waited for a likely victim. There were empty beer bottles left behind and from one bottle the Federal Bureau of Investigation was able to get fingerprints and match them to Utah Eugene Wilson, and Utah had been in the company of his brother Turman for days before the kidnapping.

The search for Utah Wilson and his brother Turman intensified when, on March 27, Dewey's nude, battered body was discovered on a gravel bar on the Wind River, fifty miles east of Vancouver. The kidnappers had abandoned two cars as they fled, one in Camas, Washington, and the second on the streets of Portland, so the FBI was brought into the case because the brothers had crossed state lines to avoid prosecution. The first abandoned automobile found was the black Buick sedan and investigators found inside human hair, blood, a button from Dewey's coat, a small piece of bone or tooth, and labels from beer bottles matching those found in Vancouver. The autopsy on Dewey revealed she had died of carbon monoxide poisoning so the investigators checked the Buick's exhaust system and found that the muffler was loose and leaked into the passenger compartment of the car.

The Wilsons had fled from Portland southward in a coupe and the description of the car was broadcast. On March 30 officers spotted the coupe in San Francisco and waited for the brothers to return. When they appeared they were arrested without resistance even though Turman, a convicted felon, had a .25-caliber automatic pistol in his pocket and officers found a six-shot revolver in the car. The brothers were charged with fleeing to avoid prosecution, kidnapping and murder, and on April 7 they were returned to Vancouver. Each prisoner had an alibi, but they conflicted.

The two prisoners were arraigned, pled not guilty, and their joint trial was set for the last week of June. On June 28 both defendants were convicted of first degree murder and Judge Eugene G. Cushing sentenced them to hang. Their attorneys, Irving Goodman and Sanford Clements, filed an appeal with the state and U.S. Supreme Courts which stayed the executions, but after a year's delay the U.S. Supreme Court rejected the appeal and the state Supreme Court affirmed the judgment and sentence of the Superior Court, and the brothers were sentenced to hang on November 30, 1951. Their attorneys then filed an appeal with the Circuit Court which resulted in a further stay so the attorneys could prepare a second appeal to the U.S. Supreme Court, but six months later that appeal was also rejected and then Judge A. L. Stephens of the Ninth Circuit Court of Appeals in San Francisco granted a stay while a third appeal was submitted. This appeal was also rejected in July 1952 and the brothers were sentenced to hang in August, but then Governor Arthur B. Langlie granted a ninety day reprieve while the American Bar Association examined several legal issues and facts of the case. The association submitted a twenty-seven page report in November and based upon their findings the governor declined to intervene, and the brothers were sentenced to hang on January 3, 1953.

During their time on death row the brothers were attended by the Reverend Frank Morgan and his wife. They had resigned themselves to their fate, and each helped the other brace up. On Friday, their last day, they were visited by their parents and two brothers. After their family left the Reverend Morgan and his wife were admitted, but by supper time only the reverend remained. The condemned men had ordered a huge and varied menu for their last meal, but when it arrived they ate sparingly, and after supper the brothers and the Reverend Morgan were moved to the small cell adjacent to the death chamber and Warden John Cranor read the death warrants. The warden retired to give the men time with their spiritual advisor but appeared again at midnight and conducted the brothers into the death chamber where they took their places on the trapdoors of twin gallows.

Their wrists and arms, knees and ankles were strapped. They were each asked if they had anything to say and both declined, so the nooses were adjusted and the black hoods were pulled over their heads. Below the gallows four guards stood with a finger poised over one of four electric buttons, three being dummies, and when signaled they simultaneously pushed the buttons and Turman Wilson's trap was sprung at 12:06 A.M. They immediately moved to a second bank of buttons beneath the second gallows while Warden Cranor distracted Utah Wilson by asking if he were ready, and he replied, "Everything is OK! I am ready." The Reverend Morgan then said, "God bless you," the signal was given, and the second trap was sprung at 12:07 A.M. Prison physician Dr. Wilmer Unterseher watched Turman as he gasped and moaned, and a trickle of blood appeared beneath the hood. When Utah's body appeared he stepped forward and alternately checked vital signs until he pronounced the brothers dead at 12:16 A.M. Turman had not broken his neck and had strangled to death but his brother's neck had been broken in the fall. The bodies were cut down and deposited in the coffins provided by their family, and later that day they were delivered to a Walla Walla funeral parlor where the family had made burial arrangements.

Minutes after the second trap was sprung a telegram signed by senior state senator Warren G. Magnuson arrived ordering a stay of execution but it was not only too late, it was a hoax to delay the hangings. The person who called in the telegram used a Seattle pay phone, and was never identified.

In April 1953 Glenn Wilson, brother of the executed brothers, was arrested in Reno, Nevada, on a charge of being a ex-felon in possession of two loaded pistols. He claimed he got a tip while at Salt Lake City, Utah, that the real murderers of Joann Dewey were in Reno and he had come to avenge his brothers. He pled guilty and was sentenced to serve one to five years in Nevada's State Prison, and arrived on May 1.

Nevada State Journal (Reno): May 1, 1953. *Record-Eagle* (Traverse City, MI): March 31, 1950. *Coshocton Tribune* (OH): January 4, 1953. *Independent* (Long Beach, CA): June 18, 1950. *Ogden Standard-Examiner* (UT): July 16, 1952. *Walla Walla Union-Bulletin* (WA): January 3–4, 1953.

Farley, Artell, Jr.
December 15, 1956

On Sunday, February 21, 1954, twenty-five-year-old Artell Farley and his girlfriend, thirty-year-old Flora E. McFarland, drove to an abandoned, partially flooded gravel pit near Tacoma, Washington. The following morning the nude body of McFarland was found floating in the pit and after she was pulled from the water the authorities found that she had been beaten, stabbed, and run over by a car at least three times. They began searching for Farley and for McFarland's automobile, and on Tuesday night they found the car parked in front of a bowling alley in Roseburg, Oregon. Inside the bowling alley the officers found Farley and he readily admitted his identity. He told Police Chief Stan Olson that he and McFarland had driven to the gravel pit, they argued, he struck her, and after that he remembered nothing. He said he returned home and then realized his clothes were bloody, so he hid them and fled south. The authorities, when they impounded the automobile for evidence, found a bloody knife jammed between the trunk and the rear bumper and many bloodstains inside the car.

The prisoner was returned to Tacoma and lodged in the county jail, arraigned, and his trial was set for late June. Farley never denied killing his sweetheart and on June 22 the jurors found him guilty of first degree murder, and fixed the penalty at death. His attorneys filed appeals with the state and then the U.S. Supreme Courts which stayed the execution until late 1956, but finally all avenues of judicial relief were exhausted. Farley's date with the hangman was set for December 15, 1956, and then a petition was sent to Governor Arthur B. Langlie asking for a commutation of sentence, but he declined to intervene.

During his months on death row Farley was attended by the Reverend James Thompson, who helped him prepare for his death. After supper on his final night he was moved from his death row cell to the small cell adjacent to the death chamber and after the warden read the death warrant he was cloistered with the Reverend Thompson until midnight. When the warden appeared, Farley, pale but composed, walked into the chamber unaided and took his place on the trapdoor. He shook hands with the Reverend Thompson and said, "Thank you," before his wrists and arms, knees and ankles were strapped. He was asked if he had anything to say but he declined, so the noose was adjusted, the black hood was pulled over his head at 12:05 A.M., and the trap was sprung immediately. He broke his neck in the fall, and prison physician Dr. J. D. Losey waited below and monitored his vital signs until he pronounced him dead thirteen minutes later. The body was then cut down, deposited in the coffin provided by the state, and the Reverend Thompson saw to his burial on prison grounds later that day.

Centralia Chronicle (WA): February 24, 1954; June 23, 1954. *Walla Walla Union Bulletin* (WA): December 16, 1956.

Collins, Harvey J.
December 3, 1957

Harvey John Collins was a twice decorated World War II veteran for his part in the invasion of Iwo Jima, but on January 6, 1954, the marine captain staged a phoney suicide attempt when he crashed his plane in Oklahoma. He was mustered out of the service and settled in Puyallup, Washington. On March 21, 1955, Collins tried to rob a motel six miles north of Tacoma using a three foot samurai sword he had taken from a Japanese officer during the war. Seventy-four-year-old Andrew Stolen, partially paralyzed, tried to pull himself to his wife to protect her and was hacked and stabbed to death, and his sixty-seven-year-old wife, Anna, was seriously wounded. Anna was able to give a description of the robber and his automobile and Collins was arrested forty minutes later.

By Wednesday, March 23, Collins admitted to slaying Stolen and also confessed to murdering twenty-five-year-old Edward Morley, who operated a service station ten miles north of Tacoma, with a single gunshot to his head during a robbery on February 7. Officers tried to link him to the killing of Edna Iona Hall at Louisville, Kentucky, on May 15, 1953, and he first denied any knowledge of that crime, but finally confessed. On March 24 the Pierce County attorney had Collins examined by two psychiatrists and he was declared sane, so the following day he was charged with Stolen's murder. His trial began in early July and, after being declared sane, his defense evolved into "temporary insanity." On July 12 the jurors found him guilty of first degree murder and fixed the penalty at death. His attorney, J. Houston Vanzant, filed an appeal which stayed the execution until late 1957, but finally all avenues of judicial relief were exhausted and his date with the hangman was set for December 3, 1957. Vanzant then petitioned Governor Albert D. Rosellini for a commutation of sentence but the governor found that there was no new or mitigating evidence, so he declined to interfere.

During Collins' time on death row he was attended by Catholic chaplain Father George McCabe, and the priest helped him resign himself to his fate. During his final day the prisoner asked to speak to Warden Robert Rhay and told him, "I am sorry for all the trouble I have caused." After supper Collins and his priest were conducted to the small cell adjacent to the death chamber and the warden read the death warrant. Collins spent his last hour with Father McCabe and at midnight he exited his cell, clutching a rosary, and walked silently into the death chamber, his face expressionless.

He took his place on the trapdoor where his wrists and arms, knees and ankles were strapped and he was asked if he had anything to say to the thirty witnesses. He whispered, almost inaudibly, "I ask forgiveness for everything I've done." The noose was adjusted and then Father McCabe presented a crucifix for Collins to kiss before the black hood was pulled over his head. The trap was sprung at 12:05 A.M. and Father McCabe began administering the last rites, while beneath the gallows prison physician Dr. J. D. Losey monitored Collins' vital signs. Dr. Losey pronounced Collins dead in twelve minutes and then the body was cut down and deposited into the coffin provided by the state. Father McCabe took charge and saw to his burial in the Catholic portion of the prison cemetery later that day.

Fairbanks News Miner (AK): March 23, 1955. *Centralia Chronicle* (WA): March 25, 1955. *Port Angeles News* (WA): December 3, 1957.

Broderson, John
June 25, 1960

Thirty-three-year-old John Broderson rented an apartment at Camas, Washington twenty miles northeast of Portland, Oregon. On November 17 he abducted fifty-one-year-old used car salesman Harold Oster and took him to his apartment. He had Oster strip to his underwear and then bound his wrists and ankles with tape and gagged him, and Broderson then murdered Oster with a fatal stab to his back. When the body was found an all-points-bulletin was broadcast for Broderson, who had fled south.

Eighty-five miles east of Portland, Oregon, Broderson's automobile broke down and he hitched a ride with Mr. and Mrs. James Tucker of Oswego, Oregon, but as soon as he was in the car he pulled out a pistol. Mrs. Tucker said, "I put my head down in my hands. He informed me I was not to cry. Evidently that upset him. I told him I wasn't going to weep. He offered to let me out of the car and told me he would take Jim with him. I said, 'No, no, no, where Jim goes, I go.' He promised me he would not harm a hair of my husband's head and he let me out of the car. We shook hands and I got out right in the middle of The Dalles." When the station wagon pulled away Mrs. Tucker immediately called the police and officer Kenneth Green started after the Tucker station wagon. Green overtook the Tucker car and pulled it to the side of the road, but Broderson got the drop on him with a .22-caliber and a 9-millimeter pistol and disarmed the officer. He then left James Tucker in his automobile and forced Green to drive him south. Meanwhile road blocks had been set up along Highway 30 and when they came to the first road block near Arlington, Oregon, Green lunged at Broderson and pinned his arms, and in the struggle Green was shot in the thigh and Broderson was shot in the leg. Other bullets went harmlessly wild before officers closed in, disarmed and subdued Broderson. The prisoner was taken to a hospital in Pendleton while Green was taken to a hospital in The Dalles, and both men recovered fully.

Broderson was returned to Vancouver in Clark County where he first said he wanted to plead guilty, but where the death penalty was a possibility he was prevented by law, so on December 14, 1959, attorneys James R. Gregg and William Boettcher were appointed to represent him. He was tried at the spring term of the Superior Court and convicted of first degree murder, and the jurors fixed the penalty at death. Broderson was sentenced to hang on June 25, 1960, and he did not want his attorneys to appeal his conviction. On Tuesday, June 22, Broderson appeared before Judge Glenn L. Bean and, after Broderson refused the services of an attorney, the judge turned down the recommendation of prison psychiatrist Dr. C. Charles Sutch for a stay pending a sanity hearing. The American Civil Liberties Union then inserted itself into the case, against Broderson's wishes, because they wanted to examine whether he needed a lawyer at the June 22 hearing. Last minute appeals and petitions were being processed in those final hours and late Friday afternoon the state Supreme Court and Governor Albert D. Rosellini rejected the ACLU's request for a stay.

During Broderson's time on death row he had been given spiritual support by Father George McCabe, the Catholic prison chaplain. On his final afternoon the priest read scriptures to the condemned man and after supper Father McCabe accompanied Borderson into the little cell adjacent to the death chamber. The warden read the death warrant to Broderson as soon as he was settled, and then retired so Father McCabe could be alone with the condemned man. The warden reappeared just before midnight and conducted Broderson into the death chamber, and the prisoner hurried up the stairs and anxiously asked, "Where do I stand?" He then took his place on the center of the trapdoor where his wrist and arms, knees and ankles were strapped and he was asked if he had anything to say. He replied, "I'm ready to die. I hope it doesn't take long." The noose was adjusted, the crucifix was pressed to his lips, the black hood was pulled over his head at 12:01 A.M., and the trap was sprung immediately. Broderson dropped, breaking his neck in the fall, and the prison physician, waiting beneath the gallows, monitored his vital signs until his heart ceased to beat and he pronounced him dead. The body was cut down, deposited into the coffin provided by the state, and Father McCabe took charge of the remains for burial in the Catholic portion of the prison cemetery later that day.

Centralia Chronicle (WA): November 18–19, 1959; December 14, 1959. *Port Angeles Evening News* (WA): June 25, 1960.

Self, Joseph C.
June 20, 1963

On Wednesday night, March 16, 1960, twenty-nine-year-old Joseph Chester Self, an ex-convict from Oregon, hired taxi cab driver Ralph J. Gemmill, Jr., to drive him to another location, but once in the taxi he pulled his pistol and ordered Gemmill to drive him toward Five Mile Lake. Once they reached a field near the lake Self shot Gemmill in the right side, then pulled him out of the taxi and bludgeoned him into unconsciousness with a flashlight. While Gemmill bled to death Self went through his pockets and took everything of value and threw his emptied wallet on the ground, then took Gemmill's taxi cab and drove to Tacoma.

Later that night four teenagers were crossing the field and found Gemmill's dead body and they called the police. A man had been seen in the vicinity of the car before it drove off and he was described as "about 25, 5 foot 6 inches, red hair, and was believed wearing a red and black blazer." Gemmill's trip record was backtracked and the police learned that the last man seen entering the taxi in Seattle matched the description of the man seen in the field. An all-points-bulletin was broadcast for the man and for Gemmill's taxi cab, and on Thursday the car was found abandoned in an industrial section of Tacoma. The car and contents were dusted for fingerprints and Self was identified from a thumb print found on the flashlight left behind. On Saturday, while Self was still a fugitive, he was charged with Gemmill's murder and the search for him had narrowed to the area around Eatonville. He was soon captured and lodged in the King County jail and his trial began at the end of May 1960.

On June 3 the jurors found him guilty of first degree murder and fixed the penalty at death, and on June 17 he was brought into court and sentenced to hang in August. His court-appointed attorneys filed a series of appeals in the state and U.S. Supreme Courts and the execution was stayed until early 1963, when they were resolved against Self. When the petition praying for a commutation of sentence was sent to Governor Albert D. Rosellini he denied it, stating, "Self's conviction was upheld twice by the state Supreme Court and once by the U.S. Supreme Court, and the decisions were unanimous in each instance."

The prison's Catholic chaplain, Father George McCabe, spent many hours with the condemned man during the time he was on death row. Self had resigned himself to his fate when, after supper that final day, he and Father McCabe were moved to the small cell adjacent to the death chamber. The warden read the death warrant and then retired leaving the priest and prisoner alone during that final hour. The warden reappeared just before midnight and conducted the prisoner into the death chamber and onto the gallows.

He took his place on the trapdoor where his wrists and arms, knees and ankles were strapped and he was asked if he had anything to say, but he declined to speak to the small group of witnesses. The noose was adjusted and, after he kissed the crucifix Father McCabe pressed to his lips, the black hood was pulled over his head. The trap was sprung at 12:01 A.M. and Self broke his neck in the fall. The prison physician waited below and monitored his vital signs until he pronounced him dead at 12:12 A.M. The body was then cut down and taken to the prison hospital. Self had willed his eyes to the Providence Hospital to restore the sight of a blind person, and the corneas were flown to Seattle that night. The body was then deposited into the coffin provided by the state and given to Father McCabe for burial in the Catholic portion of the prison cemetery that afternoon. Father McCabe later said of Self, "He died a good death."

Centralia Chronicle (WA): March 17, 1960; March 19, 1960. *Port Angeles Evening News* (WA): June 3, 1960; June 17, 1960. *Post-Register* (Idaho Falls, ID): June 20, 1963.

Dodd, Westley A.
January 5, 1993

Westley Allan Dodd was born in Washington in July 1961 and as a teenager began a pattern of child molestation and increasing violence. In November 1989 Dodd went to a Camas theater, fifteen miles east of Vancouver, Washington, looking for a victim. He abducted five-year-old James Kirk from the restroom and was carrying him off when the boy started to yell, "Help me! Help me!" The theater's owner, Cathy Asher, and several male patrons ran after them, freed the boy, and returned Dodd to theater, where they tied his wrists with a belt and held him until the authorities arrived. There had been three murders of young children near Vancouver and Dodd was immediately suspected.

On September 4 the Neer brothers, ten-year-old William and eleven-year-old Cole, had gone to the driving range near David Douglas Park to collect golf balls, which they sold back for a penny apiece. When the boys did not return home their father began searching for them and found their dead bodies in the park, William stabbed in the abdomen and Cole raped and stabbed in the heart. Dodd was charged with the murder of the Neer boys and he was also charged with the murder of four-year-old Lee Joseph Iseli. This young boy had been abducted from a school playground in Portland, Oregon, on October 29 and on November 1 his dead, nude and battered body was found west of Vancouver. Iseli had been raped and strangled to death.

As soon as Dodd was behind bars he confessed, "On September 4, 1989, I went to David Douglas Park with the premeditated intent to cause the death of another human being. I raped Cole Neer and then I killed him. Yes, I also murdered William Neer to conceal my identity. On October 29 I did kidnap Lee Iseli from Portland, Oregon, took him to my apartment in Vancouver and raped him, and on the morning of October 30 I murdered Lee Iseli. I did attempt to abduct and murder James Kirk."

His apartment was searched and the police found a torture rack he had constructed for his next victim — James Kirk. The prisoner pled not guilty when arraigned, his trial was set for June, and jury selection began on June 25, 1990. He was tried and convicted of first degree murder and he chose hanging as his means of death because, he said, "I want the same treatment I gave Lee Iseli." His attorneys filed an appeal with the state Supreme Court which stayed the execution, and the case was under considered for several years, but late in 1992 Dodd dropped all appeals and said, "I will kill and rape again and enjoy every minute of it, if I am not executed." On January 4, 1993, the state Supreme Court cleared the way for Dodd's execution to proceed.

Before midnight on January 4, 1993, the witnesses, including relatives of the murdered boys, were gathered below the gallows behind a glass partition. The prisoner was marched into the death chamber where he climbed the stairs and took his place on the trapdoor. His wrists and arms, knees and ankles were strapped and then he was asked if he had anything to say, and he gave a brief statement about his new found faith. He told the witnesses, "I was once asked by somebody, I don't remember who, if there was any way sex offenders could be stopped. I said 'No!' I was wrong. I was wrong when I said there was no hope, no peace. There is hope. There is peace. I've found both in the Lord, Jesus Christ. Look to the Lord, and you will find peace."

His head and shoulders were then covered by a long black hood, the noose was adjusted at 12:05 A.M., and the trap was immediately sprung. Dodd dropped six and one half feet, breaking his neck in the fall, and the physician in attendance pronounced him dead at 12:09. A curtain was then drawn across the window blocking the view of the witnesses before Dodd's body was cut down and placed on a stretcher. The body was shipped to Seattle for an autopsy by King County coroner Dr. Donald Reay, and after the autopsy was completed Dodd's remains were cremated and the ashes were turned over to his family.

Dispatch (Casa Grande, AZ): November 15, 1989. *Pharos-Tribune* (Logansport, IN): September 10, 1989. *Stars and Stripes* (U.S. Military): June 13, 1990. *Winnipeg Free Press* (Canada): January 6, 1993.

Campbell, Charles R.
May 27, 1994

In 1974 nineteen-year-old Charles Rodman Campbell broke into the home of twenty-three-year-old Renae Wicklund, put a knife to the throat of her baby daughter Shannah and, with threats to murder her and her daughter, he raped and sodomized the young mother. He was quickly captured and tried in the Snohomish County Superior Court. Wicklund and her neighbor, forty-three-year-old Barbara Hendrickson, testified against Campbell, he was convicted of the rape, and sentenced to serve a term of thirty years in prison. In 1982 Campbell was living at a work release house in Everett, Washington, when he went to Clearview in Snohomish County and on April 14 he once again broke into the Wicklund home. Hendrickson was visiting because Wicklund was in bed with a bronchial infection, and Hendrickson was helping eight-year-old Shannah prepare dinner. As revenge for testifying against him at the rape trial Campbell slit their throats, and Shannah was nearly beheaded. Campbell had stopped, after his crime, to drink water and he left a good set of fingerprints on the glass.

He was arrested at the work release house, charged with three counts of murder, and tried in November 1982. He was convicted of first degree murder and sentenced to die, but when it came time to choose his manner of death he refused, saying the choosing would violate his religious beliefs, so the manner defaulted to hanging over lethal injection. The first delay lasted three months while the state tried to locate a qualified hangman, but in the meantime Attorney Robert Gombiner filed an appeal with the state Supreme Court which stayed the execution. The judgment and sentence of the lower court was affirmed in 1984 but Gombiner immediately filed another appeal, and the case dragged on until March 23, 1989, when the state Supreme Court rejected his latest effort; but then on March 30 the federal court of appeals in San Francisco blocked the execution. There was more legal manipulation until the final appeal argued that hanging was cruel and unusual, but it was decided on Thursday that Campbell could hang, and then Governor Mike Lowry refused to intervene.

Campbell spent his last evening talking with friends and relatives and after they left he took his last shower. His last meal was served at 10:00 P.M. but he ate very little. When Prison Superintendent Tana Wood appeared to move him to the holding cell near the death chamber he refused to be handcuffed and he had to be doused with pepper spray before he could be subdued. When it came time for his walk to the gallows he laid on the floor of his cell and refused to rise. Officers finally strapped his limp body to a "collapse board" and carried him into the death chambe[r] and onto the trapdoor at 12:05 A.M. The curtain covering the upper window, behind which the witnesses waited, was not opened so they could see only the silhouettes of the men on the platform, and they saw Campbell rotating his head and struggling to avoid the noose.

At 12:07 Superintendent Wood announced "Mr. Campbell has declined to give any last statement." The only sound heard was th[e] shuffling of feet until at 12:08 when the trap was sprung and Campbell's body, still strapped to the board, appeared before the witnesses clearly visible through the lower window. Th[e] superintendent came down from the platform a minute later and pulled closed the lower curtain and at 12:15 A.M. Veltry Johnson, prison spokesperson, announced, "The execution of Charles Rodman Campbell by hanging ha[s] been completed. The doctor pronounced death at 12:14 A.M." The witnesses were then conducted out of the witness room and they left the prison. As the prison staff cleared out Campbell's cell they found a four inch piece of metal he was sharpening into a blade, apparently intending to commit suicide.

Chronicle-Telegram (Elyria, OH): September 13, 1989. *Sitka Sentinel* (AK): November 26, 1982. *Gleaner* (Kingston, Jamaica): March 30, 1989. *Indiana Gazette* (PA): May 27, 1994. *Winnipeg Free Press* (Manitoba, Canada): May 28, 1994.

Sagastegui, Jeremy V.
October 13, 1998

On November 18, 1995, twenty-four-year-old Jeremy Vargas Sagastegui was babysitting for three-year-old Kievan Sarbacher at the Sarbacher mobile home in Finley, Washington. Sometime after midnight on the 19th the boy began crying for his mother so Sagastegui beat, raped, stabbed, and then drowned Kievan Sarbacher. When Kievan's twenty-one-year-old mother, Melissa, and her twenty-six-year-old friend Lisa Vera-Acevado returned he shot them to death. Melissa had also left her twenty-two month old daughter Teonica with Sagastegui, but she was unharmed. Sagastegui was arrested, lodged in jail, and charged with three counts of first degree murder.

At trial in February 1996 the defendant asked the jury to sentence him to death and told them, "I killed the kid. I killed the mother and I killed her friend; and if their friends had come over, I would have killed them, too." The Benton County prosecutor and Sagastegui's attorney later agreed that "he never showed any compassion, any remorse." Sagastegui refused to appeal his execution but nevertheless on October 11, 1998, a stay of execution was granted by the 9th U.S. Circuit Court of Appeals when Sagastegui's mother, Katie Vargas, asserted that her son was mentally ill and could not make life-or-death decisions. However, the condemned man had already been found competent and by law no third party could file the appeal on his behalf, so the U.S. Supreme Court lifted the stay hours before the scheduled execution was to proceed. Governor Gary Locke then refused to intervene.

Sagastegui was the first man in Washington sentenced to die by lethal injection. Before midnight the death warrant was read to him in his cell and then he was escorted into the ten by twenty foot execution chamber. He was strapped to a gurney where medically trained personnel inserted two intravenous cannulas (IVs), one in each arm with the second a backup in case the primary IV failed. Electrodes were then attached which led to an electrocardiograph machine. The executioner took his place in the control room, where he would remain anonymous while he administered the three drug combination: sodium thiopental to induce sleep; pancuronium bromide to restrict respiration, which in time would cause death by asphyxiation; and potassium chloride to stop Sagastegui's heart.

After midnight the curtains were drawn open for the witnesses and prison superintendent John Lambert announced, "Inmate Sagastegui has no last words. The process will continue." The drugs were then administered and in minutes all sign of life had left the condemned man, and at 12:43 A.M. a doctor announced that Sagastegui was dead. The witnesses retired and then the body was removed for an autopsy, and afterwards sent to a funeral home as arranged by his mother.

Aiken Standard (SC): October 13, 1998. *Del Rio News Herald* (TX): October 13, 1998. *Seattle Post-Intelligencer* (WA): October 13, 1998. *Tri-City Herald* (WA): November 21–23, 1995, October 13, 1998.

Elledge, James H.
August 28, 2001

In 1965 James Homer Elledge served three years of a ten to fifty year sentence for kidnapping, robbery and attempted murder when he abducted an Albuquerque, New Mexico, convenience store clerk and tried to burn her to death, but after doused her with gasoline she escaped before he could set her afire. He managed to escape from the New Mexico prison on May 14, 1966, but was captured in two days. He next served a long prison term for a murder he committed in 1975 when he bludgeoned a sixty-three-year-old woman to death during a motel robbery, striking her twenty-eight times with a hammer. This time he was sentenced to serve a life term but he was paroled in 1995, and was still on parole in the fall of 1997 when he met Annette. He worked at a Boeing assembly plant and lived in an apartment below forty-seven-year-old Eloise Jane Fitzner in Lynwood, Washington. Annette and Elledge began dating but Fitzner tried to break up Elledge's relationship with his girlfriend by sending her derogatory letters, so after they were married the Elledges moved to get away from Fitzner.

On Tuesday, April 21, 1998, Elledge telephoned police and said he wanted to surrender for murdering Fitzner on Saturday, April 18. Elledge had lured Fitzner and her thirty-nine-year-old friend to the Lighthouse Church in Lynwood by promising them gifts and dinner; Elledge, a part-time janitor at the church, had previously become acquainted with Fitzner's friend when she visited the apartments. When Fitzner and her friend arrived at the church Elledge took them prisoner and bound them with nylon rope and tape, and then he murdered Fitzner by stabbing and strangling her. He told Fitzner's friend that he hated Fitzner but loved her, even though they had no prior relationship. Elledge took Fitzner's friend to his trailer, while his wife was away at a church retreat, and he repeatedly raped her and then let her go.

On Sunday evening Fitzner's body was found in the basement of the church and the police began searching for Elledge, and he was arrested at the Morgan Motel in Tacoma. He talked freely of the crime, saying, "There's something wrong with my nature. I had been able to control a lot of it by power of prayer, but the hate and the anger that was inside of me just came up, and I made my mind up that I was going to get my evens with this woman." His wife said after his arrest that she was believed he turned himself in, "because he said if anything ever happened he would commit suicide rather than go back to prison. He will always be my husband and I will always love him."

Elledge appeared in the Snohomish County Superior Court on April 22 and bail was set at one million dollars, and then Judge Thomas Fisher gave prosecutors until May 8 to file formal charges. Elledge was indicted and tried at the fall term of the court, convicted of first degree murder, and sentenced to die by lethal injection at the prison in Walla Walla. Elledge took no steps to appeal his conviction nor the sentence beyond the automatic appeals, which delayed the execution for three years. He insisted, "I made my bed and now I must lie in it."

After midnight on the day of execution Elledge was escorted into the ten by twenty foot execution chamber where he was strapped to a gurney. Eight media witnesses, two police officers, and two attorneys took their positions at the window as medically trained personnel inserted two intravenous cannulas (IVs), one in each arm with one being a back-up in case the primary IV failed, and then they attached the electrodes for the electrocardiograph machine. The drug lines led into another room where the executioner was poised to begin administering the drugs: sodium thiopental to induce sleep; pancuronium bromide to depress respiration, which in time would cause death by asphyxiation; and potassium chloride which stopped the heart and caused death quickly. The prison superintendent asked Elledge if he had anything to say but he declined, so the superintendent announced for the benefit of the witnesses and executioner, "Inmate Elledge has no last words. The process will continue."

This signaled the executioner at 12:45 A.M. to begin the administration of the drugs in sequence and as the first drug was released Elledge breathed deeply but kept his eyes closed. In seven minutes, at 12:52 A.M. Elledge's heart ceased to beat and he was pronounced dead.

Albuquerque Journal (NM): May 17, 1966. *Albuquerque Tribune* (NM): May 14, 1966. *Sitka Sentinel* (AK): April 22, 1998; August 28, 2001.

Brown, Cal Coburn
September 10, 2010

On April 9, 1977, seventeen-year-old Cal Coburn Brown assaulted a woman in a San Luis Obispo County, California, shopping center using a knife; he was captured and he pled guilty. He was free by 1981 when he committed a grand theft and on March 11 pled guilty to that crime. By 1983 Brown had moved to Corvallis, Oregon, where he met, through a babysitter, a young married woman with two small children. One day he appeared at her door wearing a backpack and limping, claiming he was hiking and had sprained his knee. He was allowed to enter while the woman called a taxi, but as she turned away Brown threw a leather thong over her head and tried to strangle her, but the thong caught on her chin. He tightened and jerked on the thong so violently he threw her six feet and she landed on her stomach, with Brown crouching over her. She managed to turn over to face him and as Brown reached for her she screamed for help. A police officer happened to be passing nearby and heard her cries for help. The officer rushed in and arrested Brown, and officers found in his backpack a long-bladed knife and a roll of duct tape. Brown was tried for the assault, found guilty on January 6, 1984, sentenced to serve seven and one half years in the Oregon State Prison, and was released on parole on March 25, 1991.

Brown then rented an apartment in Eugene, Oregon, and enrolled in college classes at the University of Oregon. Over the next two months he met with parole officer Larry Wibbenmeyer on schedule, including at least two unannounced home visits, with the last contact on May 10, 1991. Wibbenmeyer was not able to contact Brown at his apartment on May 14 and 16 and left his card, but the following day the card was still on the door indicating Brown had not returned home the previous night. At the college, the officer found Brown was absent from his 11:30 A.M. class. On May 20 the parole officer learned that Brown had bought a car and issued a bad check to pay for it, but found that there were no open cases in Eugene matching Brown's *modus operandi*. Wibbenmeyer then tried every means to contact Brown over the next three days and on May 23 a warrant was issued for his arrest.

Meanwhile Brown was prowling for a victim and on the same day the warrant was issued he saw twenty-two-year-old Holly Carol Washa driving out of the parking lot of a hotel near the Seattle–Tacoma Airport. He pointed to her tire, as if something was wrong, and when she leaned out to check he jumped into her automobile and took her prisoner at knife-point, then ordered, "Drive or die." After traveling a short distance he had Washa move to the passenger seat and handcuffed her. He beat her as he drove to her bank and forced her to withdraw more than $1000, then took her to her apartment where he stole her roommates' checks, intending to forge them later. Next he drove her to his motel room, had her disrobe, and tied her to the bed. He raped her repeatedly and tortured her for several hours, burning her with a hair dryer and cigarettes and whipping and electrocuting her with an electric cord. The following day he made Washa call her job and report her absence due to illness, again tied her to the bed and sexually assaulted her with various objects, and continued torturing her with the electric cord. After an ordeal lasting thirty-four hours, Brown carried Washa to the trunk of her car and drove her to an airport parking lot, strangled her with a cord tied around her neck, slit her throat, stabbed her repeatedly, locked her in the trunk, and abandoned the car.

Her body was discovered on May 28 after Brown, then under arrest in California, confessed and directed the police to the location of Washa's remains. Brown, after parking Washa's car, went to the airport and flew to Palm Springs, California, where he rendezvoused with Susan Schnell, whom he had met several days earlier. He was giving Schnell a back-rub when he suddenly grabbed her arms and pulled them behind her, ordered her not to scream, and when she screamed he stabbed her in the throat. He handcuffed her ankles and then brandished the knife in a threatening manner. He bandaged Susan's throat using her nylons and sanitary napkins and then raped her, but the makeshift bandage was not effective and he did not want her to bleed to death before he raided her bank account the following day. He tied her ankles to the bed and left to purchase medical supplies but Susan, whose hands were free, managed to drag herself to the phone and she called the person at the front desk, who in turn called the police. She gave officer G. A. Haas a description and he arrested Brown returning to the room, who still had the bloody knife in his right front pocket. As soon as Brown was in jail he began confessing to the attempted murder and rape of Schnell and to the murder and rape of Holly Washa, and he would confess on at least four separate occasions to Washa's murder.

On August 30, 1991, Brown pled guilty in the Riverside County Superior Court to the attempted murder of Schnell, and he was sentenced to serve a life term. He was then extradited to Washington State where his murder trial began on December 1, 1993. On December 27 he was found guilty of first degree murder, and on January 28, 1994, he was sentenced to die. The jurors considered and rejected the public defender's contention that Brown had mental problems and suffered "violent mood swings" when he failed to take his Lithium medication, prescribed while in the Oregon State Prison. A long, vigorous campaign then began to spare the life of Brown, but all efforts failed until 2005, when the Ninth Circuit Court of Appeals overturned the judgment and sentence of the King County District Court. The judgment and sentence was reinstated by the U.S. Supreme Court in 2007. On January 21, 2009, the U.S. Supreme Court denied a petition for a writ of *certiorari* and a week later a mandate was issued setting the date for Brown's execution at March 13, 2009. The campaign to save Brown's life then became frantic with two motions filed in the Washington State Supreme Court asking for stays, which were denied on March 9. On March 11, Thurston County Superior Court Judge Chris Wickham denied a motion for a stay of execution, and the following day Brown appeared before the Clemency and Pardons Board, which voted 2–2 for a stay and forwarded their recommendation to Governor Christine Gregoire. On that same day the state Supreme Court granted a stay pending the outcome of a challenge to the three drug protocol then used in lethal injections, but on July 10 the Thurston County Superior Court ruled the protocol constitutional. The state's motion to vacate the stay was filed on July 14 but denied on September 10, 2009.

In August 2009 Brown's attorneys appealed the constitutionality of the three drug protocol to the Washington State Supreme Court. Arguments were heard on March 18, 2010, but on July 29 the court dismissed the challenge as moot when the state adopted a one drug protocol in May; the justices set the date of execution for September 10, 2010. On August 18 Brown's attorneys filed a motion for a stay with Seattle's U.S. District Judge John C. Coughenour, the state responded the following day, and the stay was denied on August 31. On September 2 an emergency motion for a stay of execution was filed in the Washington State Supreme Court alleging that Brown's mental condition was downplayed during his trial but the justices denied the motion on September 8. On September 2 a motion was also filed with the Ninth Circuit Court of Appeals and a three judge panel voted 2–1 on September 4 to deny the stay. On September 3 a motion was filed in the King County Superior Court requesting a stay of execution due to the "mental illness" of the condemned man, but on September 7 Judge Sharon Armstrong denied that motion. After receiving the news of the last denial Brown's attorneys filed a petition with the U.S. Supreme Court to hear arguments on the denials of stays by all courts, and the following day the attorneys filed a motion for a rehearing in the King County Court on the denial by Judge Armstrong. On the same day, September 8, Governor Gregoire announced that she was denying clemency to Brown. On September 9 the U.S. Supreme Court announced that it would not stay Brown's execution nor hear arguments on the stays denied by lower courts. The last minute efforts failed and Brown's execution was scheduled for just after midnight on Friday, September 10.

Earlier in his final week Brown was visited by an aunt and uncle from California and on Thursday he spent most of his final hours talking on the telephone with his attorneys and his family. He had resigned himself to his fate by 4:20 P.M. when he was moved from the IMU to a special cell (in unit 6) above the injection room. At 9:00 P.M. all the prisoners were locked down as usual. Shortly after midnight Brown was removed from his cell and escorted down the stairs and into the injection chamber, a small room painted a pale institutional green with a gurney bolted to the floor and tubes coming out of one wall. Brown was placed on the gurney facing a blank wall with an arm support extended for each arm and a viewing window on his left. Five straps secured his body to the gurney and one strap secured each arm to the supports, and then an intravenous cannula [IV] was inserted into the vein of each arm. He was asked if he had any last words and Brown complained that he had not been treated fairly by the legal system, saying that men who had killed many people were now serving life terms. He said, "I only killed one victim. I cannot really see that there is true justice. Hopefully, sometime in the future that gets straightened out." He apologized to four Washa family members among the witnesses, then took the time to praise the prison staff for his treatment over the past seventeen years. When he concluded he focused on the tubes leading from the wall to his arm, and the four member injection team began the 5 gram flow of the lethal dose of sodium thiopental, the anesthetic or first drug used in the previous three drug combination. Brown's chest heaved three times and his lips quivered, and at 12:56 A.M. all movement ceased and he was pronounced dead.

Intelligencer (Doylestown, PA): January 13, 2007. *Olympian* (WA): September 3, 2010; September 7–10, 2010. *Sammamish Review* (WA): April 1, 2009. *Seattle Times* (WA): December 1, 1993; February 5, 2009; March 12, 2009; August 31, 2010. State v. Brown, King County Superior Court, Cause # 91-1-03233-1. *Tri-City Herald* (Kennewick, WA): September 2, 2010; September 6, 2010; September 9–10, 2010. *Walla Walla Union-Bulletin* (WA): August 24, 2010. Washington State Supreme Court cases 82711-7; 82742-7; 83474-1.

WYOMING

There were five major land acquisitions by the United States during America's frontier period and Wyoming benefited from four of these. Eastern Wyoming, comprising about 75 percent of the state, was acquired in the Louisiana Purchase in 1803. In 1845 a tract located in the south central portion of the region was acquired by the annexation of Texas. A northwestern tract of land was acquired when newly elected President Polk resolved the "Oregon Question" on June 15, 1846, and the United States took sole control over the Oregon Country, setting the border with Canada at the 49th parallel. Finally, the southwestern area was added as a concession in the Treaty of Guadalupe Hidalgo on February 2, 1848, following the War with Mexico. There were many explorers, mountain men, fur trappers, and immigrants in Wyoming between 1742 and 1868, the year the Wyoming Territory was organized with land which had previously belonged to the Dakota, Idaho, Oregon, and Utah territories. On July 10, 1890, Wyoming was admitted to the union as the 44th state.

Miller, Charles
April 22, 1892

Charles Miller was born in Virginia in 1875 and both his parents died when he was five years old. His mother suffered from consumption and poisoned herself to end her misery, and then his father committed suicide as a consequence of his wife's death and while in delirium tremens. Miller, with three siblings, was sent to a New York orphanage but he soon fled and made his way to Minnesota where he was taken in by a farmer's family. He managed to keep track of his siblings and after several years he left Minnesota for Kansas where two brothers were being raised by a respectable family. He apprenticed as a printer for several months but, at the age of eleven, he took to the road with tramps. He traveled northeast through New York and New Jersey, adopting the sobriquet "Kansas Charley." After spending some months in the east he returned westward to Kansas City where Miller, who had never carried a gun, acquired a six-shooter because it seemed in character that a hard case like "Kansas Charley" should be well armed. He then moved on toward Sidney, Nebraska.

Ross Fishbaugh and Charles Waldo Emerson, good boys from respectable families, left St. Joseph, Missouri, for Denver to look for work and they were beating their way on the railroad to save money. On September 25, 1890, Miller, then only fifteen years old, met the two boys and the three men rode into Sidney together. During the trip a rough gang tried to force Miller to join their ranks but, with the help of Fishbaugh and Emerson, he avoided the association. The three young men were put off the train in Sidney and separated company for a time. Later that night Miller saw a long freight train come into Sidney heading west and he climbed into a stock car, covered himself with hay, and went to sleep before the train pulled out. At dawn he arose, gathered some hay for a bed and made his way back to a boxcar, where he planned to complete the trip into Denver in greater comfort. When he entered the boxcar he found his new acquaintances Fishbaugh and Emerson, alone in the car lying on a load of railroad ties. Emerson was asleep but Fishbaugh called out, "Hello, kid." Miller knew that the two boys had some money so he moved close to Fishbaugh and, without hesitation, he pulled his six-shooter and shot him in the head. Emerson rose up at the sound of the shot, but was immediately shot in the head also, and he died instantly while Fishbaugh, mortally wounded, lay helpless while Miller went through their pockets and took $60.00. When the train stopped at Hillsdale, Wyoming, several minutes later he slipped out, begged food from a local family, and then took the passenger train into Cheyenne.

The bodies of Fishbaugh and Emerson were found by a train hand, but there was not one clue nor bit of evidence as to who had killed them. The bullet holes, one each, were at such close range that there were substantial powder burns around the entry wounds. Miller had been seen in the area but because of his youthful appearance he was not suspected, nor detained, and lawmen concentrated their search for older desperadoes.

Miller traveled east again and three weeks after the murders he was in a small Kansas town when he began bragging about the exploits of "Kansas Charley." His brother convinced him to clear his soul by confessing, and Miller did so, freely and often in great detail. His tale had enough minute facts, known only to the murderer, that the telegraph sent to Cheyenne regarding the murders convinced everyone they had the right man. Miller was brought to Cheyenne and once there he again readily talked of his crime. It was supposed that his motive for the killings was robbery and a desire for notoriety, but he claimed it was out of fear and hunger.

Miller, who was then only sixteen years old, was tried, convicted of first degree murder, and sentenced to hang. The case was reviewed by the Supreme Court and the decision of the lower court was affirmed. After his date of execution was set for April 22, 1892, petitions were circulated requesting commutation of his sentence to life imprisonment, but these were denied by Governor Amos W. Barber in a letter arriving at 8:00 A.M. the day before the execution. Throughout his confinement the youngster showed no remorse nor the slightest fear of the consequences for his crime, and he had successfully escaped twice only to be recaptured. In the first escape he was freed when friends of another convicted murderer broke him out of jail; but Miller was captured in ten hours. The second escape occurred when he joined two other prisoners in overpowering the jailor. There was a terrible blizzard raging at the time and Miller was captured in three days, stranded in a snowdrift with the dead body of another escapee.

The gallows had been built directly behind the jail within a stockade which was supposed to provide privacy, and the condemned man would exit directly into that enclosure. The trap had been devised with an automatic spring: under the trap was a post divided into three parts joined by hinges; the foot of the post rested in a socket containing a spiral spring; when the weight of the condemned man was placed upon the trapdoor it pushed the post downward and an arm, attached to the bottom, opened a valve in a rubber hose which led to a tub partly filled with water; the tub was suspended from the arm of a lever on the other end of which was suspended heavy weights, to which was attached a cord which ran over pulleys to the post under the trap. As soon as the open valve allowed enough water to escape from the bucket, the lever which balanced the weights on one end and the bucket of water on the other tipped, the weights slid from the arm and by means of the cord pulled the post from under the trapdoor. This entire operation was estimated, by testing, to take one minute.

A reporter from Cheyenne's *Leader* visited Miller, still in his night clothes, on that final morning. The prisoner quickly dressed in his jail clothes and then told the reporter that he had slept well his final night. He said that he had played cards with his death watch guard until midnight and then retired. At 8:30 A.M. deputy Harry Griffiths brought his breakfast, which had been specially prepared at the Capitol Restaurant, but he ate little as his appetite had left him, but he accepted a cigar from the newsman. At 9:00 A.M. the Reverend Father J. C. McCormack arrived to ask Miller his religious preference and the prisoner said he wanted to be baptized. The priest then propounded the catechism and administered the Catholic baptismal rites. The reporter, at Miller's request, remained while the ceremonies were conducted. After the priest concluded Miller's attorney, and the attorney's wife, arrived to console the condemned boy.

By 10:30 A.M. Miller had changed into his burial clothes, a black shirt and tie and a black cutaway suit. Several hundred people had gathered about the courthouse, twenty men had climbed Castle Dare overlooking the scaffold, and a few had mounted adjacent telegraph poles all anxious to get some glimpse of the event, and sixty invited witnesses were inside the stockade. The witnesses included five Wyoming sheriffs, one U.S. marshal and two deputy U.S. marshals interested as much in the procedure as the outcome. The first the witnesses saw of Miller was at 11:23 A.M. when he exited the side door of the jail and climbed the steps to the scaffold. Father McCormack walked beside him while the condemned man clutched a large crucifix in both his hands. He kept repeating, with the Priest, "God have mercy on me," and "Jesus save me." When he reached the platform he carefully inspected the apparatus as he was being led into one of the corners where Sheriff Albert D. Kelley and two deputies pinioned his arms and legs. The Sheriff asked, "Have you anything to say, Charley?" and he replied, "Only, God have mercy on me."

The prisoner was then led forward to the

edge of the trapdoor where the noose was slipped over his head and adjusted. He had continued praying but paused to ask the sheriff, referring to the trap, "Do you want me to stand right in the middle?" and the sheriff answered, "No, remain here for the present." The black hood was pulled over his head and then he was carefully positioned over the center of the trapdoor. Everyone drew back at the same instant and Miller was standing alone, waiting. The automatic action of the trap could be heard operating when Miller cried out, "You are choking me a little." The sheriff asked, "What's that Charley?" then hurried forward and loosened the noose slightly. Miller said, "All right now," followed by "God have mercy on me," and then with an ominous "click" the trap was sprung at a few seconds past 11:28 A.M. The condemned man dropped five feet and not a quiver passed through his body, as his neck had been broken in the fall. The attending physician, assisted by a hospital steward, monitored Miller's pulse and pronounced him dead in fifteen minutes. The body was cut down and placed in the pine box provided by the county before being taken to the county hospital. The following day Miller, who had not a dollar nor a friend, was buried in a potter's field.

Cheyenne Leader (WY): April 16–23, 1892.

Howard, Frank
December 7, 1894

Frank Howard, a blacksmith, was living with Grace Bigtold in Dixon, Wyoming, in 1893. Charley Horn, a cowboy in the employ of J. C. Kane, was interested in Grace and on New Year's eve was at Grace's house with Howard. Both men had been celebrating and, as is often the case where liquor is involved, the result was loose tongues and quick tempers. There was already jealousy between the two men and they had words earlier in the evening. At 9:00 P.M. as they waited to see in the New Year, Horn made some comment about Grace to which Howard took offense. Howard, without warning or hesitation, drew his six-shooter and sent one bullet into Horn's forehead and entirely through his brain, and Horn died instantly. Howard ran out, mounted his horse and fled south toward Colorado, but Constable Leffler heard of the killing within minutes and organized a posse to pursue the murderer. They overtook Howard fifteen miles south of Dixon where he surrendered without a fight.

Howard was brought back to Dixon, given a preliminary hearing, and held over for the grand jury. The constable took his prisoner to Rawlins on January 4, 1894, and lodged him in the county jail. Howard was indicted and tried at the May term of the District Court, found guilty of first degree murder, and sentenced to hang on November 23. An application was filed with Governor John E. Osborne praying for a commutation of the sentence to life imprisonment, so a respite of two weeks was granted so the governor would have time to consider the matter. On November 30, 1894, the governor sent a letter to Howard's attorney denying the application and also sent a letter to Sheriff Jens Hansen: "Sir: You are hereby notified that the request made by the attorneys representing Frank Howard for a commutation of the death sentence pronounced by the court to imprisonment for life has been refused. Very Respectfully, John E Osborne, Governor." This was Howard's last chance and all hope was lost.

On December 6, 1894, Howard's last night he had difficulty sleeping. He wore his clothe[s] to bed and arose at 6:00 A.M. for breakfast but ate very little. He passed the morning i[n] prayer with Father Ternes and when his tim[e] was up he leaned on the priest's arm as h[e] walked to the gallows. The scaffold was th[e] same on which Benjamin Carter had bee[n] hanged on January 26, 1888, and had bee[n] thoroughly tested. The rope used was one hal[f] inch, four strand hemp and had been teste[d] by dropping a weight of one hundred sevent[y] pounds.

Twenty witnesses were present within th[e] enclosure when Howard stepped onto th[e] trapdoor, and as he was being prepared h[e] thanked the sheriff for his kind treatment an[d] declared that he had to give up his life for the deed he had done. He said God had forgiven him; he had joined the Catholic church; and he would die a good Christian. His final words, spoken several times just before the black hood was drawn over his head, were "God have mercy on my soul!" The trap was sprung at 10:34 A.M. and the condemned man dropped six feet eleven inches, breaking his neck in the fall. His heart ceased to beat in seven minutes and he was pronounced dead, and ten minutes later at 10:51 A.M. the body was cut down and placed in the pine coffin provided by the county. He did not have a single relative known to the authorities so that afternoon his body was buried in the Rawlins cemetery at County expense.

Cheyenne Leader (WY): January 4, 1894, November 30, 1894; December 7, 1894.

Keefer, James
September 25, 1903

In early December 1902 when the weather was bitterly cold James Keefer, a tramp, drifted into the small station at Derby on the stage line between Rawlins and Lander. Charles J. Warren kept the station and tended stock for the company. Keefer asked permission to stay and Warren, a compassionate man, invited Keefer into his home. Keefer's stay stretched into many days but Warren did not object. During this time Keefer learned that Warren had over $200 at the station and decided to steal it. On December 20 Keefer borrowed a small stake from Warren and began drinking, and by evening the liquor had added confidence and bravado to his resolve. After the men retired Keefer quietly arose, took a shotgun from the wall where it hung, crept across the room and shot the sleeping station keeper in the head. The blast blew out Warren's brains killing him instantly. The murderer then searched, found the money, and fled. Throughout the night Keefer sobered and as the liquor wore off his conscience took hold so the next day he went into Big Bend, a small village near Derby station, confessed his crime and asked to be taken to Lander to surrender. He had only $5 in his possession at that time. When the party reached Lander, Keefer was questioned about the details of the killing, but he had time to think while traveling and said he knew nothing of the crime. He laid the groundwork for his defense, explaining that he had suffered a severe head injury several years previously which rendered him unaware of his acts when under the influence of liquor.

Keefer was indicted, a motion for a change of venue was denied, and he was tried at the June session of the Fremont County District Court. The defendant was convicted of first degree murder, in large part on his own testimony. He had some sympathy and support for the story of his head injury and, had he stuck to that story and said he remembered nothing, he could possibly have avoided the most serious charge. However, he changed his story and said that Warren had chased him around the station shooting at him with a rifle and that he had only fired at the station keeper as a last resort and in self-defense. This not only contradicted his first statement at Big Bend but his later claim of remembering nothing, and each version contradicted all the physical evidence at the scene. It was shown that Warren was lying in bed when killed, not chasing Keefer; the brain and skull fragments had been driven into the bed clothes perpendicularly as if someone stood over the sleeping Warren when he was shot; the rifle was rusty and had not been fired in months; and Warren's money was not at the station and was never found. Keefer was sentenced to hang by Judge Bramel but an appeal stayed the date of execution. The case was argued before the state Supreme Court on August 3 and the justices affirmed the judgment and sentence of the lower court on August 20. The date for Keefer's execution was then scheduled for September 25, 1903, and the mandate from the high court substituted as authority for the hanging in lieu of a death warrant. Keefer wrote to Governor Fenimore Chatterton asking him to review the case but after careful consideration the governor responded that he would not interfere. As the date approached Keefer again adopted the story that he could remember nothing of the crime, but it was now too late for that ruse to have any effect.

The Reverend James Leonard baptized Keefer in preparation for his death. The prisoner, who was entitled to invite six witnesses, chose to invite only three men — E. H. Fourt, his attorney; John Honrath, hotel proprietor and friend; and the Reverend Leonard. Keefer slept well and arose early on the 24th of September. He was in good spirits and spent the morning joking with his death watch guards and said, "I am ready at any time and would just as soon walk to the gallows at 10 o'clock as tomorrow morning. I know that all hope of pardon is gone and that I must die, but I have faith in the mercy of a greater and more just judge than those here and have no fears of death." As the hours dwindled away Keefer spent much of his time reading his Bible, and the Reverend Leonard was with him constantly. The sound of hammering on the gallows and fence created terror for Keefer and for another prisoner scheduled to be hanged with him, but respited at the last moment.

The gallows was surrounded by a sixteen foot board fence, completely shutting out all view except to those who would be admitted to the enclosure. The scaffold was nine feet high and ten feet square. In the middle of the platform was the trapdoor, four feet square, and the release of that trap would provide a drop of six feet. Under the platform was the trap door release which would be activated by cutting a rope and a knife was honed to razor sharpness for the purpose, but when tested this proved inadequate. A sharpened hatchet replaced the knife and the rope was run from beneath the scaffold onto the platform and stretched across a log, where the blow would be struck. The identity of the executioner was intended to be kept secret but the sheriff, who would be standing in plain view on the platform, disclosed that it was he who would severe the rope releasing the trap. The trap and rope were tested on September 24 using a two hundred pound green cottonwood log and was tested again the morning of the execution.

On his final night the prisoner was shaved and his burial clothes were delivered to his cell. He retired at 11:00 P.M. and slept soundly for six hours. He was in good spirits when he arose and dressed in his new clothes consisting of a light suit of underwear, plain black pants and a plain black negligee shirt. His ravenous appetite, which had failed him for several days, returned and he ate a hearty breakfast. The Reverend Leonard arrived at 8:00 A.M. and was sequestered with the prisoner for one hour of fervent prayer. The next hour Keefer spent alone in his cell reading his Bible and praying. At 9:40 A.M. Sheriff Charles Stough and deputy James Crouch entered the jail and told jailor Allen Axe, who was also the undersheriff, to open the cell door. The three men entered the cell and the sheriff announced, "Jim your time has come," and Keefer replied, "Well, I am ready."

Crouch and Axe stood on either side of the prisoner with the sheriff following closely behind carrying the straps and black hood. Outside the enclosure several hundred people had gathered and a few had found what they hoped would be some vantage point on a roof top, in a tree, or up a pole, but the fence effectively obscured their view. The twenty-five witnesses had been admitted at 9:30 A.M. and spent their time examining the gallows. At exactly 10:00 A.M. Keefer appeared, climbed the stairs unassisted and took his place on the trapdoor, where the sheriff immediately began to strap his wrists and arms, knees and ankles. While the sheriff worked Keefer proclaimed his innocence and blamed the judge and governor for the injustice. The sheriff finished before Keefer concluded his statement so he stood aside and waited until the prisoner said, "That is all, Charlie. I am ready now."

The sheriff took hold of the noose, firmly attached to the crossbeam five feet above Keefer's head, and adjusted it around Keefer's neck and then quickly pulled on the black hood. He hesitated long enough to check the straps, noose and cap to ensure all was in readiness, then picked up the hatchet which lay close at hand. He made one smooth stroke at the restraining cord and the trap was released at 10:12 A.M., and the drop broke Keefer's neck. After eight minutes Drs. Godfrey, Calloway and Welty examined the body and announced that Keefer was still alive, but in ten minutes more they pronounced him dead. Sheriff Stough then cut down the body and placed it in the pine coffin stored beneath the scaffold. The lid was screwed on and within minutes it was on an express wagon en route to the city cemetery for interment in a potter's field.

Cheyenne Leader (WY): September 21–25, 1903.

Horn, Thomas
November 20, 1903

Tom Horn was born into a large family in Franklin County, Missouri, in 1870. He left home at an early age and drifted to the southwest, making his living driving bull teams into Texas and New Mexico. He earned a reputation as a badman during his travels when he killed a Mexican army officer over the affections of a woman, and in New Mexico, Horn reportedly killed two sheep herders, though the law could never make the case so he was not arrested. While in New Mexico he joined the army as a scout and, in one instance, stood firm and fought off a gang of Mexicans and Indians single-handedly until his posse could rally to support him. As a scout he became close friends with Colonel W. F. "Buffalo Bill" Cody and General Nelson A. Miles. Horn was rumored to have come into Wyoming for the first time with a trail herd or with the Texans imported for the cattlemen's invasion of 1892, but he denied these claims and said he came to the territory in 1894. He took a position as a cattle detective and rode the range, intent on stopping rustlers. In that year William Powell and William Lewis were murdered at their small ranches forty-five miles north of Cheyenne when both were suspected of rustling, and every effort was made to work up the case against Horn but without success.

In 1898 Horn enlisted in the government's pack train service and went to Cuba during the Spanish-American War. He caught fever soon after arriving there and when he returned showed the ravages of the disease, and it took him some months to regain his health. On June 2, 1899, six robbers held up the Union Pacific train one mile west of Wilcox, Wyoming, and by then Horn was well enough to take the trail, and after some time he returned to claim $4,000 of the reward for killing two of the robbers, whom he said he had buried where they had fallen when shot. He was disbelieved so he led officers to the spot and dug up the remains. The evidence showed that the two men he had killed were harmless prospectors whom he had shot from ambush without warning, and he referred to that incident as his "funny mistake," but he was not arrested for the crime.

In 1900 Matt Rash and Isham Dart, small ranchers in Brown's Hole County, Colorado, were assassinated within a short period of time. Both of the men had been suspected of rustling and it happened that Horn was in the county when they were killed, and Horn had eaten supper with Dart the night before his death. A posse went out but they did not know Horn so he rode into Wyoming unmolested. At Dixon he stopped for a drink and became involved in a cutting affray with one of the posse members and received a severe cut on the back of his neck which scarred noticeably. Once he was back in Wyoming, Horn was employed as a cattle detective for the Iron Mountain Ranch Company, which operated ranches at Bosler in Albany County and Iron Mountain in Laramie County.

About this time there was a feud between the Miller family and the Nickell family in the Iron Mountain district because Kels P. Nickell had brought sheep into cattle country. At 7:00 A.M. in the morning of July 18, 1901, Willie Nickell, the fourteen-year-old son of Kels, was near the ranch wearing his father's coat and hat when he was shot in the back twice. He died instantly and, at first, the Millers were suspected. Three weeks later Kels Nickell was shot but he managed to get into his house to avoid being killed, and he was taken into Cheyenne for medical treatment and survived. He accused the Millers, Jim and Victor, of the shooting but Jim and his sixteen-year-old son proved an alibi and were released. Horn had been seen in the vicinity a few days before Willie Nickell was murdered but could not be found after the killing. He finally turned up at the Bosler Ranch and consented to testify, told of his whereabouts, and the coroner's jury again had to adjourn without a verdict.

Horn had a habit of drinking too much and when in that condition he laid claim to just about every unsolved murder and other outrageous act he could recall, but few people took his boasting seriously. In the meantime U.S. Marshal Joe Lafors had been assigned to investigate the murder of Willie Nickell and he soon became convinced that Horn was responsible. In December, Lafors had a friend write to Horn offering him a position in Montana, which required him to go to Cheyenne and meet with Lafors to make the arrangements. On January 12, 1902, Horn had been drinking heavily when he went to the office of Lafors and, while further plying him with liquor, got him to confess to the murder of the Nickell boy and also got an admission to the killing of Powell and Lewis in 1894. In the next room were witness deputy sheriff Les Snow and stenographer Charles Ohnhaus, who recorded the entire conversation. The following day Horn was arrested by Sheriff Smalley and Undersheriff Proctor. Horn had his preliminary hearing in February and his trial was set for the May term of the District Court, but his attorneys obtained a delay to the fall term.

Horn's trial began on October 24, 1902, and after thirteen days of testimony the jury found him guilty of first degree murder. A few days later Horn was sentenced to hang on January 9, 1903, and then began one of the most aggressive appeals processes ever conducted. The execution was stayed, as it took a year for the state Supreme Court to consider the facts before affirming the lower court's judgment and sentence, and in October they rescheduled the execution of Horn for November 20, 1903. The fight for Horn's life next went to Governor Fenimore Chatterton, and he was inundated with affidavits from both sides and testimony of every sort. He even received a letter from a dying man saying he was guilty of the murder and would confess on his death bed, but on November 15 the governor refused to interfere. There were many rumors that the jail would be attacked and Horn would be rescued but the only incident that materialized was Horn's escape in August 1903, and he was recaptured before he traveled two hundred yards. He had armed himself with a new automatic pistol but had not learned how to release the safety, was wounded slightly, but could not return fire.

On Horn's last night he slept soundly and arose in excellent spirits. He asked for writing materials and spent the morning writing farewell letters, except for the few minutes he spent with his religious advisor, the Reverend G. C. Rafter, and with his friend John C. Coble. He ate a hearty breakfast and enjoyed several cigars as he whiled away his last hours. He dressed in a red striped shirt with low collar, a corduroy vest, black trousers, and gaiters.

At 9:00 A.M. the number of militia men guarding the jail was greatly increased and they formed a cordon around the building to keep back the growing crowd. Many had taken up positions in windows and on rooftops, but they could see nothing of the scaffold, a design by Cheyenne architect James P. Julian improved from an earlier Wyoming gallows. At 9:45 A.M. a final test of the gallows was conducted and the upper wash tub was filled with water and then the plug was pulled. Water was drained into buckets for thirty seconds before the plug was reinstalled. These buckets, and one additional bucket of water to account for spillage and leakage, were then set aside. The ropes were attached to the supporting post and a one hundred thirty-five pound weight was placed on the trapdoor, which pushed down the post and pulled the plug, and this in turn allowed water to drain into a lower washtub. At the moment that the lever was activated and the post pulled away, the plug was reinstalled. The buckets of water were then added to the upper washtub, which again lowered the upper washtub into the raised, ready position, and a gash was made on the inside of the washtub to mark the water level. The water from the buckets would take thirty to forty seconds to drain when the fatal moment arrived, and the mark was made to ensure that the correct level of water was maintained. The water in the lower wash tub was retained as a reservoir and weight down the lower tub so it would not move. The test of the release mechanism went off without a hitch, but men were assigned to stand by at the plug and post rope in case a firm hand was needed should some difficulty arise.

The hearse from Gleason's Undertaking Parlor stood near the courthouse and attracted much attention from the crowd. At 10:55 A.M. the invited witnesses were admitted and they filed into the enclosure. Deputy Sheriff Proctor walked to the gallows and arranged the straps and black hood on the railing and stood waiting as the cell door was swung open. Horn was brought out as far as the gangway and stopped while Frank and Charlie Irwin sang a tune, which was a strange medley of railroad vernacular and sacred words, but it was inspiring. The two boys were summoned to the scaffold and they shook hands with Horn and told him to die game. Charlie Irwin asked Horn if he had confessed and the condemned man said only, "No."

When the singers left the platform Proctor secured the straps about Horn's wrists and thighs as the condemned man joked with those in his procession. Horn was led onto the platform where he examined the trapdoor carefully and remarked, "I never saw one just like that before. I've seen several of them, but that is a new one." At 11:04 A.M. the noose was put over his head and he bent forward to help Proctor get it in place easily. His knees and ankles were then bound and as the straps were cinched tight he was jerked a bit and said, "You're liable to tip me over here; somebody had better hold me. You fellows ought to have a handle on me so you could do this easier." The Reverend Rafter read a short passage from an Episcopal prayer book and as the Reverend spoke Horn moved his head about as if the rope was uncomfortable, so Proctor stepped forward and lifted the heavy hangman's knot. While in that position Horn inspected the details of the knot. When the prayer finished at 11:06 A.M. Proctor lowered the knot and pulled the black hood over Horn's smiling face. The deputy asked, "Are you ready, Tom?" and he replied, "Yes!" so Sheriff Smalley and Joe Cahill lifted the condemned man onto the trapdoor. As he was being lifted he said, "Ain't gettin' nervous, are you?" and laughed through the hood.

As soon as he was placed on the trap there was an audible "click" as his body weight activated the lever which pulled the plug from the tub. Horn stood erect with his hands clenched tightly waiting for the trap to be sprung. It took thirty-five seconds before the post was pulled and the prisoner dropped through and Horn's neck was broken in the fall, but his heart continued to beat for sixteen minutes. He hung for another four minutes before being cut down and handed over to the man from Gleason's undertaking establishment. The following morning Horn's remains were shipped to Boulder, Colorado, in the custody of Sheriff Sperry for interment. The gallows was taken down the following day and stored in the courthouse barn in the event it would be needed again.

Cheyenne Leader (WY): October 27–29, 1903; November 2–6, 1903; November 13–16, 1903; November 19–21, 1903. *San Francisco Chronicle* (CA): November 21, 1903.

Seng, Joseph
May 24, 1912

Joseph Seng was employed by the Union Pacific Railroad at Evanston, Wyoming, but on August 4, 1910, he was fired by detective William Lloyd. The firing suggested that Seng was involved in some minor criminal activity involving railroad property, but there is no record of the reason for the termination. Lloyd and his wife were walking down the street after supper at 7:10 P.M. when Seng accosted the detective and demanded to speak with him about being reinstated, but Lloyd ignored him and the couple walked on. As soon as Lloyd passed Seng pulled his revolver and, point blank, shot Lloyd in the back of his head three times killing him instantly. Seng was arrested and lodged in jail under a heavy guard, as there was talk of lynching.

On the following afternoon the remains of Lloyd were shipped to Davenport, Iowa, accompanied by his wife, where the funeral was scheduled to be conducted from his mother's home. That same day Seng waived his preliminary examination and was held over for trial, but he refused to make any comment regarding the shooting. Seng was tried at the fall term of the court, convicted of first degree murder, and sentenced to hang. He was taken to the state prison at Rawlins and lodged in a death row cell while his court appointed attorney filed a notice of appeal, which stayed the execution. The attorney began an aggressive campaign of appeals and petitions to delay the hanging of his client but by March 1912 all efforts for judicial relief or executive clemency were exhausted and the date for Seng's execution was firmly set for May 24.

Seng had resigned himself to his fate and was entirely composed when the warden appeared at his cell door at 2:30 A.M. to read the death warrant. He said he would not speak to the witnesses and was escorted, smiling, into the death house where the gallows had been erected. The "Julian gallows," the same type on which Charles Miller and Tom Horn had been hanged in Cheyenne, had been purchased by the state in 1911 and moved to the Rawlins prison where a special building was constructed to contain it. Seng climbed the stairs and his wrists and arms, knees and ankles were strapped, the noose was adjusted, and the black hood was pulled over his head. He was guided onto the center of the trapdoor where his weight activated the automatic release, a valve which drained water from a large tub. The trapdoor was sprung at 2:45 A.M. and Seng dropped straight through but, because of his light weight, he did not break his neck. The prisoner strangled to death in nine minutes and forty-five seconds and then was pronounced dead by the prison physician. The body was cut down, deposited in the coffin provided by the state, and buried in a prison plot later that day.

Nevada State Journal (Reno): August 5, 1910. *Standard* (Ogden, UT): August 6, 1910. *Ogden Examiner* (UT): May 25, 1912.

Jenkins, J. Warren
November 14, 1913

On April 14, 1912, J. Warren Jenkins took an "Indian club" and bashed in the skull of his wife, Jessie, and she died in minutes. The couple had been married less than a year but Jessie had a sizeable estate valued at about $25,000 and a $5,000 life insurance policy, and Jenkins had convinced his wife to make him the sole beneficiary in her will. The body was discovered and, though Jenkins persisted in claiming his innocence, all the circumstantial evidence pointed to him as the killer.

He was arrested and at his examination he was held over for action by the grand jury. In August he was indicted, tried, convicted of first degree murder, and sentenced to hang in October, but his court-appointed attorney filed a notice of appeal which stayed the execution. The Supreme Court considered the case for nearly a year before they affirmed the judgment and sentence of the District Court and Jenkins' execution was scheduled for November 14, 1913. In an ironic twist Jenkins had won a suit to get control of his wife's estate, Coroner C. Y. Beard was named administrator on his behalf in May 1913, and he used a substantial portion of the money to fight for his freedom. Even though he had these substantial funds there was no further judicial relief nor executive clemency to delay the proceedings.

On Jenkins' final night he ate a hearty supper at 6:00 P.M. and retired at 10:00 P.M. When the guards arrived at his cell door at 2:30 A.M. he had to be aroused from a sound sleep, but he leaped out of his bunk and quickly dressed in the regulation grey prison uniform. The death warrant was read before he stepped from his cell and then the guards pinioned his wrists and arms before he was escorted into the death house and onto the scaffold. He was asked if he wanted to speak to the witnesses and he said, "I did not kill my wife and I do not know who did." When it was clear he had concluded his remarks his knees and ankles were strapped, the noose was adjusted, and the black hood was pulled over his head. He was guided onto the center of the trapdoor where his weight activated the automatic release—a valve in a large tub of water, and when it had drained sufficiently the lever was sprung and the trapdoor fell at 2:45 A.M. Jenkins broke his neck in the fall and the prison physician in attendance said he had died almost instantly, and pronounced him dead. The body was cut down, deposited in the coffin provided by the state, and buried later that day.

Salt Lake Tribune (UT): July 28, 1912. *Fort Wayne Sentinel* (IN): May 9, 1913. *Lincoln Daily Star* (NE): November 14, 1913. *Ogden Standard* (UT): November 14, 1913. *Pinedale Roundup* (WY): November 14, 1912; December 2, 1912; August 21, 1913. *Wisconsin State Journal* (Madison): November 14, 1913.

Flanders, Willard
June 16, 1916

On July 14, 1914, Samuel Aultz and his wife visited his neighbors, Willard Flanders and his wife and their seventeen-year-old son, at their ranch near Hulett, Wyoming. When the Aultz couple arrived they found Willard choking his wife after she refused to sign a deed to property they owned in Chadron, Nebraska, which he intended to sell. Aultz intervened and then Mrs. Flanders asked to return to the Aultz farm with the couple, and they agreed. All but Willard Flanders went out and Mrs. Flanders and her son got into their vehicle and started toward Hulett behind the Aultz vehicle. As soon as they went out Willard Flanders grabbed his rifle and hurried afoot by a shortcut to a point along the road ahead of the two vehicles, and when they came into view he stepped into the road, uttered an oath toward Samuel Aultz, and shot him dead. The Aultz vehicle blocked the road so his wife could not escape and Flanders got her out, had her kneel in the road, and while she pled for her life he shot her in the head killing her instantly. He did not molest Mrs. Aultz nor his son, who ran into the woods, but returned to his ranch and awaited the arrival of officers.

He was arrested, taken into Hulett, and lodged in jail. He pled not guilty and his attorney filed a motion for a change of venue, and it was granted from Crook to Sheridan County. The trial began in Judge C. H. Parmelee's courtroom in late December and the defense admitted the killings, but relied exclusively on a claim that their client was incurably insane. The judge instructed the jury, "The law recognizes that a man may be insane on some subjects and not on others and if murder is deliberately planned and executed insanity is no defense." The case went to the jury on Christmas eve and they quickly found Flanders guilty of first degree murder, and he was sentenced to hang. His attorney filed an appeal which stayed the execution, but the judgment and sentence of the lower court was affirmed by the state Supreme Court on April 6, 1916, and Flanders was scheduled to hang on May 7. Next came the petition to the State Board of Pardons praying for a commutation of sentence to life in prison, which delayed the proceedings, but this was denied on June 9 and the date for Flanders' execution was then set at June 16.

On his final night Flanders ate a hearty supper, seemingly unconcerned with his pending doom, read a magazine until 10:45 P.M. and then retired. He was aroused from a sound sleep at 2:50 A.M. and after he dressed in his prison uniform Warden Alston read the death warrant. He was then taken from his cell, his wrists and arms were strapped, and he was marched into the death house. He took his place on the scaffold and told the witnesses, when asked if he had anything to say, "This is a poor place to do any talking." His knees and ankles were strapped, the noose was adjusted, and the black hood was pulled over his head. He was then guided onto the trapdoor where his body weight activated the automatic release. The trap was sprung at 2:54 A.M. and Flanders dropped four feet, breaking his neck. He was pronounced dead by the prison physician at 3:07 A.M. and then the body was cut down and deposited in the coffin provided by the state. He was buried later that day.

Examiner (Big Piney, WY): January 28, 1915; April 6, 1916. *Pinedale Roundup* (WY): February 18, 1915. *Reno Gazette* (NV): June 16, 1916.

Palmer, Wilbur
August 11, 1916

Thirty-four-year-old Wilbur Palmer and his wife Jessie operated a boarding house in Salt Creek, Wyoming, forty miles north of the Natrona County seat at Casper. During the late months of 1914 Palmer became obsessed with the notion that his wife had been unfaithful and began to notice every time she would talk to a male boarder or a male Salt Creek resident in a pleasant manner, or would smile at them. He suspected she was having an affair with each man and even dredged up memories of past male boarders he suspected. He became uncontrollably jealous and the couple quarreled many times during the late months of 1914, and each time Jessie insisted she had been faithful to him.

The charge of unfaithfulness was entirely a figment of Palmer's imagination, but on January 8, 1915, the couple quarreled again and Palmer suddenly grabbed Jessie, held her tightly as he drew his straight-razor across her throat cutting her from ear to ear, and watched her bleed to death. He then tried to kill himself with the same razor and, though he inflicted a severe wound, he did not cut the arteries nor the windpipe so he fully recovered. He was arrested, lodged in the jail at Salt Creek, and charged with murdering his wife. As soon as word of the murder spread a large mob formed in front of the jail and demanded the prisoner be turned over to them, and nearly managed to drag him away from the officers. The jail was heavily guarded all night and in the morning the prisoner was snuck out of the jail, put aboard an automobile, and spirited away to a jail cell in Casper.

Palmer was tried at the spring term of the Natrona County District Court, found guilty of first degree murder and the jury, under the new Wyoming law, recommended the death penalty. Palmer was sentenced to hang but he was still in the Casper jail in July, awaiting some word on the appeal which had stayed his sentence, when he again tried to commit suicide by cutting the artery on his left wrist with a safety razor blade and he lost a large amount of blood but recovered. He left a letter denying the murder of his wife and requested to be buried next to her in Salt Creek. The case dragged on in the state Supreme Court for another year and finally, on June 15, 1916, the justices affirmed the District Court's judgment and sentence and set the date for Palmer's execution at August 11, 1916. The prisoner was then taken to the state prison at Rawlins and lodged in a death row cell, and a death watch guard was placed over him to ensure he would not cheat the hangman. On the Wednesday preceding his Friday execution, Palmer, who had been weakening for days, tried to commit suicide in his prison cell by cutting his wrists with a metal button from his prison uniform, but his guards were alert and saved his life.

When Palmer failed to kill himself that third time he resigned himself to his fate. He slept fitfully that last night and at 3:00 A.M he was awakened by his guards and he quickly dressed in his prison uniform. Warden Alston arrived to read the death warrant, and he was then taken from his cell, his wrists and arms were strapped and he was escorted into the death house. He took his place on the scaffold and declined to speak to the witnesses. His knees and ankles were strapped, the noose was adjusted, and the black hood was pulled over his head. He was guided onto the trapdoor where his body weight activated the automatic release. The trap was sprung at 3:2[illegible] A.M. and Palmer dropped four feet, but th fall did not break his neck. He strangled to death in eight minutes and was pronounced dead by the prison physician at 3:30 A.M. The body was then cut down and deposited in the coffin provided by the state. According to his final wish he was taken to Salt Creek and buried in the local cemetery next to his wife.

Examiner, (Big Piney, WY): July 19, 1915; August 12, 1915; August 11, 1916. *Lincoln News* (NE): January 9, 1915. *Oakland Tribune* (CA): August 11, 1916. *Pinedale Roundup* (WY): June 15, 1916; August 24, 1916. *Reno Gazette* (NV): August 11, 1916. *Lincoln Star* (NE): August 11, 1916.

White, Oscar W.
November 16, 1916

On August 12, 1913, Oscar W. White slashed to death Anderson Coffee in a Burlington bunk car when the train was stopped at Powder River, Wyoming. Sheriff Jesse Sheffner of Natrona County investigated the murder for months and characterized it as "one of the most brutal and cowardly in the history of the state." On October 9 he arrested Oscar White at Cheyenne and his prisoner confessed immediately to the slaying, but claimed he had acted in self-defense when Coffee refused to pay a fifteen cent gambling debt. White was taken to Natrona County and lodged in the jail at Casper. He was tried at the fall term of the court, convicted, and sentenced to hang before the end of the year, but his court-appointed attorney filed an appeal which stayed the execution. The case was quickly disposed of by the state Supreme Court but then his attorney relied upon a typographical error to file an appeal in the federal courts, claiming that the official information stated the crime occurred on August 12, 19013, seventeen thousand one hundred years in the future. This matter was disposed of on June 17, 1915, and then every effort was made to delay the hanging of their client until finally all avenues of judicial relief and executive clemency were exhausted, and the date of execution was set for November 16, 1916.

White resigned himself to his fate and spent his final days singing and relaxing, and he sang all the way to the gallows. On his final night he retired and slept soundly, only to be aroused from a deep sleep after 2:30 A.M. The death warrant was read to him as he dressed in his prison uniform and then he was taken from his death row cell. His wrists and arms were strapped before he was escorted into the death chamber, and he took his place on the scaffold and declined to speak to the witnesses. His knees and ankles were strapped, the noose was adjusted, and the black hood was pulled over his head. He was then guided onto the trapdoor where his body weight activated the automatic release, and at 2:45 A.M. the trap was sprung. He dropped, breaking his neck, and the prison physician pronounced him dead in eleven minutes. The body was then cut down and deposited in the coffin provided by the state. White was buried in a prison plot later that day.

Examiner (Big Piney, WY): June 17, 1915; November 16, 1916. *Pinedale Roundup* (WY): October 9, 1913.

Yee Geow
March 11, 1921

On the afternoon of September 10, 1920, twenty-two-year-old Yee Geow was arrested by Thomas Holland and W. R. Mansfield, officers of the Immigration Inspection Board at Cheyenne, Wyoming. Geow was suspected of being a member of a tong which had smuggled him into the United States from Canada two months earlier. As they walked toward the city jail Geow suddenly pulled a pistol from his loose fitting Chinese garments and began shooting, seriously wounding Holland. He turned toward Mansfield, who was unarmed, and the officer dodged into the Pioneer Avenue firehouse. Geow pursued Mansfield through the firehouse and in the rear he met John S. Federhen, a Cheyenne fireman, and shot him to death and then fired once at another fireman, missing. Once he saw that Mansfield had escaped he surrendered and, in a fit of nervousness, fired his last bullet into the firehouse floor. He was lodged in jail and charged with murdering Federhen, and when Holland died from his wounds Geow was charged with a second murder.

Geow was indicted and tried for the murder of Holland during the summer term of Judge Mentzer's District Court, the defense of insanity failed, he was found guilty and sentenced to hang before the end of the year. At his trial he said that the two killings were incidental to his determination to kill Mansfield for interfering with his freedom, and he admitted that he always carried a pistol after being robbed in New York on his way from Canada to Wyoming. His attorney filed an appeal with the state Supreme Court, which stayed the execution, and the condemned prisoner was kept in the Laramie County jail pending the outcome of the hearing. During his stay in jail he tried, three times, to hang himself and once to starve himself to death, and his condition was badly weakened by these attempts. As 1920 came to a close the Supreme Court affirmed the judgment and sentence of the lower court and set the date for Geow's execution at March 11, 1921, and on December 27 the condemned man was taken from Cheyenne and delivered to a death row cell in the prison at Rawlins.

During his final weeks Geow was attended by Father Gerard Schellinger of St. Joseph's Church at Rawlins, who was also the Catholic chaplain at the prison, and Geow finally renounced the Buddhist religion and on March 10 he was baptized a Catholic. The priest helped Geow resign himself to his fate and stayed with him until Warden Frank A. Hadsell appeared at his cell door at midnight. The death warrant was read to him inside his cell and then he was taken out and escorted into the death house and onto the gallows by Father Schellinger. He looked up at the noose, swiped his hand across his face and said, "All'e same this." His wrists and arms, knees and ankles were strapped and the noose was adjusted, and then Warden Hadsell asked, "My boy, have you anything to say?" and he replied, "No."

The black hood was pulled over his head as the priest and prisoner prayed together. Geow was guided onto the trapdoor where his weight of barely one hundred pounds activated the automatic release. There was a delay of a half minute while water poured from a tub and at 12:24 A.M. the trap was sprung, just as Geow said, "My Jesus, Mercy." The drop was six feet and, with his light weight, it was not enough to break his neck, so it took thirteen minutes for him to strangle to death. The prison physician pronounced him dead at 12:37 and the body was cut down, placed in the coffin provided by the state, and given to Father Schellinger for burial in the Catholic portion of the Rawlins cemetery.

Examiner (Big Piney, WY): September 23, 1920; September 30, 1920. *Pharos-Tribune* (Logansport, IN): March 11, 1921. *Pinedale Roundup* (WY): January 20, 1921. *Wyoming State Tribune* (Cheyenne): March 10–11, 1921.

Brownfield, George A.
March 10, 1930

Theodore Thomas and his beautiful young wife came west from New York to Wyoming in April and made their home in a sheep wagon at Colony in northern Crook County, where Thomas was employed as a sheepherder by Hugo Cornelius. On the evening of July 28 they were visited by fifty-two-year-old George Brownfield, a sheepman, and after supper they invited him to stay the night. The young couple retired to their wagon while Brownfield slept on the ground, but after midnight Brownfield awoke Thomas and told him that he heard coyotes raiding the flock. Thomas grabbed his gun and the two men started for the flock, but as soon as they were a distance from the wagon Brownfield shot Thomas in the back, killing him instantly. Brownfield then returned to the wagon and raped Mrs. Thomas, tied her, and went to sleep. Mrs. Thomas managed to free herself and walked into Colony, where she asked citizens to call the authorities. The sheriff was notified and Brownfield was arrested on July 30 and lodged in the jail at Sundance.

He had his preliminary hearing in early August and was held over for the grand jury. The prisoner was indicted in early October and on October 7 he pled not guilty at his arraignment, and trial was set for October 28. The trial continued into the first days of November when Brownfield was convicted of first degree murder and sentenced to hang in December. An appeal was filed by defense attorneys James McGulkin and W. K. Somers, so a stay was granted. The state Supreme Court affirmed the judgment and sentence of the lower court in late January 1930 and the date for Brownfield's execution was set for March 10, 1930. His attorneys then submitted an application praying for executive clemency from Governor Frank C. Emerson, but it was denied on March 8.

Shortly before midnight the prison warden appeared at Brownfield's cell door and read the death warrant. The condemned man said he would not speak to the witnesses, then he was taken out and escorted into the death house. He climbed the stairs and had his wrists and arms, knees and ankles strapped; the noose was adjusted and the black hood was pulled over his head. He was guided onto the trapdoor where his weight activated the automatic release by opening a valve which drained water from a large tub, and when enough water was drained the lever was sprung at 12:18 A.M., and Brownfield broke his neck in the fall. Prison physician Dr. Raymond Barber waited beneath the gallows and monitored vital signs until 12:33 A.M. when he pronounced the prisoner dead. The body was cut down, deposited into the coffin provided by the state, and buried later that day.

Examiner (Big Piney, WY): November 21, 1929. *San Antonio Express* (TX): March 11, 1930. *Billings Gazette* (MT): October 8, 1929. *Ogden Standard-Examiner* (UT): March 9, 1930. *Waterloo Courier* (IA): March 11, 1930.

Aragon, Charles
May 14, 1930

On Saturday night, September 6, 1928, sixty-four-year-old Edward Large and his thirty-five-year-old son Jess were in a tent at the county fair at Riverton, Wyoming, participating in the American Legion's "49" celebration. Nellie Vandugan, Jess' ex-wife, was also in the tent as was her suitor for more than a year, thirty-three-year-old Charles Aragon, and there had been increasing animosity between Jess Large and Aragon. While Jess and his father were preoccupied with the festivities Aragon walked up behind Jess and, without warning, pulled his six-shot revolver and shot Jess three times, then turned the pistol on Ed Large and shot him twice killing him instantly, and the last bullet missed Ed Large as he fell. M. C. Burke and F. D. Wooten grabbed Aragon while George Tassi wrestled the empty pistol from his grip, and they held him for the authorities. Jess Large was rushed to the hospital but he could not be saved and he died at 3:00 A.M. the next day.

Aragon was lodged in jail and while behind bars he said that, had he seen Nellie, he would have shot her as well. On September 12 Aragon was taken before Justice of the Peace Belton and held over for the fall grand jury. In early December, Aragon was indicted, and on December 7 he was tried in Judge E. H. Fourt's Lander courtroom. After three ballots the jury returned a verdict of guilty of first degree murder and on December 9, for the first time in eight years, the death penalty was imposed and the date was set for March 29, 1929. Aragon's court appointed attorney, John D. Christie, filed a notice of appeal which stayed the execution, and then the case dragged on in the state Supreme Court for more than a year. Finally on April 29, 1930, the Supreme Court affirmed the judgment and sentence of the District Court, but as a delaying tactic petitions were filed to examine Aragon's sanity and the same petitions were filed with Governor Frank C. Emerson. The governor granted a stay to May 14 and scheduled Aragon's examination by Dr. D. L. Darche for May 10 at the state prison in Rawlins, where he was being held pending his execution. A similar petition was also filed with the county District Court which could further delay the execution and require an examination by the Carbon County lunacy commission. The commission found him sane on May 5 and on May 10 Dr. Darche also reported the condemned man sane. Aragon, who was part Arapahoe, had been resentenced to hang on May 2 and the Arapahoe Indians began "making medicine against the devil rope" which would hang Aragon, so when they heard of the stay to May 14 they felt they had succeeded. After Aragon was found sane a further request for a stay was submitted to the governor on May 10, but it was denied.

Shortly before midnight the prison warden appeared at the cell door of the condemned man, read the death warrant, and Aragon was then escorted into the death house. He climbed the stairs and his wrists and arms, knees and ankles were strapped and the noose was adjusted. He then declined to speak to the witnesses so the black hood was pulled over his head and he was guided onto the trapdoor, where his weight activated the automatic release. A valve opened which drained water from a large tub and when enough water had drained the lever was sprung and Aragon dropped, breaking his neck in the fall. Prison physician Dr. Raymond Barber waited beneath the gallows, monitored vital signs, and pronounced the prisoner dead. The body was then cut down, deposited into the coffin provided by the state, and on May 16 Aragon's remains were driven to Morton, Wyoming, in a hearse. On Sunday, May 18, hundreds viewed the remains, funeral services were then held for Aragon and he was buried in the family plot near the Kinnear bridge.

Reno Gazette (NV): May 14, 1930. *Billings Gazette* (MT): April 30, 1930; May 2, 1930; May 11, 1930; May 20, 1930. *Montana Standard* (Butte): September 12, 1928. *Pinedale Roundup* (WY): September 27, 1928. *Salt Lake Tribune* (UT): December 9, 1928

Taylor, Talton
May 11, 1933

Early on Wednesday, January 18, 1933, thirty-five-year-old William Embrey, who lived on the ranch of his father-in-law Thomas Car in the Powder River country, argued over a $10 debt with thirty-one-year-old Talton Taylor, who worked on a neighboring ranch. The following evening when Embrey went out to milk the cow he was shot three times with a high-powered rifle and Embrey died in his wife's arms after telling her it was Taylor who had shot him. Taylor submitted to arrest by Sheriff Mart Tisdale two hours after the shooting and he was lodged in the Johnson County jail at Buffalo. He was offered the opportunity to sign a confession but he refused.

On Friday, January 20, Taylor was arraigned and pled not guilty, and he was held over without bail to await action by the grand jury. In March he was indicted and his trial began in Judge James H. Burgess' District Court on March 28, and after two days of testimony he was convicted of first degree murder on the evening of March 29, after only one hour and forty-five minutes of deliberations. The jurors recommended the death penalty so Judge Burgess sentenced Taylor to hang on May 11, 1933. Taylor filed a petition with Governor Leslie A. Miller asking him to intervene, but the governor responded that unless the condemned man could produce extenuating evidence or show that he did not receive a fair trial, he would go to the gallows on May 11. Neither proof was forthcoming so the execution proceeded as planned.

Taylor had fully resigned himself to his fate with the help of Catholic chaplain Gerard Schellinger, and was baptized into the Catholic church on May 10. When the guards arrived at the death row cell at 12:15 A.M. they found Taylor and his priest kneeling in prayer, and after a few moments' delay they arose. Taylor dressed in his prison uniform, stepped out and was asked if he had anything to say, and replied, "I am sincerely sorry for having committed the crime. I thank the chaplain for all he has done for me and may God have mercy on my soul," and the chaplain responded, "I am very happy to think that I could do something for you."

The death warrant was read and Taylor entered the death chamber at 12:23 A.M. and took his place on the scaffold. While the priest prayed for his soul his wrists and arms, knees and ankles were strapped, the noose was adjusted, and the black hood was pulled over his head. He was guided onto the trapdoor where his body weight activated the automatic release, but it seemed only a few seconds before the trap was sprung. He dropped breaking his neck and was pronounced dead by the prison physician at 12:39 A.M. The body was cut down and deposited into the coffin provided by the state and he was buried in the prison cemetery later that day, following a brief service by Father Schellinger.

Billings Gazette (MT): January 22, 1933; March 31, 1933; May 3, 1933; May 12, 1933. *Ogden Standard-Examiner* (UT): January 20, 1933.

Carroll, Paul H.
August 13, 1937

Thirty-six-year-old Paul H. "Perry" Carroll, a switch tender for the Union Pacific Railroad at Laramie, was having difficulty with superintendent C. C. Barnard for over a month and on October 27, 1935, Barnard discharged him for intoxication on the job. Later that day Barnard was standing by the newspaper counter in the passenger station in Cheyenne talking with Omaha's superintendent, G. J. Adamson, when Carroll walked into the station and started toward them. When Carroll was eight feet from Barnard he pulled out a pistol and fired three times, killing Barnard instantly. Adamson rushed at Carroll but the murderer shot himself in the head twice before Adamson could grab the weapon. Carroll was taken to the hospital in critical condition and he cried out, "They were trying to make a tramp out of me." Later, after he had quieted and gained strength, Carroll said he had "planned to get Barnard for a month," and also intended "to get A. S. Kenworthy," a special agent for the railroad. A note to his sister found in Carroll's pocket read, "I hope everybody will forgive me and God help everybody also. I was just put on the tramp again."

He had recovered sufficiently to stand trial at the spring session of the District Court in Cheyenne and on March 27, 1936, the jurors began fifteen hours of deliberations, and the following day found Carroll guilty of murder after rejecting his defense of temporary insanity. The jurors made no recommendation for leniency so Carroll was sentenced to die in the gas chamber at the prison in Rawlins, the first to be executed in Wyoming by this method. The motion for a new trial was denied and then Carroll's attorney filed an appeal, which stayed the execution. The state Supreme Court affirmed the judgment and sentence of the District Court and the date for the execution was set for August 13, 1937. His attorney filed an appeal with the U.S. Supreme Court but the justices refused to hear the case. On the day preceding the execution Governor Leslie A. Miller denied the request for a commutation of the death sentence to life imprisonment.

The condemned man spent a peaceful night and arose at 5:00 A.M. on Thursday. After breakfast he was visited by his father, who returned in the afternoon and remained until 11:00 P.M. Warden Alex McPherson, at 4:00 P.M., told the prisoner he was about to be served his last meal but Carroll declined, and said he had no further requests. After his father left Carroll spent his last hour in prayer with Father William J. Short, his spiritual advisor, who was present for the reading of the death warrant. McPherson, as soon as the twenty-one witnesses were in place a few minutes before midnight, went to the cell and Carroll said, "All right, warden, I am ready to go sit in your chair."

Father Short and the warden escorted him to the chamber, clad only in shorts and smiling all the way, and blindfold him before he entered. He was guided to the steel chair where his chest and waist, wrists and ankles were securely strapped, and he asked deputy warden Frank Keifer not to make the straps so tight. The chamber door was sealed at 12:16 A.M. and the warden tripped the lever that dropped thirty-three "cyanide eggs" into three quarts of sulphuric acid in a crock beneath the chair. Carroll continued to smile until the white cloud of gas enveloped him, and then he threw his head back and breathed deeply. His head fell forward at 12:24 and the prison doctor said that he was probably dead at that moment, but he was not pronounced dead officially until 12:41 A.M. The delay was required to flush the chamber with anhydrous ammonia and then purge the chamber with fans which directed the poisonous fumes through "scrubbers" using water as a neutralizer. McPherson and Keifer entered wearing gas masks to remove the body to a wheeled stretcher, and the body was washed with a chlorine solution. The body was then placed into a hearse at 12:50 A.M. and delivered to a funeral home. Carroll's remains were embalmed and deposited into a coffin at state expense, and then shipped to his hometown of Leesville, Louisiana, for burial at his father's expense.

Ada News (OK): August 19, 1937. *Big Piney Examiner* (WY): August 12, 1937. *Billing Gazette* (MT): August 14, 1937. *Nevada State Journal* (Reno): October 28, 1935. *Ogden Standard-Examiner* (UT): March 28, 1936.

Lantzer, Stanley S.
April 19, 1940

Thirty-two-year-old Cecile Lantzer left her husband, thirty-six-year-old Stanley S. Lantzer, and moved into trailer in a tourist camp. On August 28, 1938, Stanley went to the campground and pleaded with his "beautiful, red-haired wife" to return to him but she refused. The following day he went to the camp again, pulled out a pistol, and shot her to death. Later testimony revealed that on their first meeting, Stanley, who had been crazed by his wife's adultery, threatened to shoot her and the following day did as he had threatened.

Lantzer was arrested and lodged in the Cheyenne jail where he confessed, but then refused to sign the confession. He was indicted for murder and his trial began in early December. Lantzer claimed that he had pulled out the pistol only to frighten his estranged wife, not to kill her, but the jurors rejected this defense. The case went to the jury at noon on December 7 and they found him guilty of first degree murder, without a recommendation for leniency. District Court Judge Sam Thompson then sentenced Lantzer to die in the gas chamber at the prison in Rawlins on January 20, 1939, but a notice of appeal stayed the execution. The case did not reach the state Supreme Court until April 5, 1939, where Lantzer's attorney, Allen A. Pearson, argued that the judge had erred in his instructions to the jury. It took nearly a year before the justices affirmed the judgment and sentence of the lower court and the date for Lantzer to die was set at April 19, 1940. The governor, when petitioned, refused to intervene.

During Lantzer's last days he was attended by the Reverend William Young of Brush, Wyoming, and the Reverend Clifton McGlothlan of Rawlins. The reverends were with him his final hours and after the witnesses were in place, before midnight, Warden Alonzo Roach appeared at the cell door and read the death warrant. Lantzer was then brought out and, with a faint smile and muttering prayers, he was blindfolded by a guard and guided the fifteen feet into the gas chamber. He was seated in the steel chair and his chest and waist, wrists and ankles were strapped. Lantzer and the reverends prayed and Lantzer asked for "strength to face the test ahead" and told the Reverend Young, "Kiss me, brother," and Young did and then both reverends quickly left the chamber.

The door was sealed at 12:14 A.M. and in a minute thirty-two sodium cyanide pellets dropped into the crock of sulphuric acid and the prisoner was quickly enveloped in a white cloud of hydrocyanic gas. In two minutes, ten seconds prison physician Dr. C. W. Jeffrey pronounced Lantzer dead. The chamber was then flushed with anhydrous ammonia and the fumes were evacuated by fans which directed the poison through "scrubbers" using water as a neutralizer. The body was then removed and cleansed with a chlorine solution before being sent to a funeral home.

Billings Gazette (MT): December 8, 1938; April 5, 1939. *Chester Times* (PA): April 19, 1940. *Ogden Standard-Examiner* (UT): April 19, 1940.

Brown, Cleveland, Jr.
November 17, 1944

In late 1943 twenty-seven-year-old Cleveland Brown, Jr., was employed on a railroad extra gang at Kemmerer, Lincoln County, Wyoming. On October 2, Brown waylaid eighty-seven-year-old Mrs. Elizabeth Kusnirik when she was on her way home from downtown Kemmerer. Brown beat and slashed his victim to death before robbing her, and then threw her dead body into a clump of willows. Her body was soon found and after an investigation lasting several weeks Brown was arrested and he quickly confessed.

By October 22 a charge of first degree murder was filed and Brown's trial began in mid–December. Brown was convicted, without a recommendation for leniency, so on December 17 district Judge H. R. Christmas sentenced Brown to die in the gas chamber at Rawlins on February 11, 1944. When Brown heard the sentence he could not speak but sobbed audibly. A notice of appeal was filed, which stayed the execution, but the matter was concluded within several months and Brown's date with the executioner was then set for November 17, 1944. Nothing further would delay the proceedings.

On Brown's final night the warden appeared at his cell door before midnight, after the witnesses were in place, and read the death warrant. The prisoner, stripped to his shorts, was then brought out and blindfolded by a guard. He was guided the fifteen feet into the gas chamber. At 12:17 A.M. he was seated in the steel chair where his chest and waist, wrists and ankles were securely strapped and he was asked if he had anything to say, but there is no record of a statement.

The chamber was sealed and at 12:23 the warden pulled the lever which dropped the thirty-two cyanide pellets into the crock of sulphuric acid beneath the chair, and in six minutes the chamber was filled with a cloud of white, poisonous hydrocyanic gas. Brown breathed deeply, as instructed, and two doctors in attendance pronounced him dead at 12:37 A.M. The chamber was then flushed with anhydrous ammonia and the fumes were evacuated by fans, which directed the poison gases through "scrubbers" using water as a neutralizer. The body was then removed and cleansed with a chlorine solution before being sent to a funeral home, and the body was buried in the prison cemetery.

Ogden Standard-Examiner (UT): October 22, 1943; December 18, 1943; November 17, 1944.

Ruhl, Henry
April 27, 1945

Henry Ruhl, alias Howard William Pickell, began his criminal career in Syracuse, New York, at age seven when he stole $100 from his teacher and refused to tell where it was hidden. At age 16, in 1933, Ruhl was arrested for carrying a dangerous weapon and he was sentenced to serve three years at the reformatory in Elmira, New York. In 1937 Ruhl was sentenced to serve a five to seven year prison term at Attica and he was paroled in February 1945, on the stipulation that he remain in New York State. Twenty-six-year-old Ruhl immediately left New York and made his way to Texas where he stole an automobile, and then started northwest. On June 25 he picked up hitchhiker Eugene Turner and when the youth "boasted of his conquests with women" Ruhl beat him into unconsciousness with a tire iron and then, using his knife, mutilated the body and threw it in a borrow pit near Walters, Oklahoma. Ruhl would later say, "I fixed him so he wouldn't bother any more women." Ruhl next picked up seventeen-year-old Joel McDonald hitchhiking from Bytown, Texas, and beat him into unconsciousness, but did not kill him, and left him by the side of the road.

After the second attack Ruhl drove into Walters, Oklahoma, where he abandoned the car, changed his clothes, and threw away the knife. After breakfast he hitchhiked into Colorado and then made his way to Laramie, Wyoming, arriving June 27. The next day Ruhl went to the campground on the Fort Warren Target and Maneuver Range where he saw Matt Katmo and Mrs. O. W. Larson stop their automobile to pick wild flowers. He approached them and at gunpoint ordered Katmo to give up his car keys, but when Katmo refused Ruhl riddled his body with bullets. Ruhl then beat and tied Larson and drove off in Katmo's car. He drove directly to the ranch of fifty-three-year-old Percy Cota and his forty-five-year-old wife Gertrude, a school teacher. Ruhl knocked on their door and when they answered he shot Percy in the throat and Gertrude in the head. Gertrude did not die immediately so Ruhl tied a cord around her neck to strangle her. He then took their feet and, one at a time, dragged the dead bodies to a garage one hundred feet from the house, then ransacked the house and took everything of value.

On June 30 Charles Johnson, foreman for the Alwyn Ranch, stopped at the Cota ranch and found the bodies. Within hours Sheriff Edward A. Wood of Laramie and Sheriff Norbert Tuck of Cheyenne had large posses searching for the murderer, and the deputized ranchers swore they would not take the murderer alive. Meanwhile, at midnight, deputy Charles Stevens arrested a suspicious character at Pine Bluffs, Wyoming, forty miles east of Cheyenne, on the Nebraska border. The prisoner gave the name Howard William Pickell and he was taken to Laramie where, after a brief period of questioning, he confessed to killing Katmo but denied killing the Cotas. He was arraigned on September 13 and pled guilty to killing Katmo, but there was a question of jurisdiction so the trial did not proceed until after March 5, 1944, when it was determined that Katmo was killed on federal land. Ruhl was tried in the federal Circuit Court, convicted of murder and sentenced to die, the execution to take place at the Wyoming State Prison in Rawlins using the state approved method of lethal gas. The case was appealed but the U.S. Supreme Court affirmed the judgment and sentence of the lower court, and the application for clemency sent to President Harry S. Truman was denied, so Ruhl's date with the executioner was finally set for April 27, 1945.

Ruhl refused all spiritual services while in prison, but he persisted in claiming his innocence. Before midnight on April 26 the warden read the death warrant to Ruhl in his cell and at 12:20 A.M. he was escorted into the chamber where his chest, waist, wrists and ankles were strapped to the steel chair. He was asked if he had anything to say and he replied, "I will meet all officers of the law in Hell and we will talk it over." The eye mask was then pulled on and the chamber was sealed. Within a few seconds the cyanide pellets were dropped into the crock of sulphuric acid and the white cloud of hydrocyanic gas enveloped the prisoner. Ruhl, as instructed, breathed deeply and died without a struggle. As soon as all sign of life was absent the chamber was flushed with anhydrous ammonia and then the poisonous fumes were purged using fans which directed the gases through "scrubbers" using water as a neutralizer. The body was then removed and cleansed with a chlorine solution before Drs. C. W. Jeffrey and N. E. Murad examined the remains and officially pronounced him dead at 1:00 A.M. The body was buried in the Rawlins prison cemetery later that day.

Billings Gazette (MT): July 5, 1943; April 29, 1945. *Hammond Times* (IN): April 27, 1945. *News-Herald* (Panama City, FL): July 4, 1943. *Ogden Standard-Examiner* (UT): July 19, 1943. *Salt Lake Tribune* (UT): March 5, 1944.

Pixley, Andrew
December 10, 1965

The McAuliffe family of Illinois was taking a motoring vacation across the country and stopped at the Wort Motor Hotel in Jackson, Wyoming, on the evening of August 6, 1964. Thirty-nine-year-old Robert and thirty-four-year-old Betty McAuliffe put daughters twelve-year-old Deborah, eight-year-old Cynthia, and six-year-old Susan to bed and then went downstairs to the lounge to watch a midnight floor show. They were returning to their room at 1:15 A.M. when they heard a scream, rushed to their daughters' room, and Robert had to break in the door. He found twenty-one-year-old Andrew Pixley, shirtless and lying on the floor feigning drunkenness. Deborah was bloodied and she and Cynthia were dead, but Susan was unharmed and it was her scream they heard. Deborah had been struck in the head with a rock and then strangled to death, while Cynthia was strangled but not bludgeoned. Later, at the autopsy, it would be determined that both girls had been raped after they were dead. Robert put his knee in Pixley's back, grabbed him by the neck, and yelled, "Help, Murder!" and help soon arrived. Betty rushed to her daughters and tried to wipe their faces with towels, and later said "but I saw it was too late." She tried to talk to Deborah and then covered them with a jacket. Pixley, by then, had been handcuffed and Betty saw the blood on his face and stomach, and would testify, "I could only think one thing, that's my babies' blood." Officers determined that Pixley had gained entry by removing a screen and opening the window to crawl through. He knocked Deborah unconscious, then strangled Cynthia before returning to Deborah and strangling her.

The bodies of the girls were returned to Chicago, Illinois, and buried in a single casket. Pixley was lodged in jail and charged with two counts of murder and his trial for murdering Deborah started at Worland, Wyoming, on a change of venue, and lasted three days. He was found guilty and before sentencing the court listened to psychiatrist Dr. William Karn, Jr., who described Pixley as "a sociopath [who] is sick with getting along with the outside world. He hates the human race — himself included. [Pixley] is one of the sickest we've ever seen psychopathically." Dr. Karn said "the chance for rehabilitation is absolutely nil," and when asked if he thought the girls were asleep when killed the doctor testified, "I hesitate to answer because of the presence of the parents, but it meant a lot more to Pixley to kill the girls while they were awake rather than while they were sleeping." On February 3, 1965, District Judge Donald Harkins sentenced Pixley to die at the prison in Rawlins on May 3, 1965, and the condemned man laughed when he heard the sentence. This so enraged Robert McAuliffe that he jumped up and screamed, "Laugh some more, you animal!" He had tried to attack Pixley earlier and was again restrained after the outburst. Pixley was taken to the prison and he told his attorney, James Sperry, that he did not want the sentence appealed, but an appeal was automatic. However, the case was handled so expeditiously that the execution was only delayed seven months and his new date with the executioner was set at December 10.

On the Saturday preceding his death Pixley asked to be baptized and this was accomplished in a prison bathtub by the Reverend David Griffen. On his final evening he declined to order anything special for his last meal and ate the regular prison fare. He had been moved into the death cell thirty feet from the gas chamber and before midnight Warden Lenard Meacham read the death warrant and then the prisoner was conducted into the steel chamber. He was seated in the steel chair and his chest, waist, wrists and ankles were securely strapped. There is no record of a statement.

The chamber was sealed and at 12:10 A.M. the cyanide pellets were dropped into the crock of sulphuric acid and in minutes the prisoner was enveloped in a cloud of poisonous white fumes. He took deep breaths, as instructed, and at 12:16 prison Dr. Robert Paul announced that Pixley was dead. The chamber was then flushed with anhydrous ammonia and purged by fans which directed the fumes into "scrubbers" which used water to neutralize the poison. The body was then removed and cleansed with a chlorine solution before being released to the funeral home, where Pixley's mother had made arrangements for his burial. The following year the McAuliffes brought a civil suit against the hotel to pay for Susan's psychiatric treatment.

Billings Gazette (MT): February 4, 1965. *Independent Record* (Helena, MT): December 10, 1965. *Salt Lake Tribune* (UT): August 8, 1964. *Spokesman-Review* (Spokane, WA): August 15, 1964. *Bulletin* (Bend, OR): March 19, 1966.

Hopkinson, Mark
January 22, 1992

In 1971 nineteen-year-old Mark Hopkinson was arrested in Arizona for delivering a controlled substance, convicted, and sent to a federal prison. Upon his release in 1975 he returned home to Bridger Valley, Wyoming, to find that his father was constructing a trailer park and having legal difficulties, and in two cases attorney Vincent Vehar was representing the opposition. The first case involved the Roitzes family over water rights and the Roitzes prevailed. When Mark took over construction of the trailer park from his father he tried to deal directly with Frank Roitzes and the result was that on May 6, 1976, he and his father beat Roitzes with a hammer. The county attorney was then defending the Hopkinson family in an appeal of the water rights suit, and he refused to file criminal charges.

Meanwhile another dispute arose between the Hopkinson family and the Fort Bridger Sewer and Water Board. Hopkinson wanted the trailer park annexed to the sewer district and was willing to pay the usual $100 hook-up fee per trailer space, but before action could be taken the board raised the fee to $300. Mark Hopkinson agreed to pay the increased fee but once the hook-up had been completed he refused to pay the contract price. A dispute followed between the board and the Hopkinson family and board members received threats from Mark. Vincent Vehar filed suit on January 28, 1977, on behalf of the board, which sought to force the Hopkinson family to pay the money due under the contract and also requested $50,000 in exemplary damages based upon the threats made against the board members.

Mark Hopkinson immediately began to form a plan to "punish" either Frank Roitzes or Vincent Vehar. In 1976 Mark hired twenty-three-year-old Jeffrey Lynn Green to work on various projects and later that year Green introduced Mark to Mike Hickey and Jamey Hysell. In June 1976 Hysell had been arrested for possession of marijuana because of a statement made by fifteen-year-old Kelly Wyckhuyse and Hysell wanted her killed as revenge, and Mike Hickey performed the task on June 27 and hid her body in a remote location. It was about this time that Mark Hopkinson tried to find someone to murder Frank Roitzes or Vincent Vehar. He then turned to Jeff Green and Mike Hickey, and he had leverage over the latter as he knew of the Wyckhuyse murder, and they began planning several murders.

On April 4, 1977, Green, while driving Hopkinson's car, was caught in Utah with a bomb in his possession as he was on his way to Arizona to plant the device in George Mariscal's car at Hopkinson's direction, and thereafter Green was excluded from discussions of murder. Hopkinson and Hickey continued to plan a murder and by the end of July, Hopkinson selected Vehar to be killed by throwing a bomb into the basement of the Vehar home. When Hopkinson received notice that he would be deposed by Vehar in the sewer board lawsuit on Tuesday, August 9, 1977, he ordered the murder to proceed on Saturday, August 6, and Hickey agreed. By a tragic turn of events the Vehar family — sixty-seven-year-old Vincent, his fifty-one-year-old wife Beverly, his twenty-seven-year-old son Tony, and his eighteen-year-old son John — had been in Laramie and were not due to return home until Monday morning, but Tony had business early Monday so the family decided to drive through to Evanston and arrived home shortly after midnight Sunday. Hickey got a late start for the Vehar home and was seen on August 7 at 2:45 A.M. driving toward Evanston by a highway patrolman who was investigating an accident. Hickey arrived at the Vehar home about 3:30 A.M. and after making sure it was safe for his get-away he threw the bomb through the basement window and fled. At approximately 3:35 A.M. the bomb exploded, completely demolishing the brick home and making a deep bomb crater, and the blast killed Vincent, Beverly, and John while seriously injuring Tony. On his way back to Bridger Valley Hickey picked up a hitchhiker, who later would testify that Hickey was driving away from Evanston at about 4:00 A.M., and Hickey returned to his home just after 4:30.

For days federal, state and local agencies sifted through the rubble until on August 14 they announced that the blast was "intentional from a deliberately planted device." Soon after the bombing Hickey went to California and was still there when Hysell was arrested and questioned about several larcenies, and to "make a deal" he told the authorities about Wyckhuyse's murder and guided the authorities to the body. Hickey was found in California and questioned and after his return to Wyoming he was arrested and charged in the Wyckhuyse murder. In order to save Hickey, Hopkinson conspired with Hickey and Green to blame Hysell, and this led to withdrawal of murder charges against Hickey and a murder indictment was filed against Hysell. Nevertheless, in the spring of 1978 Hickey went to prison on burglary charges. When Hysell came to trial Green weakened and decided to tell the truth, first implicating Hopkinson and Hickey in the Vehar murders and then confessing that his statements incriminating Hysell were fabricated, and that Hickey had committed the Wyckhuyse murder. When Green's confession was reported in the newspapers Hopkinson was determined to kill him before he could testify before the grand jury.

In March 1979 Hopkinson and Hickey were tried in the United States District Court in Cheyenne on federal charges arising out of Green's attempt to plant a bomb in Mariscal's car and Hopkinson was convicted and sent to the federal minimum security facility in Lompoc, California. He began a telephone campaign to have Green murdered and had a female friend send a photo of Green to Hap Russell, who recruited John Suesata, a man of dubious reputation from Salt Lake City. On the morning of May 18 Green disappeared in the company of two men and on May 20 Green's mutilated body was found, just two days before the opening of the grand jury's investigation into the Vehar bombing. Green had been tortured, with more than one hundred fifty cigarette burns on his body, and he had been shot through the head. Mike Hickey, when called to testify before the Uinta County grand jury, broke down and confessed to the Wyckhuyse killing and the Vehar bombing but, in a plea bargain, he agreed to turn state's evidence against Mark Hopkinson in the Vehar case in return for a twenty-year sentence for the Wyckhuyse murder.

Hopkinson was indicted for the murders of the Vehars and Green and his trial began on September 3, 1979. There was no defense presented so final arguments began as soon as the prosecution rested and the jurors found Hopkinson guilty on all six charges, and in the penalty phase returned a recommendation of life imprisonment for the three Vehar murders and death for the murder of Green. The judge then sentenced Mark Hopkinson to two consecutive terms of seven and one-half to ten years imprisonment for conspiracy, three consecutive terms of life imprisonment for the Vehar killings, and death for Green's murder. The convictions were appealed and every legal manipulation was used to delay the execution for thirteen years, and even up to the last minute there were three appeals pending: one to the state Supreme Court; one to the U.S. Supreme court; and one a motion before a federal judge, but all were denied. Wyoming Governor Mike Sullivan refused to commute or pardon Hopkinson, despite petitions to do so by many death penalty opponents.

Hopkinson steadfastly maintained his innocence. His execution by lethal injection, the first in Wyoming, was scheduled for after midnight on January 22, 1992. Hours earlier guards had asked the condemned man if there was anything they could get him, and he joked, "You can get me a blond and a helicopter." His last meal was pizza which he shared with his mother and other family members. When asked about witnesses he refused to have any but the official witnesses which were required, saying, "I just couldn't lie there knowing they were watching me."

After his visitors were escorted from his cell the warden read the death warrant and then Hopkinson was led out to the death chamber. He lay on a gurney and was securely strapped down. Newsmen had been allowed into the chamber and he said, "You got the wrong man. They have killed an innocent man." As the newsmen left to join the other officials, outside the chamber, medically trained personnel inserted two intravenous cannulas (IV), one in each arm with the second a back-up in case the primary IV failed. The executioner was already in place in the control room, so he would remain anonymous, and on the signal of the warden at 12:50 A.M. the three drug combination was administered: first sodium thiopental to induce sleep; then pancuronium bromide to restrict respiration, which in time would cause death by asphyxiation; and third was potassium chloride to stop his heart. Hopkinson was pronounced dead at 12:57 A.M. and after the witnesses viewed the remains the body was removed from the room and sent to a funeral home, where his mother had made arrangements for his burial.

Altoona Mirror (PA): January 22, 1992. *Cedar Rapids Gazette* (IA): January 23, 1992. *Color County Spectrum* (St. George, UT): August 14, 1977. *Herald* (Chicago, IL): January 21, 1992. *Hopkinson v. State*, 632 P.2d 79; WY, 1981. *Hopkinson v. State*, 664 P.2d 43; WY, 1983. *Hopkinson v. Shillinger*, 645 F. Supp. 374 D. WY, 1986. *Hopkinson v. State*, 708 P.2d 46; WY, 1990. *Ogden Standard-Examiner* (UT): August 10–11, 1977. *Post-Register* (Idaho Falls, ID): August 15, 1977.

Bibliography

Frye, Elnora. *Atlas of Wyoming Outlaws at the Territorial Penitentiary.* Cheyenne: Wyoming Territorial Prison Corporation, 1990.

Gibson, Elizabeth. *Outlaw Tales of Washington: True Stories of Washington's Most Nefarious Crooks, Culprits, and Cutthroats.* Guilford, CT: Globe Pequot Press, 2002.

Goeres-Gardner, Diane L. *Necktie Parties: Legal Executions in Oregon, 1851–1905.* Caldwell, ID: Caxton Press, 2005.

Hopkinson v. State, 632 P.2d 79; WY, 1981.

Hopkinson v. State, 664 P.2d 43; WY, 1983.

Hopkinson v. Shillinger, 645 F. Supp. 374 D. WY, 1986.

Hopkinson v. State, 708 P.2d 46; WY, 1990.

Meier, Gary, and Gloria Meier. *Oregon Outlaws: Tales of Old-time Desperadoes.* Boise, ID: Tamarack Books, 1996.

State of Montana vs. John H. Osnes.

State of Oregon v. F. W. Gallin, Grant County Circuit Court Case _ 1694.

Wilson, R. Michael. *Encyclopedia of Murder and Execution in the Wild West.* Las Vegas, NV: Rama Press, 2006.

_____. *Frontier Justice in the Wild West.* Guilford, CT: Globe Pequot Press, 2007.

_____. *Outlaw Tales of Wyoming.* Guilford, CT: Globe Pequot Press, 2008.

Newspapers

Aberdeen American News (SD)
Ada News (OK)
Aiken Standard (SC)
Albuquerque Morning Journal (NM)
Albuquerque Tribune (NM)
Altoona Mirror (PA)
Anaconda Standard (MT)
Anderson Herald (IN)
Argus-Leader (Sioux Falls, SD)
Ashland Tidings (OR)
Astorian (OR)
Bellingham Herald (WA)
Big Piney Examiner (WY)
Billing Gazette (MT)
Bismarck Daily Tribune (ND)
Bison Courier (SD)
Black Hills Daily Times (Deadwood, SD)
Blackfoot News (ID)
Bottineau Courant (ND)
Bremerton News (WA)
Bulletin (Bend, OR)
Bulletin (Seattle, WA)
Burlington Daily Times-News (NC)
Butte Daily Miner (MT)
Butte Inter Mountain (MT)
Capital News (Jefferson City, MO)
Capital Times (Madison, WI)
Capitol Journal (Salem, OR)
Cedar Rapids Gazette (IA)
Centralia Daily Chronicle (WA)
Charleston Daily Mail (SC)
Charleston Daily Mail (WV)
Charleston Gazette (NC)
Chehalis Bee-Nugget (WA)
Chester Times (PA)
Cheyenne Daily Leader (WY)
Chillicothe Constitution-Tribune (MO)
Chronicle-Telegram (Elyria, OH)
Citizen (IA)
Color County Spectrum (St. George, UT)
Coos Bay News (Empire City, OR)
Coos Bay News (Marshfield, OR)
Coquille City Herald (OR)
Coshocton Tribune (OH)
Council Bluffs Nonpariel (IA)
Courier (Connellsville, PA)
Cumberland Evening Times (MD)
Daily Journal (Salem, OR)
Del Rio News Herald (TX)
Dillon Examiner (MT)
Dispatch (Casa Grande, AZ)
East Oregonian (Pendleton)
Eau Claire Leader (WI)
Emporia Gazette (KS)
Eugene City Guard (OR)
Eugene Morning Register (OR)

Evening Herald (Provo, UT)
Evening Republican (Mitchell, SD)
Evening Telegram (Portland, OR)
Evening Tribune (Albert Lea, MN)
Everett Daily Herald (WA)
Everett Morning Tribune (WA)
Examiner (Big Piney, WY)
Fairbanks Daily Times (AK)
Fairbanks News-Miner (AK)
Fergus County Argus (Lewiston, MT)
Fort Wayne Sentinel (IN)
Freeport Journal-Standard (IL)
Galveston News (TX)
Garden City Telegram (KS)
Gleaner (Kingston, Jamaica)
Globe Gazette (Mason City, IA)
Grand Forks Herald (ND)
Grant County News (OR)
Great Falls Tribune (MT)
Greeley Daily Tribune (CO)
Hamilton Daily Democrat (OH)
Hamilton Journal (OH)
Hammond Times (IN)
Havre Daily News (MT)
Havre Daily News-Promoter (MT)
Hawk-Eye Gazette (Burlington, IA)
Hayward Review (CA)
Helena Independent (MT)
Herald (Chicago, IL)
Humboldt Standard (Eureka, CA)
Huronite (Huron, SD)
Idaho Falls Times (ID)
Idaho Republican (Blackfoot)
Idaho State Journal (Pocatello)
Idaho Statesman (Boise)
Idaho World (Idaho City)
Independent (Long Beach, CA)
Independent Record (Helena, MT)
Indiana Gazette (PA)
Indiana Progress (PA)
Inter Lake (Kalispell, MT)
Inter Mountain (Butte, MT)
Journal (Portland, OR)
Journal (Stevens Point, WI)
Journal-Gazette (Mattoon, IL)
La Crosse Tribune (WI)
Las Vegas Daily Optic (NM)
Lima News (OH)
Lima Times-Democrat (OH)
Lincoln Daily News (NE)
Lincoln Daily Star (NE)
Lincoln State Journal (NE)
Lincoln Sunday Journal and Star (NE)
Livingston Enterprise (MT)
Logansport Pharos (IN)
Logansport Pharos-Tribune (IN)
Logansport Press (IN)
Longview Daily News (WA)
Lowell Sun (MA)
Lowell Sun and Citizen-Leader (MA)
Mail (MD)
Mansfield News-Journal (OH)
Mason City Globe-Gazette (IA)
Meagher Republican (MT)
Minot Optic (ND)
Monroe Monitor (WA)
Montana Standard (Butte)
Morning Herald (Hagerstown, MD)
Morning Olympian (WA)
Morning Union (Walla Walla, WA)
Mountaineer (Canyon City, OR)
Muscatine Journal and News-Tribune (IA)
Nevada State Journal (Reno)
New Castle News (PA)
New York Times (NY)
News-Herald (Panama City, FL)
News-Palladium (Benton Harbor, MI)
News Standard (Uniontown, PA)
Northwest News (Portland, OR)
Northwestern (Oshkosh, WI)
Oakland Tribune (CA)
Ogden Examiner (UT)
Ogden Standard (UT)
Ogden Standard-Examiner (UT)
Olean Times (NY)
Olewein Daily Register (IA)
Oregon Argus (Oregon City)
Oregon City Courier (OR)
Oregon Daily Journal (Portland)
Oregon Mist (St. Helens)
Oregon Register (Lafayette)
Oregon Sentinel (Jacksonville)
Oregon State Journal (Eugene)
Oregon Statesman (Oregon City)
Oregon Statesman (Salem)
Oregonian (Portland)
Oxnard Daily Courier (CA)
Pharos-Tribune (Logansport, IN)
Pinedale Roundup (WY)
Pioneer-Times Extra (Deadwood, SD)
Piqua Daily Call (OH)
Plaindealer (Grand Forks, ND)
Plaindealer (Roseburg, OR)
Plainsman (Huron, SD)
Polk County Observer (Dallas, OR)
Port Angeles Evening News (WA)
Port Arthur News (WA)
Post-Register (Idaho Falls, ID)
Post-Standard (Syracuse, NY)
Press (Piqua, OH)
Progress (Clearfield, PA)
Puget Sound Semi-Weekly (WA)
Rapid City Journal (SD)
Record-Eagle (Traverse City, MI)

Reno Evening Gazette (NV)
Review (Decatur, IL)
River Press (Fort Benton, MT)
Saline Journal (KS)
Salt Lake Tribune (UT)
San Antonio Evening News (TX)
San Antonio Express (TX)
San Francisco Chronicle (CA)
San Mateo Times (CA)
Sandusky Register-Star-News (*OH*)
Santa Fe New Mexican
Seattle Daily Times (WA)
Seattle Post-Intelligencer (WA)
Seattle Star (WA)
Settler (Bismarck, ND)
Sioux City Journal (IA)
Sitka Sentinel (AK)
Skamania County Pioneer (Stevenson, WA)
Snohomish County Tribune (WA)
South Bend Journal (WA)
Spokane Daily Chronicle (WA)
Spokane Review (WA)
Spokane Times (WA)
Spokesman-Review (Spokane, WA)
Star-Mirror (Moscow, ID)
Stars and Stripes (U.S. Military)
States Rights Democrat (Albany, OR)
Statesman (Boise, ID)
Stillwell Democrat-Journal (OK)
Sturgis Weekly Record (MT)
Sunday Journal and Star (Lincoln, NE)
Syracuse Herald-Journal (NY)
Teton Chronicle (Choteau, MT)
Tillamook Headlight (OR)
Times and Daily News Leader (San Mateo, CA)
Times-Herald (Burns, OR)
Titusville Herald (PA)
Tri-city Herald (Pasco, WA)
Tucson Daily Citizen (AZ)
Tyrone Daily Herald (PA)
Umpqua Valley News (Roseburg, OR)
Union (Corvallis, OR)
Union-Bulletin (Walla Walla, WA)
Vidette-Messenger (Valparaiso, IN)
Walla Walla Daily Bulletin (WA)
Walla Walla Statesman (WA)
Waterloo Courier (IA)
Weekly Missoulian (MT)
West Side Telephone (Lafayette, OR)
Winnipeg Free Press (Manitoba, Canada)
Wisconsin State Journal (Madison)
Woodland Daily Democrat (CA)
Wyoming State Tribune (Cheyenne)
Xenia Daily Gazette and Torchlite (OH)
Yankton Press & Dakotan (SD)
Yreka Journal (CA)

Index

www.ingramcontent.com/pod-product-compliance
Ingram Content Group UK Ltd.
Pitfield, Milton Keynes, MK11 3LW, UK
UKHW051929100926
8556IPUK00022B/1447

9 780786 46126